UNITED STATES HISTORY

UNITED STATES HISTORY

A Multicultural, Interdisciplinary Guide to Information Sources
2nd Edition

Anna H. Perrault
Associate Professor
University of South Florida

and

Ron Blazek
Professor
Florida State University

LIBRARIES UNLIMITED
A Member of the Greenwood Publishing Group

Westport, Connecticut • London

Library of Congress Cataloging-in-Publication Data

Perrault, Anna H., 1944–
    United States history : a multicultural, interdisciplinary guide to information
sources / Anna H. Perrault and Ron Blazek.—2nd ed.
        p. cm.
    ISBN 1-56308-874-6
        1. United States—History—Bibliography.   2. United States—History—
    Reference books—Bibliography.   3. United States—History—Databases—
    Directories.   I. Blazek, Ron.   II. Title.
    Z1236.P45   2003
    [E178]
    016.973—dc21   2002155895

British Library Cataloguing in Publication Data is available.

Library of Congress Catalog Card Number: 2002155895
ISBN: 1–56308–874–6

First published in 2003

Libraries Unlimited
A Member of Greenwood Publishing Group, Inc.
88 Post Road West, Westport, CT 06881
www.lu.com

Printed in the United States of America

∞™

The paper used in this book complies with the
Permanent Paper Standard issued by the National
Information Standards Organization (Z39.48–1984).

10 9 8 7 6 5 4 3 2 1

CONTENTS

LIST OF ABBREVIATIONS AND SYMBOLS

ann.	annual
ann. cum.	annual cumulation
bi.	bimonthly
bienn.	biennial
bienn. cum.	biennial cumulation
col.	columns
comp.	compiler, compiled
corr.	corrected
ed.	edition, editor, edited
enl.	enlarged
et al.	additional (names) elsewhere
exp.	expanded
irreg.	irregular
mo.	monthly
q.	quarterly
quin. cum.	quinquennial cumulation
repr.	reprint, reprinted
rev.	revised
semiann.	semiannual
supp.	supplement, supplemented
wk.	weekly
*	available online or in CD-ROM

ACKNOWLEDGMENTS

It is important that authors receive the cooperation and assistance of others in doing their work. We were fortunate to benefit from the generosity of our respective employers, the Florida State University School of Information Studies and the University of South Florida School of Library and Information Science.

Dr. Perrault received a sabbatical leave from the University of South Florida for the fall 2001 semester, during which time a major portion of the work was completed. A number of students in the Information Sources and Services in the Social Sciences class at USF in fall 1999 compiled updated bibliographies of sections of the work: Tracey Covey, Barbara and Donald Davis, Carlene Jaworowski, Nancy Kocher, Xuan Luo, Salvatore Miranda, Greg Mullins, Marshall Reeves, Hilary Wagner, and Patricia Pettijohn. Graduate assistants at USF Jennifer Boucher and Monica Jenkins assisted in the early stages with manuscript preparation and indexing. Jenny Binaghi, Maureen McCartney, and Douglas Turk verified Web sites. Elisa Carlson, as editorial assistant, completed both the author-title and subject indexes and also supervised final manuscript review.

At Florida State University, no less than 19 students participated in the project over its three-year duration. These students gave freely of their time and energy in searching the literature for updated editions and reviews, and in some cases provided assistance in word processing. Their contributions were essential to the completion of this work, and they are deserving of commendation. In alphabetical sequence, they are Eric Gomez Almeida, Laura Boles, Kathleen Conerly, Susan R. Cook, Barby Cooper, Gary Crew, Bradd Geariety, William Hutchinson, Kyung-mi (Mimi) Lee, Claudia Montague, Tom Mueller, Robin G. Pavan, Robert A. Sica, Jr., Scott Snipes, Udella Spicer, Melissa Sunshine, Luigi Tavernese, Kim M. Thompson, and Chang-woo Yang.

We thank all of the people named in the paragraphs above for their assistance in making the task of producing a second edition of the *Guide* a viable project.

PREFACE

Since the publication of the first edition of this United States History *Guide* in 1994, there have been two defining historical events. The first of these was the Millennium, the transition from the twentieth to the twenty-first century. Except for the commercialism of the celebrations associated with the entry into a new century, the Millennium was rather benign in terms of change. The apprehensions of "Y2K" caused by the technological advances of the late twentieth century proved to be unfounded. The passage of the twentieth century and the beginnings of the twenty-first were not seen as traumatic as was the fin de siècle period of the nineteenth century. The prolonged Millennium period (debate as to which year was the beginning of the twenty-first century, 2000 or 2001) was still in progress when the second event occurred.

The state of relative tranquility of the Millennium was destroyed in a few cataclysmic minutes on the morning of September 11, 2001 when the New York World Trade Center Twin Towers were attacked. September 11th was a watershed in the history of the United States. It had the effect of instantly making the twentieth century history. The dividing point of September 11th ushered in a period of change in the way in which the people of the United States regarded their country and its system of government. A new patriotic fervor and an appreciation of U.S. history prevailed. Courses in U.S. history were reinserted in curricula at all levels of education and the teaching of history was encouraged through grants and new textbooks. This revised edition of the U.S. History *Guide* was already in progress before September 11th, having begun early in 2001. Its authors hope that this second edition will contribute to the renewed interest in the study of United States history and be a useful guide to those newly engaged in historical research.

PURPOSE AND SCOPE

The *Guide* is designed for a wide spectrum of users: sophisticated researchers and practicing historians; students, both graduate and undergraduate; librarians; and the general public. It is also intended to be useful as a tool in interdisciplinary research by investigators in governmental and political relations, ethnic and gender studies, popular culture, and those social sciences fields allied to historical, demographic, and sociocultural studies.

The first edition has been revised and expanded for this second edition, which presents a selective but thorough coverage of both bibliographic and informational materials. In addition to printed reference books, coverage is given to online databases, Web sites, and CD-ROM titles, as well as those in microform. Although the user will find older standard works, the emphasis has been on recent publications, with most dates ranging from the late 1980s to 2002. When the first edition of the *Guide* was prepared, the end of the Cold War, the dissolution of the USSR, and the Gulf War were very recent events. At that time, the Vietnam conflict was just beginning to be a subject for historical studies. The preparation of the second edition of the *Guide* took place at the beginning of the new century and its coverage extends through the twentieth century. A number of works were published for the Millennium reviewing the twentieth century and these have been included. It is recommended that serious researchers and reference/information personnel use this work in conjunction with the first edition to assure comprehensive coverage.

In keeping with the recent emphasis on the "New History" described in the introduction, our work offers a social science perspective and emphasizes social history in its thorough treatment of multicultural and gender influences and its recognition of various societal systems, institutions, and issues (education, religion, the law, crime, etc.). The initial edition of the *Guide* was the first of its kind to consider the gay influence and to treat genealogy in a serious manner. Chapter 6 represents nearly 60 percent of the entries. While it serves as a resource for U.S. history, the interdisciplinary nature of historical research makes this title especially useful to students in American studies, political science, ethnic and gender studies, and popular culture.

Our work hardly ignores the titles associated with the study of history in a more traditional fashion, however, as a glance at the table of contents will reveal. Political history, military history, regional history, and so forth, are treated to a degree commensurate with their available resources. Excluded from coverage are the visual arts, music, and literature from the humanities, and psychology and sociology from the social sciences. It is recommended that the researcher use other literature guides more specific to those areas.

METHOD OF SELECTION AND USEFUL SOURCES

As indicated above, both standard tools and new reference materials are included, but the emphasis is given to more recent titles. Although the *Guide* is not intended to be a Web directory, the impact of the World Wide Web is seen in the inclusion of numerous relevant sites. Selections of both print and nonprint material were made either on the basis of favorable reviews or firsthand knowledge, the rationale being to offer the very best titles for any of the intended user groups.

Most helpful for its provision of excellent reviews in history as well as other subjects is *American Reference Books Annual,* from Libraries Unlimited, which has appeared each year since 1970. The last volume of *ARBA* used for identification of titles for the *Guide* was the 2002 edition enumerating 2001 resources. Useful review journals are *Booklist* ("Reference Books Bulletin" section), *Choice, Library Journal,* and *Reference Services Review (RSR).*

The most comprehensive standard reference work for identification and description of reference tools by subject is *Guide to Reference Books,* 11th edition, edited by Robert Balay (ALA, 1996). The 11th edition did not extend coverage much beyond the first edition of our U.S. history *Guide.* The 12th edition of the *Guide to Reference Books* is projected to be available in approximately 2004 only as an online resource.

Finally, the presence of many publishers on the Web and easy access to WorldCat through the State of Florida database package enabled us to find and verify information easily. We also used the online booksellers for information and, in a few cases, reviews.

COMPOSITION AND ORGANIZATION

The introduction furnishes perspective regarding the nature of historical research and inquiry, along with the conditions of reference publishing. The section on "Electronic Reference Sources" offers suggestions for searching the literature as well as exposition of the computer environment.

The *Guide* is then divided into two major parts: part I covers the general sources (chapter 1), whereas part II covers specific topics, disciplines, and issues relevant to U.S. history (chapters 2–6).

Introductory notes are furnished for each chapter and for many sections and even subsections. These notes are likely to provide historical summaries of events and/or publishing developments related to the topic, as well as descriptions of relevant associations and their publications. Also treated in many of these passages are general indexes that cover historical writings to some degree. In certain segments, such as "Genealogy and Immigration" in chapter 6 and "Government Publications" in chapter 1, suggestions and recommendations are given for searching the literature.

In 1991, Donald O. Case reported the results of a study examining the collection and use of information by a select group of historians concerned with U.S. history.[1] He was able to confirm the continuing primacy of archival holdings and primary source material and the secondary role of reference sources in the conduct of research. All types of materials were used to some degree, although there was a surprising lack of use of bibliographic databases by historians in his study. With the development of online resources that include bibliographic material since this study was conducted, historians are now utilizing the databases for these purposes.

Case did point out the importance of presenting historical materials by *topic* in guides and bibliographies, as opposed to subdividing a large body of knowledge by format. Topical categories are perceived to be more useful to the historian than format or in most cases, chronological categories. The topics Case identified represent the subject matter of the New History and include gender, ethnicity, crime, popular culture, the Depression, and so forth.[2]

Arrangement of major sections and some subsections is topical in nature. Form divisions are utilized only in a few instances. In general, in making decisions regarding placement of entries within sections, ethnic and racial considerations are considered uppermost, followed by gender influences (e.g., a tool on African-American women is placed within "The Black Experience," and a source on women in politics is placed within "The Female Experience"). This is consistent throughout the *Guide*, except in the cases of the subcategories of "cinema" and of "theater" in chapter 6 that do include distinctive ethnic and gender titles. An attempt was made to capture alternative categories and direct the user to correct locations in the *Guide* through the indexes and through cross-references in the introductory segments to each topic.

ENTRIES AND ANNOTATIONS

There are 1,250 major entries, as well as hundreds of co-entries and minor entries that appear within the body of the annotations for major entries. This represents a 25 percent increase of titles over those treated in the first edition. This increase in number is impressive when considering the current emphasis on recent resources required the deletion of many older titles from the first edition. Major entries are given full bibliographic coverage in cases of single and dual authorship; in cases of more than two authors, only the first author is named, followed by "et al." International Standard Book Numbers (ISBNs) are given for major entries only. Minor entries and co-entries are identified in the indexes and cross-references through "n" designations following the entry numbers.

Annotations tend to be lengthy, ranging from 85 to over 250 words, and describe scope and coverage of the tool. Description may also include information on authorship, publication history, topical (historical) analysis, value to particular audience, and search strategies, as well as co-entries and minor entries. Availability as an online database or Web site, or in CD-ROM format is noted by an asterisk (*), an indicator also used in the indexes. All Web sites were current as of November 7, 2002.

NOTES

1. Donald O. Case, "The Collection and Use of Information by Some American Historians: A Study of Motives and Methods," *Library Quarterly* 61 (January 1991): 73–74.

2. Ibid., 68–79.

INTRODUCTION

NATURE OF SCHOLARSHIP AND RESEARCH TRADITIONS

Historical inquiry and its writing have passed through different stages representing different philosophical traditions through time. One of the earliest positions, espoused initially by the ancient Greeks, favored the belief in recurrent conditions or historical cycles. Subsequently, St. Augustine placed an emphasis on God and Christianity, which was followed by a growing belief in the elevation of man and his progress toward a noble future, a view characteristic of the eighteenth and nineteenth centuries. In all these philosophical orientations, the intent has been to give a complete picture of the past as a comprehensible, logical progression of events.

These attempts to depict the universality of the historical record and the presence of a guiding principle are embodied in what has now come to be called traditionalist theory. The writing of history in the traditionalist sense presents historical narrative to explain the large sweep of the past. As a discipline, history in this framework originated as part of the humanities. As such, it emphasized the importance of the high-and-mighty decision makers during the various chronological periods and gave little thought to the sentiments and activity of the common people or their impact on societal development.

During the nineteenth century, historians and philosophers in Europe, especially in Germany, began to question the theoretical and methodological assumptions upon which historical scholarship was based. The developing trend favored a more scientific and critical approach to the use of records, with more care given to their selection and to the nature of documentary evidence. It was at this time that history began to emerge as a professional discipline and theories of historical writing were developed.

Such writing remained largely within the humanistic frame and focused primarily on politics and political figures. It was not until the end of the nineteenth century and the beginning of the twentieth century that traditional history was challenged as being too narrow and exclusive. The need for inclusion of cultural, social, and economic factors in order to fully comprehend political developments was gradually accepted by modern historians in their desire to furnish an accurate picture of the past.

The influence of German scholarship diminished during the twentieth century for a number of reasons (not the least of which were the two world wars). The "New History" emerged as a challenge to the large-scale historical narrative of the past. It was given impetus by World War II, which inspired the behavioral or psychosocial approach and study of comparative relationships between people and events. Since the 1960s, this new approach has been linked to the social sciences, which encourage investigators to ask precise questions or even formulate hypotheses and then to seek answers in appropriate documents.

This process requires a certain precision of operation in enumerating assumptions, defining terms, refining strategies, and most importantly in defining the problems to be investigated. These problems relate closely to everyday life and the experience

xix

of the common man and woman. As studies embrace the social, cultural, and economic context through which political history is developed, such elements as urban history, business history, legal history, family history, women's studies, ethnic studies, popular culture, and so forth take on added significance. Indeed, the study of U.S. history has achieved primacy at the expense of the more traditional emphasis on ancient or medieval Europe.

History, today, is "less a single discipline than a family of disciplines subdivided by geography and allied fields (political science, economics, sociology, anthropology). . . . Historians are increasingly working 'at the interface' between history and one or more disciplines, collaborating with scholars from other fields . . . Definition of historical documents has broadened; historians are seeking new types of evidence, in new ways and in new places."[1] In this climate, the study of history has become highly diversified. The basic areas of inquiry, such as political history, social history, and intellectual history, still remain, but they now are aided by the knowledge generated through psychology, sociology, and demography. The recent emphasis on statistics has given birth to the "cliometrician," or statistical historian, who applies rigorous social science principles to the collection of quantifiable historical data.

Thus, history remains an exciting and fertile field of inquiry. Today it embodies a number of possible approaches with a mix of research orientations ranging from exclusively quantitative to wholly qualitative in nature. Cliometricians and traditionalists do agree on the nature of the historian's role in revealing truth about the past and the need for historical honesty in seeking to understand it. They understand the fundamental complexity of their task but seem to revel in their adoptive roles. Through it all, the search for meaning remains the universal rationale for all historical inquiry.

THE REFERENCE LITERATURE

Since the publication of the first edition of *United States History: A Selective Guide to Information Sources* in 1994, the nature of reference publication and services has changed. The publication of monograph-length bibliographies has almost ceased, and the number of separate biographical works has diminished. The reference literature now tends to favor an encyclopedic set that incorporates biographical material, topical entries, a chronology, full text of important documents, and bibliographical references either within the entries or as suggested further readings. These printed resources sometimes have an electronic edition that furnishes all types of materials including audio and video clips in one database. The electronic formats, of course, offer the searching capabilities of a search engine and the hyperlinking of entries, both within the database and externally to the Internet. While the shift to these new comprehensive resources is now evident, the publication of printed editions continues along with new titles.

ELECTRONIC REFERENCE SOURCES

When the initial edition of the *Guide* was published eight years ago, electronic databases and CD-ROMS generally were limited to a few current years of resources. Since that time, many materials formerly in microformat have been digitized, and indexes and reference databases have been extended backward in time to cover a wealth of retrospective resources. Thus, whereas in the past historians used mainly printed bibliographies, indexes and finding aids, today, as with research in any field, historical researchers now begin with a canvas of electronic databases. Many of the microform projects that were mentioned in entries in the first edition now have at least a list of titles that can be accessed through Web sites. Many popular and academic books are now available as e-books as well as in print. As an example, the first edition of this work is available as an e-book through OCLC WorldCat.

In an article in *American Libraries* in 2000, Ken Winter characterizes reference sources of that day as being "databases, not books; accessed, not acquired; erasing some limitations of printed books; mega-resources with deep content." He describes the latter as "one-stop-shopping databases combining multiple reference works with unique searching and sorting functions in a truly synergistic way."[2] Gale's *Biography Resource Center* (entry 52) is an example of this type of mega-resource. It combines 250 full-text periodicals with links to nearly 10,000 reviewed Web sites, and in partnership with Marquis provides the full text of more than 900,000 *"Who's Who"* entries. Users can create much more targeted searches. Instead of just looking up names in the *Biography Resource Center,* a user can find all biographees of a certain occupation or in a defined geographic area, or all listed graduates of a certain institution. More reference works will be offered as online resources and more will be designed in that mode from the beginning.

The historical researcher must now consult all applicable electronic databases and Web sites and then proceed to printed materials. Only after mastering the resources available electronically should the researcher turn to older bibliographies and guides.

LIBRARY NETWORK DATABASES AND SERVICES

Before the conversion of indexes and guides to electronic format, researchers were very much affected by the size and type of institution with which they were affiliated. Now, one is not limited or disenfranchised by the lack of resources at one's home institution. Many states have statewide electronic database packages available to all libraries within the state. In other network configurations, the state universities may jointly purchase electronic indexes and full-text databases. Statewide or regional multi-type consortia purchase the same resources for public and school libraries. In short, the availability of the largest and most useful databases is now widespread. The biographical, historical, literary databases, the Wilson periodical indexes, and a number of other resources are commonly a part of the electronic offerings of most libraries ranging from medium to large size. It is only the more specialized resources that are available solely through academic libraries. And most academic libraries now have "virtual libraries" through which the electronic resources can be accessed off site by those affiliated with the institution. The researcher still may need to travel to a research library to use these specialized tools on site, but this is very infrequent compared to the manner in which research had been conducted in the past.

In addition to the availability and access to all manner of digitized materials, reference service is becoming a universally offered "virtual service." The Library of

Congress and OCLC (Online Computer Library Center) have developed a subscription reference service through which clientele of a subscribing library will have reference service available 24 hours a day through the QuestionPoint Web site.

PRESERVATION AND DIGITIZATION

After World War II when new universities were being founded, there was a great demand for collections of classic works in all fields. A number of existing publishers furnished reprints of popular and important works, along with new publishers that catered specifically to that market. In the same time frame, companies or publishing divisions were formed to microfilm large collections of retrospective works based upon the classic titles identified as imprints in major bibliographies covering the periods from the fifteenth through the eighteenth and nineteenth centuries. These massive projects continued through the early 1990s. During the 1990s the companies producing large microform sets of retrospective collections of books, serials, newspapers and archival materials were subjected to the same take-over and buyout activity as was occurring throughout the publishing world.

The microfilming shifted to scanning in the last few years of the twentieth century. University Microfilms (UMI), which provided structure and apparatus for bibliographic control of dissertations, was purchased by Proquest. All of the research collections being published by UMI still continue. The complete listing of collections is now found on the Proquest Web site under the UMI section. Proquest also now owns the former DataTimes Newspaper indexing and microfilming products. Listings of those products are also on the Proquest Web site.

Another company producing research collections in microfiche, Chadwyck-Healey, had been acquired by UMI. It also can be found under the Proquest Web site, or directly at http://umi.com/chadwyck. The former Research Publications has also been subsumed under the Proquest UMI umbrella.

Congressional Information Service, which had become the primary publisher of indexes to U.S. congressional publications, and then the executive branch, had acquired Carrollton Press, an early reprinter of U.S. government catalogs and indexes. Lexis-Nexis acquired CIS in the latter 1990s. Another company, University Publications of America is also part of this group. LexisNexis was in turn acquired by the Thompson Group.

Another of the newspaper indexing and filming companies is NewsBank. It acquired Readex, which is now a division of Newsbank. Readex had filmed the *Evans Early American Imprints* series, the Shaw-Shoemaker series, *Early American Newspapers,* and a number of other retrospective collections. Information about the Newsbank and Readex collections is on the Newsbank Web site and at http://www.readex.com. It has become extremely difficult to keep track of where companies that were acquired are now residing. But the good news is that the products seem to have been continued by the new owners, and a considerable number of the acquired companies can still be found on the Web under their original names.

There has been an effort to update the entries for the large microform collections from those contained in the first edition of our *Guide.* The second edition of *Microform*

Research Collections: A Guide (Meckler, 1984), while quite old now, does contain descriptions of 370 major microform collections. The majority of the large retrospective filming projects had been initiated before the 1984 publication date so that it is still useful in identifying pertinent collections for research. The major collections received cataloging for the separate titles in the collections and those entries are in OCLC WorldCat and RLIN (Research Libraries Information Network).

Many of the individual titles in microform sets did not receive separate cataloging and must be identified through indexes and guides to these sets. An *Index to Microform Collections* (Meckler, 1984) lists the contents of 40 microform collections.

The older print reference tools have been replaced largely by catalog entries in OCLC WorldCat and RLIN, and by lists of contents on the Web sites of the companies that sell the microforms. It behooves any researcher to become familiar with all of the overlapping reference and research tools so that they may find any retrospective publications being sought.

Up until the 1980s microfilm had been thought to be the perfect preservation medium. And acting upon that assumption the aforementioned companies and many libraries engaged in preserving newspaper files, periodical runs, and monographs through microfilming. When the electronic era posed digital formatting as the perfect preservation medium, libraries, museums, archives, and commercial publishers all became engaged in digitization projects. One of the most useful digitization projects for historians is JSTOR (entry 9). The backfiles of many scholarly journals in history, the humanities, and the social sciences have been digitized by the JSTOR project.

Although digital formats were at first thought to be the solution to the preservation problems that plague paper, all film media, and audio files, at the end of the twentieth century the realization had come that digital files were not the perfect answer. Historians and archivists have joined with librarians in voicing concern about the preservation of data and resources that exist only in electronic formats. The fast pace of changing technologies continues to render hardware and software obsolete, presenting preservation challenges not experienced with paper materials. The problems of preserving manuscript drafts, data maintained only in electronic form, and government information of all types have come to the forefront, as these are the future materials for historical research. The National Archives and Records Service has formulated a plan to preserve archival resources through the continued "refreshment" of the digital files.

The computer revolution, indeed, has changed the nature of current research and scholarship. Not only are reference tools and indexes increasingly in electronic formats, but also the printed book is migrating to the e-book. The American Council of Learned Societies in collaboration with a number of other learned societies and university presses is sponsoring the History E-Book Project. While history has long been the staunch ally of the library in the acquisition of printed books and archival materials, the recognition is slowly coming that electronic publishing offers opportunities to expand the concept of the e-book. The ACLS History E-Book project plans to both convert titles of major importance to historical studies that may not be widely available to electronic format and to publish electronic works that "use new technologies to communicate the results of scholarship in new ways." In cooperation with the ACLS, the university presses will seek to identify, recruit, and solicit proposals from professional historians. The books will be published on the Web site of the ACLS History E-Book Project accessible through libraries. Thus historians are being drawn into the production of electronic works.

This reference guide attempts to look to the future of scholarship and research as well as describe the reference tools produced in recent years.

NOTES

1. Constance C. Gould et al., "Information Needs in the Humanities: An Assessment" (Stanford, CA: Research Libraries Group, 1988), 7.

2. Ken Winter, "From Wood Pulp to the Web: The Online Evolution," *American Libraries* (May 2000): 70–74.

PART I
U.S. History
General Sources

Chapter 1
Sources of General Importance to U.S. History

ELECTRONIC DATABASES, NETWORKS AND WEB SITES

Many long-running printed bibliographical series, periodical indexes, library catalogs, and guides to archival repositories are now "published" only in electronic formats. The well-known printed catalogs, such as the *National Union Catalog* and the *National Union Catalog of Manuscripts* compiled by the Library of Congress, were discontinued in printed versions in the mid 1990s. All of these major research tools were described in the first edition of this U.S. History reference *Guide*. For the most part, only the electronic versions of these old familiar tools are described in this second edition of the *Guide*. Also included, of course, are new electronic databases, which were borne of the electronic age and never had older printed counterparts.

This section is placed at the beginning of the *Guide* as now all research begins with searching the appropriate electronic resources for the subject. Those databases and electronic indexes that broadly cover the field of American history are listed in this section. Those with more specific emphases are included in the appropriate subject sections in this *Guide*. In many instances instead of specific titles, a Web site address is given for exploring all the available resources of those institutions or companies. While it is acknowledged that not every library or individual researcher will have access to all of the electronic resources covered, these resources are ubiquitous enough that enterprising individuals will be able to manage to obtain access.

*1. America: History and Life. A Guide to Periodical Literature. Santa Barbara, CA: ABC-CLIO, 1964–. Quart. ISSN 0002-7065. [Electronic database; CD-ROM]

The main index for the field of U.S. history is *America: History and Life,* which began publication in 1964. This publication broadly covers U.S. and Canadian history, area studies, popular culture, genealogy, multicultural studies, women's studies/gender studies, anthropology, and the history of science, economics, business, education, music, art, and law. As well as the print edition, *America: History and Life* is available for online searching from 1964 to the present as an online database and also from the publisher in a CD-ROM format. The capacity to combine two or more terms or descriptors makes searching in the electronic versions superior to using printed index volumes. The database indexes over 2,000 journals published worldwide, including state historical society journals. In addition to articles, 6,000 citations of book and media reviews and abstracts of dissertations are included. Also included in the electronic database are *CLIO Notes,* a research guide that has concise overviews of 22 major historical periods designed to help identify major issues and events; detailed chronologies to give context to those issues and events; and suggestions for papers and class discussions. Search strategies and guided searching using selected index terms assist the beginning researcher as well as a simple searching option. All research in U.S.

history or interdisciplinary topics in the social sciences and the humanities should begin by searching the topic in this database.

*2. **ArchivesUSA.** Ann Arbor, MI: ProQuest UMI, 1997B. ISBN 0-89887-156-5. [Electronic database; CD-ROM]. Available: http://archives.chadwyck.com.

The search for archival and manuscript collections has been greatly facilitated by this electronic database, which forms a current directory of over 5,400 repositories and over 124,000 collections of primary-source material across the United States. The repository records give detailed directory information including phone and fax numbers, hours of service, and URLs. Each collection record links to its corresponding repository record. The Web version is updated quarterly, the CD-ROM annually.

Several earlier titles have been combined into *ArchivesUSA*. The *National Union Catalog of Manuscript Collections* (*NUCMC*) was published by the Library of Congress from 1959 to 1993 in print and 1993–1995 on magnetic tape. The over 75,000 records in *NUCMC* were subsumed into the *ArchivesUSA* database in 1997. Likewise, the *National Inventory of Documentary Sources in the United States* (*NIDS*) containing information on over 42,000 collections in 300 repositories, which was published on microfiche by Chadwyck-Healey, has been continued within *ArchivesUSA*. The former *Directory of Archives and Manuscript Repositories in the United States* has been combined into the *ArchivesUSA* database along with the two bibliographic sources. The entire runs from both bibliographic titles have been "cross-collated and new records created, pooling information from both sources where available." Searching can be by keywords, name of repository, city, state, and years. Collection records include the collection name, dates, repository name, *NUCMC* record number, type and extent of the material, and a text description of the collection. There are links to more than 5,400 repository home pages and online finding aids. Material may be printed or downloaded. Repositories can submit their own information online. Updated data are also received from the Library of Congress. The database is added to continually and must be checked periodically for additions of interest as approximately 2,500 finding aids are added five times a year. This database is one of the first resources in which researchers anticipating archival research should begin.

In 1999, UMI purchased Chadwyck-Healey, which had produced the *National Inventory of Documentary Sources in the United States* since 1983. The purpose of the *NIDS* program was to film registers, catalogs, inventories, and all manner of finding aids for manuscript collections in the United States. Indexes to the finding aids were published in CD-ROM format. There was a similar project for Great Britain, the *National Inventory of Documentary Sources in the United Kingdom*. Whereas other published guides and catalogs such as the *National Union Catalog of Manuscript Collections* gave brief descriptions of collections and holdings, the *National Inventory* finding aids contain detailed listings of the contents of manuscript collections. The *National Inventory of Documentary Sources in the United States* was complementary to the *National Union Catalog of Manuscript Collections* in that it provided the on-site finding aids for many of the collections listed in the *NUCMC*. Now both have been incorporated into *ArchivesUSA*. At one point there was a separate project for oral history collections to construct a comprehensive source for finding what collections are in a particular repository and what projects and individual interviews are in a particular collection. The project reproduced on microfiche finding aids to oral history collections in universities, historical societies, state archives, and other repositories throughout North America with a printed index to the microfiche. This title has also been incorporated into *ArchivesUSA*.

Two printed works contain much the same information on repositories. *Guides to Archives and Manuscript Collections in the United States* (Greenwood Publishing Group, 1994) and *Articles Describing Archives and Manuscript Collections in the United States: An Annotated Bibliography* (Greenwood Publishing Group, 1997) are both compiled by Donald L. DeWitt. Both titles are divided into 13 general sections with several subheadings, enabling a user to identify repositories by area of interest. The first title is an annotated listing of guides to repositories, which overlaps with *ArchivesUSA*. The thorough researcher may want to use both the electronic and the print titles to ensure an exhaustive investigation.

*3. British Library. Available: http://www.bl.uk.

Bibliographic records for many of the research resources of the British Library can be accessed through the British Library Public Catalogue Web site. A "Resources for Research" page provides links to resources within the British Library and links to a variety of other online resources. These include the Department of Manuscripts, covering accessions from 1753 to the present, and the British Library Newspaper Library Web Catalogue, which has entries for over 50,000 newspaper and periodical titles from all over the world, dating from the seventeenth to the twenty-first centuries.

The *British Library General Catalogue of Printed Books to 1995* on CD-ROM is available through ProQuest UMI. This electronic catalog, originally published by Chadwyck-Healey, contains records for almost 6 million books. The database lists the largest collection of pre-1914 imprints in the world, almost every book published in the United Kingdom up to 1995, and some special foreign collections. Researchers endeavoring to locate all published materials dealing with topics in U.S. history should not overlook the possibility of the existence of non–U.S. publications dealing with the subject.

*4. CRLCATALOG. Chicago, IL: Center for Research Libraries. Available: http://crlcatalog.uchicago.edu.

The Center for Research Libraries (CRL) is a nonprofit organization founded as the Midwest Library Center in 1949 by a group of 13 research libraries for the purpose of increasing research resources available to their users. Begun as a cooperative storage facility, CRL now focuses primarily on the collection of area studies materials. Over 200 institutions are members of CRL, participating in cooperative purchasing and storage of archival and research collections. Materials housed at CRL in Chicago are loaned to member libraries for use by researchers. The *Center For Research Libraries Handbook* (1990) describes the collecting and loan policies of the center. The major collections of newspapers, microforms, government publications, archival materials, 800,000 foreign dissertations, and periodicals are described. The four area-studies collecting programs and cooperative microfilming programs for African, East Asian, South Asian, and Southeast Asian materials are also described.

CRL began contributing cataloging records to the Online Computer Library Center (OCLC) online catalog in 1981. Prior to 1981 printed catalogs for monographs (1969–1978), serials (1972–), and newspapers (1969) were issued by the center. In 1982 CRL issued a microfiche catalog of holdings up through 1981. Cataloging records since 1981 and many retrospective cataloging records from CRL are accessible through the OCLC (entry 14) and RLIN (entry 17) databases. A number of research libraries also load cataloging tapes from CRL into their local online catalogs. The CRLCATALOG is an online Web access catalog to the collections of the Center for Research Libraries in Chicago now available on the Web at http://crlcatalog.uchicago.edu. The catalog contains over 500,000 bibliographic records representing cataloged monographs, newspapers, serials, archival materials in microform, and microform sets with title analytics. In addition to the cataloged collections, CRL has a number of comprehensive collections that are not cataloged by policy; these include foreign dissertations, college catalogs, U.S. state documents, and textbooks. CRL also owns U.S. National Archives microform groups. Some of these are cataloged and some are not. Although the center in Chicago is not a library per se, on-site access to the collections is permitted. Most major research libraries are members of the Center for Research Libraries and the resources are obtained for use through interlibrary loan in those libraries.

*5. Dissertation Abstracts International. Ann Arbor, MI: Proquest/University Microfilms International, 1938–. *Humanities and Social Sciences.* Mo. *Worldwide.* Quart. ISSN 0307-6075. [Electronic database; CD-ROM].

In 1938 a program was inaugurated to bring dissertations written in universities in the United States under bibliographic control. The publication program consisted of a bibliography of dissertations, with author-written abstracts and the microfilming of the manuscript of the dissertation. In 1976 the program began international coverage. It was not until 1988, however, that 50 universities in Great Britain became involved. More than 500 doctoral-granting institutions now participate in the *Dissertation Abstracts* filming program. The database includes all U.S. dissertations from 1861 to the present, British and European dissertations, and *Masters Abstracts International* beginning in 1988.

For text-based dissertations and theses, UMI no longer requires paper submissions of electronic text. UMI now scans all print dissertations it receives and converts them to PDF files, which are available to be downloaded via the Internet for the same fee required for a print copy. The full text of over 100,000 dissertations can be purchased. The subject indexing in all UMI dissertation indexes is through keywords from the title. Access points are author, title, keyword subject, and institution. Through UMI's Current Research service, available at http://www.lib.com/cresearch/main, users can search citations and abstracts of dissertations and theses submitted by participating institutions and view 24 page previews of dissertations published after 1996. At participating institutions users can download the full text of dissertations and theses published after 1996 at no cost.

A few additional for-profit organizations are creating digital libraries of electronic theses and dissertations such as http://www.dissertations.com and the Academic Research Group. Many research libraries are now making electronic theses and dissertations from the home institution available through virtual libraries.

*6. History Resource Center. Farmington Hills, MI: Gale Group. [Electronic database] Available: http://infotrac.galenet.com.

History Resource Center is a Web-based database designed for historical research by students with specific features for instruction via distance education. The U.S. history module of the database combines documents from Primary Source Microfilms's digital archives; encyclopedic articles from Macmillan and Charles Scribner's reference works; full-text periodicals and journals; a historical bibliography; a research guide; and links to digitized special collections. There are five main search paths: person, time period, subject search, full-text, and custom search. The database blends different content by electronic searching and cross-linking. A chronology links a graphical timeline with significant events to relevant articles and shows the period in history from a world perspective. Documents, URLs, and bibliographic citations can be marked for remote access or on-site instruction. Users can e-mail search results to themselves or others and save results to a disk. There are links to special digitized collections outside the library system. Search results can be organized according to type of data such as an annotated chronology; encyclopedic and critical articles, essays, and biographies; original documents including 500 full-text monographs and articles; multimedia files of maps and images; links to full-text history journals; bibliography, abstracts, and indexes; overview information by country, era, and topic; and annotated Web links. *History Resource Center* provides integrated access to over 1,000 historical primary documents, more than 30,000 reference articles, and over 65 full-text journals covering themes, events, individuals, and periods in U.S. history from precolonial times to the present. The material also includes access to the citations for over 189 additional history journals from the Institute for Scientific Information's *Arts and Humanities Citation Index* (entry 18). The Web site brings together a broad collection of facts, primary documents, and scholarly analysis with integrated access to all.

*7.   H-Net: Humanities and Social Sciences Online. Available: http://www2.h-net.msu.edu.

The *H-Net* site acts as a clearinghouse for lists, Web sites, and multimedia projects. There are a large number of discussion lists, all beginning with AH-A, some pertaining to American history, among them H-Survey (teaching United States History Survey Sources), H-CivWar (U.S. Civil War History), H-Ethnic (Ethnic and Immigration history), H-Film (Cinema History; Uses of the Media), H-Appalachia (Appalachian History and Studies) and H-California (history and culture of California). One of the most useful of the lists is *H-Net:Reviews,* which contains scholarly reviews by subject specialists and/or academics. All reviews are signed with reviewer's affiliation listed. Reviews are lengthy and appear much in advance of the printed journal reviews. The URL just for reviews is http://www2.h-net.msu.edu/reviews/. The *H-Net* site is worth visiting for anyone who engages in historical research.

*8.   Humanities Index. New York: H.W. Wilson, June 1974–. Quart. with annual cumulations. ISSN 0095-5981. [Available as a WilsonWeb database and in WilsonDisc, a CD-ROM format from 1984 to present. *Humanities Abstracts* and full text available online from 1994]. **Social Sciences Index.** New York: H.W. Wilson, 1974–. Quart. with annual cumulations. ISSN 0094-4920. [Available as a WilsonWeb database and in WilsonDisc, a CD-ROM format from 1984 to present. *Social Sciences Abstracts* and full text from 1994].

These two indexing services grew out of the *International Index,* published from 1907 to 1965. The *International Index* became the combined *Humanities and Social Sciences Index,* and in 1974 the title was split into the separate *Humanities Index* and the *Social*

Sciences Index. Because of the interdisciplinary nature of much historical research, students and scholars may need to use one or the other, or both, of these two indexes. The *Humanities Index* covers 500 English-language journals in archaeology; area studies; art; dance; film; gender studies; literature; languages and linguistics; folklore; history; music; theater and performing arts; philosophy; and religious studies. The *Social Sciences Index* covers 500 international English-language periodicals in the fields of anthropology, economics, geography, international relations, political science, law, minority studies, public administration, sociology, and urban studies. Book reviews are in a separate section in the printed indexes. These titles would not be the primary indexes for history research, but depending upon the topic, they should be included in any thorough search for published research on topics the indexes cover.

*9. JSTOR. Ann Arbor, MI. [Electronic database]. Available: http://www.jstor.org.

JSTOR began at the University of Michigan as an effort to ease the increasing problems faced by libraries seeking to provide adequate stack space for the long runs of backfiles of scholarly journals. It was sponsored by the Andrew W. Mellon foundation in its pilot phases and was established as an independent not-for-profit organization in August 1995. The basic idea was to convert the back issues of paper journals into electronic formats that would allow savings in space while simultaneously improving access to journal content. When the contents of the journals are scanned, the images are linked as a searchable text file to the entire published record of a journal, offering a level of access not possible with print. A few of the titles germane to U.S. history already available through JSTOR are *American Historical Review, American Economic Review, American Political Science Review, Journal of Black Studies, Journal of Economic History, Journal of Southern History, Population and Development Review, Population Index, Population Studies, Reviews in American History,* and *Journal of Military History.* The database is available to libraries through membership subscription. As more titles are added to the database, JSTOR is becoming an indispensable resource for historical research, especially for those not located near research libraries likely to have the original runs of the journals.

*10. Landmark Documents in American History. New York: Facts on File [Electronic database; CD ROM]. Available: http://www.factsonfile.com/subscription.

Over 1,300 full-text primary-source documents important in U.S. history from 1492 to the present are contained in this database. The types of documents include Supreme Court decisions; party platforms; essays and literature; letters; government charters and constitutions; speeches; debates; legislation; treaties; inaugural addresses and speeches of all the Presidents; biographies; photographs; and video clips. Biographies are very brief, but provide a photograph of the subject and links to related documents and other biographies. Each document has an introduction that explains its significance and gives background information. A "Further readings," function provides users with a bibliography to inspire further research. Hypertext links facilitate navigation between related documents and to other Web sites. This electronic resource makes it easy to find and incorporate the original text of landmark documents into research papers.

Facts on File also offers a subscription Web site, *American Historical Images,* available at http://www.fofweb.com/subscription. Over 2,000 images are organized by year with a timeline, era, topic, occupations, and type. The timeline and eras are organized strictly by time frame, but the topics section is organized by 14 topical subjects. Images can be searched by type. There are 44 types of images such as advertisements, cartoons engravings, flags, and so forth. The images supplement the documents, essays, and other materials included in other Facts on File electronic products.

A similar but much broader product also published by Facts on File is *The American Multimedia Archive*. This product is based on the United States History Standards for grades 5–12. Core curriculum topics are focused on with the provision of more than 2,000 hyperlinked images that depict the most important people, places, events, and issues. Maps, critical primary-source documents, and historical audio and video clips are also included. Each volume covers the African American experience, Native Americans, women's issues, the government and the Constitution, foreign policy, immigration, and daily life and culture.

*11. LexisNexis. Dayton, OH: LexisNexis. [Electronic database]. Available: http://www.lexisnexis.com.

Lexis began in the 1970s as one of the earliest e-commerce products, "a new way to index the law." The first offerings were Ohio and New York codes and cases, and the *U.S. Code* and federal case law. Nexis began in 1979 with the licensing of the *New York Times* database. The *LexisNexis* databases were searched via proprietary software developed by the company. It was not until the products became available through the Web that researchers and the general public other than information specialists and legal personnel began to directly access the database. *Lexis* contains primary legal resources for the U.S. federal government and the 50 states. Besides the primary sources of statutes/laws, cases/opinions, court rules, and agency regulations, there are also secondary sources of encyclopedias, treatises, loose-leaf sets, legal periodicals, and finding tools—digests, indexes, and citations. The public records for the 50 states, which give access to personal information and bankruptcies, judgments and liens, civil and criminal court filings, a person locator, and driver's license and motor vehicle records, are some of the most heavily used of the *LexisNexis* information resources. While the information in the *LexisNexis* databases is intended to be up-to-the-minute, the acquisition of Congressional Information Service and University Publications in the mid 1990s added a historical dimension to the resources available online. The CIS database products are described in the appropriate subject sections of this *Guide,* but they all are subsumed under the *LexisNexis* umbrella. The company offers various modules and options for subscription to the databases. A number of different databases and resources packages are described in various sections of this U.S. History *Guide* (entries 11, 107, 121, 179, 194, 359).

LexisNexis History Universe is a suite of web products or modules which contain indexing and primary-source materials in specific subject areas. *Access to Presidential Studies* (entry 179), *Access to Women's Studies,* and *Access to African-American Studies* are subject-oriented collections under the *History Universe* umbrella. A fourth module, *Guide to Microforms,* provides access to the microform collections from University Press of America and Congressional Information Service. These collections cover thousands of primary documents in such fields as African American studies, southern history, political history, women's studies, military history and wars, immigration, labor studies, Native American studies, international relations, law and jurisprudence, FBI documents, and more. Instead of searching through printed guides to separate collections, the Boolean searching capabilities of the *History Universe* Web site enable a researcher to search multiple collections with one search. Or, the contents of one collection or even specific reels of microfilm can be searched by keyword, subject, or title. The full texts of the sources are provided. The service identifies items in the subscribing library's collections, which may be the most valuable feature because in the past, many researchers were not aware of microform materials in their home institution due to the poor bibliographic control of those collections.

Research on any topic for U.S. history should begin with LexisNexis *History Universe* if one has access.

*12. Library of Congress *American Memory Project*. Available: http://memory.loc.gov.

The *American Memory Historical Collections* are multimedia collections of digitized documents, photographs, recorded sound, moving pictures, and text from the Library of Congress's Americana collections. The site is a "gateway to rich primary-source materials relating to the history and culture of the United States." More than 7 million digital items from more than 100 historical collections can be accessed through the *American Memory* Web site. A "Collection Finder" lists broad topical categories such as Agriculture, Art and Architecture, History, Geography, Social Sciences, Technology, and Applied Sciences, which provide links to the materials in those subject areas. There are also links by time period, regions of the United States, or format of materials (e.g., maps, motion pictures, photos and prints, and sound recordings). The site provides a listing of the Divisions of the Library of Congress and also access by digital format (e.g., .JPEG, .MPEG, .MP3, and other formats). The *American Memory* site has digital collections on specialized subjects that were constructed in partnerships with other libraries and incorporates digital resources from those libraries. One such site is *The Nineteenth Century in Print: The Making of America in Books and Periodicals* (entry), which contains materials from the University of Michigan. The *American Memory* Web site should be included in any search for resources in American history.

The catalogs of the specialized collections of the Smithsonian libraries can be accessed at the Web site of the Smithsonian libraries, available at http://www.sil.si.edu. The "Galaxy of Knowledge" site contains links to many of the exhibit sites and other sites in *American Discovery*, which contain information on some of the Smithsonian's well-known and important collections. "American Indian Dress," "Elections and the Presidency," "The Horse in Blackfoot Indian Culture," "The U.S. Mexico Border," "Women and Technology," and "Women's Health" are all linked from this site. While the Smithsonian does not contain the books, maps, and archival materials that the Library of Congress has, it does have the largest collection of artifacts dealing with American history.

*13. Making of America. Available: http://moa.umdl.umich.edu.

Full texts of documents from the mid-nineteenth century, antebellum period through Reconstruction (1850–1877), are the focus of this Web site. *Making of America* began in 1995 as a collaborative project between the University of Michigan and Cornell University. The intent of the project has been to use digital technology to preserve and make accessible historical collections held at both institutions. The texts included on the site range from single images to journal articles, entire journal issues, and books. The period was chosen for the manageable size of the collections of original materials, the rapidly deteriorating condition of many of the materials, and the fact that publications from that period are in public domain status. With over a million pages of text and images from the time period, *MoA* is a significant collection of digitized books and journals.

*14. OCLC. Dublin, OH: OCLC (Online Computer Library Center, Inc.) [Network]. Available: http://www.oclc.org/home.

The first large library database, OCLC (Online Computer Library Center), was formed in 1967 by a group of academic libraries in Ohio. From a modest beginning as a statewide online union catalog, by 2002 OCLC had become an international bibliographic utility with approximately 48 million records from nearly 39,000 libraries of all types worldwide that have access to the database. The bibliographic records are for book and journal titles, government documents, musical scores, and audio-visual materials. Some archival cataloging is present. Not until the 1980s did OCLC regard this vast database of bibliographic records as anything other than a source of cataloging records for libraries and an auxiliary interlibrary loan module made possible by the library locations attached to the records. Subject searching was not possible.

In the mid 1980s OCLC began to develop a new marketing strategy aimed at the end user—the individual researcher—rather than library staff. By the early 1990s search strategies and protocols that had been developed for cataloging were revamped, and menu systems to guide the uninitiated were put in place. It is now also possible for individuals to access the entire OCLC bibliographic database (WorldCat) through the Web interface to search for specific subject terms. In many libraries, access to periodical indexes and abstracting services is provided through OCLC "FirstSearch." In addition to OCLC WorldCat bibliographic database, the FirstSearch Electronic Collections Online service includes subject periodical indexes such as the *Humanities Index* (entry 8), the *Social Sciences Index* (entry 8), and *Biography Index* (entry 58). The researcher beginning to prepare a bibliography can search these databases and download the bibliographic records. Anyone beginning research should start with a bibliographic search using FirstSearch. Although there is much retrospective material in the OCLC bibliographic database, some older works of use to the historian may not be included and, depending upon the research topic, older printed works may need to be consulted to complete the research.

*15. Periodical Contents Index. Ann Arbor, MI: Proquest/Chadwyck-Healey Products. [Electronic database; CD-ROM].

Periodical Contents Index is an electronic database with more than 200 years of fully indexed articles from journals in the arts, humanities, and social sciences providing access to more than 10 million citations. It provides abstracting and indexing for 3,035 journals from their inception to 1991. The overall dates of coverage are 1770–1991 with separate records for over 10 million journal articles. More than 1 million records are added each year. Users can search for articles by words or phrases in the title, by author, and by journal title. The search can be restricted to the language of the article, the journal's subject, the year of publication, or a range of dates. In addition, researchers can access a list of issues for each journal and a table of contents for each issue. The broad coverage of this index provides researchers access to originally published materials and to articles on historical topics.

For many of the citations in the *PCI*, UMI's *American Periodicals Series Online, 1741–1900* provides the full text. The American Periodicals series were microfilm projects begun in the 1970s: *American Periodicals I*, 1741–1800, and *American Periodicals II*, 1800–1850. The first microfilm series contained 89 titles such as Benjamin Franklin's *General Magazine* and Tom Paine's *Pennsylvania Magazine*. The 911 titles in the second series covered the issue of slavery and events leading up to the Civil War. The titles are now available in full text in the APS Online, which contains 89 journals published between 1740 and 1800, and 118 periodicals published during the Civil War and Reconstruction. Many women's and children's magazines are contained in the collection. Because the database contains digitized images of the magazine pages, researchers can see the original typography, drawings, and layouts. Together, the *Periodicals Contents Index* and the *American Periodicals Series Online* provide easy access to a broad range of periodicals important in American history. These products cover the eighteenth and nineteenth centuries up to the period in which the *Readers' Guide* (entry 16) began. There is overlap with the indexing provided by the *19ᵗʰ Century Masterfile* Web database (entry 81). Researchers will be wise to utilize both databases.

*16. Readers' Guide to Periodical Literature. New York: H. W. Wilson, 1900–. Monthly. ISSN 0034-0464. **Reader's Guide Retrospective: 1890–1982.** WilsonWeb 2002B.

Reader's Guide Abstracts. 1984. [Available as a WilsonWeb electronic database and WilsonDisc, CD-ROM format].

Although the *Readers' Guide* is regarded as a general-interest and a popular rather than scholarly resource, it is one of the few periodical indexes to cover the early years of the twentieth century. All of the major general-interest magazines and many more specialized subject periodicals are indexed in the *Readers' Guide*. Many titles of social, cultural, and intellectual prominence, such as *Scientific American, Atlantic Monthly*, and the Harper's titles, are indexed. Some years include a few government documents such as the *Bureau of Labor Statistics Bulletin*. The *Readers' Guide* is an excellent source for contemporary accounts and attitudes—social, popular, and political; or for tracing trends over a period of time. Although there are many sophisticated reference tools available for recent years, in many instances there is no substitute for the subject coverage of the printed *Readers' Guide*.

The *Reader's Guide Retrospective: 1890–1982*, which provides coverage for the complete *Reader's Guide* through WilsonWeb, is of the most interest to historians. The retrospective database contains over 1,800,000 articles in PDF format. The nineteenth-century years of *Reader's Guide* are also indexed in *19ᵗʰ Century Masterfile* (entry 81). The current years of the electronic edition are available in a full-text Mega Edition, with abstracting and indexing of 272 periodicals as far back as 1983 and full text of 148 periodicals as far back as 1994. PDF images are available from 2000 forward. The Select Edition covers 150 periodicals from as far back as 1994 with PDF images from 2000 forward. The index has an online version that begins with 1984. WilsonWeb products are updated four times a week. Any topic dealing with twentieth-century American history should be researched in the *Reader's Guide*.

*17. RLIN. Mountain View, CA: RLG (Research Libraries Group). [Network]. Available: http://www.rlg.org.

The Research Libraries Group (RLG), a consortium of large research libraries formed in the early 1970s, used the Stanford University library database, begun in the late 1960s, as the foundation for the Research Libraries Information Network (RLIN). The RLG Union Catalog is a comprehensive database that serves as a major union catalog for everything from books and serials to archives, manuscripts, maps, music scores, sound recordings, films, photographs, posters, computer files, and more. The main bibliographic catalog is noted for its strong retrospective research holdings. The Catalog extends from the advent of printing to the present, reflecting the collections of major research and academic libraries; archives and museums; law, medical, and theological libraries; art and music libraries; area studies collections; public and corporate libraries; historical societies; and book clubs. Updated daily, the Catalog included more than 40 million titles as of March 2001.

Of particular interest to the historical researcher are a number of separate files and databases within the Union Catalog. The foremost of these is the Archives and Manuscripts file, to which many research library archival collections have been contributing cataloging since the network was founded. In 1983, the Research Libraries Group began an automated system for the cataloging and retrieval of archival and manuscript records. Beginning in 1988, the current records for the *National Union Catalog of Manuscript Collections* were incorporated into the database. In 1998, RLG introduced *Archival Resources,* which integrates records from the RLG Union Catalog's Archival and Manuscripts file with online finding aids providing a single point of entry and powerful searching via the Web. Over a half a million archival and manuscript records from repositories around the world with links to finding aids and digitized material are contained in *Archival Resources.* The RLIN archival database is unique; researchers seeking archival or manuscript materials can learn of the existence and location of such materials through searching the database and many can go directly to a digitized image of the items. The majority of these records do not appear in any published source, and it has become impossible to do archival research, especially for major U.S. collections, without consulting this database.

Another RLIN database of use to U.S. historians is the *Eighteenth Century Short-Title Catalogue* (ESTC). The holdings of the American Antiquarian Society, as well as the eighteenth-century American imprints owned by British and North American libraries, are included in this ongoing project. Because of the overwhelming number of eighteenth-century imprints in English that exist worldwide, there will never be a printed catalog of the ESTC; it is available only in microfiche and through the RLIN database. Research Publications (now Proquest) began an ongoing microfilming project based on the ESTC to film at least one copy of the text of the titles.

Other specialized files in the RLIN database are musical recordings and scores, the *Avery Architectural Index,* the History of Technology, and periodical and newspaper indexing. Although almost all sizes and types of libraries are OCLC members, a smaller number of academic and special research libraries are RLG members, and access policies may vary. RLG also encourages direct access to the database by individuals. Information for access can be found at the RLG Web site, available at http://www.rlg.org.

*18. Web of Science. Philadelphia: Institute for Scientific Information. Available: http://www.isinet.com.

Arts & Humanities Citation Index. Philadelphia: Institute for Scientific Information, 1977–. ISSN 0162-8445.

Social Sciences Citation Index. Philadelphia: Institute for Scientific Information, 1977–. ISSN 0091-3707.

Both indexes now available in the electronic database Web of Science and as a CD-ROM product from the publisher.

Many topics for current historical research are broader than the indexing provided for U.S. history in *America: History and Life* (entry 1). Two indexing tools produced by the Institute for Scientific Information (ISI) both cover history and subject areas central to historical research. The *Social Sciences Citation Index* broadly covers all of the fields in the social sciences, fully indexing 1,400 journals and selectively indexing another 3,300. Subjects covered include anthropology, area studies, demography and geography, economics, ethnic group studies, international relations, political science, sociology, statistics, urban planning, and women's studies. The *Arts & Humanities Citation Index* fully covers 1,300 journals, with 5,100 selectively covered. Subjects range from archaeology and the arts, Asian studies, film, TV and radio, folklore and history, through literature, linguistics, theology, and religious studies. Both indexes include articles, book reviews, letters, editorials, notes, proceedings and meeting abstracts, excerpts from books, hardware, software, and database reviews. The printed indexes are arranged in four sections: the source index, which is an author index; the citation index; a corporate index; and the Permuterm subject index. The most unique feature of the citation indexes produced by ISI is that both the references cited in a work and other works that cite the original work are included in the indexing. Thus, it is possible to get a list of references cited in an article that is not obtainable locally. It is also possible to trace the pattern of other works citing an individual article. The subject indexing is computer-produced from keywords in the title of the work being indexed. Thus, the subject approach is by terms or concepts rather than an assigned subject descriptor. In *Web of Science,* all of the citation indexes can be searched at once. Researchers will find that the ISI citation indexes provide unique information and a different range of information than other periodical indexes that include historical topics. The indexes give a fuller inter-disciplinary perspective than other indexes that are more specific to one discipline.

GENERAL REFERENCE SOURCES

The titles described in this section are works most likely to be utilized for answering many reference questions concerning U.S. history. A number of older standard works are included, as well as more recent publications. The majority of these reference works will be useful for students, librarians, researchers, and the general public.

*19. American Heritage Dictionary of American Quotations. Margaret Miner and Hugh Rawson. New York: Penguin Books, 1997. 638p. ISBN 0-670-10002-1.

The organization of this work is chronological with contextual annotations for many of the quotations. Some 5,000 quotations are divided into 500 topics and then arranged chronologically within the topical categories. Thus it is possible to see the development of attitudes from a historical, philosophical, political, or literary perspective. Around 30 percent of the quotations have explanatory annotations, a feature not found in most standard quotation reference works. The notes are helpful in correcting misconceptions about the quotations and in explaining the context, which sometimes changes the meaning of a quotation. Many quotations are drawn from popular sources such as screenplays and advertisements. There are author and keyword indexes. The work is useful as a standard reference or to provide appropriate quotations by subject.

A different approach from the standard book of quotations format is taken in *America in Quotations: A Kaleidoscopic View of American History* (Greenwood Publishing Group, 2002), compiled and edited by Howard J. Langer. Quotations from more than 350 individuals are taken from speeches, interviews, editorials, letters, jokes, songs, and eyewitness accounts. They give what Americans thought about great events in their own lifetimes. The work includes quotations from Americans in every walk of life and covers U.S. history from pre-Columbian times through the terrorist attacks of September 11, 2001.

20. America's Historic Sites. Tracy Irons-Georges. Pasadena, CA: Salem Press, 2001. 1,272p. ISBN 0893561223.

While travel and tourist books on historic sites abound, this three-volume set has been written for American studies. The organization is by state with site essays written so as to place students at the sites where important events occurred. A total of 288 articles all have an annotated bibliography, most accompanied by at least one photograph. There are maps and charts and a subject index. Every chapter concludes with a list of "Other Historic Sites" in the state with brief annotations.

A similar work much broader in coverage is *Monuments and Historic Places of America,* in the Macmillan Profiles series (Macmillan, 2000). More than nine articles describe monuments and memorials that commemorate people and events as well as battlefields, forts, factories, homes, churches, cemeteries, and laboratories. Articles average three or four pages and are accompanied by numerous black-and-white illustrations. Timelines, definitions, brief quotes, and informational sidebars appear in outer margins. Extensive bibliographies list books, articles, and Web sites. The volume is unique in that it reflects standard social studies research topics.

21. Dictionary of American History Supplement. Robert H. Ferrell and Joan Hoff, eds. Farmington Hills, MI: Gale Group/Charles Scribner's, 1996. 2v. ISBN 0-684-19579-8.

The original edition of James Truslow Adam's *Dictionary of American History* was published in 1940. It was thoroughly revised, expanded, and updated for the bicentennial edition in 1976. The arrangement consists of alphabetical signed entries, which vary in length according to the importance of the subject. The entries are both factual and interpretative. In the revised edition, science and technology, the arts and cultural activities, Native Americans, and Afro-Americans were given greater emphasis. The index (v. 8) is a complete index to every item of information in the set, including names. The original *Dictionary of American History* and the *Dictionary of American Biography* (entry 60) were published as a coordinated effort; thus, the former does not contain biographies. There is a great deal of information, however, to be gleaned from the name index in the U.S. history set. The index includes dates and parenthetical explanatory phrases. Place names are identified by territory, city, state, or country. This eight-volume encyclopedia is a standard reference work with a reputation for accuracy and thoroughness. It is suitable for use by student and scholar alike. The two-volume *Supplement* with 757 entries brings the work up through 1995 following the format and arrangement of the eight-volume set. The first volume begins with an essay, "America and the World: 1976–1995." All entries are signed and most include a brief bibliography. *See also* references to the main set and within the *Supplement* point to related topics. The second volume contains a detailed index. The *Supplement* can stand alone or as an update to the main set.

The full texts of *Dictionary of American History* and *Supplement*; *The Presidents, A Reference History* (entry 185); *Encyclopedia of American Social History* (entry 548); and *Dictionary of American Biography* (entry 60) are contained in *Scribner's American History and Culture,* a CD-ROM product. There are over 8,000 articles and 600 photos. Also included are other sections, Timeline, Photo Gallery, and Research Ideas, which organizes U.S. history into 12 "possible report topics." There are also 75 "Selected Historical Documents." The electronic product allows advanced searching by keywords and phrases, subject area, and time period, which is the principal reason to purchase it for libraries already holding the printed sets.

American History, edited by Mark Carnes (Simon & Schuster Macmillan, 1998) is a one-volume MacMillan Compendium version of the *Dictionary of American History.* The Compendium contains over 1,000 signed essays and utilizes the same format and arrangement as the main set and the *Supplement.* Like the original set, the work does not contain biographies but the names of individuals mentioned in the essays are indexed.

To make matters confusing there is another completely different work with the same title, *Dictionary of American History,* by Thomas L. Purvis (Blackwell, 1995). This work is strong in coverage of political, military, and legal history and the eighteenth and nineteenth centuries. There is less emphasis on the twentieth century and social and cultural history. This work does contain biographical entries. One strength is its coverage of immigration from individual countries. The two, one-volume dictionaries are different enough to warrant using both.

22. Dictionary of American History: From 1763 to the Present. Peter Thompson. New York: Facts on File, 2000. 540p. (Facts on File Library of American History). ISBN 0-8160-4462-7.

Another work with *Dictionary of American History* as part of its title, this Facts on File publication has an A-Z format. The work contains 1,200 brief but informative entries covering political, diplomatic, military, economic, social, and cultural events and developments. The appendixes include maps that show the growth of the United States, presidents, Supreme Court justices, and government documents. The entries do not give sources, but there is a list of recommendations for further reading and a subject index. The work is a general ready reference suitable for all readership levels.

23. Encyclopedia of American History. Gary B. Nash. New York: Facts on File, 2002. 11v. ISBN 0816043612.

This work is worthy of the term "encyclopedia," covering chronologically in 11 volumes the history of the United States from prehistoric times up through the 2001 terrorist attacks. The *Encyclopedia* was developed and supervised by Gary B. Nash, a professor of American History at the University of California, Los Angeles, and a key author of the National Standards for United States History. Each volume is supervised by a senior scholar and corresponds to the 10 eras of the National Standards for United States History. There are both volume indexes and a comprehensive index for the set. Many entries have further reading suggestions. Each volume has a chronology and an appendix that contains excerpts of key documents of the era. Large libraries will want to own the set, but its price may keep it out of the reach of smaller school and public libraries.

Another 11-volume set is *A History of US* (Oxford University Press, 1999). Written by Joy Hakim, this series is also chronologically arranged from prehistory through 1999. The title has won numerous awards as an accurate and reliable history written in a story-telling style. The volumes are illustrated with 100 line drawings and 20 color illustrations per volume. The last volume is a sourcebook containing all or major portions of 90 significant primary documents and an index to the set. The set is priced for school and public libraries. Oxford University Press has also published a new edition of *The Oxford Companion to United States History* (2001). This one-volume work contains approximately 1,400 concise, alphabetically arranged entries written by nearly 1,000 subject specialists. The entries cover U.S. history broadly. The work is one of the best single-volume references along with *The Reader's Companion to American History* (entry 31).

24. Encyclopedia of American History. 7th ed. Richard B. Morris and Jeffrey B. Morris, eds. New York: HarperCollins, 1996. 1,296p. ISBN 0-06-270055-3.

This ready-reference work is more of a handy dictionary than an encyclopedia. The first section is a chronology of American history from the Asiatic origins of Native Americans up through the first year of the Clinton administration. The next division is a topical section with separate chronologies under headings such as population and immigration, literature, science, and technology. A third section contains brief biographies of 450 leading figures in U.S. history. The last section, on political history, gives the organization of the federal government and lists the presidents and their cabinets, Supreme Court justices, and others. The texts of the Declaration of Independence and the Constitution are included. The chronological organization makes it difficult to look up specific events or facts when the date of occurrence is not known, but there is an index. There are no references to sources, nor is there a separate bibliography. This one-volume reference is suitable for use by students and the general public.

Another one-volume work, *The American Heritage Encyclopedia of American History* (Henry Holt, 1998) is edited by John Mack Faragher. Nearly 3,000 alphabetically arranged entries cover important people, issues, genres, places, and events in government, science, arts, and religions. The contents broadly cover American life and newer aspects of U.S. social history. Longer signed entries were written by U.S. scholars and historians and contain bibliographic information for further study. There are approximately 500 black-and-white illustrations, including photographs, etchings, cartoons, maps, and portraits. A complete index is included. The work is intended for students, teachers, scholars, and history aficionados.

25. Encyclopedia of American Studies. George T. Kurian et al., eds. Danbury, CT: Grolier, 2001. 4v. ISBN 0-7172-9222-3.

American studies is an interdisciplinary field that is broader than that of American history. It includes history and culture, the arts, folklore, and ethnic studies in addition to the social, political, intellectual, and economic areas of historical research. This scholarly encyclopedia has been produced under the sponsorship of the American Studies Association. There are more than 660 signed entries arranged alphabetically by topic. The entries discuss the topics from the point of view of American culture, much of it recent. Brief biographies of the scholars who wrote the entries are provided at the end of the set. There are bibliographies and a general index. In addition there is a synoptic table of contents that arranges the entries into broad topic areas such as architecture, African American culture, and so forth. Each volume is separately paginated. The encyclopedia is useful as an overview of the field of American studies and for the information provided in the separate entries.

26. Encyclopedia USA: The Encyclopedia of the United States of America Past & Present. Gulf Breeze, FL: Academic International Press, 1983–. ISBN 0-87569-076-9.

This reference work is projected to be a 50-volume set and envisioned to encompass all major aspects of U.S. life. The arrangement consists of alphabetical entries for people, events, institutions, movements, and trends in U.S. history. Most entries are fairly lengthy and a large proportion of the entries are biographical. The most useful entries are those that give extended treatment to subjects given less attention in other reference works including many popular culture entries. The quality of the content and the clearly written entries by qualified authorities make the work interesting to read. Most entries include references to sources. The work is designed primarily for the general public and beginning researchers or as a general information source for specialists. By volume 25, published in 1998, the set had only reached the end of "E," indicating it will be much larger than the original plan of 50 volumes and many more years in progress. At the beginning of the twenty-first century a new editor, historian Donald W. Whisenhunt, began to issue supplementary volumes to those at the beginning of the alphabet published now nearly 20 years ago. The supplement to volume 3 was issued in 2000. The existing volumes make an excellent reference set, but the usefulness is limited to "A-E."

*27. Famous First Facts: A Record of First Happenings, Discoveries, and Inventions in American History. 5th ed. Joseph Nathan Kane, Steven Anzovin, and Janet Podell. New York: H.W. Wilson, 1997. 1,122p. (Wilson Facts Series). ISBN 0-8242-0930-3. Available in electronic format in both WilsonWeb and WilsonDisc.

Since 1933, over 50 years, *Kane's Famous First Facts* has been a well-known reference title. More than 9,000 inventions, discoveries, and first happenings in American history are included in the fifth edition of this ready-reference work. The fifth edition adds 1,000 new entries and has a new organization from the previous editions. The main organization is topical with entries arranged chronologically within clearly delineated subject divisions. The organization enables readers to trace new developments through the years.

A new subject index and four additional indexes enable users to trace an event by year, month, and day of occurrence; by names of persons directly or indirectly involved; and by state and municipality where the event took place. The electronic versions allow searching by subject categories, keywords, personal names, city, state, date, year, or any combination. The work is useful as a quick reference.

28. Historic Documents. Washington, D.C.: Congressional Quarterly, 1973–. Ann. **Historic Documents Index: 1972–1999.** Washington, D.C.: Congressional Quarterly, 2000. ISBN 1-56802-594-7.

The majority of the primary-source documents in this compilation are U.S. sources, although the series is not restricted to the United States. Between 50 and 100 significant documents from each year are arranged in chronological order, with an introduction placing them in historical perspective. The introductory text is presented in the form of an outline or overview. The types of documents included are presidential speeches, Supreme Court decisions, treaties, and government special studies and reports. Numerous cross-references to other volumes in the series enable a researcher to trace a particular issue through source documents over a number of years. A cumulated index also facilitates the tracing of issues over time. This series is a major reference source for primary documents since 1972. It is useful for the general public, students, and researchers.

An older but still useful work is *Documents of American History,* edited by Henry Steele Commager (Prentice-Hall, 1988. 10th ed. 2v.). The various editions of this standard reference work have been revised by retaining a core of documents, adding newer ones, and dropping a few older ones. There is no overall index that indicates which older edition a document may be found in if it is not in the latest edition. All editions have begun with the authorization for the voyage of Columbus and moved forward to modern documents. The tenth edition is divided into two volumes, the first covering the period up to 1898, the second from 1898 to the present. The last document in the tenth edition is the November 13, 1987, report of the congressional committee on the Iran-contra affair. Brief introductory notes and a short bibliography accompany each document. The set is designed to be used by students seeking the text of important papers in U.S. history; it serves this purpose for all types of users.

29. National Register of Historic Places, 1966–1994. Washington, D.C.: National Park Service, 1994.

The *Register of Historic Places* has appeared as a print publication of the National Park Service on an irregular basis since 1969. Originally, the landmarks, buildings, bridges, and other places listed were limited to resources of national significance. Succeeding editions have updated their predecessors, adding sites through the National Park Service, acts of Congress, executive orders, National Historic Landmark designation, or nomination from federal and state agencies. The National Register properties are distinguished by having been documented and evaluated according to uniform standards. These criteria recognize the accomplishments of all peoples who have contributed to the history and heritage of the United States and are designed to help state and local governments, federal agencies, and others identify important historic and archeological properties worthy of preservation and of consideration in planning and development decisions.

Listing in the *National Register* contributes to preserving historic properties in a number of ways: recognition that a property is of significance to the nation, the state, or the community; consideration in the planning for federal or federally assisted projects; eligibility for federal tax benefits; qualification for federal assistance for historic preservation, when funds are available. The National Register provides a cumulative listing of more than 75,000 sites added over more than 30 years to the register. Print publications are constantly being turned out by local and state jurisdictions. The National Park Service now maintains the *National Register* online at http://www.cr.nps.gov/nr. The Web site was created to serve as the major point of entry for searching out listed resources. Currently, the database contains 75,000 listings comprising all historic areas within the National Park Service, more than 2,300 National Historic Landmarks, and properties across the country that have been nominated for their significance to local or state history. The "NRIS" is the information system database or index containing information on each site that can be accessed on the Web. The work is available in CD ROM format as *National Register of Historic Places Index* from Buckmaster Publishing of Mineral, VA.

The National Trust for Historic Preservation Library of the University of Maryland staff compiled an *Index to Historic Preservation Periodicals,* covering the years 1979–1987 (G.K. Hall, 1988). The *Index* furnishes over 6,000 entries dealing with such topics as architectural law, restoration, real estate, and federal policy. The material represents both scholarly and popular efforts and includes the publications of the historic preservation organizations. Arrangement of entries is classified by subject heading assigned; unfortunately, there is no subject index. It is a unique and distinctive tool in terms of its coverage.

30. Opposing Viewpoints American History Series. Farmington Hills, MI: Gale Group/ Greenhaven, 1992–.

In this series, primary-source materials are placed in a pro/con format in individual volumes, each devoted to a specific issue in U.S. history. The American Revolution, immigration, slavery, and the Cold War are the topics of the first volumes in the series. Chapter introductions place each issue in a historical context. Photographs and boxes give the volumes visual appeal. Bibliographies of sources for further research are provided. The sources are selected to aid in discussion and interpretation of issues. The series is suitable for students through the college undergraduate level.

31. The Reader's Companion to American History. Eric Foner and John A. Garraty, eds. Boston: Houghton Mifflin, 1991. 1,226p. ISBN 0-395-51372-3.

Sponsored by the Society of American Historians, this single volume is an authoritative reference source for U.S. history. Three types of entries are combined into one alphabetical sequence: short factual entries, biographical entries, and thematic essays. The work was intended to be a "reader's companion," and the writing is concise, crisp, and interesting. The essays are historical overviews of pivotal events or sociological issues such as abortion, the family, and housework. The essay entries are written by scholars, are signed, and have short bibliographies. The text of the Declaration of Independence and the U.S. Constitution are included in the appendixes. Students and scholars will find it equally readable and informative.

Garraty edited *The Young Reader's Companion to American History* (Houghton Mifflin, 1994) a well-researched, well-written reference for ages 11 and up. The list of contributors is impressive. Many popular topics as well as controversial issues are included. The volume is very attractively illustrated with maps, cartoons, tables, and color plates.

A previous work by John Garraty is *1,001 Things Everyone Should Know About American History* (New York: Doubleday, 1989). This is an entertaining reference work divided into eight illustrated thematic sections. The entries are for songs, quotes, books, poems, people, slogans, battles, inventions, and more. Political and historical events are also included. There is an index. Although it is a good place to find trivia, the work is also factual and informative and an excellent complement to more scholarly works.

32. Reader's Guide to American History. Peter J. Parish, ed. Chicago: Fitzroy Dearborn, 1997. 880p. ISBN 1-884964-22-2.

Selected topics in U.S. political, social, and economic history are covered in one volume with some 600 historiographic essays written by 225 historians. The purpose of the work is to give a conceptual overview of the larger themes and topics in U.S. history from the colonial period to the Gulf War. Religion, women's history, urban history, sports, and entertainment are all covered. The discussion in each entry includes approximately 10 major works on the subject in a 1,500-word essay that attempts to summarize the major arguments of the works. In all, more than 5,000 works are reviewed. In addition to the essays there is a thematic list of topics, a booklist and a detailed general index.

Another work that provides lists of important books and articles in U.S. history written during the 1980s and 1990s is *United States History: A Bibliography of the New Writings on American History* (Manchester University Press, 1996), compiled by Louise A. Merriam and James W. Oberly. The contents are arranged in 10 chronological categories with subdivisions. Of the 4,000 bibliographic entries around two-thirds are monographs, including reference works. The remaining third are mostly review articles. An effort was made to include journal articles and books with new approaches to topics and periods. There is an author/subject index.

33. Representative American Speeches: 1937–1997. Calvin McLeod Logue, ed. New York: H.W. Wilson, 1998. 778p. ISBN 0-8242-0931-1.

Sixty years of issues as presented through the words of leading figures of the time are condensed into this one-volume work, which is a compilation of more than 150 speeches pulled from the *Representative American Speeches,* a long-running annual series. The speeches are organized around 16 interconnected themes: political community; nature and function of government; civil liberties; international affairs; war; human rights; civil rights; media; education; the arts; religion; business; industry and labor; science, technology and space; environment; urban issues; and crime and terrorism. Brief biographical information and the historical significance of each speaker are given. Introductions place each speech into context and summarize the speaker's points. There are indexes by subject and speaker name. Over 1,250 speeches published in the annual volumes of *Representative American Speeches* are a further source of historical information. While primarily aimed at students, both the compilation and the annual volumes are a ready source for the text of important speeches.

An electronic source for speeches is *History Channel: Speeches,* available at http://www.historychannel.com/speeches/index.html. Hundreds of speeches are available in audio files that can be searched by speaker, topic, or time period. A written context is provided for each speech. There is an alphabetically arranged speakers index also.

BIBLIOGRAPHIES AND CATALOGS

Throughout the latter nineteenth century and for most of the twentieth century, the energies of librarians and scholars were devoted to the identifying, cataloging, and listing of early American publications. These classic bibliographies are usually known by the names of the principal compilers and editors. As the publication universe grew throughout the nineteenth and twentieth centuries, it became impossible for any one person, and even difficult for a team, to perform the labors of love the early bibliographers accomplished. This section contains the now-famous classic bibliographies of Americana that every historian should be aware of on historical principle.

During the 1950s through the 1970s, many catalogs of libraries and special collections that hold copies of the publications of importance in American history were published. Also during this period there were many microfilming projects to film copies of the rare, original publications. Many of the microfilming projects were based upon those printed catalogs or classic bibliographies. By and large, microfilming projects have been replaced with new projects organized to digitize original texts rather than film them.

The majority of the library catalogs were compiled by photographing the card catalogs or shelflists of libraries and archival institutions. Published catalogs of library collections aid the researcher in several ways. They serve to provide information on the specific holdings of a library, special collection, or archival repository; they aid in the compilation of bibliographies by bringing new sources to the attention of the researcher; and they can assist in defining the boundaries or subtopics for subjects of research. For many of the catalogs, several supplements were subsequently published to update the base set. As the national cataloging databases grew in retrospective depth and as individual libraries converted to machine-readable cataloging, the publication of printed catalogs diminished. This section lists only a few of the major library catalogs relevant to study and research in U.S. history. There are many others for special and rare collections. Near the end of the period of published library catalogs, Bonnie R. Nelson compiled the *Guide to Published Library Catalogs* (Scarecrow, 1982). The guide lists 429 published library catalogs organized into 33 topical categories. It is useful for researchers seeking definitive bibliographical sources for specific subjects and collections. A more up-to-date listing of libraries and electronic library catalogs can be found at http://www.academicinfo.net/infoscilibcat.html. Although nearly all academic libraries and historical collections have electronic databases for their holdings, there are still many older cataloging records that have not been converted to electronic records. Thus, the historical researcher must be aware of the classic bibliographies and printed library catalogs, lest important early works escape their attention.

34. American Bibliography: A Chronological Dictionary of all Books, Pamphlets and Periodical Publications Printed in the United States of America from the Genesis of Printing in 1639 down to the Year 1800; with Bibliographical and Biographical Notes.

Charles Evans. Worcester, MA: American Antiquarian Society, 1903–1959. Repr. 1941–1967. 14v. ISBN 0-8446-1175-1.

It was Evans's ambition to bring under bibliographical control all of the titles printed in the United States from 1639 to 1800. Although his work did not achieve this goal, it is one of the monuments of early bibliography, listing almost 36,000 titles. The arrangement is chronological by date, with each title successively numbered. The number assigned to each book is referred to as the "Evans" number, and until the publication by Shipton and Mooney (below) it was the means of access to the microcard/microfiche collection, *Early American Imprints, 1689–1800* (Readex, 1955–1983), based on the bibliography. In addition to providing the bibliographical citation, Evans's work lists library locations according to abbreviations of the bibliographer's own devising. Evans died before the last volume was completed, and his work was finished by Shipton. The fourteenth volume of the set is an author-title index in one alphabetical arrangement compiled by Bristol. The Evans bibliographies have been used for research involving early American history, literature, philosophy, religion, and other topics.

As bibliographers and historians worked with the Evans bibliography, omissions were discovered. In 1970, a supplement was published that was compiled by Roger Bristol from the systematic combing of many bibliographies and lists. The *Supplement to Charles Evans' American Bibliography* (University Press of Virginia, 1970), published for the Bibliographic Society of Virginia, includes over 11,000 additional entries to the original bibliography by Evans. An index compiled by Bristol to accompany the supplement was published separately in 1971. The *Index to Supplement to Charles Evans' American Bibliography* (University Press of Virginia, 1971) includes one listing for authors and titles and another for printers, publishers, and booksellers. Bristol had previously compiled an *Index of Printers, Publishers, and Booksellers Indicated by Charles Evans in His American Bibliography* (Bibliographical Society of the University of Virginia, 1961).

In 1969, the American Antiquarian Society published the *National Index of American Imprints Through 1800: The Short-Title Evans,* compiled by Clifford Kenyon Shipton and James E. Mooney. Although the index by Shipton and Mooney is titled the "Short-Title Evans," it is actually an alphabetic guide to the Readex microprint collection *Early American Imprints, First Series (Evans), 1639–1800.* A more fitting title would be the "Shortcut to the Microform Collection," for until the publication of this index it was necessary to obtain the Evans number in order to locate a title in the microform collection. Shipton and Mooney include in one alphabetical sequence all of the entries in Evans, along with the Evans number of each. The index also includes all of the items in Bristol's supplement to Evans. Much more than a short-title index, this work further indicates errors and ghosts in the previous bibliographies. Because of its cumulative and comprehensive nature, the *National Index* replaced Evans for most research purposes. Anyone seeking the full text of pre-1800 U.S. publications should first consult this index. In addition to being listed in the *National Index,* the bibliographic records for works in the *Early American Imprints First Series* (Evans) microform collection are in the RLIN database.

A digital edition of *Series I. Evans (1639–1800)* is being produced by Readex in cooperation with the American Antiquarian Society. The Evans Digital Edition will include every item previously produced on microform plus over 1,200 additional works located, filmed, and cataloged since the completion of the filming of the microform edition of *Early*

American Imprints. Access to the Evans Digital Edition will be via the Internet. Bibliographic records created by the American Antiquarian Society will be integrated into the database as well, providing additional access points. Images will be provided in PDF format for viewing, printing and storing. When complete, the Digital Edition will be the preferred access to both the texts and the bibliographical information contained in all the former publications in the Evans line.

35. American Bibliography: A Preliminary Checklist for 1801–1819. Ralph Shaw and Richard H. Shoemaker. New York: Scarecrow, 1958–1963. 14v. **Addenda, List of Sources, Library Symbols,** v. 20. Scarecrow, 1965. **Title Index,** v. 21. Scarecrow, 1965. **Corrections, Author Index,** v. 22. Scarecrow, 1966.

The names of Ralph Shaw and Richard Shoemaker are associated with the series they inaugurated and compiled for many years. Designed to begin where Evans (entry 34) left off, with the same root title, the series consists of one volume for each imprint year, beginning in 1801. Richard Shoemaker continued the *American Bibliography* series under the title *A Checklist of American Imprints for 1820–1929* (Scarecrow, 1964–1971, 10v.). After the death of Richard Shoemaker, Gayle Cooper continued for a few years. Beginning with the 1831 imprint year (Scarecrow, 1972–), Carol Rinderknecht and Scott Bruntjen assumed the compilation of the series. The volumes for the 1840 decade began publication in 1990, with 1845 being published in 1996. The publisher plans to extend the series through the 1875 imprint year.

The 1801–1819 series was largely compiled by combing other printed works. Beginning with the volume for 1821, locations for the books were added to the bibliographical information, and the compilers examined actual copies rather than depending upon secondary sources for information. The organization is alphabetical by main entry, with title and imprint information included. The usefulness of the volumes for each imprint year has been greatly enhanced by the publication of cumulated author and title indexes. An additional index for the first decade is *Printers, Publishers, and Book Sellers Index, Geographical Index* by Frances P. Newton (Scarecrow, 1983). This index is especially valuable to historians of U.S. printing and publishing.

Beginning with the series for the 1840s there is a new entry-numbering system that gives each entry sequential numbering, with the imprint year as the prefix. For previous series the entries were sequentially numbered in each volume but did not contain the imprint year to indicate in which volume the item appeared. All series have NUC (National Union Catalog) library location symbols added to the bibliographical information. The *American Bibliography* series is much more comprehensive and accurate than earlier bibliographical catalogs such as Roorbach's (entry 39) and the *American Catalogue of Books* (entry 39n).

The microprint collection *Early American Imprints, Second Series, 1801–1819* (New York: Readex Microprint, 1964–) contains the full text of works listed in *American Bibliography, 1801–1819.* The collection is arranged in chronological and numerical order according to the Shaw/Shoemaker numbers. Bibliographic records for the titles in this series are available in both the OCLC and RLIN databases.

36. The American Historical Association's Guide to Historical Literature. Mary Beth Norton and Pamela Gerardi. New York: Oxford University Press, 1995. 2v. ISBN 0195099532.

The *AHA Guide* is comprehensive for the field of history. The third edition of the *AHA Guide* had been long-awaited as the previous edition was published in 1961. The third edition contains almost 27,000 annotated citations arranged chronologically and by national and regional history, written by hundreds of historians who provide commentary on the best and most useful works in their fields. It covers all eras internationally from prehistory through the latter years of the twentieth century. This bibliography is regarded as an authoritative source for students and researchers in American history.

*37. Americana in German Archives: A Guide to Primary Sources Concerning the History of the United States and Canada. Christof Mauch, ed. Washington, D.C.: German Historical Institute, 2001. 317p. (Reference Guides of the German Historical Institute, no. 12.) Available: http://www.ghi-dc.org.

Archives are arranged alphabetically by city in this guide to 233 federal and state, as well as city, district, church, and private archives that have significant holdings relating to the United States and Canada. Most of the records are related to German emigration to the United States and Canada, but a significant number deal with political relations between the United States and Germany. The entries provide directory information about the archives with address, contact information including Web addresses, and a brief description of the holdings. The guide is available free from the German Historical Institute and also at the Institute's Web site. This is a good introductory research guide for anyone working in German-American relations.

38. Bibliographic Guide to North American Studies. Boston: G.K. Hall, 2001. ISBN 0-7838-9214-4.

A number of bibliographic guides were begun after the closing of the New York Public Library card catalog (entry 44). The title of this guide was recently changed from *Bibliographic Guide to North American History.* The scope of the guide extends from before the European discovery of America to the present, including coverage of constitutional history, foreign relations, diplomatic history, political history, social history and the history of nationalities, Native Americans, and races in the United States. One valuable feature is that nonbook materials are included so that each bibliography fairly covers the universe of publication for the subject. The annual guides are useful for collection development and acquisitions as well as reference and research.

39. Bibliotheca Americana: A Catalogue of American Publications, Including Reprints and Original Works from 1820 to 1861. Orville Augustus Roorbach. New York: Roorbach, 1852–1861. Repr., 1939. 4v.

Until the *American Bibliography* series by Scarecrow Press (entry 35) is complete through 1875, Roorbach will remain one of the few sources for the 1840–1861 imprint years. Roorbach does contain periodical as well as monograph titles and prices.

The compilation by Roorbach is continued by the *American Catalogue of Books (Original and Reprints). Published in the United States from Jan. 1861 to Jan. 1871, with*

Date of Publication, Size, Price, and Publisher's Name (New York: Wiley, 1866–1871. Repr., 1938. 2v.) The *American Catalogue of Books* contains the same basic publication information as Roorbach's. It also contains a list of societies with their publications. Because it covers the time period of the Civil War, the *American Catalogue* is a useful research tool for pamphlets, sermons, and addresses from the war years.

A second, almost identical title is the *American Catalogue founded by F. Leypoldt, 1876–1910* (New York: Publishers Weekly, 1880–1911. Repr., 1941. 8v. in 13 parts). This second *American Catalogue* is a trade tool and can be regarded as the earliest *Books in Print* for U.S. publishing, as it covered all books published in the United States for sale at the time. It is more reliable than its two predecessors, Roorbach and the first *American Catalogue.*

40. Bibliotheca Americana: Catalogue of the John Carter Brown Library in Brown University; Books Printed 1675–1700. Providence, RI: Brown University Press, 1973. 484p. ISBN 0-87057-141-9. **Short-Title List of Additions, Books Printed 1471–1700.** Providence, RI: Brown University, 1973. 67p. ISBN 0-87057-141-9.

The scope of the collection begun by John Carter Brown was anything "printed during the colonial period, that reflects what happened as a result of the discovery and settlement of the New World." The original *Bibliotheca Americana: A Catalog of Books Relating to North and South America in the Library of the Late John Carter Brown of Providence, R.I* was published by the library between 1865 and 1871. Later catalogs published by Brown University Press largely supercede the earlier editions, which were reprinted by Kraus between 1961 and 1965. The Kraus reprint incorporates corrections and annotations by Wilberforce Eames from the New York Public Library copy of *Biblioteca Americana.* So rich are the collections that it has been estimated that roughly half of the works in the published catalogs for the fifteenth through seventeenth centuries are not listed in any other bibliography. There is a particularly high proportion of English sermons and theological titles. The catalog for 1675–1700 is arranged alphabetically, with indexes by title and subject. Many of the entries give references to other bibliographies that have more detailed descriptions of the work. The John Carter Brown Library collections are a rich resource for research in colonial U.S. history. The printed catalogs provide remote bibliographic access to these resources. The holdings of the library have been cataloged into the *Eighteenth Century Short-Title Catalogue* available as an electronic file in RLIN (entry 17).

41. Bibliotheca Americana: A Dictionary of Books Relating to America, from Its Discovery to the Present Time. Joseph Sabin, Wilberforce Eames, and R.W.G. Vail. New York: Bibliographical Society of America (and others), 1862–1892, 1928–1936. 29v.

Sabin's objective was to list all books published in the United States and those published abroad relating to the history of the entire Western Hemisphere. He combed a number of major European bibliographies and listed anything that came to his attention from publishers' flyers to company reports. The monumental dictionary began in the 1860s, and several others continued the compilation after Sabin's death. The publication eventually reached 29 volumes with 106,413 entries before its completion in 1936. One of the felicitous aspects of Sabin's *Dictionary* is the sheer pleasure one interested in U.S. history can derive from simply browsing through the work. Fugitive publications such as bylaws of organizations, railroad company reports, and excursion trip brochures abound. Many South American and European publications are listed, as are issues of serial publications. For use in conducting a systematic search, the set is much more frustrating. There is one alphabetical arrangement that spans the entire length of the publication period. The entries are mostly by author, although many books are entered under city, state, corporate entry, or title. Full bibliographic information is given, often including contents listings and notes with references to other works. In some cases reviews are cited or library locations given. Later work by others has revealed that there were many duplicate listings among the 106,000 entries.

The maddening aspects of using Sabin were greatly alleviated with the publication of J.E. Molnar's *Author-Title Index to Joseph Sabin's Dictionary of Books Relating to America* (Scarecrow, 1974, 3v.). Molnar's index is a reference work in itself, for he made an effort to identify anonymous authors. Categories indexed include editors, compilers, publishers, engravers, illustrators and cartographers, corporate authors and government agencies, main titles, half titles, and series titles. Molnar even indexed the works mentioned in the notes. The index is referenced to Sabin entry numbers. Molnar's index makes it possible to identify and use the wealth of information in the Sabin bibliography.

Proquest/UMI publishes *The Sabin Collection* in microfiche of selected works listed in Sabin. Printed guides arranged alphabetically by main entry accompany the microfiche collection.

42. British Imprints Relating to North America, 1621–1760: An Annotated Checklist.
R.C. Simmons. London: British Library, 1996. 395p. ISBN 0-7123-0363-4.

The most significant collections outside of the United States of interest to the researcher in U.S. history are in Great Britain. The scope of this checklist containing 3,212 entries is publications in Great Britain that relate to the subject of North America during the colonial era. While there are a number of bibliographies and catalogs that already cover the same imprint and subject parameters, this checklist does include additional entries not found in those earlier bibliographical works. Entries were culled from *A Short-title Catalogue of Books Printed in England, Scotland, and Ireland,* the *National Union Catalog, pre-1956 Imprints* (entry 46), Sabin's *Bibliotheca Americana* (entry 41), the card catalogs of the John Carter Brown Library (entry 40) the British Library (entry 3), the National Library of Scotland, and the Cambridge University Library. The checklist is arranged in chronological order by imprint year and then alphabetically within the year. Full bibliographic information is included as well as two locations in either British or North American libraries. The scope of publications included does not include maps, periodicals and magazines, editions of treaties, poetry, and dramatic works. A valuable feature of the work is an excellent introduction on the history of printing in England and North America with a discussion of many well-known titles published during the period covered by the checklist. Also included are a list of abbreviations and a list of library symbols for the libraries that own the titles in the checklist. There are both author and titles indexes that give the year of publication and the checklist number for each entry. The work is useful for any researcher studying the colonial period in America or Great Britain.

Another guide to collections in the British Library relating to American History is *A Guide to Americana: The American Collections in the British Library* by Gregory Palmer (K.G. Saur, 1988). Palmer's guide is divided into two distinct sections, each accomplishing a different purpose. The first section is really a history of the British Museum, now the British Library. In tracing the history of the collections that contain significant materials relating to the Americas and the United States, Palmer in effect reviews the history of the British Library with an emphasis on the collecting of Americana. The role of U.S. publishers in the development of the U.S. collections in the British Library in the nineteenth century is covered in some depth. The second section of the book guides researchers in the techniques and procedures for locating the various collections and identifying materials of use. Part 2 is arranged by format, with chapters on microfilms, newspapers, maps, music, manuscripts, and so on. The index includes personal names. Given the wealth of unique material relating to the history of the United States in the British Library, this book is a real service to historians.

Broader in scope than Palmer's guide, both in subject matter and in the number of libraries, is *The United States, a Guide to Library Holdings in the UK,* compiled by Peter Snow (British Library Lending Division in association with SCONUL; Meckler, 1982). The holdings of over 350 libraries throughout the United Kingdom are described in Snow's guide. Subject matter encompasses the arts, humanities, social sciences, and sciences. All formats are covered, including audiovisual materials. The guide covers large collections of Americana as well as collections on specific subjects, individuals, or periods. Information about the services of each library, including photocopying services, is given. There is an index listing over 1,800 microforms and multivolume works with library locations.

A companion to the guides for printed resources is *A Guide to Manuscripts Relating to America in Great Britain and Ireland,* edited by John W. Raimo (Meckler Books for the British Association for American Studies, 2nd ed.,1979). The arrangement of this guide is geographical by county according to the new county structure established in Britain in 1974. Over 100 new repositories were added in this second edition, which is 65 percent longer than the first edition. The definition of history was enlarged in the second edition to include immigration, economics, and social history. The second edition also includes information on private collections described under the National Register of Archives in London and Edinburgh, through which inquiries regarding those collections can be made. The indexing is detailed, with personal and geographical names, subjects, and archival repositories. Although it has not been updated, this guide is still a useful one because of the large number of collections it locates for the researcher.

Anyone planning to conduct research in Great Britain or researchers seeking additional sources will find these guides useful.

43. A Dictionary Catalog of American Books Pertaining to the 17th Through 19th Centuries. American Antiquarian Society Library. Westport, CT: Greenwood Press, 1971. 20v. ISBN 0-83713265-7.

The American Antiquarian Society Library is one of the premiere collections of Americana in the world. The collecting parameters are confined to the "territories that became the United States of America and to the former French and English parts of North America from the period of settlement by Europeans through the year 1876." The library was conceived and built to be a research library. It is the headquarters for the cataloging of American imprints included in the *Eighteenth Century Short-Title Catalog,* a large number of which are in the society's collections. The *Dictionary Catalog* lists the American imprints prior to 1821 and literary publications of nineteenth-century authors. It is useful for the identification and verification of scarce publications and in preparation for a site visit. *The Collections and Programs of the American Antiquarian Society: A 175th Anniversary Guide* (American Antiquarian Society, 1987) describes the more remarkable holdings. Among these are maps and atlases, sheet music, engravings and lithographs, manuscript and archival collections, pamphlets, broadsides, newspapers, hymnals, and dime novels. Together, the catalog and the guide give a fairly complete overview of the contents of the collections. All researchers in the history of the United States prior to the twentieth century will need to use this catalog as a resource. The American Antiquarian Society offers fellowships to support scholars' use of the library for research. The collections of the American Antiquarian Society are also cataloged in the *Eighteenth Century Short-Title Catalogue,* the RLIN database (entry 17).

44. Dictionary Catalog of the Research Libraries of the New York Public Library, 1911–1971. New York: New York Public Library Astor, Lenox, and Tilden Foundations; Boston: distr. by G.K. Hall, 1979. 800v. ISBN 0-8161-0320-8.

The collections of the New York Public Research Libraries are rich in materials on the history of New York, the theater, natural history, technology, local history and genealogy, tobacco, the growth of U.S. business, and cartographic materials, to mention only a few prominent subjects. The 800-volume dictionary catalog was published after the NYPL closed its card catalog and implemented an online catalog. Two supplements have been published to the original 800-volume edition: one for the years 1972–1980, published in 1980 in 64 volumes, and a second for the years 1981–1988 published in 1988 in 73 volumes.

The *Dictionary Catalog* includes the three largest collections for general research—history and the humanities; economics and public affairs; and science and technology. The catalog also includes the American History and the Local History and Genealogy collections. It is especially valuable for the subject approach made possible by the dictionary arrangement. There are also many analytic entries for journal articles, a feature not found in most library catalogs. Because of the comprehensiveness of the catalog and the depth of the NYPL collections, researchers who have access to this catalog should make it an essential part of their research strategy.

A number of special subject catalogs from the New York Public library collections were also produced. One of these is the *Dictionary Catalog of the History of the Americas* (G.K. Hall, 1961, 28v.), which covers the history of the Western Hemisphere from the prehistory and archaeology of Native Americans through the period of exploration and discovery of the New World, settlement and contact with the white man, and down to the modern period. The collection is strong in cartography from the fifteenth through the eighteenth centuries. There is even material on Hawaii, the Philippines, and Oceania. As is the case with all New York Public Library dictionary catalogs, there are helpful analytics provided for periodical articles and chapters in books. All of the holdings of the New York Public Library prior to the beginning of the online catalog were not retrospectively converted so that the printed catalogs are still useful for historical research.

45. European Americana: A Chronological Guide to Works Printed in Europe Relating to the Americas, 1493–1776. John Alden, ed., with Dennis C. Landis. New York:

Readex Books, 1980–1988. ISBN 0-918414-03-2 (v. 1) 1980; 0-918414-09-1 (v. 2) 1982; 0-317-59108-8 (v. 5) 1987; 0-918414-02-4 (v. 6) 1988. 0-918414-00-8 (series).

The quincentenary of the discovery of America was the impetus for the compilation of this bibliographical work. The objective of the set is to document, year by year, the growing impact of the New World on the old European consciousness. Whereas Sabin's dictionary (entry 41) is arranged by author (or main entry), this bibliography, which covers the same time period and many of the same works, is arranged chronologically by imprint year. This alternative approach enables researchers to focus on publications that reflect the social and political milieu of a particular time period.

The purpose of this bibliography is to list those books that were printed in Europe and reflect the European view of the Americas. The chronological listing makes it possible to know what contemporaries were reading at the time. Many works not listed in Sabin are identified in this bibliography, which broadly covers subject areas in the sciences and literature as well as political and cultural texts. The entries in the main chronological listing contain full bibliographic information, with all editions of a work listed. Other bibliographical references are also cited, and Library of Congress locations symbols are given. There is a separate index of printers and booksellers by geographical location, with chronological listings of their publications. There is also an alphabetical index of printers and booksellers, giving their geographical location. The final index is an author, title, and subject index. This is a key bibliography for historians of the exploration and colonial period of the Americas. The indexes for printers and booksellers make it indispensable for those researching the history of the printing and publishing trades as well. As with other bibliographies and library catalogs for this period, cataloging and location records are available in the RLIN file for the *Eighteenth Century Short-Title Catalog* (entry 17) and the cataloging projects imprints from the earlier centuries.

46. National Union Catalog, Pre-1956 Imprints. A Cumulative Author List Representing Library of Congress Printed Cards and Titles Reported by Other American Libraries. London: Mansell, 1968–1980. 685v. ISBN 0-7201-1562-0. **Supp.** 1980–1981. v. 686–754. ISBN 0-7201-1947-2.

The Library of Congress (LC) is one of the largest libraries in the world. It was founded to be exactly what it is named, a library for the Congress of the United States. Although it has never been designated as the national library, it is the U.S. library of copyright and receives every copyrighted publication. Throughout the nineteenth and twentieth centuries the library has grown into one of the foremost research libraries in the world, collecting in all subject areas except the agricultural and medical sciences.

The Library of Congress began publishing a book catalog in 1942. In 1952 the title was changed to the *National Union Catalog,* signifying that records and location symbols for other libraries had been incorporated into the work. The set known as "pre-1956," or "Mansell," is the most useful to historians because it contains works published before 1956 that were cataloged by the Library of Congress and other major U.S. research libraries. The arrangement is alphabetical by author or main entry. There is no subject approach in the main catalogs. *Library of Congress Catalog, Books, Subjects,* a series of catalogs organized by Library of Congress subject headings, provides the only subject approach. A number of cumulative sets for the Library of Congress catalogs have been published by trade publishers. *Library of Congress National Union Catalog Author Lists, 1942–1962* (Detroit: Gale, 1969–1971. 152v.) is one such cumulation.

Because the main entry is the only access point in the Library of Congress author catalogs, it is often difficult to locate anonymous, corporate, governmental, or other works not having a personal author. The Carrollton Press performed a service to all who have struggled to locate materials in the Library of Congress catalogs when it published the *Cumulative Title Index to the Library of Congress Shelflist* (1983, 158v.). This bibliographic aid makes it much easier to locate and verify titles for which the complete bibliographic information is not known.

The Library of Congress (LC) discontinued printed publication of all of its various union catalogs in the 1990s. The LC and union catalog records are now available at http://www.loc.gov. Many bibliographic records were converted to machine-readable form, but one can never tell if there are gems left in the printed catalogs that were never converted to electronic format.

47. The New Sabin: Books Described by Joseph Sabin and His Successors, Now Described Again on the Basis of Examination of Original and Fully Indexed by Title, Subject, Joint Authors, and Institutions and Agencies. 10v. Lawrence S. Thompson. Troy, NY: Whitson Publishing, 1974–1986. **Cumulative Index. Volumes I-X.** 1986. 497p. ISBN 0-87875-330-3.

Although titled *The New Sabin,* the work by Thompson is not a revised edition of Sabin's *Dictionary of Books.* Many of the works listed in the original Sabin are included in the Thompson work, and many others from the same time period were added. The bibliographical information includes author, title, size, and volume/page numbers. The original Sabin number is not given, nor are LC card numbers or library locations. The entries are numbered consecutively within the 10 volumes. The *New Sabin* is an additional source for publications on the exploration of America from the sixteenth to the nineteenth centuries.

A worthy successor to the eclectic original Sabin is *U.S. Reference-iana (1481–1899): A Concise Guide to Over 4000 Books and Articles . . .,* published by Thomas Truxtun Moebs in 1989. The antique style of the title of this work almost obviates the need for further elaboration. Moebs, an antiquarian bookseller, compiled a very useful annotated listing of reference works and bibliographies by subject categories. This work is primarily focused on information sources about collectibles of all types and formats. Although Moebs does not specifically mention historians or researchers in his title, many of the 4,000 items listed in *U.S. Reference-iana* may be of value in a comprehensive scholarly search.

48. The Printed Catalogues of the Harvard College Library, 1723–1790. W.H. Bond and Hugh Amory, eds. New Castle, DE: Oak Knoll Press, 1996. 710p. ISBN 0-9620737-3-3.

These reproductions of three catalogs from the Harvard College Library in the eighteenth century were printed via a digital remastering process. The original catalogs were digitized and the resulting images enhanced to make them more readable. Thus, the old is made new. The first catalog, from 1723 with some 2,300 entries, is the first library catalog published in the now United States. It is valuable because the library burned in 1764 and that catalog is a partial record of what was lost. The second catalog is from 1773 and is not a full catalog of the library but only that of the undergraduate collection. It was compiled by John Winthrop. The third catalog is from 1790 and contains approximately 9,800 entries. The editors for this reproduction have supplied an "Index and Concordance" to facilitate use of the catalogs that are not in modern alphabetical order and do not follow modern bibliographic conventions. Researchers on the colonial period, of education in the eighteenth century, and book historians will find the catalogs useful.

49. Writings on American History. Washington, D.C.: American Historical Association, 1902–1961; Millwood, NJ: Kraus-Thomson. 1902–1961. ISBN 0364-2887.

Writings on American History is a title with a rather tangled history. The American Historical Association began publishing *Writings on American History* in 1902. For a number of years the title was published as part of the association's annual report. It was not published during the years 1904–1905 and 1941–1947. When publication resumed in 1948, the scope was narrowed to include only books and articles directly on the subject of United States history, and reviews for the entries were no longer cited. The organization is a classified subject arrangement with titles in chronological order according to the date of the subject matter with author, title, and subject indexes. This series ceased publication in 1961. Until it ceased, *Writings on American History* was the only indexing tool for U.S. history and still must be used for the years 1902–1954, when coverage by *America: History and Life* (entry 1) begins.

A new series annual with the same title, *Writings on American History,* began in 1973–1974 as a publication of the American Historical Association's bibliographical series. The basis for this annual bibliography was *Recently Published Articles,* which, until 1975, was a section of the quarterly *American Historical Review. Recently Published Articles* ceased publication in 1990, and *Writings on American History* ceased with the 1989/1990 volume.

The second series of *Writings* is organized into a general section, a chronological section, a geographical section, and a subject section. Articles are listed under all applicable headings. Over 4,000 journals were consulted in compiling the 1989/1990 volume, including many foreign journal titles. Although it was somewhat easier to use, *Writings* overlapped with the larger, more comprehensive *America: History and Life* (entry 1), which began publication in 1964.

A retrospective cumulation, *Writings on American History, 1962–73: A Subject Bibliography of Articles,* was published by KTO Press in 1975. This set was compiled by James J. Dougherty and sponsored by the American Historical Association. A companion set, *Writings on American History 1962–73, a Subject Bibliography of Books and Monographs* . . . , was also published by Kraus in 1985. Both of these publications fill in the years between the old and new series of *Writings on American History.* Although these retrospective sets overlap with *America: History and Life,* they are valuable as cumulations and for the difference in subject classifications they offer.

Somewhat of an update to the Writings on American History series is *United States History: A Bibliography of the New Writings on American History,* by Louise A. Merriam and James Warren Oberly (Manchester University Press, 1995). The 4,000 entries in this bibliography are mainly for publications from the 1980s and early 1990s. The compilers made an effort to select the most important books and articles published within that time frame. The entries are arranged in 10 chronological chapters by historical period and then subdivided by topics within the chapters. The topics are the same for each chapter so that the user can compile a selective bibliography across chapters. Because the scope of the bibliography is restricted to slightly over 10 years, there are many topics that do not have entries whereas other topics of great interest have many entries. Entries for monographs are annotated but not those for periodical articles. There are subject and author indexes. The bibliography provides a useful reference that pulls topics together, but the same results might be obtained through a database search.

BIOGRAPHICAL SOURCES

Biography is central to the study of history. Biographical sources for prominent persons have long existed, but the researcher making new history or the genealogist establishing family chronologies is searching for the not-so-famous, even the obscure. The hunt for biographical information has been made easier and faster with electronic databases that have eliminated the need to consult a large number of printed biographical sources.

The electronic databases have completely changed the search for biographical information. Nearly all of the long-running print titles are now available in online versions, many of them aggregated into large biographical resource databases. In addition to very large biographical databases published by leading reference publishers, there are many Web sites with biographical information. *Biography.com* is based on the popular A&E Biography series. It offers basic biographical information on more than 25,000 famous and notable persons and is available at http://biography.com. A private site, *Lives, the Biography Resource* (available at http://amillionlives.com) is maintained by Kenneth P. Lanxner. This is mainly a listing of links to other biographical sites, but it covers people who are no longer living. The site also contains an interesting section of articles on biographical criticism for scholars.

This section describes comprehensive biographical indexes available in electronic formats with separate entries for the printed titles. A few older, classic biographical sources are also included. The biographical research process in American history should start with either the printed or online version of the *ANB* (entry 50), the *Biography Reference Bank* (entry 51) or the *Biography Resource Center* (entry 52), after which more specialized reference sources can be consulted.

ELECTRONIC RESOURCES

*50. ANB Online. Oxford University Press, 2002B. [Electronic database]. Available: http://www.anb.org.

The 1995, 24-volume edition of *American National Biography* (entry 56) is available in an online database that takes the original print edition past the 1995 cutoff date. The *ANB* Web site features a powerful search interface with 80,000 hyperlinks between entries. Searching can be done by full text, subject name, gender, occupation, birth date and place, death date, bibliographic citations, and contributor name. The search capabilities of the site received rave reviews from *Library Journal* and *Reference Books Bulletin* for its design and power.

*51. Biography Reference Bank. H.W. Wilson, 2001B. [WilsonWeb electronic database]. Available: http://www.hwwilson.com.

Some 195,000 names from antiquity to present day are included in the Wilson *Biography Reference Bank,* which is an all-in-one comprehensive database combining Wilson *Biographies Plus Illustrated, Biography Index* (entry 58), and more. The biographies are quality profiles from articles in a wide range of periodicals and include PDF images, full-text articles, and abstracts. Searching can be by name, profession, gender, ethnicity, date of birth, place or origin, and more, making this database especially good for history, ethnic and gender studies, and other areas beyond straight biographical research. The database is updated weekly. This database does not index the contents of biographical dictionaries, but provides the full text of biographies that appear in periodicals; thus it is necessary to use this database in addition to the *Biography Resource Center* (entry 52) and the *ANB Online* (entry 50).

Another biographical database from H.W. Wilson is *Current Biography Illustrated,* available through WilsonWeb. This database contains the long-running print title *Current Biography,* 1940 to present (entry 59). More than 24,000 articles and more than 21,000 photographs, reflecting more than a half century of coverage are contained in the database. It provides biographies and obituaries of politicians, business people, journalists, actors, sports figures, artists, scientists, and other prominent figures from 1940 to the present. Approximately 3,000 word profiles give information on the subject's life and career, including his or her views, attitudes, and opinions, plus factual data and further readings. The database is updated with 200 profiles a year.

*52. Biography Resource Center. Farmington Hill, MI: Gale Group. [Electronic Database].

More than 50 of the most frequently consulted Gale biographical databases with nearly 250 full-text periodicals and over 1 million thumbnail biographies from the Marquis *Who's Who* are combined in the *Biography Resource Center* (entry 52) database. The major Gale printed sources *Encyclopedia of World Biography* and the *Scribner Encyclopedia of American Lives* (*SEAL,* entry 61) are included. The online biographical resources published by Gale have been incorporated into one database that includes the Marquis *Who's Who* (entry 62) publications through a partnership with that publisher. The database includes the *Biography and Genealogy Master Index* (entry 57). *Biography Resource Center* is a comprehensive source for detailed biographical information on notable individuals worldwide and throughout history. Brief biographies, narrative biographies, and full-text magazine and newspaper articles are included. There are links to related biographies and periodical articles within the database and to Web sites that provide citations to the texts. Titles held by the subscribing library are indicated. The coverage for most periodical titles dates from the 1970s and 1980s. Searching can be by name, birth/death years, places, nationality, ethnicity, occupation, and gender. This electronic resource is a good starting place for biographical information.

*53. NameBase: A Cumulative Index of Books and Clippings. Arlington, VA: Public Information Research. [Electronic Database]. Available: http://www.namebase.org or http://www.pir.org/nbhome.html.

Now a Web database, *Namebase* was started in the 1960s by New Left activist Daniel Brandt who incorporated Public Information Research in the 1980s to continue the work. The database includes over 100,000 names with over 260,000 citations drawn from books and serials with a few documents obtained under the Freedom of Information Act. Individuals are not identified in the usual biographical sense; the database simply provides citations to where the individuals' names have been found. The database uses data mining techniques to establish relationships, creating a social network diagram by using cluster analysis. Thus the researcher can obtain information about the people that a person has associated with. There is a country search capability and a document scan that will look up Web pages, another way to establish individual affiliations. *Namebase* is most useful to journalists and researchers tracking down investigative reports or looking for connections between names. It provides access to the intelligence community and is useful for alternative approaches to historical interpretation of events. Undoubtedly it provides information not accessed in other periodical indexes and databases.

PRINT INDEXES AND COLLECTIVE BIOGRAPHY

54. The American Biographical Archive. New York: K.G. Saur, 1986–1989. 1,842 microfiche. Accompanied by 6v. index titled **American Biographical Index.** Printed **Index,** 19v. ISBN 0-86291-0 (set). Series II, 730 microfiche, 1995.

Biographical dictionaries and encyclopedias originally published between 1702 and 1920 in the United States, Canada, and England are reproduced in this microfiche collection. The 367 biographical works cover 300,000 individuals from the earliest period of North American history through the early twentieth century. All men and women of local, national, or international importance who resided in or were associated with the United States and Canada are included. The sources were reproduced, annotated, cross-referenced, and cumulated into one alphabetical sequence. The coverage of the collection is 15 times greater than the *Dictionary of American Biography* (entry 60). A printed index accompanies the microfiche collection. The index is a reference work in itself, giving birth and death dates, occupation, and a list of sources in which the individual appears, as well as the fiche number and frames where the full text of the entries is reproduced. A second series published in 1995 includes twentieth-century biographical works. It is likely the *American Biographical Archive* will be found only in large research libraries because it is an expensive acquisition. In those institutions in which it is available, it forms a comprehensive biographical resource for U.S. history that has not entirely been superceded by online databases.

55. American Diaries: An Annotated Bibliography of Published American Diaries and Journals. Laura Arksey et al. Detroit: Gale, 1983–1987. **Diaries Written from 1492–1864,** v. 1. 1983. 311p. ISBN 0-8103-1800-8. **Diaries Written from 1845–1980,** v. 2. 1987. 501p. ISBN 0-8103-1801-6.

The time span covered and the number of entries make this two-volume set a major source for determining the existence of published diaries and journals. The first volume is a revision and expansion of *American Diaries, an Annotated Bibliography of American Diaries Written Prior to the Year 1861* by William Matthews (University of California Press, 1945). The first volume contains 2,780 entries, and the second volume has 3,263 items. The introduction explains the types of personal journals included and the sources used in compiling the bibliography. The definition of "American" is very broad, including material from all 50 states and Spanish American sites. The arrangement is chronological by the year in which the diary was begun, then alphabetical by author. The diaries cited are both separate publications and those published in periodicals or parts of larger works. The indexing is extensive, with subjects, geographical names, and names of primary authors, as well as persons mentioned in the annotations. Many of the diaries are by individuals prominent in U.S. history, but others are not well known. This bibliography is of use to anyone seeking personal accounts for specific geographical regions, time periods, or specific individuals.

A similar publication is *American Autobiography, 1945–1980: A Bibliography* edited by Mary Louise Briscoe (University of Wisconsin Press, 1983). This title continues an earlier work by Louis Kaplan, *A Bibliography of American Autobiographies* (University of Wisconsin Press, 1961), which included autobiographies published before 1945. The Briscoe bibliography begins with 1945 imprints but also includes earlier items not in Kaplan. Together these two bibliographies list over 11,000 autobiographies published in book form by private and trade presses. The definition of "autobiography" is very broad, encompassing all manner of personal accounts: diaries, journals, memoirs, and collections of letters. The arrangement is alphabetical by author in both bibliographies, with subject indexes by occupation, place, subject, and personal name. These bibliographies are useful for anyone seeking published first-person accounts by occupation, subject, locale, or specific individual.

Broader coverage is provided by *Biographical Books, 1876–1949* (New York: Bowker, 1983; *1950–1980,* 1980). The database for the retrospective and cumulative edition of *American Book Publishing Record Cumulative, 1876–1949* and later supplements is the source for the entries in the *Biographical Books* bibliographies. The term "biographical" is broadly defined to encompass all manner of works containing biographical material, including directories and juvenile literature. The entries give basic publication information on the books indexed. One feature of these compilations is the vocation index, which allows for research on occupations or areas of interest as well as individuals. There is a great deal of overlap between the Bowker bibliographies and those of Arksey and Briscoe above. All are useful depending upon their availability in local libraries.

*56. American National Biography. John A. Garraty and Mark C. Carnes, eds. New York: Oxford University Press, 1999. 24v. ISBN 0-19-520635-5. **Supplement 1.** Paul Betz and Mark C. Carnes, eds. 2002. 900 p. ISBN 0-19-515063-5. **ANB Online.** Available: http://www.anb.org. (entry 50).

The *ANB* is a completely new biographical work that has not entirely replaced the *DAB* (*Dictionary of American Biography,* entry 60) but offers a new alternative to that work. As in the case of the *DAB,* the new *ANB* has been compiled under the auspices of the American Council of Learned Societies, a federation of scholarly societies in the humanities and social sciences, which decided an entirely new biographical work was needed to incorporate new historical perspectives, research methods, and emphases on new fields and occupations. The general editors, Garraty and Carnes, were previously affiliated with the DAB. Contributors of the signed entries are scholars and specialists. The *ANB* includes about 17,450 notables from every field of endeavor who died before 1996. The term "American" is defined broadly as a person whose significance, achievement, fame, or influence occurred during residence within what is now the United States, or whose life or career directly influenced the course of U.S. history. The editors included new scholarship and people who were missed in the *DAB,* especially women and ethnic minorities. The work offers readable, informative, and critical biographies for each subject, the location of their papers, and selective bibliographies. In addition to the usual factual biographical information, the concluding paragraph of each entry attempts to assess the individual's contributions from the perspective of the late twentieth century. There are indexes by subject, contributor, place of birth, and occupation. The *ANB* is a premier single, authoritative printed source of high quality for historical biographical research. An online version begun in 2002 takes the print edition past the 1995 cutoff date to include biographies of recently deceased figures (entry 50).

Also edited by John A. Garraty, the *Encyclopedia of American Biography,* 2nd ed., (Harper/Collins, 1996) is a one-volume work providing information on over 1,000 significant and famous Americans. Entries are evaluative of the subject's contributions and accomplishments, a feature not found in most biographical works.

Another one-volume biographical work is *The Cambridge Dictionary of American Biography,* edited by John Bowman (Cambridge University Press, 1995). Intended to be a comprehensive biographical reference work of Americans, living and dead, it contains 9,000 brief biographies. It covers all careers and all history of the United States from colonial times to the present. Special attention has been paid to providing coverage of worthy individuals belonging to groups often neglected in the past, such as women, African Americans, and other minority groups.

*57. Biography and Genealogy Master Index. 2nd ed. Barbara McNeil. Detroit: Gale, 1980. 8v. Ann. supp. with five-year cumulations, 1981–. ISSN 0730-1316. 1996–2000 cumulation. 4v. 1999. ISBN 0-8103-1618-8.

The first edition of this compilation in 1975 had the title *Biographical Dictionaries Master Index.* The second edition indexed the biographies in over 350 current and retrospective reference works. Prior to the publication of the first edition it was necessary to consult all of these works individually. By the end of the twentieth century, the *Master Index* contained over 11 million entries from 150 volumes and editions of 80 collective biographies, biographical dictionaries, subject encyclopedias, indexes, and works of literary criticism. The emphasis is on U.S. individuals, but a number of foreign biographical tools are also included. Names are listed in one alphabetical sequence. For each name, abbreviated citations of biographical sources are listed. Variant forms of names have not been reconciled, so a person may be listed more than once. Some entries include birth and death dates. When this information is missing, it is difficult to distinguish between individuals with identical names. Entries indicate when a portrait is included with the biography. Gale Group has continued to issue two-volume printed updates with five-year annual cumulations. The database for the *Master Index* is used to produce other biographical indexes by occupations and subject fields.

Prior to the second edition of the *Master Index,* which contains retrospective works, the *Historical Biographical Dictionaries Master Index* was published in 1980 (Gale). Thirty-four of the principal retrospective biographical reference works are indexed in this set. At the time, there were some living individuals in the historical index because of the sources included. A number of works are covered in both of the sources, such as the *Dictionary of*

American Biography (entry 60). Others, such as *Appleton's Cyclopedia,* are indexed only in the *Historical Biographical Dictionaries Master Index.* Not all retrospective reference works are in the historical index, so historical researchers must use both the *Historical Biographical Dictionaries Master Index* and the *Biography and Genealogy Master Index.*

The *Biography and Genealogy Master Index* is available online in the Gale *Biography Resource Center* database (entry 52). The database can be searched by names and variant names, birth or death years, source publication, year of publication, and portrait availability.

A less expensive version of the *Biography and Genealogy Master Index* is produced in microfiche under the title *Bio-Base. Bio-Base 2000 Master Cumulation* provides more than 12.7 million citations from more than 1,250 biographical dictionaries and who's whos. The 2001 edition contains a bibliographic listing of all the sources indexed in *Bio-Base 2000 Master Cumulation.*

*58. Biography Index. New York: H.W. Wilson. v. 1–, 1946–. Quart. with ann. cumulations. ISSN 0006-3053. [WilsonWeb Electronic database; CD-ROM].

This work indexes biographical information from periodicals, collected biographical works, and biographical and nonbiographical monographs. It is a general biographical source not limited to U.S. figures. Over 2,500 English-language books are indexed annually, including works of individual and collective biography, autobiographical memoirs, diaries, letters, bibliographies, biographical novels, drama, poetry, and juvenile literature. The index is arranged alphabetically by the names of the subjects. A list by occupation or profession is also included. Basic bibliographic information on monographs indexed is given in a list of those works included in each issue. The number of years this index has been published makes it useful for historical research. Coverage in the online database dates from the mid-1980s.

*59. Current Biography. New York: H.W. Wilson. 1940–. ISSN 0011-3344. **Current Biography Cumulated Index: 1940–2000.** 2001. ISBN 0-8242-0997. [WilsonWeb electronic database; CD-ROM].

The number of years this title has been published makes it useful for historical research despite its title. The biographies in this monthly periodical are taken mainly from news articles. A photograph is included with the majority of the sketches. Although the purpose of the periodical is to give current biographical information on newsworthy individuals, short obituaries are also included. A cumulative index covers 1940–2000. The WilsonDisc CD-ROM version of *Current Biography* permits searching by name, profession, keyword, place of origin, gender, race/ethnicity, and birth/death dates to access the full text of biographies and obituaries that have appeared in the periodical. The title is also available as an online database.

*60. Dictionary of American Biography. New York: Scribner's, 1996. 21v. (10 base volumes, 10 supp. with index), 1996. ISBN 0-684-80540-5. [CD-ROM].

This title is the best known of U.S. biographical reference tools, one reason being its similarity to the well-known British *Dictionary of National Biography* (*DNB*). The scholarly *DAB* was first published as a set with over 13,000 entries, sponsored by the American

Council of Learned Societies. Supplements have brought the number of entries to over 19,000. The first set, published 1928–1937, contains biographies with both career and personal information, but beginning with the fifth supplement the personal information has been excluded. Persons included are judged to have made significant contributions to U.S. history through politics or career achievements. Anyone who has resided in the United States or its territories may be included. The biographical articles feature a bibliography. The reprint edition has an errata section of corrections to the original first edition. The comprehensive index published in 1996 contains six separate listings: 1) names of biographees with authors; 2) contributors with the subjects of their articles; 3) birthplaces arranged by state or foreign country; 4) educational institutions attended by the biographees; 5) an occupations index; and 6) a topical index. The *DAB* is also indexed in the *Biography and Genealogy Master Index* (entry 57).

The *DAB* was published under the auspices of the American Council of Learned Societies, which decided to discontinue its sponsorship. A lawsuit between the ACLS and Scribner's, the publisher of the *DAB,* was settled in 1997. The *DAB* name can no longer be used for future publication so the set has been closed out. Scribner's now publishes the *Scribner Encyclopedia of American Lives (SEAL,* entry 61), which has continued the pattern of the five-year supplements to the DAB. *American National Biography* is a completely new work being published by Oxford University Press under the auspices of the ACLS (entry 56).

A CD-ROM version of the *DAB* contains all 19,1973 entries from the printed work and supplements. Searches can be conducted by name, birthplace, occupation, birth/death dates, sex, or keywords. The CD-ROM forms an index to the printed work through cross-reference to the printed set.

61. The Scribner Encyclopedia of American Lives. Kenneth T. Jackson, Karen Markoe, and Arnold Markoe, eds. New York: Macmillan Library Reference/Simon & Schuster Macmillan, 1998–1999. (v. 1) 1998. 930p. ISBN 0-684-80492-1; (v. 2) 1999. 967p. ISBN 0-684-80491-3.

Scribner's envisions the *Encyclopedia of American Lives (SEAL)* as a continuation of the *Dictionary of American Biography* (entry 60). The new title began with volume 1 published in 1998. The new title bears a great deal of resemblance to the DAB. The last supplement to the DAB contained biographies of persons who died 1976–80. The first *SEAL* volume contains biographies of persons who died between January 1981 and December 1985. Each volume in the series presents original scholarly biographies of notable Americans. Persons from a wide variety of backgrounds who made significant contributions in politics, business, scholarship, education, sports, popular culture, and the arts and entertainment are included. The essays contain traditional biographical data with an opening paragraph highlighting the individual's achievements and placing them in historical context. Each essay ends with a note on sources that supplies information for further research. Most of the biographies are accompanied by photographs. The volumes have an occupations index and a directory of contributors. Researchers will have to use both the new *ANB* and *SEAL* as there will be overlap, but also different individuals included in each work.

*62. Who Was Who in America with World Notables: Index, 1607–1993. 12v. including index. Chicago: Marquis Who's Who, 1993. 272p. ISBN 0-8379-0218-5.

Marquis Who's Who has been a major publisher of current biographical source works for nearly a century, producing *Who's Who in America* and a number of regional and specialized subject *Who's Who* volumes. The emphasis in the Marquis publications is on career achievement, and the entries contain brief factual information. *Who's Who in America* began publication in 1899 and can be used for historical research. The necessity of consulting many older volumes of *Who's Who in America* was eliminated when *Who Was Who in America* was published. The first volume, containing only deceased subjects, *Who Was Who in America: 1897–1942,* was published in 1943, with subsequent volumes pulling information from the current *Who's Who* sources as individuals died. A *Who Was Who in America: Historical Volume, 1607–1896* was published in 1963. It contains biographical information on individuals from the United States and other countries that played some role in U.S. history. All of the *Who's Who* titles, both current and historical, are grouped by the publisher under an umbrella title, *Who's Who in American History.* The index volume for all of the *Who Was Who* volumes and the historical volume is titled *Who Was Who in America with World Notables.* This latter set continues to update the *Who Was Who* series, with the addition of a cumulative index for volumes already published. The Marquis *Who's Who* publications are also indexed in the *Biography and Genealogy Master Index* (entry 57) and are incorporated into the *Gale Biography Resource Center* (entry 52). The Marquis index to the *Who Was Who* series is a time saver for any student or researcher using those volumes.

The current *Who's Who in America* is supplemented by a number of regional biographical dictionaries begun in the 1940s. Separate publications focus on subject or professional specialties.

Over one million entries from the Marquis Who's Who publications are available as a section of the GaleGroup *Biography Resource Center* (entry 52).

CHRONOLOGIES AND ERAS

The chronology has been a long-established historical format. The end of the twentieth century occasioned a number of works that focused on the events and personalities of specific centuries or decades. Many of the new works were volumes in a series and are grouped together in this section. The first section contains general works not for a specific time frame. The following two sections are divided into pre-twentieth and the twentieth century.

GENERAL SOURCES

63. Album of American History. New York: Scribner's, 1960–1969. 6v. **Supp.** 1968–1982. Scribner's, 1985. ISBN 0-684-17440-5.

The six-volume edition of this pictorial work is divided into historical periods. Within the chronological framework there are headings relating to major political occurrences, news events, or social and cultural trends of the period. The photographs are selected to best convey the emotional impact of events. All are reproduced in black and white with credits. The short descriptions or captions combine with the illustrations to give an excellent visual impression of the various periods in history. There is an index to facilitate searching for photographs on specific subjects or incidents. The supplement updates the coverage through 1982 and is organized into 10 topical chapters. The presidency, Vietnam, social consciousness, business, ecological awareness, entertainment, and milestones are some of the subjects portrayed. The *Album of American History* is a perfect companion to assigned readings in both high school and undergraduate courses or for use by anyone seeking illustrations for historic events. It affords an overview of U.S. history through contemporary illustrations.

An older pictorial work is *Pageant of America: A Pictorial History of the United States* (New Haven: Yale University Press, 1925–29. 15v.). Although it has not been updated since its first publication, this standard multivolume work is a great source for older photographs. Unlike the *Album of American History,* the *Pageant of America* contains considerable text, both reference information and interpretation of the events depicted. An effort was made to secure contemporary photographs rather than later reproductions; the grainy early photographs evoke the era of the historical events. The set is organized in a chronological progression for the first nine volumes. The last six volumes each focus on a different theme or subject: religion, literature, art, architecture, the theater, and sports. Because of the different eras in which the *Album of American History* and the *Pageant of America* were compiled and the different editorial approaches they take, each is unique and valuable for historical study. The *Pageant of America* is also available as a microfiche collection from Proquest/University Microfilms, Inc.

64. Almanacs of American Life. New York: Facts on File. **Revolutionary America.** Thomas L. Purvis. 1995. 383p. ISBN 0-8160-2528-2. **Victorian America, 1876 to 1913.** Crandall Shifflett. 1996. 408p. ISBN 0-8160-2534-2. **Modern America 1914 to 1945.** Ross Gregory. 1995. 455p. ISBN 0-8160-2532-0. **Colonial America to 1763.** Thomas L. Purvis. 1999. 381p. ISBN 0-8160-2527-4.

The titles in this Facts on File series each cover a period in U.S. history beginning with *Colonial America to 1763.* An interdisciplinary approach is used in these volumes. The works are organized topically with individual chapters devoted to climate, natural history, Native Americans, the economy, population, religion, government, education, literature, science and technology, sports and popular culture, and crime. Both the positive and negative aspects of American life during the time periods covered are presented. Accounts of life by persons living at the time are often used. There are many boxed lists and tables. A thematic bibliography, an appendix of tables, and an index complete the volumes. One of the outstanding features of these titles is the amount of statistical information that is analyzed and interpreted. The titles do not dwell on covering major historical events but contain much detail on other aspects of the time period. The almanacs are designed for a student audience and present information in an attractive and interesting format.

65. American Book of Days. Stephen G. Christianson. Bronx, NY: H.W. Wilson, 2000. 945p. ISBN 0-8242-0954-0.

This has been a long-running reference title since the first edition by G.W. Douglas in 1937. The third edition was published in 1978. The fourth edition had almost double the number of articles as that of the previous edition. Older articles have been extensively revised with new essays covering important events that have occurred since the third edition. The emphasis has altered from holidays and festivals to the diversity of U.S. heritage. The organization is chronological by day and month. Both well-known and obscure events are included. Several substantial essays explore significant events of military, scientific, ethnic, or cultural significance. Most days have three to five events, which can be battles, disasters, holidays, treaties, birthdays, and historical political events. There are excellent indexes and appendixes that contain historical information as well as cross-referencing.

A much larger number of entries are contained in *This Day in American History* by Ernie Gross (McFarland, 2000) than in the *American Book of Days.* The book grew out of the author's career as a radio news writer. The approach is a "what happened when," historical event for each day of the year. Topics covered are as much popular as political and historical. There is a one-sentence summary for each of the entries. There is less background and descriptive information about the events than the *American Book of Days,* but the difference in the number of entries and selectivity between the two works makes them both useful because they do not cover exactly the same set of events. Also by the same author is *The American Years: A Chronology of United States History* (Scribner's Sons/Macmillan Library Reference, 1999). The arrangement of this work is by year and within the years by topical lists. The emphasis is on popular culture. The entries are again brief. The work is useful as an overview of trends by year, but more authoritative sources should be used to verify information.

66. American Eras. Gretchen D. Starr-Lebreau et al. Farmington Hills, MI: Gale Research, 1997–1998. 8v. ISBN 0-7876-1477-7 (set). **Development of the Industrial United States, 1878–1899.** Vincent Tompkins, ed. 1997. 455p. ISBN 0-7876-1485-8. **Civil War and Reconstruction, 1850–1877.** Thomas J. Brown, ed. 433p. 1997. ISBN 0-7876-1484-X. **The Colonial Era, 1600–1754.** Jessica Kross, ed. 1998. 455p. ISBN 0-7876-1479-3. **The Reform Era and Eastern U.S. Development, 1815–1850.** Gerald J. Prokopowicz. 1998. 379p. ISBN 0-7876-1482-3. **Development of a Nation, 1783–1815.** Robert J. Allison, ed. 1997. 423p. ISBN 0-7876-1484-X. **The Revolutionary Era, 1754–1783.** Robert J. Allison, ed. 1998. 394p. ISBN 0-7876-1480-7. **Westward Expansion, 1800–1861.** 1998. ISBN 0-7876-1483-1. **Early American Civilizations and Exploration, Prehistory to 1600.** 1998. ISBN 0-7876-1478-5.

The history of the United States up through the nineteenth century is covered by eras in this eight-volume series. Each volume is organized around topical chapters such as world events; the arts; business and the economy; communication; education; government and politics; law and justice; lifestyles; social trends; fashion; religion; science and medicine; and sports and recreations. Each subject chapter begins with a chronology of events, followed by an essay with an overview of the topic. More specific aspects of the topic are then covered. Each section has a brief bibliography and short biographies of notable people with bibliographies for those. The volumes are heavily illustrated with pages of historical documents, contemporary illustrations of events, portraits, and photographs. At the end of each chapter there is an annotated bibliography of contemporary publications. A bibliography at the end of each volume contains sources for further study. Each volume has an index of photographs and a general subject index. The *American Eras* volumes gather together information on social and cultural history and provide a sense of the spirit of the eras. The intent of the set is to make history interesting to students.

Two similar series for students are published by Oxford University Press. The individual volumes in the series *Student Companions to American History* are comprehensive A-Z guides to major historical periods or themes written by scholars. Further reading lists, cross-references, a chronology, and a full index are contained in each volume. *Pages from History* provides primary documents of historical significance in an attractive format with headnotes, extended captions, sidebars, and introductory essays to provide the essential contexts that frame the documents.

67. Chronicle of America. Rev. ed. New York: DK Publishing, 1997. 1016p. ISBN 0-7894-2091-0.

The attractive "newspaper" format of this work makes it easy and quick to use. American history, pre-1492 through 1997, is covered in one-page spreads for each year after 1764. Besides persons, places, and events, cultural and social topics are also covered. In addition there is an illustrated list of facts about the presidents, information on each of the 50 states, an organization chart of the federal government, and a comprehensive index. In the index there are four columns of "books, fiction," listed in the order of coverage. For students researching a certain period, or readers just browsing, this work can be both enjoyable and useful for many purposes.

Another reference work with a similar title is *An American Chronology* by Jerry Bornstein (Neal-Schuman, 2000). The author was an archivist and researcher in the Reference Library at NBC news and was frequently asked for historical chronological information. The arrangement is chronological year by year within 119 topical lists. Categories include the armed forces, wars and military interventions, sports, politics, crime, science, religion, business, the arts and fashions, and award winners. There are also chronologies for each state. The information has been gleaned from standard reference works and the sources of information are provided. Again, the selections of entries may differ from those in other chronologies and the work can be useful in consultation with other reference works.

*68. Daily Life through History Series. Westport, CT: Greenwood Press. Available in CD-ROM (ISBN 0-313-31367-9) and as an electronic database (ISBN: 0-313-31525-6). **Daily Life In Civil War America.** Dorothy Denneen Volo and James M. Volo. 1998. 321p. ISBN 0-313-30516-1. **Daily Life on the Nineteenth Century American Frontier.** Mary Ellen Jones. 1998. 288p. ISBN 0-313-29634-0. **Daily Life in the United States, 1960–1990: Decades of Discord.** Myron A. Marty. 1997. 400p. ISBN 0-313-29554-9. **Daily Life in the United States, 1940–1959: Shifting Worlds.** Eugenia Kaledin. 2000. ISBN 0-313-29786-X.

A number of works beginning with "Daily Life in . . . " have been published by Greenwood Press. These include *Daily Life on the Nineteenth Century American Frontier, Daily Life in Civil War America, Daily Life in the United States, 1940–59,* and *Daily Life in the United States, 1960–1990.* Other works in the series pertain to topics or specific aspects of world history and culture. These works are intended to provide an accurate account of what daily life would have been like for individuals living during the respective time periods. Each work begins with a chronology and concludes with a bibliography and an index. All include some period photographs, illustrations, and original artwork. The series is clearly meant to supplement factual and interpretive histories of the time periods covered. The works are not just chronologies of the time, but provide examples that make the facts more real. The series is available in print, on CD-ROM, and as an online database.

A one-volume work with a similar theme is *Advances and Innovations in American Daily Life, 1600's–1930s* by Ernie Gross (McFarland, 2002). Twenty broad thematic main sections are further subdivided into the appropriate advances and innovations for the each topic. Examples of the broad themes are agriculture, arts and music, clothing, energy, public service, shelter and domestic furnishing, sports, and transportation. Many aspects of daily life in America are described through the innovations that made life easier.

*69. Early Encounters in North America: Peoples, Cultures, and the Environment. Alexandria, VA: Alexander Street Press, 2002. [Electronic database; CD-ROM]. Available: http://www.alexanderstreetpress.com.

The digitized collections of documents in *Early Encounters in North America* are divided into four geographical sections that show the relationships between the peoples and the environment in North American from 1534 to 1850. The documents range widely from published to unpublished accounts including narratives, diaries, journals, and letters, and provide the perspectives of both genders and all walks of life. The interactions between the variety of cultures in early North America—Dutch, English, French, Spanish, Italian, Portuguese, African, and native peoples—are revealed through the documents. The collection includes thousands of descriptions of the fauna and flora of the regions. A unique index allows users to browse and search for specific animals and plants. Index fields can be combined to restrict searches to specific places and times. Starting with an electronic, annotated bibliography that identifies original sources, these are then indexed using no fewer than eight controlled vocabularies that were created for the database. The indexing identifies each letter, diary entry, or chapter of the material by a variety of subject headings, including a field that identifies descriptions of first-time encounters, which makes it possible to compare original descriptions of an area with later observations. The wealth of original source materials in this database make it useful for nearly any topic dealing with the time period covered.

70. The Encyclopedia of American Facts and Dates, 10th ed. Gorton Carruth. New York: Harper & Row, 1997. 1,104p. ISBN 0-06-270192-4.

More than 15,000 facts, events, and dates are contained in an arrangement of four parallel columns, which provides both a concurrent list horizontally and a chronological list vertically. The organization is first chronological by year. Within each year are four subject categories: governmental affairs; the arts and entertainment; business, science, philosophy, and religion; and sports, social issues, and crime. The four sections are arranged in columns that list chronological events by date and offer short accounts of significant inventions or issues that can be attributed to a year but not a specific date. Thus, not every event in U.S. history has a dated entry. The emphasis is on a flow of history rather than on a daily recounting of unconnected events. The arts, entertainment, popular customs, and the like receive as much coverage as governmental and political events. Columns can be read down in chronological order or across to get a broader picture of the events of a particular year. This work is useful for scanning through time periods or specific years. The attention given social and cultural issues makes this one-volume encyclopedia a good source for an overview of these aspects of U.S. history. It is the most comprehensive of U.S. chronologies. The work is suitable for students and the general reader.

A similar work by Ted Yanak and Pam Cornelison is *The Great American History Fact-Finder* (Houghton Mifflin, 1993). The work contains more than 2,000 brief alphabetically arranged entries. While political and military leaders and events are predominant, important figures and developments from science, business, the arts, sports, and entertainment are included.

71. Events That Changed America Series. Westport, CT: Greenwood Press. **Events That Changed America Through the Seventeenth Century.** John E. Findling and Frank Thackeray, eds. 2000. ISBN 0-313-29083-0. **Events That Changed America in the Eighteenth Century.** John E. Findling and Frank Thackeray, eds. 1998. 224p. ISBN 0-313-29082-2. **Events That Changed America in the Nineteenth Century.** John E. Findling and Frank Thackeray, eds. 1997. 232p. ISBN 0-313-029081-4. **Events That Changed America in the Twentieth Century.** John E. Findling and Frank Thackeray, eds. 1996. 256p. ISBN 0-313-29080-6.

Another series of separate titles covering different periods in American history is the Events That Changed America series. Greenwood also publishes an Events that Changed the World series. The topical chapters in these titles focus on 10 seminal events and are usually divided into two parts: the first gives an objective description of the time period and the second is a longer interpretive essay written on the period by a scholar. Appendixes are a glossary, a chronology, and lists of U.S. government officials with terms in office.

Major Issues in American History is another series from Greenwood Publishing Group begun in 2002, with Randall Miller as series editor. The volumes are on topical themes, such as federalism, immigration, war and peace, freedom of expression, and westward expansion, rather than by historical period. Each volume is written by a subject specialist and is a complete resources guide to a pivotal event in American history. In each volume there is an introductory narrative and a timeline of events. The entries on each event contain a comprehensive discussion and analysis of the event with the text of several primary documents from the time, presenting a variety of viewpoints and an introduction to each document. Each volume also has an annotated research guide including books, recommended Web sites, and videos. Both of these Greenwood series are useful as research guides for students or as supplementary texts for studies in American history.

72. Great Events from History: North American Series. Frank Magill and John L. Loos. Pasadena, CA: Salem Press, 1997. 4v. ISBN 0-89356-429-X.

The revised edition of this set contains entries from the first title, *Great Events from History: American Series* (1975) and also selected articles from *Great Events from History: Worldwide Twentieth Century Series* (1980) plus 325 completely new entries. In all, there are 665 articles arranged chronologically with the names of the original authors and the revisers. Each entry includes the date, the locale, subject descriptor categories, key figures, a summary, and a short annotated bibliography with *see also* references. The articles provide coverage of all of North America including Mexico, Canada, and the Caribbean as well as coverage of Native Americans, African Americans, Asian Americans, and Latinos. The time frame is from the 15,000 B.C. Bering Strait migrations up to the Internet in 1996. Each volume has a keyword index for titles and a category list of 31 different topics for all four volumes of the set. The last volume has a "Personages Index," which lists key individuals discussed throughout the work. There is also a subject index. As with all Magill reference works, this set is designed for students and is well suited for beginning research.

The Timetables of American History, edited by Laurence Urdang (Simon and Schuster, 1996), is also divided by subject. The emphasis in this work is on placing events in U.S. history in a time frame alongside significant happenings in world history. Sections are titled History and Politics; the Arts, Sciences and Technology; and Miscellaneous. Each section is further divided into subsections for the United States and "elsewhere." The introduction from the earlier editions by the noted historian Henry Steele Commager is retained with a new foreword by Arthur Schlesinger, Jr. There is an index by name and subject.

73. Historical Dictionary of . . . Series. Westport, CT: Greenwood Press. **Historical Dictionary of Reconstruction.** Hans L. Trefousse. 1991. 284p. ISBN 0-313-25862-7 (entry 78). **Historical Dictionary of the 1950s.** James S. Olson, ed. 2000. 353p. ISBN 0-313-30619-2. **Historical Dictionary of the 1960s.** James S. Olson, ed. 1999. 560p. ISBN 0-313-29271-X. **Historical Dictionary of the 1970s.** James S. Olson, ed. 1999. 424p. ISBN 0-313-30543-9. **Historical Dictionary of the Great Depression, 1929–1940.** James S. Olson, ed. 2002. 0-313-30618-4 (entry 356).

These historical dictionaries contain brief, concise entries on prominent people, organizations, events, issues, and controversies of the decades, as well as the culture of the era. Groups, including women, blacks, Native Americans, and Hispanics, as well as social movements, are well represented. Entries usually include at least one reference. There is a chronology and a selected bibliography in each title in the series. The dictionaries are straight text with not much in the way of eye-catching display devices. The various titles offer a quick overview of important segments of American history, providing a solid introduction to the period.

COLONIAL THROUGH NINETEENTH CENTURY

74. Books on Early American History and Culture, 1986–1990. Raymond D. Irwin. Westport, CT: Greenwood Press, 2001. 328p. 0-313-31430-6. **Books On Early American History and Culture, 1991–1995.** Raymond D. Irwin. Greenwood Press, 2000.

These bibliographies cover scholarship on early American history, including North American and the Caribbean from 1492 to 1815. Although each is restricted to a short publication period, they survey over 1,000 monographs, essay collections, exhibition catalogs, scholarly journals, and reference works published during the 10-year time span. The organization is in thematic sections covering such topics as colonizations, rural life and agriculture, and religion. The arrangement is topical by broad subjects such as "Race," "Gender," "Religion," and "Education." While a database search could yield a listing covering a longer publication time span the annotated entries in the bibliographies have been subjected to qualitative review. The two bibliographies gather much of the scholarship for the period together in one place with thematic coverage.

75. Cultural Encyclopedia of the 1850s in America. Robert L. Gale. Westport, CT: Greenwood Press, 1993. 472p. ISBN 0-313-28524-1.

The scope of this work is actually from 1849 to 1861 covering the period between the Mexican Revolution and the American Civil War. Presidents during the time period were Taylor, Fillmore, Pierce, and Buchanan. Literary figures were Emerson, Hawthorne, Thoreau, and Melville; cultural figures included Stephen Foster, P.T. Barnum, and Jenny Lind. In 437 entries on all aspects of the period, both political and cultural, personages and events are covered. A year-by-year chronology, which contains key events and literary publications, begins the work. Coverage of the literature of the time is extensive with summaries of books and essays. The work is especially strong in coverage of women, as well as popular culture. There is an overall bibliography for the volume, and a thorough index. Entries are listed both alphabetically and topically. The focus on the period before the Civil War in one volume shows the changes shaping the destiny of the United States at that time.

76. Encyclopedia of the North American Colonies. William J. Eccles and Jacob E. Cook, eds. Farmington Hills, MI: Gale Group, 1993. 2397p. ISBN 0-684-19269-1.

The scope of this three-volume work is from the eleventh-century Norse settlers in Newfoundland to the Spanish in New Mexico and the Russians in 1850 Alaska. The aim of the work is "to provide a fuller understanding of our colonial heritage by incorporating recent literature on previously neglected areas of colonial history." The 274 signed essays are by scholars from the United States, Canada, Great Britain, and Western Europe in history, anthropology, sociology, and folklore. The topical essays cover all aspects of political, social, economic, and cultural life. There are bibliographies, some annotated, and cross-references. There is a detailed chronology, maps, and an index in volume 3. The set succeeds in covering the settlement and expansion into North America through the colonization by Europeans, enslavement of Africans, and the subjugation of native peoples. It presents recent and competing historiographical perspectives on these topics and is an excellent starting place for research.

The three-volume *Encyclopedia* has been adapted for young adults as a four-volume set, *North America in Colonial Times: an Encyclopedia for Students* (Scribner's, 1998). The language has been revised for a younger audience and the set's layout has been changed to make it more attractive and easy to use. There are 200 illustrations, 16 maps, 16 color plates, and an overall index.

An earlier one-volume work is *The Encyclopedia of Colonial and Revolutionary America* by John Mack Faragher (Facts on File, 1990). This work provides information on individuals and topics in 1,500 brief, alphabetical entries. The articles are written by a team of scholars, but most are not signed. The encyclopedia explains political, social, economic, and cultural terms, with many biographies of major and lesser-known figures. There are 26 topical guides for broad themes or subjects such as women, agriculture, colonial government, Spanish colonies, and so forth. These guides have a brief overview of the subject and lists of related terms, themes, references to biographies elsewhere in the volume, and a brief bibliography. Some of the articles give further bibliographic references. There are maps and illustrations. The work is a good, quick reference tool for students, scholars, and the general public, but does not provide the scholarly depth of coverage of the more recent three-volume *Encyclopedia of the North American Colonies.*

77. Encyclopedia of the United States in the Nineteenth Century. Paul Finkelman, ed. New York: Charles Scribner's Sons, 2000. 1500p. ISBN 0-684-80500-6.

The aim of this three-volume set is to cover all aspects of United States history in the nineteenth century. The changes the United States underwent in the nineteenth century, including territorial and population expansion, social upheaval, the Civil War, and foreign policy, are explored in more than 600 A-Z articles. The articles, written by scholars, have bibliographic references and cover such topics as the frontier and Native Americans, immigration, slavery and sectional conflict, the Gilded Age, industrialization, the women's movement, labor laws, and the American Empire. There are over 400 black-and-white drawings, cartoons, photographs, and other illustrations including 30 maps. The set includes an exhaustive year-by-year chronology, original documents, and tables with a complete index. The set is suitable for the general reader and researcher as well.

The same time period is covered in *The United States in the 19th Century* by David Rubel (Scholastic, 1996). This work is organized in chapters, each for a different era. Each chapter has an introduction that provides an overview of the age. The chapters are divided into topical categories, such as arts and entertainment, daily life, social movements, and politics. Within the topical sections the information is organized as a timeline to enable the reader to understand the relationships between events. More than 300 illustrations and photographs, a glossary, and a comprehensive index make the work easy to use and attractive. The Rubel work is more of a chronology whereas the *Encyclopedia* provides more interpretation for an understanding of the history of the United States in the nineteenth century.

78. Historical Dictionary of Reconstruction. Hans L. Trefousse. (Historical Dictionaries series). Westport, CT: Greenwood Press, 1991. 284p. ISBN 0-313-25862-7.

The Reconstruction period in U.S. history covered in this dictionary is 1862–1896. Reconstruction was a program undertaken by the federal government to rule and then rehabilitate the Southern states that had been members of the Confederacy. The topics covered in this reference work by a distinguished historian of the period are politics, race relations, major figures, and the restoration of the states. All entries include bibliographic references, many to nineteenth-century sources. A chronology of the period is another feature of the dictionary. Because of the dictionary arrangement there are no indexes, but there are numerous cross-references. The viewpoint of the period expressed is that of current historical scholarship. This volume not only defines the terms and events of the Reconstruction period, it also provides a complete overview and interpretation of the period. It is useful for both students and researchers.

Another work on the same period is *The ABC-CLIO Companion to American Reconstruction, 1862–1877* (ABC-CLIO, 1996) by William L. Richter. This is a scholarly work with a historiographical essay covering changes in thought regarding the Reconstruction period. There is a dictionary of descriptive essays on important people, events, institutions, legislation, and ideas relating to the period. Voting rights for African Americans and Confederate soldiers, states' rights, corruption and scandal, economic recovery, and political leadership are all covered. A chronology and subject index complete the volume. While the Trefousse dictionary is useful for reference, the Richter work is more suitable for research.

79. James Madison and the American Nation 1751–1836: An Encyclopedia. Robert A. Rutland, ed. New York: Macmillan/Simon & Schuster Academic Reference Division, 1994. 509p. ISBN 0-13-508425-3.

Although the fourth U.S. President, James Madison, is the focal point of this work, the scope of the book covers the Early National Period in American history. Edited by a Madison scholar, the work has 400 signed articles by 88 expert contributors. The entries on the life, times, and influence of James Madison cover the people, institutions, and events during his life and include biographical articles on important Madison contemporaries. The entries include a bibliography. A chronology that compares events in Madison's life with events in the United States and the world is provided. The book also provides a detailed overview of the Constitutional Convention of 1787, the Constitution, and Bill of Rights. The work is well illustrated with portraits and facsimiles. There are cross-references, an index, and a synoptic outline of contents. This scholarly work provides a thorough treatment of the Madisonian era.

*80. Nineteenth Century Documents Project. Available: http://www.furman.edu/~benson/docs/.

Maintained by Lloyd Benson, a professor of history at Furman University, this site is especially strong in primary texts focusing on the causes, events, and debates preceding the U.S. Civil War. The bulk of the texts are public-domain documents arranged under broad subjects. All documents were scanned and proofed for accuracy. The site has search capabilities and is recommended for students and researchers looking for documents of the period.

*81. 19th Century Masterfile. Paratext Resources. [Electronic database]. Available: http://paratext.com.

19th Century Masterfile is a comprehensive electronic resource on the nineteenth century. Series I (Multi-title Indexes) contains: *Poole's Index to Periodical Literature* (1802–1907), 497,000 citations; Stead's *Index to Periodicals, 1890–1902,* ed. W.T. Stead, 265,000 citations; *Cumulative Index to a Selected List of Periodicals* (1896–1899), 150,000 citations; an *Alphabetical Subject Index and Index Encyclopedia to Periodical Articles on Religion 1890–1899,* ed. E.C. Richardson, 1907, 80,000 citations; and many in other languages. Series II indexes books. Series III includes the *New York Times Index* (1851–1912), 1.2 million citations, and the *New York Daily Tribune Index* (1875–1906), 780,000 citations. Also included in Series III are the *Index to Harper's Magazine* (1850–1892), 80,000 citations, and the *Index to Library Journal* (1876–1897), 40,000 citations. Series IV indexes individual periodicals and Series V indexes government document indexes. Documents indexes include the *Descriptive Catalogue of the Government Publications of the U.S., 1774–1881* and Ames' *Comprehensive Index to Publications of the United States Government, 1881–1893.* Not only are these important indexes and periodicals of the nineteenth century now indexed electronically, but they also are all presented in one product. Anyone researching any subject for the nineteenth century and prior centuries must search using the *19th Century Masterfile.*

The main periodical index for the nineteenth century is *Poole's Index to Periodical Literature* (Boston: Houghton, 1891. Rev. ed, 2v.; Supp. 1881–January 1, 1907, pub. 1887–

1898 in 5v.). The set was reprinted in 1938 and in 1963 by Peter Smith. Poole's index covers 105 years of U.S. and English periodicals. A *Cumulative Author Index for Poole's Index to Periodical Literature, 1802–1906* was compiled by C. Edward Wall and others (Ann Arbor, MI: Pierian Press, 1971). Because Poole's original work is a subject index, it has no author entries. The *Cumulative Index* greatly facilitates use of Poole's, but as many of the entries in the original are of questionable accuracy, the *Cumulative Index* must be used with caution. Another aid to use is *Poole's Index, Date and Volume Key,* compiled by Marion V. Bell and Jean C. Bacon (Chicago: American Library Association, 1957). The *19th Century Masterfile* now replaces the printed Poole's indexes. It also includes the *Reader's Guide,* 1890–1899 (entry 16).

82. Sources for U.S. History: Nineteenth-Century Communities. W.B. Stephens. New York: Cambridge University, 1991. 558p. ISBN 0-521-35315-7.

Various sources, both primary and secondary (manuscripts, records, books), are listed in bibliographic narratives arranged topically by chapter. Chapter headings include demography, ethnicity and race, land use and settlement, religion, education, politics and local government, industry, trade and transportation, and poverty, health, and crime. Entries are treated as footnotes within the bibliographical essays. The work surveys the literature to furnish an important source of information for the study of nineteenth-century local, regional, and state history in this country. The focus on nineteenth-century communities reflects a unique perspective. A helpful segment on the use of primary sources is designed to aid the novice. A topical index furnishes access.

TWENTIETH CENTURY

83. America in the 20th Century. Paul Humphrey et al., ed. New York: Marshall Cavendish, 1995. 11v. ISBN 1-85435-736-0.

Each decade in the twentieth century is the focus of a separate volume in this set with the eleventh volume being an exhaustive index. The coverage of the decades is topical with common themes such as health and medicine, the media, literature and the arts, education, family life, sports, crime, the environment, and demographic change. The changes in U.S. society and popular culture can be easily seen through the chronological arrangement. Each volume has a list of key dates, suggestions for further reading, and an index. Much of the indexing is repeated and culminates in the eleventh volume, which contains indexes to people, science and scientists, places, civil rights, women and minorities, laws and treaties, popular culture, and the arts. The set is designed for the general reader and is heavily illustrated with photographs, political cartoons, and advertisements. There are brief biographies of prominent figures from each era and quotations in sidebars. The coverage is not in-depth. The set is suitable for students and supplementary for research on a variety of topics relating to twentieth-century life in the United States.

Term Paper Resource Guide to Twentieth-Century United States History (Greenwood Press, 1999), by Robert Muccigrosso, Ron Blazek, and Teri Maggio, presents entries on 100 of the most important events and developments in the twentieth century organized in chronological order. Each entry consists of a short description of the event, followed by a wide-ranging bibliography of books, articles, videos, and Web sites for further research. Up-to-date materials as well as landmark works and primary sources are given.

84. American Decades. Farmington Hills, MI: Gale Group. **American Decades 1900–1909.** Vincent Tompkins, ed. 1996. 589p. ISBN 0-8103-5722-4. **American Decades 1910–1919.** Vincent Tompkins, ed. 1996. 632p. ISBN 0-8103-5723-2. **American Decades 1920–1929.** Judith S. Baughman, ed. 1996. 554p. ISBN 0-8103-5724-0. **American Decades 1930–1939.** Victor Bondi, ed. 1995. 612p. ISBN 0-8103-5725-9. **American Decades 1940–1949.** Victor Bondi, ed. 1995. 641p. ISBN 0-8103-5726-7. **American Decades 1960–1969.** Richard Layman and James W. Hipp, eds. 1994. 595p. ISBN 0-8103-8883-9. **American Decades 1970–1979.** Victor Bondi, ed. 1995. 623p. ISBN 0-8103-8882-0. **American Decades 1980–1989.** Victor Bondi, ed. 1996. 774p. ISBN 0-8103-8881-2. **American Decades 1990–1999.** Tandy McConnell, ed. 1996. 673p. ISBN 0-7876-4030-1.

The American Decades series treats a single decade of the twentieth century in each volume. The organizational format is the same as the American Eras set, which treats U.S. history pre-twentieth century. In each volume there are thirteen broad categories in alphabetical order covering such aspects as the arts, business and the economy, education, law and justice, lifestyle and social trends, medicine and health, religion, science and technology, and sports. Each volume begins with a chronological listing of world events, providing context for the American events. Each chapter also has a chronology; an essay overview and discussion of particular aspects of the subject area; brief biographies of headline makers and notices of significant accomplishments by prominent people; biographies of eminent people and those who died with the decade; and a listing of important publications relating to the subject area. There are black-and-white illustrations and sidebars with interesting tidbits. A list of contributors, an index to the photographs, and a general index conclude the volumes. The treatment of issues is clear and balanced. The volumes in the series are suitable for persons seeking an overview of the significant people, events, and issues of the decades.

A CD-ROM product with the same title, *American Decades on CD* (Gale Group) includes 1,500 subject-specific and overview essays. There is a timeline, the texts of more than 100 primary documents, and more than 1,000 biographies. There are a variety of lists and tables, including such information as award winners, obituaries, wage and price information, popular songs, films, and literature. The database includes images and audio and visual clips on twentieth-century American history and life. It can be used in conjunction with the printed volumes in the series or as a stand-alone resource.

A more narrowly focused work is *Twentieth-Century Teen Culture by the Decades: a Reference Guide* by Lucy Rollin (Greenwood Press, 1999). This work was not written for teens, but it is not a scholarly treatment either. Changes in slang, music, fashion, work, and other aspects of teenage life can be seen from the beginning to the end of the twentieth century. The work adds additional information to other references on life in the twentieth century.

85. Atlas of the Baby Boom Generation. Neil A. Hamilton. Detroit: Macmillan Reference USA, 2000. 256p. ISBN 0-02-865008-5.

The "Baby Boom" generation spanning the latter half of the twentieth century became a transforming force in American social and cultural life. The birthrate after World War II precipitated a booming economy toward the end of the century. This atlas presents the "Baby Boom" generation in a decade-by-decade chronology from the Cold War through the 1990s. The events included span political and social issues, arts, music, sports, and other cultural aspects. Each chapter examines current events, biographical profiles, trends, science and technology, television, and protests. There are maps and graphs of demographic and other information. A statistical appendix organized by decade, a bibliography, and an index complete the volume.

The largest generation in American history has been the subject of much corporate and marketing attention. *The Baby Boom: Americans Aged 35 to 54* (2nd ed. by Cheryl Russell, Ithaca, NY: New Strategist, 1999) is a marketing guide that looks at the demographics of the generation that represents the largest, best-educated group of potential customers for products and services. The data are drawn primarily from federal statistical series—the Census Bureau, the Bureau of Labor Statistics, the National Center for Health Statistics, and the National Center for Education Statistics. Findings from major public opinion polls from 1972 to 1996 are also utilized. Nine topical categories—attitudes and behavior, education, health, income, labor force, living arrangements, population, spending, and wealth—have broad highlights summarized at the beginning of each chapter. Tables have been constructed to show trends and differences between Boomers and other generations.

A similar work is *American Generations: Who They Are. How they Live. What They Think* by Susan Mitchell (3rd ed, New Strategist, 2000). Five generations of the twentieth century are covered in 11 chapters. Chapter 1 provides an overview of the generations and their characteristics. Chapters 2–11 cover the topics of attitudes and behavior, education, health, household, housing, income, labor force, populations, spending, and wealth. Tables and charts from government information analyzed by the author illustrate trends and future projections. The work is most useful for the data and analysis provided by the author.

86. The Columbia Chronicles of American Life, 1910–1992. Lois Gordon and Alan Gordon. New York: Columbia University Press, 1995. 837p. ISBN 0-231-08100-6.

This title is a revision and updating of *American Chronicle* (Atheneum, 1987; Crown, 1990) by the same authors. The newer title covers a longer time span, 1910–1992. In this year-by-year chronology, each year is a chapter divided into topical sections. A record of the significant cultural, political, and social trends and events over the majority of the twentieth century is provided. Much of the subject matter is covered through facts and figures, headlines, quotes, ads, anecdotes, and black-and-white photographs from the Library of Congress, the National Archives, and the Smithsonian. There is an extensive index for names and titles, and a general index. As with *America in the 20th Century* (entry 83), the emphasis is on popular culture. While the subjects are much the same, the presentation and selection of topics differ in the two works.

87. Lifetimes: The Great War to the Stock Market Crash: American History Through Biography and Primary Documents. Neil A. Hamilton, ed. Westport, CT: Greenwood Publishing Group, 2002. 366p. ISBN 0-313-317999-2.

The time period from the end of World War I until the market crash of 1929 saw the United States become a world leader in agriculture, business, military, and scientific fields. This period is shown through biographies of 60 of its most famous individuals. Photographs, text, and primary documents are combined to give comprehensive accounts of each subjects' life, work, and reputations, and how each contributed to the advancement of the United States on the world stage in the time period after World War I.

88. Encyclopedia of the United States in the Twentieth Century. Stanley I. Kutler et al., eds. New York: Scribner's/ Simon & Schuster Macmillan, 1996. 4v. ISBN 0-13-210535-7.

The organization of this set is in six topical sections ("The American People," "Politics," "Global America," "Science, Technology, and Medicine," "The Economy," and "Culture"). For these sections 80 historians have written 74 interpretative essays based on current scholarship. The thorough bibliographical essays analyze the major themes and subtopics such as regionalism, gender issues, Congress, health and disease, bureaucracy, nontraditional religions, mass culture, and industrial research. The demographic changes from the beginning of the century when the population was concentrated in the Northeast to the end of the century with pluralism and multiculturalism reflected in the populations of the two largest states, Texas and California, are analyzed and explained. The way average Americans worked, lived, played, and worshiped, is pictured against the backdrop of political and social change. Illustrations and photographs accompany the essays. A chronology corresponds to the six topical areas enabling the reader to follow trends throughout the century. This excellent reference work is useful for all levels of research.

Growing Up in Twentieth Century America: a History and Reference Guide by Elliott West (Greenwood Press, 1996) is a more narrowly focused work. It presents U.S. history from the viewpoint of the roles and significance of childhood in American society. The work is organized into 20-year blocks revolving around recurring familial themes and changes affecting home, work, school, health, and law. It looks at children in light of technological and social changes in American life and assesses the home, school, and work environments from 1900 to the present. As an example, toys, and money spent on toys and their influence are analyzed. Historical and statistical data such as the birth rate are analyzed. The interpretations and analyses in this work are thoughtful and insightful.

89. Encyclopedia of the Reagan-Bush Years. Peter B. Levy. Westport, CT: Greenwood Press, 1996p. 442p. ISBN 0-313-29018-0.

The more than 250 entries in this work are alphabetically arranged and include suggested readings and cross-references. The focus is on the presidential administrations, but the coverage encompasses the sociocultural milieu of the period from 1980 to 1992 as well. Written only a few years after the end of the era, the treatment is factual and summative, rather than interpretative. The volume contains ample illustrations, tables, charts, economic graphs, and photographs. There is a timeline and a statistical appendix of Gallup poll approval ratings follow the entries. The index is substantial. The work is a good reference source for the time period.

A more narrowly focused work is *The Reagan Years A to Z: An Alphabetical History of Ronald Reagan's Presidency* (Lowell House, 1996). Kenneth Franklin Kurz has compiled a guide of short essays on important events, people, and political matters during the Reagan era. The entries do not have indications of the source of the information. There is an index and a selected bibliography to the volume.

90. The First Measured Century: An Illustrated Guide to Trends in America, 1900–2000. Theodore Caplow et al. Washington, D.C.: AEI Press, 2001. 318p. ISBN 0-8447-4137-X.

The purpose of this work is to identify and interpret trends through the use of historical statistical data. The book is organized by subject categories such as population, work, and health. The format presents text on one page with the accompanying statistics in chart form on the opposing page.

*91. Guides to Historic Events of the Twentieth Century. Westport, CT: Greenwood Press. Online sourcebooks available through GEM (Greenwood Electronic Media) Available: http://www.gem.greenwood.com.

This is a series that contains many titles by different authors. The format for the series volumes is a historical overview of a period, such as the *War in Vietnam* or *Japan's Emergence as a Global Power*. The volumes usually have a chronology of events, biographies of key persons, and primary documents related to the topic. The guides are available as online sourcebooks.

*92. ResourceLink 20th-Century American History. Santa Barbara, CA: ABC-CLIO, 1998. [CD-ROM]. ISBN 1-57607-013-1.

This CD-ROM product is a digital encyclopedia containing primary sources and reference information. More than 1,500 resources are presented in both text and audio/visual formats. Texts include articles, definitions, biographical sketches, documents, and quotations. Still photographs, flags, animations, maps, documents, statistical tables, and audio and video clips are formats included. There is more material on the second half of the century. The search features make the product easy to use. The user can locate sources by topic through a lists feature, type of sources/format, or keyword. While not a comprehensive encyclopedia, the product is an excellent supplement to more thorough printed works.

93. The Roaring Twenties. Tom Streissguth. New York: Facts on File, 2001. (An Eyewitness History). ISBN 0-8160-4023-0.

Intended for a general audience, this is a highly readable work that chronicles the decade of the 1920s. The author probes past popular perceptions of the decade. The main feature of the work is a chronology of events and observations from the "eyewitnesses" of the period. Many of the quotes are by political figures, but others such as William Jennings Bryan and H.L. Mencken are included on the Scopes Trial and Senator Henry Cabot Lodge on the League of Nations. Three appendixes contain documents of the period, brief biographies, and data tables and maps. The volume is amply illustrated with photographs throughout and an exhaustive index. The work provides an excellent overview of the decade.

94. Twentieth-Century America: A Primary Source Collection from the Associated Press. Associated Press. Danbury, CT: Grolier, 1995. 10v. ISBN 0-7172-7494-2.

The reader gets a true sense of the time period in this set. The contents consist of articles reprinted from the Associated Press wire service of news provided to subscribing newspapers and radio and television stations. The articles are reprinted in their entirety with dates, headlines, and bylines. Thus, history as it was happening is presented in this 10-

volume set, which includes original news photographs as well. The only retrospective commentary is notes that summarize the subsequent impact of some of the events. The stories are organized into broad topics and presented chronologically within the topics. Articles on the significant events are held together in serial fashion in order that the development of the situation can be followed. Each volume begins with a timeline and detailed tables of contents and has its own index. Volume 10 contains a cumulative index to the set including the illustrations. Many details on events that are only found in news coverage can be gleaned from this unique set. It makes an excellent supplement to scholarly works.

A similar series based upon news reports is the Facts on File series Day by Day. These titles cover both international events and U.S. history in atlas-sized volumes for decades in the twentieth century. The extensive chronologies are gleaned from the *Facts on File Yearbooks,* which are compiled from news media reports. Each volume begins with a brief preface followed by an introduction that provides an overview of the decade. For each day there are 10 topical columns: five cover events by geographic location, three are for U.S. topics, and the two remaining treat science and culture. There are name and subject indexes, which are arranged alphabetically and chronologically. Each index entry includes the year, month, day, and column location in the volumes. The Day by Day volumes are useful for ready reference and for an overview of the events of the decade.

America's Century: Year by Year from 1900–2000 (DK Publishing, 2000) is a popular treatment of significant events and personalities. The twentieth century is divided into three blocks: 1900–1916, 1917–1945, and 1946–1999. Within each of the time periods, key events are listed chronologically by year. The format is newspaper-style, attractively illustrated and arranged. There were a number of similar chronologies published at the end of the twentieth century that are useful for students and the general reader but do not contain much of research value.

95. U.S.A. Sixties. Edward Horton and Matthew Turner, ed. Danbury, CT: Grolier, 2001. 6v. ISBN 0-7172-9503-6.

The focus of this set is primarily the United States, but international events that had world impact also are included. As with all Grolier publications this one is aimed for junior and senior high school students. The work covers all aspects of society, politics, and life in the decade that saw great changes in culture and mores from the years immediately after World War II.

The Columbia Guide to America in the 1960s (Columbia University Press, 2001) by David Farber and Beth Bailey is similar. The work is organized in three main sections with one containing brief topical essays, a second part with an alphabetized list of events, personalities, and organizations, and the last a section of data on attitudes, elections, education and more. The turbulence of the times is brought out in the civil rights struggle and the consumerism that followed WWII. The cultural contribution and changing mores of the time are seen through television shows. The work is an excellent and scholarly overview of the decade.

NEWSPAPERS

Because of their immediacy, newspaper accounts have been central to the historical research process. Contemporary newspaper stories and the publication in that format of official governmental records have made newspapers essential to historical research. In direct juxtaposition to their importance, the stock on which newspapers are produced, newsprint, is one of the most impermanent of materials. Moreover, indexing for individual newspapers had not been available on any large scale until the advent of the computer age. Thus, newspapers have been both the boon and the bane of a historical researcher's existence.

It was not until the advent of microfilming technology in the 1930s that newspaper files became widely available. Large research libraries began converting stacks of newsprint to the more permanent medium of microfilm. Location tools were compiled to aid the researcher in finding the files of microfilm. Although the microfilming of newspapers has come under fire because the process includes destroying and not retaining the original newsprint editions, were it not for microfilming the majority of historical research needing newspapers could not have been conducted.

Not only were newspaper runs difficult to obtain, but until the 1970s only the *London Times,* the *New York Times,* and a very few other newspapers had their own published indexes. In the 1970s commercial indexing was begun for major U.S. newspapers. Separate printed indexes were published for the *Christian Science Monitor,* the *Wall Street Journal,* the *Washington Post,* the *Chicago Tribune,* and newspapers from other major cities.

The availability of newspaper indexes has greatly increased, and now virtually all indexing is electronic. For researchers needing newspaper references for recent history of the last 30 years, the availability of newspaper indexing is much greater than for the history of the U.S. prior to the 1970s. In the mid-1980s DataTimes began an online database of newspaper indexing. Another newspaper indexing service is produced by Newsbank Inc., indexing over 250 U.S. newspapers, with the text in microfiche (entry 98). The printed indexes begun in the 1970s for major city and nationally distributed newspapers are now available in database formats.

Electronic databases have now replaced microform as a means of preservation and access to the full text of newspapers. Current issues of many newspapers are now available online through LexisNexis, Proquest, and other electronic database services. Although the newspaper indexes have not been extended retrospectively to the years in which the publications began, databases are being built to provide historical indexing. The Proquest *Historical Newspapers* project has begun indexing complete runs of the *New York Times, Washington Post, Wall Street Journal,* and *Christian Science Monitor* (entry 102).

The historical researcher needs to follow the major electronic indexing and full-text imaging projects. But thousands of reels of microfilm are housed in libraries and archival repositories still providing the only access to newspaper files from the past. This section endeavors to pull together the current situation with regard to newspaper indexing and preservation. The majority of the entries are for electronic databases.

96. History and Bibliography of American Newspapers, 1690–1820. Clarence S. Brigham. Worcester, MA: American Antiquarian Society, 1947. 2v. Repr. Greenwood Press, 1975. ISBN 0-8371-8677-3.

This work, originally published in the *Proceedings of the American Antiquarian Society 1913–1927,* was revised, augmented, and published as a monograph in 1947. A further supplemental revision, *Additions and Corrections to History and Bibliography of American Newspapers, 1690–1820,* was published by the American Antiquarian Society in 1961. The work has been reprinted several times, the latest by Greenwood Press in 1975. It is still the most comprehensive printed source for the history of the 2,120 U.S. newspapers it lists for the time period before 1820, arranged alphabetically by state and then by city. The information given includes beginning dates and all changes of title with exact dates, editors, and publishers. Indexes of titles and publishers are included. Although other tools provide location information for microfilmed newspapers, the locations in Brigham are given for original copies in newsprint as well as microfilm. It is still a necessary location tool for issues that have never been filmed.

Another work covering the same time period and complementary to Brigham's history is *Chronological Tables of American Newspapers, 1690–1820,* compiled by Edward Latham (American Antiquarian Society, 1972). Latham's work provides locations by date of issues for the newspapers listed in Brigham's history.

The continuation of the history of U.S. newspapers beyond 1820 can be found in *American Newspapers, 1821–1936: A Union List of Files Available in the United States and Canada,* edited by Winifred Gregory and published under the sponsorship of the Bibliographical Society of America by H.W. Wilson in 1937. The emphasis in Gregory's *American Newspapers* is locational rather than historical. The purpose of the work was to locate and list holdings of U.S. and Canadian newspapers in those countries. The organizational pattern is the same one used in Brigham: alphabetical by state and then city, with title, frequencies, and changes of titles. Library of Congress *National Union Catalog* symbols are used to indicate holdings. As with Brigham, the locations for issues that have not been microfilmed can be found in Gregory.

The problem of locating newspaper files for research has been greatly alleviated by commercial microform companies. There are two microfilm collections titled *Early American Newspapers.* The first one was begun in 1962 by Readex Microprint Corporation to publish on microprint all 2,000 newspapers listed in Brigham. The collection was filmed in cooperation with the American Antiquarian Society and complements the *Early American Imprints* collection (entry 34n). The newspaper filming was completed in 1970, and the company began converting the microprint format to microfilm in 1979. Readex is now a division of Newsbank, Inc. A listing of the newspapers in the Readex *Early American Newspapers* collection can be found on the Web site at http://www.readex.com.

University Microfilms International, now a division of Proquest Learning and Information, also has a series titled *Early American Newspapers, 1789–1949,* which includes papers of journalistic and historical importance from the eighteenth, nineteenth, and early twentieth centuries.

*97. New York Times Index, 1851–. New York: New York Times, 1913–. ISSN 0147-538X.

The most well-known and comprehensive newspaper index in existence is that of the *New York Times.* The index matches the reputation and caliber of the newspaper it indexes. Publication of the index began in 1913, with annual cumulations beginning in 1930. A

"Prior Series" index of 15 volumes covering the time period 1851–1912 was published by Bowker, 1966–1977. The Prior Series is compiled from a combination of in-house indexing already in existence and retrospective indexing. The handwritten in-house index for 1851–1858 is reproduced in facsimile. Although the indexes for the pre-1912 time period form a set, the indexing is not cumulative but is simply produced as it existed year by year. There is also a microfilm version of the Prior Series that was filmed before the series was printed.

The *New York Times Index* is very thorough in the information given. Exact references are provided for date, page, and column, including a brief indication of the contents of the article. The references are to the edition of the newspaper that was microfilmed. The *New York Times* has its own established subject headings, and there are many cross-references.

Guide to the Incomparable New York Times Index (New York: Fleet Academic Editions, 1980) by Grant W. Morse leads the user through the intricacies of the printed index and the microfilm. This handy pamphlet gives a brief history of the index and explanations of all the elements of the citations and the parts of the newspaper.

The *New York Times Biographical File* has been produced by the New York Times Company since June 1980 and is available online. The *Biographical File* contains the full text of selected articles, interviews, and obituaries.

In addition to the long-running main index to the *New York Times,* several complementary indexes have been published. The *Personal Name Index, 1851–1974* was published by Roxbury Data Interface in 22 volumes from 1976 to 1983. This finding aid was compiled from the *New York Times Index* volumes and not directly from the newspaper. Additional names were added. A supplement for the years 1875–1989 was published in 1990–1991 in five volumes.

One of the areas for which the newspaper has always been renowned is book reviews. An index to the book reviews in the *New York Times* was published by Arno Press in 1973 in five volumes, *The New York Times Book Review Index, 1896–1970.* This printed set indexes the *New York Times Book Review* comprehensively—that is, not only are the reviews indexed, but so are other essays, biographical sketches, letters to the editor, and so on. The five-volume set was produced as an index to a 125-volume set that reprinted the entire *New York Times Book Review* from 1896–1970. The *Index* can be used with either the reprint set or the newspaper microfilm. Each volume provides a different access point. Volume 1 is the author index (the author of the book being reviewed). Volume 2 is the title index. Volume 3 is a byline index that includes the authors of the reviews and the authors of the non-review pieces. Volume 4 is a subject index that uses the *Times Thesaurus of Descriptors* as the subject authority. The fifth volume is labeled a "Category Index," in which works are classed into genre categories such as children's fiction, nature and wildlife books, and poetry. This set is a major reference work, not only for the access it provides to individual book reviews but also because of the importance of *The New York Times Book Review* itself in its coverage of the cultural, literary, artistic, social, and political life of the United States. The *New York Times Book Review* is indexed on a current basis in several online databases and CD-ROM products, which index the *New York Times.*

The *New York Times Index* is a major research tool, useful not only for the primary indexing of the newspaper but also for establishing dates for which to consult other newspaper sources. It is remarkable as an index for its coverage of the political, intellectual, and social life of the United States for nearly 150 years.

Indexing for the *New York Times* is available in several online databases, some including full text. Availability will vary according to which databases are provided locally, but the majority of researchers should have no problem obtaining electronic access to the *New York Times.*

*98. Newsbank, Inc. Available: http://www.newsbank.com.

Newsbank provides current, ongoing cover-to-cover indexing of over 250 domestic newspapers. The listing of newspapers is maintained on the company Web site. Of interest to U.S. historians is the *Chicago Tribune Historical Archive,* which is a digitized collection of over 150 years of the *Chicago Tribune.* Published since 1849, the *Chicago Tribune* is one of the nation's oldest continuing publications. In addition to news coverage of the Chicago and the Midwest, the *Tribune* also provides major coverage of the wars of the twentieth century and is useful for social, political, and historical research. The Newsbank digital edition of the *Chicago Tribune* adds to the national historical news coverage available to researchers.

99. Newspaper Indexes: A Location and Subject Guide for Researchers. Anita Cheek Milner. Metuchen, NJ: Scarecrow, 1977–1982. 3v. ISBN 0-8108-1244-4.

Until the advent of computerized indexing, only a small number of newspapers with national or international reputations had their own separately published indexes. For many newspapers, however, there is unpublished indexing available through locally maintained indexes or clipping files. The Milner work is a compilation of information on locally available indexing obtained through questionnaires sent to public, college, and society libraries. The publication follows a geographic arrangement by state and then by city. There are separate listings of the institutions included in the index, which give information on services provided and photocopy rates. Although this publication did not continue, it is valuable for its identification and listing of existing newspaper indexes at the local level.

A similar guide is the *Lathrop Report on Newspaper Indexes: An Illustrated Guide to Published and Unpublished Newspaper Indexes in the United States and Canada* (Wooster, OH: Lathrop Enterprises, 1979). This loose-leaf service was short-lived, but it listed over 500 indexes and clipping files, most of which are in existence and valuable for historical research.

*100. Newspapers in Microform. United States, 1948–1983. Washington, D.C.: Library of Congress, 1984. 2v. ISSN 0097-9627.

The Library of Congress began to gather information on the location of microfilmed newspaper files from libraries and publishers in 1948. The publication of this union list of microform holdings began in 1948 and has been updated and cumulated in several editions, the latest through 1983. Arrangement is by state and then city. There are separate U.S./ Canadian and foreign newspaper sections. Publication information is provided for each title with dates and changes of title. Locations for microform files are indicated by Library of Congress *NUC* symbol. *NIM* was the first and most indispensable reference source for verifying titles and dates and determining the location of holdings for U.S. and foreign newspapers. It is one of a handful of reference tools no historical researcher can manage without. Much of the location information has been incorporated into the *United States Newspaper Program National Union List* (entry 103) but for historians who want to be certain, *NIM* still needs to be consulted.

As is the case with other catalogs and union lists published by the Library of Congress, *Newspapers in Microform* is now an online tool for the location of microform holdings of U.S. newspapers from the colonial period to the present. *NIM* is maintained as an electronic database by UMI and is found at http://www.umi.com. The information contained in the early printed indexing and location tools for newspapers can now be found in the UMI electronic edition of *NIM.*

*101. Nexis. LexisNexis. [Electronic database]. Available: http://www.nexis.com.

Nexis began in 1979 with the licensing of the *New York Times* online. The primary mission of *Nexis* is to provide up-to-the minute news and business information, U.S. and international. The database includes public records from 50 states. Category divisions from the *Nexis* home page are Advertising & Marketing; Agriculture, Forestry & Fishing; Automotive; Banking & Financial Services; Business & Management; Chemicals, Plastics & Rubber; Government & Politics; Insurance, Law & Legislation; Manufacturing & Mining; Media, Publishing & Entertainment; and Medicine & Health. Although the emphasis is current information, the number of newspapers, magazines, broadcast transcripts, and information on individual states makes the database useful for researching historical articles or information contained in those sources, the majority in English. Although *Lexis* and *Nexis* are available through separate subscription, the most common arrangement is that libraries or networks and consortia subscribe to an electronic database package that includes both databases.

*102. ProQuest Historical Newspapers. Proquest/UMI. Available: http://www.umi.com/pq-product.shtml.

The Proquest project is digitizing the *New York Times,* 1851–1999, the *Wall Street Journal,* 1889–1985, the *Christian Science Monitor,* and the *Washington Post,* from its first issue in 1877. The *London Times* has been digitized from 1785–1870, the period covered by *Palmer's Index to the Times.* For most of the titles, the collection includes digital reproductions of every page from every issue—cover to cover. These full-text digital image databases have largely obviated the need for indexes as they are searchable by keyword for the full text.

Another database that provides full text of news articles is *FACTS.com* offered by the World Almanac Education Group. *FACTS.com* contains worldwide news from October 1940 to the present on public policy issues and many other topics. It includes the World Almanac Reference Database.

*103. United States Newspaper Program National Union List. 5th ed. Dublin OH: OCLC, 1999. 102 microfiche in binder with booklet. ISBN 1-555653-281-4 (microfiche).

The United States Newspaper Program began in 1976 with a grant from the National Endowment for the Humanities (NEH). It is an ambitious project that has as its goal the identification and cataloging of all U.S. newspapers and the microfilming for preservation of those titles considered important for research. From its inception, the objective of the project has been to compile within the OCLC database an online union catalog of holdings of U.S. newspapers. A printed union list was first issued in 1985 in eight volumes. The second edition was issued in microfiche in 1987, a third microfiche edition in 1989, and a fourth edition in 1993. Organization is alphabetical by masthead title rather than the customary geographic arrangement of other compilations of newspaper holdings. A guide that accompanies the microfiche editions includes a preface, an overview of the set, a list of intended-audience terms, and a key to institution codes. The codes are OCLC location symbols, not the Library of Congress *NUC* symbols. The microfiche sets include four indexes: a beginning/ending date index; an intended-audience index; a language index; and a place of publication/printing index. The NEH has funded a number of state newspaper program projects; for those states the information in the *Newspaper Program National Union List* is very comprehensive. Any researcher making extensive use of U.S. newspapers is advised to become proficient at searching the OCLC online newspaper union list, which is being updated on a daily basis and is preferable to using the microfiche editions.

GOVERNMENT PUBLICATIONS

One of the most difficult areas for the researcher to master is that of government publications. The phenomenal growth of the federal bureaucracy in the twentieth century produced a voluminous array of publications to identify, classify, and index. Bibliographical control of U.S. federal government publications has not been comprehensive until very recent years. State and local government publications have usually been even more difficult for the researcher to identify and locate. The earlier catalogs and indexes that list historically significant documents have been, for the most part, very inadequate. First microform and then computer technology have aided in bibliographic control of both historical and current government publications.

The first edition of this *Guide* listed the historical catalogs of U.S. government documents. Up until the electronic era, there were a number of catalogs and indexes issued to provide bibliographic access to U.S. government publications. Many of these are classic catalogs and indexes that have only been superceded in the latter years of the twentieth century. The indexing by CIS and now electronic access provide such complete bibliographical information that a researcher rarely has to resort to the early finding aids. Thus, these classics have not been included in this second edition of the *Guide*.

Many periodical indexes, such as the *Readers' Guide* (entry 16), and *PAIS International* (entry 373), include a small number of government periodicals. The *American Statistics Index* (entry 121n) covers U.S. government serial titles for statistical data. The most comprehensive article indexing was provided by the *Index to U.S. Government Periodicals (IUSGP)* (Chicago: Infodata International, Inc., 1974–). Nearly 200 government periodicals are indexed by author and subject from 1970 forward. The IUSGP is available online. The index, unfortunately, has not maintained a current schedule and is several years behind. LexisNexis began an electronic index to the publications of the federal government in 2001, *Government Periodicals Universe* (entry 107).

Only the broad, general indexes to government publications are described in this section. For statistical information sources, see the section in this chapter headed "Geographical, Statistical, and Demographic Sources." Guides and indexes for specific branches of the federal government and for state and local government are in chapter 2, "Politics and Government." The resources described in this chapter give an overview of the reference tools for locating U.S. government publications. Any researcher who must constantly use documents is advised to acquire a guide to federal publications for in-depth and step-by-step guidance.

ELECTRONIC ACCESS

Governmental agencies began "publishing" in electronic formats in the 1990s. Nearly all government agencies now have at least a home page. A number of electronic "gateways" have been created to facilitate finding government information online. The majority of these access Web sites are free, but a number of publishers have also constructed subscription sites. The gateways to United States government information are described in this section and electronic indexes to federal government publications are described in this section.

*104. Catalog of United States Government Publications. Washington, D.C.: United States Government Printing Office. Available: http://www.access.gpo.gov/su_docs/locators/ cgp/index.html (Web version of the *Monthly Catalog* [entry 112]).

CGP, the Internet version of *MOCAT* (the *Monthly Catalog,* an abbreviation born in the electronic era) begins with bibliographic records published in *MOCAT* since 1994. New and updated records are added on a daily basis and appear in the Web catalog before appearing in the printed *MOCAT.* Searches can be conducted by a multiplicity of access points including names of authors, editors, and organizations; keywords in a title or series; by format terms such as microfiche, computer file, or video; precise word order; and truncation. Search results include relevance rankings and location of the document in a depository library. The results include a summary with title, date, issuing entity, SuDocs class, depository item number, GPO stock number, and the option to select a hypertext link to the document. Historical researchers will still need to use the printed *Monthly Catalog* (entry 112).

*105. FirstGov. Available: http://www.firstgov.gov.

FirstGov was created as a partnership between the U.S. government and private enterprise. It became operational in 2000. The goal of the gateway was to be the "first resource to any government information on the Internet." Besides providing links to government Web sites, the main feature of *FirstGov* is a search engine. The organization is topical, much like the popular Internet portals. It was intended for use by the average person and small businesses, not like the agency Web sites such as *EDGAR* and the Census Bureau, which were designed more with information specialists and power users in mind. The intended focus of *FirstGov* is the most popular sites and pages. The top level has 16 broad topics with a decided consumer orientation. Although the stated aim was to access "any government information on the internet," the portal does not reach that goal. It is, however, still a useful starting point for anyone attempting to identify the many sources of information from government agencies. Those more familiar with the organization of the federal government and specific agencies will probably prefer to go straight to those Web sites.

*106. GPO Access. Washington, D.C.: United States Government Printing Office. Available: http://www.access.gpo.gov.

The United States Government Printing Office (GPO), established in 1860, sells about 12,000 different publications of government agencies, administers the depository library program in 1,400 libraries, and provides more than 70 federal publications online. The GPO created *GPO Access* to enable the public to reach free U.S. government information on the Internet. From the beginning in the mid-1990s, the *Code of Federal Regulations, Congressional Record* (entry 193), the *Federal Register* (entry 169), *Commerce Business Daily,* the *US Code* and public laws, and the agency's own MOCAT (entries 104, 112) could be accessed through the *GPO Access* gateway. *GPO Access* provides public access at no charge to over 70 agency databases. There is also subject searching of specific databases. Other publications available are the *U.S. Government Manual* (entry 155), the *Statistical Abstract of the United States* (entry 122), GAO reports, and congressional and presidential documents. While the majority of the information in electronic form is recent and current information, it is important that any researcher be aware of the major gateways to government information and be capable of navigating the systems.

*107. LexisNexis Government Periodicals Universe. Dayton, OH: LexisNexis, 2001–.

Although retrospective coverage is only back to 1988, *LexisNexis Government Periodicals Universe* indexes over 125,000 periodical articles from a selective list of U.S. federal government publications. Hyperlinks are included within the index for about half of the publications covered. Approximately 10,000 articles will be included annually from more than 160 periodicals. Articles can be accessed by title, author, issuing agency, SuDoc number, or GPO item number. The subject indexing employs a controlled vocabulary of over 4,400 terms. Searching can be by Boolean operators, controlled vocabulary, or segment searching. Indexed titles of interest to those engaged in historical research include the *Naval War College Review, Soldiers,* and the *Federal Archeology Report.*

*108. National Archives Information Locator. Washington, D.C.: National Archives and Records Administration. Available: http://www.nara.gov.

The Strategic Plan of the National Archives and Records Administration provides for the development of an online catalog that will describe 100 percent of the agency's archival holdings by 2007. The *National Archives Information Locator (NAIL)* will be the electronic, virtual catalog of all NARA holdings. The most popular and highly requested documents have been digitized and made available on the Web site. The National Archives and Records Administration has 33 facilities with over 22 million cubic feet of textual materials; 300,000 reels of motion picture files; more than 5 million maps, charts, and architectural drawings; more than 14 million still pictures and posters; 9 million aerial photographs; and nearly 8,000 computer datasets. *NAIL* will enable researchers to determine which facility holds the materials desired and to access directly those materials in electronic format. *NAIL* will be a boon for genealogical researchers who make up a significant portion of the users of archival and records data. *NAIL* can be searched from the *NARA* Web site. Its coverage of NARA holdings is significant, particularly in the area of photographic and motion picture holdings.

BIBLIOGRAPHIES, CATALOGS, AND RESEARCH GUIDES

109. Government Information on the Internet. 3d ed. Greg R. Notess. Lanham, MD: Bernan Associates, 2000. 833p. ISBN 0-89059-247-0.

This work broadly covers government information, both U.S. and international. There are 250 sites from international governmental organizations and foreign countries, 150 U.S. state government sites, 2,500 sites for U.S. city and county governments, and the Web sites and e-mail addresses for members of the U.S. Congress. The arrangement is topical in 19 chapters by broad subject category. In all there are approximately 5,000 Web sites given. There are indexes for URL's; SuDocs numbers for U.S. federal publications; and a master index for subject, sponsor, titles, and acronyms. The indexes are the best feature of the work as the Web addresses can be found in a number of sources. A subscription Web site was inaugurated in 2001 with the same title as the Internet guide. The Web site provides a search engine to locate and find sites and documents with keyword searching and filed searches by agency, subject, title, and more. The site provides direct links to full text government documents searchable by title or SuDoc stem. Over 5,000 live links to state, local, international, and intergovernmental sites are maintained and kept current.

A similar guide is *Government Online: One-click Access to 3,400 Federal and State Web Sites,* edited by John Maxymuk (Neal-Schuman, 2001). The Web sites are described in 12 topical chapters. Compiled by subject area experts, each chapter begins with an overview of the most useful Web sites. Entries include the URL, a brief description of the site, and highlights designed to answer most commonly asked questions. The advantage of this guide is the accompanying CD-ROM, which allows direct access, the "one-click," to the 2,200 federal government and over 1,200 state Web sites described in the book.

One of the earliest Internet guides is by Bruce Maxwell, *How to Access Federal Government on the Internet* (Congressional Quarterly, 4th ed. 1999). This guide is organized topically covering over 900 sites offering information from the federal government. The focus is on free information. Sites maintained by university faculty and libraries and archives are also included. There is a comprehensive index.

110. Guide to U.S. Government Publications. Donna Batten. Detroit: Gale Group, 2002. 1690p. ISBN 0-78765-455-8.

The publication history of this title, long referred to as "Andriot," is rather complicated, but it is one of the best-known and relied-upon sources among government documents librarians. Begun by John Andriot as a loose-leaf publication in 1975 with the title *Guide to U.S. Serials and Periodicals,* it became an annual in 1981. The guide is valued for its completeness in the listing of government serial publications, including historical and bibliographic information. It lists titles that have ceased as well as those currently being published. There are indexes by agency and by publication title. One of the most valuable features for historical research is the "Agency Class Chronology," which lists the changes undergone through the years in SuDocs classification numbers for each agency and the changes in agency name. Once a researcher learns to utilize the unique features of this guide, it becomes an indispensable resource.

Guide to Popular U.S. Government Publications by Frank W. Hoffmann and Richard J. Wood has proven to be a popular publication itself (Libraries Unlimited, 5th ed. 1998). This handy guide is organized by subject with each entry containing full SuDocs bibliographic apparatus. The more general and practical publications are indexed, but even those conducting historical research may find leads in this user-friendly reference.

Bibliographic Guide to Government Publications-U.S. (G.K. Hall) began publication in 1975. It includes publications from federal, state, and local governmental sources. It is particularly useful for nonfederal government publications, many of which are hard to verify. The subject organization makes it an excellent source for finding new citations.

111. Introduction to United States Government Information Sources. 6th ed. Joe Morehead. Englewood, CO: Libraries Unlimited, 1999. 491p. (Library Science Text Series). ISBN 1-56308-734-0.

One of the best introductory works for librarians and researchers alike is this library science text. The rapidly evolving nature of government publication into near total provision of current information only in electronic form has made keeping this standard work up-to-date a formidable challenge. The sixth edition begins with a chapter on "The Transformation of Government Information," which traces the history of the Internet and which, after all, is a child of the U.S. government with its beginnings in the ARPANET in the Department of Defense. The narrative begins with an overview of the issues, themes, and problems associated with the migration of federal government information to the Internet. Detailed chapters on the Government Printing Office (GPO), the Office of the Superintendent of Documents, and the Depository Library System introduce the student and researcher to the complicated apparatus and procedures of the government publications system. There is a section devoted to the general catalogs, indexes, and bibliographies produced for accessing federal publications. The legislative, the presidency, administrative law, legal information sources, statistical sources, intellectual property, selected departments and agencies, and geographic information sources are all covered in separate chapters. Electronic databases and Web sites are covered. This guide is very thorough in its explication of the organization and bibliographic apparatus of the federal publication universe. While the migration to electronic provision of information is covered in the sixth edition, changes in the organization of the agencies for the preservation and dissemination of government information at the beginning of the twenty-first century have already made some of the information in the work outdated. But the Morehead work remains the most comprehensive introduction to U.S. government information. Most valuable for the historian is the attention paid to historical publication and early titles in the attempts at bibliographical control of federal publication and documents. The fourth edition of this guide was the last edition to include the history of many executive branch agencies and departments. Those needing to conduct extensive research using U.S. government publications would do well to own this handbook.

A new addition to the repertoire of texts concerning government information sources from Libraries Unlimited is *United States Government Information: Policies and Sources* by Peter Hernon et al. (2002). The work is designed to give students an understanding of the importance of policy and how it is formulated. It traces policies and sources from the founding of the U.S. government to the emergence of electronic government resulting from the advent of the Internet. Chapters cover the Freedom of Information Act, PaperWork Reduction, Privacy Protection, the three branches of government, statistical and GIS sources and policies, and more. There is a companion CD-ROM with study questions by Joe Morehead, key documents, tutorials, and exercises. The URL's are updated through the Libraries Unlimited Web site (available at www.lu.com).

*112. Monthly Catalog of United States Government Publications. Washington, D.C.: Government Printing Office, January 1895–. ISSN 0362-6830.

Although the bibliography of U.S. government publications did not begin with the *Monthly Catalog,* its comprehensiveness and long publication history make it the core resource to which others relate. The *Monthly Catalog* (or more recent abbreviation *MOCAT*) began in 1895 and has undergone several title changes since then. The most sweeping change in its bibliographical history came in 1976, when it was converted to AACR2 cataloging rules and machine-readable format in order to be entered into the OCLC online catalog database. Prior to 1976 the *Monthly Catalog* was arranged alphabetically by government agency, with one index for authors, titles, and subjects. Beginning in 1976, arrangement was by SuDocs number. There were also separate indexes by author, title, subjects (LC subject headings), title keyword, series/report numbers, and GPO stock numbers. A SuDocs classification number was included in the semiannual and annual indexes. An annual *Serials Supplement* listed current periodical titles.

In 1995, the GPO began issuing *MOCAT* on CD-ROM and the print version was scaled back with one index and abbreviated descriptions of the records on the CD-ROM. The printed version now resembles the pre-1976 *Monthly Catalog,* while the CD-ROM contains fuller information and of course, has the enhanced capacity of electronic keyword searching. The *Monthly Catalog* is available for online searching through major database vendors and as a CD-ROM database from several private companies. Magnetic tapes for loading into local online catalogs can be purchased from the Library of Congress or Marcive. Readex, a division of NewsBank, Inc. continues to offer full-text microfiche copies of publications indexed in *MOCAT.*

The Internet version of *MOCAT* has been titled *Catalog of United States Government Publications* because it is updated constantly and does not have the monthly frequency. The Web version can be accessed through the GPO access gateway at http://www.access. gpo.gov/ (entry 104).

Researchers will still need to consult the older printed *Monthly Catalog,* but much of the bibliographic information for U.S. documents and publications has been converted to electronic format.

*113. The Sourcebook to Public Record Information: The Comprehensive Guide to County, State, & Federal Public Records Sources. 3rd ed. Tempe, AZ: BRB, 2002. 1542p. ISBN 1-879792-64-8. **Public Record Research System.** [CD-ROM].

BRB has concentrated on publishing guides to the location of public records. The collective title for all of the guides is *Public Record Research Library.* Although these guides are mainly for locating current information, they are useful to the historical researcher. One of the advantages to the historical researcher is that the guides contain explanations of the types of public records, defining the differences between various types of public records, assisting the researcher in identifying the type of records needed or type of records available. Another advantage of these guides is that they give current contact information for states, counties, and cities that in many instances are the appropriate place to begin searching for historical records.

The Sourcebook to Public Record Information consolidates into one publication the information which was formerly published in four different sourcebooks: *The Sourcebook of County Asset/Lien Records, The Sourcebook of County Court Records, The Sourcebook of Federal Court Records,* and *The Sourcebook of State Public Records.* There is a CD-ROM product containing the same information, *Public Record Research System.* The guide instructs on finding public records whether or not available through the Internet. The public record primer explains how to search and where categories of records can be found. The individual state chapters give agency facts, record access, fees and methods of payment, and miscellaneous information such as how to purchase databases.

In addition to the *Sourcebook to Public Record Information,* a number of more-specialized guides have been published by BRB. *The Librarian's Guide to Public Records 2000: The Complete State, County & Courthouse Locator* deals with locating court records only. This is a directory of state-by-state listings of state agencies, county courts and recording offices and federal courts. It contains information on free Internet access to public records, private online sources of public records, and other useful Web sites.

Another title by the same publisher is *The Sourcebook of Local County Record Retrievers 2000: The Definitive Guide to Searching for Public Record Information at the State Level* (6th ed. BRB, 2000). The titles of all the sourcebooks are very similar, but this one provides information on companies and individuals who will perform public records searches for a fee. The purpose of the work is to help the researcher retrieve public information at the state level. The two main sections of the work organize the information differently. The first section is a geographical finding aid by state and then county. The second section "Retriever Profiles," is organized alphabetically by the name of the company or individual retriever. Information is given on how to choose a competent retriever and on the Code of Professional Conduct for members of the Public Record Retriever Network. The work is a handy guide for those needing research performed in a distant locale. The information is also included in the *Public Record Research System* CD-ROM.

114. Subject Guide to U.S. Government Reference Sources. 2nd ed. Gayle J. Hardy and Judith Schiek Robinson. Englewood, CO: Libraries Unlimited, 1996. 358p. ISBN 0-58508-038-0.

This guide is a revision of an earlier work of the same title by Sally Wynkoop published by Libraries Unlimited in 1972. A broad range of reference sources is included from bibliographies to numeric databases. The 1,324 annotated entries are arranged into the four broad subject categories of general, social sciences, humanities, and science and technology. For those using the guide as an acquisition tool, GPO stock number, LC card number, and OCLC numbers are given. For research use, this subject guide lists SuDocs classification and is indexed by title, topic, and place name. There are a large number of bibliographies available for the myriad agency publications, making it necessary to consult a guide such as this one when first approaching a research topic using government publications.

A similar but more selective publication is the *Subject Guide to Major United States Government Publications* by Wiley J. Williams (American Library Association, 1987, 2nd ed.). Also a revision of an earlier (1968) guide, this work lists sources under a much more detailed subject breakdown than that used in the Hardy/Robinson guide. In the main section are the selective lists of sources organized under 250 topics based on Library of Congress subject headings. Entries provide complete bibliographic information with annotations. Supplemental notes provide historical information and additional sources. The two appendixes are valuable aids to the researcher. The first lists additional guides, catalogs, indexes, and directories useful for obtaining government information. The second lists the bibliographies issued in the Subject Bibliographies series for sale by the GPO.

115. Tapping the Government Grapevine: The User-friendly Guide to U.S. Government Information Sources. 3rd. ed. Judith Schiek Robinson. Phoenix: Oryx Press, 1998. 286p. ISBN 1-573-56024-3.

As its title implies, this guide is meant for the ordinary library user and beginning researcher. It is an excellent introduction to the use of government publications, covering the organization of government agencies; the publication, distribution, and servicing of government publications; and how-to instructions for common uses of government information. The third edition focuses on electronic resources and the changing world of government information in 15 chapters. The URL is listed for each government Web site and a cumulative list appears in an appendix. There is one chapter by Karen Smith that focuses on international/foreign and state government publications. This guide makes an excellent place to begin for anyone who has a need for government information. The writing style is as lively as the title suggests, and it accomplishes the purpose of simplifying the complex organization and bibliographic apparatus of government publications. Visual explanations in the form of charts, illustrations, and summary tables further aid in the simplification process. An index provides keyword access and six appendixes offer lists such as "Abbreviations and Popular names." Students and researchers who find library organization and terminology bewildering will be enthusiastic about this publication, which makes it all so easy to understand.

116. Using Government Information Sources: Electronic and Print. 3rd ed. Jean L. Sears and Marilyn K. Moody. Phoenix: Oryx Press, 2001. 550p. ISBN 1-57356-288-2.

The first edition of this work, titled *Using Government Publications,* became known for its approach, which emphasized search strategies, and that approach has been continued through the second and third editions. The sources are still explained in the context of research strategies, although the third edition has been extensively revised including a new title that emphasizes the electronic. Each chapter is grouped into four search-strategy categories: the subject search, the agency search, the statistical search, and special techniques. Among the subjects covered are tax and copyright information, audiovisual information, climate, elections, maps, genealogy, agriculture, education, health, the environment, and travel information. In the second edition, research sources for astronomy and space, transportation statistics, and judicial reports were added. The "Special Techniques" covers legislative histories, technical reports, patents and trademarks, standards and specifications, and other difficult materials. The third edition has a chapter on "Housing and Construction Statistics." Two appendixes include addresses for government agencies and commercial firms. There are indexes by author, title, and SuDoc classification numbers. This source is extremely useful for anyone who needs to be guided through the steps involved in searching for specific types of information. The chapters can be utilized separately as the need arises.

117. U.S. Government on the Web: Getting the Information You Need. Peter Hernon, Robert E. Dugan and John A. Schuler. 2nd ed. Englewood, CO: Libraries Unlimited, 2001. 405p. ISBN 1-56308-886-X.

As the title implies, this work is a guide to finding current information on the Web. It is useful for historical research in that it gives URLs for most federal government agencies. The beginning chapters introduce government information, its importance and the structure and types of publications, and how search engines work. After these chapters, the work is organized according to the organization of the federal government and then topically in the last few chapters. Additional features in the second edition include a detailed analysis of information policies governing e-government; expanded coverage of the Freedom of Information Act and Web sites devoted to it; direction to sites that provide subject-specific statistics; and more. The work makes an excellent complement to Morehead (entry 111) as it contains more Web sites but the organization is roughly parallel to Morehead, making it easy to use the two together. The URLs are highlighted in blue and those given in each chapter are repeated in a "blue pages" list of Web sites at the end of each chapter. In addition to federal government Web sites there are also relevant and helpful Web pages from universities, libraries, and public-interest groups in an appendix. There is a "Government Body Index" and a "Selected Title Index." An accompanying Web site at http://www.lu.com updates URLs monthly. As many federal agencies now publish only on the Internet, a guide is essential to finding government information. This work is not just a listing of Web addresses, but a how-to in finding government information through the use of search engines and directly through specific agencies.

A similar work is *The Internet Blue Pages: The Guide to Federal Government Web Sites* compiled by Laurie Andriot (Information Today, 2000). Web addresses for more than 1,800 federal government offices and agencies are provided along with a brief description of the contents of the Web site and links from the site. The organization of this guide follows the format of the *United States Government Manual* (entry 155) arranged by legislative, judicial, and executive agencies grouped and other agencies listed alphabetically. A Web site has been created to update the contents of the printed work (available at http://www.fedweb.com).

STATISTICAL, GEOGRAPHICAL, AND DEMOGRAPHIC SOURCES

The U.S. government is the principal and largest collector of statistical data for the United States. In many instances, the federal government is mandated by law to collect data, such as the decennial census, and is the only agency with the legal authority to do so. Although the data are produced by the government, many of the major access tools are maintained by private enterprise.

Current data are increasingly produced only in electronic formats. Beginning with the 1980 Census, much of the detailed data were never printed but were available only in electronic form. For the 1990 Census, more information for detailed geographic areas was provided on CD-ROM disks than in printed summary reports. Since the mid-1990s, current statistical and demographic information has more often been produced only in electronic formats. Such databases as STAT-USA, CenStats, FedStats, and the National Agricultural Statistics Service (NASS) are all provided electronically from the agencies' Web sites.

This section includes the most basic indexes and the long-running statistical publications that are most suitable for historical research. A fuller listing of statistical sources and datafiles produced by the federal government are included in the research guides and reference sources listed in the "Government Publications" section of this reference guide. *Introduction to United States Government Information Sources* by Morehead (entry 111) describes government statistical sources. Both *Tapping the Government Grapevine* by Judith Schiek Robinson (entry 115) and *Using Government Information Sources* by Sears and Moody (entry 116) have explanatory sections on the use of government statistical sources, which are numerous and complex. These reference works may be used to identify additional sources to those described in this section.

STATISTICAL SOURCES

*118. Census Catalog and Guide. Washington, D.C.: U.S. Department of Commerce, Bureau of the Census. 1985B-Ann.

A large proportion of the statistical data generated by the federal government is the responsibility of the Bureau of the Census. The most well known of these responsibilities is the decennial population census, which is mandated by law to establish population shifts for the redistricting of Congress. The bureau also gathers, compiles, and publishes statistical data in the areas of agriculture, government, economics, and business. The business statistics are extensive, covering wholesale and retail trade, manufacturing and transportation, construction, mineral industries, and service enterprises. Most of these statistics are gathered every five years. The Bureau of the Census produces databases of current demographic data by zip code and economic and agricultural data. Current data and information, most since the mid 1990s, are available on the Bureau's Web site (available at http://www.census.gov). The 2000 census information is being made available on the Web site. An "Access Tools" section helps users navigate the census data. The "Census Tract Street Locator" allows the user to very quickly identify the tract the user lives in by simply entering his/her address. The entire Census site is keyword searchable. In the future, historians will have it much easier locating and using census information.

The *Census Catalog and Guide* is still printed annually with a somewhat varying format. In some years the *Catalog* just updates the previous year. Preceding the annual *Catalog* were a number of cumulative publications. The *Catalog of Publications, 1790–1972* consists of two parts. The first part is a reissue of the *Catalog of United States Census Publications, 1790–1945* by Henry J. Dubester (Government Printing Office, 1950), and the second part is the *General Catalog of Publications, 1946–1972,* which cumulates the annual Bureau of the Census catalogs for those years. Each section has its own index. This one-volume catalog forms a comprehensive historical bibliography of over 60,000 publications of the bureau. The *Catalog of Publications* will be of use to any student or researcher endeavoring to identify and locate earlier publications of the Bureau of the Census. The historical volume is updated annually by the *Census Catalog and Guide.*

Also of use in identifying census bureau publications are the *Catalogs of the Bureau of the Census Library.* The 20-volume catalog was published in 1976 by G.K. Hall with a five-volume supplement in 1979. The Bureau of the Census Library was established in 1952. It contains a large collection of population surveys, census data, and government reports, both U.S. and foreign. The collecting emphases of the library are in economics, populations, state and local government finance, urban studies, statistical methodology, and data processing. The library also contains a strong retrospective collection of U.S. census publications from 1790 to the present, with materials covering census history, operations, and products. The catalogs are useful for identifying publications and statistical sources for historical research.

The Congressional Information Service has a number of microfiche collections that reproduce census publications. The collection of *Non-Decennial Census Publications* follows the two parts of the Bureau of the Census *Catalog of Publications, 1790–1972*, which have been reprinted by Greenwood Press to correspond to the microfiche collections. An index has been added to the second part that cross-references the catalog listings to the documents in microform. Separate collections for the 1970, 1980, and 1990 censuses are available in microfiche from CIS. These collections are drawn from the *American Statistics Index* (entry 121n) and the documents are accessible through the *ASI*.

The *Encyclopedia of the U.S. Census* (CQ Press, 2000) edited by Margo J. Anderson contains articles covering a wide range of topics from historical overviews of the decennial censuses since 1790 to preparations for Census 2000. There are articles on population-related topics such as immigration and characteristics of ethnic groups. Each article is signed and accompanied by a short bibliography. There are period photographs and appendixes with sample census questionnaires and costs related to taking the census.

*119. Guide to Social Science Data Preparation and Archiving. Ann Arbor, MI: Inter-University Consortium for Political and Social Research, 2000. Available: http://www. icpsr.umich.edu.

The foremost agency in the academic sector for the gathering and dissemination of social sciences statistical data is the Inter-University Consortium for Political and Social Research. The ICPSR was founded in 1962 at the Survey Research Center of the University of Michigan to advance the theory and research use of quantitative data in the social sciences. The ICPSR database contains social, economic, political, historical, demographic, census survey, international relations, and cross-national data from the U.S. and foreign sources. ICPSR receives, processes, maintains, and distributes social sciences data. Information is received from other research centers and individual researchers, with ICPSR functioning as a central repository for maintenance and dissemination. Data for research on specific topics such as the aging process, leisure activities, and crime and criminal justice are gathered and maintained. In addition, the center provides training in the use of quantitative analysis and computer technology in the social sciences. Local access to ICPSR datafiles formerly had to be obtained through a library, computer center, research center, or university academic department. In the late 1990s, ICPSR began to move toward total availability through the World Wide Web and began conversion of older data files to electronic format. A redesigned Web site was related in February 2001 with an enhanced search capability to allow those looking for data to find what they need with greater speed and accuracy. An ambitious program to scan and convert paper codebooks to digital format was also begun in 2001. And ICPSR began expanding services to members, enlarging the archive, engaging in new partnerships with archives and data distributors worldwide and helping to establish standards for the preservation and documentation of digital archives. A listing of available datafiles and studies indexed by researcher, subject, and ICPSR number can now be obtained from the ICPSR Web site replacing the annual *Guide to Resources and Services.* In 2000 ICPSR began offering unmediated access to datafiles for researchers through *ICPSR Direct.* Any researcher seeking statistical data needs to explore the datafiles available through ICPSR.

120. Guide to U.S. Government Statistics. Jay Andriot. Manassas, VA: Documents Index, 1998. 1,384p. ISSN 0434-9067.

Libraries that cannot afford the much more comprehensive (and much more expensive) *American Statistics Index* (entry 121n) or have little need for it have an alternative source in the *Guide to U.S. Government Statistics.* This guide is a single-volume index to the statistical publications of federal government entities. The entries are arranged by SuDocs number and contain SuDocs class stem, title, depository item number, beginning and ending dates of the publication, frequency of publication, and earlier or later SuDocs numbers. The "Agency Class Chronology" feature is useful for tracing agency name and organization changes, as well as SuDocs author symbol changes. If a researcher wants to locate particular publications for a certain span of time or ascertain the publications of a certain agency, this guide can be useful. It can be used in conjunction with the *ASI* but does not substitute for the *ASI* when that index is also available.

*121. LexisNexis Statistical Universe. Dayton, OH: LexisNexis. Available: http://www.lexisnexis.com.

Three products that are produced by Congressional Information Services have been combined into the *LexisNexis Statistical Universe* database. Inaugurated by CIS in the early 1970s and 1980s, the three printed indexes had accompanying full text available in microfiche. Those same services have become electronic databases with full text, although the printed versions are still available. The three indexes are the *American Statistics Index, Statistical Reference Index,* and *Index to International Statistics.*

Publication of the *American Statistics Index* was begun in 1974 by Congressional Information Service. It is the most comprehensive index to United States federal government statistical data. The *ASI* covers every type of statistical publication from hundreds of federal government agencies, including congressional committees, regulatory agencies, commissions and boards, judicial offices, statistical and research agencies, and special councils. Both depository and nondepository publications are indexed. The organization of the printed *ASI* is that of an abstracting tool. Data are indexed by subject, names, titles, categories or type of data breakdown (including demographic and geographic), and agency report number. These indexes refer to the abstract volumes that contain the bibliographic citation with SuDocs, ordering information, and an abstract that describes the organization, currency, and sources of the information. For statistical indexing prior to 1974, CIS published a three-volume *Annual and Retrospective Edition,* which selectively indexed publications back to the early 1960s. Complete copies of the statistical sources are contained in the *ASI Microfiche Library* and available individually through an on-demand ordering service.

Since 1980 the *Statistical Reference Index* has been the counterpart to the federal *American Statistics Index.* Statistical data published by state governments and the private sector are indexed in the *SRI*. Publications from associations and institutes, universities, research centers, state governments, and the commercial sector are indexed.

Index to International Statistics is the third index that was inaugurated and published by CIS. Begun in 1983, it is devoted to some 2,000 key statistical titles from approximately 100 international governmental organizations. Among these are the United Nations, the European Union, the Organization for Economic Cooperation and Development, leading commodity organizations, development banks, and more.

LexisNexis Statistical Universe is the tool of first choice for anyone seeking statistical data, either historical or current. Searching is by a feature called PowerTables or by abstract modules. PowerTables gives quick access to individually indexed tables. Searches can be conducted based on the data contained in the tables, on assigned subject descriptors, or on bibliographic information. An advanced Research Edition includes detailed data for geographic areas and industries from government and private sector sources, over 130,000 tables. The Abstracts Module offers a much broader scope of statistical information than is available in PowerTables. The abstracts in LexisNexis *Statistical Universe* describe the content of a publication, specifying what data are presented, the source of the data, and the publication's relationship to other statistical series. Every table in PowerTables is linked to an abstract, which in turn contains links to the full text and all individual tables covered by these abstracts, plus hundreds of thousand more.

*122. Statistical Abstract of the United States. U.S. Bureau of the Census. Washington, D.C.: Government Printing Office, 1878–. Ann. ISSN 0081-4741. Available: http://www.census.gov/statab/www.

If there were one indispensable statistical compilation, the *Statistical Abstract of the United States* would be that source. It presents summary tables of usually 10 to 20 years of social, political, and economic data drawn from federal statistical reports and publications. The coverage of topics is broad, ranging from information on business and economics, labor, vital statistics, education, energy, science, and transportation to social insurance and welfare services. Not only does the *Statistical Abstract* provide a wealth of recent statistical data, the tables are referenced as to the source of data, and there is a "Guide to Sources" bibliography at the end, as well as a guide to state statistical abstracts. The *Statistical Abstract* is also a major source for historical data, having begun publication in 1878.

Historical Statistics of the United States from Colonial Times to 1970 (2v., Government Printing Office, 1975; repr. Kraus International, 1989; Cambridge University Press, 1997 CD-ROM) is published as a supplement to the *Statistical Abstract*. Revised every few years, this compilation of over 1,000 pages contains data on the social, economic, political, and geographic development of the United States. A separate chapter contains colonial and pre-federal statistics. Notes at the beginning of the chapters explain the sources for and reliability of the data. Many of the tables are constructed in the same manner and categories as the *Statistical Abstract,* making the time series data compatible. An appendix in the annual *Statistical Abstract* serves as an index to many of the *SA* tables that continue *Historical Statistics* tables. There are indexes by time period and by subject. Researchers seeking historical data should first consult the two-volume *Historical Statistics* issued by the Bureau of the Census. Bernan Press publishes *Datapedia of the United States, 1790–2005* (2001), which updates the *Historical Statistics* with projections for the future. Printed editions of the *Statistical Abstract* are also published by Bernan Press and Hoover's Inc.

Another publication of use to historians is *International Historical Statistics: The Americas 1750–1993* by B.R. Mitchell (Stockton Press'/Groves dictionaries, 1998). The first edition of this work appeared in 1982. The arrangement of the tables is topical with population and vital statistics, labor force, agriculture, industry, external trade, finance, prices, and national accounts.

Another supplement to the *Statistical Abstract* is the *County and City Data Book* (Washington, D.C.: U.S. Department of Commerce, Bureau of the Census). First issued in 1949, this compilation combined two earlier separate titles, one for county and one for city data. The compilation has usually been updated every five years from census data. Every county in the United States is covered, as are over 300 standard metropolitan areas, cities of over 25,000 population, and a few other regional categories. For the geographic areas covered, the statistical information in this publication is more detailed than the summary data in the main *Statistical Abstract*. Since 1988 the *County and City Data Book* has been available in CD-ROM format.

*123. Statistical Resources on the Web. University of Michigan Library Documents Center. Available: http://www.lib.umich.edu/govdocs/statsnew.html.

The University of Michigan Documents Center maintains this comprehensive portal to statistics. Statistical Resources on the Web includes information on agriculture, business and industry, consumers, cost of living, demographics, economics, education, energy, environment, finance and currency, foreign economics, foreign trade, government finances, health, housing, labor, military, politics, science, sociology, transportation, and weather. The site has a choice of search engines and an alphabetical "quick jump" index and a broad subject directory of topics. The site has won numerous awards and is an alternative to the government maintained gateways.

POPULATION AND DEMOGRAPHIC INFORMATION

*124. AmeriStat. Population Reference Bureau and Social Science Data Analysis Network. Available: http://www.ameristat.org.

This site is described as a "one-stop source for U.S. publication data." It covers 13 broad subject areas, such as education, migration, income and poverty, and mortality. From the broad subject areas the user is given a list of subtopics that leads to the data in text, charts, and tables. As could be expected, the source of most of the data is the U.S. Census Bureau. Sources of the data are listed at the bottom of the Web page and key concepts are linked to definitions. One reason to use the site is the explanatory text that accompanies the data making it easier to interpret.

125. Bibliography of American Demographic History: The Literature from 1984 to 1994. David R. Gerhan, comp. Westport, CT: Greenwood Press, 1995. 339p. (Bibliographies and Indexes in American History, no. 30). ISBN 0-313-26677-8.

Gerhan is responsible for the earlier, *Retrospective Bibliography of American Demographic History from Colonial Times to 1983* (Greenwood Press, 1989). Together these bibliographies form a comprehensive listing of books and journal articles on American demographic history. The emphasis is on historical studies that concentrate on demographic changes over a period of time. The earlier work has over 3,800 citations to books and journal articles, including many from state and local history publications. It is divided into six sections: general background; marriage and fertility; health and death; migration, pluralism, and local patterns; family and demographic history; and population, economics, and society. Within each section there are three chronological divisions for the early United States, the nineteenth century, and the modern United States. Indexes are by subject, author, and geographic names.

The second, more recent title has nearly 9,000 citations following the same organizational pattern. All six chapters begin with an overview section. Each subsection begins with an explanation of its scope and nature followed by relevant citations. The books and articles are primarily U.S. publications, but the increasingly international scholarship on American history is reflected in entries from many countries, especially European. Besides author, place, and topical indexes, there is also an ethnicity and national origin index. These bibliographies will provide a basis for research in sociology, political science, geography, economics, and history. These bibliographies are most useful to students and scholars in the social sciences with some knowledge of demographic history.

126. Federal Population Censuses, 1790–1890: A Catalog of Microfilm Copies of the Schedules. Washington, D.C.: U.S. National Archives and Records Service, 1979. 96p. ISBN 0-911333-63-9. **1900 Federal Population Census,** 1978. 84p. ISBN 0-911333-14-2. **1910 Federal Population Census,** 1982. 56p. ISBN 0-9911333-15-0. **1920 Federal Population Census,** 1991. 96p. ISBN 0-911333-86-X.

The U.S. National Archives and Records Service sells or rents positive microfilm copies of the original schedules of the first 15 federal population censuses. The last to be released was 1930 in 2002. These pamphlets list the schedules in chronological order, with prices. Microfilm may be purchased through the Publications Services Branch.

Research Publications, Inc. also sells microfilm of decennial population census publications for the 1790–1970 censuses. The *Bibliography and Reel Index* (1975, 276p.) serves as a bibliography to the original publications and as a reel guide to the microfilm collection.

127. Population History of Eastern U.S. Cities and Towns, 1790–1870. Riley Moffat. Metuchen, NJ: Scarecrow, 1992. 242p. ISBN 0-8108-2553-8.

Population History of Western U.S. Cities and Towns, 1850–1990. Riley Moffat. Scarecrow, 1996. 344p. ISBN 0-81008-3033-7.

The U.S. Bureau of the Census reported population data only by county and incorporated townships until 1870. Constructing population histories for cities and towns that were unincorporated during this time period is very difficult. This first work contains population figures for almost 7,000 cities and towns in the eastern portion of the United States from the Atlantic Ocean to Louisiana and Minnesota. The western work covers 19 states west of North Dakota and south to Texas. The compilation includes the U.S. Census decennial population figures for all incorporated cities and towns, as well as states, territorial, and special censuses where available, as are estimates for communities that never incorporated, or waited many years to incorporate, when available. The two titles are of use to historians, geographers, and genealogists.

Two other reference works that contain historical data are *Township Atlas of the United States, Named Townships,* 2nd ed. (McLean, VA: Andriot Associates, 1979, Supp. McLean, VA: Documents Index, 1987) and the companion title, *Population Abstract of the United States* (Andriot Associates, 1983, 2v.). The atlas covers the 22 states that still have townships as civil divisions of the state. The maps are by individual state, with accompanying lists and indexes of incorporated and unincorporated places of 1,000 or more population. The *Population Abstract* gives population totals for states, counties, and cities with a population of 10,000 or more. Historical population statistics are included for the states, cities, and towns.

128. Population in Nineteenth Century Census Volumes. Suzanne Schulze. Phoenix: Oryx Press, 1983. 446p. ISBN 0-89774-122-6. **Population Information in Twentieth Century Census Volumes, 1900–1940.** Oryx Press, 1985. 274p. ISBN 0-89774-164-1. **Population Information in Twentieth Century Census Volumes, 1950–1980.** Oryx Press, 1988. 317p. ISBN 0-89774-400-4.

This three-volume set has been a boon to researchers trying to locate population information in census publications. The first volume covers the 11 censuses from 1790 to 1890. The first half of the twentieth century (up to World War II) is covered in the second volume. These two volumes use the Dubester number as the basic index number. Henry Dubester's *Catalog of United States Census Publications: 1790–1945* (Government Printing Office, 1950) has been one of the reference works most often used for identifying census publications. The years covered by the third volume are beyond the coverage of the Dubester catalog.

The Schulze volumes greatly simplify the process of identifying, locating, and retrieving printed population census information. One easy feature is the location of guides on inside covers, which serve as the first index to consult. The subjects are cross-referenced to the census year, volume, and part. The researcher proceeds to the citation for the appropriate census and volume for more detailed information. Complete bibliographic information for each part includes SuDocs number, Serial Set number, and availability in microform collections. Each decennial census is described in an essay providing history, scope, manner in which data were gathered, and unique features. Also included are lists of the subject inquiries of each census; congressional serial volumes containing census reports; and state censuses for the period. There is a section with definitions of terminology by census. This set forms the best and easiest-to-use index to census publications. It is the preferred reference tool for anyone seeking population information from the U.S. census.

129. The Population of the United States: Historical Trends and Future Projections. Donald J. Bogue. New York: Free Press/Macmillan, 1985. 728p. ISBN 0-02-904700-5.

Social and economic trends as seen in population shifts from 1790 to 1980 are shown in this reference work. The 20 chapters are topically organized and include statistical tables, graphs, pie charts, and definitions of terms. The first chapter provides an overview of the U.S. population growth and distribution. A second section is devoted to population changes and includes figures on birth and death, marriages, divorces, and migration. Social and economic factors are covered in two separate chapters and include ethnicity, education levels, the labor force, income, and unemployment. The chapter on special topics contains information on Puerto Rico, religious affiliations, and political demography. There are many references to the source documents, and bibliographies and an index are included. This work emphasizes the years since 1960; an earlier work, *The Population of the United States* (Free Press, 1959), emphasized the years preceding and following World War II. Although the data are drawn from Census Bureau publications, this work is interpretative and analytical.

A similar work is *Twentieth-Century History of United States Population* by Russell O. Wright (Scarecrow Press, 1996). Besides presenting census statistical data, the compiler of this work analyzed growth in population of the states and major cities for each census between 1900 and 1990. Considerable attention is focused on growth by regions. The social and political implications of population shifts are analyzed. The book does not have an index. It is particularly useful for the analyses it contains, as the data are available in many other sources.

An earlier publication that concentrates on the eighteenth and nineteenth centuries is *A Century of Population Growth: From the First Census of the United States to the Twelfth, 1790–1900* (Genealogical Publishing, repr. 1989, 303p.) This work was originally published by the Bureau of the Census in 1909 and has been reprinted several times. It reproduces much valuable data on the early population patterns of the United States. Besides data on age, race, sex, family characteristics, and social and economic factors, there are a number of statistics on slaves. Maps showing county boundary changes in the original 13 states plus Kentucky and Tennessee are given. Another interesting feature is a table of 4,000 surnames found in the 1790 census with spelling variations. There is much of historical value in this one volume that is useful for students and researchers.

130. Researcher's Guide to United States Census Availability, 1790–1900, 2nd ed. Ann B. Hamilton. Bowie, MD: Heritage Books, 1992. 134p. ISBN 1-155613-066-X.

This publication is a guide to U.S. census records on a county-by-county basis. The 1790–1900 U.S. censuses and indexes to those censuses are arranged by state and then by county. An introduction gives the type of data collected in each federal census. There is information on the existence of county histories and whether courthouse records were destroyed and have been reconstructed, plus a bibliography of publications issued by state and regional genealogical societies. This index can be used in conjunction with the *Map Guide to U.S. Federal Censuses, 1790–1920,* which traces county boundary changes (William Thorndale and William Dollarhide. Baltimore: Genealogical, 1987). The *Map Guide* uses the present county boundaries in each state and shows changes to the county boundaries by each census up through the 1920 census. Aside from the maps, there is a complete list of county names for each state that traces changes in names and spelling, including defunct counties. The availability of census information is also indicated. The introduction to the work gives historical information on the U.S. censuses and the records for each census. Both guides are useful for state and local historians, genealogists, geographers, political scientists, and anyone else studying changes in demography.

ATLASES AND GEOGRAPHICAL SOURCES

The study of history often involves the need for reference works that present geographical or spatial information to assist in visualizing distances or terrain. Historical maps help the student and researcher enter the mind-set of people in the time period under study. Historical atlases present information that does not become obsolete.

U.S. libraries did not extensively collect maps until after World War II, according to Cobb in his introduction to *Guide to U.S. Map Resources* (entry 134). In the electronic age, static maps that the user must interpret are being replaced by electronic geographic information systems (GIS). Geographic, census, and demographic data can be combined to create thematic maps to study growth patterns of a region, site businesses, and create new maps. Computer imaging techniques have been used to create three-dimensional battlefield maps. The historian now has the power of enhanced visual imaging for the study of life and events from the past.

131. Atlas of Historical County Boundaries. John H. Long, ed. New York: Macmillan Reference Library/Charles Scribner's Sons, 1993–. **Alabama.** ISBN 0-13-309568-1. **Delaware, Maryland, Washington, D.C.** ISBN 0-13-366337-X. **Florida.** Peggy Tuck Sinko and Kathryn Ford Thorne, comps. John H. Long, ed. 1997. 323p. ISBN 0-13-366329-9. **Illinois.** ISBN 0-13-366402-3. **Indiana.** John H. Long, ed. Peggy Tuck Sinko, comp. 1996. 394p. ISBN 0-13-309550-9. **Iowa.** ISBN 0-13-366386-8. **Kentucky.** ISBN 0-13-309543-6. **Connecticut, Maine, Massachusetts, [and] Rhode Island.** John H. Long, comp. and ed. Gordon DenBoer, comp. 1994. 412p. ISBN 0-13-051947-2. **Michigan.** ISBN 0-13-366311-6. **Mississippi.** ISBN 0-13-051970-7. **New Hampshire [and] Vermont.** John H. Long, ed., and Gordon DenBoer with George E. Goodridge Jr., comps. 1993. 216p. ISBN 0-13-151954-5. **New York.** ISBN 0-13-051962-6. **North Carolina.** ISBN 0-13-366469-4. **Ohio.** ISBN 0-13-366394-9. **South Carolina.** ISBN 0-13-366360-4. **Pennsylvania.** ISBN 0-13-315532-3. **Tennessee.** ISBN 0-13-366451-1. **Virginia, West Virginia.** ISBN 0-13-366345-0. **Wisconsin.** ISBN 0-13-366352-3.

A projected 40-volume set that will cover all states except Alaska, which does not have counties, this series has become the definitive atlas on the subject. Long previously served as an assistant editor of the *Atlas of Early American History: The Revolutionary Era, 1760–1790* and editor of the *Historical Atlas and Chronology of County Boundaries, 1788–1980* (G.K. Hall, 1984), both of which the present series will replace. The atlases are based on original research in legal documents and cover changes of county boundaries from colonial times or origin of the state to 1990. The information is presented in both maps and text. The historical boundaries are marked on special versions of U.S. Geological Survey state base maps for each state. A consolidated boundary chronology covers all boundary changes, in chronological order, for the whole state. A section of individual county chronologies, maps, and areas provides a detailed look at each county. An introduction describes the purpose, audience, scope and editorial decisions on the series. Each introduction also has unique state-specific information. Each volume has a bibliography. The project has received funding from the National Endowment for the Humanities. The atlases are useful for historians, genealogists, geographers, political scientists, students of state and local government, county clerks, librarians, and social scientists. Although a monumental undertaking, this well-researched, well-documented series will remain the definitive resource for many years.

132. Atlas of the Historical Geography of the United States. Charles Oscar Paullin. John K. Wright, ed. Washington, D.C., and New York: Carnegie Institution of Washington and the American Geographical Society, 1932. Repr. Greenwood Press, 1975.

This atlas has been a standard for many years and has never been replaced as a basic historical atlas for U.S. history. The atlas is divided into two parts. The first contains the text, which refers to the plates contained in the second part. The first section of text covers geographical and geological features, plus temperature and climate. The next section, on cartography, reprints in very small format the early maps from 1492 up to Colton's map of 1867. There are sections on Indian tribes, the exploration of the West, population, political parties and opinion, religions, military history, and boundaries. The text contains a wealth of historical information. The reproductions are adequate. Any type of user can consult this atlas when more recent publications do not contain the historical information sought.

133. Guide to Cartographic Records in the National Archives. U.S. National Archives and Records Service. Washington, D.C.: Government Printing Office, 1971. 444p. ISBN 0-911333-19-3.

Since the founding of the nation, the U.S. federal government has extensively engaged in cartographic activities of a military, geographical, geological, and agricultural nature. The extent of the mapping activities can only be realized when the guide to 1.6 million maps and 9,000 aerial photographs in the collections of the National Archives Cartographic and Architectural Branch is perused. The introduction briefly traces the development of exploration, surveying, and mapping activities from 1777 to the present. The organization of the guide is by government branches and agencies. A brief historical account of each agency's responsibility and activities is given. The information includes record group title and number, with series subheadings showing inclusive dates and the number of items. Military maps for all wars are included, as well as peacetime aerial photography by the Department of Agriculture. The indexing in the guide was produced from a database and gives entry number, a list of major classifications by page numbers, and the inclusive dates of groups covered in the text.

Other extensive collections of maps in the federal sector are in the collections of the Library of Congress, which has published several catalogs and lists of these collections. *A List of Geographical Atlases in the Library of Congress with Bibliographical Notes* (1909–1974, 8v.) is the most comprehensive inventory. For U.S. history there is a separate *List of Maps of America in the Library* (1901; repr. B. Franklin, 1974), which describes many old state and county maps and city plans in the library's Map Division. Another is *United States Atlases: A List of National State, County, City and Regional Atlases in the Library of Congress* (1950–1953, 2v. Repr. Arno, 1971). The second volume of this title also lists atlases held by 180 other libraries with locations.

An interesting Web site of the Library of Congress is Panoramic Maps, 1847–1909A based upon information from John R. Hebert and Patrick E. Dempsey's *Panoramic Maps of Cities in the United States and Canada,* 2nd ed. (1984). "Panoramic maps are non-photographic representations of cities portrayed as if viewed from above at an oblique angle.

Although not generally drawn to scale, they show street patterns, individual buildings, and major landscape features in perspective." Access is available through http://www.loc.gov.

The researcher will need to use all published lists and finding aids in endeavoring to make use of the vast cartographic resources of the National Archives and the Library of Congress.

134. Guide to U.S. Map Resources. 2nd ed. David A. Cobb, comp. Chicago: American Library Association, 1990. 495p. ISBN 0-8389-0547-0.

The ALA Map and Geography Round Table sponsors the compilation of this directory. The organization is alphabetical by state, city, and institution. Collections of 975 map libraries and their holdings are described, including chronological coverage, hours, and access policies. The first edition was criticized for the lack of subject indexing. This revised edition has greatly expanded indexing, adding a "Collection Strengths Index" with access points by area, name of special collection, and subject according to the Library of Congress map classification. There is a "Library Institution Index" that gives addresses and telephone numbers. The information was gathered by a questionnaire sent to academic, geoscience, private, public, and federal libraries. Because the maps in many collections do not appear individually cataloged in databases, ascertaining which institutions collect certain subjects may be the first step in finding maps for research.

There is another directory of map collections published by the Special Libraries Association, *Map Collections in the United States and Canada: A Directory* (4th ed., 1985). The two directories give much the same information; 805 collections are indexed in the Special Libraries directory edited by David K. Carrington and Richard W. Stephenson. Either directory can be used.

135. Historical Atlas of the United States. Rev. ed. National Geographic Society. Washington, D.C.: National Geographic Society, 1994. 289p. ISBN 0-87044-970-2.

The revised edition of the historical atlas was produced in celebration of the Society's centennial and 35,000 copies were given to U.S. high schools. The intent of the volume was to provide the first comprehensive atlas of U.S. history from a geographic perspective in 50 years. It contains 380 maps, 450 photographs, and considerable text, all very attractively formatted. The arrangement is in six broad areas, with additional chronological chapters by time period. The areas are the land, the people, boundaries, the economy, transport and communications, and communities. There are clear, concise timelines. There is a bibliography for the text and the sources of the illustrations. A subject index also covers text and illustrations.

136. Historical Maps of North America. "Michael Smith." London, PRC Publishing; distr., New York: Sterling Publishing, 2001. 144p. ISBN 1-8648-592-7.

The maps reproduced in this work are from the collections of the Public Record Office at Kew. The oversized volume contains 154 maps, the majority tinted or in multiple colors. The maps range from the seventeenth through the nineteenth centuries with one from the twentieth century. A few are from Canada, Mexico, and Central America. The majority is by British cartographers, but there are several by U.S. and French and Dutch cartographers. There is an introduction by "Michael Swift," a pen name of the author. Because the maps are not produced with dimensions, scales, or bibliographic descriptions, the volume is more useful for general reference and as information on their existence for locating the originals.

137. Mapping America's Past: A Historical Atlas. Mark C. Carnes, and John A. Garraty, with Patrick Williams. New York: Henry Holt, 1996. 288p. ISBN 0-8050-4927-4.

The emphasis in this historical atlas is on social and cultural history. There are nearly 200 maps on American history but also nearly 100 maps of other countries from which people immigrated to the United States. The volume is divided by broad historical period beginning with pre-Columbian America and ending with "America, Evolving Superpower." There are extensive bibliographical sources, notes, and an index. The maps illuminate often-obscure aspects of American life. Many moments of American history—from slavery to immigration, cholera to race riots are explicated. The work is useful for the general reader, students, and researchers.

138. Maps Contained in the Publications of the *American Bibliography,* **1639–1819; An Index and Checklist.** Jim Walsh. Metuchen, NJ: Scarecrow, 1988. 367p. ISBN 0-8108-2193-1.

Both separate maps and maps within books are listed and indexed in this work, which is divided into three sections. The first section contains the maps in Evans's *American Bibliography* (entry 34), 1639–1800, arranged by Evans number. The next section covers the Shaw and Shoemaker *American Bibliography* (entry 35) for the years 1801–1819, arranged by Shaw/Shoemaker number. The last section is made up of six indexes by date of publication, place of publication, personal and corporate name, book title, map title, and geographic name. Anyone searching for maps of the Americas and the United States should use this time-saving tool.

*139. Omni Gazetteer of the United States of America. Frank R. Abate. Detroit: Omnigraphics, 1991. 11v. ISBN 1-55888-336-3. [Available as a CD-ROM product from the publisher].

Approximately one and a half million place names in the United States and territories are briefly described in this gazetteer, organized into nine regional volumes and by states within the regions. The regional volumes cover counties, cities, towns, islands, rivers, swamps, creeks, parks, churches, cemeteries, and historic buildings. Descriptions in the entries include the names and variants, zip code, county where located, map coordinates, and U.S. Geological Survey (USGS) topographic map in which the place name can be found. Sources of information are given. An index to the set provides access by geographic names. The last volume, *U.S. Data Sourcebook,* contains seven appendixes, including an index to USGS maps and list of U.S. airports, Indian reservations, and items on the National Register of Historic Places. There is a section titled "Acquiring and Using Maps and Other Topographic Resources." This is the most comprehensive U.S. gazetteer ever published and is of use to geographers, historians, and genealogists.

The *Omni Gazetteer* is derived from the U.S. Geological Survey GNIS (Geographic Names Information System) database. Now the GNIS has in excess of 2 million names and can be accessed at http://mapping.usgs.gov/www/gnis. *The National Gazetteer of the United*

States of America (NG) is an ambitious long-range project of the USGS proceeding on a state-by-state basis. The states that have been covered thus far are available in CD-ROM.

A one-volume work is *The Cambridge Gazetteer of the United States and Canada: A Dictionary of Places* (Cambridge University Press, 1995). Although not as complete as the authoritative U.S. sources, this makes a handy ready-reference work for smaller libraries.

An older but still useful work is the *Bibliography of Place-Name Literature: United States and Canada,* (American Library Association, 3rd ed. 1982.) The literature of place-names furnishes exposition of origins, meanings, correct spellings, nicknames, pronunciations of sites, geographical features, regions, and cities located throughout the United States. The third edition furnishes a listing of over 4,800 books and journal articles, along with manuscript compilations located in various libraries with brief notes accompanying some of the entries. Author and subject indexes aid access.

140. The Routledge Atlas of American History. Martin Gilbert. 3rd ed. New York: Routledge, 1995. 138p. ISBN 0-4151-3627.

The multicultural history of the United States is covered in 138 maps in this atlas. From the origin of settlement in America to the Persian Gulf War and Somalia, the political, military, social, transport, and economic history of the country are covered. Topics include the War of Independence; World War I, World War II and the subsequent conflicts; the development of the railroads; immigration trends; voting rights for women and African Americans; farming and industry; and much more.

Another more recent work with the same title, *Atlas of American History,* is by Robert H. Ferrell and Richard Natkiel (Facts on File, 1997). This atlas is designed for instruction and each chapter contains three to six pages of written narrative providing teachers with a new way to summarize historical events. The aim is to present a brief, but historically thorough, political picture of American history from the beginning to 1992. The work is visually pleasing with maps, illustrations, and historical photographs.

*141. U.S. National Park Service "Mapping History Using GIS." Available: http://www2.cr.nps.gov/gis/knoerl.htm.

The National Park Service maintains the Mapping and Preservation Inventory Tool (MAPIT), which is a database with sophisticated mapping capabilities that combines information about where historic properties are located with information about how these properties look. MAPIT displays inventory information as a map, chart, or table. Through the MAPIT database standard survey forms, National Register of Historic Places nomination forms, and other forms used by preservationists can be generated.

PART II
U.S. History
Topics and Issues

Chapter 2
Politics and Government

The current state of affairs in politics and government is the province of political scientists and international relations and governmental affairs experts. The historian studies a longer time span. The current awareness tools do become retrospective files as they age, so that materials for historic research overlap with those of the present. Since the advent of the computer age, disciplines in the social sciences have become increasingly data oriented. Political scientists make extensive use of election data, both current and historical. Because this is a guide to reference sources for historical research, a number of long-running current awareness services and data sources produced mainly for the political science, communications, and sociology fields have been included in this chapter. For the most part, reference tools have been omitted if they do not contain information dating at least as far back as 1970. A few exceptions are new tools that within a few years will contain a substantial amount of historical information.

Political science was indexed for many years by the former *ABC POL SCI* index. Cambridge Scientific acquired the title and in 2002 began a merged database of the international serials literature in political science and its complementary fields, including international relations, law, and public administration/policy. Although researchers in the fields of political science, policy studies, and public administration do not use the same approach as those engaged in historical research, the reference tools employed in these fields are also of use to the historian.

Another political science index also available online is *United States Political Science Documents* (USPSD), compiled at the University of Pittsburgh. The database contains citations and abstracts from 150 scholarly U.S. journals dealing with political and social sciences including education, domestic and foreign policy, international relations, behavioral sciences, public administration, economics, law and contemporary problems, and world politics.

This chapter is organized into a general section, followed by a section on the U.S. Federal government, including the Constitution and then subdivided by the three constitutional branches. There is a section devoted to state, local, regional, and territorial government, which includes other governmental entities outside of the federal sector. A last section is devoted to political campaigns and elections.

GENERAL SOURCES

142. American Political Leaders 1789–2000. Washington, D.C.: CQ Press, 2000. 560p. ISBN 1-56802-562-9.

Basic biographical facts about America's political leaders are included in the entries organized by six chapters: presidents, vice presidents, cabinet members, Supreme Court justices, members of congress, and governors. Also included is descriptive and analytical text on topics such as presidential disability and succession, first ladies, presidential affiliations, ethnic and gender makeup of Congress. Appendixes include additional reference tables on Congress. The volume is organized as a quick reference guide and thoroughly indexed to provide easy access to names and facts.

An earlier similar title to the CQ work is *American Political Leaders from Colonial Times to the Present* (ABC-CLIO, 1991). Although selective, rather than comprehensive, this is an excellent biographical work. It includes over 400 individuals, some of whom are lesser known but who had an important political role in U.S. history. The biographies not only give the pertinent facts about the individual, they also are well written and stress the significance of the individual to U.S. history. Brief bibliographies accompany the biographies, and some entries have portraits. Besides including all major-party presidential candidates, the work also includes a selection of third-party candidates, all vice presidents, speakers of the house, chief justices of the Supreme Court, and secretaries of state. Not all of the persons included were officeholders. For those individuals profiled, *American Political Leaders* is a superior source to the standard biographical dictionaries.

U.S. Government Leaders (Salem Press, 1997) updates 124 biographies from two other Magill's series. The leaders are the foremost names in American government including all U.S. presidents as well as various leaders during colonial and the early Republic period. Current political figures are also included. The entries are lengthy and provide analysis on accomplishments and significance of the individual with short annotated bibliographies. A chronology lists the individuals included in the set. There is an index. The set is designed for students.

143. Atlas of American Politics, 1960–2000. J. Clark Archer et al. Washington, D.C.: CQ Press, 2002. 350p. ISBN 1-56802-665-X.

District, state, and federal information provides comprehensive coverage of U.S. political administrations from the 1960s forward. More than 200 maps with narrative provide analysis of political party control of Congress, state legislatures, and governorships; presidential voting patterns; Supreme Court confirmation votes; origins of Supreme Court cases by state; and a variety of other political, social, economic, and demographic issues. The entire time span of 1960–2000 in the title is actually covered only in the chapters on national politics, allowing readers to trace trends over that time span. Other chapters on the state and foreign policy do not contain coverage for the 40 years. The text begins with background on contemporary politics and government and includes the impact of political administration since the 1960s on American life. The political maps are useful to historians and students alike.

144. Biographical Dictionary of Public Administration. Patricia Moss Wigfall and Behrooz Kalantari. Westport, CT: Greenwood Publishing Group, 2001. 184p. ISBN 0-3313-30203-0.

The foreword to this work is written by Paula Quick Hall. It is designed to introduce individuals who originated or had a significant impact on the major theories of public administration. The coverage is cross-disciplinary with individuals from organizational theory, personnel, and budgeting. Each short biography includes a personal history followed by the subject's major contribution to the discipline and a bibliography of his or her works on the subject.

A complementary earlier work is *Public Administration in American Society: A Guide to Information Sources* by John Edward Rouse, Jr. (Gale, 1980) The concentration in this bibliography is on the decade of the 1970s and the growth of the field of public administration and governmental bureaucracies. The bibliography of over 1,000 annotated entries also selectively covers the history of public administration since the end of the nineteenth century. The majority of the sources are articles in scholarly and professional journals from the fields of history, sociology, psychology, political science, business, management, and economics. Author, title, and subject indexes are included. Although the bibliography is not up-to-date, it serves as a historical overview of the development of the field of public administration and is a useful source for historians of government policy.

145. Congressional Quarterly's Desk Reference on American Government. 2nd ed. Bruce Wetterau. Washington, D.C.: Congressional Quarterly, 2000. 344p. ISBN 1-56802-548-3.

Intended as a current ready-reference source, this title is updated every four to five years. Although currency is maintained, the information covers the U.S. government from 1789 to the present. The text is arranged in five sections: the government, presidency, Congress, campaigns and elections, and the Supreme Court. The format is question-and-answer, with the answers having source bibliographies and directing the reader to other related subjects. There are also lists of firsts and charts that analyze information not found elsewhere. The text of the U.S. Constitution is included. There is a bibliography of the sources from the text and an exhaustive index. The publication is attractive and an excellent first source to consult.

*146. CQ's Electronic Encyclopedia of American Government. Washington, D.C.: CQ Press. [Electronic database] Available: http://library.cqpress.com.

The electronic database from CQ consolidates the information in a number of CQ print reference works. The database contains biographies of American leaders; the complete text of the U.S. Constitution, articles, and amendments; *CQ's Guide to the U.S. Constitution* (entry 159); and U.S. Supreme Court cases and decisions. Contained within the database are information on how the U.S. government is organized and works, the division of powers, and political parties in America. The electronic encyclopedia is very user friendly with search capabilities by subject, branch of government, or 1 of 10 Quick Search Topics. There are also Simple or Boolean searches within or across all subject areas as well as full-text searches. Browsing is by contents, alphabetical entries, branches of government, elections, or illustrations. Current reference titles now online are *CQ Researcher* and *CQ Weekly*.

Another database in the CQ electronic Library is the *CQ Public Affairs Collection*. Even though this is a current affairs and public policy database, it does have statistical and historical analyses, the full text of historic documents, and primary source materials. There is a similar electronic database for the *Supreme Court Collection* (entry 209). These databases make an excellent starting point for students and ready reference.

Facts on File maintains a Web site, *Government on File* (available at http://www.fofweb.com/subscription), which is an online resource of data on the U.S. government.

The site is designed for students with textual and visual materials covering the structure and function of the federal government. The entries discuss American democracy, the Constitution and its amendments, and how the American political system works. There is also a print version.

ABC-CLIO also has an online database, *American Government* (available: http://americangovernment.abc-clio.com). This site is designed to function as a resource tool for enhancement of instruction. It can be searched for reference as a database, which includes more than 10,000 entries all connected with cross-references. In addition to the entries, there are bibliographies, chronologies, directories, timelines, statistics, and a glossary.

147. Encyclopedia of American Government. Joseph M. Bessette and R. Kent Rasmussen, eds. Englewood Cliffs, NJ: Salem Press, 1998. 4v. ISBN 0-89356-117-7.

This four-volume reference work was developed for students in middle and secondary schools. There are 200 alphabetical entries that cover the basics of the organization and functioning of the U.S. government. Contemporary social issues that are in the forefront of public policy are well covered and reflect an awareness of gender and minority issues. The coverage is broad including international politics. Each entry has a short bibliography with references, mostly from the 1990s. The last volume includes the text of the Constitution and its amendments. There is a glossary and a comprehensive index.

A similar title compiled for student use is *How Government Works* (Macmillan, 1999). This title is in the *Macmillan Compendium* series and is drawn from other Macmillan reference titles on the presidency, Congress, the Constitution, and the judicial system. The articles have not been updated from original publication. The purpose of the volume is to provide a one-volume compendium of information on all aspects of U.S. government.

The focus of *American Government at Work* edited by Richard C. Remy (Grolier, 2001) is issues that pertain to young adults. This nine-volume work explains the inner working of American government in a question-and-answer format in patriotic red, white, and blue.

148. Encyclopedia of American Political History. Paul Finkelman and Peter Wallenstein. Washington, D.C.: CQ Press, 2001. 494p. ISBN 1-56802-511-4.

More than 255 signed, original articles by prominent scholars of American political history make up this new volume. The articles are organized alphabetically and cross-referenced by subject with a bibliography of further readings. In addition to a timeline with explanatory text that helps to establish a context for key figures, events, and concepts, there is a glossary of frequently used abbreviations, an index, and a bibliography. The volume has over 150 photographs, illustrations, maps, and tables. It is a general encyclopedia for all levels of reference use.

The CQ encyclopedia is similar to an earlier work with the same title—*Encyclopedia of American Political History: Studies of the Principal Movements and Ideas,* edited by Jack P. Greene (Scribner's, 1984. 3v.) The work contains 90 essays, each written by a noted scholar in the field. The introductory essay is "Historiography of American Political History." It is important to note the subtitle of the work, as it emphasizes ideology, issues, movements, and trends. This is not a work one goes to for facts or short historical accounts. The articles average 10 pages in length and are arranged, not in topical order, but alphabetically by title from "Agricultural Policy" to "Women's Rights." There is an index, which includes subjects and personal names. Annotated bibliographies are included with each chapter, although these vary somewhat in length.

A visual record of U.S. politics is provided by *American Political Prints 1766–1876: A Catalog of the Collections in the Library of Congress* (G.K. Hall, 1991). Bernard F. Reilly, Jr., has selected prints from the Library of Congress collections to form a history and political commentary through editorial cartoons. U.S. presidents, other prominent politicians, businessmen, and minorities are lampooned and vilified but seldom praised. Political cartoons are usually biased and vitriolic. The work has notes and text to accompany the cartoons and is of interest to journalists, political scientists, and historians.

149. Encyclopedia of American Political Reform. Richard A. Clucas. Santa Barbara, CA: ABC-CLIO, 1996. 346p. ISBN 0-874-36855-3.

The time span covered by this one-volume reference work is from 1962 to 1996. The focus is at the federal and state levels. The term "reform" is broadly defined and divided into four subtopics: economic reform, increased political participation, more effective government, and government ethics. The entries cover issues and concepts that fostered reform, investigations, lawsuits, movements, terms, places, and people. There is an introduction, which provides an overview of the period and discusses themes and issues. A chronology for the time period by year follows. There is a bibliography that includes books and journal articles. The work is useful to political scientists and historians.

150. Ethics in U.S. Government: an Encyclopedia of Investigations, Scandals, Reforms, and Legislation. Robert North Roberts. Westport, CT: Greenwood Press, 2001. 367p. ISBN 0-313-31198-6.

The scope of this work includes a timeline from the beginnings of the United States as a nation. The topics of ethics, scandals, and reform are covered in 264 entries written by the author. Each entry gives pertinent details along with the final outcome of the case and contains a bibliography of suggested readings that include many periodical and newspaper articles and a few Web sites. The volume is illustrated with photographs from the National Archives, the Library of Congress, presidential libraries, and other sources. This useful work gathers incidents treated separately elsewhere into one volume in which the entire span of such incidents can be viewed.

*151. Famous First Facts About American Politics. Steven Anzovin, and Janet Podell. Bronx, NY: H.W. Wilson, 2001. 756. ISBN 0-8242-0971-0. [WilsonWeb electronic database and WilsonDisc CD-ROM].

Since 1933, over 50 years, *Kane's Famous First Facts* has been a well-known reference title. The *Famous First Facts* title has been slightly changed in the latest edition and the number of entries scaled back to 4,000 facts related to American politics very broadly defined. Traditional topics in politics such as elections, elected and appointed officials, government at all levels, courts, legislation, and political parties are covered. Five separate indexes by subject, year, month and day, personal name, and geography, make the volume easy to use.

The fifth edition of *Famous First Facts: A Record of First Happenings, Discoveries, and Inventions in American History* was published in 1997 edited by Joseph Nathan Kane, Steven Anzovin, and Janet Podell. More than 9,000 inventions, discoveries, and first happenings in American history are included in the fifth edition, which has a new organization from the previous editions. The main organization is topical with entries arranged chronologically within clearly delineated subject divisions. The organization enables readers to trace new developments through the years. A new subject index and four additional indexes enable users to trace an event by year, month, and day of occurrence, by names of persons directly or indirectly involved, and by state and municipality where the event took place. The electronic versions allow searching by subject categories, keywords, personal names, city, state, date, year, or any combination.

152. The Facts on File Dictionary of American Politics. Kathleen Thompson Hill and Gerald N. Hill. New York: Facts on File, 2001. 448p. ISBN 0-816-04519-4.

The purpose of this reference with more than 1,600 up-to-date entries is to "demystify politics, shatter traditional beliefs, and promote a greater understanding of the people, terms, and language associated with the American political system." Much like earlier dictionaries of American politics, short definitions are included for terms, phrases, agencies and organizations, slang, specific legal cases, locations, and acronyms. Appendixes contain the text of key historic documents, presidential election results from 1789–2000, presidential and vice presidential biographies, a listing of presidents and vice presidents that includes terms of office, party affiliation, and birth and death dates.

A more scholarly work is *The HarperCollins Dictionary of American Government and Politics* by Jay M. Shafritz (HarperCollins, 1992). Former editions of the *HarperCollins Dictionary* were titled the *Dorsey Dictionary*. The work has more than 4,000 entries covering U.S. politics and government at the federal, state, and local levels. Entries range from significant Supreme Court decisions to political slang. Brief biographies, major federal laws, journals and professional associations, and bibliographic references are included. The format is attractive, with illustrations, charts, and diagrams. Boxes treat specific events such as Great Society legislation, presidential vetoes and congressional overrides of vetoes between 1961 and 1985, and turnouts in presidential elections, 1920–1984. Five appendixes include the text of the U.S. Constitution with annotations, a guide to federal government documents, information on online databases and statistical information, and an index that places all of the entries in the dictionary into concept lists by subject.

Another similar, more recent work is *The American Political Dictionary* by Jack C. Plano and Milton Greenberg (Harcourt Brace College Publishers, 1996). This standard dictionary was first published in 1962 and has been updated periodically. It is classified by subject, with a comprehensive alphabetical index included to facilitate location of particular terms. One of the strengths of this dictionary is the coverage of important court cases and statutes. Each entry begins with a definition, followed by an explanation of the significance of the term or event. Chapters cover the U.S. Constitution, civil rights, the legislative and judicial processes, business and labor, health, education, foreign policy, and state and local government. It is an excellent ready-reference source.

*153. Guide to the Federal Records in the National Archives of the United States. National Archives and Records Administration, 1995. **National Archives of the United States.** Available: http://www.nara.gov.

The National Archives are the official repository of U.S. historical records from the First Continental Congress forward, including the records of all three branches of the U.S. government. There is no one main tool for identifying the vast collections of the U.S. National Archives, which has issued numerous finding aids and publications dealing with specific groups of collections.

Collections in the National Archives are organized according to record groups, which are numbered according to accession order. The guide provides comprehensive coverage of NARA holdings of federal records at the records group level. Its purpose is to assist researchers in identifying which record groups may have material relevant to their research topics. The arrangement is by government branch, then bureau or agency. The descriptions in the guide are very brief, and the index provides access not by collection or subject, but according to the terms in the descriptions. The guide is now available in both printed and electronic versions. The Web version incorporates descriptive information about federal records acquired by the National Archives after the 1995 edition went to press and it is regularly updated with new acquisitions. The electronic version can be accessed on the National Archives site.

The records in the National Archives created in, or relating to, the period before the Constitution went into effect on March 4, 1789, are described in *A Guide to Pre-Federal Records in the National Archives* (NARA, 1989). These documents include those of the Continental and Confederation congresses, the Constitutional Convention, and the Continental Army and Navy. Records are included for the period of the Revolutionary War pertaining to commerce, Indian affairs, postal and customs operations, and land, pension, and other claims arising out of the military and civilian activities for the period. Diplomatic, fiscal, and judicial records for the Revolutionary War era are included. Information on each record group includes a brief history and describes the organization of the records, indicates availability in microform with reel numbers, and notes the existence of finding aids. There is a subject index that includes names, offices, places, and topics.

One of the more useful tools for research using National Archives materials is *National Archives Microfilm Resources for Research: A Comprehensive Catalog* (1986). The National Archives has an extensive microfilming program that has greatly facilitated access to the collections. This catalog lists the materials available for purchase and gives the "M" and "T" numbers by which microfilm is ordered. Arrangement is by government department or agency, with keyword and geographical indexes. Another series, titled *Select Catalog of National Archives Microfilm Publications,* includes catalogs for individual collections such as black studies, American Indians, genealogy and biographical research, immigrant and passenger arrivals, military service records, and diplomatic records.

One of the most indispensable guides is not a publication of the National Archives and Records Service. *The Archives: A Guide to the National Archives Field Branches* (Salt Lake City: Ancestry Publishing, 1988) provides information on materials in the 11 field branches of the National Archives, which were created to house regional documents, including district court records. Records of a number of specific agencies (such as the Bureau of Indian Affairs and the surgeon general's office) and personnel and military records are located in field branches. In addition to storing original documents, the field branches contain duplicate microfilm collections of census records and other records pertinent to the region. The guide gives information on the holdings and services of each branch, both holdings shared by other branches and those unique to that branch. The guide also describes over 150 record groups, with information on published finding aids and the record groups availability of microfilm.

A special publication is the *Guide to the Holdings of the Still Picture Branch of the National Archives* compiled by Barbara Lewis Burger (NARA, 1990). There are over 6 million photographs and graphic images in the National Archives Still Picture Branch. The guide is arranged according to record group with descriptions of the photographs by topic, the name of the photographer, date range, and medium. There is a name and subject index.

The Trust Fund Board of the National Archives and Records Administration publishes the journal *Prologue*. The purpose of the journal is to inform the public about the collections and resources of the National Archives. It contains articles about the collections of the various libraries and archival repositories under the administration of the National Archives and Records Service, with illustrations of some of the materials. The periodical also contains news on accessions, declassification of records, and other current information about the archives.

154. The Oxford Guide to the United States Government. John J. Patrick et al. New York: Oxford University Press, 2001. 802p. ISBN 0-19-514273-X.

The scope of this work includes all branches of the U.S. federal government. Articles include biographies of presidents; vice presidents; Supreme Court justices; some, but not all, first ladies; some members of Congress; and profiles of significant groups in American politics. Most, but not all, executive departments and agencies, as well as event, terms, issues, and concepts are included. Major Supreme Court and presidential decisions are also included. Each entry contains a short bibliography and cross-references to other entries. There are seven appendixes, a general bibliography, and an index. The work is useful for ready reference.

155. United States Government Manual. Washington, D.C.: Government Printing Office, 1935–. Ann. ISSN 0887-8064. **United States Government Manual** (1995–1996 through 1999–2000). Available: http://www.access.gpo.gov/nara/nara001.html.

Although it is designed to be a current information source, the *Manual* began publication in 1935, and earlier editions are useful for historical information. The *Manual* contains current information on the organization and personnel of the United States government and quasi-official agencies organized according to branches of government. All of the executive agencies are defined and described. Also included are international organizations in which the United States participates. There is a brief description and history of each agency, including its role and functions within the federal government. Key personnel are listed with addresses and telephone numbers, and electronic access. Additional information can include publications, grants and contracts, and other appropriate information specific to a particular agency. Appendixes contain abbreviations and acronyms, organization charts, lists of abolished agencies or transferred functions, and citations to agencies in the *Code of Federal Regulations*. There is an index by name, subject, and agency. This is one of the most useful and basic sources of information on the federal government. More detailed information on the organizational structure, regulatory documents of an agency, or presidential documents is published in the *Federal Register* (entry 169). Now that the *Manual* is available electronically it is searchable and the information can be downloaded. A useful Internet site organized along the lines of the manual is the listing for U.S. Federal Government Agencies (available: http://www.lib.lsu.edu/gov/fedgov.html) provided by Louisiana State University.

THE CONSTITUTION

A number of reference works were issued in observance of the bicentennial of the U.S. Constitution in 1987. Many of these works are interpretative and analytical, with essays written by scholars. Several recent reference works focus on constitutional law in light of social issues since World War II. Only those sources that broadly cover the writing and historical development of the U.S. Constitution are described in this section. Reference sources for state constitutions are listed in the section headed "State, Local, Regional, and Territorial Government."

156. The American Constitution: An Annotated Bibliography. Robert J. Janosik. Pasadena, CA: Salem Press, 1991. 254p. (Magill Bibliographies). ISBN 0-89356-665-9.

The compiler's intent with this bibliography is to provide source material for the study of the U.S. Constitution for students from the high school to university level and to present a diversity of viewpoints on the major issues in constitutional law. The bibliography contains citations to secondary-source material written since 1970. The work is divided into four categories: reference works; the text of the Constitution; federal government institutions; and the individual and the Constitution. Like all products of Salem Press, this bibliography is an excellent basic reference tool that must be supplemented by more in-depth research for serious scholarship.

157. A Companion to the United States Constitution and Its Amendments. 2nd ed. John R. Vile. Westport, CT: Greenwood Press, 1997. 288p. ISBN 0-275-95785-3.

John R. Vile is a political scientist responsible for several reference works on the U.S. Constitution. This *Companion* is his contribution to the numerous guides that have been published. One of the best features of Vile's work is that he has endeavored to explain the historical roots of the Constitution, the idea of equality of human rights, and the various plans that formed the basis of the Constitution. The Declaration of Independence and the Articles of Confederation are each the subject of a chapter as the foundation documents of the Constitution. Then the parts of executive, judicial, and congressional branches are focused on. Each section of the Constitution is taken up with explanations of it meaning. The remainder of the book deals with the amendments. Each chapter has extensive references to source materials, including court cases and readings. The work is aimed at students or the general reader and is clearly written.

Another work by Vile published in the same time frame is *Encyclopedia of Constitutional Amendments, Proposed Amendments, and Amending Issues, 1789–1995* (ABC-CLIO, 1996). This title is devoted solely to the amendments to the Constitution and provides a history and analysis of amendments that have been proposed and ratified. Since 2001 it has been available from the publisher as an e-book. There are 400 alphabetically arranged entries covering the 27 amendments in short useful essays. Nearly 11,000 amendments are grouped by topic such as the Equal Rights for Women amendment and school prayer. Many entries have brief bibliographies and there is a general bibliography as well. Several appendixes contain the text of the Constitution; dates amendments were proposed and ratified; approximate number of proposed amendments by decade; and a chronology from 1683 to the present that lists important moments in amendment history and the number of amendments proposed by year. There is a comprehensive subject index. This is a definitive reference work on the history of amendments to the Constitution and makes an excellent supplement to the *Companion to the United States Constitution* by the same author.

John R. Vile has also authored *The United States Constitution: Questions and Answers* (Greenwood Press, 1998). Intended for high school students, the aim of this work is to illustrate basic facts and principles of the U.S. Constitution, its amendments, and its history.

Words and phrases in the U.S. Constitution and the Bill of Rights are the focus of *The Language of the Constitution: A Sourcebook and Guide to the Ideas, Terms, and Vocabulary Used by the Framers of the United States Constitution* (Greenwood Press, 1991) by Thurston Greene. The two documents, plus other political writings and documents from the colonial period that may have influenced the framers of the Constitution, were scanned and made into a database, from which the passages containing 85 seminal words and phrases were extracted. Each extract is accompanied by a citation to the source. The purpose of the work is to set the words and phrases into the context of the time so that the contemporary meanings can be understood in the present. The work has a subject/source index. An 1872 "Concordance to the Constitution" by Charles W. Stearns is included as an appendix. The work is of use to students and scholars studying the formation of the Constitution.

In 2002, Greenwood inaugurated a new series, *Reference Guides to the United States Constitution,* with Jack Stark as editor, projected to have over 35 books dealing with major topics such as Federalism, privileges and immunities, due process, freedom of the press, presidential powers and state sovereign immunity. Each of the books will have a brief history of the topic, lengthy and sophisticated analyses of the current state of the law on the topic, a bibliographical essay that organizes and evaluates scholarly material to facilitate further research, a table of cases, and an index.

158. The Complete Bill of Rights: The Drafts, Debates, Sources, & Origins. Neil H. Cogan, ed. New York: Oxford University Press, 1997. 705p. ISBN 0-19-51-322-X.

The purpose of this work is to provide and interpret the documentary record for the first 10 amendments to the U.S. Constitution. It does not supercede or replace the *Founder's Constitution* (entry 163) an earlier, similar reference set. John R. Vile's *Encyclopedia of Constitutional Amendments, Proposed Amendments, and Amending Issues, 1789–1995* (entry 157n) also overlaps with this work. The book is arranged in 10 chapters by amendment. The original documents included are excerpts of colonial charters and laws and preliminary drafts and proposals from state conventions; discussions of drafts and proposals, debates, commentary from contemporary newspapers and pamphlets; and letters and diaries from the founders and others. The work is useful as a compact source for original documents relating to the drafting of the Bill of Rights.

159. CQ's Guide to the U.S. Constitution: History, Text, Index, Glossary. Ralph Mitchell. Washington, D.C.: Congressional Quarterly, 1986. 108p. ISBN 0-87187-392-3.

A revised edition of *An Index to the Constitution of the United States with Glossary* (CQ, 1980), this guide gathers a number of elements into a single source. Both the text and a history of the Constitution are included. The history explains the importance of each of the major components of the Constitution and the historical currents and philosophy behind their incorporation into the document. The index in the guide gives references to the exact article or amendment, section, and paragraph. The glossary of terms is helpful in understanding the language of the Constitution. This guide is useful for teaching the Constitution and as a quick reference for students and researchers in all types of libraries.

Many reference works on the Constitution contain the text with the amendments. An authoritative compilation is the *Constitution of the United States of America, Analysis and Interpretation,* which is issued every 10 years by the Congressional Research Service of the Library of Congress, with biennial supplements between editions. The volume is known as the *Constitution Annotated* because every article and section is explicated, with citations to Supreme Court decisions. Tables are also included that list constitutional amendments with status (i.e., pending or ratified); acts of Congress and state and local laws that have been held unconstitutional by the Supreme Court; and Supreme Court decisions that were later overturned. There is an index.

160. The Constitution and Its Amendments. Roger K. Newman, ed. New York: Macmillan Library Reference/Simon & Schuster Macmillan, 1999. 4v. ISBN 0-02-864858-7.

The emphasis in this four-volume work is on an integrated view of the history of the Constitution from political, social, and judicial issues. The set is attractively formatted with black-and-white photographs, illustrations, and political cartoons. Terms are defined in sidebars and are cumulated in a glossary in the fourth volume. There are 165 essays written by more than 120 constitutional experts from the law, academe, and journalism. The essays examine the key institutions and clauses that make up the Constitution's seven articles and 27 amendments. Related Supreme Court decisions receive coverage. The essays clarify each article with explanations of the intent of the founders and examples of applications throughout U.S. history. The first three volumes cover the Constitution and Bill of Rights. The last volume covers the remaining amendments. Each volume is separately indexed. There is a comprehensive index but not a general bibliography. The set is suitable for students or anyone studying the Constitution for the first time. It provides a clear introduction to the background and history of the Constitution.

Constitutional Amendments: From Freedom of Speech to Flag Burning, edited by Elizabeth Shaw Grunow (Gale, 2001) is designed to provide a comprehensive discussion of all the Constitutional Amendments for students. Each of the 27 amendments is covered in its own chapter, which gives historical context on what made the amendment necessary, its ratification, and its interpretation through Supreme Court case decisions. Simple examples are provided to explain complex legal issues. The work is an excellent text for middle school students.

161. The Constitutional Law Dictionary. Ralph C. Chandler et al. Santa Barbara, CA: ABC-CLIO, 1985–1987. 2v. ISBN 0-87436-031-5 (v. 1); ISBN 0-87436-440-X (v. 2).

Supp. v. 1, 1984–1986. 1987. ISBN 0-87436-484-1; 1991. ISBN 0-87436-758-1; 1995. ISBN 0-87436-598-8. Vol. 2 supp. 1, 1998. ISBN 0-87436-925-8.

This reference work has been published in two base volumes, with supplements that update the volumes. Volume 1 is titled "Individual Rights" and volume 2, "Governmental Powers." Chapters 1 and 8 of volume 1 have a dictionary arrangement and cover constitutionalism and legal words and phrases. The remainder of the volume, chapters 2–7, concerns amendments to the Constitution, with introductory essay material and significant court cases. Approximately 300 landmark Supreme Court cases are covered in volume 1. Volume 2 covers over 200 cases affecting governmental powers. The emphasis is on recent decisions and the current thinking of the Court, but the definitions of concepts and the tracing of cases that shaped the law make the set useful for historical research. There is considerable overlap with the *Encyclopedia of the American Constitution* (entry 162), but both sources offer enough unique material to justify consulting each of them.

162. Encyclopedia of the American Constitution. 2nd ed. Leonard W. Levy and Kenneth L. Karst, eds. New York: Macmillan Library Reference USA/Gale Group, 2000. 6v. ISBN 0-02-864880-3.

The emphasis in this set is on currency. There are over 2,750 signed entries by political scientists, lawyers, judges, and historians concerning constitutional law cases and legislative developments relating to constitutional issues. The second edition has 361 new entries and over 180 updated articles. The entries are thorough essays on practical and theoretical topics dealing with every aspect of constitutional law in the United States from the Constitutional Convention in 1787 to the impeachment of President Clinton. For a number of current topics there are two essays that present contrasting views. The writing makes the set useful to students as well as researchers. Most entries contain brief bibliographies. The set is intended to assist in research and the entries on relevant Supreme Court cases provide the legal citation to the decision in the U.S. Reports series. Included in the appendixes are outlines of the development of constitutional law, the history of the Constitution, the Articles of Confederation, and the text of the Constitution. A glossary, case index, name index, and subject index are included.

Macmillan also produces a CD-ROM version of the *Encyclopedia.* Unfortunately, the CD-ROM is a digitized version of the first edition and it supplements, not the second edition. If the emphasis in providing the CD-ROM is for historical rather than current research, then the electronic version offers ease of use over the printed set. Cross-references in the printed version are hypertext links in the CD-ROM. The usual searching capabilities are present allowing keyword and Boolean searching. The CD-ROM is also less expensive than the printed set.

The Gale subsidiary Primary Source Media has created a Web-based collection of primary-source materials relating to U.S. history called *American Journey.* One module of this collection is dedicated to the Constitution, the documents that helped originally shape it, and court cases that have refined it.

*163. The Founder's Constitution. Philip B. Kurland and Ralph Lerner, eds. Indianapolis, IN: Liberty Fund, 2000. 5v. ISBN 0-86597-279-6. [Electronic database; CD-ROM]

The purpose of this work is to reproduce documents that trace the writing of the Constitution and shed light on its philosophical underpinnings. Many of the documents are famous and well known, but there are also more obscure texts reprinted. Most of the *Federalist Papers* are included, as well as letters from Jefferson, Madison, Hamilton, Adams, and Washington. The first volume has a theme arrangement, with documents reproduced according to their relevance to a particular concept or theme in U.S. government. Essays on each theme place the documents in historical context. The remaining volumes follow the organization of the Constitution arranged by article, section, and clause of the U.S. Constitution, from the Preamble through Article Seven and continuing through the first twelve amendments, with each document accompanying a particular article in the Constitution or the Bill of Rights. Some texts are reprinted more than once, and sometimes cross-references are given instead of text. The work succeeds in tracing the history of the Constitution through the documents involved in its preparation and ratification. It is not designed to be a quick reference work but rather one for the study of the historical development of the Constitution. Originally published by the University of Chicago Press to commemorate the bicentennial of the United States Constitution, Liberty Press has prepared a new online edition of the entire work at http://press-pubs.uchicago.edu/founders.

Also by Liberty Press is *The Federalist: The Gideon Edition,* edited by George W. Carcy and James McClellan (2001); *Friends of the Constitution: Writings of the Author Federalists, 1787–1788,* edited by Colleen A. Sheehan and Gary L. McDowell (1998); and *Colonial Origins of the American Constitution: A Documentary History* by Donald S. Lutz (1998). Together these publications provide the documentary history of the origins of the constitution and the arguments of those who advocated its ratification.

164. Impeachable Offenses: A Documentary History from 1787 to the Present. Emily Van Tassel and Paul Finkelman. Washington, D.C.: Congressional Quarterly, 1999. 326p. ISBN 1-56802-479-7; 1-56802-480-0 pa.

The impeachment of President Clinton in 1998 stirred considerable interest in the subject. This reference covers 16 cases of impeachment from the proceedings against Senator William Blount in 1797 to that of President Clinton in 1998. All federal impeachments, including those for members of Congress, the judiciary, and the cabinet, as well as the president are reviewed. The work explores the frequency and reasons impeachment articles have and have not emerged from House investigations in the past 200 years. The authors provide analysis, trace the evolution of impeachment, and outline the Senate's trial procedures. Primary documents are provided on all 16 times articles of impeachment have been drawn up. The outcomes of investigations that did not lead to impeachment are also included. The phrase, "high crimes and misdemeanors," is defined and discussed. The catalog of potentially impeachable offenses in the Starr Report is also included. The volume has a brief bibliography and an index. It is attractively formatted with illustrations and photographs. This is an excellent work on a topic that received much attention in the latter 1990s.

A more specific reference for an earlier presidential scandal also by CQ Press is *Watergate: Chronology of a Crisis* (1999). Exhaustive coverage is provided of all aspects of the period and the crisis.

165. States' Rights and American Federalism: A Documentary History. Frederick D. Drake and Lynn R. Nelson, eds. Westport, CT: Greenwood Press, 1999. 232p. (Primary Documents in American History and Contemporary Issues). ISBN 0-313-30573-0.

The intent of this work is to provide in one volume the full text of key documents on the relationship between states' rights and the American system of Federalism. Seventy-two documents are arranged chronologically in five parts. Part 1 examines the founding era (1620–1789), the drafting of the constitution, and the related debates between Federalists and anti-Federalists. Part 2 continues through the period 1789–1835 from the writing of the Bill of Rights through the time the Tenth Amendment was debated. Part 3 covers the antebellum and Civil War periods, a time of heated debate between advocates of states' rights and Federalists. Part 4 from the Civil War to the New Deal (1940) highlights the rights of women and African Americans as citizens. Part 5 focuses on the issues of state's rights and Federalism from the New Deal to the present. The documents are presented in full, unless very long, and include Supreme Court and lower-court decisions, speeches, letters, position papers, news stories, and statutes. Brief essays with bibliographies for further reading introduce each document. The work brings out important themes, setting the documents and issues in historical context. The treatment of the subject is more thorough than broader works on the Constitution. There is a comprehensive name and subject index. This work is suitable for anyone researching the subject.

BRANCHES OF THE FEDERAL GOVERNMENT

THE EXECUTIVE

The executive branch and departments other than the presidency are described in this section. There are not a large number of reference works that deal with these offices and agencies. A number of very specialized works focused on one agency such as *The FBI: A Comprehensive Reference Guide* (Oryx, 1999) have not been included in this reference guide. Only more general sources on the executive branch are included in this section.

General Sources

166. CIS Index to U.S. Executive Branch Documents, 1789–1909: Guide to Documents Listed in Checklist of U.S. Public Documents, 1789–1909, Not Printed in the U.S. Serial Set. Bethesda, MD: Congressional Information Service, 1990–1996. 7v. ISBN 0-88692-202-X. **CIS Index to U.S. Executive Branch Documents, 1910–1932, 1996–.**

The *CIS Index to U.S. Executive Branch Documents, 1789–1909* and a second project for the years 1910–1932 will make available indexing and full text on microfiche of the largest and most important of the executive branch agencies. The set for 1789–1909 was completed in 1996 with the 1910–1932 set for completion in 2002. The value of the first set is twofold: the set serves as a subject index to the *1909 Checklist,* and lists documents not in that publication. The *1909 Checklist* was compiled from the shelflist of the Public Documents Library and is thus a record of the holdings of that institution. During the process of locating documents for filming, other documents not in the original *1909 Checklist* were located, indexed, and filmed. The printed resources are divided into index and reference bibliography volumes. There are indexes by subject/name, SuDocs number, title, and agency report number. The reference bibliography volumes give the dates of publication, pagination, frequency for serial publications, SuDocs number, report number, and subject descriptors. It also tells whether or not the title is indexed and whether or not the item is in the accompanying microfiche collection. Because CIS has an index and microfiche collection for the *U.S. Serial Set* (entry 194n), those documents already filmed for that collection are not repeated in the executive branch collection. The SuDocs index provides the number for the documents in the *Serial Set.*

The second set for the years 1910–1932 will consist of seven parts: part 1, Treasury Department, Smithsonian Institution, Tariff Commission, Veterans Bureau, Veterans Administration, and Vocational Education Board; part 2, Commerce Department; part 3, the War Department and War Trade Board; part 4, Interior, Justice, and Labor Departments and Interstate Commerce Commission; part 5, Agriculture Department; part 6, the Navy Department, Library of Congress and other agencies; part 7, the State Department, Post Office Department, Pan American Union, Shipping Board, Philippine Government, and other agencies. These are detailed indexes—including subject, personal author, issuing agency, SuDoc number, title, and agency report number. A Reference Bibliography brings together the various series of each department or agency. *The CIS Index to U.S. Executive Branch Documents* and accompanying microfiche collections have greatly facilitated the identification and location of early executive branch records for research. The indexes provide authoritative, reliable access to important source documents produced by the various departments and agencies of the federal government. Current information about the project can be obtained at the LexisNexis Web site, (available at http://www.lexisnexis.com) under the Congressional Information Service area of the site.

167. Encyclopedia of the United States Cabinet. Mark Grossman. Santa Barbara, CA: ABC-CLIO, 2000. 3v. ISBN 0-87436-977-0.

The history of each cabinet department and all of the individuals who served as secretaries from George Washington through the Clinton administration are profiled in this three-volume reference work. Organized into 20 chapters, all cabinet departments and offices, including those that no longer exist or have been merged, are discussed. A final section furnishes similar information on the Confederate cabinet. Arranged alphabetically, each entry opens with an overview of the department or office and is followed by detailed biographic and historical entries relating to each individual who held the top position in that department. The essays and the entries chart the history of the departments, and provide insight into the political maneuvering that preceded the creation of some departments, evaluate the importance of each office at key periods in history, and significant achievements. The biographical entries include an analysis of the person's background for the post, an examination of successes and failures, and changes that occurred in the department during their administration. Each entry has bibliographic references at the end. Each volume has a table of contents for the set and a "Chronological List of Cabinet Members" in the front. The last volume has four appendixes: "Cabinet Officers by Administration," "Cabinet Members Who Died in Office," "Failed Nominations for the Cabinet, 1834–Present," and "Withdrawn Nominations for the Cabinet, 1801–1969." The set is a comprehensive reference on the U.S. Cabinet, which provides an understanding of the historical context and the role of the cabinet members in influencing policymaking in government.

Biographical Dictionary of the United States Secretaries of the Treasury, 1789–1995 edited by Bernard S. Katz and C. Daniel Vencill (Greenwood Press, 1996) includes the 69 men who had served as Secretary of the Treasury up to 1995. The coverage begins with a list by presidential administration of the names and years of office for the secretaries. Next are biographies of the secretaries. Each biography contains pertinent factual information and also the problems faced and an assessment of the person's contributions. The biographies stress the theme of fiscal management as exercised by the Department of the Treasury. The editors have published a similar work, *Biographical Dictionary of the Board of Governors of the Federal Reserve* (Greenwood Press, 1992). Works on other cabinet secretaries are *Principal Officers of the Department of State and United States Chief of Mission, 1778–1986* (U.S. Department of State, Office of the Historian, 1986) and *The Secretaries of the Department of the Interior, 1848–1969* (Washington, D.C.: National Anthropological Archives, 1975).

168. The Executive Branch of the U.S. Government: A Bibliography. Robert Goehlert and Hugh Reynolds, comps. New York: Greenwood Press, 1989. 380p. (Bibliographies and Indexes in Law and Political Science, no. 11). ISBN 0-313-26568-2.

The focus of this bibliography is toward the executive branch in general, particularly the departments other than the presidency and the White House. The bibliography contains 4,000 entries, including monographs, periodical articles, reports, and dissertations. The entries are not annotated. Because of the large number of entries, the bibliography will be useful for students and researchers seeking a fuller range of sources than those afforded by selective annotated bibliographies.

*169. Federal Register. Washington, D.C.: Office of the Federal Register, 1936–. ISSN 0097-6326. [Electronic database] Available: http://www.access.gpo.gov/nara.

The *Federal Register* is the official publication of the U.S. government, in which all proposed and final texts of rules, regulations, notices, and orders issued by executive departments and agencies are published. Once a final notice is published it has the force of law. The Office of the *Federal Register* is a component of the National Archives and Records Administration and the *FR* Web site is at http://www.access.gpo.gov/nara. In 1984, CIS began publishing an index to the *Federal Register*. The index provides detailed and comprehensive access to the more than 35,000 items published annually in the *Federal Register*. The complete text from the beginning of the publication in 1936 is available on microfiche. There are also indexes prepared by the Office of the Federal Register. The earlier years of the *Federal Register* are useful for historical research concerning particular agencies or government regulations. Just as the *Congressional Record* is now regarded as an online electronic resource, so too is the *Federal Register*. There are numerous CD-ROM products of the *FR* and it is also available online in the major commercial databases, *LexisNexis,* and *Westlaw.*

170. Historical Encyclopedia of U.S. Independent Counsel Investigations. Gerald S. Greenberg. Westport, CT: Greenwood Press, 2000. 415p. ISBN 0-313-3070-735-0.

The appointment of special prosecutors is traced from Ulysses Grant's appointment to investigate the St. Louis Whiskey Scandal in 1875 up through the Whitewater investigation during the Clinton administration. The emphasis is on the time period from 1978 when the independent counsel statute became law up through 1999. The entries include individuals who have served as independent counsel; those who have been targets of investigations; all attorneys general who have called for appointment of special prosecutors; all presidents during whose terms of office such prosecutors served; and all legal cases relating to the constitutionality of the statute.

A similar work is *Independent Counsel: the Law and the Investigations* by Charles Johnson and Danette Brickman (CQ Press, 2001). The work provides an overview of the investigations into misconduct by public officials through the presidencies of Richard Nixon, Ronald Reagan, and Bill Clinton. The authors trace the development of the independent counsel law and what worked and what did not work. All of the investigations since 1978 are briefly summarized. An appendix explains the independent counsel law and provides text from the most important Supreme Court cases.

171. A Historical Guide to the U.S. Government. George Thomas Kurian et al. New York: Oxford University Press, 1998. 741p. ISBN 0-19-510230-4.

The history of many departments and agencies in the federal government is hard to trace. This source provides a brief history (ranging in length from a single paragraph to two pages) for many bureaus, departments, offices and agencies of the U.S. executive branch. Congress and the judiciary are excluded except in cases in which authority spans more than one of the three main branches of government. In 183 alphabetical entries there is a discussion of the present mission, structure, and history of the agency. Many entries include a brief bibliography. Cross-references are plentiful. In addition to the agencies, key terms and processes receive treatment. An appendix contains key texts from 26 pieces of legislation or executive orders that established various agencies or significantly affected the evolution of public administration in the US. Earlier editions of Morehead's *Introduction to United States Government Information Sources* (entry 111) contained much historical information on the executive branch agencies. This reference work is a good, single reference work on the topic.

The Presidency

The presidency and individual presidents have quite naturally been the subjects of a voluminous amount of research. Consequently, the number of reference works in this subject area is also quite large. The works annotated in this section are recent publications pertaining to the office of the presidency in general. This guide does not list reference works on individual presidents. The works cited have been selected for their comprehensive coverage, currency, and usefulness in the research process. A large number of less-scholarly reference works have been omitted. For works dealing with presidential campaigns see "Political Parties and Elections" in this chapter.

*172. The American Presidency. Danbury, CT: Grolier Interactive, 1996. [CD-ROM]. ISBN 0-717-723367-7.

The information contained in this CD-ROM product was culled from three Grolier reference sets: *New Book of Knowledge, Academic American Encyclopedia,* and the *Encyclopedia Americana,* all published for student-level research. More than 800 biographies, general-interest articles, facts, data, and document texts are included. Perhaps the most interesting features are those that take advantage of multimedia technology. For example, "Hail to the Chief" plays when the user clicks on the opening screen. There are many video clips of the presidents. For teachers there are built-in quizzes. Although the product is not scholarly in treatment, it is useful as a ready-reference source. The product incorporates the encyclopedias into a multimedia format, but they are still discrete reference sources. There is a "Presidential Assistant" to take users on a tour of the disk, but there is not a Boolean search capability. Users of the CD-ROM products should be encouraged to pursue research in more scholarly reference works.

173. The American Presidency: Origins and Development, 1776–1998. 3rd ed. Sidney M. Milkis and Michael Nelson. Washington, D.C.: Congressional Quarterly, 1999. 474p. ISBN 1-56802-432-0.

The focus of this one-volume reference work is the historical development of the office of the presidency of the United States. It examines the constitutional precepts that underlie the U.S. presidency and the social, economic, political, and international conditions that continue to shape it. Written at the close of the twentieth century, the authors argue that the modern power of the presidency began not with Franklin D. Roosevelt, but during the time of Theodore Roosevelt and Woodrow Wilson. The first chapter examines the Constitutional Convention and the conceptual framework that set up the presidential office. The second chapter examines the various organizational structures that characterize the institution. The remaining chapters are centered on a dominant political philosophy or party or an age dominated by a particular president. The history is through the election of 1996 and the impeachment of President Clinton. The last chapter is devoted to the office of the vice president. The authors take into account new scholarship on the presidency to make this an outstanding explication of the history of the presidency. It provides a chronological survey of the American presidency. The Constitution of the United States is included in an appendix as well as a listing of all presidents and vice presidents. There is a comprehensive index. This well-written work is an excellent handbook on the office of the presidency.

The *American Presidents Reference Series* is published by CQ Press. Each president has a separate volume. The format of each book follows the same organization and includes a biographical sketch, campaign and electoral strategies, an A-Z of key figures in the administration, policies, crises, and relationship with major institutions. There are a timeline, a bibliography and an index in each volume.

*174. CIS Index to Presidential Executive Orders & Proclamations. Bethesda, MD: Congressional Information Service, 1987. 20v. **Supp.** March 4, 1921–December 31, 1983; 1987, 2v. ISBN 0-88692-106-6. [Online in *LexisNexis History Universe,* entry 11].

This 22-volume index covers presidential documents issued between 1789 and 1983. It lists more than 75,000 documents and is organized chronologically into two parts. Part I covers the administrations of Washington through Wilson (1789–1921). Part II begins with Harding and ends in 1983, at which point the *CIS Federal Register Index* provides access to executive orders and proclamations. There is a two-volume supplement that includes another 5,300 documents located after the publication of part II. Each part of the index contains five separate approaches to the documents. There are indexes by subjects and organizations; an index by personal names; a chronological day-by-day list of all documents; a cross-reference of all executive orders that affect or are affected by other executive orders; and an index by site and document number. This tool may be used with the hard-copy publications or with the *CIS Presidential Executive Orders & Proclamations on Microfiche* collection. The microfiche collection contains the full texts of over 70,000 documents, plus over 3,000 maps and other descriptive attachments. The index and accompanying microfiche collection bring together and provide access for the first time to all numbered and unnumbered executive orders and proclamations. The set is useful to historians, political scientists, and legal researchers. The *Index to Presidential Executive Orders & Proclamations* can be accessed online in *LexisNexis History Universe: Access to Presidential Studies* (entry 179).

175. Encyclopedia of the American Presidency. Leonard W. Levy and Louis Fisher, eds. New York: Simon & Schuster, 1998. 4v. ISBN 0-13275-983-7.

This four-volume work contains over 1,000 essays by 335 contributors covering all aspects of the executive branch of government. The comprehensiveness of the coverage and the evaluative nature of the entries have made this work one of the most highly regarded reference works on the presidency and the executive branch. The contributors were encouraged to express "opinions and judgements." The entries have extensive cross-references and bibliographies at the end. In addition to the entries there are a quick-reference table of presidential cabinets, a table of other key presidential appointed officials, and a synoptic outline of the contents of the set. There are also an index to legal cases and a keyword index. Anyone researching the presidency or the workings of American government should consult this reference.

176. Facts About the Presidents. Steven Anzovin and Janet Podell. New York: H.W. Wilson, 2001. 7th ed. 729p. ISBN 0-8242-1007-7.

The *Presidential Fact Book* was a long-running title by Joseph Nathan Kane. The seventh edition has a revised title. Designed to be a single, in-depth reference source about presidents and the Executive Office, this work delivers an abundance of information. Part I includes a chapter on each president, arranged chronologically according to dates of office. Included are biographical information and family history, data on elections, congressional sessions, the Cabinet, Supreme Court appointments, and the vice president and first lady. Part II provides comparative statistics on the individuals. This title has been a staple on reference shelves for many years.

The Complete American Presidents Sourcebook by Roger Matuz (U*X*L/Gale, 2001) is chronologically arranged with a section on each president that contains a general overview of his life, events during his presidency, facts, and a summary. There are profiles of the 44 first ladies and at least one primary-source document for each president.

177. Guide to the Presidency. Michael Nelson, ed. 3rd ed. Washington, D.C.: CQ Press, 2002. 2v. 1706p. ISBN 1-56802-714-1.

The first edition of the *Guide to the Presidency* was published in 1989 in one volume. The third edition has been expanded to two volumes and covers the presidency through early days of President George W. Bush and the September 11, 2001, terrorist attacks. The authors of the third edition set these events in the context of the history and evolution of the presidency. The historical development of the office, the selection and removal of the president, the powers of the presidency, and the relationships within the executive branch and with other governmental agencies are all explored in an essay-chapter arrangement. Much factual information is presented in the form of tables, charts, sidebars, and boxes with lists. These features, plus the numerous photographs and illustrations, make the work very attractive. There is a section for biographies of presidents, vice presidents, and first ladies. Other features are the reprinting of the text of selected documents relating to the presidency, approval ratings for presidents, lists of party nominees, cabinet appointments and other officials. The essays are all written by experts in their fields. Each chapter is referenced and includes an extensive bibliography. There is an index in each volume. This easy-to-read guide is suitable for beginning research on the office of the presidency by historians, political scientists, and students of international relations.

The full texts of many seminal documents in U.S. history are reprinted in *Historic Documents of the Presidency: 1776–1989* (Congressional Quarterly, 1989). Nearly 80 documents are reproduced, including the Articles of Confederation, the Monroe Doctrine, Roosevelt's "Four Freedoms" speech, Nixon's "Checkers" speech and the "smoking gun" transcript, and Carter's Camp David accords. Each document is prefaced by an introduction on its historical significance. This publication will be of use to anyone seeking a ready source for the text of historical documents. Presidential documents are now in the CQ Press annual series *Historic Documents* (entry 28).

178. How to Research the Presidency. Fenton S. Martin and Robert U. Goehlert. Washington, D.C.: Congressional Quarterly, 1996. 134p. ISBN 1-56802-029-5; 1-56802-028-7pa.

Martin and Goehlert have written a series of guides for the three branches of the U.S. government. The "How to" guides are designed for beginning researchers. The introductory essay explains basic searching procedures with a step-by-step research strategy. The first part of each book contains concise descriptions of secondary references and finding tools. The volume explains how to find platforms, oral histories, and public opinion polls as well as speeches, papers, and vetoes. Although Internet, CD-ROM, and database resources are included, as well as printed materials, government publications and periodicals, the electronic resources may have changed as the publication is several years old. The final part is a selected bibliography of books. The volume on the presidency is arranged by both subject and individual president. There are two appendixes that list, in tabular format, all presidents and vice presidents and background data. There is an author and a title index.

Two earlier enumerative bibliographies by the authors of *How to Research the Presidency,* although somewhat dated may still be useful. *The American Presidency: A Bibliography.* (Congressional Quarterly, 1987) and *American Presidents: A Bibliography* (CQ, 1987) have very similar titles. The two bibliographies were designed to be used in tandem. *The American Presidency* contains approximately 8,500 citations relating to the office of the presidency: "its history, development, powers, and relations with other branches of the federal government." The second work, *The American Presidents* is devoted to the individual presidents and contains over 13,000 entries. There is no overlap between the two titles. One of the advantages of these bibliographies is that the publication period of the entries spans 1885–1986. These are research-oriented bibliographies, with references to scholarly monographs, journal articles, and dissertations. Government documents are excluded. Each contains an author index and a subject index. The entries are not annotated, so judging the relevance of sources may be a problem and even though they have not been updated, the comprehensiveness of these bibliographies makes them useful for scholarly research.

*179. LexisNexis History Universe: Access to Presidential Studies. Dayton, OH: LexisNexis. Available: http://www.lexisnexis.com.

Access to Presidential Studies is a module of the *History Universe* suite of Web services for historical research. Much of the material included in this electronic product is drawn from Congressional Information Service's indexes and microfilm collections. The site brings together key primary and secondary presidential resources including full text of scholarly articles on specific presidents; autobiographies and contemporary accounts; manuscripts such as letters and office diaries; speeches, including all inaugural addresses; and all State of the Union messages and executive orders and proclamations. There is in-depth coverage of presidencies with documents of key events. A feature of the *History Universe* site is that documents may be viewed as HTML or PDF files, meaning that a "photo" of the actual original document can be viewed or a transcribed version of the text can be downloaded. The wealth of information and full-text resources make this site one of the major places to search for presidential materials.

180. The Politics of the Presidency. Joseph A. Pika et al. Washington, D.C.: CQ Press, 2001. 5th ed. 472p. ISBN 1-56802-419-3.

The emphasis in this work is not on individual presidents, but upon the office of the presidency. The institution of the presidency, the individuals who have served, the president's interaction with other government branches and the public, and the president's impact on public policy are all analyzed in this work. The coverage goes through George W. Bush's first 100 days in office. The authors show how the effectiveness of a president has varied with the character, political style, and performance in the politicized environment of the White House. The book is a good accompaniment to more factual reference works.

*181. POTUS: Presidents of the United States. Available: http://www.ipl.org/ref/potus.

Staffers at the Internet Public Library have compiled links for all presidents, with their terms of office, background information, election results, lists of cabinet members, and notable events during each administration. Current biographical material is provided via links to the White House's official Web site (available: http://www.whitehouse.gov) and other sources. Links to complete inaugural addresses and other key speeches are also provided.

182. The Presidency A to Z: CQ's Ready Reference Encyclopedia of American Government. 2nd ed. Washington, D.C.: Congressional Quarterly, 1998. 650 p. (CQ's Encyclopedia of American Government, v. 2) ISBN 1-56802-359-6.

This work is volume 2 in CQ's *Encyclopedia of American Government*. It is a comprehensive one-volume reference work of 300 easy-to-read entries alphabetically arranged. The essays explain concepts and relationships such as constitutional powers and the budget process, relations with Congress, the Supreme Court, the bureaucracy, the media, interest groups, and the public. Shorter entries define terms, procedures, and the like. Biographies for all presidents, vice presidents, and other important figures are also included. There are numerous charts, tables, lists, photographs, cartoons and the like. Some entries have bibliographies and there are cross-references. The second edition has an annotated list of four comprehensive Internet directories of federal Web sites. The *A to Z* is designed to be easier and quicker to use than the *Guide to the Presidency* (entry 177). Of the two, *A to Z* is more suitable for quick reference and as a starting point for research. The more in-depth essays and bibliographies in the *Guide* make it a suitable next step after consulting the *A to Z.*

An accompanying reference to the *A to Z* for students is *Congressional Quarterly's Desk Reference on the Presidency* (CQ, 2000). Despite the title, this work is not organized as a reference work. It contains 500 questions and answers on the presidency and vice presidency. The questions and answers are divided under six major headings and then subdivided into more specific categories. There are cross-references and a comprehensive subject and name index. The work is designed for students and not researchers.

183. The Presidential-Congressional Political Dictionary. Jeffrey M. Elliot and Sheikh R. Ali. San Bernandino, CA: Borgo Press, 1998. 366 p. ISBN 0-80950-706-4.

Although designed as a current information tool, this reference work is also suitable for use in historical studies. Over 750 terms dealing with the relationship between the presidency and Congress are defined. The terms are arranged into topical chapters evenly divided between the presidency and allied executive agencies on one hand and Congress with its committees and staff on the other. Each term has a paragraph of definition or identification followed by a second paragraph on the significance of the term both currently and historically. A detailed index facilitates access to the entries. Appendixes contain organization charts and tables of popular and electoral voting totals for president. The reference work can be used by students, the general public, and scholars seeking to learn more about the current and historical relationship between the president and Congress.

184. Presidential Vetoes, 1789–1988. U.S. Senate Library, comp. Washington, D.C.: Government Printing Office, 1992. 595p.

A bill becomes law if the president does not veto it within 10 days after it has been presented to him. The Senate Library compiles a cumulative listing of vetoes. The arrangement is chronological by presidential administration and then by Congress within the administrative term. Each veto is numbered, and the index refers to the numbers. Information on the veto includes the date the legislation was returned to Congress; the reasons given for the veto; and the disposition of the matter by Congress (i.e., whether the veto was unchallenged, overridden, or sustained). There are a list of bills vetoed by each president and an index of names and subjects. This volume is useful in research pertaining to presidential administrations and in tracing the history of particular legislation. It is updated periodically, but this base volume is the most useful to the historian.

185. The Presidents: A Reference History. Henry F. Graff, ed. New York: Diane Publishing Co., 1999. 815 p. ISBN 0-78816-394-9.

The first edition of this work was published in 1984. Since that edition, the work has been updated through the 1996 presidential election and the Clinton presidency. The biographical essays on presidents from Washington through Clinton summarize the accomplishments of each administration. Each essay is written by a well-qualified historian or political scientist. The essays are analytical and attempt to assess the impact of key policies and events in the administration. Each essay has a brief bibliography and there is a general bibliography for the volume. The second edition in 1996 added an essay and annotated bibliography on First Ladies, discussing the demands on First Ladies and the influence a "wife/confidant" can have on the presidency. An appendix table gives biographical, political, and historical data for each president; election results; major appointments; and key events. Another appendix describes the activities of the Executive Office of the President. The essays are not referenced, but each is accompanied by an annotated bibliography. This work is not a factual reference source, but an excellent overview source for students.

Another work similar in scope and objectives to the Graff volume is *The American Presidents: The Office and the Men,* edited by Frank N. Magill (Salem Press, 1986, 3v.). The essays are written by academics and focus on the impact made upon the presidency by each holder of the office. The work is illustrated, including official portraits. It is most useful to students as another source of information on the impact of individual presidents.

186. The Presidents, First Ladies, & Vice Presidents: White House Biographies, 1789– 2001. Daniel G. Diller and Stephen L. Robertson. Washington, D.C.: CQ Press, 2001. 281 p. ISBN 1-56802-574-2.

This title is written in a popular vein for a general audience. Biographies examine the early lives and important events that occurred while the subjects held office. All biographies include portraits. Biographies for vice presidents and first ladies are shorter. Vice presidents who became president have longer essays. The profiles of the first ladies include personal data and cover their personal lives as well as their role as first lady. This work is in an attractive format similar to other CQ publications. There are comparative tables and a detailed index to help readers easily trace names, places, and events from the early days of the presidency to the present.

A similar work is *Presidents: A Biographical Dictionary* by Neil Hamilton (Facts on File, 2001). Besides factual information, the work aims to "examine the hopes and disappointments, the victories, and defeats, and the integrity and perfidy of the leader of this country . . . " It contains 42 black-and-white photographs and illustrations, appendixes, a bibliography, chronologies, and an index.

A somewhat more scholarly treatment of biographies of the vice presidents is *The Vice Presidents,* edited by L. Edward Prucell (Facts on File, 2001). The work is essentially an update to the previous edition published in 1998. Each entry is several pages long and includes a short bibliography. Yet another work is *the Vice Presidents: Biographies of the 45 Men Who Have Held the Second Highest Office in the United States,* by Carole Chandler Waldrup (McFarland, 1996). This work is useful for a quick introduction to the lives and careers of the vice presidents.

187. The President's Position: Debating the Issues in Pro and Con Primary Documents. Mark Byrnes, series editor. Westport, CT: Greenwood Publishing Group, 2002B. **Presidents from Washington through Monroe, 1789–1825.** Amy H. Sturgis. 2002. 240p. ISBN 0-313-31387-3. **Presidents from Taylor through Grant, 1849–1877.** Jeffrey W. Coker. 2002. 248p. ISBN 0-313-31551-5. **Presidents from Theodore Roosevelt through**

Coolidge, 1901–1929. Francine Sanders Romero. 2002. 280p. ISBN 0-313-31388-1. **Presidents from Hoover through Truman, 1929–1953.** John E. Moser. 2002. 256p. ISBN 0-313-31441-1. **Presidents from Nixon through Carter, 1969–1981.** Aimee D. Shouse. 2002. 296p. ISBN 0-313-31529-9. **Presidents from Reagan through Clinton, 1981–2001.** Lane Crothers and Nancy S. Lind. 2002. 320 p. ISBN 0-313-31411-X.

Each book in the *President's Position* series has a narrative summary of the issue and a capsule description of both the president's position and that of the opposition. The description is followed by a statement by the president voicing his position and then a statement by a member of the opposition. Each issue concludes with a list of suggested readings for further study. The series is designed for students to debate the key issues that shaped each U.S. presidency. Introductions place the issues in political context. Primary documents include presidential memoirs, speeches, and letters, congressional speeches, Supreme Court decisions, newspaper editorials, statements by opposition groups, and comments from prominent private citizens. The books in the series are useful for students in both history and debate classes.

188. Public Papers of the Presidents of the United States, Containing the Public Messages, Speeches and Statements of the President. Washington, D.C.: Office of the Federal Register, 1957–. Ann. ISSN 0079-7626.

The forerunner to the *Public Papers* annual series is a 20-volume set, *A Compilation of the Messages and Papers of the Presidents . . .* (New York Bureau of National Literature, 1917). This title, originally published by the Government Printing Office from 1896 to 1899, covered the years 1789–1897, from George Washington to William McKinley. The compilation was updated to include administrations through the term of Calvin Coolidge in 1929, at which point the *Public Papers* series begins.

In 1958, the Office of the Federal Register began publishing an annual compilation in chronological order of the public statements of the president. This series is the *Public Papers of the Presidents of the United States.* Subsequently, retrospective annual volumes were published, beginning with the Hoover administration in 1929. In 1965, the Federal Register also began publishing the *Weekly Compilation of Presidential Documents,* which contains the text of proclamations and executive orders, letters, messages, communications with Congress, news conferences, and so forth. Beginning in 1977 the annual *Public Papers* began cumulating all material from the *Weekly Compilation.* These publications provide a day-to-day account of history in the making and a comprehensive record of each presidential administration. Since January 1997, the WCPD has been available in an Internet version on the GPO Access Web site at http://www.access.gpo.gov/nara/pubpaps/srchpaps.html.

The *Cumulated Indexes to the Public Papers of the Presidents of the United States* 1977– were published by Kraus International and are currently being published by Bernan Press. The *Cumulated Indexes* series contains a chronological compilation of papers, speeches, and writings of each president beginning with Harry S. Truman. The *Cumulated Indexes* series compiles the annual volumes of the *Public Papers* into a set for each presidential administration. In the compilations, "see" and "see also" references have been added. The cumulated set also has references to the page numbers in the original annual series. The cumulated indexes enable a researcher to locate material on one president much faster than by using each annual volume of the *Public Papers* series individually. The *Cumulated*

Indexes for both the Reagan and the first Bush presidency were published in 1995. Anyone conducting research on a president or the presidency must be aware of the *Public Papers* and *Cumulated Indexes* series.

189. Presidential Scandals. Jeffrey D. Schultz. Washington, D.C.: CQ Press, 1999. 300p. ISBN 1-56802-414-2.

Every incident or event that was considered scandalous at the time or that was uncovered and regarded as scandalous later is covered in this book. The author looks at the behavior and public image of every president and puts the scandals into perspective. The book is written in a lively, popular style. It pulls together information on scandals and makes a handy reference work on the topic.

190. Records of the Presidency: Presidential Papers and Libraries from Washington to Reagan. Frank L. Schick et al. Phoenix: Oryx Press, 1989. 309p. ISBN 0-89774-277-X.

Most reference works on the presidents are arranged in chronological order by presidential administration. This guide is arranged according to the type of institution in which presidential papers and records are to be found. The types are: agencies responsible for the maintenance of presidential records, legislation relating to presidential libraries, guides to presidential records, and presidential book collections at historic sites; presidential papers in the Manuscript Division of the Library of Congress; presidential papers in historical societies and special libraries; and the presidential libraries administered by the National Archives. Appendixes provide statistical tables on the presidential libraries, directories of major presidential record collections and historic sites, and an explanation of the White House filing system. There are short biographies and bibliographies for each president and outlines of the collections. This guide is a useful overview of the organization and distribution of presidential papers and records. More detailed collection guides from the Library of Congress, the National Archives, and the individual presidential libraries will need to be consulted for specific research.

Separate indexes have been prepared to the microfilmed collections of presidential papers in the Manuscript Division of the Library of Congress. These indexes are not publications, but are collectively referred to as the *Presidential Papers Index Series* (Library of Congress, 1960–1976). An index has been prepared to the papers of 23 presidents: Washington, Jefferson, Madison, Monroe, Jackson, Van Buren, William Henry Harrison, Tyler, Polk, Taylor, Pierce, Lincoln, Andrew Johnson, Grant, Garfield, Arthur, Cleveland, Benjamin Harrison, McKinley, Theodore Roosevelt, Taft, Wilson, and Coolidge. The indexes are arranged by correspondent and by date with no subject approach. These indexes are useful in searching for correspondence of particular individuals.

Seven presidential libraries, from presidents Herbert Hoover to Gerald Ford, are included in *A Guide to Manuscripts in the Presidential Libraries,* (College Park, MD: Research Materials Corporation, 1985). Much of the information is drawn from the published guides to the individual libraries, but it is useful to have it all collected into one publication. The collections of each library are described, including manuscripts, microfilm, and oral history archives. Descriptions include the name, size, reference number, and National Union Catalog of Manuscript Collections (NUCMC) number, plus information about the contents of the collections and opening hours of the libraries. There is a subject and name index. Any researcher needing access to presidential papers should consult this guide.

The Internet site *President* (available at http://sunsite.unc.edu/lia/president/pres-home.html) provides access to varying amounts of material in the libraries of the Presidents Hoover through George H. Bush, (with other types of links for Clinton), including speeches and historical documents. Many links to useful collection finding aids are provided to assist the serious researcher.

A less research-oriented work is *Presidential Libraries and Museums: an Illustrated Guide* (CQ, 1995). The focus in this handbook is on the libraries and museums as tourist attractions. It describes the 10 presidential libraries administered by the National Archives, as well as the privately operated Rutherford B. Hayes Library.

191. Speeches of the American Presidents. Janet Podell and Steven Anzovin, eds. New York: H.W. Wilson, 2001. 1,057p. ISBN 0-8242-1006-9.

Most of the orations in this volume are reproduced in full. Each president is the subject of a separate chapter, with the number of speeches varying from 4 to 10. Background information is given for each address. An introductory chapter gives an overview on the general subject of presidential speeches. The speeches were selected to provide insight into the growth of speech making as a political tool, to illustrate the president's character, and to cover as many of the important issues of each administration as possible. This work contains a total of 200 speeches by 43 different presidents, making it a handy reference for students.

The Presidents Speak: the Inaugural Addresses of the American Presidents, compiled by Davis Newton Lott (Olive Grove Publishing, 2002) is more limited in scope. The contents of this reference are obvious from its title, but the Declaration of Independence, the Articles of Confederation, the Constitution, the Mayflower Compact, and a chronological chart of presidents and vice presidents are also included. It is a handy ready reference work for schools and public libraries.

192. Vital Statistics on the Presidency: Washington to Clinton. Rev. ed. Lyn Ragsdale. Washington, D.C.: Congressional Quarterly, 1998. 464p. ISBN 1-56802-393-6; 1-56802-427-4 pa.

The title gives the rationale for this work. It is designed to bring together in one volume data on the office of the presidency. The emphasis is not upon the individual administrations of each president, but to show how a quantitative analysis can broaden and enhance understanding of institutional behavior and explain how the statistics may highlight trends and issues regarding the executive office. The work does not just present data in tables. There are introductory essays to each of the nine chapters that give historical context and examine current research trends associated with the presidency. The essays provide a descriptive interpretation of the data and highlight key issues. Thus, even though the emphasis is on quantitative data and analysis, the essays are one of the best features of the work because the data can be found elsewhere. Sources of the data are given for all tables.

LEGISLATIVE

As the federal government bureaucracy expanded in the twentieth century, it created an ever-growing universe of publications to acquire and index. Beginning in the 1970s, there were great improvements in access and bibliographic control of congressional publications and documents mainly emanating from the private sector. With the advent of the Internet, the Government Printing Office and various government agencies including Congress began to provide current and historical information via the Web. By the beginning of the twenty-first century, the majority of current U.S. government information was being disseminated and accessed electronically. Official government Web sites are mentioned throughout this *Guide* with those pertaining to Congress and legislative and legal activities appearing in this section.

The foremost Web sites to be mentioned in this section are those sponsored directly by the two houses of Congress and by the Library of Congress. The first Web site for congressional information was THOMAS (entry 195). Web sites are maintained by both the House (available at http://www.house.gov) and Senate (available at http://www.senate.gov). The Web site of the Clerk of the House (available at http://clerk.house.gov/index.php) contains a number of useful history links: session dates, 1789–present; floor leaders of the House, 1899–present; resumes of congressional activity, 91st through 105th congresses; political divisions of the Senate and House, 1855–present; electoral college results, 1789–present; and House and Senate elections, 1920–1998.

The Congressional Information Service's indexing products, which were both printed and in CD-ROM, have been incorporated into the online database services of LexisNexis (entry 194). While CIS continues to issue printed versions of the major indexes, the preferred mode of access for students and researchers has become the electronic databases. The printed indexes have been retained in this *Guide* as separate entries as not all researchers have access to the databases through their home institutions.

Long one of the major publishers of guides to Congress, CQ Press (Congressional Quarterly) has numerous publications, most of them for current information. *CQ Weekly* and *CQ Researcher* are available online by subscription. The publisher has a Web site where publications not treated here, or more up-to-date information, can be found at (available at http://www.cqpress.com).

The major electronic resources are listed first in this section followed by an alphabetical listing of printed reference sources.

Electronic Resources

*193. Congressional Record. Washington, D.C.: Government Printing Office, March 1, 1873–. Daily with bound editions for each Congress. Electronic access through THOMAS, available: http://thomas.loc.gov; GPO Access, available: http://www.access.gpo.gov; Library of Congress, available: http://lcweb.loc.gov; *LexisNexis Congressional Universe,* and *Westlaw.*

The *Congressional Record* provides a complete account of the debates on the floor of Congress. It also includes many items placed "on the record" by members of Congress, texts of bills, presidential messages, treaties, and other materials relevant to the legislative process. The *CR* is divided into four sections: proceedings of the House (H) and Senate (S);

the Extensions of remarks (E); and the Daily Digest (D), which summarizes the day's proceedings in both houses and their committees. The bound edition is available only to regional depository libraries from the GPO in printed and microfiche formats. The Congressional Information Service films the bound edition, which is considered to be the authoritative version for legal purposes. All volumes from 1873 to the present are available in the CIS microfiche collection. The predecessors of the *Congressional Record,* the *Annals of Congress* (1789–1824), the *Register of Debates* (1824–1837), and the *Congressional Globe* (1833–1873), have also been microfilmed. Indexing for the *Congressional Record* has been provided by the GPO and also commercial firms.

CIS also offers microfiche collections of *U.S. Congressional Journals* and *Congressional Bills, Resolutions, and Laws.* The collection of journals covers the years 1789–1978. The bills, resolutions, and laws are available from the 73rd Congress (1933–1934) forward.

Although the current *Congressional Record* is now regarded as an electronic publication, depository librarians have lobbied to have the *CR* continue to be issued in print for preservation purposes. The distribution of the printed version has been greatly scaled back, whereas the electronic *CR* is widely available. The electronic editions of the *CR* do not all have the same beginning dates for the electronic backfile. A number of services have retrospectively converted back years to electronic format and the availability in electronic format will probably continue to stretch backward for greater historical use.

*194. LexisNexis Congressional Universe. Dayton, OH: LexisNexis. [Electronic database] Available: http://www.lexisnexis.com.

Congressional Universe is a current-awareness subscription database. Through *Congressional Universe* researchers can monitor legislation and public policy on almost any topic; learn the current makeup and mission of Congressional committees; find out how members of congress voted on legislation; find expert testimony on the leading issues of the day; and search "Hot Bills" and other topics of Congress. Most useful for historical research is the legislative history feature. Also included within *Congressional Universe* is the complete text to the 200 volumes of the *U.S. Statutes at Large,* searchable back to 1789. Finding aids let users search by public law number, citation, title, and popular name. The scanned pages include all the marginal notes, footnotes, maps, and tables. Using the electronic version, an original law and all its amendments can be tracked.

State Capital Universe provides the same resources for the 50 states that *Congressional Universe* provides for the federal level. Bill tracking, statutes, full text of state regulations, administrative codes and state registers, directory information, and more are included in the database.

Although its primary purpose is to provide resources on the Congress presently in session, *Congressional Universe* does contain a wealth of historical documentation. The source of the historical information is in the product line of Congressional Information Service. Although various GPO publications have indexed government documents, the indexing in many cases is not thorough, does not cover all years, and/or is contained in a number of different publications. CIS began indexing congressional proceedings and documents on a current basis in the early 1970s. The need to fill in many gaps in the provision of historical documents was quickly realized. The company became the primary commercial provider of indexing and microfiche copies of historical congressional documents. Now a part of LexisNexis, much of the retrospective indexing by CIS is now available through the LexisNexis *Congressional Universe* database with links to the full text of some documents. One of the main advantages of the CIS indexes is that they have eliminated the necessity for using a number of different sources; in addition, they have supplied information not previously available. The CIS indexes are grouped together here under the *Congressional Universe* entry to make clear the relationship between the various indexes and that the CIS indexes are now modules of the *Congressional Universe* database package.

The *CIS Index* was inaugurated by Congressional Information Service in 1970 and continues as the current index to congressional documents. Since 1970 CIS has collected, analyzed, indexed, and microfilmed the publications generated by congressional committees, including hearings, reports, documents, and other miscellaneous publications. The indexes come out monthly, with annual cumulations accompanied by abstracts. The indexing is cumulated every five years, but the abstracts are not reprinted. The electronic database, of course, has the advantage in that all indexing is available and the search engine "cumulates" it. This comprehensive index is useful to attorneys, historians, political scientists, students, and researchers in a variety of fields.

Congressional Indexes, 1789–1969. *LexisNexis Congressional Universe.* Although *Congressional Universe* only indexes from the mid 1980s and in some cases 1995 forward, earlier indexing is available in *Congressional Universe* through a separate module, *Congressional Indexes 1789–1969.* The Web version of the print CIS indexes to the historical document collections microfiche texts available through CIS have been enhanced through corrections, provision of House and Senate bill number indexing for reports issued as documents through the 29th Congress, and the regularization of subject and name indexing. The CIS indexes and microfiche collections, which can be accessed through *Congressional Indexes 1789–1969,* are listed below. Entries for the printed versions of the CIS congressional indexes have been retained in this *Guide* and they can still be found in with accompanying microfiche in many academic and public libraries. Access to the Web version is through an institution that subscribes to the electronic database.

CIS U.S. Serial Set Index, 1789–1969. Bethesda, MD: Congressional Information Service, 1986. Pts. 1–12, 3v. per pt. ISBN 0-812380-26-8.

Unique in the variety and comprehensiveness of the publications it includes, the *Serial Set* begins with the first session of Congress in 1789. Congressional publications such as committee reports, legislative journals, directories, manuals, and other publications have been included in the *Serial Set* over the years. Also included are departmental and agency reports, serial publications, and nongovernmental publications such as reprints of newspaper, magazine, and journal articles. Over 330,000 congressional reports and documents together with reported bill number indexing to more than 1 million committee reports on public and private bills are searchable through the electronic index. Also *House and Senate Journal* for the years covered, numerous committee investigations, directories and rule manuals, and histories of Congress and the Capitol are included. The *American State Papers,* 1789–1830s are also included.

This wealth of information has historically been poorly indexed, and very few libraries own complete runs of the *Serial Set.* The printed index to the *Serial Set* published by CIS is in three volumes divided into 12 chronological parts. An alphabetical index contains some 2 million names and keyword subject terms derived from the titles of the publications indexed. There is a separate index for proper names that concern private legislation in the "Private Relief and Related Actions Index of Names of Individuals and Organizations." The *Serial Set* reference number for all House and Senate reports and documents is given in the "Numerical List of Reports and Documents." There is a shelflist-order index for each *Serial Set* volume, which allows the review of the contents of each volume. Both the shelflist index and the numerical list give full information on the publication—Congress and session, publication type, volume, report or document number, and serial number. For those documents in the *Serial Set,* the *CIS U.S. Serial Set Index* for the most part replaces the early document indexes of Poore, Ames, the *Document Catalog* and the *Monthly Catalog* (entry 112). The *Serial Set's* coverage ends with the first session of Congress in 1969, coinciding with the beginning of the current index for congressional publications, the *CIS Index.* The *CIS U.S. Serial Set Index* is the major retrospective index to government publications for historians and all other researchers. The complete *Serial Set Index* is a module of *Congressional Universe.*

CIS U.S. Congressional Committee Hearings Index (1833–1969). Bethesda, MD: Congressional Information Service, 1981. 8 pts. ISBN 0-88692-050-7.

More than 40,000 titles published between 1833 and 1969 are indexed in the *CIS Congressional Committee Hearings Index,* with the full text reproduced in the accompanying microfiche collection. The transcripts of testimony and supporting documentation of witnesses appearing before congressional committees are a gold mine of information on a wide variety of subjects. The index contains a reference bibliography that provides full information for locating printed hearings. Information on the hearing may include a description of the subject matter, bills considered, a list of witnesses and their affiliations, and the subject descriptors assigned to the hearing. There are indexes by title, subject, and organization; personal names; bill number; report and document number; and SuDocs number. As with the other retrospective indexes, the *Committee Hearing Index* has been continued since 1970 on a current basis by the *CIS Index.*

CIS Index to Unpublished U.S. Senate Committee Hearings (1823–1972); CIS Index to Unpublished US House of Representatives Committee Hearings (1833–1964).

The testimony and proceedings of many hearings were not made public for a variety of reasons, usually dealing with national security or the confidentiality of witnesses. A vast array of 22,000 uncataloged and unindexed materials were filmed and indexed by CIS and made accessible to researchers for the first time. New segments are published as the documents are opened by the Senate and House and become available for filming.

CIS U.S. Congressional Committee Prints Index.

Similar to the unpublished committee hearing reports are congressional committee prints. These are issued in limited numbers by the congressional committee and synthesize the research and issues germane to a given set of hearings. They are prepared by committee research staffs or by the Library of Congress Congressional Research Service, written as background papers for the members of Congress to be informed on important national and international issues, and they contain statistical, bibliographical, and other reference information. Committee prints for the years 1830–1969 have been gathered, filmed, and indexed.

CIS Index to Senate Executive Documents and Reports (1817–1969).
Senate executive documents and reports, like committee prints, if not classified as secret, have been distributed in very limited quantities. Through executive documents and reports, the U.S. Senate acts on treaties, nominations, and other matters of national concern that the president submits. Some 4,000 publications are indexed and reproduced in this collection.
This lengthy entry has only included the congressional modules of the LexisNexis database lineup. Historical resources and indexing other than for the U.S. Congress and state legislatures are included in LexisNexis *History Universe* (entry 11n).

*195. THOMAS. Washington, D.C.: Library of Congress. Available: http://thomas.loc.gov.
One of the very first U.S. government Web sites created for the public, *THOMAS* is named after Thomas Jefferson. Inaugurated January 5, 1995, *THOMAS* was created in order that the public could find online the text, current status of bills and roll call votes. Bill summary and status are searchable by bill number or keyword/phrase. The site is a gateway with links to all of the congressional Web sites. The full text of the *Congressional Record* since 1989 and the index since 1994 are available on the site. Also the texts of "How Our Laws Are Made" and "Enactment of a Law," two pamphlets that explain the legislative process are available. One of the major links provided on the site is to the University of Michigan Documents Center collection and guide to "Legislative Histories" (available at http://www.lib.umich.edu/govdocs/legishis.html).
While there is duplication of congressional information between *THOMAS* and *GPO Access, THOMAS* is a service of the Library of Congress maintained for Congress and the public, whereas *GPO Access* is an all-inclusive gateway to U.S. government information in electronic form.

Print Resources

*196. Biographical Directory of the United States Congress, 1774–1989. Washington, D.C.: Government Printing Office, 1971. 1,972p. S/N 5271-0249.
The *Biographical Directory* has been a long-running title from 1859 to 1989, the last edition being published by the GPO to commemorate the 200th anniversary of Congress (Senate Document 100-34, serial volume 13849). Historians revised many entries in the bicentennial edition for accuracy and historical scholarship. The *Biographical Directory* is updated by the *Official Congressional Directory,* issued biennially. An updated and expanded version of the *Directory* is available on the Web at http://bioguide.congress.gov. The Web site includes information previously published by the House in the *Guide to Research Papers of Former Members.* Similar information is also maintained for the Senate. In addition to a brief biography, useful bibliography and research collection links are also provided for many members of Congress.
The title, *Biographical Directory of the American Congress, 1774–1997* (Alexandria, VA: CQ Staff Directories Ltd., 1996) is a commercial publication of the government direc-

tory. The CQ 16th edition in 1996 updated the bicentennial edition. It contains personal and career information on 11,400 men and women who served in the U.S. and Continental Congresses, as well as a complete listing of Congresses and Cabinet members. Each entry contains date and place of birth, education, employment (prior to and after governmental service), record of governmental service, party affiliation, and date and place of death. Beginning with the 79th Congress (1945–1947), information includes the political division of the Congresses, district numbers for representatives, and party affiliations for all members. In the case of legislation named after a member, a brief description of the legislation has been added.

A number of biographical works on women in Congress have been published. *Biographical Dictionary of Congressional Women* by Karen Foerstel (Greenwood Press, 1999) contains 200 biographies of women who served through the end of the twentieth century. There are a number of similar works published earlier that do not contain as many entries. The book begins with an overview of women in Congress. There are two tables listing the chairs of committees and the number of women by Congress. The work is useful for supplementing the information in the CQ *Directory.*

A good complement to the biographical reference works is *Members of Congress: A Bibliography* by Robert U. Goehlert, Fenton S. Martin, and John R. Sayre (Congressional Quarterly, 1996). This unannotated bibliography lists more than 9,000 journal articles, books, dissertations, and essays from collected works that cover the public and private lives of members of Congress. The intent of the work is to provide "an extensive listing of biographical references of individuals who have served in the U.S. Congress from 1774–1995." Government publications, popular articles, newspaper articles, and obituaries are not included. The chief value in this bibliography is for researching lesser-known members of Congress, as the better-known will be found in many reference works. It is a comprehensive work in that it is the only recent bibliography to cover everyone who has served in Congress.

197. Committees in the U.S. Congress, 1789–1946. Washington, D.C.: CQ Press, 2002. 4v. ISBN 1-56802-2.

The volumes in this set cumulate titles that have been issued over a number of years. An earlier set with the same title, which covered the years 1947–1992, was published in 1993. A total of seven volumes cover the assignments from the First Congress in 1789 through 1992. For the 1789–1946 time period, volumes 1 and 2 cover the House and Senate. Volume 3 lists committee membership. Volume 4 lists select committees in Congress. Much of Congress's business was conducted through these special committees until the modern period. The works lists the membership of standing committees in the House and Senate, as well as the length of tenure and leadership positions held by each member. Often assignments are indicators of career progress, status, and chance of future advancement in Congress. Lists are organized by committee and then by individual members of Congress, giving the committee members' assignments throughout his or her career. The work is the most comprehensive printed reference for congressional committees.

An earlier work published by Greenwood covers much the same material, *Congressional Committees, 1789–1982: A Checklist,* compiled by Walter Stubbs (1985). This checklist enables a researcher to use a subject approach, listing committees alphabetically according to a keyword in the committee name. A subject index is also provided, with references to entry numbers. More than 1,500 standing, select, and special committees are listed. Besides the name of the committee, information given includes the legislation (with citation) creating the committee; the dates of establishment and termination; SuDocs number if the committee was assigned one; and serial set number and volume if a report was issued. A chronological list of committees by date of establishment provides another reference approach. There is a bibliography included. This checklist gathers information on congressional committees into one volume and is useful for those seeking citations to committee reports or information for committees dealing with particular topics.

198. CQ Almanac. 57th ed. Washington, D.C.: CQ Press, 2001. 1,000p. ISBN 1-56802-637-4.

The *Almanac* has been published for each session of Congress since 1949. It provides analysis and detailed coverage of legislative developments and congressional events including national party conventions and results of presidential and congressional elections. The treatment is current, but the older volumes are useful for historical studies. The current volumes begin with an overview of developments for that session of Congress, focusing on significant legislation regardless of whether it passed or not. Appendixes include a glossary of terms; rosters of congressional members and their committee assignments; voting records of members on key issues; and the text of important documents. The publication is known for objective analysis and coverage of key events and legislation.

A similar title published for current reference by CQ Press is *Congress and the Nation*. In its 10th volume in 2002, the work covers the post–World War II era and the 10 presidencies from Truman through Clinton. Each volume is a general survey of the politics of the period. The title is significant for historical research in that each volume was written close to the time period of the actual events and provides insight into contemporary thinking.

199. Congressional Quarterly's Guide to Congress. 5th ed. Washington, D.C.: Congressional Quarterly, 1999. 2v. 1,354p. ISBN 1-56802-477-0.

The first edition of this guide was published in 1971. Each subsequent edition has emphasized the changes occurring in Congress since the previous edition. Each edition also has as its first section historical information on the origins and development of Congress. The second section reviews the powers of Congress; the third explains congressional procedures. A complete listing of members of Congress is included in each edition. Other sections vary according to the edition and the issues prominent in the time period covered. Taken as a series of editions, the *Guide to Congress* is both a current information tool and a historical reference work with an interpretative perspective. It is thoroughly indexed and includes hundreds of charts and tables. It is a reference that should be utilized by anyone studying the federal legislative process or researching any aspect of Congress.

Congress A to Z: A Ready Reference Encyclopedia (3rd ed. CQ Press, 1999) contains much the same information as the *Guide to Congress*. The format of the *A to Z* makes it much easier to use than the guide. The majority of the entries are brief historical or biographical sketches. Despite the encyclopedic approach, the emphasis is still on the role of Congress in the U.S. government and its historical development and influence. There are a number of longer essays on the committee system, the budget process, the legislative process, war powers, and Watergate. There are cross-references and an index of names and subjects. Besides photographs and charts there are appendixes that list members of Congress by various categories. There are also lists dealing with congressional actions such as vetoes and overrides. There are maps and organization charts for Congress and the U.S. government. A bibliography is provided for further research. The arrangement and format of the *A to Z* make it ideal for ready reference, students, and the general public.

A newer work is *American Congressional Dictionary* (3rd ed. CQ Press, 2001). Terms and phrases such as "balanced budget" are defined and explained in this comprehensive dictionary. Many of the explanations give the historical origins of the words. The work is an expansion of the glossaries in the back of several CQ publications. It will be a handy reference to use along with the other CQ Congressional guides.

200. Directory of Congressional Voting Scores and Interest Group Ratings. 3rd ed. Michael J. Sharp. Washington, D.C.: Congressional Quarterly, 2000. 2v. ISBN 1-56802-565-3.

The data in this two-volume work are drawn from other Congressional Quarterly publications. The angle in this work is that the votes by members of Congress are not rated by specific issues, but according to whether they voted in accordance with policies being espoused by various interest groups, their political party, or the position of the president. Participation in roll call votes is also given. Votes are compiled by year and compared to the position of various groups such as Americans for Democratic Action, the American Civil Liberties Union, League of Conservation Voters, and others. Brief biographical entries are followed by tables of annual scores and ratings for every member since 1947. Four voting scores indicate support of the Conservative coalition, alliance with the member's party, support of the president's position, and recorded votes. Interest-group ratings represent the percentage of votes on which each member voted in favor of a special group's position. From the analysis the conservative or liberal leanings and how the votes of the members of Congress align with their party and the president can be seen. There are a number of guides that provide voting records but this is the only work to connect how a member voted to particular interests.

201. The Encyclopedia of the United States Congress. Donald C. Bacon et al., eds. New York: Simon & Schuster Academic Reference Division, 1995. 4v. ISBN 0-13-276361-3.

This reference work is most useful for historical research as it focuses on the development of Congress from 1789 to 1995. Other reference works on Congress are more factual, with tables and lists, and the focus tends to be on the current Congress. In over 1,000 alphabetical entries written by 550 experts, mainly academics or government researchers, the history, functions, and relationships of Congress are explained. All articles have bibliographies that include all formats, even media, but no Internet sites. In four volumes, this title provides comprehensive coverage. Topics include Congress's record in important public policy areas, such as civil rights, the environment, social welfare and taxation, and women's issues. Less-expected topics include the portrayal of Congress in literature and the movies. The work is attractively formatted with more than 900 illustrations, tables, charts, and graphs. There are a comprehensive index and a glossary of terms. The work is suitable for students and researchers alike.

A more thorough treatment of laws passed by Congress is the purpose of a new Greenwood series begun in 2002, *Student's Guide to Landmark Congressional Laws,* edited by John R. Vile. Separate volumes are devoted to laws on Civil Rights, Social Security and Welfare, Laws on Youth, the First Amendment, and Education. Each volume has a discussion of the law's intent and purpose; a summary of the substance of the law, including a explanation of difficult terms and concepts; examination of the politics and legislative history of the law; a summary of the law's impact; and an edited text of the law.

202. Facts About the Congress. Stephen G. Christianson. New York: H.W. Wilson, 1996. 635p. ISBN 0-8242-0883-8.

The workings of Congress including its committee structures, leadership and seniority, and relationships with the president are covered in the opening section of this work. Each congressional session from the first in 1789 through the 104th in 1995 is covered. Each chapter has information on the background of the historical events during the session, the leaders in both the Senate and the House, a chronology of major actions and bills passed, with a table of key votes, important failed legislation, constitutional amendments, impeachments, and scandals. The introduction is written by Richard Baker, Historian of the U.S. Senate. The work is a well-organized presentation of the structure, function, and history of Congress.

203. Guide to Research Collections of Former United States Senators, 1789–1982. Kathryn Allamong Jacob, ed. Washington, D.C.: Historical Office, U.S. Senate, 1983. 352p. (U.S. Senate Bicentennial Publication no. 1). Reprint, Gale, 1986. ISBN 0-8103-3334-2.

Parallel to the *Guide to Research Collections* for senators is *A Guide to Research Collections of Former Members of the United States House of Representatives, 1789–1987* (U.S. House of Representatives, Office of the Bicentennial, 1988), edited by Cynthia Pease Miller. Together these guides cover 3,000 House members and 1,800 senators. They are arranged alphabetically by names of congressmen and congresswomen. Collections of primary materials, including papers, oral histories, photographs, and other archival materials, are identified by repository. There are brief descriptions of the collections. Repositories are listed by state in the appendices. These guides are the only sources specifically devoted to location information on the papers of members of both houses of Congress. They serve as a starting point for a more thorough search for archival materials on specific individuals.

204. The Historical Atlas of State Power in Congress, 1790–1990. Kenneth C. Martis. and Gregory A. Elmes. Washington, D.C.: Congressional Quarterly, 1993. 190p. ISBN 0-87187-742-2.

This title is the third political atlas by Kenneth Martis and updates *The Historical Atlas of United States Congressional Districts, 1789–1983* (Free Press/Macmillan, 1982) and *The Historical Atlas of Political Parties in the United States Congress, 1789–1989* (Macmillan, 1989). The atlases concentrate on the changes in Congress that have occurred after each census and how reapportionment affects the strategy of presidential campaigns. A historical introduction explains congressional reapportionment. The second part of the volume shows congressional reapportionment by decade. The third part treats major geographical trends showing when power shifts took place, how the balance of power swung from slave states to free states, how the West emerged as a separate region, and the growth of the Sunbelt. The atlas contains 33 color maps and 70 charts that analyze the changes in seat allocations and power shifts from 1790–1990. Overviews and case studies supplement the information in the graphic analyses and explicate the historical relationship between geography and public policy. This atlas is of interest to political historians, geographers, political scientists, journalists, and sociologists.

Congressional Quarterly has also published two other works on congressional redistricting: *Congressional Districts in the 1980s* (1983) and *Congressional Districts in the 1990s* (1994). Both trace the distribution and redistribution of political power in the U.S. House of Representatives, state by state, district by district, in text, maps, and census data. The series will be useful in the future for historical research.

An earlier similar work is *United States Congressional Districts, 1788–1841,* by Stanley B. Parsons, William W. Beach, and Dan Hermann. (Greenwood Press, 1978). Two further volumes have been published with slightly different titles: *United States Congressional Districts and Data, 1843–1883* (Greenwood Press, 1986) and *United States Congressional Districts, 1883–1913* (Greenwood Press, 1990). The intent of the series is to enable researchers to analyze an individual legislator's behavior according to the socioeconomic and political makeup of the representative's district. In each of the volumes, data are organized into the decade breakdowns corresponding to the U.S. Census from which the data are derived. Although census data were not consistently collected for the same variables over the years, an effort has been made to make the data categories as similar as possible to allow comparison across decades. Data on variables are presented in tabular format by state and then county. There are state maps showing congressional district boundaries by congressional session, and there are political subdivision maps for cities or counties having more than one congressional district. These volumes can be used in conjunction with the Martis atlases and the concomitant congressional publications.

205. How to Research Congress. Robert U. Goehlert and Fenton S. Martin. Washington, D.C.: Congressional Quarterly, 1996. 107p. ISBN 0-87187-870-4; 0-87187-869-0.

This title supplants the earlier *Congress and Law-Making: Researching the Legislative Process* by the same authors published by ABC-CLIO. It is designed to provide a foundation for developing a research topic and to describe key sources of information for researching the legislative process. The work is a clearly written explication of the complex of publications, agencies, and procedures involved. The introduction gives an overview of legal resources and a discussion on how to design a research strategy. Concise descriptions are given of major primary and secondary sources for bills, reports, debates, and so forth. Sources of oral histories, archives and data files as well as specialized sources issued by organizations that rate the votes of member of Congress, and campaign finance data sources included. Electronic sources are indicated throughout. A major part of the work is devoted to tracing the legislative process through both houses of Congress. The final section is composed of a bibliography of books arranged by subject and a glossary. This guide shows the relationship between the steps in the legislative process and the concomitant congressional publications. Those who discover it will carry it along as a companion in the research process.

Another CQ title with much the same information is *How Congress Works* (3rd ed. 1998). The emphasis in this work is on the leadership, the legislative process, and the committee system. It goes into more depth on the legislative process than other reference works with sections on House and Senate procedures in committees and floor action. Each edition has also focused on the changes that have taken place in Congress and there are historical perspectives. As with all CQ titles, there are plentiful graphics and boxes. The volume is written in an easy-to-understand style.

Supplementing the research guides is another CQ Press publication *Landmark Documents on the U.S. Congress* (1999). The work includes materials on the conduct of senators and representatives, the origins and development of the Congress, and congressional procedures and reform efforts. The editor, Raymond W. Smock, a former historian of the U.S. House of Representatives, has selected key documents, edited them, and placed them in historical context. More than 150 documents are arranged in chronological order with head notes that offer valuable interpretation and context. The work includes an introductory essay, a bibliography on Congress, and an index.

206. Index, The Papers of the Continental Congress, 1774–1789. John P. Butler, comp. Washington, D.C.: National Archives and Records Service, 1978. 5v. ISBN 0-911333-56-8.

The National Archives produced this five-volume index as a bicentennial project. The documents indexed are available on microfilm from the National Archives and include the records of the two Continental Congresses, the Confederation Congress, and the Constitutional Convention, as well as the Declaration of Independence and the Articles of Confederation. The documents are organized not by congress but by type: Journals, committee reports, correspondence, and so forth are grouped together. There is a separately published index for the journals, *Index to the Journals of the Continental Congress, 1774–1769* (National Archives, 1976). Indexing for persons, places, and subjects is in one alphabetical sequence. Volume 5 is a chronological listing of all the documents, with originator and recipient of the document, number of pages, and location in the microfilm provided.

Since the publication of the two indexes by the National Archives in the late 1970s, a microfiche collection of *U.S. Congressional Journals* has been published by CIS. This collection is available in two components: one of all congressional journals from 1789 to 1978, and another that contains only those journals not in the *CIS U.S. Serial Set Index.* Researchers trying to locate congressional journals can inquire into the availability of the National Archives microfilm or the CIS microfiche publication. LexisNexis *Congressional Universe* also contains the CIS indexing.

207. Members of Congress: A Checklist of Their Papers in the Manuscript Division, Library of Congress. John J. McDonough, comp. Washington, D.C.: Library of Congress, 1980. 217p. ISBN 0-8444-0272-9.

The papers of the members of Congress are not all deposited with the Library of Congress, but this is a useful source for quickly determining which collections are there. A total of 894 members of Congress are included, from the Continental Congress to the 95th Congress. Many of the collections listed have only a few items, but other collections are quite extensive. Each entry contains brief biographical information and a description of the holdings of the collection. A useful feature is a summary of microfilmed manuscripts from other repositories held by the Library of Congress, thus providing leads to collections with materials pertaining to the same individual. The entry notes of the collection appears in the *National Union Catalog of Manuscript Collections.* There is also a listing of the members of Congress by state as well as by the Congress in which the member served. This checklist will be useful to the researcher seeking to locate personal papers of members of Congress.

208. The United States Congress: An Annotated Bibliography. Robert U. Goehlert and Fenton S. Martin. Washington, D.C: Congressional Quarterly, 1995. 640p. ISBN 0-87187-810-0.

It is rare in the age of electronic databases to see printed bibliographies updated. This bibliography updates the earlier work by the same authors, which was published in 1982. That bibliography of over 5,600 entries was not annotated. The organization of this newer work is similar to the earlier one. Scholarly books, articles, dissertations, essays and research reports are included, but not popular works or biographical works. The entries are arranged in topical sections. An introduction written for the new work is actually a guide arranged by format that describes reference sources for researching Congress. There are author and subject indexes. The work is a useful accompaniment to the many guides to Congress and is comprehensive for scholarly literature in English before the Internet became so popular.

A work with a more restricted scope is *The Speakers of the U.S. House of Representatives: A Bibliography, 1789–1984,* edited by Donald R. Kennon (John Hopkins University Press, 1986). Both the individuals who have been Speaker of the House of Representatives and the office itself are thoroughly covered in this bibliography of over 4,000 articles, books, speeches, and dissertations. The first section concerns the office; the second part is devoted to individual speakers and is divided into four time periods. Each begins with a biographical section, followed by information on the location of manuscripts. The bibliography is divided into sections for writings or publications by the individual, and another section lists secondary materials. There are separate subject and author indexes. This volume is a comprehensive treatment of the office of Speaker of the House of Representatives and would be useful for students and researchers interested in the topic.

THE JUDICIAL

Throughout history, the Supreme Court, in its role as the third branch of the U.S. government, has counterbalanced the other two branches. Many controversial issues dealing with states' rights, attacks on freedom of speech, desegregation, and abortion, insolvable through the legislative process, have come before the high court. Rulings on such volatile issues have kept the Court and its members before the public during periods of intense unrest in the history of the United States.

In 1974 the Supreme Court Historical Society was founded. It now has upward of 3,500 members, both individuals and institutions, which engage in historical research and the collection and preservation of artifacts dealing with the history of the Supreme Court. The society sponsors lectures, research projects, and the publication of historical studies, including an index to judicial opinions. It publishes a newsletter and yearbook, as well as the *Annual Lecture Reprints* (111 Second St. NE, Washington, DC, 20002, (202) 543-0400).

The bicentennial of the Supreme Court was the impetus for the publication of a number of reference works. The majority of the works described in this section are recent publications. Law in the United States is covered more broadly in the section "Law and Crime" in chapter 6.

*209. CQ Supreme Court Collection. [Electronic database]. Washington, D.C.: CQ Press, 2002–. Available: http://library.cqpress.com.

Information from the printed CQ products on the Supreme Court is gathered into one place with this Web site, which blends historical analysis with current updates and expert commentary on Supreme Court decisions, biographies, history of the Court and the U.S. Constitution. The site includes summaries and analysis of more than 4,000 major decisions including all cases in which a written opinion was issued from 1969 to the present. There are biographies of every justice with an analysis of their major opinions and judicial philosophies. Tables and statistics are included analyzing voting records, political alliances, and institutional data. There are timelines for major cases, justices, and key events in U.S. history. Bibliographies, texts of primary documents, and a glossary are included. The Web site supports basic and advanced searching with navigational and browse features. Links to other governmental and non-governmental Web sites are included. For those who have access to the site, its all-inclusiveness makes it the best starting point for research.

210. Encyclopedia of the U.S. Supreme Court. Thomas T. Lewis and others, ed. Hackensack, NJ: Salem Press, 2001. 3v. ISBN 0-89356-097-9.

The organization of the encyclopedia is an A–Z of topical entries. The entries are written by approximately 220 contributors and range from 250 to 3,000 words. Headers briefly describe the topic and summarize its significance. There are numerous illustrations including portraits. Topics are wide ranging from specific cases to eras and issues. Appendixes include a timeline, a list of justices in order of appointment, a glossary, a bibliography, and a listing of the entries by broad subject category. There are both a general index and an index of all cases referenced in the text. The work is designed for a general audience.

211. A Guide to the Early Reports of the Supreme Court of the United States. Morris L. Cohen and Sharon Hamby O'Connor. Littleton, CO: Fred B. Rothman, 1995. 237p. ISBN 0-8377-0486-5.

This work sets out to explain why there are no Supreme Court cases in volume 1 of the *Reports of the Supreme Court of the United States.* The answer lies in the early process of reporting Supreme Court cases. This reference work provides historical, biographical, and bibliographical information on the first 90 volumes, 1790–1876 of the *Reports of the Supreme Court of the United States.* The process of reporting as developed by Alexander J. Dallas from 1790–1807 is explained. Biographies of seven early court reporters are included. The majority of the volume is a detailed bibliography of the sources in which the early cases are to be found. The bibliography takes the reader through the different printings and editions of the *United States Reports.* There are indexes to memorials and rules and orders and lists of related publications and research resources. This is a unique reference work and one that provides information not provided elsewhere. Given the subject and the detailed treatment, it is most useful to the legal scholar or researcher of the period of the early judiciary in the United States.

212. Guide to the U.S. Supreme Court. 3rd ed. Joan Biskupic and Elder Witt. Washington, D.C.: Congressional Quarterly, 1997. 2v. ISBN 1-56802-130-5.

Of the reference works on the Supreme Court published by CQ Press, this guide offers the best historical treatment. In two volumes of more than 1,100 pages, the origins of the Court and how it functions, people who have shaped it and the impact decisions have made on American life are all covered. The guide covers the history of the Court, its operations, its power in relation to other branches of government, major decisions affecting the other branches, the states' and individual rights, and biographies of all the justices. Entries include extensive notes and a selected bibliography of additional sources. The third edition is current through the 1996 Court term. In addition there are two lengthy appendixes, "Chronology of Documents and Texts" and "Tables, Lists, and Geographical Data," which provide lists of nominees, a glossary of legal terms, and related events pertaining to the Court. The full text of five landmark rulings and chronological summaries of some 400 major decisions are provided. The format is typical CQ with numerous boxes, editorial cartoons, drawing, maps, and photographs. One valuable feature is the section "Sources of Supreme Court Decisions," which shows readers how to access major Court opinions using the Internet. A case index includes every decision mentioned in the work, along with the complete legal citation for each case. This reference work is a good place to begin any research on the Supreme Court. The guide is updated by *The Supreme Court Yearbook,* which *Congressional Quarterly* began publishing in 1991 with the 1989–1990 year.

The Supreme Court A-Z, also published by CQ Press is designed to be a ready-reference work on the subject (2nd ed. 1998). It compliments the more in-depth treatment of the *Guide* with a simplified approach. A great deal of information is contained in more than 300 essay entries or lists. Entries are written for general readers and include definitions of legal terms and procedures, background of landmark cases, discussions of controversial topics both historical and recent, and short biographies of justices. Appendixes include online sources of opinions, a seating chart, a list of nominees, and how to read a court citation. The volume is one of four in CQ's *Encyclopedia of American Government,* the other three on the Congress, the presidency, and elections. The work is more appropriate for students and the general reader than the researcher.

Yet another publication on the Supreme Court by CQ Press is *The Supreme Court Compendium: Data, Decisions, and Developments* (2002). The emphasis in this work is on data and facts, rather than discussion. It brings together data on judges and judicial staff, petitions and decisions, political climate, public opinion, and more. The tabular organization of the data makes possible longitudinal analysis and research. The data are divided into nine topical chapters with suggested methods of using the information. For individual justices, such topics as political party affiliation, public support of opinions, backgrounds, nominations, and confirmations can be researched. Other aspects of the Court include its history and development as an institution, workload, cases, decision trends, and impact on society. The volume has a detailed index and can be used by lay readers. As with the other two CQ Supreme Court titles, current Web sites are provided for further information. This title is designed for research and supplements the information given in the other reference works.

213. How to Research the Supreme Court. Fenton S. Martin and Robert U. Goehlert. Washington, D.C.: Congressional Quarterly, 1992. 140p. ISBN 0-47187-497-3.

Both general research resources and advanced legal research tools are covered in this guide. It is useful for students and members of the general public with little knowledge of the research process and for advanced researchers in law, history, and political science. In addition to listing the resources according to format category, this guide describes the best use of the resources for the type of research being conducted. Bibliographies on the history of the Court and its relations with the other branches of government are included, as well as reference tables listing justices, appointments, and nominations. This guide is obligatory as a beginning point for research on the Supreme Court.

The authors of the research guide have also produced a bibliography emphasizing scholarly research sources. *The U.S. Supreme Court: A Bibliography* (Congressional Quarterly, 1990) can be used in conjunction with the research guide. It is an extensive, although not annotated bibliography that covers research monographs, journal articles, and dissertations. Government documents have been excluded. Subject sections include the history, work, and organization of the Court; civil liberties; equal rights; due process; regulation; and education. This bibliography is useful for anyone beginning research on the Supreme Court or sociopolitical topics.

Another title from CQ is *Illustrated Great Decisions of the Supreme Court* by Anthony Mauro (CQ Press, 2000). This is a ready reference for the general reader. Nearly 100 cases are summarized with background and facts of the case; the vote and highlights of the decision with excerpts from the opinion; and a discussion of the impact of the decision on the law and society. The goal of the work is not to provide comprehensive coverage, but to illustrate the impact the court decisions have on American society. Appendixes include the Constitution, a list of all the justices, a succession chart of court seats underscoring the historical makeup and leanings of the Court, and a comprehensive bibliography. Cases are arranged alphabetically, but a topical list provides quick access to the impact of rulings in particular areas of law. Most of the cases are civil and First Amendment decisions between 1824 and 1999. There are photographs, portraits, political cartoons, and drawings. For each case the citation is given and the FindLaw Web site address. The most valuable aspect of the work is Mauro's impact summaries.

214. Landmark Supreme Court Cases: A Reference Guide. Donald E. Lively. Westport, CT: Greenwood Press, 1999. 384p. ISBN 0-313-30602-8.

Seventy-four cases are divided into four general topic areas in this guide: the distribution of powers, the relationship between the federal government and the states, equality, and individual rights. Each part treats a set of legal topics addressed by the Court and begins with a summary of the issues and the times. Cases were selected for their impact on society and the future and are presented in chronological order so that changes in legal thought over time can be seen. Each case has a fact box for quickly identifying the issues, year of decision, outcome, vote, and author of the opinion. The narrative discussion of each case puts it in historical perspective and examines the background and constitutional issue involved, the case itself, why it is a landmark case, and its significance and impact. *US Reports* citations are given and brief bibliographies follow the case summaries. The work concludes with a glossary, the U.S. Constitution, a table of cases, and an index. The cases most often sought by undergraduates are included with more in-depth discussion than other reference works.

Also published by Greenwood Publishing Group is *Dictionary of American Criminal Justice: Key Terms and Major Supreme Court Cases* (2002). The work is in two parts. Part One is a dictionary that applies an interdisciplinary approach to enhance its effectiveness in explaining the American criminal justice system. Part Two provides examples to further explicate the terms and concepts in Part One. Recent and significant Supreme Court cases are utilized. Each case has an account of the events leading up to the case and the rationale used in each decision. The work can be used both as a reference work and a study guide on significant cases in criminal justice.

*215. LexisNexis. Dayton, OH: LexisNexis. [Electronic database] Available: http://www.lexisnexis.com.

LexisNexis is included in a number of different sections of this U.S. History guide (entries 11, 107, 121, 179, 194, 359). As a legal database designed for research as well as current awareness it naturally includes the Supreme Court and the federal judiciary of U.S. Courts of Appeal cases and decisions as well as legislative histories. The coverage includes federal case law and state/territorial case law; federal statutory materials and statutory materials for all 50 states and the District of Columbia; the Code of Federal Regulations; U.S. patents; and law reviews and periodicals. Within *LexisNexis* is the Shepard's Citations Service for identifying cases and articles that have cited the case under study. Both *LexisNexis* and *Westlaw* are comprehensive databases for all federal, state, and district courts. Both offer the ability to Shepardize cases.

216. The Oxford Guide to United States Supreme Court Decisions. Kermit L. Hall, ed. New York: Oxford University Press, 1999. 448p. ISBN 0-19-511883-9.

The material for this work is drawn from the earlier title by Hall, *The Oxford Companion to the Supreme Court of the United States* (Oxford University Press, 1992). The entries for over 400 landmark decisions cover the particulars of the case, the legal and social background, the reasoning behind the Court's decision, and the case's impact on American society. The guide includes a case index, a topical index, the text of the Constitution, an appendix on the justices, and a legal glossary. It is a suitable reference work for laypersons, written in nontechnical language.

Kelly S. Janousek has compiled *United States Supreme Court Decisions, 1778–1996: An Index to Excerpts, Reprints, and Discussion, 1980–1995* (Scarecrow, 2001), an update to an earlier work by Nancy Anderman Guenther with the same base title published in 1983 covering the years 1960–1980. The emphasis in these works is on providing students with citations to easily accessible publications that discuss or reprint specific Supreme Court decisions. The citations are to book and journal articles and are arranged in chronological order of publications. Each entry contains the case name, date of the decision, citations to the decision as published in the *U.S. Reports* and other case reporters, and abbreviations of the journal or books that are included in the bibliographical citations. Instructions for use at the beginning of the volume explain the entries and how to use the four indexes in the volume.

Supreme Court Drama: Cases that Changed America is another title from Gale Group (2001). This four-volume set contains entries of three to five pages on 150 major Supreme Court decisions that have had significant impact on American society.

217. The Personal Papers of the Supreme Court Justices: A Descriptive Guide. Alexandra K. Wigdor. New York: Garland, 1986. 226p. (Garland Reference Library of Social Science, v. 327). ISBN 0-8240-8696-1.

All of the justices of the Supreme Court, up to and including Chief Justice Warren Burger, are listed in this reference work. Justices for whom no personal or judicial papers have been found are listed with that indication. Arrangement is alphabetical by justice. Information given on collections includes location, size, access restrictions, provenance, and a description of the collection as to correspondence and legal papers. The source of the information on the collections is also given. This work gathers much scattered information into one highly useful volume. Those researching the Supreme Court, individual justices, and broad topics in constitutional history will find this particularly useful.

*218. Search FLITE Supreme Court Decisions. Available: http://www.access.gpo.gov/su_docs/supcrt/index.html.

The Air Force, in cooperation with the GPO, has mounted the full text and summaries of Supreme Court decisions from 1937 to 1975 at the FLITE Web site. Though a disclaimer states that this site is simply "a finding aid" and "not an official version of the Supreme Court's opinions," it is searchable by keyword, case name, and case number.

Another useful free source of the text of actual cases is the Legal Information Institute at Cornell University Law School (available at http://supct.law.cornell.edu/supct/cases/historic.htm). This site provides the text from over 600 cases from 1794 to 1998 and is searchable by topic, party name, or opinion writer. A very affordable CD-ROM of this database is also available for purchase.

The OYEZ Project at Northwestern University is a major Web site featuring a multimedia U.S. Supreme Court database (available at http://oyez.at.nwu.edu). The site contains both transcripts and full audio versions of recent U.S. Supreme Court decisions with full transcripts dating as far back as 1935. An attraction is a virtual tour of the Supreme Court. There is also biographical information for each of the current justices.

219. The Supreme Court. Philip Weinberg, ed. New York: Macmillan Reference USA/Gale Group, 1999. 1028p. (Macmillan Compendium). ISBN 0-02-865369-6.

Another in the *MacMillan Compendium* series, this encyclopedia is based on the Supreme Court articles from the four-volume *Encyclopedia of the American Constitution* and its 1992 supplement. Historical periods, public acts (statutes, treaties, and executive orders), and individual people and decisions of the Supreme Court are covered. The articles are signed with cross-references and bibliographic references. New articles have been added and others updated. The arrangement is alphabetical with a detailed subject index. The format is attractive with illustrations, sidebars, and marginal quotations.

Those looking for a chronological approach can use, *Facts About the Supreme Court of the United States,* by Lisa Paddock (H.W. Wilson, 1996). The work covers the Supreme

Court from its beginnings, 1790 to 1995, providing case citations, date argued, date decided, basis for review, vote, and legal significance.

220. Supreme Court Cases on Gender and Sexual Equality, 1787–2001. Christopher A. Anzalone, ed. Armonk, NY: M.E. Sharpe, 2002. 707p. ISBN 0-7656-0683-6.

More than 200 cases are divided into eight topical categories in this volume: civic and social rights; educational import; employment or career; sexual harassment; procreation; family and marriage; morality and sexual ethics; and orientation issues. Within the topical areas the cases are arranged chronologically, discussed and analyzed, so that the historical context and development can be seen. Appendixes include a table of all cases, keyword indexes, a bibliography, and the Constitution. This work is essential for any research and study on the judicial treatment of gender and sexual equality issues.

Two similar titles by the same editor and publisher are *Encyclopedia of Supreme Court Quotations* (2000) and *Supreme Court Cases on Political Representation, 1787–2001* (2002). Approximately 900 excerpts from Supreme Court decisions are arranged into 13 topical chapters in the *Encyclopedia of Supreme Court Quotations*. The quotations run the gamut both in terms of time span and subject. The excerpts were chosen for precedent, historical, or research value. Within chapters, passages are arranged chronologically, with entries including the name of the case, primary citation, year, author, type of decision, and keywords under which the passage is indexed. The keywords are often too general to allow finding specific cases and there is no other indexing approach by subject. *Supreme Court Cases on Political Representation, 1787–2001* includes every case relevant to elections and political representation from the Court's beginnings through 2001. It is a primary document reference book organized into 16 topical chapters. Every case is included either as a full opinion, extensive excerpts of the opinion, or a detailed description of the case.

221. The Supreme Court in American Life. George J. Lankevich, ed. Millwood, NY: Associated Faculty Press. 1986–1987. 9v. ISBN 0-86733-060-0.

The volumes in this series are divided into nine historical periods: volume 1, *The Federal Court, 1781–1801;* volume 2, *The Marshall Court, 1801–1835;* volume 3, *The Taney Court, 1836–1864;* volume 4, *The Reconstruction Court, 1864–1888;* volume 5, *The Fuller Court, 1888–1910;* volume 6, *The Conservative Court, 1910–1930;* volume 7, *The Court and the American Crises, 1930–1952;* volume 8, *The Warren Court, 1953–1969;* volume 9, *The Burger Court, 1968–1984.* Each volume follows the same format. There is a foreword by the author giving a historical overview of the period covered, focusing on significant events and issues of the period. The first part of the text proper is a chronology of major events, which provides a context for the issues and decisions of the Court. The second part, "Decisions and Documents," includes portions of the arguments in landmark decisions, dissenting opinions, constitutional amendments, and other documents pertinent to the founding and evolution of the Court. There is a biographical section with basic facts and portraits or photographs of the justices. The last section in each volume is a selective bibliography of scholarly articles and treatises pertaining to the era of the Court covered by the volume. The series and its division by historical period are intended to place the decisions of the Supreme Court into a historical context and to assess the impact of those decisions on the country. The volumes succeed in both presenting information and the prevailing philosophy of the Court in each period. The set is useful for students and the general public.

ABC-CLIO has a series of Supreme Court handbooks. Each handbook is devoted to one chief justice and has a section with essays on the period, the justices, major decisions, and the legacy. The second section is devoted to reference materials and includes brief alphabetically arranged entries on key people, laws, and events; a chronology; a table of cases; a glossary; and an annotated bibliography.

222. The Supreme Court Justices: Illustrated Biographies, 1789–1995. Clare Cushman, ed. Washington, D.C.: CQ Press, 1996. 588p. ISBN 1-56-802-126-7.

This work, produced under the auspices of the Supreme Court Historical Society, is the first single-volume reference to provide in-depth biographies of each of the justices who have served on the Court. Besides presenting standard biographical information, the biographies describe the legal philosophy of each justice and the major issues on which each passed judgment. The volume is suitable for general audiences and students and will be used often for research on the justices of the Supreme Court.

Several other works with similar titles and contents have been published. *Supreme Court Justices: A Biographical Dictionary* by Timothy L. Hall (Facts on File, 2001) is an attractively formatted ready-reference work containing 108 black-and-white photographs, appendixes, a bibliography, chronologies, and an index. The main text of each entry is two to three pages containing a narrative of the justice's life and career, along with major highlights of their court service, their role in major cases, and the political, social, and religious philosophies that may have guided their decisions.

Biographical Directory of the Federal Judiciary 1789–2000 (Bernan Associates, 2001) contains brief biographies with directory-type information. The most valuable features of the work include a detailed list of manuscript locations for many of the entries; information on circuits courts, even those that were abolished in 1912 and replaced by the U.S. district courts; a list of appointments for each court; and legislative histories for each court. In all, information covers about 80 federal courts, including the Supreme Court, circuit courts, courts of appeals, and district courts.

223. Supreme Court of the United States, 1789–1980: An Index to Opinions Arranged by Justice. Linda A. Blandford and Patricia Russell Evans, eds. Millwood, NJ: Kraus International, 1983. 2v. ISBN 0-527-27952-8.

Certain types of reference works fulfill a distinct need and once published do not have to be revised. This index to opinions of Supreme Court justices is one such work. With its publication, it became no longer necessary to search legal source materials repeatedly for the opinions. The editors have included an introduction and a handy "Note to Users." The introduction explains the seven categories into which the opinions have been classified. The complete case name and citation are provided for each opinion. The arrangement is alphabetical by justice and then within the seven categories. Historians, political scientists, legal scholars, and students interested in issues placed before the Supreme Court will find this index useful. It forms a base for more current research, which can be conducted through database searching as well as printed sources.

*224. Westlaw. Eagan, MN: West Group. [Electronic database] Available: http://www.westgroup.com.

John B. West founded the West Publishing Group (now West Group, a Thomson company), over 130 years ago. West introduced a classification of American law that became the standard model for citing law cases. In the early days of the Internet, the classification scheme was challenged because West considered it to be propriety. Subsequently West Group developed a new classification system. While *Lexis* was developed for a wider user audience than the courts system and the law, *Westlaw* was mainly used within the legal and courts system until the beginning of the twenty-first century. The electronic entity *Westlaw* contains cases, statutes and administrative materials, law reviews and treatises, attorney profiles and business information, and forms. Within *Westlaw* are 15,000 databases, more than 1 billion public records, more than 6,800 news and business publications, Dow-Jones Interactive, and more than 700 law reviews. There is international as well as U.S. coverage. In recent years, the West Group has begun marketing *Westlaw* to a wider audience. It is now available in many academic libraries as well as law libraries. Because of depth and breadth of the legal materials, court reporters, and case law, the *Westlaw* database is useful for historical case research.

STATE, LOCAL, AND REGIONAL GOVERNMENT

This section is divided into sources for state and local government, urban politics, and regional/territorial resources. The study of state, local, and urban politics has not traditionally enjoyed as high a status for academic historians as the study of federal government policies and national issues and trends. Much state and local history has been carried out by genealogists and public or nonacademic historians. An important organization is the American Association for State and Local History (available at http://www.aaslh.org) with its numerous publications.

STATE AND LOCAL SOURCES

225. American Legislative Leaders 1850–1910. Charles F. Ritter et al. New York: Greenwood Press, 1989. 1,090p. ISBN 0-313-23943-6. **American Legislative Leaders in the Midwest, 1911–1994.** Nancy Weatherly-Sharp and James R. Sharp, ed. Westport, CT: Greenwood Press, 1997. 376p. ISBN 0-313-30214-6. **American Legislative Leaders in the Northeast, 1911–1994.** Kevin G. Atwater. Westport, CT: Greenwood Press, 2000. 352p. ISBN 0-313-30215-4. **American Legislative Leaders in the South, 1911–1994.** James R. Sharp and Nancy Weatherly-Sharp, ed. Westport, CT: Greenwood Press, 1999. 361p. ISBN 0-313-30213-8. **American Legislative Leaders in the West.** Nancy Weatherly-Sharp and James R. Sharp, ed. Westport, CT: Greenwood Press, 1997. 396p. ISBN 0-313-30212-X.

The 1989 volume on legislative leaders from 1850–1910 serves as a base volume with coverage continued by a number of other titles with regional scope. In each of the volumes there is an introductory essay in which the editors describe and analyze personal and professional data about the speakers. The essay sets the state legislatures and their leaders into historical perspective. Appendixes offer tabular data on each legislator arranged by topic, state, and name on issues such as gender, race, birth and death, political party affiliation, education, and religion. The individual biographies do not highlight the accomplishments or influence of the legislators. A summary bibliography of sources is also included. From the data presented, the editors are able to make important commentaries on shifts in state politics and political party alignments over most of the twentieth century. The volume for the Northeast includes 315 biographies for legislative leaders from Connecticut, Delaware, Maine, Massachusetts, New Hampshire, New Jersey, New York, Pennsylvania, Rhode Island, and Vermont. The volume for the South includes the states of Alabama, Arkansas, Florida, Georgia, Kentucky, Louisiana, Maryland, Mississippi, North Carolina, Oklahoma, South Carolina, Tennessee, Texas, Virginia, and West Virginia. The Midwest includes the states of Illinois, Indiana, Iowa, Kansas, Michigan, Minnesota, Missouri, Nebraska, North Dakota, Ohio, South Dakota, and Wisconsin. The West volume includes the states of Alaska, Arizona, California, Colorado, Hawaii, Idaho, Montana, Nevada, New Mexico, Oregon, Utah, Washington, and Wyoming. Although many of the leaders profiled can be found in other biographical sources, these volumes gather the information by state and in addition provide state analyses for a number of important elements.

226. Bibliographies of the States of the United States. Westport, CT: Greenwood Press, 1992–.Vol. 1. **Kansas History: An Annotated Bibliography.** Virgil W. Dean, ed. 1992. 616p. ISBN 0-313-28238-2. Vol. 2. **South Dakota History: An Annotated Bibliography.** Herbert T. Hoover and Christopher J. Hoover, ed. 1993. 552p. ISBN 0-313-28263-3. Vol. 3. **North Carolina History: An Annotated Bibliography.** H.G. Jones, comp. 1995. 796p. ISBN 0-313-28255-2. Vol. 4. **Illinois History: An Annotated Bibliography.** Ellen M. Whitney et al., comps. 1995. 603p. ISBN 0-313-28235-8. Vol. 5. **Arkansas History: An Annotated Bibliography.** Michael B. Dougan et al., comps. 1995. 365p. ISBN 0-313-28226-9. Vol. 6. **Nebraska History: An Annotated Bibliography.** Michael L. Tate, comp. 1995. 549p. ISBN 0-313-28249-8. Vol. 7. **Alabama History: An Annotated Bibliography.** Lynda W. Brown et al., comps. 1998. 438p. ISBN 0-313-28223-4. Vol. 8. **Wisconsin History: An Annotated Bibliography.** Barbara D. Paul and Justus F. Paul, comps. 428p. ISBN 0-313-28271-4. Vol. 9. **Kentucky History: An Annotated Bibliography.** Ron D. Bryant, comp. 2000. 553p. ISBN 0-313-28239-0.

Greenwood Press is publishing this series of annotated bibliographies by state designed to "systematically review the components of local, state, and regional history within the chronological framework of the states' histories." Each work has been compiled by authors from that state, many of them academics. A number of the works have cosponsorship by the state historical society or state library. All have received very favorable reviews. The organization of the works is either chronological or topical. They are not all of one template, in a "cookie cutter" format; there is some individuality within an overall format. The topical sections are determined by the history of the particular state and usually are broad in scope ranging from standard political and economic studies to social and environmental histories, local studies, and regional studies with special significance to the state. Each work provides comprehensive coverage of secondary materials on the state as well as information on major archival and manuscript collections. All are indexed. For many states the bibliography is the first publication of a resource for the state. For many the currency and comprehensiveness of the works make the title the best resource available for research on the state.

An earlier similar series by state was also published by Greenwood beginning in 1982, *Reference Guides to State History and Research.* States are covered individually in separately published works that follow a standardized coverage beginning with part I, which contains historical essays divided by chronological periods or themes. These survey the important literature and identify materials of various types. The second part of the work describes archival repositories and sources of information containing state history materials. Beginning in 1983 with *A Guide to the History of Louisiana,* edited by Light Townsend Cummins and Glen Jeansonne, the series included *A Guide to the History of Massachusetts* (Martin Kaufman et al., eds., 1988); *A Guide to the History of Texas* (Cummins and Alvin R. Bailey, Jr., eds.,1988); *A Guide to the History of Florida* (Paul S. George, ed., 1989); *A Guide to the History of California* (Doyce R. Nunis, Jr. and Gloria R. Lothrop, eds., 1989); and *A Guide to the History of Illinois* (John Hoffman, ed., 1991). For those states with works in the earlier series, the guides and the bibliographical works complement each other.

227. Biographical Directory of the Governors of the United States, 1888–1994. Marie M. Mullaney. Westport, CT: Greenwood Press, 1994. 425p. ISBN 0-313-28312-5.

A continuing biographical series is formed through this title, which updates earlier volumes on governors of the United States. The first title is *Biographical Directory of American Colonial and Revolutionary Governors,* by John W. Raimo (Westport, CT: Meckler, 1980). The next title is *Biographical Directory of the Governors of the United States, 1789–1978,* edited by Robert Sobel and John Raimo (Meckler, 1978). After 1978, supplementary volumes have been published to this set: one, released in 1985, updates the work through 1983, and a second supplement, from 1989, covers men and women who were governors during the years 1983–1988 elections. In 1984 another title, *Biographical Directory of American Territorial Governors* by Thomas A. McMullin and David A. Walker, was published by Meckler. An earlier work updated by Mullaney in 1988 is *American Governors and Gubernatorial Elections, 1979–1987,* which originated with Roy R. Glashan's work of the same title covering 1775–1978.

Within this the succession of Meckler and then Greenwood titles for gubernatorial biographies, persons who served as governors in all states and territories of the United States from the colonial era to the 1990s are profiled. Arrangement is geographical and then chronological by date of office. The standard biographical information is given, with fuller information when it is available. Many entries include a photograph. In the Colonial volume, persons who held other positions of authority are included. Theses reference works include individuals not found in the standard, better-known biographical works such as the *Dictionary of American Biography* (entry 60). There are bibliographies for each state or colony and for individuals. A name index is provided. The history of the states and territories can be followed through the accomplishments and assessments of the terms in office of the governors. Although much of the information in these directories is gleaned from other sources, the accumulation of the information and its organization into one continuous set makes these directories a major reference tool.

Another reference source with biographical information is *The Governors of the American States, Commonwealths, and Territories, 1900–1980* (Council of State Governments, 1980). This volume contains much the same information as the Meckler and Greenwood directories in the same geographic organization, but the biographies are much briefer.

228. The Book of the States. Lexington, KY: Council of State Governments, 1935–. Bienn. ISSN 0968-0125.

The longevity of this publication makes it suitable for historical as well as current research. Much of the contents consists of contemporaneous directory information on members of the executive, legislative, judicial branches, and government services agencies, with addresses and telephone numbers. Historical and statistical data are provided for each state, with an emphasis on government affairs within the two years preceding the year of publication. The introductory essays and special feature articles are written by the staff of the Council of State Governments. These articles address issues in state government, such as consumer protection, education, and reapportionment. Thus, this reference work is valuable not only for directory and factual information but also for the comparative perspectives it provides for the handling of issues by state governments.

A similar publication is *Congressional Quarterly's Desk Reference on the States,* which began in 1999. This title is a current information reference source, but it does contain sections of historical information. Many of the current issues such as abortion are covered from a historical perspective. The final question in each chapter cites and annotates various pertinent reference works. Whereas the *Book of the States* will give contemporary presentation and interpretation of the facts, the CQ gives a current interpretation of historical events.

There are several other titles with similar information: *Facts About the States* by Joseph Nathan Kane, Steven Anzovin, and Janet Podell (H.W. Wilson, 1994); *The 50 States* edited by R.K. Rasmussen (Salem Press, 2000); and *Worldmark Encyclopedia of the States* (5th ed. Gale, 2001).

229. Encyclopedia of the American Legislative System. Joel H. Silbey, ed. Gale Group, 1994. ISBN 0-684-19243-8.

Federal, state, and to a lesser degree, local legislative structures from colonial times to the present are covered in this three-volume reference work. Ninety-eight experts in history and political science have written 91 original essays divided into six subject areas: history; recruitment, personnel, and elections; structures and processes; behavior; specific policy issues; and relationships with non legislative entities. Topics such as early territorial and state legislatures, the party allegiance, ethics, the role of individual committees, budget process, pressure groups and lobbyists, civil rights and vetoes are covered. Each essay has a short bibliography and *see* references. There is no overall index.

The Third House: Lobbyists and Lobbying in the States by Alan Rosenthal (2nd ed. CQ Press, 2001) is a thorough treatment of the lobbying at the state level. The author discusses the role and influence of lobbyists, their behavior and practices, the types of issues and interests, and the strategies and tactics employed. Although not a historical treatment, the work will be useful in the future for historical study of the topic.

230. Home Rule in America. Dale Krane et al. Washington, D.C.: CQ Press, 2000. 350p. ISBN: 1-56802-281-6.

Although it is a primary tenet in the relationship of states to the local governmental jurisdictions within a state, home rule powers vary by state. This one-volume reference examines the powers and functions of municipalities and counties that operate under home rule within each state. Covered are the actions that local governments can, and cannot, pursue; states where power is centralized at the capital and where it is not; and trends in important issues such as taxes, land annexation, and citizen access. The volume has three main parts: an overview of home rule, including its history; a state-by-state description of home rule authority; and 16 tabular appendixes that allow readers a quick comparative reference source of powers by state. A scholar or governmental expert in each state prepared the state descriptions. This single source on the subject of home rule is written for researchers and students.

231. State Constitutions of the United States. Robert L. Maddex. Washington, D.C.: Congressional Quarterly, 1998. 518p. ISBN 1-56802-373-1.

The constitutions of the 50 states and three U.S. territories are profiled in this reference work. The full texts of the constitutions are not given; the attention is on the amendments to the constitutions. Introductory material provides perspective on the significant role of the state constitutions in U.S. history and recent years. After the introduction there is a set of tables that include state government structure, state constitutions and amendments, and new states rights and special provisions. From these tables the terms of state officials, whether item veto power exists, the memberships of the upper and lower houses, court size, and whether officials are elected or appointed can be determined. The state constitution table presents the date of statehood and the effective date of the current constitution along with amendments. The major portion of the work is an alphabetically arranged seven-to-nine page profile on each constitution. Basic data on the state and the origin and historical highlights of the document appear at the beginning. A readable summary of each article or section follows in excerpts or summary form. The years the sections were added or amended and pertinent court decisions are noted. Division of powers, the legislative, executive, and judicial branches; amendment procedures; and provisions concerning such critical issues and policies as direct democracy, education, environment, health and welfare, local government, and taxation and finance are covered. Comparative charts, a glossary, a bibliography of print and Internet sources, an appendix containing the U.S. and model state constitutions, and an index make this work the best one-volume reference on state constitutions for the student and general researcher.

Greenwood Publishing Group also has a series by state, *Reference Guides to the State Constitutions of the United States,* in which the history of the constitutions of individual states is traced.

232. State Constitutional Conventions from Independence to the Completion of the Present Union, 1776–1959: A Bibliography. Cynthia E. Browne, comp. Westport, CT: Greenwood Press, 1973. 250p.

This title is the first in a series of bibliographies that accompany and index the microfiche collection *State Constitutional Conventions* begun by Greenwood and now published by CIS. The complete collection covers documents from 1776–1988, plus relevant documents from before 1776. The bibliography and part 1 of the microform collection cover all 50 states. The official documents from the state conventions include the enabling legislation, journals, proceedings, resolutions and rules, the proposed draft of the constitution, and the final ratified constitution. Additional parts of the microfilm collection contain material produced by conventions and commissions between 1959 **and** 1988. An updated two-volume bibliography for the years 1959–1978 published by CIS accompanies parts 2–4 of the microform collection. Volume 1 provides full bibliographic information arranged by state and time period; volume 2 is arranged alphabetically by author and title within each state. There is also a separate annotated bibliography for the 1979–1988 time period accompanying part 5 of the microfiche collection. The bibliographies and microform collections are essential sources for those researching state constitutional conventions.

233. State Document Checklists: A Historical Bibliography. Susan L. Dow. Buffalo, NY: William S. Hein, 2000. 280p. ISBN 1-57588-617-0.

Bibliographic control of state documents has varied considerably among the states. Dow has compiled a bibliography by state that lists all the state checklists in chronological order according to publication date. Checklists dating back to the eighteenth century are included. The bibliography is evaluative as well as enumerative. Information is given on the scope and time span covered for each checklist. For the current checklists, ordering and full cataloging information are given. A title index is provided. In addition to the bibliography by state, there is an introductory essay on the history of the bibliographic control of state publications. Historians making extensive use of state documents will find this work helpful.

234. State Legislatures: A Bibliography. Robert Goehlert and Frederick W. Musto. Santa Barbara, CA: ABC-CLIO, 1985. 229p. ISBN 0-87436-422-1.

A compilation of scholarly writings concerning state legislatures, this bibliography includes dissertations, books, articles, and selected documents published between 1945 and 1984. The work contains 2,532 citations divided into two parts. The first part contains studies about state legislative processes, arranged by subject, and the second part contains studies of individual state legislatures, arranged by state. There are separate subject and author indexes. The only bibliography of its kind, this reference work is indispensable for historical research on state legislatures.

235. State Names, Seals, Flags and Symbols. 3rd ed. Benjamin F. Shearer and Barbara S. Shearer. Westport, CT: Greenwood Press, 2001. 495p. ISBN 0-313-31534-5.

The third edition of this title has been revised and expanded to include the District of Columbia and all U.S. territories and possessions. The work provides the only single reference source for information about state symbols and features over 300 information updates plus three new chapters, updated license plate illustrations, and a new format for ease of use. There are new chapters on state and territory universities, state and territory governors throughout U.S. history, state professional sports teams, and a complete revision of the chapter on state and territory fairs and festivals. Legal authority is cited and color illustrations are provided for official state birds, flowers, trees, flags, seals, songs, postage stamps, and more. Historical background is provided and also a bibliography of state and territory histories. There is an index. Although the information can be found in many sources, this work provides it all in one volume.

URBAN STUDIES

The city has been the setting for a number of U.S. novels and motion pictures, and it has been both damned and praised for its role in fostering the energies that shaped the lives of the heroes and heroines. It has been either credited with harboring the forces that lead to progress or blamed for encouraging the processes of decline and decay. Cities have served as "melting pots" of ethnic acculturation and were frequently the predetermined destinations of past generations of immigrants. Political party affiliations formed along the lines of labor, as opposed to farm or entrepreneurial interests, and the Democratic Party gained a strong foothold in the early decades of this century.

The study of urban politics is a new field that formed in the latter half of the twentieth century. The research is carried out mainly by political scientists, sociologists, and public-policy experts. The formation of the field can be seen in the beginning publication dates of the two main indexes, which began in the 1970s. The first is the *Index to Current Urban Documents* published by Greenwood Press in 1972 (entry 240). The other index is *Sage Urban Studies Abstracts* (Sage, 1973–). Several histories have been written on the subject, but relatively few reference books are available, as shown by the paucity of selections in this segment.

236. Biographical Dictionary of American Mayors, 1820–1980: Big City Mayors. Melvin G. Holli and Peter d'Alroy Jones. Westport, CT: Greenwood Press, 1981. 451p. ISBN 0-313-21134-5.

Biographies of 647 mayors from 15 of the largest U.S. cities are included in this dictionary. The cities are Baltimore, Boston, Buffalo, Chicago, Cincinnati, Cleveland, Detroit, Los Angeles, Milwaukee, New Orleans, New York, Philadelphia, Pittsburgh, San Francisco, and St. Louis. The biographies are written by over 100 scholars who used local libraries and archives for their research. The arrangement is alphabetical by individual, but an appendix provides chronological listings by city. Other appendixes list the mayors by place of birth, religious and party affiliations, and ethnic background. Each entry is signed and includes a list of sources. Standard biographical information is included as well as dates of terms in office. This work was thoroughly researched and provides information on individuals not found in previously published sources.

A more recent work by Holli, which builds upon the biographical dictionary, is *The American Mayor: the Best & Worst of Big City Leaders* (Pennsylvania State University Press, 1999). A survey of historians, biographers, and social scientists was taken to provide the selection of 730 of the best and worst mayors of 15 big cities. Holli explains the results of the survey, gives biographical sketches of the 10 best mayors, as well as some attention to the worst, and then uses the findings of modern leadership studies to explore mayoral success and failure. Although not strictly a reference work, the book makes a nice complement to the biographical dictionary.

237. City Directories of the United States, 1860–1901: Guide to the Microfilm Collection. Woodbridge, CT: Research Publications, 1984. 487p. ISBN 0-89235-081-4.

In the past, Research Publications has prepared microfilm copies of thousands of city directories and with this work now offers a guide to its massive collections. This directory and resource guide describe the three segments of the massive microform project. It is organized chronologically under city; entries enumerate the directories' time period and give bibliographic data. There is an index by state, region, and city. Scholars, students, and genealogists profit from the tool.

The microform project itself is titled *City Directories of the United States.* Segment 1, which furnishes complete copies of city, state, and regional directories published prior to 1860, was issued in nearly 6,300 microfiche. Segment 2 places the directories published between 1861 and 1881 on about 365 reels of microfilm. Segment 3 provides coverage from 1882 through 1901 on roughly 750 microfilm reels. Segment 4, which is not covered in the guide, offers additional coverage from 1902 through 1935. Research Publications became part of the Proquest/UMI group.

238. Encyclopedia of Urban America: The Cities and Suburbs. Neil L. Shumsky, ed. Santa Barbara, CA: ABC-CLIO, 1998. 974p. ISBN 0-87436-846-4.

The expected arrangement for an encyclopedia on U.S. cities might be by city. This work is an A-Z encyclopedic topical arrangement that allows the commonalities of urban life across different metropolitan areas to be seen and understood. Thus the emphasis is not on particular cities and cities are not often named throughout the entries. The work begins with an introductory essay before the 547 entries by 126 thematic subject areas. The entries by 374 contributors, almost all academics, are signed and include a bibliography. The entries cover a broad spectrum. There is good coverage of issues of race, ethnicity, women, and immigration. Other coverage includes profiles of key political, architectural, and artistic figures associated with the development of urban America; historical descriptions of major cities, suburbia, and neighborhoods; descriptions of social and cultural issues closely identified with urban life such as social welfare; descriptions of city infrastructures, such as subways, and their impact on city planning; environmental issues such as air and water pollution; and the urban-built environment and its impact on public policy. Concepts and terms are defined. The focus is primarily twentieth-century growth of urban areas. A selected bibliography, a detailed subject and general index and a list of entries by 16 thematic subjects are included. ABC-CLIO also issued the *Encyclopedia of Rural America* in 1997.

Cities of the United States: A Compilation of Current Information on Economic, Cultural, Geographic, and Social Conditions (3rd ed. Linda Schmittroth, ed., Gale, 1998. 4v) is a reference to consult for current information. The organization of this four-volume set is by regions of the United States: the South, the West, the Midwest, and the Northeast. Each volume covers over 40 cities for a total of 179 cities. Information included is directory, bibliographic, and illustrations.

239. Fire Insurance Maps in the Library of Congress: Plans of North American Cities and Towns Produced by the Sanborn Map Company. Library of Congress. Geography and Map Division. Reference and Bibliography Section. Washington, D.C.: U.S. Government Printing Office, 1981. 773p. ISBN 0-8444-0337-7.

This resource represents a real benefit for scholars and serious students. Insurance maps generally serve as excellent indicators of the physical condition, construction, and composition of dwellings and commercial buildings of the various geographic regions. The work is a checklist or guide to thousands of maps and sheets on nearly 10,000 cities and towns prepared by the Sanborn Map Company, one of the leading cartographers of U.S.

cities and towns. Maps date from 1867 and furnish information on details of construction and locations of such features as exits, windows, and water mains. Valuable detail is given regarding boundaries, block numbers, and construction features, as these were prepared to help determine the degree of risk and hazard for insurance purposes. Arrangement of entries is by state, with indexes of counties and cities.

An earlier work, *Union List of Sanborn Fire Insurance Maps Held by Institutions in the United States and Canada* (Western Association of Map Librarians, 1976–1977) is a two-volume source complementary to the Library of Congress checklist that furnishes listings of maps held by over 160 U.S. and Canadian libraries.

The most comprehensive collection of Sanborn maps is contained in the *Digital Sanborn Maps, 1867–1970,* collection produced on CD-ROM by Chadwyck-Healey (now owned by Proquest). The collection charts the growth and development of more than 12,000 American towns and cities for over a century. There are more than 660,000 maps in the collection.

*240. Index to Current Urban Documents. Greenwood Press, 1972–. **ICUD.** Greenwood Press, 2001. [Electronic database]

Although by its title, this is an index for current awareness, it has a long enough publication history to be used for historical research. Since 1972, the *Index to Current Urban Documents* has been the only comprehensive index to local government documents with text of the documents available in microfiche. The *Index* covers the documents produced by 500 of the largest cities in the United States and Canada. Documents in the electronic ICUD are available in PDF format. More than 2,400 documents are indexed yearly across 3,000 subjects. There are Web links to the originating jurisdiction for the documents. The full subscription includes an annual print index and archive CD-ROM with full documents. Regional subscriptions are also available. Anyone researching aspects of municipal government or local reactions to national trends will need to use this index.

*Sage Urban Studies Abstracts is a current quarterly service that has been issued since 1973 by Sage Publications. It abstracts a wealth of materials (books, articles, dissertations, speeches) on a variety of topics, including urban history.

241. The Municipal Year Book. Ann. Washington, D.C.: International City/County Management Association, 1934. ISSN 0077-2186.

Similar to the *Book of the States, The Municipal Year Book* has been published for many years and the early volumes are useful for historical research. Each edition has comprehensive directory information on local government officials and statistical tables for cities as small as 2,500. In addition, the various editions have essays on topics of importance to municipal government at the time, written by scholars and practitioners, well documented and illustrated.

242. Urban Politics Dictionary. John Smith W. Santa Barbara, CA: ABC-CLIO, 1990. ISBN 0-8743-6534-1.

Some 600 terms pertinent to urban politics and those involved are arranged alphabetically. The entries contain brief descriptions and explanations of the significance of the terms. About one-third have a suggested reading list. The emphasis in the work is on urban policy and administrative development and it provides an overview of successful and unsuccessful programs over the last half of the twentieth century. The volume includes a subject index and is useful for historians, political scientists, and urban planners.

243. Urban Sprawl: A Reference Handbook. Donald C. Williams. Santa Barbara, CA: ABC-CLIO, 2000. 264p. (Contemporary World Issues). ISBN 1-57607-225-8.

Although this work is in a world issues series, the contents have an almost exclusively American focus. The work covers the issues of urban sprawl with the associated economic and social challenges that sprawl has wrought. An introductory essay, which covers the major policy issues, is followed by a chronology that traces the events in the growth of urban sprawl historically. There are also biographical sketches of persons who called for the need to control urban growth. Chapter 4 contains statistical tables, polls results, and quotes that show the dominant trends in growth. Texts of documents, which illustrate some of the suggestions for controlling sprawl, are contained in chapter 5. Organizations, governmental agencies, and advocacy groups are listed in chapter 6 with directory information. The work strives to present a balanced view of both advocates for growth and those who see urban sprawl as an evil that needs to be controlled. The work ends with bibliographies of print and electronic resources, a glossary of terms, and a comprehensive index.

REGIONAL HISTORY

With the rise of sectionalism in the United States over the first half of the nineteenth century, the burning issues that divided the nation, states' rights, and the practice of slavery, were inextricably linked to geography and the resulting economic systems. The growing disaffection and alienation climaxed in the most troubling single event in this nation's history, the War Between the States. The War settled the slavery issue once and for all, but sectionalism has remained a political and economic reality for those elected to serve their constituencies.

General works on regionalism precede divisions by regions in this section of the chapter.

244. The Facts on File Dictionary of American Regionalisms: Local Terms and Expressions from Coast to Coast. Robert Hendrickson. New York: Facts on File, 2000. 755p. ISBN 0-8160-4156-3.

There are a number of dictionaries of slang, but this work is different from those in that the emphasis is on the regional aspects of the expressions and dialect contained therein. The organization is by region. Most sections contain a general discussion of the regional language or dialect followed by the alphabetized words and phrases with brief definitions. The dictionary does cover the continental states and Hawaii. The one-volume work is a condensation of an earlier five-volume edition.

245. Region and Regionalism in the United States: A Source Book for the Humanities and Social Sciences. Michael Steiner and Clarence Mondale. New York: Garland, 1988. 495p. (Garland Reference Library of Social Science, v. 204). ISBN 0-8240-9048-9.

A unique work that furnishes a framework for the interdisciplinary study of regionalism in the United States, this annotated bibliography of some 1,600 entries includes both books and periodical articles. It is divided into 14 subject areas, each of which contains materials relevant to the study of major thinkers, trends and developments, and schools of thought. Each discipline addresses the concepts of region and regionalism in its own way, and together they form a revealing package for broader understanding. In addition to history and geography, fields included are American studies, anthropology, architecture, art, economics, folk studies, language, literature, philosophy, and religion, political service, psychology, and sociology. Annotations are descriptive and range from 150 to 200 words; some entries are repeated in various sections. This is a valuable work for all inquirers; unfortunately, there is only an author index.

246. Researcher's Guide to Archives and Regional History Sources. John C. Larsen, ed. Hamden, CT: Library Professional Publications/Shoe String, 1988. 167p. ISBN 0-20802-144-2.

This guide consists of a collection of 14 essays written by various archivists and dealing with issues important to the utilization of archival and regional history resources. It serves the needs of both beginning researchers and serious inquirers by presenting a cohesive body of information, beginning with the first chapter, which covers the nature of archival research and the various types of materials and techniques. The work offers an interesting blend of general bibliographic awareness and practical information for conducting studies. Specialized types of materials are described in various areas, such as business, religion, and genealogy. There is a notes and bibliography section that furnishes references to sources with more in-depth topical coverage. The work serves as both a manual/textbook and a bibliographic source useful in preparing for archival work with regional materials. Topical treatment is given to ethics, preservation, oral history, and so forth.

New England

The states in New England all have strong historical identities. There is not a pronounced focus on the region in study and publication, but a few series and reference works for the region have separate treatments for each state.

The Society for the Preservation of New England Antiquities (available at http://www.spnea.org), located in Boston, was founded in 1910 and has 3,000 members. It publishes *Historic Houses in New England* annually and issues a quarterly newsletter.

247. Bibliographies of New England History. Committee for a New England Bibliography. Hanover, NH: University Press of New England, 1976–2000. v. 1–10. (In progress). ISBN 0-8161-1212-6 (v. 1).

The Committee for a New England Bibliography was created in 1969 to respond to the need for organization of the wealth of historical material available in the region. It was decided to produce individual state bibliographies as part of a projected seven-volume series. That projection was exceeded with the recent publication of the eighth volume, and others are still to come. Volume 1, *Massachusetts: A Bibliography of Its History,* edited by John Haskell (1976), established the pattern for the series as an alphabetical arrangement of books, periodicals, and articles under geographical units (state, county, or city). Location symbols are given if materials are not in the *National Union Catalog.* The cutoff date for inclusion is 1972. Works span the entire history of the state from its earliest development to the present. Volume 2, *Maine: A Bibliography of Its History* (1977), with a cutoff date of 1975, was also edited by Haskell. Volume 3, *New Hampshire: A Bibliography of Its History,* edited by Haskell and T.D. Seymour Bassett, was issued in 1979, with a cutoff date of 1977. Bassett edited volume 4, *Vermont: A Bibliography of Its History* in 1981, with 1979 as the cutoff date. Since then, Roger N. Parks has taken over the editorship and produced the following: volume 5, *Rhode Island: A Bibliography of Its History,* in 1983, with the cutoff date being 1981; volume 6, *Connecticut: A Bibliography of Its History* (1986); and volume 7, *New England: A Bibliography of Its History* (1989). Volume 8 (1989) and subsequent issues provide additions and corrections to the state bibliographies. They are volume 9 (1995), volume 10A (1998), and volume 10B (2000).

248. The Encyclopedia of New England. Robert O'Brien and Richard D. Brown, eds. New York: Facts on File, 1985. 613p. ISBN 0-87196-759-6.

From Facts on File comes this effort as part of the plan to furnish one-volume encyclopedias targeting the different regions of the country (see also entries 254, 264, 270). Similar in format to the others, this effort furnishes about 2,500 articles alphabetically arranged and covering various events, personalities, and places associated with the six states of the New England region (Connecticut, Maine, Massachusetts, New Hampshire, Rhode Island, and Vermont). Entries tend to be brief rather than giving in-depth coverage to topics; therefore, it is best used by the general public rather than the serious student. Coverage is given to what is considered to be cultural information in describing people's lives, institutions, historical events, demographics, climate, and politics. Definitions are given and geographical information provided, along with cross-references, maps, photographs, a bibliography, and an index.

249. New England in U. S. Government Publications, 1789–1849: An Annotated Bibliography. Suzanne M. Clark, comp. Westport, CT: Greenwood Press, 1998. 598p. (Bibliographies and Indexes in American History, no. 36). ISBN 0-313-28128-9.

The main virtue of this work is that the compiler has gathered together in one volume all of the resources for the seminal period in the beginnings of United States history for the states of Connecticut, Maine, Massachusetts, New Hampshire, Rhode Island, and Vermont. The organization is by state, enabling the researcher to concentrate on one state, or to get an overview of the entire region. Through government publications issued during the first 30 Congresses in the 1789–1849 time period, the origin of the social, fiscal, and foreign policies that were developed during the period are traced. These include the development of the postal system and the Treasury Department, the distribution of public lands, boundary disputes, and the origin of the divisive differences between the South and North over tariffs and slavery. Through speeches from New England representatives and senators their views and that of their constituents on the issues of the day can be discerned. The volume has chapters on each state, and within each chapter, the entries are arranged chronologically by Congress and session. The work is useful to anyone studying the time period as well as the region or states within the region.

The South

The South continues to draw the attention of historians, writers, and reporters seeking to furnish enlightenment and understanding of its almost mystical way of life. It has been revered and castigated, praised and condemned, serenely described and bitterly rendered by commentators and observers. No section of the country has inspired such polarization. The materials included here treat both the Old South (genteel, romantic, slow-paced, hospitable, but defensive and even violent in its protection of its way of life) and the New South (urban, sophisticated, and politically aware in pursuing its interests).

The Southern Historical Association (available at http://www.uga.edu/sha) was founded in 1934 and operates out of the Department of History at the University of Georgia in Athens. The organization has 4,500 members and has published the *Journal of Southern History* on a quarterly basis since 1935.

250. French and Spanish Records of Louisiana: A Bibliographical Guide to Archive and Manuscript Sources. Henry P. Beers. Baton Rouge, LA: LSU Press, 1989. 371p. ISBN 0-8071-1444-8.

Early Louisiana was a region composed of the present states of Alabama, Arkansas, Louisiana, Mississippi, and Missouri and administered by Spain, England, and France during successive time periods. Historical inquiries have been aided considerably with the publication of this comprehensive bibliographical guide to relevant materials. The author was a noted archivist, historian, and bibliographer and has produced a first-rate tool for scholars and serious students. The area was initially discovered and claimed by Spain and then settled by France, leaving a rich historical tradition in this region. Arrangement of the bibliography is in five chapters, each devoted to a state. The chapters furnish a documentary history and give locations of important collections (including European archives), reproductions, documents, publications, parish/county records, and so on. There are extensive footnotes, plus a detailed bibliography and a good index.

251. Index to Southern Periodicals. Sam G. Riley, comp. Westport, CT: Greenwood Press, 1986. 456p. (Historical Guides to the World's Periodicals and Newspapers). ISBN 0-313-24515-0.

The compiler is a professor of communication and has furnished a helpful resource tool for the study of magazine history in the South and topical coverage of events treated in the popular periodical literature. The South is defined in terms of the states of the Confederacy (Alabama, Arkansas, Florida, Georgia, Louisiana, Mississippi, North Carolina, South Carolina, Texas, and Kentucky). Maryland is excluded after the onset of the Civil War. Coverage includes about 90 periodicals published over a period of 120 years beginning in 1764 and emphasizes publications with general appeal rather than those considered the most scholarly. Those specific to black interests or to religious interests are excluded. Arrangement of entries is alphabetical; entries furnish a summary of the title's history, editorial policy, and content. Appendixes identify titles by founding date and by location; indexing is furnished.

252. Encyclopedia of Southern Culture. Charles R. Wilson and William Ferris, eds. Chapel Hill: University of North Carolina, 1989. 1,634p. ISBN 0-8078-1823-2.

This one-volume encyclopedia is considered an excellent survey of Southern tradition and culture prepared by two academicians. Twelve years in the making and the product of the combined efforts of 800 authorities who contributed entries, it is a special work without peer in its breadth of coverage. There are more than 1,300 entries, with bibliographies arranged under 24 topical sections varying in length from around 30 to 130 pages. Topics include agriculture, environment, violence, and women's life. About 250 of the entries cover personalities, both living and dead, who are representative of the topical element being covered. Each section begins with an introductory essay, followed by thematic articles, then by biographical entries. An extensive general index facilitates the search for specific information.

An earlier work is *The Encyclopedia of Southern History,* David C. Roller and Robert W. Twyman (LSU Press, 1979). The editors, both history professors, developed this one-volume encyclopedia to furnish answers to the most frequently asked questions about the South. The South is defined as the section of the country that accepted slavery in 1860 and includes Washington, D.C., Delaware, Arkansas, West Virginia, and Missouri, as well as the states of the Confederacy. Designed for the full array of inquirers, from scholars and serious students to the general public, the work consists of 2,900 articles written by the editors and 1,100 contributors, who have signed their entries. Coverage is given to personalities, events, definitions of terms, and places over a period of time from the beginnings to the present day. Most noteworthy are the lengthier treatments given to each of the 16 states and to archival materials with descriptions of state holdings. An index is furnished.

253. Encyclopedia of the Antebellum South. James M. Volo and Dorothy D. Volo. Westport, CT: Greenwood Press, 2000. 390p. ISBN 0-313-30886-1.

Designed for students, this one-volume ready-reference work broadly covers the period 1810–1860 and regions of the South. In nearly 300 entries, all aspects of political, economic, military, social, and cultural history of what was an exceedingly complex period in American history are covered. The overarching theme is that there was much seething beneath the "genteel" exterior of the South. Slave life and conditions, plantation society, political and reform movements, revolts, industrialization, profiles with statistics of each Southern state, and biographical profiles of 90 key individuals of the periods are included. Each entry concludes with a bibliography of reading suitable for students. A chronology of events and more than 45 illustrations from the period enliven the volume. The work is suitable as a starting place for more in-depth research.

254. The Encyclopedia of the South. Robert O'Brien and Harold H. Martin, ed. New York: Facts on File, 1985; Reprint, New York: Smithmark, 1992. 568p. ISBN 0-83172-768-3.

Another of the Facts on File regional one-volume encyclopedias, this, like the others in line, is designed primarily for the relatively unsophisticated user. Therefore, the brief unsigned entries, ranging in length from a paragraph to a full page and providing somewhat scanty coverage of topics, are less useful to scholars and serious students than are other works of this type (entries 252, 253). Nevertheless, there is a place for this effort in its coverage of 15 states (the Confederacy plus Arkansas, Kentucky, Maryland, Missouri, and West Virginia). Entries are alphabetically arranged and treat personalities, institutions, places, events, and products. The intent is to be inclusive and furnish brief information of cultural, geographic, statistical, political, and topical aspects. The work is illustrated with nearly 90 black-and-white pictures. A detailed index is furnished.

255. Routledge Historical Atlas of the American South. Andrew K. Frank. New York: Routledge, 1999. 144p. ISBN 0-415-92141-4.

The South is described as the "nation's most distinctive region" in this work which is divided into five historical periods: "The Nascent South," covering the seventeenth and eighteenth centuries; "The Antebellum South," "The Confederate South," "The New South," and "The Modern South," from 1930 forward. Specific topics include the mound builders, European settlement, slavery, the Trail of Tears, battles of the Civil War, industrialization, the Great Migration, the New Deal, and the Freedom Rides. The contents are attractively arranged in two-page spreads that contain maps, photographs, tables, and essays conveying the diversity of the people, places, and events of the region. There is a chronology, a list of suggestions for further reading, and an index. The atlas makes an excellent companion to the several dictionaries and encyclopedias on the history of the South.

256. The Urban South: A Bibliography. Catherine L. Brown. New York: Greenwood Press, 1989. 455p. (Bibliographies and Indexes in American History, no. 12). ISBN 0-313-26514-7.

Targeting urban development and urban life in the South, this work furnishes more than 7,000 entries of various types of materials representing the interests of social, economic, political, and cultural historians of the region. "Southern" is defined along the lines set by the Census Bureau: all states south of Delaware and the Ohio River west to Texas and Oklahoma. "Urban" is broadly interpreted and suggests all types of gatherings or clusters of people and buildings, including Indian settlements and ghost towns. Nearly 4,500 of the entries are articles from 275 different periodicals, followed by just over 2,000 monographs and nearly 900 dissertations; dates range from the mid-nineteenth century to 1987. Arrangement of entries is by format then by subject. Geographic and subject indexes are given.

The West

Similar to the South in the romantic and mystical manner in which it has been treated by observers and reporters, the West is the most heavily documented of regions. In the image of the cowboy, the admirable U.S. characteristics of rugged individualism, hardy pioneering spirit, and a sense of fair play are represented. Westerners have been perceived as courageous, unassuming, and full of virtue. The lure that the region has had for historians and writers is reflected in the number of bibliographic sources created as reference tools. The West is broadly defined in this section to include the early West beyond the Appalachians and the Louisiana Purchase up to the present-day Midwest. More attention has been given to the Southwest in research and publication, with far less concern shown for the Midwest and the Pacific Northwest.

The Western History Association was founded in 1962 at the University of New Mexico in Albuquerque and has 2,000 members. It publishes *Western Historical Quarterly,* among other titles. The Midwest Archives Conference, based in Evanston, Illinois, has produced *The Midwestern Archivist,* a semiannual journal, since 1976. Founded in 1972, the conference has 1,100 members at present.

257. Atlas of Western Expansion. Alan Wexler. New York: Facts on File, 1995. 240p. ISBN 0-8160-2660-2.

The development of the United States is traced through the eyes of western expansion in this well-conceived reference work. One hundred full and part maps arranged in chronological order are accompanied by well-written historical text that traces the expansion of the United Sates from the Alleghenies to the Pacific, bringing the story up to the beginnings of the twentieth century with the Indian Territory and Oklahoma land openings. Explorations, conquests, treaties, tribal wars, trade routes, land rushes, the French and Indian War, the Lewis and Clark expedition, and the Mormon exodus to the West are all covered. In addition to the maps there are photographs and original pen-and-ink drawings of everyday objects such as a Blackfoot bow and arrow, a gentleman's beaver hat, and a gold digger's shovel. Side boxes cover more single topics such as the Army Camel Brigade begun by Jefferson Davis. A final chapter, "The Real Significance of the Frontier," highlights the expansion westward taking place among the conflicts of North versus South, West versus East, and individuals versus big government and big business. There are two appendixes listing the states as they entered the Union and a chronology of the principal events from 1750 **to** 1917 that affected westward expansion. The volume ends with a three-page bibliography and an index of names and subjects. The work can be used alone as a ready reference or as an accompaniment to other historical works on western expansion. It is suitable for all levels of readers and researchers.

The Gale Group has published a *Westward Expansion Reference Library* consisting of three volumes, and *Almanac* (2000), *Biographies* (2001), and *Primary Sources* (2001). The *Almanac* is a chronological approach to the events that created the mythology of the pioneers who settled the wilderness. Many colorful characters are featured in biographical essays. Texts and excerpts from diaries, books, letters, and other sources are in the *Primary Sources* volume. The set is designed for students and general readers.

258. Atlas of the Lewis and Clark Expedition. Gary E. Moulton, ed. Lincoln: University of Nebraska, 1983; Reprint, 1999. 196p. (The Journals of the Lewis and Clark Expedition, v. 1). ISBN 0-8032-2861-9.

Through the efforts and support of President Thomas Jefferson, the Lewis and Clark expedition represented an official activity designed to explore the territory acquired by Jefferson through the Louisiana Purchase. The trip took two and a half years (1804–1806) and traced the Missouri River to its source, then crossed the northern Rockies. The charts, maps, and surveys developed during the expedition are reproduced in this work of historical interest. It represents the first definitive edition, furnishing 134 maps (most of them at their full original size), including 42 that have never been published. Joint sponsorship by the University of Nebraska and the American Philosophical Society made it possible for this important work to be produced.

More contemporary coverage is given in the seventh edition of *Atlas of the Pacific Northwest,* edited by A. Jon Kimmerling and Philip L. Jackson (Oregon State University,

1985). The source is unique in its coverage of the region, which includes Idaho, Oregon, and Washington State. It contains authoritative historical maps among the 167 offered.

259. Borderline: A Bibliography of the United States-Mexico Borderlands. Barbara G. Valk et al. Los Angeles: UCLA Latin American Center, 1988. 711p. (Reference Series, v. 12). ISBN 0-87903-112-3.

One of the more noteworthy bibliographical publications is this comprehensive listing of 9,000 books, serials, journal articles, technical reports, government documents, dissertations, maps, and conference proceedings about the borderlands published between 1960 and 1985. These lands are identified as California, Arizona, New Mexico, and Texas, as well as six Mexican states, including Baja, California. The work originated as a database at UCLA formatted in the MARC style of the Library of Congress, from which conversion was made to a print bibliography organized into 26 subject areas with geographical and form divisions. Library locations are given with respect to about 35 major institutions. There is an author index.

The *Borderlands Sourcebook: A Guide to the Literature on Northern Mexico and the American Southwest,* edited by Ellwyn Stoddard et al. (University of Oklahoma, 1983), is similar in scope and furnishes 60 bibliographic essays covering societal aspects of the region (culture, history, sociology, religion, politics). A composite bibliography is furnished from materials in the essays. Maps and charts are included.

260. Chronology of the American West. Scott C. Zeman. Santa Barbara, CA: ABC-CLIO, 2002. 350p. ISBN 1-57607-207-X.

The time frame covered is from the opening of the Canadian ice corridor, c. 30,000 B.C. to the present. The chronology is divided into four eras: The Native West, (c. 30,000 B.C.E.–1500 C.E.); the Imperial West (1500–1840); the Incorporated West (1841–1932); and the Contested West (1932–2001). Each section contains an overview of the major events and historical trends of the period. The chronology contains critical points in the social and cultural history of the region, examining the multiethnic character of the region. There are numerous sidebars that offer biographical portraits of important figures and further extend the analysis of important events. Maps and other illustrations accompany the text.

261. The Cowboy Encyclopedia. Richard W. Slatta. Santa Barbara, CA: ABC-CLIO, 1994. 474p. ISBN 0-87436-738-7.

The cowboy myth and its influence on the culture of the United States are treated in some 1,300 entries. Topics include people, places, equipment and dress, historical events, terminology, and cultural imagery surrounding the cowboys of both North and South America. The majority of the entries are for the United States, some brief definitions and some essay length. Both the myth and the reality are treated in an exploration of how and why the romantic cowboy image came into being. The role of cowboys in art, literature, and film is explored. Appendixes list films, periodicals, and museums. The work is very readable and the subject fascinating.

Also by Richard Slatta is *In the Spotlight: the Mythical West: An Encyclopedia of Legend, Lore, and Popular Culture* (ABC-CLIO, 2001). The culture, history, and folklore of the West are explicated in this one-volume A-Z reference work, which includes a chronology, a bibliography and an index. The entries are both factual and interpretative. The work also offers hundreds of Internet sites and references to radio, film, television, and popular culture.

*262. Encyclopedia of Frontier Biography. Dan L. Thrapp. Glendale, CA: A. H. Clark, 1988. 3v. ISBN 0-87062-191-2. **Supp** (v. 4). 1994. ISBN 0-870-62222-6. [In CD-ROM, Lincoln: University of Nebraska, 1995. ISBN 0-803-24425-8.]

This three-volume effort presents biographical sketches of about 4,500 frontiersmen and American Indians. The intent is to cover all people who achieved to a significant degree or who generated interest in the playing out of the drama of the U.S. West. Personalities are varied and include traders, cowboys, scouts, explorers, settlers, politicians, trappers, and outlaws. Excluded are people in the mining industry and those whose marks were made solely through the conduct of wars. Most articles run about one-fourth of a double-columned page and furnish enough detail to describe the person's role and significance. Arrangement is alphabetical by name. There are no illustrations, but a bibliography is given for each biographee. There is a detailed index identifying both topics and names of biographees, as well as personalities associated with them. The complete set was issued in CD-ROM under the same title in 1995 by the University of Nebraska Press.

263. Encyclopedia of the American West. Charles Phillips and Alan Axelrod, eds. New York: Macmillan Library Reference/Simon & Schuster Macmillan, 1996. 4v. ISBN 0-02-897495-6.

This four-volume work offers a comprehensive treatment of the westward expansion, examining events, organizations, persons, and social customs that shaped the American West. More than 1,000 alphabetically arranged entries define the concerns of the traditional West within the broader framework of social history. The work includes numerous photographs and is intended for readers at all levels.

264. The Encyclopedia of the Central West. Allan Carpenter. New York: Facts on File, 1990. 544p. ISBN 0-8160-1661-5.

Another of the Facts on File efforts to furnish one-volume encyclopedias of the different regions, this is the fourth in the series and covers 10 states: Colorado, Kansas, Montana, Nebraska, New Mexico, North Dakota, Oklahoma, South Dakota, Texas, and Wyoming. Like others in the series, the work is intended to meet the needs of the general public rather than those of the scholar or serious student. Of course, serious inquirers will utilize the work for less-sophisticated purposes because it offers a convenient package of information. Entries are arranged alphabetically and briefly describe places, events, institutions, and topical material. States receive the most detailed treatment, with entries revealing population, other statistics, archaeology, and history.

An earlier entry in the same series by the same author is *The Encyclopedia of the Midwest* (Facts on File, 1989). The strength of this particular work is its uniqueness as a source of information on a region that, plainly, has been ignored by bibliographers, editors, and publishers in the past. Other than that, the title is subject to the same type of criticism lodged against the other Facts on File efforts. Coverage of the 2,500 entries is brief rather than in-depth; the descriptions of personalities, historical events, institutions, climate, and politics are better utilized by the general public than by those with a scholarly or serious interest. The states of Illinois, Indiana, Iowa, Michigan, Minnesota, Missouri, Ohio, and Wisconsin are treated. Cross-references are included, as are photographs; there is a bibliography and a general index.

In the series also by Carpenter, is *The Encyclopedia of the Far West* (1991). Covered here are nine states: Alaska, Arizona, California, Hawaii, Idaho, Nevada, Oregon, Utah, and Washington, as well as the U.S. Pacific territories.

265. Historical Atlas of the American West. Warren A. Beck and Ynez D. Haase. Norman: University of Oklahoma Press, 1989; Reprint, 1992. 156p. ISBN 0-8061-2456-3.

This atlas furnishes nearly 80 maps covering 17 western states from the 100th meridian westward. Coverage is thorough and furnishes excellent historical perspective, reinforced by narratives accompanying each map. These descriptions provide exposition of major points on the map in some detail and indicate causes and origins of various phenomena. A wide range of information is furnished, along with such elements as World War II prisoner-of-war maps and Great Salt Lake elevations. Most of the maps have a legend to aid in their comprehension. An especially useful feature is the bibliography or list of references used for each map. These are listed near the end under the appropriate map number. A detailed index of names concludes the work.

266. The Louisiana Purchase: A Historical and Geographical Encyclopedia. Junius P. Rodriguez. Santa Barbara, CA: ABC-CLIO, 2002. 500p. ISBN 1-57607-188-X.

The Louisiana Purchase more than doubled the geographical area of the United States in one fell swoop, adding territory that stretched from Canada in the north to the mouth of the Mississippi River and the Gulf of Mexico in the south. The bicentennial of the event, which will be celebrated in 2003, sparked a number of new reference works. This encyclopedia includes signed articles by experts, which cover important historical figures, concepts, the reactions of individual states, the frontier, Native Americans, and the benefits and costs of westward expansion. The negative effects of the Purchase such as the depopulation of indigenous peoples are dealt with. There is a brief chronology of events and a bibliography of print and nonprint sources. Over 50 documents relating to the time period are included along with maps and illustrations.

A similar work has been issued by CQ Press, *the Louisiana Purchase: Emergence of an American Nation,* edited by Peter J. Kastor (2002). The work combines documents and analytical essays to explain why the United States acquired the massive territory; the profound social and political changes that came in the wake of the purchase; and how major historical figures like Thomas Jefferson, Aaron Burr, and James Madison were influenced by the purchase.

267. Maps of Texas and the Southwest, 1513–1900. James C. Martin and Robert S. Martin. University of New Mexico, for the Amon Carter Museum, 1984. 174p. Reprint, Austin, TX: Texas State Historical Association, 1999. 190p. ISBN 0-876-11169-X.

This is an attractive, useful atlas of high quality furnishing reproductions of nearly 60 maps developed over a period of nearly 400 years and relating to the southwestern region. More than a simple atlas, the work furnishes in its first half an interesting and informative

historical description of the development of European cartography. The period of exploration and settlement in this country is then interpreted through the examination of maps and
reports of regions extending from Florida to California and up to the Canadian borders. The
second major segment contains 50 black-and-white and 9 color maps, arranged chronologically and covering the Mexican-U.S. border regions of the West. Reproductions are excellent and together with the expository material make for an important tool. Also furnished
are a bibliography and suggested readings, along with an index to provide access.

268. Museums and Historic Sites of the American West. Victor J. Danilov. Greenwood
Publishing Group, 2002. 840p. ISBN 0-313-30908-6.

More than 1,500 museums and historic sites in 38 states and the District of Columbia
are included in this comprehensive reference on the American West. The author examines
both the real and mythic history of the trans-Mississippi region from the mid-1800s to the
early 1900s. Included are missions, trading posts, trails, landmark military forts, battlefields,
railroads, ghost towns, and early Native American villages. Details on exhibits and artifacts
are given. The work is useful both as a guidebook and an information source for historical
research.

269. The New Encyclopedia of the American West. Howard R. Lamar, ed. New Haven,
CT: Yale University Press, 1998. 1324p. ISBN 0-300-07088-8.

This work is a limited revision of the earlier *Reader's Encyclopedia of the American
West* (2nd ed., Harper Collins, 1977) by the same editor. The new edition consists of more
than 2,400 entries by more than 300 contributors with over 600 illustrations and maps. The
material in the previous edition seems to remain with some updates attached to the end of
the entries. The new articles cover topics from the time period since the first publication of
the work. The usual topics on the history of the American West are covered with the biographies being a particularly strong area. A number of lesser-known topics are also covered
such as territorial governments, environment, mining, transportation, legislation, and notable
western historians. There are also many articles on cultural aspects such as films, literature,
photography, myths, and artists and writers. The bibliographies have been updated for all
the articles with citations as recent as 1997. More illustrations were added to give the volume
greater appeal. The work is a reasonably priced one-volume reference work suitable for
students at all levels.

270. The Old West: Day by Day. Mike Flanagan. New York; Facts on File, 1995. 498p.
ISBN 0-8160-2689-0.

The chronological format of this work includes brief entries from the period 1840–
1890, the peak years of westward expansion from the discovery of gold in California to the
massacre at Wounded Knee. The entries were culled mainly from newspapers of the plains
states of the period and deal with historic persons, places, and events. A 26-page prologue
covers the period of 50,000 B.C. up to 1848. After the main body of day-by-day events, an
epilogue brings the coverage from 1890 to the Waco, Texas, disaster in 1993. In addition
to the day-to-day listings, there are boxes with more detailed information on important and
interesting events. The work complements other dictionaries and encyclopedias of the period.

271. Platte River Road Narratives: A Descriptive Bibliography of Travel Over the Great Central Overland Route to Oregon, California, Utah, Colorado, Montana, and Other Western States and Territories, 1812–1866. Merrill J. Mattes. Urbana: University of Illinois, 1988. 632p. ISBN 0-252-01342-5.

The Platte River Road ran from St. Joseph, Missouri, to Fort Laramie, Wyoming, and from 1812 to 1866 it was this country's greatest trail for western migration. The author has made a lifelong study of the region and in 1969 furnished an excellent historical study of the road. This bibliography contains listings of more than 2,000 travel accounts written on that passage during that time period. The purpose is to include all known overland accounts relating to the Platte River during the 50 years prior to the transcontinental railroad, which eventually caused the demise of wagon travel. Entries are arranged chronologically, then by name of traveler, and furnish author, document type (letter, diary, journal, memoir), library location, route and chronology of the journey, highlights of the trip, and evaluation of the document's importance.

A similar work is *Overland on the California Trail, 1846–1859: A Bibliography of Manuscript and Printed Travel Narratives* by Marlin L. Heckman (Glendale, CA: A.H. Clark, 1984). This is a unique work of excellent quality identifying both published and unpublished accounts of the movement to California during a period of 13 years. More than 400 diaries and journals are identified, forming a nucleus of primary-source material that is invaluable to historical inquiry in this area. Scholars and serious students benefit most, although the notes and descriptive matter are of interest to the western history buff as well. Arrangement of entries is alphabetical by name of author, although most names will not be familiar to the general reader. These travel narratives were written in a variety of circumstances and for a variety of reasons. Holdings of libraries and public archival agencies are identified. Entries furnish title, year, places at which the journey began and ended, format, location, and references from sources that identify the items. There is a name and subject index.

272. Six-guns and Saddle Leather: A Bibliography of Books and Pamphlets on Western Outlaws and Gunmen. 2nd ed. rev. and enl. Ramon F. Adams. Norman: University of Oklahoma Press, 1969; Reprint, Mineloa, NY: Dover, 1998. 808p. ISBN 0-486-40035-2.

Through all his extensive bibliographic work during the 1950s and 1960s, Adams considered himself a collector and tailored his effort to the needs of librarians and collectors, hoping it might also be useful for historians. Originally published in 1954, it was revised 15 years later and contains listings for nearly 2,500 titles, more than doubling the coverage of the earlier edition. Bibliographic description is full; evaluative commentary is insightful. Adams attempts to set the record straight historically and does not hesitate to render his thoughts regarding the quality and accuracy of the accounts.

A similar effort is Adams's *Burrs Under the Saddle: A Second Look at Books and Histories of the West* (University of Oklahoma, 1964), which was reprinted as a paperback in 1989. This is recognized as an important contribution in its detailed descriptions of over 400 books on gunmen, peace officers, outlaws, and generally notorious individuals. Carefully researched, it, too, sets the record straight.

273. The Trail West: A Bibliography-Index to Western American Trails, 1841–1869.
John M. Townley. Reno, NV: Jamison Station, 1988. 309p. ISBN 0-913381-05-5.

This work, as its title suggests, is both a bibliography and an index to important trails utilized for westward migration for a period of nearly 30 years during the nineteenth century. Both published and unpublished sources are listed and include diaries, articles, theses, books, and reminiscences, many of which are evaluated for their utility. The period of coverage begins with the first wave of settlers bound for California in 1841 and ends with the completion of the transcontinental railroad in 1869. The work is divided into two major parts, the first of which furnishes an alphabetical listing by author. Entries give locations, dates, trails, and a rating of quality. The second part furnishes indexes by chronology, subject, and trail segment. The latter contains descriptions of locations and features. Both researchers and students benefit from this source.

Territories and Dependencies

The acquisition and governance of territories, although not specifically granted as a right in the Constitution, has been inferred through other expressed powers, such as the right to make war and conclude treaties. Thus, such activity has always been a cause for debate and sometimes heated emotion, the most recent example being the controversy surrounding the independence accorded the Panama Canal Zone by President Jimmy Carter in planned stages. Alaska and Hawaii most recently shed their territorial status to become states. Others, like the Philippines, have achieved independence. Today, our affiliates are found in both the Atlantic and Pacific, and theoretically include even our nation's capital.

Of the territories past and present, Puerto Rico has received the most attention by publishers, although in recent years there has been more interest in the others. This section reflects that imbalance by giving a subsection to Puerto Rico alone, whereas the other segment embraces the remainder of the territories.

Puerto Rico

Puerto Rico, like Guam and the Philippines, was ceded to the United States by Spain in 1898 and was administered as a territory. In 1952, it was granted independence as a Commonwealth of the United States. For coverage of Puerto Ricans in the Continental United States, see "The Hispanic Experience," in chapter 5.

274. Annotated Bibliography of Puerto Rican Bibliographies. Fay Fowlie-Flores. New York: Greenwood Press, 1990. 167p. (Bibliographies and Indexes in Ethnic Studies, no. 1). ISBN 0-313-26124-5.

The first issue of a new Greenwood series, this work furnishes a listing of bibliographies that have covered topics important to the study of Puerto Rico. Subject matter varies and includes personalities, broad topics, and specific issues. The compiler, a librarian at the University of Puerto Rico, is an important contributor to Puerto Rican studies, having completed other bibliographic efforts (entry 275). The work opens with an introduction describing the development of bibliographical research on the area. The major part of the text contains an annotated bibliography of bibliographies arranged in classified manner under topics and subjects. Bibliographies contain both Spanish- and English-language publications compiled between 1877 and 1989. Annotations vary in length with the value or complexity of the entry. There are author, title, and subject indexes.

Although the work was published in 1932, *Bibliografia Puertorriqueña (1493–1930)* by Antonio S. Pedreira (Madrid: Imprenta de la Libreria y Casa Editorial Hernando, 1932; Reprint, New York: B. Franklin, 1974) has been the standard bibliography on Puerto Rico. It has been reprinted because of its comprehensive nature and value for study and research. Covering more than 400 years, from 1493 to 1930, publications include both monographs and journal articles. There are approximately 10,000 entries that include works about Puerto Rico and its traditions and works by Puerto Ricans on a variety of topics. Entries are arranged under format (bibliographical sources, general information) or topical categories (natural history, public health, political and administrative history). Of special interest is the section titled "History of Puerto Rico," which lists materials furnishing a broad perspective. The work is designed well as a reference tool, with access facilitated by both a detailed table of contents and author and subject indexes.

Another older but still valuable bibliography is *The Puerto Ricans: An Annotated Bibliography* (Paquita Vivo, ed., Bowker, for Puerto Rican Research and Resources Center, 1973). This work is considered to be one of the better bibliographic efforts and has succeeded in its purpose, furnishing a source of readily available material useful to a wide variety of inquirers. It represents a selective annotated bibliography that covers Puerto Rican history in comprehensive fashion, touching on all aspects of Puerto Rican existence. There are about 2,600 entries in Spanish and English. Arrangement of entries is within four major format segments: books, pamphlets, and dissertations; government documents; periodical literature; and audio-visual materials. The work was carefully developed and employed the resources of major library collections, among them the Library of Congress, University of Puerto Rico, New York Public Library, and Instituto de Cultura Puertorriqueño. An excellent feature is the listing given of the various publishers able to furnish the titles listed. There is both an author/title index and a subject index.

275. Index to Puerto Rican Collective Biography. Fay Fowlie-Flores, comp. New York: Greenwood Press, 1987. 214p. (Bibliographies and Indexes in American History, no. 5). ISBN 0-313-25193-2.

As part of the Greenwood Press series, this work represents another useful index to published biographies of Puerto Rican people. In all, 146 titles are indexed, 22 of which are in English. These works have all been published prior to 1986 and furnish at least three biographies each. No journal articles are used, but books represent varied types: collective biographies, collections of essays, histories, and anthologies. Entries furnish name, dates, and citation/reference, including volume, page numbers, and presence of illustrations in sources. Personalities are both historical and contemporary, dating from the colonial period to the present.

A complementary source is *Index to Spanish American Collective Biography* by Sara de la Mundo Lo (G.K. Hall, 1981–). Volume 3 of this valuable work was issued in 1983 and covers the Central American and Caribbean countries. This tool is arranged by subject, and indexes 186 biographical works (100 of which are also indexed by the Fowlie-Flores effort). Subjects range from art to religion and medicine. It is well indexed for easy access.

276. Puerto Rican Government and Politics: A Comprehensive Bibliography. Edgardo Melendez. Boulder, CO: Lynne Rienner Publishers, 2000. 356p. ISBN 1-55587-894-6.

This bibliography is divided into the two major periods of Puerto Rico's history. The first part is politics under the Spanish regime until 1898 and the second is the territorial rule under the United States during the twentieth century. The 17 thematic chapters cover political parties, ideologies and movements, government institutions and policies, culture and identity, gender, race, class, economic relations, and more. The more than 6,000 unannotated entries are for both Spanish- and English-language materials. The work is an important recent addition to reference works on the history of Puerto Rico.

277. Puerto Rico, Past and Present: An Encyclopedia. Ronald Fernandez, Serafin Mendez Mendez, and Gail Cueto. Westport, CT; Greenwood Press, 1998. 375p. ISBN 0-313-29822-X.

The historical coverage of this one-volume English-language work concentrates on the recent past half-century of the island. The work provides a guide for reading and interpreting the localized and frequently opaque references that appear in Puerto Rican newspapers though the definition of many Puerto Rican terms. From African roots to El Yunque, this encyclopedia has nearly 300 substantive entries on important people, places, events, social and political issues, legislation, movements, organizations, and terms and concepts. Entries vary in length from one paragraph to several pages and select bibliographies accompany each entry. The work is especially strong in biographies of important artists, intellectuals, and politicians. There are relatively few reference works on Puerto Rico and this one is an authoritative and up-to-date work.

278. Puerto Rico: A Political and Cultural History. Arturo M. Carrion, ed. Nashville: American Association for State and Local History [1983]; Reprint, New York: Norton, 1984. 384p. ISBN 0-393-30193-1.

This is one of the better histories of Puerto Rico. The editor and five other contributors develop a well-structured, cohesive description and interpretation of Puerto Rican tradition and development. All contributors are Puerto Rican and have succeeded in furnishing an accurate perspective of the essence and flavor of Puerto Rico as a distinctive Caribbean entity and a cultural nationality. As a mix of Indian, Hispanic, and African ethnic influences merged within a Spanish culture and language, the Puerto Rican experience unfolds from the colonial period through the dependency phase to eventual recognition as a commonwealth; each contributor covers a different stage. Illustrations accompany the text and aid comprehension of the descriptive material. Suggestions for further readings are given that should be helpful; an index furnishes access.

Other Regions

279. Pacific Island Studies: A Survey of the Literature. Miles M. Jackson, ed. in chief. New York: Greenwood Press, 1986. (Bibliographies and Indexes in Sociology, no. 7). ISBN 0-313-23528-7.

A useful set of bibliographic essays identifying important English-language monographs and journal articles organized into four major divisions are contained in this work. Polynesia is composed of the Pacific Islands and Hawaii; Micronesia includes the Caroline,

Marshall, and Mariana Islands administered by the United States as a trust for the United Nations. Also covered are Melanesia and Australia, with special attention given to the Aborigines and the Torres Straits islanders. A composite author-title-subject index furnishes access to the 2,000 entries.

Similar coverage is given in Gerald Fry's *Pacific Basin and Oceania* (ABC-CLIO, 1987), which identifies over 1,175 recent books and articles in the English language, many of which are by natives and residents of the regions covered (Melanesia, Micronesia, and Polynesia). Emphasis is given to the 1975–1985 period in terms of publications; there is a composite index to furnish access.

280. Panama. Rev. ed. Eleanor D. Langstaff. Santa Barbara, CA: CLIO, 2000. 225p. (World Bibliographical Series, v. 14). ISBN1-851-09251-X.

Originally published in 1982, the earlier bibliography has been supplemented through this work. In the earlier effort, a good portion of the 640 entries dealt with the history and development of the Canal. Historians will find the inclusion of older items, including those examining French involvement, to be useful. Much of the research included among the books, articles, and government documents is of contemporary nature and will be welcomed by both researchers and students in developing an awareness of prevailing conditions during different stages of growth and management. The current effort supplies an additional 750 items with emphasis on writings since 1985. Both volumes should be used to identify writings on Panama's history, geography, environment, recreations, and physical nature treated under a topical arrangement. Annotations are brief but informative. There is an index of authors, titles, and subjects.

281. Philippines. Jim Richardson, comp. Santa Barbara, CA: ABC-CLIO, 1989. 372p. (World Bibliographical Series, v. 106). ISBN 1-85109-077-0.

Like Puerto Rico and Guam, the Philippines was ceded to the United States in 1898 as a result of the Spanish-American War and administered as a territory until 1946, when the country achieved independence as a republic. This bibliography includes over 950 entries, primarily monographs in the English language but also journal articles, census reports, and other varied items. Emphasis is given to contemporary publications, although some older materials are included as well; arrangement is by broad topic. The entries are annotated and furnish informative content description; the work is of value to inquirers at all levels but is especially useful to students. There are author, title, and subject indexes.

282. Samoan Islands Bibliography. Lowell D. Holmes, comp. and ed. Wichita, KS: Poly Concepts, 1984. 329p. ISBN 0-915203-00-6.

Formerly called the Navigators Islands, Samoa today comprises two segments of islands. Western Samoa is independent, but the eastern segment, American Samoa, is administered as a territory. Most of the islands were ceded to the United States between 1900 and 1904 by their chiefs; Swains Island was annexed in 1925. This comprehensive bibliography enumerates all materials found on the island chain. Included here are books, chapters, articles from periodicals and newspapers, dissertations and theses, films, manuscripts and archives, government documents, and publications of international organizations in various languages. Arrangement of entries is under 44 subject divisions that range from broad to specific in nature. As with any huge project of this type, there are omissions and oversights; most serious in this case is the absence of an index. Scholars and students will need to take the time necessary to access the relevant material.

POLITICAL PARTIES AND ELECTIONS

As the capacity to analyze huge amounts of data has evolved, the study of political parties and campaigns has become focused more on socioeconomic factors than on political strategies. Traditionally, campaign elements such as slogans, songs, speeches, and newspaper coverage played a major role in campaign strategy. Since the 1960s, political campaigns have become ever more media-intensive, with predictive polls and sociopolitical strategies taking on increasing importance. Like the sections on politics and government, this section does not describe many contemporaneous publications for election statistics. Rather, the sources mainly concern historical campaign tools and tactics on the study of political parties in the United States.

PARTIES AND CAMPAIGNS

283. Campaign and Election Reform: A Reference Handbook. Glenn H. Utter and Ruth Ann Strickland. Santa Barbara, CA: ABC CLIO, 1997. 351p. (Contemporary World Issues Series). ISBN 0-87436-862-6.

The subject of campaign and election reform from the colonial period to the present is covered thoroughly in this volume. An introductory essay reviews the history of reform efforts and discusses key issues. It is followed by a chronology of events associated with the topic and a section of biographical sketches of 28 individuals who made significant contributions to reform efforts. Another section summarizes public opinion data and major Supreme Court cases. There are numerous quotations from the *Congressional Record* and other sources. The last section is a directory of organizations and agencies associated with various aspects of political reform. There is an annotated list of sources divided into six topics and also a list of nonprint resources including Web sites. The book also has a glossary and an index by title, subject, and name.

A more specialized work published by Congressional Quarterly is *Congressional Campaign Finances* (1992). Through a combination of chronology and narrative text, this work follows the issues in campaign finance reform from the Teapot Dome scandal to the present. Contributions and expenditures, political action committees (PACs), and political parties are included.

284. Campaign Speeches of American Presidential Candidates, 1948–1984. Gregory Bush, ed. New York: Ungar, 1985. 343p. ISBN 0-8044-1137-9.

This volume contains the text of selected campaign speeches. Included are nomination acceptance speeches and several other representative campaign speeches for the major-party presidential candidates. Third-party candidates are represented by one speech each. There is some essay commentary providing background information on the major campaign issues. An earlier volume, *Campaign Speeches of American Presidential Candidates, 1929–1972* (Ungar, 1976) provides the text of speeches for elections before 1948. The full text of speeches can be difficult to find. This publication is a useful source for students in history, political science, and communications.

Presidential Election Campaign Documents, 1868–1900 is a microfilm collection that focuses on political issues in the period following the Civil War. The collection of 14 reels published by Proquest/University Microfilms contains a wealth of political pamphlets and speeches and is another major resource for the study of presidential election campaigns.

285. Encyclopedia of American Parties, Campaigns, and Elections. William C. Binning et al. Westport, CT: Greenwood Publishing Group, 1999. 467p. ISBN 0-3133-0312-6.

The focus of this work is on contemporary American politics, but historical events and terminology are included. A 64-page section titled "Elections," provides detailed accounts of presidential elections and campaigns from 1789 to 1996. Following that are more than 450 entries written by three political science scholars. The entries include terminology, political figures, parties, organizations, legislation, and relevant Supreme Court cases. Examples are frequently offered to help clarify definitions. Particular attention is given to the ever-changing organizational structure of parties and contemporary electoral systems. Brief biographies of important political figures such as presidents, vice presidents, and congressional and party leaders are also included, along with a concise summary of every presidential election since 1789.

Less general in its focus is *Political Parties and Civic Action Groups,* by Edward L. Schapsmeier and Frederick H. Schapsmeier (Greenwood Press, 1981). Approximately 300 political organizations that had national influence at some point in U.S. history are included in this reference source. Many of the groups are familiar: the Women's Christian Temperance Union, Common Cause, the Gray Panthers. Some of the groups are still active, others defunct. In addition to descriptive and historical information on the origins, goals, and accomplishments of the organizations, citations for organizational publications and references to other sources of information are given. Appendixes include a glossary of 200 terms; a subject listing of the organizations according to mission or function; and a chronology by founding dates. This reference source is useful to students and researchers in a broad range of disciplines in the social sciences.

286. The Encyclopedia of the Republican and the Encyclopedia of the Democratic Party. George Thomas Kurian and Jeffrey D. Schultz, eds. Armonk, NY: M.E. Sharpe, 1997. 4v. ISBN 1-56324-729-1. **Supplement to the Encyclopedia of the Republican party** and **Supplement to the Encyclopedia of the Democratic Party.** George Thomas Kurian, ed. Armonk, NY: M.E. Sharpe, 2001. 2v. ISBN 0-7656-8031-9.

This encyclopedia is a comprehensive reference work on the two major political parties in the United States in four volumes with a two-volume supplement. In the base set, each party is treated in two volumes with like organization. Coverage ranges from extended signed essays with bibliographies to shorter entries. The first volume begins with a historical essay of the development of the party through various presidents, political events, and movements ending with a bibliography. The first section is followed by approximately 50 signed essays that treat party positions on a wide variety of topics. The issues discussed in relation to each party are very similar, but unique events and issues are covered for each party. The signed essays are one of the best features of the set. These essays contain cross-references and a short bibliography. The next section consists of signed biographies of presidential candidates, presidents, vice presidents, speakers of the House and other notable party members with lists of the party's members of Congress and governors. The second volume treats the party conventions, platforms and elections. The majority of these volumes reprint the text of the party platforms, one of the few reference works to do so. Appendixes present party rules, party headquarters, committee chairs, and statistical information. Each party's second volume has indexes—general, biographical, geographical, and an index of women and minorities. The *Supplement* brings the set up through the 2000 presidential election and the 2001–2002 Congress. This encyclopedia is a must for anyone researching the two major political parties in the United States.

287. Encyclopedia of Third Parties in America. Immanuel Ness and James Climent, eds. Armonk, NY: M.E. Sharpe, 2000. 3v. ISBN 0-7656-8020-3.

This three-volume work is the most comprehensive reference on alternative political parties in the United States. Written by historians and political scientists, it presents the history of all major and minor third political parties and independent candidacies from 1789 through the 1990s. Also included are major parties prior to the formation of the Republican Party in 1856 and minor parties that never ran a candidate for office. There are four main sections. The first is a chronological survey by historical epochs in which eight essays trace the evolution of political parties in the United States. The second section contains alphabetically arranged entries for over 100 parties with cross-references. The next section contains biographies of major figures in those parties. A section of 40 color-coded maps illustrate prominent third and independent candidate strength by county in presidential elections, 1880–1996. There are also illustrations, a glossary of terms, cross-references, an extensive, broad-ranging bibliography, and a list of Web sites about third parties. There are three complete indexes—subject, biographical, and geographical.

An earlier and more limited work on the same topic is *Encyclopedia of Third Parties in the United States* by Earl R. Kruschke (ABC-CLIO, 1991). This reference work is more useful to students than researchers, both for identifying third parties in the United States and getting basic information about them. The historical information on 81 parties includes the founding of the party; the origin of the name; the party platform or agenda the party is identified with; personalities associated with the movement; and what became of the party. Candidates supported or elected are mentioned and pertinent election statistics provided. There is information on the type of materials published or distributed by the party.

288. Historical Dictionary of Political Communication in the United States. Guido H. Stempel III and Jacqueline Nash Gifford, eds. Westport, CT: Greenwood Press, 1999. 171p. ISBN 0-313-29545-X.

Written by leading academics in departments of journalism and communications, this dictionary approaches political communication from the point of view of those fields. Political communication is defined broadly to include court cases, debates and theories, publications, groups and organizations. The alphabetically arranged entries include brief bibliographies. Given the increasing influence of the media in twentieth century politics, this is a useful reference work for historians and political scientists who are not expert in the communications field.

289. Historical Dictionary of United States Political Parties. Bass F. Harold, Jr. Lanham, MD: Scarecrow, 2000. 389p. (Historical Dictionaries of Religions, Philosophies, and Movements, no. 29). ISBN 0-8108-3736-6.

As the title implies, this one-volume work is a compact compilation of information about political parties in the United States. The emphasis is national. Entries provide brief biographical sketches of all presidents and vice presidents, anyone who received presidential votes in the Electoral College, key national party leaders, and others who played important roles in shaping the political party system. The work is most useful for definitions of terminology, conceptual terminology, technical terminology, and idioms concerning all aspects of the political party system. Entries clarify jargon with clear definitions, often in historical context. There is an introductory essay that gives an overview of the development of the political party system in the United States. Following the alphabetical entries, there are 14 appendixes that are primarily lists of presidents and vice presidents, speakers of the House, floor leaders of both houses, chairs of both major and minor political parties, and statistical summaries of both popular and electoral votes back to the eighteenth century. There is a 30-page bibliography arranged by subject and chronological period.

290. National Party Conventions, 1831–2000. Washington, D.C.: CQ Press, 2000. 297p. ISBN 1-56802-2563-7.

This reference work is updated after each national election. The main part of the book consists of a "Convention Chronology," brief histories of all major political party conventions from 1831 to the most recent convention. Each convention receives a description that includes the major issues, platforms, and results of any votes taken. The candidates are profiled, with photographs and biographical information also presented. All parties that held conventions are included, as well as excerpts from party platforms. Tables list state-by-state breakdowns of key convention ballots for the presidential nominees and votes on rules and procedures disputes. Also examined are the pre-convention nominating process, a brief history, and details concerning American political parties. The information is fuller for the twentieth-century meetings than for those held in earlier years. Although not as comprehensive as the *Encyclopedia of the Republican and the Encyclopedia of the Democratic Party* (entry 286), the work is a good one-volume source useful for students and researchers of the electoral process.

291. The People's Voice: An Annotated Bibliography of American Presidential Campaign Newspapers, 1828–1984. William Miles, comp. New York: Greenwood Press, 1987. 210p. ISBN 0-313-23976-2.

Before the advent of radio and television, the primary campaign medium was the newspaper. The history and influence of the campaign press are discussed in the introduction to *The People's Voice*. The bibliography is chronological by election year and then subdivided by political party or candidate. Masthead title and slogan, beginning and ending dates, frequency, publisher, and place of publication are given for each newspaper. One of the most valuable features for researchers is the location and holdings information for the newspaper files. Anyone conducting research involving U.S. presidential campaigns will need to consult this work.

292. Political Parties & Elections in the United States: An Encyclopedia. Sandy L. Maisel and Charles Bassett, eds. Hamden, CT, and New York: Garland, 1991. 2v. (Garland Reference Library of Social Science, v. 498). ISBN 0-8240-7975-2.

Although this reference work covers much the same information as several more recent publications, it contains over 1,100 entries written by a group of 250 scholars. The scope is broad, covering political parties and elections from colonial times to the present. One strong point is that it gives more attention to some less-prominent figures and terms than do other sources. The detailed index makes location of terms easy. This encyclopedia can be used in conjunction with other similar reference tools by inquirers at all levels.

An anthology containing nine analytical essays (some updated) from *Political Parties and Elections in the United States: An Encyclopedia,* edited by L. Sandy Maisel, was published in 1994 (Garland). The volume contains three original essays, as well as one significant revision of an encyclopedia article. The essays examine the origins, development, and growth of political parties, party organization at all levels of government, the appeal of parties to the electorate, and the functioning of parties within the halls of government. There is no index.

293. Presidential Also-Rans and Running Mates, 1788 Through 1996. Leslie H. Southwick, comp. Jefferson, NC: McFarland & Company, 1998. 808p. ISBN 0-7864-0310-1.

Although it is easy to find information on the winners of presidential elections, it is often not easy to even find the names of those who were not victorious in their quest for office. The first edition of this work, which appeared in 1984, was highly acclaimed. Now greatly expanded and with illustrations, it provides detailed biographies of the 95 major-party and 41 significant third-party nominees who were never elected president or vice president. The arrangement is chronological by date of election, from 1788 through 1996. The 1861 election for the Confederacy is also included. Most of the biographical profiles begin with a summary of facts about the person, including birth, education, religion, ancestry, occupation, and family, followed by the career journeys of the candidates, the election, and the person's career afterward. The profiles are analytical and substantive, ranging in length from two pages for John A. Brooks, 1888 vice presidential candidate for the Prohibition Party, to approximately eight pages each for Hubert Humphrey, George Wallace, and many others. At the conclusion of many sketches there is a balanced and forthright "Analysis of Qualifications," providing insight into what the presidency (or vice presidency) would have brought. Biographies of persons who served at some time as president or vice president are not included. Each entry includes a brief bibliography, with a general biography at the back of the volume. This edition adds a list of historical sites and movies about the candidates. A comprehensive index concludes the volume. The work is a major contribution to the understanding of presidential elections.

294. Presidential Winners and Losers: Words of Victory and Concession. John R. Vile. Washington, D.C.: CQ Press, 2002. Aprox. 400 p. ISBN 1-56802-755-9.

More than 500 speeches and other documents, from George Washington to George W. Bush, that relate to the outcome of elections are collected in this one volume. The materials relate to victory and concessions following races for the White House. Private letters, diary entries, interviews, and newspaper and journal articles are included as well as formal speeches. While much attention has been focused on winning candidates, there has been less attention to those who did not win. The volume begins with an analytical essay that shows how victory and concessions speeches developed and evolved throughout the late nineteenth and the twentieth centuries, and how the study of these speeches affords an understanding of the American political system. The organization is by presidential elections, each with a commentary setting the context for the speeches and other materials. The volume includes a lengthy bibliography; an appendix elections chart to help track election years, candidates, states, and parties; and a complete index. While numerous reference works have been published containing presidential speeches, the specific focus of this work makes it likely that it contains the text of documents difficult to find in other sources. This work makes an excellent companion to entry 293 above, *Presidential Also-Rans and Running Mates.*

An earlier work on elections produced by Congressional Quarterly is *Historic Documents on Presidential Elections 1787–1988* (1991). Editor Michael Nelson has selected 70 key speeches and documents that highlight developments in the presidential election process. The documents are preceded by a brief essay that sets the text in a historical context. Topics such as third parties, important party platforms, debates, and landmark speeches are included. The work is useful for students and teachers. The full text of documents is continued in the *Historic Documents* annual series produced by CQ Press (entry 28).

295. Running for President: The Candidates and Their Images: 1900–1992. Arthur Meier Schlesinger et al., eds. Farmington Hills, MI: MacMillan Library Reference, 1994. 2v. ISBN 0-1330-3371-6.

This illustrated history of American presidential elections includes a strange juxtaposition of illustrations of the cultural materials of campaigns and a number of short essays by leading scholars. The focus is on campaign images that have been conveyed every four years through such artifacts as posters, buttons, and bumper stickers. For each election, a half-dozen pages of text and several pages of color photographs of artifacts provide a feeling for the mood of the times. Each campaign, from the first in 1789 through the most recent in 1992, is treated separately in a lively essay by a historian, political scientist, or journalist. The contributors describe the significance of television, the decline of print journalism, the proliferation of polls, and the emergence of consultants since the 1940s. Each volume has a bibliography arranged by election and its own index. An introduction by Schlesinger is repeated in each volume. Users seeking to understand presidential elections through popular culture will find much enjoyment as they browse through the more than 1,000 attractive photographs of such housewares as pitchers and tankards, umbrellas, medals, banners, ribbons, snuffboxes, sheet music, and other memorabilia, from the collection of David and Janice Frent, all in full color. Each item is clearly identified. The popular images conveyed through the memorabilia are what make this book unique.

Although dated, *The Image Makers: A Bibliography of American Presidential Campaign Biographies* (Scarecrow, 1979) by William Miles is still useful for identifying campaign biographies. The comparison of campaign biographies to known biographical facts is an interesting exercise as campaign biographers endeavor to portray the candidate in the best possible light. This bibliography is not exhaustive, but it covers a broad range of sources and topics, including both favorable and unfavorable satirical material. All serious candidates for office, successful and unsuccessful, are included. As with most presidential campaign reference works, the organization is chronological by election year, beginning with 1824. The decline in the number of official campaign biographies in the latter half of the twentieth century is apparent from the number of entries. Campaign newspapers are not included in this bibliography. *The Image Makers,* a microfilm collection based on the Miles bibliography, has been published by University Microfilms. The bibliography is of interest to political scientists, media specialists, and historians.

296. Songs, Odes, Glees, and Ballads: A Bibliography of American Presidential Campaign Songsters. William Miles. Westport, CT: Greenwood Press, 1990. 200p. (Music Reference Collection, no. 27). ISBN 0-313-27697-8.

Before the electronic media age, campaign songs were a prominent feature of election campaigns. This work contains an introductory overview of the place of the song in election campaigns, which makes for entertaining reading. The main part of the work is a bibliography of anthologies containing campaign songs from 1840 to 1964. Location of copies of the works cited is facilitated by the inclusion of the OCLC database accession number in the bibliographic information. Lists of secondary sources and discographies are in the appendixes. There are indexes by name, title, and publisher. This bibliography will be of interest to historians, political scientists, and musicologists.

297. U.S. Presidential Candidates and the Elections: A Biographical and Historical Guide. James T. Havel. New York: Macmillan Library Reference/Simon & Schuster Macmillan, 1996. 2v. ISBN 0-02-897134-5.

This two-volume work is organized into a volume of biographies and a volume of election results. Volume 1 is an alphabetical directory of candidates for office. The biographical entries include U.S. presidential and vice presidential candidates and third-party leaders. The entries consist mainly of standard factual information. The second volume provides summaries of each national election, highlighting important events, parties, conventions, and platforms. Primary, general, and Electoral College balloting are given. There is an introductory essay on the early presidential nominating and election processes and a bibliography. The information contained in this reference work can be found in a number of other works, but it is a useful source and in some cases a more concise presentation.

American Presidential Campaigns and Elections, edited by William Gerald Shade and Ballard Campbell (M.E. Sharpe, 2002) covers much the same material as similar reference works. The three-volume work is illustrated and includes fact boxes with detailed information on every candidate, winners and losers, presidents and vice presidents. All articles are written in a lively style by leading historians and signed. Complete election returns of both popular and electoral votes by state are presented in both chart and map formats. The set is up-to-date through the 2000 presidential election.

POLLS AND ELECTIONS

298. America at the Polls, 1960–1996 Kennedy to Clinton: a Handbook of American Presidential Election Statistics. Richard M. Scammon and Alice V. McGillivray. Washington, D.C.: Congressional Quarterly, 1998. 1002p. ISBN 1-56802-322-7.

Like the original *America at the Polls* (1965), which covered presidential elections from Warren Harding (1920) to Lyndon Johnson (1964), this volume presents comparable statistics for each county in the United States from 1960 (Kennedy) to Clinton's second-term election, 1996. It is an update of the second volume of *America at the Polls* published in two volumes in 1994. As with previous editions, national summary of the state-by-state vote and the Electoral College vote is provided for each election from 1920 to 1996. Republican, Democratic, and minor-party votes; major-party pluralities and percentages; totals for both counties and states; and analysis, in terminal notes, of the states' minor-party votes are provided. Maps of county boundaries in each state (and wards in the District of Columbia), population of each county from the most recent census, national and statewide summaries of popular and electoral votes from 1920 to 1984, and presidential primary statistics from 1968 through 1984 are included. This reference provides the only readily available timeline of election results stretching over more than seven decades. The wealth of information that Scammon and McGillivray have assembled from state election agencies, and the useful way in which it is presented, make this an important source for any quantitative study of American politics.

299. America Votes. New York: Congressional Quarterly, 1956–. Bienn. ISSN 0065-678X.

This biennial publication is the longest-running series of election information available for presidential, congressional, and gubernatorial elections. The organization is by state, and within each state by county, with separate tables for major cities. Winner/loser percentages are calculated. Statewide vote tables for governors and senators since 1945 offer a historical perspective for state voting patterns. Population statistics are given along with the election results. Congressional district maps are included. The 1991 volume gave presidential election results on a state-by-state basis from 1920 to 1988 and the results of elections for governor and senator since World War II. Primaries and special elections are also included. One disadvantage of the biennial format is that much of the information is not cumulated, although there are cumulations on different variables from time to time. This title does not attempt to analyze voting results in any way; it is strictly a reporting of election results.

Another tool for recent election data is *Election Results Directory,* begun in 1993 by the National Conference of State Legislatures and issued again for the 1995 election results. The first section of this tool, "The Election in Perspective," includes articles reprinted from the journal *State Legislatures,* which highlight trends and changes on such topics as women and minorities, redistricting, term limits, and party control. The second section is for federal elections and the third for state elections. If continued this title will be a good resource for historical research.

300. American National Election Studies Data Sourcebook, 1952–1986. Warren E. Miller and Santa Traugott. Cambridge, MA: Harvard University Press, 1989. 375p. ISBN 0-674-02636-5.

This sourcebook is not a compilation of voting statistics but rather the results of surveys of voter opinion conducted biennially by the University of Michigan Center for Election Studies. The first publication contained data from 1952 to 1978. This edition updates the original through the 1986 national elections. Public opinion on issues such as abortion and school busing are analyzed over the time period the data have been collected. Voter demographics are also analyzed by party, race, income, and so forth. The last chapter synthesizes the information into a profile of issues that most influenced the voters on Election Day. Not only is the volume useful for the data it contains, it also serves as an index to portions of the raw data available from ICPSR (the Inter-University Consortium for Political and Social Research, entry 119) at the University of Michigan. This work is one of the best sources for tracing changes in public opinion on national issues since the 1950s.

Another source that discusses issues and the role of political parties in the United States is *The People Speak: American Elections in Focus* (Congressional Quarterly, 1990). This work covers elections since 1945, with the concentration on the 1980s.

301. Election Day: A Documentary History. Robert J. Dinkin. Greenwood Publishing Group, 2002. 256p. ISBN 0-313-32220-1.

The story of how Election Day has evolved since the beginnings of the Republic is told through the use of contemporary documents in this work. The elaborate celebrations of the early republic, the virtues and abuses of the electoral system, and the struggles of African Americans, Native Americans, and women to win the right to vote are all covered. The documents give a flavor of the excitement of Election Day throughout the history of the United States. The work makes an excellent companion to compilations of election statistics.

*302. The Gallup Poll Public Opinion, 1935–1997. [CD-ROM] Wilmington, DE: Scholarly Resources, 2000.

Public opinion research has been a major tool for setting public affairs agendas and evaluating government programs, and it has also become the primary tool of data collection for most social scientists. The Gallup Poll reports have been released to the media one to four times a week since October 29, 1935. The Poll is underwritten by daily newspapers and CNN. The *Gallup Poll* questions cover five major areas: the public's response to major news events; measuring support for political candidates; societal issues, lifestyle trends; and gauging the mood of the public. In 1999, an index for the years 1935–1997 was published by Scholarly Resources. That work indexes results from 60,000-plus questions asked over a 60-year time span contained in 25 years of the publication. In 2000, Scholarly Resources released a CD-ROM of the cumulated index. The complete results of all Gallup public opinion polls conducted over 62 years are contained on the CD-ROM. Users can conduct quick searches by topic, comprehensive searches of the full-text cumulative index, and searches by year. Answers to poll questions can be broken down by age, race, gender, level of education, geographic region, political affiliation, and other factors. The capability of comparing poll results with events that preceded or followed the polls exists for the years 1972–1997. Trend questions can also be tracked over time to ascertain changes in public opinion on topics such as quality of life, job satisfaction, and the economy. The CD-ROM provides a wealth of information for researchers in cultural anthropology, history, and political science. Libraries that do not own the 25 years of the published volumes of the *Gallup Poll,* which the Cumulated Index indexes, can now own all of the set in the full-text CD-ROM.

303. Guide to U.S. Elections. 4th ed. Washington, D.C.: CQ Press, 2001. 2v. ISBN 1-56802-603-X.

The purpose of this publication is to gather all statistics on U.S. presidential, congressional, and gubernatorial elections into one reference source. This updated edition incorporates data on all federal and gubernatorial elections from 1945 to 2000. New features include an expanded discussion of American political parties and their historical development; a new chapter on election campaign financing; and a new chapter that describes the evolution of American elections with particular emphasis on the modern period that began with President Roosevelt's New Deal political coalition. The work not only contains elections data, but also narrative explanations and interpretations of the context of elections and the evolution of political parties. The presidential and senatorial data begin with the year 1789. Data for U.S. House of Representatives begin in 1824. Returns are given by state and not analyzed by further breakdowns. In addition to the data, topics such as the origins of the Electoral College, nominating conventions, and southern primaries are addressed in narrative format, thus giving a look at the historical development of the election process. The work is well written and organized with bibliographic references, charts and election maps containing a variety of information, such as the number of U.S. immigrants by country of origin. Candidate indexes are for primaries and general elections and include major and minor parties. This title is an excellent source of historical election statistics and information on the electoral process for all types of users.

A broader treatment is contained in another CQ publication, *Elections A to Z* by John L. Moore (1999). Part of Congressional Quarterly's *Encyclopedia of American Government* and other A-Z volumes (Congress, The Presidency, and the Supreme Court), this ready-reference work has over 200 entries. The title provides information on key concepts, issues, and political parties that define the act or process of electing individuals to office in the United States. Entries include the roles of political consultants, the media, debates, term limits, amendments, voting rights, and court cases that have shaped elections. One feature of the work is a clear explanation of the Electoral College system. Coverage of political parties is inclusive, not just a concentration on the major parties. There are 25 appendixes of election data as well as maps and photographs. There is a brief bibliography and a subject index. The work is useful for all levels of readership in all types of libraries.

304. Presidential Elections 1789–1996. 4th ed. Washington, D.C.: Congressional Quarterly, 1997. 280p. ISBN 1-56802-0658-1.

This work updates an earlier title *Presidential Elections Since 1789*. While much of the information is also contained in the Congressional Quarterly *Guide to U.S. Elections* (entry 303) the emphasis in this title is historical rather than current. It provides all data necessary to understand presidential elections: electoral votes and electoral maps from 1789, popular votes from 1824, and primary votes from 1912. Explanations of the Electoral College, the popular vote and voter turnout, primaries and caucuses, and national party conventions set the data in context. Tables, maps, and figures aid in understanding the data. Also included are a biographical directory of presidential and vice presidential candidates, texts of major election laws. There are a bibliography and an index.

The Routledge Historical Atlas of Presidential Elections by Yanek Mieczkowski (Routledge, 2001) traces every presidential election from 1789 through 2000. Graphs and color illustrations show local and regional trends and major themes in electoral politics. Such topics as the role of status, voter anxiety, ethnic conflicts, and the role of corporate and campaign contributions are all examined.

Another compilation of presidential election results is *A Statistical History of the American Presidential Election Results* (Greenwood Press, 1981). This edition contains more than 100 tables of votes and percentages by state and by election from 1789–1980. The strength and usefulness of this work are in the information provided for each historical party.

The Pursuit of the White House by G. Scott Thomas (Greenwood Press, 1987) emphasizes statistics less than does either of the two publications above. The Thomas work contains both statistical election information organized by period, with biographical information on candidates. It repeats information found in a number of other sources.

305. Public Opinion Polls and Survey Research: A Selective Annotated Bibliography of U.S. Guides and Studies from the 1980s. Graham R. Waldon. Garland, 1990. ISBN 0-8240-5732-5.

Two bibliographies by Graham R. Waldon form a useful accompaniment to the *Gallup Poll* CD-ROM (entry 302). The focus of the bibliographies is the major methodological issues in survey research. The first bibliography includes sources from the 1980s organized into chapters dealing with the various survey techniques. The items were chosen for the quality of their research and significant philosophical and/or critical evaluations. Included are books, chapters, articles, U.S. government documents, dissertations, and seminar papers. Subsequent to this publication, the compiler produced a complementary work, *Polling and Survey Research Methods, 1935–1979: An Annotated Bibliography* (Greenwood Press, 1996). The history of the Gallup and Roper polls, which were among the first to use scientific sampling in polling and survey research, is covered in this bibliography. Information is provided on over 1,000 items under headings such as polling organizations, design and planning, sampling, interviewer, interviewing, mixed-mode data collection methods, respondents, responses, analysis, special topics, and humor. Although it only covers the literature up to 1979, this work will be useful to those interested in the history of the development of polls and surveys.

306. United States Congressional Elections, 1788–1997: The Official Results of the Elections of the 1st through 105th Congresses. Michael J. Dubin. McFarland, 1998. 1,005p. ISBN 0-7864-0283-0.

This volume comprehensively provides complete popular vote returns for 97 percent of nearly 37,000 elections, using many original sources to form a historical record of the elections to the U.S. House and Senate from the nation's beginning. Dubin conducted extensive research to gather the data, going to the primary sources in the states in many cases. He uses hundreds of sources including political almanacs, federal documents, federal and state archives, newspapers, and returns published by the states since 1970. Runoffs and special elections are included, but primaries generally are not. The results are arranged by Congress, then by state, giving the date of each election, the names of the candidates, the party, the number of votes cast, and the percent each candidate received. Each congressional section ends with a statistical summary that includes any incomplete returns and gives notes explaining causes of vacancies. Sources list materials used to compile the data for each session's election results. A statistical overview of the entire 210 years summarizes the numbers of regular, runoff, special, and contested elections; the number of incumbents reelected and defeated; districts contested; members serving their first term; and the names of members whose terms exceeded 35 years. A brief history of U.S. elections, an explanation of election returns and terminology, and four pages of party abbreviations are included. There are indexes of political parties and candidates. There are similar compilations, but none as comprehensive. CQ's *Guide to U.S. Elections* (entry 303) gives House popular votes 1824–1993 but Senate votes only from 1913, and excludes both candidates receiving less than five percent of the vote and primaries. *America Votes* (entry 299) records votes by county but only began with the 1950 elections. The compilation will be very useful for specific facts and for analyzing election data. Given the thoroughness of the coverage, this source is the most definitive for congressional election results.

307. United States Presidential Primary Elections 1968–1996: A Handbook of Election Statistics. Rhodes Cook. Washington, D.C.: Congressional Quarterly, 2000. 825p. ISBN 1-56802-451-7.

In 1968 there were presidential primaries held in 15 states. By 1992, there were 42 primaries with major party candidates entered in almost every one. The certified results of these primaries are compiled into one volume organized by state and county breakdowns. The author, a political reporter, has provided an excellent introduction describing the evolution of the nominating process with trend analyses that provide insights into the voting habits of different parties and regions. The introduction is supplemented by a brief chronology, maps showing the growth of presidential primaries, summaries of Democratic and Republican nominee winners by state, and national primary results and vote summary maps. The remainder of the volume is devoted to the state-by-state results for each primary. This is the only comprehensive reference work on presidential primaries.

Chapter 3
Economic History

After political, social, and possibly moral convictions, economic self-interest is an important fuel for the engine that drives the actions of the nation and its regions, states, and cities. Liberal or conservative, hawk or dove, Democrat or Republican, every American seems to share the same needs regarding employment, housing, education, and health care.

The Economic History Association, now operating out of the Department of History at George Washington University in Washington, D.C., was founded in 1941 and has 3,300 members. The *Journal of Economic History* (available at http://eh.net/EHA), its quarterly publication, has been issued from the organization's beginning.

There are relatively few reference tools that focus on economic history. In business and industry the focus is naturally on current information. The stock market bubble of the 1990s made up-to-the-minute news a necessity for online databases and the media. Sections of this chapter furnish coverage of the major sectors or components of economic life, following the general introductory section.

GENERAL SOURCES

Tools in this section treat the economy in general rather than targeting any particular component of it. Succeeding sections furnish coverage specific to a sector of the total economy.

308. Children and Adolescents in the Market Place: Twenty-five Years of Academic Research. Tomasita M. Chandler and Barbara M. Heinzerling, eds. Ann Arbor, MI: Pierian Press, 1999. ISBN 0-87650-383-0.

Children and adolescents as consumers in the marketplace are the focus of this annotated bibliography, which covers publications in academic journals and proceedings from 1970 to 1995. The research had to include children ages 3 to 18 and the marketplace had to be directly referenced. There is an author and title index. Each of the six chapters has introductory material followed by the 836 annotated entries. The bibliography is suitable for researchers in marketing, child development, and sociological studies of consumer behavior.

309. Encyclopedia of American Economic History: Studies of the Principal Movements and Ideas. New York: Scribner's, 1980. 3v. ISBN 0-684-16271-7.

The value of this older work lies in its examination of concepts, themes, trends, and developments germane to economic history but related to political, social, educational, and technological progress. There are 72 commissioned articles treating the U.S. economy from the nineteenth century through the 1970s. Arrangement is under five major sections: "The Historiography of American Economic History;" "The Chronology of American History;"

"The Framework of American Economic Growth;" "The Institutional Framework;" and "The Social Framework." Articles furnish in-depth analyses, descriptions, and interpretations of topics. All entries provide an extensive bibliography useful to the student and to the general public. There is a general index in volume 3.

310. Encyclopedia of the Consumer Movement. Stephen Brobeck, ed. Santa Barbara, CA: ABC-CLIO, 1997. 659p. ISBN 0-87436-987-8.

The focus of this work is not restricted to the United States, but the majority of the 198 entries, written by academics and practitioners, deal with consumer issues in the United States. There is an A-Z arrangement of information on leaders, impacts, activities, laws, and regulations intended to protect consumers, and movement-related institutions. The origins and history of the consumer movement are traced in the work. This is the first reference work of its kind dealing specifically with the consumer movement.

311. Gale Encyclopedia of U.S. Economic History. Thomas Carson and Mary Bonk, eds. Farmington Hill, MI: Gale, 2000. 2v. ISBN 0-7876-3888-9.

Although this encyclopedia was designed for high school and lower-division undergraduates, it is well written and can serve as a reference and introduction to U.S. economic history for all readers. The organizational approach is mainly by eras; there is a contents list divided into 10 eras with an overview of each era prepared by a scholar. A detailed, 33-page chronology, helps to place events into their historical context. The index is lengthy, allowing access to the contents, which are not organized in the usual A-Z arrangement. The emphasis is on the nineteenth and twentieth centuries. The longer entries consist of "overviews, issues, biographies, state economic histories, historical events, and company and industry histories." Short further reading lists are included.

312. The Topline Encyclopedia of Historical Charts. Boulder, CO: Topline Investment Graphics, 1997. 3v.

The *Topline* three volumes consist of 30 charts in loose-leaf binders. The format is designed to make the charts easy to photocopy. The charts range from economic measures, such as interest rates and consumer prices in various countries, to foreign currency exchange rates, stock indexes, bonds, commodities, precious metals, and more. Each set of charts begins with an explanation of what the chart represents and how the data were obtained and computed. Although the set is designed for investors, the historical charts will be useful for researchers of economic trends in the U.S. The set gathers a wealth of statistical and historical economic data together in one place.

BUSINESS, INDUSTRY, AND BANKING

Since Calvin Coolidge's pronouncement that the business of this country is business, we have seen ample evidence of that philosophy in the types of legislation generally pursued by the Republican Party. The country has come through various periods of socioeconomic change, progressing from the Herbert Spencer laissez-faire policies of the late nineteenth century to the adoption of the income tax in 1913 and its attempt to redistribute wealth in line with a growing belief in the virtue of social welfare. In the past two decades, the pendulum has swung back, illustrated by a type of uneasy alliance of the worker with the entrepreneur through profit-sharing and incentive plans. Most recently, there have been troubled times, with the specter of the Japanese and their economic emergence in the face of industrial decline and growing unemployment in this country.

Business and industry (along with labor) have received much attention from publishers of reference books. Certain business sectors or segments, such as the railroads, have received an inordinate share of total publication.

The Business History Conference (available at http://www.eh.net/bhc) was founded in 1954 at the College of William and Mary in Williamsburg, Virginia. It presently has 450 members. *Business and Economic History,* its annual journal, has been issued since 1975. Another organization, the American Truck Historical Society (available at http://www.aths.org), was founded in 1971 and is headquartered in Birmingham, Alabama. It has 12,000 members and has published a bimonthly journal, *Wheels of Time,* since 1980. The Steamship Historical Society of Providence, Rhode Island (available at http://www.sshsa.org), was formed in 1935 and has 3,300 members. Its official quarterly journal, *Steamboat Bill,* has been issued since 1940. The National Railway Historical Society (available at http://www.nrhs.com) was founded in Philadelphia in 1935 and has 19,000 members. The *National Railway Bulletin,* a bimonthly journal, has been produced from the society's beginning.

*313. American Business Leaders: From Colonial Times to the Present. Santa Barbara, CA: ABC-CLIO, 1999. 2v. ISBN 1-57607-002-6. [CD ROM]

Many of the 400 business leaders profiled in this reference work can be found in the standard biographical tools. The virtue of gathering them together is that the biographies uniformly place the subjects within the context of their times, and reading through the entries the social forces that shaped economic development can be discerned. The work includes men and women who created new industries, developed resources, or took original ideas and molded them into enterprises that changed our way of life. The majority of the biographees are well known, however, there are a number of relatively obscure leaders. Although an effort toward diversity is made, there are only 24 women, four African American, one Asian, and one Hispanic. The second volume has a list of the individuals arranged by fields or types of business. There are bibliographies for further reference in most of the entries. The set is most useful for high school and undergraduate students. A CD-ROM version makes searching for commonalities or comparative information among the biographies easy.

Another earlier biographical work is *Biographical Dictionary of American Business Leaders,* by John N. Ingham (Greenwood Press, 1983. 4v.). Greenwood Press commissioned historian John Ingham to produce a large-scale retrospective biographical dictionary. Ingham wrote all the entries himself, unusual for a work of this sort, and submitted them for review by a panel of historians. The intent was to treat historically significant business leaders; therefore, most personalities are deceased. (Lee Iacocca and a few other living persons are included.) Biographical sketches are based on secondary sources but serve adequately to identify and describe the biographees. More than 1,100 personalities are covered, with descriptions ranging from a single paragraph to several pages in length. A bibliography is supplied for each one. Appendixes furnish listings by industry, company, birthplace, place of business, religion, ethnicity, birth date, and gender. Although there are several misrepresentations in the index concerning names of foreign firms, the work is generally accurate.

314. The Automobile in American History and Culture: A Reference Guide. Michael L. Berger. Westport, CT: Greenwood Publishing Group, 2001. 512p. ISBN 0-313-24558-4.

The history of the automobile is covered in 12 thematic chapters with bibliographic essays in this reference guide. Included are general histories of the vehicle and the growth of the industry to manufacture automobiles and biographies of famous automotive personalities. Various social aspects are examined including labor-management relations. Following the thematic chapters are an overview of reference works and periodicals and a description of selected research collections. The work is useful for beginning research on the topic for all types of readers.

315. Banking in the U.S.: An Annotated Bibliography. Jean Deuss. Metuchen, NJ: Scarecrow, 1990. 164p. ISBN 0-8108-2348-9.

The study of banking and the attitudes of Americans toward the industry remains one of the most interesting areas in economic history. This bibliography was developed by a specialist in business information to illustrate the possible need for restructuring of the industry because of competition from abroad and the impact of automation. Nearly 400 entries are furnished, representing a wide variety of materials, including texts, histories, statistics, abstracts, bibliographies, legislation, serials, and information on the Federal Reserve System. Emphasis is given to recent conditions. The entries represent publications issued between 1984 and 1989. Coverage is given to the management and operation of commercial banks, savings institutions, and investment banking. Annotations are critical in nature. Appendixes provide a list of abbreviations, a chronology, and listings of agencies and associations. Author and title indexes furnish access.

*316. Business Periodicals Index. New York: H.W. Wilson, 1958-B . **Wilson Business Full Text** [Electronic database; WilsonDisc CD-ROM.]

The *Business Periodicals Index,* which has been published since 1958, was for many years the main index to business periodicals. Abstracts and indexing are provided for 527 English-language periodicals and trade journals covering all aspects of business and industry. Business was one of the first areas in which online databases for current information were developed. The electronic version is *Wilson Business Full Text.* In addition to abstracting and indexing going back to 1982, the full texts of 260 publications are provided as far back as 1995. The retrospective file of the index are useful for research into the development and trends in U.S. business and industry since 1958.

Other major business databases designed for current awareness are not usually consulted for historical research. The leading ones include the *Dow Jones Interactive and Business Directory, LexisNexis,* various stock market sites, and the Internet providers.

317. A Century of American Icons: 100 products and Slogans from the 20ᵗʰ Century Consumer Culture. Ed. Mary Cross. Westport: CT: Greenwood Publishing Group, 2002. 224p. ISBN 0-313-314810.

How consumer culture reflected changing attitudes, priorities, and value in America during the twentieth century is shown through 100 consumer products in this work. The story is told by decade with 10 products in each decade. The rise of consumer culture in the United States is traced through these popular products, their slogans and symbols. Such familiar ad campaigns as the Morton Salt Girl, "Got Milk," and the Burma Shave roadside signs are included.

An earlier, similar work is *Symbols of America,* by Hal Morgan (Viking, 1986). This entertaining and informative book treats trademarks and logos associated with U.S. products over the years. In the period of business development and merchandising, it was important to develop a symbol that would serve to distinguish a product or service. Hundreds of these are treated, with their origin and development traced; in some cases, one is able to see the changes over the years in well-known symbols (such as that of Morton's salt). There are two major sections: "Visions of America," subdivided by subjects; and "Symbols of Commerce," subdivided by product. Photographs and illustrations in black and white serve to enhance the narrative. There are bibliographic notes and a brand-name index. Both works are aimed at the general public as well as students and researchers interested in the advertising business.

318. Directory of Business Archives in the United States and Canada. 4th ed. Rev. Chicago: Society of American Archivists, 1993. 96p.

This directory was started in the late 1960s as a pamphlet of less than 40 pages by the Business Archives Committee of the Society of American Archivists. Through succeeding publications, it has added listings and presently offers a work of nearly 100 pages published under the auspices of the Business Archives Section of the SAA. It remains a highly useful listing of business archival collections in the United States and Canada and is possibly the best source with which to identify holdings of private business organizations and firms. Entries furnish the usual directory-style information, enumerating name, address, and telephone number of the organization, along with the name of the archivist or librarian. Content of the collection is described briefly, as are any restrictions in use.

319. Encyclopedia of the Industrial Revolution in the United States. James S. Olson. Westport, CT: Greenwood Publishing Group, 2002. 344p. ISBN 0-313-30830-6.

Economic, political, and social developments of the Industrial Revolution in the United States from 1750–1920 are covered in this ready-reference work. The more than 200 substantial entries cover key individuals, significant technologies, court cases, companies, political institutions, economic events, and legislation. All aspects of the American economy including water and rail transportation, agriculture, manufacturing, mass production, the labor movement, big government, and the key inventions that changed the American economy are covered. More than 50 historical illustration and photographs enliven the text.

A more limited work is *The Industrial Belt: An Annotated Bibliography* by Thomas J. Schlereth (Garland, 1987). The region covered in this bibliography is western Pennsylvania, Ohio, Indiana, Michigan, western New York, and northern Illinois. Coverage is given to major cities such as Pittsburgh, Detroit, Cleveland, and Chicago. In general, there is an emphasis on the nineteenth and twentieth centuries, tracing the rise to prominence and subsequent decline of U.S. industrial strength and development. The bibliography concentrates primarily on books but also lists dissertations and journal articles on the Industrial Belt Publications, which, for the most part, were issued in the 20 years prior to publication of the bibliography. Entries are organized under 10 sections, most of which are topical: e.g., physical environment, economic activities, social history. Two of the sections identify general sources, including bibliographies and institutions. There are author, geographic, and subject indexes.

320. The Dow Jones Averages, 1885–1995. Phyllis S. Pierce, ed. Burr Ridge, IL: Irwin Professional Publishing, 1996. 1v. (unpagd.) ISBN 0-7863-0974-1.

The 100th anniversary of the Dow was the occasion for the publication of a history of the Dow Jones Averages. The work has an introduction written by an editor of the Wall Street Journal followed by a comprehensive graph showing the monthly averages from 1940 to 1990. The most recent five years are each covered in a separate graph, 1991–1995. There is a chronology that traces all of the stocks listed in the index from the first publication on July 3, 1884, to September 18, 1995. The remainder of the volume is occupied by monthly and annual charts showing the daily highs, lows, and averages, for each month from 1885 to 1995. Charles Dow was a journalist, a fact that might surprise some today. He began by figuring stock performance averages on a group of 11 issues, mostly railroads, the dominant industry of the time. Industrials were separated from railroads in 1896 and the two indexes issued in the first Dow Jones listing in 1887. The work offers the most detailed listings and provides the dates when stocks were first listed. It serves both as an authoritative research source and a source of delight for stock market enthusiasts.

Chronology of the Stock Market, by Russell O. Wright (McFarland, 2002), covers the early trading and the evolution of the stock exchange in the United States. Also covered are the establishment of the various market indexes, the development of market regulation, and how the market was affected by historical events. The New York Stock Exchange naturally figures prominently. Other topics covered are investment topics such as risk, long-term stock market drops, evaluating stocks, and axioms of the stock market. There are appendixes, a bibliography, and an index. Both works are useful to students and researchers in economic and social history.

321. A Financial History of the United States. Jerry W. Markham. Armonk, NY: M.E. Sharpe, 2001. 3v. ISBN 0-7656-0730-1.

The history of the United States is traced through the growth and expansion of banking, securities, and insurance in this three-volume work. The influence of Old World policies and attitudes are shown in the founding and development of the United States, especially as financial concerns gave impetus to the American Revolution. The author shows how the Civil War began the transformation of the United States from a small nation largely dependent upon foreign capital into an economic superpower in the twentieth century. The growth and shaping of the U.S. economy in the last century are analyzed through the stock market boom of the 1990s and up to the 2001 attack on the World Trade Center. The set is written to be understood by undergraduate students and the general reader. It provides a comprehensive overview of the history of the growth of American business.

A much larger, more ambitious history is being published by Facts on File, *Encyclopedia of American Business History and Biography.* Begun in 1988, the title was projected to be 50 volumes. Each volume is edited by a specialist in the field, aided by various historians who have contributed the signed articles. Entries cover personalities, events, corporations, legislation, and various topics and issues relevant to the theme of each particular volume. The work has been recognized as a valuable contribution, and both students and scholars profit from its excellent coverage. No new titles have appeared since the early 1990s. The volumes that have been published are: *Railroads in the Age of Regulation, 1900–1980*, Keith L. Bryant, ed. (1988); *Railroads in the Nineteenth Century*, Robert L. Frey, ed. (1988); *Iron and Steel in the Nineteenth Century*, Paul F. Paskoff, ed. (1989); *The Automobile Industry, 1925–1980*, George S. May, ed. (1989); *Banking and Finance to 1913*, Larry Schweikart, ed. (1990); *The Automobile Industry, 1896–1920*, George S. May, ed. (1990); *Banking and Finance, 1913–1989*, Larry Schweikart, ed. (1990); *Iron and Steel in the Twentieth Century*, Paul F. Paskoff, ed. (1991); and *The Airline Industry*, William M. Leary, ed. (1992).

322. Handbook of American Business History. David O. Whitten and Bessie E. Whitten, eds. Westport, CT: Greenwood Press. Vol. 1. **Manufacturing: a Historiographical and Bibliographical Guide.** 1990. 503p. ISBN 0-313-251983. Vol. 2. **Extractives, Manufacturing, and Services: A Historiographical and Bibliographical Guide.** 1997. 532p. ISBN 0-313-25199-1. Vol. 3. **Infrastructure and Services: A Historiographical and Bibliographical Guide.** 2000. 600p. ISBN 0-313-25198-3.

The volumes in the collective title, *Handbook of American Business History*, have been published over a 10-year time span. The *Handbook* is intended to be a history of business in the United States, but not every industry is included. The original volume focused on 23 manufacturing industries and the second volume added 16 industries, including printing and publishing, and four chapters on transportation. The last volume covers 21 more. Volume 1 is divided into 23 chapters, each furnishing bibliographical and historical essays on one of the various manufacturing industries identified by the Enterprise Standard Industrial Classification Code (ESIC). There is an introductory chapter on business history in the United States in general that describes useful books and articles, followed by the chapters on specific manufacturing segments. The other two follow the same format. Articles are signed and a list of contributors with their credentials is included. The editors and contributors are all academics and the guides are intended for researchers. Each chapter provides a concise history of the industry with an emphasis on bibliographies. There is a very good detailed index by subject and publication title. There are few publications devoted to the history of business in the United States and this set serves as an excellent starting place for research.

323. The Historical Guide to North American Railroads. 2nd ed. George H. Drury, comp. Waukesha, WI: Kalmbach Books, 2000. 480p. ISBN 0-89024-356-5.

An introductory segment furnishes a historical overview and exposition of railroading. The compiler has served as the librarian for *Train* magazine and during the 1980s published interesting reference books on the topic. This historical guide treats 160 railroads that either vanished or were merged with other lines between 1930 and 1985. These railroads all had lines of track exceeding 50 miles in length and were noteworthy, long lived, or historically important. This set of criteria eliminates the numerous tiny lines that appeared and disappeared in routine manner. Each entry furnishes a brief history describing the railroad's origin and development, statistics on mileage and rolling stock for 1929 and for its final year, a map for the line in 1930, and a black-and-white photograph. Biographies are given for the owners. There is a glossary of terms and a detailed index.

A companion work by the same author is *The Trainwatcher's Guide to North American Railroads: Significant Facts, Figures, and Features of Over 140 Railroads in the U.S., Canada, and Mexico* (Kalmbach, 1984; Reprint, 1988). Similar in format to the more recent effort, this also is an alphabetical listing of railroads. Entries furnish descriptions, illustrations, maps, and suggested readings. A glossary and an index are supplied.

The Routledge Historical Atlas of the American Railroads (2001) is a necessary companion to the two reference works above. John Stover has blended 50 full-color maps with an excellent text in this illustrated atlas that traces U.S. railroads from the 1830s up to the founding of Amtrak in 1970. It explores the geographical expansion of America made possible by the U.S. railways system.

Early railroad maps in the Library of Congress are reproduced in *Railroad Maps of North America: The First Hundred Years* by Andrew M. Modelski (Library of Congress, 1984). This important large-size volume of early railroad maps of the United States, Canada, and Mexico, was carefully developed and well designed for use by both scholars and students. Included are over 90 maps taken from the Geography and Map Division of the library, including survey maps, general-purpose maps, regional maps, and terminal maps, among others. Although most are in black and white, five are in color; all are fine examples of the mapmaker's art and show cartographic techniques and styles. They are clearly drawn and described in accompanying text. There are nearly 200 illustrations of trains, crews, depots, and even advertising material. An excellent introduction describes the history of railroad cartography. There is a comprehensive index of subjects, places, and persons.

An earlier publication for the Library of Congress is Modelski's *Railroad Maps for the United States: A Selective Annotated Bibliography of Original 19th Century Maps in the Geography and Map Division of the Library of Congress* (1975). This book identifies and describes over 600 maps separately held by the Library of Congress but does not reproduce the maps themselves.

324. Methodology and Method in History: A Bibliography. Lee D. Parker and O. Finley Graves, eds. New York: Garland, 1989. 246p. (Accounting History and Thought). ISBN 0-8240-3323-X.

Prepared through the efforts of the Accounting History Research Methodology Committee of the Academy of Accounting Historians, this work was developed in order to furnish a basis for methodological approaches. The work is organized within a classification schedule of 13 areas. Within these classes, bibliographic references are arranged alphabetically by author. Bibliographic descriptions are full; there is an annotated bibliography of selective nature. The work is a collaborative effort, and selections were made on the basis of a consensus of committee members. The title should be useful to all inquirers professing interest in historical research in accounting and should furnish enlightenment to beginning researchers in the field as well as to scholars from outside the field.

325. Notable Corporate Chronologies. 2nd ed. Kimberly N. Hunt and AnnaMarie L. Sheldon, eds. Farmington Hills, MI: Gale, 1999. 2v. ISBN 0-8103-9500-2.

Alphabetically arranged timelines are provided for 1,152 significant corporations currently operating in the United States or abroad. The timelines describe 30 or more significant events in the history of an industrial, commercial or financial firm. Both private and public companies are represented, 60 percent U.S. corporations. Events include the founding of the business, reorganizations, major financial events, the tenure of leading managers, products and the introduction of new products, newsworthy events, and even scandals. Short lists of further readings are provided. Several indexes provide access to the contents: a master chronology, 1770–1990, a geographical index, an alphabetical index, and an anniversary index. The work is very useful in providing short histories with historical perspective on a large number of U.S. corporations in one handy volume.

326. Railroads of North America: A Complete Listing of All North American Railroads, 1827–1986. Joseph Gross, comp. Spencerport, NY: Joseph Gross, 1986. 275p. ISBN 0-9616476-0-4. **Supplement,** 1988. **Supplement #2, 1990.**

An interesting and well-conceived tool for inquirers at all levels is this alphabetically arranged handbook of railroad companies in North America over two centuries. The nineteenth century witnessed the introduction, expansion, and development of the railroad as a major segment of the U.S. economy. This work furnishes brief histories of railroad lines in Canada, Mexico, and Alaska. Included along with common carriers are construction railroads (developed as dummy operations to build the lines but then absorbed by the parent corporation) and private industrial railroads offering some public access. Entries furnish name, reporting marks, maximum mileage, beginning and ending dates, and disposition of assets, when available. There is an index of reporting marks.

A less-comprehensive work is *Railroad Names: A Directory of Common Carrier Railroads Operating in the United States 1826–1989* by William D. Edson (Edson, 1989), which is limited to common carrier railroads in the continental United States. Although much of the material is duplicated, there is also much unique information in each title.

327. Trade Catalogs at Winterthur: A Guide to the Literature of Merchandising, 1750–1980. E. Richard McKinstry, comp. New York: Garland, 1984. 438p. (A Winterthur Book; Garland Reference Library of Social Science, v. 241.) ISBN 0-8240-8952-9. Reprint, Bethesda, MD: University Publications of America, 1993. ISBN 1-55655-480-X.

The introductory section of this useful catalog of catalogs furnishes a good description of important collections of such publications and will be useful to the business historian. The Winterthur Museum is devoted to the preservation and study not only of the decorative arts and horticulture but also of American material culture and historical objects. Housed here are nearly 1,900 trade catalogs from U.S. firms spanning a period of 230 years beginning in 1750. Arrangement of entries in this catalog is under 30 different subject categories— art supplies, clothing and accessories; food and refrigeration; stoves; paintings and prints; and so on. Entries describe the catalogs, which were generally furnished to retailers and merchandisers, and display the company lines. Mail-order varieties are also held. Indexes provide chronological, geographical, and name access.

328. Type Foundaries of America and Their Catalogs. Rev. ed. Maurice Annenberg, comp. Rev. by Stephen O. Saxe. New Castle, DL: Oak Knoll Books, 1994. 286p. ISBN 1-884718-06-X.

The first edition of this bibliography was published in a limited edition of 500 copies in 1975 and quickly became an item on the antiquarian book market. The original edition contained the history of 67 firms that produced foundry types with a list of specimen type books for each firm. The revised edition contains one additional type foundry and an additional 73 type specimen books. The books are described in detail in both editions. Saxe has added a brief biography of Annenberg and appendixes that describe the type specimen holdings in the New York Public Library, the Smithsonian Institution, and his own personal collections. There is a bibliography and many of the entries are illustrated. The work provides an overview of an important industry in the history of printing and publishing in the United States.

329. United States Business History, 1602–1988: A Chronology. Richard Robinson, comp. Westport, CT: Greenwood Press, 1990. 643p. (Garland Reference Library of Social Science, v. 807.) ISBN 0-313-26095-8.

This is an interesting and informative chronology of U.S. business over a period of nearly 400 years beginning with the arrival of the earliest settlers from Europe. It will be welcomed by inquirers at all levels for its breadth of coverage. It identifies major events on a year-to-year basis, with each year divided into two major sections. "General Events" identifies changes in living conditions and social structure; "Business Events" highlights activities and developments of both general and specific nature in the corporate world. The chronology is a marvel of detail and factual presentation that should prove advantageous to those searching for obscure information. Coverage includes such diverse personalities as Al Capone and Marilyn Monroe; events and organizations also vary considerably. There is a detailed index of names of people and organizations.

330. United States Corporation Histories: A Bibliography, 1965–1990. 2nd ed. Wahib Nasrallah. New York: Garland, 1991. 511p. (Garland Reference Library of Social Science, v. 807.) ISBN 0-8153-0639-3.

The second edition of this bibliography of business identifies some 3,000 business histories of various types. Included are books, articles from periodicals and newspapers, and dissertations, as well as corporate histories derived from annual reports of the companies. The first edition was published only four years earlier and furnished coverage of publications issued between 1965 and 1985. The second edition extends the coverage through 1990. Arrangement of entries is alphabetical by name of corporation; their level of suitability ranges from those of popular general appeal to those of scholarly nature. Included are biographies of prominent executives, who receive varied coverage dependent upon their fame or notoriety. Full bibliographic information is supplied; no annotations are given. The work is indexed by author, chief executive, and industry.

331. The Value of a Dollar 1860–1999: Prices and Incomes in the United States. 2nd ed. Scott Derks, ed. Lakeville, CT: Grey House Publishing, 1999. 495p. ISBN 1-891482-49-1.

The approach used in this work is like the current Consumer Price Index. Standard prices for a selection of representative items were tracked annually. Income was obtained from job ads in major newspapers. The data are divided into five chronological chapters with each chapter divided into five-year segments except the first chapter covering the Civil War period up to the end of the nineteenth century. The other chapters, (1900–1919, 1920–1939, 1940–1959, and 1960–1989) consist of a brief historical overview, followed by tables listing consumer expenditures, investments, income, food prices, and so forth. More than 500 sources were consulted: trade cards, newspapers and magazines, catalogs, letters, posters. Illustrations from advertisements are interspersed among the tables. The data in this work are useful in many kinds of historical studies; the historical prices of household necessities, wage levels, and comparisons with what a dollar bought in the past versus the present. One drawback, there is no index.

AGRICULTURE, FORESTRY, AND CONSERVATION

Agriculture has remained an important factor in economic history since the beginning of this nation. There have been major problems requiring resolution: slavery as an institution, states' rights, bank charters, railroad kickbacks, tariffs, and labor and trade unionism, to name only a few. In the latter decades of the twentieth century there was the crisis regarding the foreclosure of family farms.

In addition to works on agriculture, included in this section are tools on conservation, forestry, and reclamation of land. The Nonpartisan League is treated here, but one should consult the next section, "Labor," for treatment of unions, including the United Farm Workers.

The Forest History Society was founded in 1946 in Durham, North Carolina, and has 1,750 members. It publishes *Forest History Cruiser* on a quarterly basis. The Agricultural History Society, headquartered in Washington, D.C., was founded in 1919 and has 1,400 members. Its quarterly journal, *Agricultural History,* has been issued since 1927. The Historical Farm Association was founded in 1971 and operates out of Stroudsburg, Pennsylvania. There are 1,200 members; a newsletter is issued.

332. Agricultural Crisis in America: A Reference Handbook. Santa Barbara, CA: ABC-CLIO, 1999. 270p. (Contemporary World Issues). ISBN 0-87436-737-9.

The issues and concerns about agriculture in the United States in the latter decades of the twentieth century are summarized in this reference source. There is a chronology of the history of agriculture in the United States with biographical sketches of a few of the most important or visible figures. The author delineates seven areas he perceives as aspects of a crisis in agriculture: the survival of farms and ranches, modern technological changes in agriculture, a growing world to feed, safe drinking water and food, environmental concern in agricultural management, urbanization, and conflicts with city "outsiders" moving into the country. The crises are presented in some detail with an excellent concluding essay. There is a "Facts and Figures" chapter that contains tables linked to the seven crises with information drawn from government, popular, technical, and Internet sources. A selective list of agriculture organizations and an annotated list of books are provided as well as useful Internet sites for information on associations, government agencies, and agricultural policies.

A glossary of terms and an index are also provided. The reference source is useful to students and researchers alike.

333. The American Farm Crisis: An Annotated Bibliography with Analytical Introduction. Harold D. Guither and Harold G. Halcrow. Ann Arbor, MI: Pierian, 1988. 164p. ISBN 0-87650-240-0.

This bibliography materials, most of which date to the mid-1980s, furnishes the historian and student with an excellent historical perspective of today's farming crisis, the causes of which are certain to be studied for the next few years. The work identifies 465 annotated entries covering government documents, journal articles, books, and reports of state agricultural extension agencies. These are arranged into eight chapters that categorize the issues for both understanding and ultimate management. These chapters cover the farm in transition, the scientific and technological revolution, business management, markets and marketing, farms and rural communities, government commodity programs, necessary policy changes, and the use of information and education. Annotations furnish ample descriptions of content. There is a chronology of important dates and a glossary of terms; author and title indexes provide access. Although not up-to-date, the works makes a good accompaniment to *Agricultural Crisis in America: A Reference Handbook* (entry 332).

334. Atlas of American Agriculture: The American Cornucopia. New York: Macmillan Library Reference/Simon & Schuster Macmillan, 1996. 278p. ISBN 0-02-897333-X.

A statistical and historical overview of U.S. agriculture is provided in this atlas. The organization is by 12 regions defined according to three criteria: crops, technology and farming strategies, and environment. In the first section, "The American Agricultural Scene," charts the history of U.S. agriculture and describes agriculture today. Also covered are farm ownership patterns, conservation, agricultural economics, and marketing. "Cornucopia's Regions," discusses the regions in depth with a focus on the ways in which agricultural production is linked to the region's geography, culture, demography, ethnicity, economy, history, and society. "Cornucopia's Abundance," covers 24 crops with regard to their regional context and their effects on peoples and cultures. Each crop chapter has a table listing the counties that are leading producers of that commodity. The text highlights changes in agriculture over the years. Interspersed are county views and boxes with statistics on representative agricultural counties. Maps are thematic, of specific crops and of agricultural regions. Charts and tables provide historical data. Included are important names in the history of agriculture and food processing and large agribusinesses. Developments in irrigation and the control of crop diseases are also covered. The volume concludes with an extensive bibliography, a general, index, and a place-name index.

For those searching for early publications, *Agriculture in America, 1622–1860: Printed Works in the Collections of the American Philosophical Society, the Historical Society of Pennsylvania, The Library Company of Philadelphia* (Garland, 1984) furnishes a union list of the holdings of three important Philadelphia libraries. The agricultural publications span a 240-year history prior to the Civil War. The catalog serves the interests of scholars and serious students in its emphasis on broadsides, trade catalogs, prospectuses, circular letters, almanacs, printed speeches, and society transactions. The work begins with an introductory history and contains about 2,000 alphabetically arranged entries, a chronology of publications and detailed appendixes that include an index by subject and institution. Other bibliographies in the series cover philanthropy (entry 980), natural history (entry 1077), and education (entry 990).

335. Conservation and the Law: A Dictionary. Debra L. Donahue. Santa Barbara, CA: ABC-CLIO, 1998. 347p. ISBN 0-87436-771-9.

Although the purpose of this work is to be a current resource, it does contain the principal federal constitutional doctrines, statutes, regulations, and judicial opinions as well as selected state laws all concerning conservation. The focus is the conservation of natural resources on U.S. federal public lands and secondarily on the conservation of private lands and resources. Topics such as national forests, the Bureau of Land Management, national parks and monuments, wilderness areas, and national wildlife refuges are covered. The protection and use of common resources such as minerals, forest, soil, and wilderness are set within the legal context of state, federal, tribal, and international law. This is a good introductory reference work on the topic; those who includes conservation in their research agenda would do well to own a copy of the work.

336. The Contemporary and Historical Literature of Food Science and Human Nutrition. Jennie Brogdon and Wallace C. Olsen, eds. Ithaca, NY: Cornell University Press, 1995. 296p. ISBN 0-8014-3096-8.

This bibliography is divided into eight chapters that cover development and trends in food science; knowledge and changing concerns in human nutrition; determination of core publications and monographs; primary journals and serials; databases of nutrient composition; daily intake and food adulteration; reference updates; and primary historical literature from 1850–1950. The work is useful for a foundation on how the discipline of food science and human nutrition has evolved and an introduction to research for students in the field. It is not up-to-date or specific enough for in-depth research.

337. Encyclopedia of American Farm Implements and Antiques. C.H. Wendel. Iola, WI: Krause Publications, 1997. 395p. ISBN 0-87341-507-8.

Many inventions came from the farm as the economy of the United States was based on agriculture in the nineteenth century. This volume includes nearly 2,000 photographs of all manner of farm implements and an array of trademarks. It is not a price guide, but rather a comprehensive work on the business of farming as seen through the constant striving for improvement in the equipment used to produce crops and commodities. It gathers in one work a wide variety of information useful for historical studies.

338. Encyclopedia of American Forest and Conservation History. Richard C. Davis, ed. Macmillan, 1983. 2v. ISBN 0-02-907350-2.

The goal of this two-volume effort was to produce the standard, authoritative guide and reference to the history of U.S. forestry conservation, forest industries, and related subjects. It contains over 400 articles signed by specialists and covers a broad range of topics, such as biographies of naturalists, national parks, government agencies, legislation, various organizations, related industries, associations, even ecological processes. More than 200 scholars and specialists contributed to the effort, for which the entries are arranged alphabetically by topic. Selection of entries was determined by a panel of experts. The title is useful to inquirers at all levels, because of both its comprehensive nature and its careful execution. Numerous photographs accompany the text. There are five appendixes that furnish chronologies and listings and an index to provide access.

339. Historical Directory of American Agricultural Fairs. Donald B. Marti. New York: Greenwood Press, 1986. 300p. ISBN 0-313-24184-0.

Agricultural fairs represent a historical tradition in the study of rural life and have been major gala events for many years. It has been reported that attendance at these fairs today exceeds 125 million people a year. This is a directory of over 2,000 fairs; the most important ones are described in some detail. All types of agricultural fairs are treated, including livestock shows, state fairs, county fairs, 4-H events, and Future Farmers of America–sponsored fairs. The work opens with an introductory narrative describing the nature of fairs and giving the history of U.S. agricultural fairs as well as the role of the Grange. A bibliography is furnished. The 205 major fairs are listed alphabetically and described in terms of origin and history as well as attractions. The appendix lists another 2,000 fairs. There is an index of names and subjects.

340. The Nonpartisan League, 1915–1922: An Annotated Bibliography. Patrick K. Coleman and Charles R. Lamb, comps. St. Paul, MN: Historical Press, 1985. 86p. ISBN 0-87351-189-1.

The history of the Nonpartisan League is documented in this bibliography of books, manuscript collections, pamphlets, articles, papers, court cases, and government documents available in 18 U.S. and Canadian libraries. Although it can serve as a union list, the title has been developed as a bibliography important to the needs of scholars and serious students in furnishing over 1,000 annotated entries. Also included are black-and-white photographs and political cartoons of the time. The league began in 1915 in North Dakota and was especially influential in the Plains states and the mountain states, where it served as a political party promoting the economic interest of the farmer. This title, recognized as the most complete bibliographic work on the subject, is divided into eight format categories (e.g., books, periodical articles, archival and manuscript collections). It builds on a bibliographic base provided by an earlier history of the league described below.

Robert L. Morlan's *Political Prairie Fire: The Nonpartisan League, 1915–1922* (University of Minnesota, 1955; Reprint, Minnesota Historical Society, 1985), is a balanced and detailed history of the league and its leader, Arthur Townley. The work is well documented, and prior to publication of the Coleman and Lamb title was considered the top bibliography of the movement.

LABOR

Because of the multifaceted nature of its struggle and emergence, U.S. labor has inspired the curiosity of reporters and the scrutiny of historians more than any other single element or factor of economic history. The labor movement embraces political, social, moral, and humanitarian issues, furnishing incentive for inquiry and documentation on a large scale and from different perspectives. These range from the perception of, on the one hand, a noble struggle waged by a valiant and exploited underdog element striving for social justice to, on the other hand, a selfish and self-serving power wielder determined to control the operations of its employers. The working class, its unions, and its activities are revealed in these reference sources.

The Committee of Industrial Relations Librarians (CIRL) maintains a Web site on labor collections at http://www.ilr.cornell.edu/CIRL/. Archival collections are The Kheel Center at Cornell (available at http://www.ilr.cornell.edu/library/kheelcenter/); the Holt Labor Library (available at http://www.holtlaborlibrary.org); the Institute of Labor and Industrial Relations Library (available at http://www.library.uiuc.edu/irx/); and the Southern Labor Archives (available at http://www.library.gsu.edu/spcoll/labor/).

341. American Federation of Labor and Congress of Industrial Organizations Pamphlets, 1889–1955: A Bibliography and Subject Index to the Pamphlets Held in the AFL-CIO Library. Mark E. Woodbridge, comp. Westport, CT: Greenwood Press, 1977. 73p. ISBN 0-8371-9686-8.

Prepared as a printed guide to primary source material, this unannotated listing of titles is available at the AFL-CIO Library in Washington, D.C. These pamphlets were created to draw the attention of the general public as well as union members to the major issues and problems of the day, serving as a convenient means by which to publicize union programs. There are more than 750 AFL pamphlets issued between 1889 and 1955 and nearly 300 issued by the CIO between 1935 and 1955, thus offering an excellent perspective on labor history in this country. Arrangement is chronological by year, then alphabetical by title. Entries generally furnish author, title, and pagination, except in cases of reprints of journal articles, for which reference is given to periodical titles and months. Foreign-language items are included. A subject index is furnished.

A major effort from Greenwood Press is the actual source material published on 19 microfilm reels as *AFL and CIO Pamphlets, 1889–December 1955: Held in the AFL-CIO Library*. It is useful to labor historians.

342. Bureau of Labor Statistics. U.S. Department of Labor. [Web site] Available: http://stats.bls.gov.

Although this site is for current information on the unemployment rate, the Consumer Price Index, the Producer Price Index, and other economic and statistical data, there are also past and current statistics for the U.S. economy. Economic data for individual states can also be obtained.

An important online tool is *Laborlaw,* published by the Bureau of National Affairs and available through DIALOG. It is made up of seven subfiles and furnishes summaries of decisions as well as references to determinations regarding labor relations, fair employment, and similar issues. Some of the rulings go back to 1938.

343. Biographical Dictionary of American Labor. 2nd ed. Rev. and exp. Gary M. Fink, ed. in chief. Westport, CT: Greenwood Press, 1984. 767p. ISBN 0-313-22865-5.

This is a revision and expansion of the editor's initial edition of 1974, which treated 500 figures. The second edition furnishes over 725 biographical sketches of personalities representative of the diversity within the labor movement in this country. There is a conscious effort to include women and minorities; much care has been taken in the revision of previously used entries. The change in emphasis from the "leaders" covered in the first edition to the representative figures of this one has made it possible to include a good percentage of the rank-and-file membership, along with the addition of previously omitted leaders, making it a more comprehensive work for purposes of identification. Appendixes furnish listings by union affiliation, religion, birthplace, and public office held. The bibliography was updated for the second edition; there is a detailed index.

344. A Guide to the Archives of Labor History and Urban Affairs, Wayne State University. Warner W. Pflug, comp. and ed. Detroit: Wayne State University, 1974. 195p. ISBN 0-8143-1501-1.

The collection at Wayne State University, with the generous support of Walter Reuther and the United Automobile, Aerospace, and Agricultural Implement Workers Union, has achieved national prominence for the study of labor history. By the mid-1970s, the library had acquired over 230 collections of personal papers of important leaders, activists, and government officials. In addition, there are records of prominent labor organizations: the Air Line Pilots Association, the American Federation of Teachers, the Newspaper Guild, the United Auto Workers, the United Farm Workers, the Congress of Industrial Organizations (CIO), and others. The urban affairs materials generally emphasize the Detroit area and represent a more recent collecting specialty.

Not all of the materials at Wayne State are from big industry. An important collection at Wayne State University is that of the United Farm Workers. Published in the same time frame as the guide to the archives is *Cesar Chavez and the United Farm Workers: A Selective Bibliography,* by Beverly Fodell (Wayne State University, 1974). From the archivist of this important collection comes this useful, concise bibliography of Cesar Chavez, whose impact on the farm labor movement was monumental. This work represents a revised and expanded edition of the initial publication in 1970 and furnishes an annotated bibliography of books, articles, pamphlets, newspaper pieces, government documents, theses and dissertations, and unpublished source material. Articles are drawn from a variety of periodicals and represent general-interest magazines, scholarly journals, and union, grower, and even church publications. In the mid-1970s, the UFW was much in the news, and inquirers at all levels profit from this effort. Emphasis is given to the organizing efforts of the time. Annotations are descriptive of content and, although brief, are informative.

These guides to the archives published in 1974 have not been updated, but the library now maintains a Web site (available at http://www.reuther.wayne.edu). The Walter P. Reuther Library receives regular deposits from 10 large unions. The library contained over 75,000 linear feet of records within 1,600 individual collections as well as an audiovisual collection of 2 million items by the end of the twentieth century.

345. First Facts of American Labor: A Comprehensive Collection of Labor Firsts in the United States Arranged by Subject. Philip S. Foner, comp. New York: Holmes & Meier, 1984. ISBN 0-8419-0742-0.

This is a detailed chronology of "firsts" in U.S. labor history, beginning as early as 1526 with a slave revolt in present-day South Carolina and progressing to the signing of a first union contract by the J.P. Stevens Company of North Carolina in 1980. Research for this work entailed the use of union histories, biographical works, and newspapers, as well as monographs on specific topics. Entries are arranged alphabetically under broad subject categories. They vary in length and generally are concise but informative. Access is furnished by a detailed index of names, events, and titles.

Similar in scope is *The Labor Almanac* by Adrian A. Paradis and Grace D. Paradis (Libraries Unlimited, 1983). Important events, aspects, topics, and leaders are rendered along with definitions in an eight-part treatment beginning with a chronology. There are listings of unions, labor leaders, legislation, government agencies, information sources, and activities. A comprehensive index furnishes access.

346. The Immigrant Labor Press in North America, 1840s–1970s: An Annotated Bibliography. Dirk Hoerder and Christiane Harzig, eds. New York: Greenwood Press, 1987. 3v. (Bibliographies and Indexes in American History, no. 4, 7–8.) ISBN 0-313-24638-6 (v. 1).

This work represents an important contribution to researchers at all levels. Volume 1, *Migrants from Northern Europe,* furnishes a listing of labor publications produced in the United States by individuals from the Nordic countries (Iceland, Norway, Denmark, Sweden, and Finland). Volume 2, *Migrants from Eastern and Southeastern Europe,* covers the labor publications of those from Byelorussia, Russia, Lithuania, Latvia, Estonia, Czechoslovakia, Hungary, the Ukraine, Yugoslavia, Bulgaria, Albania, Romania, and Greece, as well as those of Jewish persuasion. Volume 3, *Migrants from Southern and Western Europe,* treats the publications of former Italians, Spaniards, British, Dutch, French, and Germans. Entries in all volumes furnish title, place of publication, duration, languages, first edition and publisher, circulation, dates, frequency, and so forth. Introductory essays open each volume; indexes of titles, places, and dates conclude the efforts.

347. Labor Arbitration: An Annotated Bibliography. Charles J. Coleman and Theodora T. Haynes, eds. Ithaca, NY: ILR Press, 1994. 271p. (Cornell Industrial and Labor Relations Bibliography Series, no. 17). ISBN 0-87546-322-3.

Entries from nearly 1,200 articles and proceedings in professional and academic journals and 154 books are listed chronologically and briefly annotated in this specialized bibliography. There are separate sections for books and articles, each subdivided into subject areas such as arbitrator characteristics, advocacy, discipline and discharge, arbitration and the courts, and arbitration in selected industries. The work begins with an excellent overview of the legal foundations of grievance arbitration. The bibliography surveys the major case law emerging from four key Supreme Court cases in the 1960s. The work is designed to be used by professionals in the field, but can be useful for historical research on the topic.

348. Labor Conflict in the United States: An Encyclopedia. Ronald L. Filippelli, ed. New York: Garland, 1990. 609p. (Garland Reference Library of Social Science, v. 697.) ISBN 0-8240-7968-X.

This one-volume encyclopedia furnishes comprehensive coverage of events, personalities, and issues relevant to labor conflict in this country over a period of about 330 years from the Virginia indentured servants strike in 1661 to the Eastern Airlines workers strike in 1989. The violence or intensity of the altercations varies considerably from the major struggles involving the Pullman Company, Homestead strikers, and Haymarket "rioters" to milder demonstrations waged by a variety of workers in different industries, crafts, and trades throughout the country at different times. Contributors are varied and include trade unionists, labor historians, and graduate students who have all signed their articles. Entries average two to three pages in length and are arranged alphabetically. There are a chronology of events, a table of contents, a glossary of terms, a bibliography, and an index.

349. Lexicon of Labor: More Than 500 Key Terms, Biographical Sketches, and Historical Insights Concerning Labor in America. Emmett R. Murray. New York: New Press, 1998. 207p. ISBN 1-56584-456-4.

The focus of this work is organized labor. The entries are generally brief, providing concise definitions of commonly used terms, sketches of important figures, descriptions of organizations, and information about key events in labor history. The women's movement and African American labor leaders are covered. There is also good coverage of the nineteenth century. The volume is not meant to be comprehensive, but provides a good introduction to the labor movement in industry.

350. The U.S. Labor Movement: References and Resources. Robert N. Stern et al. New York: G.K. Hall; Simon & Schuster Macmillan, 1996. 356p. (Reference Publications on American Social Movements.) ISBN 0-8161-7277.

The literature of U.S. labor from 1942 to 1994 is covered in 1,500-plus annotated numbered entries arranged by author within subject sections. This bibliography replaces many earlier works published in the 1970s and 1980s. The aim of the authors was to "provide a comprehensive guide to the literature that will connect researchers to the diverse sources of material on the study of the labor movement as a social movement." Covering the period from World War II to the end of the twentieth century, the work reflects the different disciplines that have an interest in the labor movement—economics, political science, psychology, and sociology. The first chapter provides an overview of the work with the remaining eight chapters covering the literature by topical areas including social movement theory, the organizational structure of the labor movement, movement mobilization, labor and politics, the impact of the labor movement on social inequality, antilabor countermovements, the labor movement in relation to other social movements, and data sources and reference works. The chapters are further divided into subchapters with each section beginning with a brief essay. The bibliography will be useful to researchers in a broad number of fields.

351. Women & Children of the Mills: An Annotated Guide to Nineteenth Century American Textile Factory Literature. Judith A. Ranta. Westport, CT: Greenwood Publishing Group, 1999. 352p. (Bibliographies and indexes in American literature, 28). ISBN 0-313-30860-8.

Not only is this work a bibliography, but it also serves as a partial index to a number of nineteenth-century periodicals that were primarily women's magazines. Thirty-six of the entries are by mill workers and nearly half of that are by women. The entries include broadside ballads, labor periodicals, story papers, dime novels, and children's literature. Other genres includes, novels, novellas, poetry, songs, drama, short stories, tales, allegories, narratives, dream visions, and dialogues, drawn from newspapers, magazines, trade publisher monographs, Sunday school tracts, and crime pamphlets. The annotated entries are arranged by topics such as women in the workplace, education, labor periodicals, social class, sex discrimination, violence, child labor abuse, occupational hazards, and labor-management conflict. In addition to the bibliographic citation, most entries include brief author identification, genre, setting, synopsis, and other notes on content. Most annotations include library locations and availability of microform or reprints.

Child Labor: An American History by Hugh D. Hindman (M.E. Sharpe, 2002) is a broader treatment of the problem of child labor. The first section discusses child labor as a social and economic problem in America from a historical and theoretical perspective. The second part concerns child labor in the major American industries and occupations, including coal mines, cotton textile mills, and sweatshops in the early 1900s. The concluding section attempts to analyze the present day situation in the U.S. and the world today.

352. Working Americans, 1880–1999. Scott Derks. Vol. 1. **The Working Class.** Lakeville, CT: Grey House, 2000. Vol. 2. **The Middle Class. 2001.** 2001. 591p. ISBN 1-891482-72-6.

The story of the American working class is told decade by decade between 1880 and 1999 when the country was shifting from an agrarian to an industrial economy. Profiles of families, data on budgets, and excerpts from contemporary periodicals and advertisements present the economics of daily life. There are many tables and lists of sources, quantitative analyses of government surveys and economics to create an appreciation of ordinary working-class Americans in volume one and middle-class professionals and small businessmen in volume two. There are no footnotes, but there is attribution to sources of data and information.

353. Working in America: An Eyewitness History. Catherine Reef. New York: Facts on File, 2000. 418p. ISBN 0-8160-4022-2.

The purpose of this work is to provide personal firsthand accounts that illustrate how historical events appeared to those who lived through them, but it also comprises a history of major trends in the American working experience from the colonial period to the end of the twentieth century. Each chapter begins with an overview describing the important historical events affecting workers during the period and a chronology, then followed by the eyewitness accounts from that period. The topics include agriculture, industry, mining, cattle breeding, and cowboy activities. There is an emphasis on labor, work conditions, organization, and the poor quality of life of working people. The struggles of blacks and women to achieve equality are detailed.

There are many black-and-white photographs. The book has appendixes that provide additional documentary materials, brief biographical sketches of significant historical figures, and a set of maps. The documentary materials include the Emancipation Proclamation, the Preamble to the Constitution of the Industrial Workers of the World, and the text of Section 7(a) of the National Industrial Recovery Act. The volume concludes with an extensive bibliography listing basic references in the field. The work provides a useful overview of the subject for students and can serve as a pointer to primary resources for the researcher.

DEPRESSION AND RECESSION

Economic downturns are part of the cycle of a free trade economy and are influenced by certain fundamentals or factors. Severity ranges from the mildest recessions to the Great Depression of the 1920s–1930s. Out of that tragic circumstance came a number of reforms packaged in President Roosevelt's New Deal. In this section are books relating both to the Great Depression and the reform measures adopted to combat it. Materials on public works can be found in chapter 6 under the heading "Social Welfare and Philanthropy."

354. Encyclopedia of the Great Depression and the New Deal. James Ciment, ed. Armonk, NY: M.E. Sharpe, 2001. 2v. ISBN 0-7656-8033-5.

The era between the two world wars that formed a watershed period in American economic history is covered in this scholarly two-volume work. The main organization is six separate sections. The first, part 1, contains five long thematic essays with bibliographies to provide historic context on the broad areas of "Government and Politics," "Business and Economy, "Labor and Unions," "Daily Life," and "International Affairs." The second section contains an alphabetic listing of 144 short entries on more specific topics on sociological, cultural, and economic aspects. Part 3 is focused on governmental programs and issues of New Deal legislation, the Emergency Banking Act, the Tennessee Valley Authority, and so forth. There are 30 entries in part 4, which focuses on international affairs leading up to World War II. The last main section is biographical with 222 entries. The last section is devoted to the text of 56 primary source documents and contains Roosevelt's "Fireside Chat on the European War" in 1939 and other important documents of the period. The set includes a glossary of terms and acronyms, a bibliography, and subject, biographical, and legal indexes. The work is very attractive with graphs and maps and large illustrations. It is an excellent beginning point for research on the period.

Depression America (Grolier, 2001) is a six-volume set for high schools and public libraries. There are many photographs and illustrations. The writing conveys both the darker side of the depression and the many new programs and successes, which lifted the country out of the economic downturn. There is an emphasis on daily life rather than government and politics. Each volume has a glossary and a timeline and is indexed. The index for the entire set is repeated in each volume.

355. The Great Depression: America, 1929–1941. Rev. ed. Robert S. McElvaine. New York: Times Books, 1994. 402p. ISBN 0-8129-2327-8.

This is a historical account furnishing an interesting interpretation of the causes and factors associated with the Great Depression of 1929. Both the scholar and the student will benefit from its scrutiny in developing a better understanding of the phenomenon. In this work, both social and political conditions are examined; interpretations are given of the motives and values of decision makers and the common folk. The work is divided into 15 chapters covering such aspects as President Hoover's policies, President Roosevelt's charisma, and the growing militancy of the Congress of Industrial Organizations (CIO), with its demands for a sympathetic government response to the needs of labor. The author sees the major cause of the Depression as the inequity in distribution of income and regards the Roosevelt administration's support of labor as a political rather than ideological decision. This work appeals to inquirers at all levels.

356. Historical Dictionary of the Great Depression, 1929–1940. James S. Olson, ed. Westport, CT: Greenwood Publishing Group, 2001. 368p. ISBN 0-313030618-4.

The period of the Great Depression is covered from many points of view in over 500 entries in this reference work. Not just the economic problems, but also diplomacy, popular culture, intellectual life, public policy issues, and prominent individuals of the era are covered. The shifting of the responsibility for maintaining full employment and stable prices to the federal government made the period of the Great Depression a watershed in U.S. history. The "New Deal" reshaped the economy and politics of the country.

Also edited by James S. Olson is *Historical Dictionary of the New Deal: From Inauguration to Preparation for War* (Greenwood Press, 1985). This effort contains about 700 entries covering personalities, laws, agencies, court cases, political groups, and miscellaneous topics, such as "Greenbelt Towns." As in other dictionaries edited by Olson, a number of contributors have aided his effort. Entries vary in length from a half page to two pages, depending upon the significance of the topic, and reflect the important aspects of the nation's domestic policy between 1933 and 1940. Arrangement of entries is alphabetical; four appendixes furnish a chronology, a bibliography, and listings of personnel and of acronyms. Both titles are useful to scholars, students, and the general public because of the comprehensive coverage of relevant concerns and issues.

Also published by Greenwood is *New Day/New Deal: A Bibliography of the Great American Depression, 1929–1941* (1988), compiled by David E. Kyvig et al. Although no longer current, this is an extensive bibliography of over 4,600 unannotated entries organized into 13 chapters, such as "Overviews and General Histories," "Participant Accounts," "The Hoover Administration," and "The Roosevelt Administration." These are subdivided by topic, then by format. Of the total, 2,500 are articles; there are 1,300 books and 800 dissertations. All works are in English; emphasis is given to publications of the 25 years preceding the publication date. Omission of contemporaneous publications from the 1930s has been noted by reviewers. An author index is provided.

*357. New Deal Network: a Guide to the Great Depression of the 1930s and the Roosevelt Administration. Available: http://newdeal.feri.org/.

This Web site, designed for student research, was jointly developed by the Franklin and Eleanor Roosevelt Institute and the Institute for Learning Technologies at Columbia University's Teachers College. The site has a photo gallery with over 4,000 images and a documents section that provides access to more than 700 articles, speeches, letters, and other texts organized by subject, date, and author. There are links to other collections and sources.

358. Pickaxe and Pencil: References for the Study of the WPA. Marguerite D. Bloxom. Washington, D.C.: Library of Congress, 1982; distr. by the Superintendent of Documents, Government Printing Office. 87p. ISBN 0-8444-0384-9.

The Works Progress Administration was the New Deal agency designed to boost the economy by creating employment through government projects. It became the Works Projects Administration in 1939 and was terminated in 1942. Throughout its brief history, it was most influential in administering funds designated for recovery from the Depression. This bibliography covers the entire history of the operation with almost 400 entries identifying books and articles. There is a separate listing of dissertations. Entries are organized into nine chapters, the first three of which give background information, followed by chapters on individual projects, such as the Federal Writers Project and the Federal Theatre Project. Entries are subdivided into time categories of publication: those prior to 1943 and those from 1943 to 1980. Brief annotations are furnished, and each section is given an introductory narrative. Photographs are included; there is an author index.

Several archival microfilm collections and digitized collection on the Web are available on the WPA. Primary Source Microfilm of the Gale Group has a 13-reel collection. *Archives of the Work Projects Administration and Predecessors, 1933–1943* and the *Final State Reports, 1943. By the People, For the People: Posters from the WPA, 1936–1943* are on the American Memory site of the Library of Congress (available at http://memory. loc.gov/ammem/wpaposters/wpahome.html). The collection consists of 907 original posters produced as part of Franklin Delano Roosevelt's New Deal. Of the 2,000 WPA posters known to exist, the Library of Congress's collection of more than 900 is the largest. The posters were designed to publicize health and safety programs; cultural programs including art exhibitions, theatrical, and musical performances; travel and tourism; and educational programs; and community activities in seventeen states and the District of Columbia.

Chapter 4
Diplomatic History and Foreign Affairs

The study of diplomatic history and foreign relations is one of the oldest categories of historical research. As in other areas of political history, government documents and archival materials are integral to research in the history of foreign policy.

For many years, the major indexing title in international relations and foreign affairs has been *PAIS, the *Public Affairs Information Service.* This index includes many U.S. and foreign government documents as well as articles from foreign journals and other publications. The title is now published by OCLC, Inc. and is available in print and online (entry 373). A newer database, *CIAO,* in political science and international affairs, is published by Columbia University Press (entry 362).

There are many reference works on the government and politics of individual countries. Only a few reference works are available that are devoted to specific time periods or geographic areas. This section on foreign affairs is limited to reference works dealing directly with U.S. foreign policy and relations with other countries.

GENERAL SOURCES

359. American Foreign Policy and Treaty Index. Congressional Information Service of LexisNexis. Quart. 1993–B. ISSN 1070–1583.

Congressional Information Service began The *American Foreign Policy Index* as a comprehensive guide to the foreign relations of the U.S. government. The index is quarterly with annual cumulations. The aim is to locate U.S. documents dealing with foreign policy that are not indexed in other CIS indexes and to cover major unclassified publications and all printed or duplicated materials issued by the federal government. Included are those publications that analyze or record U.S. foreign policy and relevant conditions abroad, culled from agencies in all branches of government. The listing itself is in order by agency, and the index, under separate cover, has entries for names and subjects. This current information source will in the future form a thorough index for historical research. There is an accompanying microfiche collection that contains the text of documents listed in the *American Foreign Policy Index.*

Another current publication that will be useful for historical research in the future is *Diplomatic Record,* an annual begun in 1989, just before the Persian Gulf War (Georgetown University Institute). The year's events and diplomatic actions by all countries having an effect on U.S. foreign relations are reviewed in essays and a chronology.

360. American Foreign Policy Current Documents, 1950/55–. Washington, D.C.: U.S. Department of State, 1956–. Ann. ISSN 0501-9811.

The title and frequency of this publication can be misleading for users seeking current information. The Department of State began publishing this annual containing the text of important documents relating to foreign affairs in 1956, with the first volume containing documents from the five previous years. The annual publication takes up after the publication of *A Decade of American Foreign Policy: Basic Documents, 1941–1949* (Senate document 123, 81st Congress, 1st Sess.). The annual series has continued to publish documents on a retrospective basis, with approximately a five-year time lag. Since 1981, the printed text has been supplemented by accompanying microfiche with the full text of longer documents. The organization of the publication is topical/chronological. The principal foreign policy messages and congressional testimony by the executive branch make up the majority of the documents reproduced. The series is useful to researchers for topics in U.S. foreign relations since 1941.

A publication with a similar purpose and scope that also includes official statements and documents is *American Foreign Relations* (World Peace Foundation 1939–1952; Council on Foreign Relations, 1952–). This publication is more useful to those seeking a current awareness tool. For retrospective research, earlier years published under the title *Documents on American Foreign Relations* (1938/39–1973) are available in microform.

361. Chronological History of United States Foreign Relations 1776 to January 20, 1981. Lester H. Brune. New York: Garland, 1985–1991. 3v. (Garland Reference Library of Social Science, v. 196.) ISBN 0-8240-9056-X (v. 1–2); 0-8240-5690-6 (v. 3).

The first two volumes of this work, from 1776 to the beginning of the Reagan presidency, form an overview of U.S. foreign relations, not just a chronological listing of events. Both historical and diplomatic significance are given in the descriptions, which vary in length according to the importance of the incident but can be as much as a page long. The author recommends a two-year approach when following specific events, the year preceding and the year following. The work is organized into four parts according to eras, each with an overview essay: "The Early Republic," "The Emergence of the United States in the Western Hemisphere," "Becoming a Global Power," and "The Nuclear Age." Political, economic, and national security issues are included. Over half of the chronology is made up of twentieth-century events. The closing event is the return of the hostages from Iran at the beginning of the Reagan administration. There are 24 outline maps and a 12-page bibliography. A third volume covering the Reagan years was published in 1991. This well-researched chronology is appropriate for general reference, students and researchers.

*362. CIAO: Columbia International Affairs Online. Available: http://www.ciaonet.org/.

The stated purpose of *CIAO,* inaugurated in 1995, is to be "the most comprehensive source for theory and research in international affairs." It is a current awareness database that provides full-text resources including the working papers of organizations, unpublished papers and reports, and conference proceedings. It includes contents listings and article abstracts for the current issues of journals, and the full text of books published by Columbia University Press. Links variously titled "Country and Map Information" or "Map Information" connect to a current edition of the CIA's World Factbook (available: http://www.odci.gov/cia/publications/factbook/). A search engine is provided and lists of most types of full-text materials by subject, author, and title help convey the scope of the collection and make it possible to browse. *CIAO* is most useful to political science faculty and graduate students, because the working papers and conference reports are not widely held by libraries, but the site does not replace basic periodical indexes in the field. As the database grows and contains more retrospective materials it will also be useful for historical research.

363. Contemporary U.S. Foreign Policy: Documents & Commentary. Elmer Plischke. Westport, CT: Greenwood Publishing Group, 1991. 872p. ISBN 0-313-26032-X.

The time period covered in this one-volume work ranges from the end of WWII to the later 1980s. A selection of documents, each accompanied by commentary, are arranged under topical sections that include the conduct of foreign affairs, general foreign policy principles and presidential doctrines, crisis diplomacy, and regional issues. The documents chosen, many of which are excerpted, lead to representation of foreign policy as seen from the U.S. point of view. The work does address the most significant aspects of U.S. foreign policy and how it is made. It provides a good accompaniment to reference works not containing the text of the documents described.

A longer time span is covered in *Two Centuries of U.S. Foreign Policy: The Documentary Record,* edited by Stephen J. Valone (Greenwood Press, 1995). Primary source documents from the late eighteenth century to the late twentieth century are collected in this one-volume work designed for students. It supplements general reference works on U.S. foreign policy.

364. Dictionary of American Foreign Affairs. Stephen Flanders. New York: Macmillan, 1993. 993p. ISBN 0-02-897146-9.

This one-volume reference work attempts an overview of American foreign policy since 1776 up to 1992 in a single volume. It is broader in scope than many references for U.S. foreign policy in that the authors include space, technological, and environmental issues as well as traditional foreign policy. U.S. immigration policy and relations with Native American tribes are also included. There is more emphasis on the presidents, setting foreign affairs within the context of domestic issues and policies. There is a bibliographic essay, but not suggested readings for each entry. Appendixes contain listings of diplomatic personnel, conferences, and summits. Maps and a glossary of diplomatic terms are provided. An extensive timeline highlights the major developments in U.S. agencies within the executive branch of government.

A narrower work with a dictionary arrangement that focuses on foreign-policy events subsequent to World War II is *A Concise Overview of Foreign Policy (1945–1985)* (Melbourne, FL: Krieger, 1986) by Kenneth L. Hill. The title briefly describes 174 events and can be used to supplement more extensive works such as the *Chronological History of United States Foreign Relations* (entry 361).

365. Documents of American Diplomacy: From the American Revolution to the Present. Michael D. Gambone. Westport, CT: Greenwood Publishing Group, 2001. 600p. ISBN 0-313-31064-5.

The evolution of American diplomacy from its revolutionary roots to the present is examined in one comprehensive volume. The work includes documents from every major period of American history. Political decisions regarding Europe, Asia, the Middle East, and

Latin America are covered. Not only necessary classic statements that are found in many reference works, but also other lesser-known, critical documents from the Cold War era and other statements addressing terrorism, instability in eastern Europe and nuclear proliferation are included. The work is a handbook to accompany any studies in U.S. foreign relations.

366. Encyclopedia of American Foreign Policy: Studies of Principal Movements and Ideas. 2nd ed. New York: Scribner's, 2001.

The 1978 first edition of this encyclopedia has been revised and expanded. The original articles on concepts and themes in U.S. foreign policy have been revised: 33 by new contributors and 43 by the original contributors. Forty-four new essays are included in the second edition. The essays, all written by respected post–Cold War scholars, analyze the development of ideas, theories, and policies and explore the significance of major events in U.S. foreign policy such as "Isolationism," "The Marshall Plan," and "Revisionism," among others. The encyclopedia does not function as a reference work for consultation on specific events, but volume 3 has a biographical section with information culled from standard biographical sources such as the *DAB* (entry 60). Each article has a bibliographical essay at the end. There is an extensive name and subject index. This work gives a scholarly overview of the field of U.S. foreign policy. It is suitable for supplemental reading at the college level or beginning research on the topics covered.

367. Encyclopedia of U.S. Foreign Relations. Bruce W. Jentleson and Thomas G. Paterson, eds. New York: Oxford University Press, 1997. 4v. ISBN 0-19-511055-2.

In the introductory article to this four-volume work, the editors define eight distinct periods in U.S. diplomatic history since 1776, identify five core goals that have been the foundation of U.S. foreign policy and explain how U.S. foreign policy can be understood. The arrangement is alphabetical with over 1,000 articles having been written by 373 scholars and foreign-policy analysts, including Arthur Schlesinger, who attempts to provide historical perspectives on foreign-policy issues. Names, events, countries, and concepts are included along with economic, cultural, military, and political activities. Each article has a bibliography. The topics are linked by extensive cross-referencing and a comprehensive index to biographical profiles and articles about countries, regions, and key characteristics and themes. The encyclopedia concludes with an extensive chronology of U.S. foreign relations, national data on 185 United Nations members, and an extensive bibliography arranged by subject. The encyclopedia was prepared under the auspices of the Council on Foreign Relations. The coverage is broad and scholarly, especially of theoretical aspects of world politics.

368. Foreign Relations of the United States: Diplomatic Papers, 1861–. Washington, D.C.: U.S. Department of State, 1861–. Ann. ISSN 0780-9779.

As with *American Foreign Policy Current Documents* (entry 360), the years covered by this publication of the U.S. Department of State do not correspond to the publication year. For those researchers seeking diplomatic correspondence between the United States and foreign countries, this is the primary source. Also included are the text of treaties, the presidents' annual messages to Congress, and special messages on foreign subjects. *FRUS* was published annually from 1861 to 1951 and then triennially thereafter. The years 1861–

1956 are also available in microform. An index in two volumes was published covering the years 1861–1899 and 1900–1918 (Government Printing Office, 1902–1941). Kraus International published *The Cumulated Index to the U.S. Department of State Papers Relating to the Foreign Relations of the United States, 1939–1945* (1980, 2v.). The Kraus index includes the regular annual volumes for the 1939–1945 period and the special volumes on China and the conferences attended by Presidents Roosevelt and Truman. The publication of documents lags approximately 30 years. Volumes in progress are from the administrations of Kennedy, Johnson, and Nixon. The Office of the Historian has a Web site (available at http://www.state.gov/r/pa/ho) that includes information about the series with summaries of recently released volumes, volumes online, and those available from the Superintendent of Documents.

369. Historical Dictionary of Terrorism: Second Edition. Sean K. Anderson and Stephen Sloan. Landham, MD: 2002. 632 p. ISBN 0-8108-4101-0.

Although the second edition of this title concentrates on actions the U.S. government has taken since September 11th, the work does trace the acts of terrorism from the roots of Middle Eastern conflicts in the first century. The work offers insights into how and why present-day leftist, rightist, and fundamentalist militant groups originated. There is an extensive bibliography and sections devoted to U.S. government documents and Internet resources. It can be used as a current reference tool or as background historical information for political scientists and historians.

370. Historical Encyclopedia of U.S. Presidential Use of Force, 1789–2000. Karl R. DeRouen, Jr., ed. Westport, CT: Greenwood Publishing Group, 2001. 328p. ISBN 0-313-30732-6.

The president is empowered to use military force without a declaration of war by Congress. Throughout the latter half of the twentieth century, the use of force became an increasingly more relevant foreign policy action. The entries in this encyclopedia study the use of force from a variety of angles: domestic politics, which includes Congress, executive-congressional relations, ethics, multilateralism, and theories on the use of force. The volume includes a list of important concepts and terms. There are suggested readings following each entry as well as a selective bibliography. There is an index. The work is one of the few reference works to concentrate on the subject of Presidential use of force and will be useful for most studies in U.S. diplomatic history.

371. The Lords of Foggy Bottom: American Secretaries of State and the World They Shaped. Tom Lansford. Baldwin Place, NY: Encyclopedia Society, 2001. 540p. ISBN 0-914746-55-X.

The author's aim is to provide biographical and career information on the 62 American secretaries of state, from Thomas Jefferson to Colin Powell. Each secretary has three to seven pages devoted to him, including a portrait and a bibliography. In addition to factual information, the essays cover historical and political events, setting the context for understanding the successes and failures of those profiled.

372. Notable U.S. Ambassadors Since 1775: A Biographical Dictionary. Cathal J. Nolan, ed. Westport, CT: Greenwood Press, 1997. 430p. ISBN 0-313-29195-0.

The purpose of this biographical work is to examine the careers of 58 U.S. Ambassadors selected for their contributions to U.S. foreign policy and diplomatic interests. Among those selected are Madeline Albright, Benjamin Franklin, John Kenneth Galbraith, George Kennan, Jeanne Kirkpatrick, Thomas Jefferson, and Adlai Stevenson. The articles are well written and analytical. The articles point out the pressures the ambassadors worked under, assessing their influence, successes or failures. Many foreign concerns and domestic issues are covered in evaluating the methods each ambassador used to advance policy interests. The entries include a brief bibliography of works by and about the ambassadors. An introduction by the editor covers the history of the role of ambassadors with some attention to the key personalities and activities in U.S. diplomatic history. The early ambassadors established the institutions and culture of U.S. diplomacy and the careers of later ones reflect the widening global interests of the United States. A select bibliography of primary and secondary courses concludes the volume. This work is valuable for further reading beyond the standard biographical sources for the insights that it provides.

*373. PAIS International. OCLC PAIS. Quart. 1915–. [Electronic database; CD ROM]. ISSN 0898-2201 Available: http://www.pais.org.

The *PAIS International* database, produced by OCLC PAIS, is a global public policy and public affairs database containing over 480,000 records. Formerly titled *Public Affairs Information Service,* it has been available through the OCLC FirstSearch service since 1992 and indexes publications from over 120 countries. It covers a variety of sources including journal articles, books, government documents, statistical compendia, directories research reports, gray literature, publications of international agencies, and Internet resources in a variety of languages. The records for each *PAIS International* entry contain a complete bibliographic citation, Internet addresses for electronic documents, a short abstract, up to nine subject headings, language of publication, and type of publication. The editors have identified over 2,600 Web sites important to the field of public affairs and inserted records for them with hot links. The special features field provides information about the nature, content, and other important aspects of a Web site, which could eliminate the need for a user to examine each site. The printed index began publication in 1915 and the long run of this index makes it valuable for historical research.

374. A Reference Guide to United States Department of State Special Files. Gerald K. Haines. Westport, CT: Greenwood Press, 1985. 393p. ISBN 0-313-22750-0.

The archival files described in this guide include materials in the National Archives and materials in the files within the Department of State. The bulk of the entries are for files from the 1940s and 1950s. The guide is arranged into 17 geographical and subject sections, mainly following the organization of the Department of State. For each entry there is a description of the file that includes the arrangement of the records, the existence of finding aids, the physical volume of the records in boxes or cubic feet, and information on the exact location of the records. For National Archives records the access number is given, along with any restrictions on access. In addition to conveying factual information, many of the descriptions give background on the file, including committees or individuals responsible for its generation. There are name, subject, and file number indexes. This reference guide is essential for those seeking information from Department of State files because the files are not all located in the National Archives.

Another archival collection covering the next decade from the Department of State files is *National Security Files, 1961–1969.* Over 150,000 pages of declassified archival materials from the Kennedy and Johnson presidential libraries have been microfilmed for the *National Security Files, 1961–1969* under the editorship of George C. Herring (University Publications of America, 1989–1991). The series is divided into separate collections for Latin America, Africa, Vietnam, Asia and the Pacific, the Middle East, Western Europe, the USSR and Eastern Europe, and the United States. International crises such as the Bay of Pigs, the Cuban Missile Crisis, Laos, Berlin, the Congo, the Six-Day War, and Vietnam took place in the 1961–1969 time period. The *National Security Files* contain primary-source materials on national security, international relations, and the affairs of U.S. allies and adversaries worldwide. Each portion has a printed guide that contains document-by-document descriptions listing type of document, sender, recipient, brief description of subject matter, date of document, original classification, number of pages, and date declassified. There is also a comprehensive analytical subject index. The *National Security Files* microfilm collection makes an enormous volume of diverse documents available for research. The collection contains essential source materials for the study of U.S. foreign policy in the decade of the 1960s.

375. Treaties and Other International Agreements of the United States of America, 1776–1949. Charles I. Bevans, comp. Washington, D.C.: Government Printing Office, 1968–1976. 13v.

The compilation supervised by Bevans contains the text and an index for those agreements entered into by the United States in the 1776–1949 period. The Bevans set updates an earlier compilation by Mallow et al., which covered the 1776–1927 time period. Before 1950 when the U.S. Department of State began publishing *United States Treaties and Other International Agreements* (*UST*), the official texts of treaties and agreements were only found in the *United States Statutes at Large* or published in pamphlets in the *Treaties and other International Acts* (TIAS), as of Dec. 27, 1945– series (Government Printing Office, 1946–). Thus, the Bevans set gathers together the text of treaties from a number of different sources. The first four volumes of the Bevans work contain multilateral treaties arranged chronologically. The next eight volumes contain bilateral treaties arranged alphabetically by country. The last volume is the general index. The Bevans volumes reproduce the treaties whether they are presently in force or not; thus the set is suitable for historical research. The work is useful for students and researchers seeking the text of treaties for the 1776–1949 time period.

United Nations treaties in which the United States is a signatory are available on the United Nations Web site (available at http://www.un.org).

Oceana Publications also issues quarterly, *Consolidated Treaties & International Agreements* (*CTIA*), which consists of *CITA: Current Document Service–United States, Index: CTIA,* and a CD-ROM. The Oceana treaties from 1783 are also online in *LexisNexis. Westlaw* has coverage from 1979 of treaties and agreements.

376. U.S. Department of State: A Reference History. Elmer Plischke. Westport, CT: Greenwood Press, 1999. 763p. ISBN 0-313-29126-8.

Although this work is more of a history and less of a reference book, it does provide a comprehensive overview of the history of the Department of State. Plischke has produced a number of reference works on U.S. diplomatic history and foreign service. The narrative, which occupies most of the volume, traces the Department's history in four chronological chapters by historical era. The chapter for 1861 to WWI traces how the Department was reoriented to reflect the United States's newfound role in international politics. The final chapter explores the future and the Department's role in foreign policy-making in the twenty-first century. The tables outlining treaties in force and bilateral agreements are especially helpful as reference aids to a very confusing subject. The reference matter is contained in tables in each chapter, a glossary of terms, and a list of symbols and abbreviations. The appendixes provide a chronological list of principle statutes and executive orders concerning the department and foreign service, a summary of laws concerning the conduct of U.S. foreign relations, and a table of U.S. territorial expansion.

Plischke is also responsible for an earlier work, *U.S. Foreign Relations: A Guide to Information Sources* (Gale, 1980). This work is organized into four main sections: diplomacy and diplomats; conduct of U.S. foreign relations; official sources and resources; and memoirs and biographical material. Each major section is subdivided into chapters on more specific aspects of the general topic. Analytical, descriptive, and documentary sources from British and U.S. scholarship and some foreign-language works are included. The annotated guide was prepared to assist serious students in doing research in U.S. foreign relations.

A later research guide is *The Department of State and American Diplomacy: A Bibliography,* by Robert U. Goehlert and Elizabeth R. Hoffmeister (Garland, 1986). In the introduction to this bibliographical work, reference sources and research guides are listed, along with the publications of the Department of State and guides to U.S. government documents. The bibliography is divided both topically and geographically. The first chapter covers the functions of the Department of State and historical studies. The second chapter deals with the conduct of U.S. foreign policy, relations with the president and Congress, and so on. The third chapter is organized geographically and covers U.S. relations with other countries. The fourth chapter lists biographical source material on diplomats and members of the foreign service, with a separate section for the secretaries of state. The bibliography includes only English-language items published between 1945 and 1984. There are author and subject indexes. The work is useful for students at all levels and for researchers seeking information on any aspect of U.S. foreign policy.

377. United States Treaty Index, 1776–1990 Consolidation. Igor I. Kavass, ed. Buffalo, NY: W.S. Hein, 1992. 11v. ISBN 0-89941-770-1.

The *Consolidation* has replaced a number of treaty indexes published by W.S. Hein as it consolidates the information in the previous indexes. The set provides access to *TIAS* number, country or countries, and time frame. Unpublished acts from 1776 to 1950 and treaties and agreements from 1950 to 1990 not yet published are included. The first volume explains the five different treaty series and gives reference sources for U.S. and international treaties. Chronological lists of U.S. treaties from 1776 forward begin in volume 6. In volumes 8 and 9 treaties are listed chronologically by country, group of countries, or organization. Series citation and classification cross-references are given. The last two volumes make up the subject index to the set including agreements by names of individuals and negotiating organizations. For historical research of U.S. treaties the *Consolidation* is now the starting point. *Current Treaty Index: Supplement to the United States Treaty Index: 1776–1990 Consolidation* is a semi-annual supplement edited by Kavass. It is available in print and on CD-ROM. A current microfiche service provides the text of indexed documents.

378. Unperfected Treaties of the United States of America, 1776–1976. Christian L. Wiktor. Dobbs Ferry, NY: Oceana, 1976–1984. 6v. ISBN 0-3790-0560-3.

The majority of reference aids for researching treaties and agreements are for those that were officially put in force. This unique reference work is an aid to those searching for information and the text of treaties that never went into force, the exclusions being Indian treaties and postal agreements. The text of the proposed agreements is accompanied by information on the parties involved, the place and date of signature, Senate actions, the location of the text of the treaty in the National Archives, and other historical details. The table of contents in each volume lists the treaties. There is a listing of works cited and an index. The last volume has a cumulative index for the set. This reference set will undoubtedly be of interest to diplomatic historians and other researchers concerned with U.S. foreign policy.

INTELLIGENCE AND SECURITY

379. Conducting Post–World War II National Security Research in Executive Branch Records: A Comprehensive Guide. James E. David. Westport, CT: Greenwood Publishing Group, 2001. 266p. ISBN 0-313-31986-3.

Records pertaining to the post–WWII period are scattered throughout various agencies, repositories, and libraries, many of them not in Washington, D.C. This book provides considerable detail on the accessibility of records in the National Archives, Federal records centers, presidential libraries, and the agencies themselves. Smaller repositories are also included. This up-to-date guide will be a primary tool for any researcher in the subject of U.S. intelligence.

A Web site that supplements the information in the David guide and provides links to the appropriate agencies is at http://www.loyola.edu/dept/politics/intel.html. This directory of sites relating to intelligence and investigative bodies, including the CIA, FBI, Naval Intelligence, and international organizations. The links connect to full-text essays, declassified articles, and government documents. The page also links to Military Intelligence, and Economic Intelligence directory pages, for different perspectives on the intelligence community.

Over 150,000 pages of declassified archival materials from the Kennedy and Johnson presidential libraries have been microfilmed for the *National Security Files, 1961–1969* (University Publications of America, 1989–1991). The series is divided into separate collections for Latin America, Africa, Vietnam, Asia and the Pacific, the Middle East, Western Europe, the USSR and Eastern Europe, and the United States. International crises such as the Bay of Pigs, the Cuban Missile Crisis, Laos, Berlin, the Congo, the Six-Day War, and Vietnam took place in the 1961–1969 time period. The *National Security Files* contain primary-source materials on national security, international relations, and the affairs of U.S. allies and adversaries worldwide. Each portion has a printed guide that contains document-by-document descriptions listing type of document, sender, recipient, brief description of subject matter, date of document, original classification, number of pages, and date declassified. There is also a comprehensive analytical subject index. The *National Security Files* microfilm collection makes an enormous volume of diverse documents available for research. The collection contains essential source materials for the study of U.S. foreign policy in the decade of the 1960s.

380. Dictionary of the United States Intelligence Services: Over 1500 Terms, Programs, and Agencies. William Wilson. Jefferson, NC: McFarland, 1996. 191p. ISBN 0-7864-0180-X.

The branches of the armed services and the intelligence community are legendary for their use of abbreviations, acronyms, and code words. There are four sections to this work: an introduction, a comprehensive list of abbreviations, a dictionary of terms, and a bibliography. The aim is to define and explain the intelligence agencies, their operations and procedures, and their language. In the introduction, the author, a retired Army intelligence officer, explains the scope of the work and the changing nature of intelligence work since the end of the Cold War. The bibliography contains unclassified works published from 1975 to 1995 and the focus is terms and concepts used since the Vietnam War. The work is for specialists and laypersons alike.

381. United States Intelligence: An Encyclopedia. Bruce W. Watson et al. New York: Garland Publishing, 1990. 896p. ISBN 0-8240-3713-8.

The period since World War II is the focus of *United States Intelligence: An Encyclopedia*. Short entries are given for over 3,000 acronyms, terms, persons, agencies, and programs. The emphasis is on military and weapons systems. Most entries have references to sources, and there is a complete bibliography to all sources at the end of the work. There is no index. A chronology of significant events in the U.S. intelligence sphere since 1941 is included. Appendixes offer 25 "verbatim reproductions of virtually all of the most significant Executive and congressional statements regarding the Intelligence community after World War II." This encyclopedia furnishes comprehensive coverage of the modern intelligence operations of the United States.

382. The U.S. Intelligence Community: An Annotated Bibliography. Mark M. Lowenthal. Hamden, CT: Garland, 1994. 206p. (Organizations and Interest Groups, v. 11; Garland Reference Library of the Humanities, v. 1765.) ISBN 0-8153-1423-X.

The 225 entries in this bibliography are divided into three thematic chapters, a section on published document collections, and a general bibliography. Publications include books, journal articles, and government documents. The annotations are brief but evaluative. Both military and nonmilitary intelligence gathering are covered. The author aims at providing an overview of intelligence theory and the role of intelligence, espionage, and covert operations in U.S. policy. Over one-half of the book is devoted to the text of primary documents, a list of the directors of the Central Intelligence Agency, and the organization of the U.S. intelligence community. There are both author and subject indexes.

Another bibliography on the same subject is *American Intelligence Operations: 1775–1990: A Bibliographic Guide* by Neal H. Petersen (Regina Books, 1992). The guide is organized into 13 chapters, mainly by historical period and contains over 6,000 citations to biographies, monographs, journal articles, and dissertations that deal with various aspects of intelligence operations from the American Revolution through the Cold War.

AFRICA/MIDEAST

383. United States Foreign Policy and the Middle East/North Africa: A Bibliography of Twentieth-Century Research. Sanford R. Silverburg and Bernard Reich. New York: Garland, 1990. 407p. (Garland Reference Library of Social Science, v. 570.) ISBN 0-8240-4613-7. **US Foreign Relations with the Middle East and North Africa: A Bibliography, Supplement, 1998.** Lanham, MD: Scarecrow, 1999. 518p. (Scarecrow Area bibliographies, no. 19.) ISBN 0-8108-3615-7.

Silverburg and Reich have updated their earlier bibliography published in 1990. The *Supplement* more than doubles the number of entries when added to the first volume. The geographic areas included in this selective bibliography are defined as all Arab nations plus the non-Arab nations of Iran, Israel, and Turkey. The introduction provides an overview of U.S. involvement in this area of the world, beginning in the late nineteenth century. The majority of the works cited are English-language sources published after 1960. Monographs, journal articles, government publications, and doctoral dissertations are included. The arrangement in the first work is alphabetical by author, but there is a subject index. The 1998 supplement contains more than 3,500 sources organized by topical descriptors. In addition to books, journal articles, and government publications, electronic sources including Web sites and CD-ROMs are included. The supplement has an author and subject index. The bibliography is a current source of use mainly to those interested in developments in the Middle East since 1960. It is a good basic reference source for students and beginning researchers.

384. The United States in Africa: A Historical Dictionary. David Shavit. Westport, CT: Greenwood Press, 1989. 298p. ISBN 0-313-25887-2.

Shavit has produced a number of dictionaries, each concentrating on a specific geographic region (entries 385, 388n, 395, 400) As with most of the dictionaries of this type, the majority of the entries are for individuals involved in establishing relationships between the U.S. and African countries. There are a considerable number of entries, however, devoted to institutions, organizations, and businesses. The entries are well written and contain references for further research including manuscript material. There are lists by occupation and profession, including authors, explorers, hunters, diplomats, and engineers. The dictionary functions as a basic information source on the relationship between the United States and African countries from 1600s to the present and is suitable for use by all types of library users.

385. The United States in the Middle East: A Historical Dictionary. David Shavit. Westport, CT: Greenwood Press, 1988. 441p. ISBN 0-313-25341-2.

This work on the Middle East covers approximately 200 years of U.S. involvement in that region. The entries are mainly biographical, but institutions, events, and businesses, mainly oil companies, are included. The biographical information on individuals includes dates, education, role in the Middle East, length and places of service, and locations of archival materials. Each entry includes a list of further references. In addition to the alphabetical entries, there is a bibliographical essay on the role Americans and American institutions have played in the Middle East relations; a list of modern place-names with historical equivalents; a chronology of events from 1787 to 1986; a list of U.S. chiefs of mission in the Middle East from 1831–1936; and lists of biographees by occupation or profession such as explorers, engineers, and more. The dictionary for the Middle East is an excellent information source for general readers, students, and researchers.

The Middle East: A Political Dictionary by Lawrence Ziring (ABC-CLIO, 1992) is similar to the Shavit work. The emphasis is more current, although this title also covers historical terms and events. The reference work is another in ABC-CLIO's dictionaries in political science series, a feature of which is the two-part entry: one paragraph for definition, one for significance. The work is helpful for understanding the history of many of the tangled relationships between nations and factions in the Middle East.

386. U. S. Relations with South Africa: An Annotated Bibliography. Y. G-M. Lulat. Boulder, CO: Westview Press, 1991. 2v. ISBN 0-8133-7138-4 (v. 1); 0-8133-7747-1 (v. 2).

The most comprehensive work on the subject to date, this bibliography of over 4,500 books, articles, government documents, reports of nongovernmental organizations, and dissertations includes English-language sources from the last 100 years. The organization of the bibliography is somewhat complex, with sources arranged by publication type and then by subject within those two groupings. Only about 40 percent of the entries are annotated, but those provide abstracts, tables of contents, and, for some important works, citations to book reviews. The main index lists authors, organizations, and subjects. There is a separate list of periodical titles. In addition, there is a "Guide to Sources of Current Information on U.S. Relations with South Africa." The recent publication date of this bibliography makes it useful to those seeking up-to-date information as well as those engaged in historical research.

ASIA

387. East Asia and the United States: An Encyclopedia of Relations Since 1784. 2v. James I. Matray, ed. Westport, CT: Greenwood Publishing Group, 2002. 1,044 p. ISBN 0-313-30557-9.

The coverage of relations between the United States and the nations of East Asia over the last 200 years in this two-volume set is comprehensive. The essays, many written by distinguished scholars from over nine countries, reflect current scholarship. The responses of the United States to diplomatic, economic, political, military, and cultural developments in East Asia are described. The major countries of China, Japan, Korea, and Vietnam naturally receive the most attention, but all the other countries in East Asia are also covered. The encyclopedia will be useful to Asian specialists and students as well as to scholars in the broader fields of international history and foreign relations.

388. Security, Arms Control, & Conflict Reduction in East Asia & the Pacific. Andrew McLean, comp. Westport, CT: Greenwood Press, 1993. 576p. ISBN 0-313-27539-4.

The organization of this extensive bibliography is by 27 country and regional chapters. The chapters on Japan and China are the largest with other chapters on U.S. relations between Australia, New Zealand, and Russia. Within the chapters subtopics such as human rights, foreign relations, terrorism, trade, and security provide further specificity. The 12,645 selectively annotated entries include books, articles, dissertations, official documents, and working papers. An appendix provides a directory of research institutions, which published many of the entries listed in the bibliography. There is an author and subject index.

Two earlier, more specific bibliographies may still be useful although needing updating. *The Allied Occupation of Japan, 1945–1952: An Annotated Bibliography of Western Language Materials,* by Robert Edward Ward and others (Chicago: American Library Association, 1974) was prepared under the sponsorship of The Joint Committee on Japanese Studies of the Social Science Research Council of the American Council for Learned Societies and the Center for Japanese Studies at the University of Michigan. The work lists over 3,100 items—books, periodical and newspaper articles, government documents, and archival materials, mainly in English. All aspects of the period of occupation are included. The arrangement is by topical sections. There is a list of "High Ranking Personnel," a list of periodical titles, and an author index. The bibliography is a definitive work on the subject, of use to scholars and students for research on the period of the occupation of Japan.

Philippine-American Relations: A Guide to Manuscript Sources in the United States by Shiro Saito (Greenwood Press, 1982) lists primary resource materials for the study of U.S.-Philippine relations from the mid-nineteenth century to the 1970s. Materials located in the United States that contain contemporary descriptions of the relations between the two countries include manuscripts, official records, and other unpublished papers. Although there is material from the nineteenth century, items pertaining to internal affairs and the Spanish period of the Philippines (1521–1898) are not included; only material for U.S. involvement with the Philippines is examined. The first section of the book lists the collections alphabetically by person or institution. Descriptive information includes title and date of source material; size, scope, and contents of the collection, with evaluative comments; location of the material; and other sources of information about the material. The second section of the work is a geographical listing (by state) to manuscript sources. The last section includes a chronology, a general index, and an index by repository. This is a useful guide to primary source materials for a specialized area of research.

389. The United States in Asia: An Historical Dictionary. David Shavit. New York: Greenwood, 1990, 620p. ISBN 0-313-26788-X.

A basic information source on U.S.-Asian relations, this work follows the same organizational pattern as the other Shavit historical dictionaries (entries 384, 385, 395, 400). The entries consist mostly of biographical sketches on individuals, with some entries for events and institutions. Although Shavit states in the preface of the work that military personnel who fought in World War II and the Korean and Vietnam conflicts are not included, there are a number of prominent military leaders profiled. As in the other Shavit works, sources to manuscript materials and other biographical sources are included with each biography. The entries range from the early trade and missionary contacts between the United States and Asia up to the present. The work provides a list of biographees by occupation and a list of the leaders of U.S. diplomatic missions in Asia from 1843–1989. It also includes a bibliographic essay on the development of U.S.-Asian relations. The dictionary is a useful reference work for all type of library users and a good basic information tool for students and researchers.

EUROPE

*390. Cold War International History Project (CWIHP): Document Library. Washington, D.C.: Woodrow Wilson International Center for Scholars. Available: http://cwihp/si.edu.

This project established in 1991 has as its purpose to disseminate new information and perspective on Cold War history, and to prompt the release of historical materials by governments on all sides of the Cold War, including previously unavailable archival records from former communist bloc countries. The site contains papers on the arms race, Cold War crises, Cold War leaders, intelligence, individual countries, the Khrushchev Era, the Reagan Era, and the rise and fall of détente.

The New York Times' 20th Century in Review: The Cold War (Fitzroy Dearborn, 2002) is a compilation of more than 500 articles and 100 illustrations in two volumes. The material originally appeared in *The New York Times* and first illuminates the origins of the East-West conflict through the two World Wars and then moves on to the growing tensions of the post-war period, the great crises of the 1950 and 1960s, and the eras of détente and glasnost.

391. The Cold War 1945–1991. Benjamin Frankel, ed. Detroit: Gale, 1992. 3v. ISBN 0-8103-8927-4.

This reference was published just one year after the dissolution of the Soviet Union. Edited by Benjamin Frankel, a specialist on U.S. national security, foreign policy, and international relations, this three-volume encyclopedia is a definitive work on the Cold War period. The first two volumes are devoted to examining the careers and explaining the significance of individuals who played key roles in the Cold War including spies and scientists as well as political and governmental figures. Volume 1 has in-depth biographical information on more than 140 American and Western European figures who played leadership or other key roles during the era. Volume 2 covers Eastern figures who played leadership or other key roles. The third volume discusses themes and events that had a major impact on the period. It contains aids for further research, including a 120-page history of the Cold War, a chronology of events, a listing of manuscript and oral history collections, and a selective bibliographical guide to additional research sources. The set is amply illustrated with photographs, maps, and diagrams. It will be consulted by experts and general readers alike.

Frankel is also editing a series *The Cold War* (London: St. James Press, 2000B). The first volume of this series contains a pro-and-con approach to scholarly interpretations of many Cold War events, such as Kennan's containment, détente, the Berlin crisis, and more.

392. The Columbia Guide to the Cold War. Michael Kort. New York: Columbia University Press, 1998. 366p. (Columbia Guides to American History and Cultures). ISBN 0-231-10772-2.

One of the most valuable features of this one-volume guide is the narrative survey of the Cold War period, which forms an introduction to the topic. The book is divided into four sections: a narrative describing the causes of the Cold War; entries on key events, policies, and people; a chronology of major developments from 1945 to 1991; and an annotated resource guide arranged by topics includes books, journals, archival collections,

Web sites, novels, and films. The survey explains the major historiographical debates. References are identified as to which school of thought they reflect. Not only does the work provide information, it provides historical context and unbiased interpretations of events. The volume ends with an appendix on the costs of the Cold War. It is an excellent introduction to the history of the period for students.

Another one-volume work is *The Cold War Encyclopedia* by Thomas Parrish (Henry Holt, 1996). The volume contains well-written and concise entries and a chronology of the events of the Cold War.

A similar work with the same title is *The Cold War* by Katherine Sibley (Greenwood Press, 1998). The intent of this work is to introduce the subject of the Cold War to students. There is a chronology of events, a historical narrative, a glossary, and an annotated bibliography.

Cold War Chronology: Soviet-American Relations 1945–1991 by Kenneth Hill (CQ, 1993) is also designed for a young adult audience. Some 2,000 brief chronological entries describe the significant events in Soviet-American relations during the last half of the twentieth century.

393. Encyclopedia of Cold War Politics. Brandon Toropov. New York: Facts on File, 2000. 242p. ISBN 0-8160-3574-1.

The focus of this work is not the global nature of the Cold War, but American domestic events and issues during the second half of the twentieth century that were affected by the international scene. In 700 entries, events, individuals, organizations and institutions, ideas and concepts, publications, and documents are covered in a generally nonpartisan tone. The work includes popular phrases and figures that other reference works with an international focus do not cover. Many of the entries include black-and-white photographs. The work serves as an introduction to the era.

394. Historical Dictionary of the Cold War. Joseph Smith and Simon Davis. Lanham, MD: Scarecrow Press, 2000. 329p. ISBN 0-8108-3709-9.

One of the most recent of the Cold War reference works, this one volume offers brief descriptions of people places, events, concepts, and organizations, which attempt to place each subject in the historical context of the period. There is a 27-page introduction that provides a narrative history of the period's main themes and events. The authors are specialists, Smith in U.S. relations with Latin American and Davis in Anglo-American relations. There is a long chronology from the German invasion of Poland in 1939 to the dissolution of the Soviet Union in 1991. There is also list of acronyms and abbreviations, and a lengthy 33-page bibliography. Cross-references are embedded in the text but there is no index. The work has the advantage of being farther removed from the period of the end of the Cold War than those reference works published during the 1990s.

395. United States Relations with Russia & the Soviet Union: A Historical Dictionary. David Shavit. Westport, CT: Greenwood Press, 1993. 256p. ISBN 0-313-28469-5.

Another of the Shavit historical dictionaries from Greenwood, this volume follows the same format as the others. There is a bibliographical essay, short entries in an alphabetical arrangement of people, organizations, and events involved in relations between the two superpowers. Most entries have references to the sources of the information. Appendixes include a "List of Individuals by Profession and Occupation." This work pulls together information found in a variety of sources. The biographies do not add any information that cannot be found in the standard biographical sets. The bibliographic essay that concludes the book provides a list of basic works on the subject.

An earlier bibliography which may partially supplement the resources cited in the Shavit work is *Origins, Evolution, and Nature of the Cold War: An Annotated Bibliographic Guide* by J.L. Black (ABC-CLIO, 1986). The focus of this scholarly bibliography is the 1938–1950 time span, which covers the origins of the Cold War. The bibliography is divided into 13 topical sections, each with an introductory note. The approximately 1,300 entries include books, journal articles, dissertations, and government publications. Strengths of the work are chapters on the Soviet perspective and the historiography of the Cold War. There are author and subject indexes.

LATIN AMERICA AND THE CARIBBEAN

Latin America as a region and the individual countries it encompasses have been subjects of intense study. There are many reference works and bibliographic guides for Latin American studies. The most comprehensive and well known is the annual *Handbook of Latin American Studies* edited at the Hispanic Division of the Library of Congress and published by the University of Texas Press. The handbook is an annotated bibliography with introductory essays that evaluate the research and literature in specialized areas. It alternates each year between the humanities and the social sciences in the focus of the bibliography. It is a comprehensive resource for students and scholars of any aspect of Latin American studies. It is now online at http://lcweb2.loc.gov/hlas/.

This section contains only works directly related to the historical study of U.S. relations with Latin America. Works on individual countries not concerned directly with U.S. foreign relations are not included.

396. Cuba and the United States: A Chronological History. Jane Franklin. New York: Ocean Press, 1997. 416p. ISBN 1-875284-92-3.

The relations between Cuba and the United States have continued to simmer since the Cuban Missile crisis in 1962 with occasional flare-ups. This chronology traces the relations between the two countries from the Cuban revolution in 1959 through 1995. An introductory section reviews the history of Cuba from the arrival of Christopher Columbus. The narrative relates the major crises with seemingly minor episodes covering the turbulent and controversial relationship.

An earlier, scholarly and still useful work is *The Missile Crisis of October 1962: A Review of Issues and References* by Lester H. Brune (Claremont, CA: Regina Books, 1985). In the beginning of this reference work there are several essay chapters giving the historical background and events leading up to the crisis and the sequence of events that took place during it. Brune analyzes the reactions of both Washington and Moscow and the maneuvers that defused the crisis. The second half of the book is a bibliographic essay referencing both contemporary accounts of the incident and later analyses of it. Both primary and secondary materials are cited, including news magazines and scholarly articles. The citations are annotated as to the significance of the source and the interpretations put forth in them. This is an excellent basic source for the historical background, understanding of the issues, and the later interpretations of the events. It is useful for all audiences with an interest in research on the subject of the Cuban Missile Crisis.

397. Early U.S.-Hispanic Relations 1776–1860: an Annotated Bibliography. Rafael E. Tarrago. Metuchen, NJ: Scarecrow, 1994. 171p. ISBN 0-8108-2882-0.

Although the title of this work indicates a broad scope, the emphasis is on relations with Central and South American countries. In beginning with the founding of the United States as a nation, the events that led up to the promulgation of the Monroe doctrine and the development of foreign relations in the Western Hemisphere can be traced. In addition to the Louisiana Purchase and relations and trade with Spain, the wars of independence of the Kingdoms of the Indies are included. The development of the countries in Central and South America are followed up to the beginning of the U.S. Civil War. There are 800 entries including many primary sources. The bibliography is a good reference companion for those beginning research on the geographical regions and time period covered.

398. The Legacy of the Monroe Doctrine: A Reference Guide to U.S. Involvement in Latin America and the Caribbean. David W. Dent. Westport, CT: Greenwood Press, 1999. 418p. ISBN 0-313-30109-3.

U.S. foreign relations with 24 countries are covered in separate chapters for each country. An introductory essay and all of the chapters were written by Dent, a professor of political science. Each chapter has a timeline and is organized around major events and issues. The essays are scholarly with references and lists of suggested readings at the end. The essays give an appraisal of U.S. policy. While the emphasis is on the influence of the Monroe Doctrine, the essays cover U.S. relations with the 24 countries up through the Reagan years. An appendix contains excerpts from the Monroe Doctrine. There are also a number of editorial cartoons by Thomas Flannery of the *Baltimore Sun.* There is a glossary and an extensive index.

An earlier work by Dent is *U.S.-Latin American Policymaking: A Reference Handbook* (Greenwood Press, 1995). An introductory essay by Dent has the title of the work. The main contents are 19 thematic essays written by leading scholars in Latin American diplomatic history covering the subject since the 1960s. Chapters cover the United States and international economic organizations, interest groups and the media, and who makes Latin American policy. This work also contains an appendix of political cartoons. There is an index. In spite of its title, the work is more of an overview of the topic than a reference book.

399. The United States and Latin America: A Select Bibliography. John A. Britton. Pasadena, CA: Salem Press and Lanham, MD: Scarecrow, 1997. 277p. (Magill Bibliographies). ISBN 0-8108-3248-8.

The Magill series is made up of reference tools designed to assist students and beginning researchers. This annotated bibliography provides a solid overview of the background and present history of U.S.-Latin American relations. The first two chapters provide a background on traditional diplomatic history and the new international history. Works that cover several countries or regions are included in these chapters. The remaining chapters cover the nineteenth century and twentieth century international relations dealing with drugs, immigration, armed forces in Latin America, and the North American Free Trade Agreement. The bibliography is a useful reference tool for its coverage of the changes in U.S.-Latin American relations from the Monroe Doctrine to the end of the twentieth century.

400. The United States in Latin America: A Historical Dictionary. David Shavit. New York: Greenwood Press, 1992. 471p. ISBN 0-313-27595-5.

The format of this dictionary is the same as for the other historical dictionaries David Shavit has authored (entries 384, 385, 388n, 395). The work is an alphabetical listing of definitions and biographies for people, terms, issues, and events in history of U.S. relations with the countries of Latin America. All countries south of the United States are covered, including the Caribbean islands and Mexico, with the exception of places that were annexed to the United States. The entries include biographical and bibliographical references. Appendixes include a list of chiefs of U.S. diplomatic missions in Latin America, 1823–1990, and a list of biographees by profession and occupation. There is an index of names and subjects. This is a basic work suitable for all levels of library users and sound enough for use by scholars.

A work with a more current emphasis is *Latin America: A Political Dictionary* by Ernest E. Rossi and Jack C. Plano (ABC-CLIO, 2nd ed., 1992). The current and historical significance are explained for the terms and events in this reference. It can be used in conjunction with the Shavit work for research on U.S.-Latin American relations.

Although not specifically focused on U.S. and Latin American relations, a recent work provides an excellent background in Latin American Studies. *Latin America and the Caribbean: A Critical Guide to Research Sources* (Greenwood Press, 1993) edited by Paula H. Covington. A section on electronic resources for Latin American research in the United States, Latin America, and Europe is particularly useful.

401. U.S. Mexican Treaties. Richard A. Westin, comp. Buffalo, NY: William S. Hein, 1996. 11v. ISBN 0-89941-985-2.

It may come as a surprise that the treaties between the United States and the United Mexican States would occupy 12 volumes. The William S. Hein Company has been publishing sets of United States treaties for many years and has done a valuable service for those in international law and political science as well as historians by issuing this compilation. The first 11 volumes containing bilateral and multilateral treaties were issued as a set in 1996. These volumes contain only treaties in force from the Treaty of Guadalupe Hidalgo in 1848 through 1994. The 12th volume issued in 1999 contains previously unavailable treaties and newly ratified treaties since the publication of the set. The compiler has provided a short description of each treaty preceding the full text of the treaty. Each volume has a chronology and subject index at the front of the volume. The indexes give the signing date, the short title, and the treaty numbers and their location within the set. References to the *TIAS* (*Treaties and Other International Agreements Series,* entry 375) or *UST* (*U.S. Treaties and Other International Agreements*) and also the *Statutes at Large* are given. Those who conduct research into the history of U.S.-Mexican relations will find it convenient to have the treaties and agreements between the two nations pulled together in one set.

Chapter 5
Military History

The course of history has largely been determined by wars and military conquests. The Revolutionary War, the Civil War, and World War II stand out as the major conflicts in terms of military, diplomatic, and political history of the United States. These wars were the major focus of U.S. history until the redirection toward social history. The Vietnam conflict is now generally regarded as a turning point in the history of the United States. The Vietnam conflict, which was so divisive, has brought the political and social aspects of war to the forefront of research, pushing aside to some degree the study of troop movements, battle strategies, and military leaders. The effect of the increased interest in social issues is seen in the lack of development of tools for military research.

Publications concerning specific branches of the armed services have not been as numerous as those dealing with particular wars. There has not been a large number of new bibliographies and research guides produced in the last 20 years concentrating on the armed forces. The exception is U.S. naval history; it is being thoroughly covered by the Naval Institute Press which has published a number of bibliographical and biographical reference works.

The equipment, weapons, vessels, and technology for waging war have been the object of much amateur and professional interest. However, works dealing specifically with military equipment have been excluded from this reference guide, with a few exceptions. Naval vessels have been treated. None of the excellent standard reference works in the *Jane's* series have been included as they are too numerous and are well known to buffs and scholars alike.

This chapter begins with a section of works on military history and the armed forces in general. The next section contains works focused on specific branches of the U.S. armed services. The wars or armed conflicts in which the United States has participated follow chronologically. Works on branches of the services concentrating on a particular war are in the section pertaining to that war.

GENERAL SOURCES

*402. Air University Library Index to Military Periodicals. Maxwell Air Force Base, AL: Air University Library, 1949–. ISSN 0002-2586. Back issues available in microfiche from U.S. Supt. of Documents. After 1999 only available online at http://www.dtic.mil/search97doc/aulimp/main.htm.

AULIMP is the *Air University Library Index to Military Periodicals*. It contains citations to articles in English-language military journals. Air University Library (AUL) has been producing the index since 1949. Issues covering the years 1990 to the present are available on the Web. The specialized subject focus of this periodical index is both an advantage and disadvantage. The scope is confined to military affairs, aeronautics, arms technology, and international relations. Sixty percent of the periodicals covered are not indexed anywhere else, and the other 40 percent are scattered over a wide variety of indexing tools. The emphasis is on the U.S. armed forces and military affairs. Even though many of the articles indexed are on narrow military topics, the thorough coverage of the field and the numerous citations make this index an excellent source for the serious researcher in defense policy and international relations. One disadvantage is that the periodicals indexed may not be carried in many libraries. The specialized nature of the index makes it the best—in some cases, the *only*—available source to consult for many of the topics covered.

Another source for military publications is *The Dougherty Collection of Military Newspapers* produced on microfilm by Proquest/University Microfilms. Nearly 2,500 military newspapers are represented, most of them dating from World War II. Titles from all branches of the military are included, as well as some from the defense industries. A brief history of the collection and a printed guide written by Walter S. Dougherty accompany the 58 reels of microfilm. The collection complements those publications indexed in the *Air University Library Index to Military Periodicals* and will be of interest to researchers in military history, military science, and political science.

403. American Military History: A Guide to Reference and Information Sources. Daniel K. Blewett. Englewood, CO: Libraries Unlimited, 1995. 295p. ISBN 1-56308-035-4.

Blewett is a librarian and he has provided a well-organized guide to all types of resources for research in U.S. military history. Over 1,000 annotated references to English-language resources are presented in a chronological arrangement in 14 chapters covering armed conflicts from the colonial era through the Persian Gulf War. Another nine chapters are topically oriented for such subjects as terrorism, and libraries, archives, organizations, and journals specializing in military history. The guide begins with a long chapter on materials covering U.S. military history in general. All types and formats of works are included. There are subject and author/title indexes. This work is the best guide for an overview of research in U.S. military history. It should be used as a starting place for any topic in military history. It complements the Higham and Mrozek guide (entry 412), which is written by historians with bibliographic essays.

404. America's Military Adversaries: From Colonial Times to the Present America's Military. John C. Fredriksen. Santa Barbara: CA, 2001. 621p. ISBN 1-57607-603-2.

The lives and accomplishments of over 200 persons who fought against the United States in some fashion are included in this work. The work is heavily illustrated and each entry contains a lengthy bibliography. The biographies take the reader through all of the wars and conflicts in which U.S. forces have been involved. Among the biographees included are Indian warriors, spies, German and Japanese fighter pilots, Confederates, and admirals of opposing navies. While the majority of those included are familiar names, there are lesser figures on which full biographical information may be hard to find.

405. A Bibliography of Military Name Lists from Pre-1675 to 1900: A Guide to Genealogical Sources. Lois Horowitz. Metuchen, NJ: Scarecrow, 1990. 1,080p. ISBN 0-8108-2166-4.

The arrangement of this bibliography is by time period and then locality. There are no indexes for branch of service, war, and so on. Both published and unpublished lists, including war records, rolls of servicemen, lists of veterans and pensioners, reports, journals, and histories are included in the bibliography. The work is most useful to genealogists, but it is also useful to other researchers tracing individuals who served in the military.

406. A Dictionary of Soldier Talk. John R. Elting et al. New York: Scribner's, 1984. 383p. ISBN 0-684-17862-1.

The definitions in this dictionary compiled by former U.S. Army personnel are linguistically valid. The work is entertaining and substantial. The main body of the dictionary presents Army slang and terminology, but there is also a section for Navy and Marine Corps terminology. The definitions cover the period from the beginnings of the U.S. military to the present. The dictionary is especially strong in post–World War II terminology. Both definitions and etymology are given, with references in appropriate contexts. The number of acronyms has been limited to avoid having the work become a dictionary of acronyms. The dictionary will be useful in all types of libraries for any user seeking definitions to military terms.

407. Encyclopedia of the American Military: Studies of the History, Traditions, Policies, Institutions, and Roles of the Armed Forces in War and Peace. John E. Jessup and Louise B. Ketz, eds. New York: Scribner, 1994. 2,255p. ISBN 0-684-19255-1.

Seventy lengthy signed essays by historians and political scientists form the core of this three-volume reference work. Each essay contains a comprehensive bibliography. The essays are divided into six thematic sections. Each war is covered in the section on "The American Military in War and Peace." Other sections deal with "The Formulation of American Military Policy," "The Role of the Armed Forces," "Military Arts and Sciences," and "Military Practices." In addition to the essays there is an extensive chronology divided into columns for key leaders, general American history, and American military history. The set is illustrated with maps and charts and has an index. This excellent reference work is useful for students and researchers alike.

408. Encyclopedia of American War Literature. Philip K. Jason and Mark A. Graves, eds. 440p. Westport, CT: Greenwood Publishing Group: 2001. ISBN 0-313-30648-6.

Both fiction and nonfiction, and prose and poetry about major conflicts from before the Revolutionary War through the Vietnam War are included in alphabetically arranged entries. The major writers and texts that have imaginatively represented the American experience of war are covered in critical commentary. The literature included deals with subjects such as Indian captivity narratives, women's diaries of the Civil War, the literature of the Spanish-American War, and African American war literature. All entries are written by experts and provide bibliographical references. There is a bibliography for further reading at the end of the volume.

409. Encyclopedia of Battles in North America: 1571 to 1916. Edward L. Purcell and Sarah J. Purcell. New York: Facts on File, 2000. 383p. ISBN 0-8160-3350-1.

There are more than 350 entries for all the wars and conflicts in North America during the years covered. The battles and skirmishes are placed in context with descriptions of the combatants, outcomes, casualties, and significance with further readings. The broad definition of battle allows the inclusion of many conflicts not found in works of narrower scope. Battles between Native Americans are included as well as naval engagements within 250 miles of the coasts. The work includes several appendixes, which list the battles alphabetically, chronologically, and by war. There are also lists of historic battlefield sites alphabetically and by region. Many entries have maps and there are a bibliography and a subject index. The book is written in clear language for the nonspecialist. It is suitable for students and the general reader.

410. Encyclopedia of Historic Forts: The Military, Pioneer, and Trading Posts of the United States. Robert B. Roberts. New York: Macmillan, 1988. 894p. ISBN 0-02-926880-X.

More than 3,000 military posts and forts are listed alphabetically by state in this comprehensive work. Not limited to a particular time period, region, or conflict, the work gives the history of each fort, along with present visiting status and preservation efforts. Historical information includes major historical events; commanders; dates of construction, destruction, and reconstruction; architectural innovations; and name changes. The book concludes with a selective bibliography and listing of state archives and libraries for further research. There is an index of forts by name, but no chronological or geographical listings are given. There are maps and illustrations accompanying the text. Because of its comprehensiveness, this resource can be consulted before going to more specialized references on the subject.

411. Facts About the American Wars. John S. Bowman, ed. Bronx, NY: H.W. Wilson, 1998. 750p. (Wilson Facts Series). ISBN 0-8242-0929-X.

This work is a one-source place to look for information on 26 U.S. military wars and conflicts. In one volume it provides an overview and historical perspective on U.S. military conflicts from the Franco-Spanish War in Florida in the sixteenth century to the Persian Gulf War in 1991. It is well organized as a reference book. The entries compiled by six contributors are standardized and include the dates, alternate names, the causes and combatants, geographic and strategic considerations, the battles and campaigns, negotiations and the peace treaty, the war's results and historical perspectives and a brief bibliography. Also included are notable phrases, songs, legends, and trivia. In addition to the chapters on the wars, there are a preface and introduction, good illustrations and maps, a glossary of military terms, a general bibliography, and an index. The title is suitable for the student or researcher in all types of libraries.

A broader, less-scholarly work is *Wars of the Americas: A Chronology of Armed Conflict in the New World, 1492 to the Present* by David F. Marley (ABC-CLIO, 1998). The aim of this work is to provide a complete chronology of all wars and armed conflicts in the Americas, both north, south, and the Caribbean from the time of Columbus to the present. The brief entries are in chronological order and then according to geographic area. There are numerous illustrations and the volume is indexed. It is useful in conjunction with more scholarly historical treatments.

412. Guide to the Sources of United States Military History. Robin Higham. Hamden, CT: Archon Books, 1975. 559p. ISBN 0-208-01499-3. **Supps. I-III,** Robin Higham and Donald Mrozek, eds. **Supp. I.** 1981. ISBN 0-208-01750-X. **Supp. II.** 1986. ISBN 0-208-02072-1. **Supp. III.** 1992. ISBN 0-208-02214-7.

The bibliographical essay is the format for this guide and its supplements. The initial publication covers U.S. military history from colonial times to 1972. The first supplement updates the work to 1978, the second supplement to 1983, and the third supplement up through the Persian Gulf War. The third supplement updates all previous chapters from the original edition and the first two supplements, then offers three new chapters. The original publication contains 18 essay chapters written by scholars, most of them well-known military historians. Each chapter provides a broad survey of the literature of the subject, with an emphasis on primary materials. Social, political, and economic aspects are covered. Each essay includes suggestions for further research and about 300 selective bibliographic citations. The arrangement is chronological by historical period, with additional topical essays on military medicine, Defense Department policies, and museums as historical resources. The supplements, in addition to updating the bibliographies for the original topics, have new sections on nuclear war, military law, the Coast Guard, and the Corps of Engineers. There are no indexes. These bibliographies have long been regarded as a major resource for the study of military history. They are an important starting place for students and researchers.

Another work by Higham is *Official Military Historical Offices and Sources* (Greenwood Press, 2000). The first volume of this, work which covers Europe, Africa, and the Middle East, was published in 1970. It is being reissued with volume 2, which covers the Western Hemisphere and the Pacific Rim. Essays on the bibliographic resources of each country have been written by historians or military staff. Even though there are gaps and the coverage is very uneven, there is not another work that gathers this information together in one place. It is useful for researchers seeking source materials from other countries.

413. Intervention and Counterinsurgency: An Annotated Bibliography. Benjamin R. Beede. New York: Garland, 1985. 312p. (Wars of the United States, v. 5; Garland Reference Library of Social Science, v. 251.) ISBN 0-8240-8944-8.

The subject of this annotated bibliography is the small wars of the United States, the military interventions or occupations undertaken "under executive authority." The organization is by action, beginning with the Boxer Rebellion (1898–1901) and ending with Grenada in the 1980s. There are over 30 confrontations covered, including the *Pueblo* seizure and the *Mayaguez* incident. Excluded are political actions that did not involve the discharging of weapons. The more than 1,200 citations are to English-language books, periodical articles, dissertations, and documents, the majority of which are U.S. publications. An introduction defines the confrontations and provides general background; each section also has prefatory background material. There are author and subject indexes. This bibliography is the only source on the subjects covered. It is suitable for students and the general public, but the serious researcher will need to seek foreign source material in addition.

414. The Military History of the United States. Christopher Chant. North Bellmore, NY: Marshall Cavendish, 1992. 16v. ISBN 1-85435-361-9.

The striking illustrations contribute to the effectiveness of this 16-volume work. The volumes are chronologically arranged and trace U.S. military history from the Revolutionary War to the Persian Gulf War in 1991. The text is authoritative in this set by Chant, who has produced several other works of military history. More than 1,500 illustrations from various media-photographs, engravings, contemporary paintings, maps, and drawings-adorn the set. Each volume has a bibliography and an index. Volume 16 contains an index for the entire set and a glossary. The bibliographies from the individual volumes are repeated in volume 16. This attractive work is an up-to-date military history of the United States that will be of use to students, scholars, and the general reader.

415. Oxford Companion to American Military History. John Whiteclay Chambers, ed. New York: Oxford University Press, 2000. 960p. ISBN 0-19-507198-0.

Ranging from brief pieces to extensive essays, the over 1,000 entries in *The Oxford Companion to American Military History* are written by more than 500 distinguished contributors. Major pieces are by such recognizable names such as James M. McPherson (Battle of Antietam), Stephen E. Ambrose (D-Day landing), Mark A. Noll (religion and war), and Jean Bethke Elshtain (Jane Addams) and David S. Wyman (Holocaust). The scope of coverage is every major war from the American Revolution to the Persian Gulf. The usual political and military people, places, battles, and weapons are included but other topics make the work broad ranging. War is viewed through the interdisciplinary fields of anthropology, economics, gender, and psychology as well as the cultural lenses of film, literature, music, and photography. Concepts, theories, and peace and antiwar movements are covered as well. Supplementary materials include a list of U.S. casualties for 12 major wars and a table of ranks and insignias for the U.S. armed forces. There are extensive cross-references, suggestions for further reading, and a detailed index.

416. Shield of the Republic, Sword of Empire: A Bibliography of United States Military Affairs, 1783–1846. John C. Fredriksen, comp. New York: Greenwood Press, 1990. (Bibliographies and Indexes in American History, no. 15). ISBN 0-313-25384-6.

Over 6,800 entries make up this specialized bibliography, including almost 2,000 citations to biographical materials. The majority of the sources cited are secondary sources, but the section on military campaigns lists a number of personal narratives. The bibliography includes books, articles from both scholarly and popular sources, dissertations, and state and local history publications. There are name and subject indexes as well as extensive cross-references. The bibliography is suitable for beginning research on the early development of the armed forces in the United States and U.S. military history from 1783 to 1846.

417. The U.S. Defense and Military Fact Book. C.W. Borklund. Santa Barbara, CA: ABC-CLIO, 1991. 293p. ISBN 0-87436-593-7.

This work is an account of the growth of the U.S. Department of Defense and the military establishment since the end of World War II. There is a chronology of events influencing the department and an appendix of documents relating to its organization. There are also lists of personnel, with brief biographies. The section on the defense budget goes into detail on the makeup of military spending and the congressional appropriations process. The growth of expenditures since 1945 is traced in budgetary and statistical tables. Some sources are not given nor cited exactly, but references to the U.S. Code—the official publication of public laws in force that incorporates amendments and deletes repealed portions of the law—are complete. There is a selective bibliography. This reference work is appropriate for students, business people, and researchers.

418. War and American Popular Culture: A Historical Encyclopedia. M. Paul Holsinger, ed. Westport, CT: Greenwood Press, 1999. 496p. ISBN 0-313-29908-0.

Although this work is principally about American popular culture it is arranged into 13 chapters according to periods of war experience. The first chapter is "Colonial American Wars, 1565–1765," and the last is "The United States Military since 1975." Each chapter has an essay about the time period followed by brief entries on popular songs, movies, television programs, best-sellers, and other phenomena of the period. The emphasis is on the latter half of the twentieth century and the author had to be selective in the items to be included. The national consciousness was necessarily consumed with WWII, but other conflicts occupied less of the public's attention. This work sets the context of ordinary life in the United States and complements those works of a strictly military nature. Historians of popular culture, students, and the general public will find it interesting work, especially good for trivia hunts.

419. Warbirds: An Illustrated Guide to U.S. Military Aircraft, 1915–2000. John C. Fredriksen. Santa Barbara, CA: ABC-CLIO, 1999. 363p. ISBN 1-57607-131-6.

Fredriksen is a recognized authority on the War of 1812 and is the author/compiler of several military reference works. This reference work is an introductory source to U.S. military aircraft from WWI to the latest planes in development at the end of the twentieth century. It includes all types of military aircraft, not just fighters and bombers, but helicopters, transports, trainers, flying boats, reconnaissance aircraft and several other lesser-known types deployed by military or naval units. The entries are arranged alphabetically by manufacturer and then by name of the craft. Information given includes a black-and-white photograph plus the physical dimensions, engines, performance, armament, service dates, and a brief narrative. The book includes two bibliographies. The first lists books and articles on specific aircraft and is arranged like the body of the work by manufacturer and aircraft. The second is a general military aircraft bibliography of three pages. The useful appendixes include a listing of aircraft by function, a chronological listing by historical period, a listing of U.S. and Canadian aircraft museums, and a listing of aircraft journals and magazines. The work is not indexed nor is it as comprehensive or detailed as the *Jane's* titles, but it is intended for a more general audience. Libraries that cannot afford the *Jane's* titles will find it to be a current source with adequate coverage of the subject.

420. Wars of the Americas: A Chronology of Armed Conflict in the New World, 1492 to the Present. David F. Marley. Santa Barbara, CA: ABC-CLIO, 1998. 722p. ISBN 0-87436-837-5.

The broad scope of this work makes it easy to place wars and events in the United States within the context of what was happening in the Western Hemisphere during the same time frame. The chronological listing of every war and conflict is arranged by time period and then geographic area. The text is informal in style and there are numerous maps and illustrations. Reviewers caution there are a few factual errors so the volume should be used along with more authoritative works. There is a bibliography of suggested readings and an index.

421. The West Point Atlas of American Wars. Vincent J. Esposito, ed. New York: Praeger, 1959. 2v. Rev. ed H. Holt, v. 1, 1995, v. 2, 1997.

The West Point atlas was prepared for military cadets to study the conduct of battles. It remains a standard reference source. The reissue in the 1990s contains a new foreword, slight revisions in text, and an updated bibliography. There are over 400, black-and-white maps with troop movements in red and blue for every campaign from the colonial era through the War of 1898. The two volumes are divided chronologically: volume 1, 1689–1900; volume 2, 1900–1953. The Civil War section of 137 maps has also been separately published (entry 468n). Although primarily an atlas of land operations, the book also includes naval battles. Not all battles are covered for every war. The atlas ends with the Korean conflict. This atlas remains one of the best available U.S. military atlases.

BIOGRAPHICAL SOURCES

422. American Military Leaders: from Colonial times to the Present. John C. Fredriksen. Santa Barbara, CA: ABC-CLIO, 1999. 2v. ISBN 1-57607-001-8.

Although it is written for high school students and undergraduates, a number of features make this work the best of the reference works on military biography. It includes biographies of over 400 persons who have played significant roles in American military history. The term "leader" is interpreted broadly and includes Native Americans, women, and civilian or political figures who had influence or connection with the military services. The work includes forgotten leaders as well as prominent men and women of the military and is especially strong on early American military leaders. The arrangement is alphabetical with each entry between one and two pages in length containing both birth and death dates with places. At the end of each entry is a current bibliography of books, articles, and theses. Many entries have small photographs. Both a subject index and a list of leaders organized by their military titles are included. Fredriksen has written numerous books on nineteenth-century American military history. (Entries 404, 416, 419, 422, and 457) This work updates the three-volume *Dictionary of American Military Biography* by Roger Spiller (Greenwood Press, 1984) and *Webster's American Military Biographies,* by Robert McHenry (Dover, 1984).

423. Fallen in Battle: American General Officer Combat Fatalities from 1775. Russell K. Brown. Westport, CT: Greenwood Press, 1988. 243p. ISBN 0-313-26242-X.

The criteria for inclusion in this biographical work make it very specialized. The 221 U.S. officers profiled held at death, previously held, or were posthumously awarded general or flag officer rank and died in combat or of wounds, were executed or died as prisoners of war, or became missing in action from the Revolutionary War through Vietnam. Officers of the Confederacy are included, along with an explanation of the criteria that determined officer ranks in the Confederacy. Almost three-fourths of the biographees died in the Civil War. Basic biographical facts about the officer are given, as well as a list of sources. Appendixes include lists of officers killed, wounded, or captured according to the war, branch of service, and battles. One appendix lists officers who were noncombat fatalities during wartime. The author combed biographical works; service, unit and campaign accounts; and other reference works to compile the biographies. Almost two-thirds of the officers are not found in the *Dictionary of American Biography* (entry 60). This work is useful to genealogists, students, and military historians.

424. How to Locate Anyone Who Is or Has Been in the Military: Armed Forces Locator Guide. 8th ed. Richard S. Johnson and Debra Johnson Knox. Spartanburg, SC: MIE Publishing, 1999. 299p. ISBN 1-877639-50-8.

The first edition of this work was published in 1988 and it has undergone considerable expansion since then. It has become the most well-known guide for locating persons who have at any time served in a military unit in the United States. It is not merely a listing of sources of information, but a guide to formulating appropriate search strategies, conducting searches, and utilizing the sources described. The eighth edition provides information on how to search for military personnel with attention to different categories such as women veterans who have changed their name, tracing service by members of families and other special cases. A number of the chapters are by service unit. In addition to the how to search information there are appendexes that provide listings of contact information for U.S. military bases worldwide as well as Navy ships. There are also listings of state veteran's offices, state reserve and National Guard headquarters, and veteran's associations. The work is a complete one-source reference for finding military personnel, past and present. It is used extensively by genealogists and is useful for students and researchers as well.

425. Medal of Honor Recipients 1863–1994. George Lang et al., comps. New York: Facts of File, 1995. 2v. ISBN 0-8160-3259-9.

Although there have been earlier compilations of Medal of Honor recipients, this two-volume work is the most current and contains information not found in the earlier works. In addition to name, rank, birth date, military unit, where honoree entered service, and the citation for the Medal of Honor, places of death and burial are also given. The over 3,400 entries are arranged chronologically and grouped by war or military operation ending in 1994. Indexes are provided by name, state of enlistment, and birth. The work is a handy one-volume reference on the subject.

426. They Also Served: Military Biographies of Uncommon Americans. Scott Baron. Spartanburg, SC: MIE Publishing, 1998. 333p. ISBN 1-877639-37-0.

The organization of this work is topical rather than alphabetical. There are capsule biographical sketches of over 500 Americans who served in the military. The entries are under 11 headings mostly according to occupation, but with a few other categories such as "idealists," and "notorious." This is a great trivia reference book that provides information not found in most scholarly references on the military.

BRANCHES OF THE ARMED FORCES

THE AIR FORCE

The Air Force is the youngest of the branches of the U.S. armed forces, having begun as a unit of the U.S. Army in 1907. It did not become a separate branch of the services until

1947. In 1954 the Air Force Historical Foundation (available at http://www.theaha.org/ affiliates/air_force_his1_found.htm) was founded for the purpose of preserving the history of the U.S. Air Force and other units or subjects connected with U.S. air power. The foundation has 5,000 members and publishes the quarterly *Air Power History,* which covers all aspects of aerospace history.

Since World War II, a number of organizations have formed based on specific fighter units of the Air Force and Army Air Corps. The 17th Bomb Group, the 43rd Bomb Group, the 401st and 494th Bombardment Groups, the 381st Bomb Group, and the 304th and 369th Fighter Squadrons have associations for veterans. Many of these groups maintain memorials and biographical archives and promote research in the history of the unit and military history.

Many illustrated volumes on aircraft have been published, but such works are not listed in this reference guide. The subject of space exploration is also not covered. The Air Force History Support Office in Washington (available at http://www.airforcehistory.hq. af.mil) has published a number of reference works for the study of Air Force history and one has been listed (entry 429).

427. Historical Dictionary of the U.S. Air Force. Charles D. Bright, ed. New York: Greenwood Press, 1992. 768p. ISBN 0-313-25928-3.

The comprehensiveness and inclusiveness of this one-volume reference work make it suitable for users at all levels. There are over 1,000 entries for persons, events, terms, and concepts, all relating to the U.S. Air Force. Included are acronyms, battles, campaigns, air bases, equipment, famous units, movies and television shows, slang, and songs. Although many popular subjects are included, the work is authoritative. The time span ranges from the beginnings of aviation in 1907 to Operation Desert Storm. Entries range in length from short definitions to longer signed articles with references to other sources of information. There are numerous cross-references, including asterisks within articles marking terms that have a separate entry. This work is a current source for all inquirers seeking information about the U.S. Air Force.

428. Historical Dictionary of the United States Air Force and Its Antecedents. Michael Robert Terry. Lanham, MD: Scarecrow, 1999. 460p. (Historical Dictionaries of War, Revolution, and Civil Unrest, no. 11). ISBN 0-8108-3631-9.

In addition to the entries in the dictionary portion of this work, there is a chronology, which begins with the Wright first flight in 1903 and ends with Kosovo in 1998. The 22-page introduction gives a history of the Air Force from 1914 to the present. The entries encompass every aircraft used in combat operations and all major officers. There is an extensive bibliography and 10 appendixes, 5 of which identify aces of the air wars. The work is useful as a quick reference or for historical research.

The United States Air Force: A Dictionary edited by Charles Bright (Greenwood Press, 1992) is a more limited work concentrating on terminology from World War II to 1992. More of a true dictionary, it attempts to discuss the major Air Force terms currently in use. There are over 1,000 entries for person, events, terms, and concepts, all relating to the U.S. Air Force. The provision of sources is one of the most useful features of the work. Sources for the definitions of the terms are overwhelmingly from U.S. Air Force or Department of Defense publications.

429. United States Air Force History: A Guide to Documentary Sources. Lawrence J. Paszek, comp. Washington, D.C.: Office of Air Force History, 1986. 245p. S/N 0870-00322.

Over 700 collections that have documents relating to the Air Force and historical material on aviation as far back as the use of balloons in the Civil War are described in this research guide. The organization is in five sections, divided according to type of repository. The first section lists Air Force official depositories. The second section describes the collections of the National Archives, presidential libraries, and federal records centers. Academic library collections occupy the third section. The Library of Congress, other federal and local government depositories, and historical societies are the subject of the fourth section. The last section describes other collections that have primary or secondary materials relating to the development of aviation in general. There is a general index and an index by name of depository. This guide is useful for historians and researchers interested in aviation history and the history of the U.S. Air Force.

THE ARMY

The Army (Web site available at http://www.army.mil) is the oldest branch of the U.S. armed services, dating back to June 14, 1775, when the Continental Congress created the Continental Army. A number of U.S. presidents served in the Army, including its first commander, George Washington; Ulysses S. Grant; and Dwight D. Eisenhower. The history of the U.S. Army is also one of technological evolution, from muskets to missiles with telegraph, radio, and satellite communications. There are numerous associations of Army infantry and other units. The majority of these are veterans organizations formed to honor those who fought with distinction in the world wars. A few of the associations do maintain museums or libraries.

Because of the Army's long history, there have been a number of reference works compiled on some aspect of it, although there have not been many new works in recent years. A few of the most useful reference works on the U.S. Army are listed in this section.

430. Encyclopedia of United States Army Insignia and Uniforms. William K. Emerson. Norman, OK: University of Oklahoma Press, 1996. 674p. ISBN 0-8061-2622-1.

This is a definitive work encompassing U.S. Army uniforms and insignia from 1782 to the present in detailed text with 2,000 black-and-white photographs. A third of the book is devoted to uniforms and two-thirds to insignia. All branches of the Army are covered including support branches of chaplins, medical personnel, musicians, foreign units, Indian scouts, and more. Men's and women's uniforms and insignia are covered thoroughly. Illustrations are placed alongside the text for ease of identification. The work provides a comprehensive history of the development of uniforms and insignia in the U.S. Army. There is an index with *see* and *see also* references. There is also a bibliography that lists books, government documents, periodicals, and catalogs. This well-documented work will be of use to researchers, history buffs, genealogists, collectors, curators, and costume specialists.

Two more specialized works have been produced by Barry Jason Stein and published by the University of South Carolina Press. *U. S. Army Heraldic Crests: A Complete Illustrated History of Authorized Distinctive Unit Insignia* (1993) and *U.S. Army Patches: An Illustrated Encyclopedia of Cloth Unit Insignia* (1997). The first title identifies more than 3,100 heraldic crests. For each crest the unit, the date adopted, the motto, and a summary of unit action are included. There are 129 color plates with small reproductions of the crests. The second title depicts more than 1,800 patches from World War I to the present in full color. Information on the army units includes its origins, current status, decorations, battle campaigns, and the historical and heraldic significance of the patch(es). There are a glossary of terms, a brief bibliography and an index. Both works are prepared to high standards and are definitive for the subject.

431. The Late 19th Century U.S. Army, 1865–1898: A Research Guide. Joseph G. Dawson, III. Westport, CT: Greenwood Press, 1990. 252p. (Research Guides in Military Studies, no. 3). ISBN 0-313-26146-6.

The period covered in this research guide is that of the Old West and the Indian wars, a time span in which there were no major foreign conflicts. An excellent overview of the time period and the state of the Army introduces the guide. The first chapter describes manuscript collections, government documents, and the personal papers of such major military figures of the period as Ulysses S. Grant, William Tecumseh Sherman, and George Custer. The second chapter covers the reference literature. The ensuing chapters cover the phases of the Army and reconstruction, the Indian-fighting Army, and the Army in the late nineteenth century. Another chapter lists personal accounts of officers, wives, and others connected with Army life. Other chapters cover post life, coastal defense, and fictional depictions. Each chapter has an introductory bibliographical essay. The research guide is an excellent survey of the sources available for research on this period in the history of the U.S. Army. It is useful for students, researchers, and members of the general public interested in the Old West and U.S. Army history.

432. On the Trail of the Buffalo Soldier: Biographies of African Americans in the U.S. Army, 1866–1917. Frank N. Schubert, comp. Wilmington, Del.: Scholarly Resources, 1995. 519p. ISBN 0-8420-2482-4.

The scope of this work is the 50 years between the end of the Civil War and the beginnings of World War I. Thus, it does not cover one of the major wars in American history, but may be more valuable because it covers an interim period. The nickname, "Buffalo Soldier," refers to African American troops fighting in the conflicts with Native Americans in the West. The basic biographical information for almost 8,000 individuals is given on each person, birthplace, rank and unit, and their service history. For those individuals with more information available, their circumstances prior to emancipation and family information are included. Sources of the information are given in most entries. The bibliography includes a wide range of materials: books, articles, newspapers, archival collections and manuscripts, military and Veterans Administration records. Appendixes give data on the number of black men enlisted in the army, dates of service of sergeants major of the black cavalry regiments, soldiers killed in action, recipients of the medal of Honor, and dates and locations of the various regimental headquarters. This unique work is of use to genealogists, historians, and students.

433. The Peacetime Army, 1900–1941: A Research Guide. Marvin Fletcher. Westport, CT: Greenwood Press, 1988. 177p. (Research Guides in Military Studies, no. 1). ISBN 0-313-25987-9.

The emphasis in this guide is on the development of the U.S. Army during the first part of the century preceding World War II. Because the focus is on peacetime changes, no references are included for the wars occurring during the time span covered, the Spanish-American War and World War I. The annotated references are to articles, books, and dissertations written since the end of World War II. The bibliography is divided into two time periods, before and after World War I. The chapters are topically subdivided into sections such as biography, management, technology, strategy, and political and social issues. There is an introductory essay and a chronology. Research ideas and an author/subject index are also provided. This work is an excellent introduction to sources and research in the history of the U.S. Army in the years before World War II.

434. U.S. Army Center of Military History. Available: http://www.army.mil/cmh-pg/.

The Center of Military History, headquartered in Washington, D.C., is responsible for "the appropriate use of History throughout the U.S. Army." The site contains an extensive range of material including changing exhibits. Some topics have been "Native Americans in the U.S. Army," "Remembering Desert Shield/Desert Storm 10 Years later," and "Remembering the Korean War." There is helpful information for researching service records and unit histories. There is a chronologically arranged list of Medal of Honor recipients from all services with the history of the medal and a list of Black World War II recipients. Of recent interest is a bibliography on Afghanistan with primary and secondary resources including online publications and Web sites as well as print materials. The site is extensive and anyone researching U.S. military history should visit.

Another U.S. Army history site is maintained at the US Army Military History Institute at Carlisle Barracks, Pennsylvania. The Web site provides access to the electronic catalog, reference bibliographies, unit history bibliographies, Civil War biographical bibliographies, and more. There are a number of digitized historical materials on the site, but it mainly provides information on the extensive collections available for use on site. The online finding aids are continually being added to. *A Guide to the Study and Use of Military History* by John E. Jessup, Jr. and Robert W. Coakley was published by the Center of Military History (1979). This bibliography is based on the extensive holdings of the U.S. Military Institute Library. The first section of the work is a general one on military history and sources. The major portion of the work is part II, which contains seven bibliographical essays on U.S. military history by period from 1607 to the early 1970s. The remaining two sections are devoted to the U.S. Army. The work is indexed. Anyone researching U.S. military history should not overlook the fine collections at the US Army Military History Institute (available at http://carlisle-www.army.mil/usamhi/).

THE MARINES

The U.S. Marine Corps (Web sites available at http://www.marines.com and http://www.usmc.mil) grew out of two sharpshooter battalions in 1775 into the branch of the armed services that specializes in amphibious assault operations. The Marine Corps has an especially proud history, but an organization devoted to the Corps was not founded until relatively recently, in 1979. The Marine Corps Historical Foundation, now called the Marine Corps Heritage Foundation (available at http://www.marineheritage.org), has a membership of 2,000 individuals and institutions. The foundation promotes the study and preservation of the history and traditions of the U.S. Marine Corps. It supports a museum; sponsors fellowships for thesis and dissertation work and a research grant fund; and underwrites publications and displays of manuscripts and artifacts focusing on the history of the Marine Corps.

Other organizations related to the Marine Corps for veterans and families are the 1st Marine Division Association; Loyal Escorts of the Green Garter (available at http://www. womenmarines.org/auxiliary.htm); Marine Corps League Auxiliary (available at http:// www.pos.net/Marine/Auxiliary.html); Military Order Devil Dog Fleas (available at http:// www.pos.net/Marine/DevilDogs.html); Devil Pups; the Second Marine Division Association (available at http://www.independentproject.com/SMDA); and the Women Marines Association (available at http://www.womenmarines.org).

There have been few reference works specifically focused on the Marine Corps.

435. An Annotated Bibliography of U.S. Marine Corps History. Paolo E. Coletta. Lanham, MD: University Press of America, 1986. 417p. ISBN 0-8191-5218-8.

The 4,000-plus entries in this bibliography make it a major source for materials on the history of the U.S. Marine Corps. The annotated entries include books, articles, documents, dissertations and theses, and films. Fictional works are included, as well as informational materials. The bibliography is divided by historical period and subdivided by format. In addition there is a subject section covering aviation, education, logistics, music, uniforms, women Marines, and division histories. There is a list of the personal papers of over 1,000 individuals that are deposited at the History and Museums Division at Marine Corps Headquarters in Washington, D.C. An unusual feature is the inclusion of classification numbers for the Marine Corps Historical Center Library. There is an author/subject index to the volume. This bibliography is of use to anyone beginning to search for information on the history of the U.S. Marine Corps.

An earlier, similar bibliography is *Creating a Legend: The Complete Record of the United States Marine Corps,* compiled and self-published by a former Marine officer, John B. Moran (Moran/Andrews, 1973). The work lists all Marine Corps publications and a selection of articles from Marine Corps periodicals. The compiler endeavored to produce a comprehensive bibliography on the Marine Corps and uncritically included fiction, films, plays, and songs as well as standard book and periodical sources. The organization is by subject and title, with an author index. The bibliography may not be on hand in many libraries, but where available it can be used in conjunction with other bibliographies such as the entry above.

THE NAVY

Interest has always been high in the history of naval warfare. The Naval Historical Foundation (available at http://www.mil.org/navyhist/) was founded in 1926. It is open to members of the U.S. Navy, Marine Corps, and Coast Guard, and to civilians interested in U.S. naval history. The foundation has over 1,000 members. It maintains a library and has placed an extensive manuscript collection on deposit with the Library of Congress. It publishes *Pull Together,* a semiannual newsletter; the *Naval Historical Foundation Manuscript Collection Catalog;* and occasional monographs.

There are many other organizations focused on the history of the U.S. naval forces, including those for specific units or vessels. A few of the more general organizations are the United States Navy Memorial Foundation (available at http://www.lonesailor.org), the American Battleship Association (PO Box 711247, San Diego, CA 92171, (619) 271-6106), the Naval Order of the United States (4404 Anderson Ave., Oakland, CA 94619, (510) 531-6797), the Tin Can Sailors (available at http://www.destroyers.org), and the Waves National (available at http://www.onceawave.org).

The literature of naval warfare and the history of naval vessels are extensive. This reference guide does not attempt to cover the many popular and technical publications on naval vessels and aircraft. Only those reference works dealing with the history of the U.S. Navy are included.

The U.S. Navy (Web site available at http://www.navy.mil) is the only branch of the armed forces that has its own press, publishing high-quality research and reference works. Trade publishers have also recently produced a number of reference works pertaining to the history of U.S. naval forces.

436. American Naval History: An Illustrated Chronology of the U.S. Navy and Marine Corps, 1775–Present. 2nd ed. Jack Sweetman. Naval Institute Press, 1991. 376p. ISBN 1-55750-785-6.

The entries in this illustrated chronology include battles, explorations, personnel, ships, technological developments, and events that influenced the development of the Navy in some way. The entries have very brief commentaries that explain the significance or consequences of events. This edition updates the 1984 work and includes the recent naval operations in the Persian Gulf War. Maps and a bibliography are included at the end. There is an index by vessel; a general index of persons, events, and subjects; and a calendar index for each day of the year. The illustrations make the work very attractive. This resource will be useful to any inquirer seeking an overview of naval history and specific facts about the U.S. Navy and Marine Corps.

437. Battleships: United States Battleships, 1935–1992. Rev. ed. William H. Garzke, Jr. and Robert O. Dulin, Jr. Annapolis, MD: Naval Institute Press, 1995. 386p. ISBN 1-55750-174-2.

The revised edition of the first edition published in 1976 brings the coverage up through 1992. Thus the work is both historical and a reference for vessels still in service. The revision includes not just updated material, but also revision and updating of the first edition. Of historical significance is a new appendix, which discusses the role of President Franklin D. Roosevelt in battleship design and construction. The work covers the technical physical characteristics of the ships as well as the design, development, and operational history. There are ample illustrations and photographs. In all, this is a comprehensive reference work on the fast battleships, those built since 1935. A similar work more limited in coverage is Norman Friedman's *U.S. Battleships: An Illustrated Design History* (Naval Institute Press, 1985). Both works are suitable for researchers as well as the general reader.

***438. Dictionary of American Naval Fighting Ships.** Washington, D.C.: U.S. Department of the Navy. Naval Historical Center, 1959–1991. 9v. S/N 008-046-00101-4.

Naval vessels in both the Continental and the U.S. Navy are listed in this alphabetical reference work. Information on the ships includes service history, statistical description, and a discussion of the role and missions of the ship. The work is especially valuable because of the information on minor vessels, which is not to be found in most reference sources. Besides an alphabetical listing of the ships, each volume contains appendexes and statistical tables. Chronological listings by type of vessel begin in volume 1 and continue throughout the eight volumes. Volume 2 includes Confederate vessels. New ships and aircraft are in volume 5. There is a wealth of information on naval vessels in this comprehensive set, which will be useful for anyone seeking a description of a specific vessel or an historic overview of the naval fleet.

The DANFS is now online (available at http://www.uss-salem.org/danfs/). The files are transcribed from the printed work without updating or corrections.

439. Historical Dictionary of the United States Marine Corps. Harry A. Gailey. Lanham, MD: Scarecrow, 1998. 253p. (Historical Dictionaries of Wars, Revolution, and Civil Unrest, no. 5). ISBN 0-8108-3401-4.

The arrangement in this work is alphabetical with a "Chronology section" and a section on "Abbreviations and Acronyms." The scope of the work is the Marine Corps from its beginnings as the Continental Marines during the American Revolution up through the Gulf War to its 1994 mission in Haiti. Individuals, weaponry, wars and conflicts are included in the dictionary. There are six black-and-white maps and a bibliography. It is useful as a background work or quick reference, but researchers may want to verify the information.

440. Historical Dictionary of the United States Navy. James M. Morris and Patricia M. Kearns. Lanham, MD: Scarecrow, 1998. 405p. (Historical Dictionaries of War, Revolution, and Civil Unrest, no. 4). ISBN 0-8108-3406-5.

The majority of the entries in this work are brief. Included are ship type designations, major ship types by class, every type of airplane and airship, weapons used by the Navy from its beginnings to the present, every secretary of the Navy, other persons who played important roles, and significant battles and conflicts in which the Navy took part. Front matter includes lists of acronyms and abbreviations, ship type designations, and a chronology from 1775 to 1997. There is an unannotated bibliography at the end arranged by subject and time period. This is a useful work for students and quick reference, compiled by a historian and a librarian, but researchers may want to verify the ship information.

A fuller biographical treatment is given in *American Secretaries of the Navy* (Naval Institute Press, 1980. 2v.) The chapters in this work are all written by naval historians and contain references to sources. The lives and influence of 60 secretaries of the Navy are covered, beginning with the first-ever secretary of the Navy (appointed by President Adams) and continuing up to the term of President Nixon. Portraits are included along with biographical information. The sketches cover the abilities of each secretary, his influence upon the administration in which he served, and the impact his programs and policies had upon the navy. The biographies are arranged chronologically in the two volumes; the second volume begins with World War I. An introduction describes the role of the office within the executive branch. This is a useful reference work for those seeking biographical information on secretaries of the Navy or a historical overview of the office.

441. The Naval Institute Guide to the Ships and Aircraft of the U.S. Fleet. 17th ed. Norman Polmar. Annapolis, MD: Naval Institute Press, 2001. 657p. ISBN 1-55750-656-6.

Although this work deals with the current state of the U.S. Fleet, it is the 17th edition in a long line of such works dating back to 1939 begun by James C. Fahey. This entry is viewed as the most current in a long running series. The latest edition contains historical background leading up to current naval conditions. The emphasis is naturally on current information and the work contains the latest technical data on the U.S. Navy's current ship aircraft, missile, and electronics programs. The earlier editions of this work will be of interest to those researching the U.S. Naval Fleet, providing a contemporary point of view on the state of the Fleet.

442. The Naval Institute Historical Atlas of the U.S. Navy. Craig L. Symonds. Annapolis, MD: Naval Institute Press, 1995. 241p. ISBN 1-55750-797-X.

Two hundred years of U.S. naval history are documented through 94 maps arranged into 10 chronological sections from the American Revolution to "The Pax Americana, 1980–1994." The maps show deployment of ships and their tracks. In addition to the maps or charts, each section begins with a historical essay on the period. The volume has an index and an epilogue on the U.S. Navy in the twenty-first century. This is a fine resource to use in conjunction with narrative histories.

A full treatment of the major battles making an excellent companion to the atlas is *Great American Naval Battles* (Naval Institute, 1998), edited by Jack Sweetman. Noted naval historians have written the chapters on each battle. Schematic outlines of each battle as well as tables of naval units and armaments for the antagonists are included for every conflict from the American Revolution to the Gulf War.

A more specialized work is *Civil and Merchant Vessel Encounters with United States Navy Ships, 1800–2000* (McFarland, 2002). The work is authored by Greg H. Williams with a foreword by Channing M. Zucker, Captain, U.S. Navy (Ret.). Contacts or incidents occurring between nearly 1,000 United States Navy ships and nearly 900 merchant vessels, yachts, workboats, and other craft during peacetime and wartime throughout the history of the Navy are the subject of this reference work. The disposition of disputes and official reports are included in the information on the contacts.

443. A Selective and Annotated Bibliography of American Naval History. Rev. ed. Paolo E. Coletta. Landham, MD: University Press of America, 1988. 523p. ISBN 0-8181-7111-5.

This is an update of a bibliography by the same author published by the Naval Institute Press in 1981. The first title, *A Bibliography of American Naval History,* listed over 4,800 sources, with very brief imprint information and short opinion phrases rather than full annotations. The revised edition updates the first bibliography up to 1987. The arrangement for both bibliographies is chronological by historical period beginning in 1689 and ending with the present. Sources include books, both fiction and nonfiction, articles, dissertations and theses, and government documents. A useful feature is that oral histories are also listed. The U.S. Marine Corps, Coast Guard, and other subjects as related to the U.S. Navy are also included. There are author and subject indexes; the latter includes biographies. These two bibliographies are adequate for students but not for serious research.

SPECIAL FORCES AND OTHER SERVICE BRANCHES

444. Special Operations and Elite Units, 1939–1988: A Research Guide. Roger Beaumont. Westport, CT: Greenwood Press, 1988. 258p. ISBN 0-313-26001-X.

The preface to this work reveals the compiler's personal interest in the subject of special forces. A substantial introduction traces and describes the use of special forces and units in wars and intelligence operations since 1939. The annotated bibliography is divided into 10 topical sections arranged by author. The sources cited include popular and scholarly books and periodical articles as well as military field manuals and reports. Four appendixes list current elite units, elite forces since 1939, counter-terrorist operations since World War II, and principal airborne combat operations. There are separate indexes by author, title, and subject. This bibliography is unique among military reference works and will be of general interest as well as research use in military history and foreign affairs.

THE WARS

This section of the reference guide is organized chronologically. Most information resources for a particular historical period are included in the "Chronologies and Eras" section of the *Guide* in chapter 1. Sources that pertain to wartime periods are included in this section.

The number of reference works on each war varies, as would be expected, according to the magnitude of the conflict in the history of the United States. There has been a number of new reference tools published in recent years dealing with specific wars. A few older, classic reference works are also included when they are still the most useful works for research.

PRE-REVOLUTIONARY

445. Colonial Wars of North America, 1512–1763: An Encyclopedia. Alan Gallay, ed. New York: Garland, 1996. 856p. ISBN 0-8240-7208-1.

The term "colonial" is defined to include all of the territories that subsequently became part of the United States, including Alaska and the Caribbean. During the time period covered by this reference work, these geographic areas underwent numerous changes in government as wars and treaties among the European powers swapped territory. Both the military and the diplomatic aspects of the period are considered. The beginning date is the discovery by Juan Ponce de Leon of Florida and the ending point is the French and Indian War. The signed entries are contributed by historians from several countries. The work contains much little-known information and is a contribution to the history of the period covered. The 700 cross-referenced entries, including approximately 150 biographical sketches, vary in length. In addition to entries for wars, battles, treaties, forts, and geopolitically significant locales, analytical essays explore the diplomatic and military history of some 50 Native American groups, as well as Dutch, English, French, Spanish, and Swiss colonies. There are black-and-white illustrations, maps, battle plans, a chronology, and a very detailed index. This is an excellent reference work for the general reader, students, and researchers.

Colonial America is a five-volume set in the middle school reference series U*X*L by Gale Group (2000). Its coverage and scope are similar to *Colonial Wars of North Amer-*

ica. The first two volumes are the *Almanac,* spanning 1565–1760, which contains chapters on such topics as Native Americans, Spanish exploration, and social and political issues and daily life in the colonies. There are two biography volumes. The final volume is *Primary Sources,* which contains contemporary documents. The reference set is designed to draw students into further research.

REVOLUTIONARY WAR (1775–1783)

The Revolutionary War has quite naturally been the focus of much historical research. The Revolutionary period was the founding period of the country, when the American colonists fought to break away from England and, having been successful, formulated a new system of government. The major historical societies focused on the Revolutionary period are those for descendants of the original colonists or those who fought in the War of Independence. These include the Daughters of the American Revolution (available at http://www.dar.org), the Sons of the American Revolution (available at www.sar.org), the Society of Loyalist Descendants (PO Box 848, Rockingham, NC 28380, (910) 997-6641), the Society of the Descendants of Washington's Army (PO Box 915, Valley Forge, PA 19482, (610) 647-5532), and the Black Revolutionary War Patriots Foundation (available at http://www.blackpatriots.org). Many of these organizations sponsor high school essay contests, scholarships and publications; raise funds for memorials and the preservation of historic sites; maintain historical/genealogical libraries; and sponsor activities to foster patriotism in U.S. society.

The bicentennial of the United States, celebrated in 1976, was the impetus for many historical publications and reference works. Interest in the Revolutionary period has tapered off somewhat since then, but new reference materials have been published in the years since the bicentennial. Those of most significance for historical research are described in this section.

446. The American Revolution 1775–1783: An Encyclopedia. Richard L. Blanco, ed. Hamden, CT: Garland, 1993. 2v. (Military History of the United States, v. 1; Garland Reference Library of the Humanities, v. 933.) ISBN 0-8240-5623-X.

The emphasis in this work is on the military aspects of the American Revolution. The format is a series of essays of varying length, written by over 130 contributors who provide a thorough overview of the war. The essays do include some information on political, social, and cultural topics. In that vein, efforts were made to include the role and contributions of Native Americans, women, and African Americans. Very detailed information is provided on battles, weaponry, ships, and the specifics of war. A chronology and maps are included. The index is not comprehensive. This two-volume work is more valuable for information on the military aspects of war and as background reading for research. It is not suitable as a general reference source.

447. The American Revolution in the Southern Colonies. David Lee Russell. Jefferson, NC: McFarland, 2000. 367p. ISBN 0-7864-0783-2.

The five southern colonies of Maryland, Virginia, North Carolina, South Carolina and Georgia are the focus of this work. While the most well-known battles were fought in the northern colonies, the southern colonies played a critical role in the war and the shaping of the new country. The work includes an essay on the origins of the five colonies beginning with the English settlers in 1585 and including the introduction of slavery into the colonies. The number of slaves, conditions, runaways, and the theft of slaves by the British are discussed. The main focus is on the period 1763–1783. The important battles in the South are covered along with the broader implications as they influenced the overall efforts of the revolutionaries. The volume contains reproductions of historical maps and biographical sketches of the principal leaders in the Revolution. There is a bibliography and a detailed index. This is a scholarly treatment of the topic more than a reference work.

448. American Revolutionary War Sites, Memorials, Museums, and Library Collections: A State-by-State Guidebook to Places Open to the Public. Doug Gelbert. Jefferson, NC: McFarland, 1998. 255p. ISBN 0-7864-0494-9.

The main advantage of this guide is that it includes libraries and museums along with historical sites. There are many tourist guides to historical sites, but finding all of these venues in one guide is unusual. There are a number of older guides that are still useful in terms of the locations, but this guide contains updated information. It does not entirely replace the Boatner *Landmarks of the American Revolution,* which was issued for the Bicentennial in 1976, as the older guide contains information not found in this one. *American Revolutionary War Sites* is more suited to general audiences.

449. The Blackwell Encyclopedia of the American Revolution. Jack P. Greene and J.R. Pole, eds. Cambridge, MA: Basil Blackwell, 1991. 845p. ISBN 1-55786-244-3.

Ninety-six scholars from the United States and Europe contributed to this authoritative encyclopedia reflecting recent scholarly thinking on the Revolutionary period. The major part of the work is 75 signed, thematic essays covering the military, political, social, economic, and religious underpinnings of the American Revolution. The first nine essays examine such aspects of colonial history as the family, population, and cultural development; the next 17 follow events leading up to the war; the following 20 focus on events after 1776. The last 12 essays deal with concepts such as equality, sovereignty, suffrage, and nationalism. Following the essays is a section of signed biographical sketches of major participants and lesser-known figures, including a number of women. The last section is a chronology from 1688 to 1790. There is an index to the essay and biography sections that allows use of the volume for reference queries. The essay format of this encyclopedia presents a coherent view of the entire Revolutionary period. It is one of the best sources for high school and university students and has much to offer for researchers also.

A number of reference works have been published specifically for middle and high school students in American history, civics, and political science classes. Another in the U*X*L reference series by Gale Group (2000) designed for middle school students, The *American Revolution* set is four volumes following the format for the series with an *Almanac,* two volumes of *Biographies* and a volume of *Primary Sources.* The first volume gives information about the colonies, daily life during colonial times, and the political situation. Preliminary material in each chapter includes a timeline and a glossary of terms. Each chapter has a bibliography including Web sources. The *Biographies* contain information on many unknown figures of the period. The *Primary Sources* include letters and speeches as well as the major historical documents of the time. The set is well illustrated and attractive. A separately published cumulative index is available free.

The Revolutionary War by James R. Arnold and Roberta Wiener (Grolier, 2002) had been produced for young people. The contents of the 10 slim volumes are arranged chronologically and cover causes, important strategies and battles, political disagreements and foreign relations, and the struggle to construct a new country after the war. The work is heavily illustrated. Each volume contains the index to the set, a glossary, and a list of additional resources including Web sites.

450. Encyclopedia of Colonial and Revolutionary America. John Mack Faragher, ed. New York: Facts on File, 1989. 484p. ISBN 0-8160-1744-1.

This one-volume encyclopedia covers the time period from the colonial period up to 1785. The work is strong on economic, political, and social history rather than emphasizing the military aspects of the Revolution. Thus it has numerous entries on people, ethnic and gender groups, religious themes, geography and culture. In addition to the alphabetical entries there are 16 topic guides covering such subjects as agriculture, colonial government, Spanish colonies, and women. There are illustrations and maps, cross-references, and brief bibliographies. This encyclopedia is an ideal introduction to themes for further research and provides a balance to many reference works that deal with the period and emphasize the military.

Revolutionary America, 1763–1800 by Thomas L. Purvis (Facts on File, 1995) makes an excellent factual companion to the *Encyclopedia*. It is an almanac with broad scope covering a wealth of nonmilitary topics such as climate, banking and finance, property holdings, literacy rates, and crime and violence. The contents include biographies and statistical data drawn from a wide range of government and scholarly publications. There are also lists of city, state, and federal officeholders. This one-volume work gathers together information scattered over a wide range of sources and makes an excellent quick reference work.

A more recent addition to the Facts on File offerings is *The American Revolution: An Eyewitness History* by David F. Burg (2001). The Revolutionary era is covered in nine chapters, each with a historical overview, a chronology of events, followed by excerpts from published eyewitness accounts. A citation is given for each excerpt, but there is no explanatory text. There is an index, a brief bibliography, and three appendixes with documents, short biographies of major figures and eight maps. It is best used in conjunction with the other two Facts on File titles for a more complete picture of the era.

451. Guide to the Sol Feinstone Collection of the David Library of the American Revolution. David J. Fowler. Washington Crossing, PA: David Library of the American Revolution, 1994. 515p. ISBN 0-9643693-0-3.

The David Library of the American Revolution, located in Washington Crossing, Pennsylvania, is part of a foundation endowed by Sol Feinstone. The foundation is a leading research center for the study of the Revolutionary era. Feinstone, a businessman and philanthropist, built the collection over a span of 50 years. The guide to the collection is thorough and detailed with nearly 2,500 numbered entries for every document in the collection, giving writers, date written, location written, recipient's name, the number of pages, and an abstract and subject headings. The item numbers correspond to the organization of microfilm of the original documents in the collection. There is a chronological arrangement of the item numbers in an appendix. The guide includes notes on Feinstone's life in Lithuania and the United States. There is a thorough subject index. The guide is useful for all researchers of the period.

452. The Historical Atlas of the American Revolution. Ian Barnes and Charles Royster, eds. New York: Routledge, 2000. 208p. ISBN 0-4159-2243-7.

More than just an atlas, the scope of this work is much broader, covering political, social, and religious factors of the period. The time frame covered is from colonial settlement until 1820, the founding period of the United States. Each chapter contains an overview, followed by two-page spreads on land and sea battles. There are also portraits and other illustrations. A concluding section contains biographical sketches. The political dimensions of the Revolutionary War abroad in the British Empire and Europe receive attention as well as immigrants, the slave trade, and relations with Native Americans. The aftermath of the American Revolution is also represented and includes the subsequent Anglo-American conflict in the War of 1812. The atlas is attractive and of high quality with many color-plates. The compiler was assisted by Charles Royster, a leading historian of the eighteenth and nineteenth centuries. Two earlier atlases—Nebenzahl (Rand McNally, 1974) and Symonds (below) published at the time of the Bicentennial, are not superceded by this one. *The Historical Atlas of the American Revolution* is an excellent, modern reference source.

A Battlefield Atlas of the American Revolution, by Craig L. Symonds (Nautical & Aviation Publishing, 1986) is a longtime standard. If the researcher is seeking illustrations of troop movements, this atlas is the best reference to consult. The major battles of the American Revolution are analyzed, with symbols delineating the action. There are 41 black-and-white maps, with forces depicted in two shades of blue and movements shown by dotted lines. The maps are divided chronologically into four sections, each beginning with an overview: "Early Campaigns," "1777: The Turning Point," "A Global War," and "The War Moves South." Each map has explanatory text on a facing page. There is no index, but references for suggested reading are included with each map. The atlas clearly sets forth the military dimensions of the American Revolution. It is useful for students and all but the most specialized researcher.

453. Historical Dictionary of the American Revolution. Terry M. Mays. Lanham, MD: Scarecrow, 1999. 555p. (Historical Dictionaries of Wars, Revolutions, and Civil Unrest, no. 7). ISBN 0-8108-3404-9.

The title of this work aptly describes the format. There are over 1,000 brief entries covering the Revolutionary period from 1765 to 1783. The arrangement is alphabetical, with a general introduction, a chronology, and an appendix containing six documents. There is a lengthy bibliography. There are numerous cross-references but no index to the volume. Although social and political issues, people, and countries are covered, the emphasis is on the military aspects of the Revolution. The work is suitable for quick reference, but not in-depth research.

454. Uniforms of the American Revolution, in Color. John Mollo. New York: Macmillan, 1975. Reprint, New York: Sterling, 1991. 228p. ISBN 0-8069-8240-3.

Uniforms and equipment for the major armies—the American, French, and British—as well as other groups—Loyalists, Indians, and German troops—are depicted in this small volume. There are 334 numbered plates, followed by a section of text arranged primarily by campaigns describing the military action and the uniforms and equipment from the plates. There is an introduction for each of the major armies. Mollo engaged in considerable archival research to present a wider range of reconstructed uniforms than has any previous work on the subject. A bibliography of sources completes the volume. There is no index. This work is of interest to students, military historians, enactors, and others seeking information on military dress and equipment during the Revolutionary War.

455. Who Was Who in the American Revolution. Edward Purcell. New York: Facts on File, 1998. 548p. ISBN 0-8160-2107-4.

Biographical information on more than 1,500 men and women who played a major or supporting role in the American Revolution including French allies, British military and government officeholders, diplomats, politicians, and citizens from both sides are all included in this reference work. There is an introduction providing an overview of the period. The alphabetically arranged entries include birth and death dates and all pertinent biographical information. Many entries include a brief bibliography and cross-references. The major figures are, of course, covered in the *DAB* and other standard biographical works, but the information on minor figures is particularly useful. The work is illustrated with 200 line drawings and there is a brief index.

A more specialized work is *Naval Officers of the American Revolution: A Concise Biographical Dictionary* by Charles E. Claghorn (Scarecrow, 1988). The information in this dictionary is gleaned from a variety of published sources and state and federal records. The names of 3,500 U.S. and French naval officers and privateers are listed. Other data are given when found, such as date and place of birth, commissioning, the ships served aboard, battles, and captures and rescues participated in. Date of death is not included unless death was military-related. This work brings information from a variety of sources together and indicates the sources along with the biographical data. It is useful for researchers, genealogists, and others pursuing such information.

WAR OF 1812 (1812–1814)

Although it is not regarded as a war of major proportions in the scheme of U.S. history, the War of 1812 has at least three patriotic societies that still perpetuate the memory of those who served in the conflict. The General Society of the War of 1812 (c/o Forrest R. Schaeffer, Box 106, Mendenhall, PA 19357, (610) 444-8492) is for male descendants of the veterans; the National Society, United States Daughters of 1812 (1461 Rhode Island Ave. NW, Washington, DC 20005-5402, (202)745-1812, (305) 251-6532) is obviously for the women descendants of those who rendered service; a smaller organization is the Society of the War of 1812 in the Commonwealth of Pennsylvania (c/o Richard R. De Stefano, 425 Haverford Rd., Wynnewood, PA 19096, (610) 896-9229). There have not been a large number of reference sources published for the War of 1812, but two new resources were published in 1997.

456. Encyclopedia of the War of 1812. David S. Heidler and Jeanne T. Heidler, eds. Santa Barbara, CA: ABC-CLIO, 1997. 636p. ISBN: 0-87436-968-1.

The Heidlers have produced a thorough and scholarly work on the historical period of the War of 1812. Some 500 signed essays are written by 70 contributors, including leading authorities on the War. Each entry includes cross-references and a list for further reading. All military engagements are covered, but the work also includes the political and social history of the period. The work begins with a broad introductory overview of the war. The book is well illustrated and includes 25 maps. A daily chronology is supplied which begins in May 1805 and lists, political, diplomatic and military actions through 1815. There is an up-to-date 24-page bibliography. One of the best features of the work is the three appendixes: "12th Congress Vote on Declaration of War;" "Executive Officers of the Federal Government during the Madison Presidency;" and "Documents." The latter contains the text of 10 documents including "The Berlin Decree, 21 November 1806," "Treaty of Ghent, 24 December 1814," and "President Madison's War Message of 1812."

The War of 1812, also by the Heidlers (Greenwood Publishing Group, 2002), is one in a series of guides designed as an introduction to the topic for students. This work contains seven essays on specific topics related to the war, biographies of the major players, 10 important primary documents, and a timeline. There is an introductory overview essays providing historical background to the war.

Another on volume reference for students similarly titled *War of 1812* is involved in the conflict. Biographies of key figures and excerpts from primary source materials, maps, a chronology of events, and sidebars with additional features, a glossary and a list of further readings are all included.

THE TEXAS REVOLUTION AND THE UNITED STATES-MEXICAN WAR (1830–1848)

The 150th anniversary of the ending of the Mexican-American War, 1846–1848, and the Treaty of Guadalupe Hidalgo, prompted a number of reference books dealing with the period from 1830–1848. In the fall of the Alamo in 1836, Mexico retained the southwest territory. But those lands were lost to the United States in the Mexican-American War. The Treaty of Guadalupe officially ended the war and transferred the lands of Texas, California, New Mexico, Arizona, Nevada, Utah, and parts of three other states to the United States. The conflict cost Mexico half of its territory and provided battle training for many officers who served in the Civil War.

457. Encyclopedia of the Alamo and the Texas Revolution. Thom Hatch. Jefferson, NC: McFarland, 1999. 229p. ISBN 0-7864-0593-7.

While concentrating on the siege of the Alamo, this work covers the period from the settlement of Texas through the forming of the Republic. A chronology of the Texas Revolution is included to place the Alamo in the context of the period. The entry for the siege of the Alamo runs 20 pages and includes a day-by-day account of the 13-day siege. There are biographies of each of the 188 Alamo defenders and articles on as many of the Mexican forces as could be found. Other battles are covered in depth, some with chronologies, maps, and troop strengths. The work endeavors to be historically accurate and deals with the folklore that has grown up around the event. A bibliography of both U.S. and Mexican resources and a detailed index complete the volume. This work is a comprehensive guide providing thorough coverage of an important period.

458. Encyclopedia of the Mexican-American War. Mark Crawford. Santa Barbara, CA: ABC-CLIO, 1999. 400p. ISBN 1-57607-059-X.

An introductory essay provides political, geographical, economic, and social background to the Mexican-American War. The works also contain a summary of major events and an analysis of the causes of the war. The 459 entries include subjects, persons, battles, places and factors such as disease, weapons, and treaties. The entries contain cross-references and suggestions for further reading. There are four maps prepared specifically for the work but judged to be inadequate by several reviewers. The entries are accompanied by numerous black-and-white illustrations and a few lithographs from contemporary newspapers. A special feature is the inclusion of excerpts from a number of eyewitness accounts by soldiers and war correspondents that bring out the day-to-day reality of war. A six-page chronology from 1830–1848 and an extensive, 25-page bibliography of titles in English and Spanish are provided. The compilers endeavored to produce an unbiased work but acknowledge the difficulty of documenting the Mexican side of the conflict.

Another work on the same subject is *United States and Mexico at War* (Macmillan, 1998). Nearly 600 entries cover the time period 1821–1854. It is more scholarly and comprehensive than the other two titles above.

459. Historical Dictionary of the United States-Mexican War. Edward H. Moseley and Paul C. Clark, Jr. Lanham, MD: Scarecrow, 1997. 345p. (Historical Dictionaries of Wars, Revolution, and Civil Unrest, v. 2.) ISBN 0-8108-3334-4.

Compiled by two Latin American history scholars, this work covers the decade of the 1840s. A bibliographic essay provides an overview of the war for student and researcher alike. The essay examines the justification of the war from the U.S. point of view and explains the war from Mexico's perspective as an unjustified invasion and ultimately annexation of its territory. The essay identifies both Mexican and U.S. primary sources and archival collections. Over a dozen maps were drawn for the book depicting major battlefields from the first engagement to the last and the broader distances over which the armies moved. The entries are well researched with the biographical entries being the most useful feature. The work also contains a chronology, bibliography, and subject index.

460. War of 1812 Eyewitness Accounts: An Annotated Bibliography. John C. Fredriksen, comp. Westport, CT: Greenwood Press, 1997. 311p. (Bibliographical and Indexes in Military Studies, no. 8). ISBN 0-313-30291-X.

This is a specialized work that describes sources of primary narratives from the period of the War of 1812. It is organized into sections by country for military and naval accounts by U.S., British, American, and Canadian personnel, and civilian accounts by American, British, and foreign persons. The latter include narratives by politicians, merchants, women, and Native Americans. Annotations to the entries include the agency or body with which the writer was affiliated, detailed descriptions of the contents of the narratives, and quotes from the texts. There are indexes by editor and subject.

Fredriksen has produced many reference works. The *Eyewitness Accounts* may have been an outgrowth of a bibliography of the period published in 1985, *Free Trade and Sailor's Rights* . . . (Greenwood Press). The main value of this bibliography on the War of 1812 is in the chapter on manuscript collections, which describes over 100 groupings of personal papers in libraries in the United States and Canada. The bibliography also contains books and journal articles, a chronology of the war, a list of military regiments that were active, and a list of wartime newspapers. Dwight Smith also published in 1985 *The War of 1812: An Annotated Bibliography* (Garland). The Smith work is more comprehensive and covers a wider range of source materials than the Fredriksen book. Both bibliographies are now outdated, but can be used in conjunction with the *Encyclopedia of the War of 1812*.

CIVIL WAR (1861–1865)

The war between the North and the South, the Union and the Confederacy, has been one of the most romanticized wars in history. It has been the subject of many publications, both of a popular and a scholarly nature. The character and personalities of the leading figures have been, and continue to be, the subject of biographical works.

There are a number of societies and organizations focused on preserving battlefields and conducting research in Civil War history. One of the most well known is the Civil War Round Table Associates. This organization of 1,500 members was not founded until 1968, after the Civil War centennial in 1961. The Civil War Round Table has been active in the preservation of Civil War battlefields and historic sites. It holds an annual congress and operates the Confederate Historical Institute near a Civil War battlefield. The monthly *Civil War Round Table Digest* is a newsletter relating to the study and preservation of Civil War historic sites (contact at PO Box 7388, Little Rock, AK, 72217).

A similar group is the Civil War Society, a relatively young organization founded in 1975 that now has 3,500 members interested in the history of the U.S. Civil War. The society raises funds for the preservation of Civil War battlefields; sponsors lectures, workshops, and walking tours; conducts a high school essay contest; and bestows awards. It publishes *Civil War,* a bimonthly magazine (contact at 33756 Black Mountain Rd., Tollhouse, CA 93667-9604, (540) 955-1176).

Another organization that emphasizes the Civil War is the 2,000-member Confederate Memorial Association, founded in 1872. Composed of individuals interested in the literature and culture of the South and the Civil War, the association maintains the Confederate Memorial Hall museum and library in Washington, D.C. It operates a speakers' bureau and bestows awards in addition to sponsoring the Confederate Embassy Honor Guard and Confederate Cavalry (contact at Confederate Memorial Hall, PO Box 610, Washington, DC 20005, (202) 483-5700).

Preservation, patriotism, and reenactments are the foci of the American Civil War Association (ACWA), founded in 1988. The ACWA encourages understanding and appreciation of the American Civil War, encourages research in American history of the Civil War era, assists individuals and organizations that reenact Civil War battles, and helps members to attend reenactments.

Two specialized organizations are the Civil War Press Corps and the Confederate Memorial Literary Society. The Civil War Press Corps, founded in 1958, is composed of authors, artists, journalists, and others interested in the Civil War and concerned that the war receives "fair treatment" in the U.S. media. The Corps (7674 Heriot Drive, Fayetteville, NC, 26311, (919) 488-0598) sponsors a speakers' bureau, maintains a library and biographical archives, and publishes *Civil War Byline*. The Confederate Memorial Literary Society, founded in 1890, presents annual literary awards for historical research and writing on the Confederacy. It maintains a library that includes the Jefferson Davis collection. The society (Web site available at http://www.moc.org) has 8,000 members, including authors, educators, students, and others interested in the study of Confederate history and culture. It maintains a museum of Confederate uniforms, weapons, flags, and espionage.

The Civil War also has a number of organizations for descendants of veterans: the Military Order of the Stars and Bars (available at http://www.mosbihg.org); United Daughters of the Confederacy (328 N. Blvd., Richmond, VA 23220-4057, (804) 355-1636); Sons of Confederate Veterans (c/o Randy Beeson, 4300 S. Aspen Place, Broken Arrow, OK 74011); Military Order of the Loyal Legion of the United States (c/o Herbert K. Zearfoss, 532 Candace Ln., Villanova, PA 19085-1702); Dames of the Loyal Legion of the United States of America (1805 Pine St., Philadelphia, PA 19103); Daughters of Union Veterans of the Civil War (503 S. Walnut St., Springfield, IL 62704-1932, (217) 544-0616); and Hood's Texas Brigade Association (Box 619, Hillsboro, TX 76645, (254) 582-2555).

The centennial of the Civil War was observed from 1961 to 1965. At that time the Civil War was a prominent area of academic specialization, and several classic reference works in the field had already been published. The Civil War has traditionally been treated more from the perspective of military history than social history, and this approach is reflected in the resources considered essential to the field. During the 1960s the focus of historical studies began to shift away from the war's political and military aspects toward social, economic, and urban issues. Increasingly, voices from the many research areas of the new social history have become major contributors to the dialogue on the Civil War, especially from the field of African American studies. Much of this goes beyond a revision to include new resources, and instead involves a reconsideration of perspective and approach to the time period and era of the Civil War. The Civil War is best approached in context, which requires the inclusion of resources on and about slavery and Reconstruction. Changes in the way historians view the Civil War era, along with technology-driven changes in information communication, access, preservation and storage, have changed Civil War Studies, both in terms of content, and of process. Historians, while still dependent on archival research, increasingly look to online collections of archival sources. Of interest is the fact that many of these digital collections are selective, and represent only a part of the archival collection. Similarly, historians make increasing use of both primary and secondary sources of selected materials in areas newly included in the canon of Civil War Research, especially studies of slavery, African American history, and Reconstruction.

The organization of the Civil War section is not the same as in other sections of this guide. The first subsection is devoted to electronic resources, many of which are tied to the older, classic compilations of records of the period. The old and new are treated together so that the relationships between them can be readily seen. Much is available online, but much more remains to be digitized. Many micrographic collections are being made available online as parts of proprietary databases, available to academic researchers through library database subscriptions. The electronic resources have literally revolutionized the search process on records and primary documents from the war.

Electronic Resources

*461. The American Civil War: Letters and Diaries. Alexandria, VA: Alexander Street Press, 2001B. [Electronic database] Available at http://www.alexanderstreetpress.com.

The American Civil War is a collection being published electronically. It is available by subscription for Web site access or for purchase to load into local online systems or virtual libraries. The collection is projected for release in five parts with each part including more than 20,000 pages of materials, associated bibliographies, biographical notes, a detailed chronology, and selected manuscripts in facsimile form. The collection includes approximately 100,000 pages of published memoirs, letters and diaries from individuals plus 4,000 pages of previously unpublished materials, drawn from more than 500 sources. More than 1,000 biographies are also included. The bibliography for the collection is freely available and searchable on the Web. A thesaurus of Civil War terms built specifically for the collection enables researchers to quickly find references to individuals, battles, theaters of war, and activities. New indexes and controlled vocabularies have been created for the collection, allowing faster, more precise access and the ability to browse tables of contents. Both the letters and diaries include biographical notes to provide context for the material. Photographs are included when available. A detailed chronology of events allows the user to see multiple perspectives surrounding a particular event. The letters and diaries give both the Northern and Southern perspectives and those of foreign observers as well. *The American Civil War* is a rich collection of resources for researching all aspects of the time period. Other collections by Alexander Street Press are entries 600n, 799, 1166.

*462. The American Civil War Homepage. University of Tennessee. Available: http://www.sunsite.utk.edu/civil-war/.

Many of the best Web presences are academic, maintained or affiliated with Civil War Research Centers, library special collections, and academic societies. The *American Civil War Homepage,* a project that began as a Library and Information Science class Project at the University of Tennessee School of Library & Information Science, is a frequently revised, well-designed site with well-maintained subject directories of hyperlinks to documents, directories, images, organizations, e-mail lists, and electronic files of all kinds. It is part of the Civil War Virtual Archives Ring, a Web ring of over 300 member sites, most containing primary research material on the Civil War era (available at http://www.geocities.com/Athens/Forum/1867/cwring.html).

The United States Civil War Center at Louisiana State University is another site with a good selection of subject indexed hyperlinks, with access to full text and data (available at http://www.cwc.lus.edu/cwc/index.htm) The University of Virginia Library has a collection of digitized texts at http://etext.lib.virginia.edu/civilwar/. Other sites of interest include The Center for the Study of the Civil War, Web site of the George Tyler Moore Center for The Study of the Civil War, offering online regional maps, e-journal articles, and the Civil War Soldiers Database at http://www.shepherd.wvnet.edu/gtmcweb/cwcenter.htm.

*463. American Memory Project. Washington, D.C.: Library of Congress Available: http://memory.loc.gov/ammem/cwphtml/cwphome.html.

The Library of Congress has made important collections of pictorial material available online through the *American Memory Project,* including *The Civil War Photograph*

Collection, available for duplication from the LC Photo-duplication Service. About 1,100 images were digitized and online in November of 1999. These photographs include materials from larger LC collections, including the Brady Collection of photographs of camp and military life at two Library of Congress sites: and (http://lcweb.loc.gov/rr/print. Also at the *American Memory* site is the collection *Civil War Maps: American Treasures of the Library of Congress,* an example of the sampling style common to online exhibits, where the small number of images serves more as a marketing tool than a research tool (available at lcweb.loc.gov/exhibits/treasures/trm010.html). Additional digital Civil Wars maps will be added. The American Memory Collection Search (available at http://memory.loc.gov/ammem/ammemhome.html) allows searching across all 60 digital databases, with optional limiting by subject area (history), and with a large number of electronic databases. Materials include primary historic data, documents, photographs, recorded sound, moving pictures, and text. The Library of Congress has created a Civil War Pathfinder to LC documents available online in diverse collections, with hyperlinks to over 15 collections, such as *African American Perspectives, 1818–1907* and *Narratives of the American South, 1860–1920* (available at http://memory.loc.gov/ammem/ndlpedu/collections/index.html). A similar pathfinder, for Civil War bibliographies, maps, and books available from the U.S. Government Printing Office can be found at http://www.access.gpo.gov/su%5fdocs/sale/sb-192.html. This includes a bibliography of available documents, tours, oral histories, and military bibliographies from the National Park Service, stewards of the Civil War Battlefields and Historical Parks. These resources are also available from the GPO as publications.

*464. The Civil War CD-ROM. Carmel, IN: Guild Press, 1996. ISBN 1-878208-76-4.

There are a number of separate CD-ROM products issued by Guild Press of Civil War resource materials. The first grouping is those which center around the monumental printed set *The War of the Rebellion: A Compilation of the Official Records of the Union and Confederate Armies* originally published in 128 volumes from 1881 to 1900. The main CD-ROM, *The Civil War,* contains the text of the 128 volume set plus two other sets: Frederick Dyer's three-volume *A Compendium of the American Civil War (1861–1865)* published in 1908, and William F. Fox's *Regimental Losses in the American Civil War (1861–1865)* published in 1889. Dyer's *Compendium* (entry 477) contains statistical data and capsule histories of all Union Army Regiments. Fox's work provides almost 600 pages of text and statistics on losses of Union and some Confederate regiments. The *Compilation of Official Records* is most often referred to as the *OR* and Alan and Barbara Aimone's *A User's Guide to the Official Records of the American Civil War* is included on the CD-ROM. Also included is *Military Operations of the Civil War: A Guide Index to the Official Records of the Union and Confederate Armies,* an indexing effort by the National Archives issued in 1968 in five volumes. The electronic search features of the *Civil War* on CD-ROM allow retrieval results, which could not be obtained by even the most arduous searching through the printed volumes. Searching can be performed on a single volume of a set, the entire set, or the contents of all the sets at once. The CD-ROM acts as an index, but it must be remembered that it also contains the full text of documents from the *OR*.

Two other separately issued CD-ROMS by Guild Press supplement the base product. *Civil War CD-ROM II: Official Records of the Union and Confederate Navies in the War of the Rebellion* (1999) is a companion to the voluminous records of the land war. The naval forces of both sides did play crucial roles in the war. In many instances the army, which was supported by naval forces, was able to dominate the conflict. In tandem with the *OR,* both sets comprise the majority of the available primary documents that report the conduct of the war. Electronic full-text searching makes it possible to find terms and topics highlighted within documents. Field searching also allows document retrieval by writer, addressee, date sent, or date ranges.

The second supplemental title to the *OR* is *Atlas of the Official Records of the Civil War,* which was published in 1891 by the U.S. War Department and has been reprinted several times. The *Atlas* was published on CD-ROM by Guild Press in 1999. The military maps are contemporary from the war, many drawn on the spot and used in battles or to accompany action reports written by commanders. The *Atlas* contains multicolor military maps showing the entire theater of the war, military divisions and departments, military field operations, campaigns, battle, and skirmishes. The maps are reproduced in the same size and color in the CD-ROM as the printed work. The maps are useful for studying the geographic features of the terrain at the time of the war, not just the military aspects. In addition to the maps, there are many illustrations showing details of Union and Confederate uniforms, weapons, medical equipment, flags, plans of forts and defensive structures. In contrast to modern maps drawn to explicate and illustrate battle strategies, the maps in the *Official Military Atlas* reproduce original source material and will never be replaced as a definitive resource for research on Civil War military strategy. A geographic and topical index provides locations in both the maps and illustrations. There is also an index to maps that are not on the CD-ROM.

Guild Press also has several other CD-ROMs with a Civil War focus. *Campaigns of the Civil War* (1999) contains the text of a number of published books, which include accounts by Union Army and Navy participants written in the decades after the war. The 19 volumes contained on the CD-ROM provide a military history with an almost exclusively northern point of view. The Confederate side of the Civil War is reflected in the CD-ROM containing the *Southern Historical Society Papers* (Guild Press, 1998). From 1876 until 1959 the Southern Historical Society published an annual volume of records of the Confederate side of the Civil War. Among the records published were the proceedings of the Confederate Congress and the roster of the 26,300 soldiers who surrendered at Appomattox. The contents of the series included essays, biographies, diaries, rosters, correspondence, speeches, statistics, and even lengthy monographs.

Altogether, these CD-ROM products by Guild Press provide coverage of all of the major printed works that pulled together primary documents, records, rosters of names and regiments for both sides of the war. They enable libraries and individuals who were unable to acquire the printed sets to now have them all inexpensively with the added capability of electronic data retrieval.

465. The Civil War on the Web: A Guide to the Very Best Sites. William G. Thomas and Alice E. Carter. Wilmington, DE: Scholarly Resources, 2000. 220p. ISBN 0-8420-2848-X.

Although guides to Web sites date very quickly, this is an excellent handbook that anyone interested in the Civil War would like to own. It includes a foreword by Gary W.

Gallagher, an introduction, and a user's guide. There are annotated listings of recommended sites, illustrations from the Web sites, and suggested readings.

*466. USCivilWar.Net. Society for Online Civil War Research. Available: http://www.cwresearch.org.

The large and active community of Civil War scholars and affiliated amateurs, from re-enactors to collectors, are ubiquitous on the Web. Among the better of these Web sites is the Society for Online Civil War Research, a non-profit research group whose online presence is underwritten by USCivilWar.Net, a large network of Civil War related sites of all kinds: commercial, nonprofit, and individual sites, scholarly and popular. At this site are a small number of full-text books and articles online.

The U.S. Army Military Institute at Carlisle Barracks, Pennsylvania, has an extensive collection of Civil War materials including photographs. The Institute's Web site has a photograph database containing about one third of the photographs. Information about on-site finding aids the collections and catalog of the Institute can be found on the Web site (available at http://carlisle-www.army.mil/usamhi/).

The United States Colored Troops in the Civil War, by Bennie J. McRae, Jr., includes links to articles, chronologies, and databases of and about African American soldiers (available at http://www.coax.net/people/lwf/data.htm). A useful research guide to women's roles, status, and history during the Civil War is at http://frank.mtsu.edu/˜kmiddlet/history/women/wh-cwar.html.

Print Resources

467. The American Civil War: A Handbook of Literature and Research. Steven E. Woodworth, ed. Westport, CT: Greenwood Press, 1996. 754p. ISBN 0-313-29019-9.

In the 1960s, during the Civil War Centennial commemoration, a number of excellent bibliographies compiled by scholars were published. Until recently there had been little activity. Of the recent scholarly bibliographies of Civil War resources, *American Civil War* is the most comprehensive. The organization consists of 47 bibliographic essays divided into 11 subject areas, each written by a specialist. The essays cover every aspect of the war—strategy, tactics, battles, logistics, intelligence, supply, and prisoner of war camps. Besides the strictly military, other topics include civilian leaders, the economy, causes of the War, international relations, the African American experience, social conditions, medical activities, and aspects of Reconstruction. In all 3,960 sources are covered in the essays which range from 10 to 20 pages in length with bibliographies at the end with full citations of published and nonpublished sources. The essays show trends and changes in interpretations in Civil War scholarship and sometimes even mention areas in need of further research. The essays are particularly strong in the area of musical and narrative recordings. Even fictional works and film and television productions are covered. The focus is on works published after 1970. The volume contains an appendix providing current information on 516 publishers and vendors of Civil War literature. There is an index by subject, name and title. This is a high-quality, extensive reference source useful for the general reader and specialists alike.

Another set with the same title is *American Civil War* in the U-X-L series by Gale Group (2000) which is specifically for middle and high school students. This set covers the basic facts of the Civil War in four volumes. The *Almanac* provides a concise overview of the war; there are two biography volumes, and a final volume of *Primary Sources* with first-person accounts. The set is a handy reference source that serves to introduce the topic.

468. The Atlas of the Civil War. James M. McPherson, ed. New York: Macmillan/Simon & Schuster, 1994. 223p. ISBN 0-02-579050-1.

There was a long hiatus between the Civil War Centennial and the publication of several new atlases. The *Atlas of the Civil War* is the work of James M. McPherson and nine other historians. McPherson has produced a number of Civil War reference works and is a Pulitzer prize-winning author. Besides being authoritative this atlas is attractive with over 200 full-color maps specially prepared for the work. In addition, there are another 200 illustrations, some also in color. The work is organized chronologically into five sections, one for each year of the war. Each section contains a narrative account of the year written by McPherson. Each battle or campaign is described in a two-page spread that includes a narrative description, timeline, and maps that show troop movements, and the progress of the battle. Additional insights are provided through quotes and photographs. Each battle map is cross-referenced to communications and locator maps that place the fighting as it swept the country. This atlas includes many inset maps of minor skirmishes that are not covered in other similar atlases. Expert reviewers have pointed out a number of minor errors. As in any historical research, consulting more than one source is advisable.

An earlier impressive and attractive set edited by James M. McPherson is *Battle Chronicles of the Civil War* (Macmillan, 1989). This six-volume guide describes the course of every battle from 1861 to 1865, explaining strategies, tactics, and outcomes.

Another newer atlas is *Civil War Atlas* published by William R. Scaife (Atlanta, 1995), a one-volume unpaged work with battlefield maps.

The West Point Atlas of the Civil War, edition by Vincent J. Esposito (Praeger, 1962), has been accepted as the standard military atlas of the Civil War since its publication. The atlas was extracted from the larger *West Point Atlas of American Wars* developed for instructional use at the U.S. Military Academy. The Civil War atlas shows troop movements in great detail, even down to the hour of the day, through the use of symbols in color. Other details include troop strength, landmarks, topography, and fortifications. Although it is very detailed, the atlas is also clear and easy to understand. The accompanying text explains and evaluates the tactics and strategies of the opposing forces. There is an annotated bibliography, which is now quite out-of-date. The atlas is useful for students and all others interested in military strategy of the Civil War.

469. The Civil War Battlefield Guide. Frances H. Kennedy. Boston: Houghton Mifflin, 1990. 317p. ISBN 0-395-52282-X.

The Conservation Fund is the sponsor of this chronological survey of 58 major Civil War battlefields. There is a summary account of each battle giving the events leading up to it, as well as the strategies and their significance to the outcomes. There is also a map for each battle showing the positions of the forces, the Union in blue and the Confederate in red. One purpose of this guide is to urge the preservation of battlefields that are not under public ownership. The maps show the boundaries for the portions that are publicly owned. Modern features that impact the sites, such as buildings and roads, are included in the maps.

An older standard work, *A Battlefield Atlas of the Civil War* by Craig L. Symonds (Annapolis, MD: Nautical and Aviation Publishing Co., 1983) has been reissued in a third edition (1993). The new edition is attractive, with portraits and photographs illustrating the text. Arrangement is in four chronological sections: "The Amateur Armies," "The Organized War," "Confederate High Tide," and "Total War." The maps are drawn to scale and use a simple scheme of symbols to show the placement, number, and kinds of troops. The 43 maps form a concise topographical survey of the major Civil War campaigns. Opposite each map is a brief essay that clearly explains the strategy and outcome of the event. The discussions of the battles are lively, with references to the numbered positions on the maps. A list of suggested readings is provided at the end. The atlas is suitable for use by anyone with an interest in Civil War battles.

Symonds's battlefield atlas is much more suitable for the study of the battles, but *The Civil War Battlefield Guide* gives a broader perspective on the significance of the battles. The two works make excellent companions and should be used in conjunction with other reference works on the Civil War.

470. Civil War Eyewitnesses: An Annotated Bibliography of Books and Articles, 1955–1986. Garold L. Cole. Columbia, SC: University of South Carolina Press, 1988. 351p. ISBN 0-87249-545-0. **1986–1996.** 2000. 271p. ISBN 1-57003-327-7.

The first edition of this highly acclaimed bibliography has been updated by an additional volume bringing the coverage of published personal narratives up through 1996. The advantage of these bibliographies is that they cite recent materials, the majority published after the Civil War centennial in the 1960s. The first volume contains 1,395 items and the update catalogs 596 firsthand accounts. The bibliographies are divided into three subject categories: the North; the South; and anthologies, studies and foreign travelers. The entries include name of author, editor, publication information, rank and unit if military, original form, major battles the author participated in, and civilian occupation. Sources include books, collected essays, memoirs, autobiographies, and periodical articles. The annotations are evaluative and insightful identifying the activities of the eyewitnesses and providing a "glimpse of their feelings and attitudes about the war and themselves." An extensive index provides access to the entries by author, title, and subject. The two volumes provide a guide to the many published eyewitness accounts. It is useful for researchers of all levels.

An earlier standard bibliography that has not been superceded is *Travels in the Confederate States: A Bibliography* by Merton E. Coulter (University of Oklahoma Press, 1948). This classic reference has been reprinted several times. The bibliography is a selective listing of 500 diaries, letters, regimental histories, and other personal accounts of life and conditions during the Civil War, written during the conflict and after by military figures and civilians, including foreign travelers. Researchers seeking personal accounts of the Civil War will need to use this bibliography and the Cole work cited above. The texts of works cited in *Travels in the Confederate States* have been published in a microform collection, with the same title available from Proquest/UMI.

Another type of "eyewitness account" is found in newspapers. Proquest/University Microfilms has a collection of *Civil War Newspapers,* an invaluable source for news of battle actions, casualty reports, troop movement notices, and reports on the economic disruptions and political decisions that affected the course of the conflict. *Frank Leslie's Illustrated Newspaper* published nearly 3,000 pictures of battles, sieges, and other war scenes sketched by Leslie's artists at the front. There is no bibliography for the Civil War newspaper microfilm collection, but the UMI Web site lists film collections and titles (available at http://www.umi.com).

Some digital resources, such as *The Civil War: A Newspaper Perspective,* once on microfilm, are newly available as full-text proprietary databases from Accessible Archives (available at http://www.accessible.com). With more than 11,000 records, this database contains major articles from over 2,500 issues of *The New York Herald, The Charleston Mercury,* and *The Richmond Enquirer* between 1860 and 1865. Although the coverage is selective, not inclusive, recognition of current research interests is clearly included: "A great effort has been made also to include articles which describe other than military concerns of the day. These include such topics as travel, arts and leisure, geographical descriptions, sports and sporting, social events, etc."

471. The Civil War in Books: An Analytical Bibliography. David J. Eicher. Champaign, IL: University of Illinois Press, 1997. 407p. ISBN 0-252-02273-4.

In the 1960s during the Civil War Centennial commemoration, several excellent bibliographies were compiled by distinguished scholars. Until recently, these works had not been updated or superceded by newer works. *The Civil War in Books* is a scholarly analytical bibliography covering 1,100 major works ranging in publication date from 1965 to 1995. The books span the range of Civil War literature and include fiction. The titles were selected with the help of an editorial board of scholars to be the most important, current, or representative of a topic. About 27 percent of the titles were published after 1981. Thus, the bibliography provides an overview of both recent and retrospective literature on the Civil War. The annotations written by Eicher are descriptive and critical following the style of scholarly historical journals. Broad categories, such as "Battles and Campaigns," or "Unit Histories," are further subdivided. Battle literature is listed chronologically. Biographical works are divided by Union and Confederacy. Information about the authors of the works is given when known, such as birth and death dates, literary awards, and other pertinent information. There are author/editor and title indexes. There are two appendixes: one of Civil War Publishers and the other "A Short List of Civil War Bibliographies."

Guide to Civil War Books by Domenica M. Barbuto and Martha Kreisel (ALA, 1995) includes 320 books published since 1981. The books are grouped into 31 subject categories. Each entry follows a uniform format with complete bibliographic citations and detailed annotations. There are citations to reviews of the works. The coverage of social aspects of the war is particularly strong with outstanding annotations. There are separate author, title, and subject indexes. Although more limited in scope than the Eichler bibliography, the work provides in-depth coverage of the best of the literature in the past 20 years.

Both *The Civil War in Books* and the *Guide to Civil War Books* update the older, classic *Civil War Books* by Nevins et al. (Baton Rouge, LA: Published for the U.S. Civil War Centennial Commission by LSU Press, 1967–1969. 2v. Repr, Wilmington, N.C. Broadfoot Publishing, 1996). The Nevins work was published for the Civil War Centennial and contains information on monographic publications prior to 1960. The bibliography includes some 6,000 books selected and annotated by 15 historians. The entries are arranged in 15 subject sections. Volume 1 includes three sections on military aspects of the War. Volume 2 includes general works, biographies, memoirs, and collective works, with three sections each on the Union and the Confederacy. A cumulative author, title, and subject index covers both volumes. The bibliography is useful for monographic publications on the Civil War written prior to the 1960s, but anyone researching the period will need to search more recent compilations.

472. Civil War Manuscripts: A Guide to Collections in the Manuscript Division of the Library of Congress. John R. Sellers, comp. Washington, D.C.: Library of Congress, 1986. 391p. ISBN 0-8444-0381-4.

The 1,064 collections of personal papers described in this guide are mainly from Northern sources. The individuals are both military and nonmilitary figures. The entries are alphabetical by name, with birth and death dates, occupation, and rank given for each individual if available. The number and type of items are given, along with a brief description of the scope and contents, for each collection. The size of the collections varies widely. Information is given on finding aids if they exist. There is an extensive name/subject index. This guide will be useful for researchers searching for primary materials dealing with the Civil War.

Chadwyck-Healey has published a microfilm collection, *A People at War,* of the papers of more than 350 Civil War era figures from the Library of Congress Manuscript Division. The collection contains papers of political and military figures from both sides. Included are noncombatants, women, freedmen, wives of soldiers, artists and photographers, and people from many other walks of life. The collection gives researchers access to a vast amount of original manuscript material without requiring them to visit the Library of Congress. The published index/guide to the collection has the same title (available at http://www.chadwyck.com).

473. Civil War Maps: An Annotated List of Maps and Atlases in the Library of Congress. 2nd ed. Richard W. Stephenson, comp. Washington, D.C.: Geography and Map Division, Library of Congress, 1989. 410p. ISBN 0-8444-0598-1.

Originally issued for the Civil War centennial in 1961, this guide has been expanded in its second edition. The volume is an attractive one, with reproductions from maps in the collections. The 2,240 maps and 76 atlases are indexed by title, battle, cartographer, place, subject, printer, and engraver, among other things. One of the largest groups in the collection is the Hotchkiss Map Collection of 341 Confederate maps from the Army of Northern Virginia. Another collection, which belonged to General William T. Sherman, consists of 210 maps and three atlases showing fortifications and troop movements. The Library of Congress has an extensive collection of maps from the Civil War, and this list enables researchers to ascertain which maps are in the collection. It will be of interest to cartographers and Civil War historians, both amateur and professional. The *American Memory Project* of the Library of Congress (entry 12) has a selection of digitized images of Civil War maps (available at http://lcweb.loc.gov/exhibits/treasures/trm010.html).

474. Civil War Newspaper Maps: A Cartobibliography of the Northern Daily Press.
David Bosse comp. Westport, CT: Greenwood Press, 1993. 253p. (Bibliographies and Indexes in Military Studies, no. 5). ISBN 0-313-28705-8.

Bosse has authored two works on maps in newspapers during the Civil War. The second title is *Civil War Newspaper Maps: A Historical Atlas* (Johns Hopkins, 1993). The *Cartobibliography* identifies more than 2,000 maps of military engagements and field positions which appeared in 20 Northern daily newspapers. The maps are grouped by issuing newspaper and arranged chronologically. Each entry contains the title, dimensions, scale, author, engraver, and notes on sources used to produce the maps. A detailed geographical, personal name, and subject index provides access to the maps. An appendix lists any missing issues of newspapers that could not be examined by the compiler.

In *Civil War Newspaper Maps: A Historical Atlas,* Bosse covers the development and distribution of maps through newspapers of the day. Eight essays deal with the development of journalistic mapmaking, the design and production of maps, and the problems of accuracy and timely reporting. The volume contains 45 maps chronologically arranged. The maps illustrate design and production techniques and also illustrate reporting styles. Each map is accompanied by a brief summary of the military operation and a commentary on the design and accuracy of the map. There is a bibliography that includes primary archival sources. Newspapers often carried the first maps to appear after a battle and were sometimes the only source of maps for lesser engagements. Both of these works are unique in being the only references devoted to maps in newspapers.

475. Civil War Sites, Memorials, Museums, and Library Collections: A State-by-State Guidebook to Places Open to the Public. Doug Gelbert. Jefferson, NC: McFarland, 1997. 201p. ISBN 0-7864-031905.

Civil War battle sites, memorials, and library/museum/archival collections are all included in this extensive guidebook. The arrangement is by 43 states and the District of Columbia then alphabetically by city or site within the states. For each state, a brief description of its role in the war, the 1860 populations, number of troops provided, the sites of action, and a timeline are provided. For collections and sites the location, hours, and contact information are given. Also included is the fee schedule if any, and information on reenactments. An appendix of gravesites of significant individuals gives the name of the person and city or state. The index consists mostly of names of individuals. The work is mainly useful as a guidebook for visiting the sites and collections listed, but one can get an overview of a state's role and participation in the war.

A similar work is *Civil War Battlefields: a Touring Guide* (Dallas, TX: Taylor Publishing, 1995). This guide by David Eicher was written from in-person visits and research into 12 major battlefields. Although it is intended as a guide to the battlefields, it is useful for research as well as site visits. The narrative on each battle ties the conduct of the engagement with the terrain and sites to be visited. There are 40 detailed maps and many photographs. Those interested in knowing more than just a few salient facts and making more than just a short visit will want to take this guide along for an in-depth exploration of the battle sites.

476. Compendium of the Confederate Armies. Stewart Sifakis. New York: Facts on File, 1991–1995. 11 vols.

Those who have studied the Confederate forces during the Civil War have longed for a reference comparable to that of Frederick Dyer's *Compendium of the War of the Rebellion* (entry 477), which presents statistics and historical material on each unit in the Union Army. At last there is a series on military units that fought in the Confederate Army. The series contains 11 volumes arranged by state and a last volume that comprises tables of brigades and higher commands. Entries for each unit include organizational information, history, and final disposition; the name of the first colonel of the regiment, with an alphabetical listing of the field command; the higher assignments of the unit with dates; the service of the unit in the field; and a listing of available histories, memoirs, biographies, and diaries dealing with the unit. Each volume has an extensive bibliography and an alphabetical index of battles and names. The Confederate compendium will be a much-used and essential reference source for all students, genealogists, and local and Civil War historians for many years to come. Unlike the earlier *OR* and Dyer's *Compendium,* the contents of these volumes are not included in an electronic database.

477. Compendium of the War of the Rebellion, Compiled and Arranged from Official Records of the Federal and Confederate Armies . . . Frederick H. Dyer, comp. Dayton, OH: National Historical Society, in cooperation with the Press of Morningside Bookshop, 1979. 2v. Repr. of the 1908 ed. (Torch Press).

Dyer's *Compendium of the War of the Rebellion* has long been a unique reference for the study of the Union forces during the Civil War. Originally published in 1908 in one volume of 1,796 pages, it has been reprinted several times. An introduction by Civil War historian Bell Irvin Wiley was added in 1959 to the reprint by Thomas Yoseloff. The work is divided into three large sections. Part 1 is statistical, with numbers and organization; compositions and leaders of departments, armies, corps, division, and brigades; locations of national cemeteries; and sketches arranged numerically by state. In part 2 are lists taken from other sources of engagements and losses arranged by both state and chronology. Over 10,400 conflicts are also arranged by actions, battles, campaigns, and so on. The largest section is part 3, "Regimental Histories," consisting of a concise statement for each regiment and lesser unit telling where the units were organized and where they fought; service records and losses are included. In compiling the work, Dyer examined hundreds of original muster rolls, talked with thousands of veterans, and examined all available printed sources, including the 128 volumes of the *War of the Rebellion: Official Records of the Union and Confederate Armies* (U.S. War Department, 1880–1901). The Dyer work is an encyclopedia of federal units and actions. Archivists, researchers, and writers have consulted it constantly since 1908, and it remains the only source of its kind. Dyer's *Compendium* is now included in the Guild Press Civil War CD-ROM product.

478. Confederate Imprints: A Bibliography of Southern Publications from Secession to Surrender. T. Michael Parrish and Robert H. Willingham, Jr. Austin, TX: Jenkins; Katonah, NY: Gary A Foster, n.d. 991p. ISBN 0-8363-0712-3.

There is no publication date on the piece, but this bibliography was published in 1987, 30 years after those by Crandall and Harwell in the next entry, 479. There are 40 percent more Confederate imprints listed in this bibliography than were listed in Crandall and Harwell. The organization remains the same as the earlier volumes: official and unofficial publications. The official publications include the Confederate government departments and the states of the Confederacy. The 4,781 unofficial publications are divided into nine sections by format and subjects: military; politics; economics and social issues; science and medicine; maps and prints; belles-lettres; music and entertainment; sheet music; education and religion. Bibliographic information is complete, including page numbers and size. Holdings are recorded for over 400 libraries and private collections. Entry numbers are given for those items listed in Crandall and Harwell. An extensive index provides access by author, title, subject, name on broadside, place of publication, name of printer and publisher, and class of publication. There are illustrations of title pages and broadsides. This much-needed update to Crandall and Harwell replaces the two earlier bibliographies and smaller, separate publications for the most part. All researchers concerned with the Confederacy during the Civil War will have to make extensive use of the bibliography.

A microform collection of the texts, *Confederate Imprints, 1861–1865,* has been published by Research Publications now available through ProquestUMI. There is a reel index to the 144-reel set. The items have also been cataloged in the OCLC database. The bibliographies and the microfilm collection are central to any research on the Civil War period.

479. Confederate Imprints: A Check List Based Principally on the Collection of the Boston Athenaeum. Marjorie Lyle Crandall. Boston: Boston Athenaeum, 1955. 2v. (Robert Charles Billings Fund publication no. 11).

Marjorie Crandall's two-volume bibliography was the first of a number of lists of Confederate imprints and has long been regarded as a classic in the field, not having been updated until 1987. The first volume lists official publications. The second volume lists unofficial publications and has a section of sheet music complied by Richard Harwell. Richard Harwell also compiled *More Confederate Imprints* (Virginia State Library, 1957, 2v.), a supplement with 1,773 additional items arranged in the same categories as the first checklist. Another compilation by Harwell is *Confederate Imprints in the University of Georgia Library* (University of Georgia, 1964). A number of other libraries with extensive collections of Confederate imprints have published lists of holdings. Although these bibliographies have been largely superceded by the 1987 update to *Confederate Imprints,* they are still useful as guides to the holdings of particular libraries.

480. Encyclopedia of the American Civil War: A Political, Social, and Military History. David S. Heidler, Jeanne T. Heidler, and David J. Coles, eds. Santa Barbara, CA: ABC-CLIO, 2000. 5v. ISBN 1-57607-066-2.

A comprehensive reference work on the Civil War did not exist until the publication of this five-volume work. The set consists of five oversized volumes, liberally illustrated with contemporary photographs, lithographs, maps, and drawings. The encyclopedic part of the work has over 1,600 signed articles by over 300 specialist contributors which range from a column to several pages in length. The topics covered are the gamut of military, diplomatic, political, social and cultural subjects, people, and events. Full biographies of all major and many minor figures are included as well as descriptions of 60 major engagements and skirmishes. Collectively, the entries cover the history and conduct of the war and the consequences in a political, military and social context, making it apparent that no aspect of America was unaffected by the war. The text is readable and accurate. Each essay contains see also references as well as extensive suggested readings for further research. The last volume contains an overall index and five appendixes. One of the helpful features of the set for students is the full text of 250 documents. Included are the major speeches of President Lincoln, the Jefferson Davis "Proclamation of 1861," Lee's farewell address, legislation, military and civilian correspondence, editorials, and eyewitness accounts. The appendixes list the officers of both armies and officials of the governments. There is a directory of Civil War battlefield sites with maps, addresses and contact information. Following the appendixes is a "Civil War Chronology," which shows the relationship between the military, political, and social/cultural events. A glossary defines contemporary terms. An extensive bibliography contains all of the sources listed throughout the articles. The index includes illustrations as well as the text. This set will be the first reference work consulted in those libraries that own it. It is clearly organized and written, encompassing the broad sweep of the era in detailed articles.

481. Encyclopedia of the Confederacy. Richard N. Current and Paul D. Escott, eds. Farmington Hills, MI: Macmillan, 1993. 4v. ISBN 0-13-275991-8.

This work is the first of its kind to focus exclusively on the Confederacy. Compiled by a prominent Civil War historian, the four volumes contain more than 1,400 alphabetically arranged signed articles written by more than 300 well-known scholars. The encyclopedia is broad in scope treating the Confederacy as a nation unto itself. The set covers all aspects of the Confederacy, including social, cultural, military, economic, and political issues. It is amply illustrated with contemporary photographs and etchings, maps, and photographs of equipment and uniforms. Each article includes a bibliography. Volume 4 contains an extensive index, a synoptic outline of contents and nine appendixes. There is no other comparable reference work. It is an excellent modern accompaniment to the various printed compilations of records from the period.

482. Everything Civil War: The Ultimate Guide to Civil War Products, Services, Places of Interest, Organizations, Archives, Accommodations. Spencer Kope, ed. Silverdale, WA: Willow Creek Press, 1996. 304p. (Everything Books). ISBN 0-9657183-1-6.

Although not in the title, this is an encyclopedic work of a sort. The publisher gathered the information in this guide through requests to over 1,000 companies, museums, organizations, and other agencies. Each chapter in the book focuses on a different type of product or service. Each chapter is self-contained with its own index, but there is also an index for the entire volume. Some of the types of information contained in the work are addresses for Internet sites, historic inns, sources of authentic reproduction clothing and accessories. The catalog is not so much for research as for the tourist, reenactors, and others seeking current information. It does contain descriptions of Civil War associations and the Internet sites can provide leads for the researcher.

483. [Guides]. Washington, D.C. National Archives and Records Administration.

The Confederacy: A Guide to the Archives of the Government of the Confederate States of America. Henry Putney Beers. Washington, D.C.: National Archives and Records Administration, 1986. 536p. Repr. of the 1968 ed. ISBN 0-911333-18-5. **Guide to Civil War Maps in the National Archives.** 2nd ed. Washington, D.C.: National Archives and Records Administration, 1986. 139p. ISBN 0-911333-36-2. **The Union: A Guide to Federal Archives Relating to the Civil War.** Kenneth W. Munden and Henry Putney Beers. Washington, D.C.: National Archives and Records Administration, 1986. 721p. ISBN 0-911333-46-0.

These three guides all originate in the same time frame. Although they have not been updated in many years, they are still useful to indicate primary source materials from the Civil War in the National Archives. The two guides "The Confederacy" and "The Union" are usually mentioned in tandem. The guide for the Confederacy includes collections in the Library of Congress and 29 other library and archival collections, plus additional information from guides and bibliographies to other sets of material. The 1968 edition was reprinted with a new introduction by Frank G. Burke. The guide is arranged by governmental agency and lists records, finding aids, and other bibliographic references. Because the guide for the Confederacy has not been updated in over 30 years, researchers may find more up-to-date information in *Confederate Research Sources: A Guide to Archive Collections* (Ancestry, 1986) by James C. Neagles. Used together, these two guides will provide the researcher with information on the major collections of Confederate government records.

The majority of the records in the guide to the Union are in the National Archives, but those in federal records centers and other agencies are also included. It lists and describes federal records from the Civil War period and records relating to the war created in subsequent years. The 11 chapters describe records of a major branch or agency of the federal government, with subdivisions for the various bureaus, offices, and other units. Each chapter begins with a historical analysis of the department's organization and wartime functions, with bibliographical references included. The guide then describes those records relating to the department as a whole and cites finding aids and items pertinent to the use of the records. Major collections of related records in the Library of Congress and historical societies are indicated. An appendix lists all groups of federal records relating to the Civil War, cross-referenced to the page in the guide where the records are described. There is also an index.

The *Guide to Civil War Maps in the National Archives* (2nd ed., 1986) lists over 8,000 Civil War maps, charts, and plans held by the National Archives. The largest collection of cartographic records in the world pertaining to the Civil War is located in the Cartographic and Architectural Branch of the National Archives. The second edition includes maps from the War Department Collection of Confederate Records and is divided into two parts. The first part is a general guide organized by classification scheme with entry numbers. The map file number, which is necessary for ordering copies from the National Archives and Records Service, is supplied for each item. The second part describes 267 maps in greater detail. There is an index that includes geographical and personal names mentioned in the descriptions. The cartographic records described are useful in geographical, topographical, historical, and genealogical research.

The three NARA guides together are useful for determining the extent of records on the Civil War in the National Archives.

484. Historical Atlas of the Congresses of the Confederate States of America: 1861–1865. Kenneth C. Martis. Simon & Schuster, 1994. 158p. ISBN 0-13-389115-1.

Martis, recognized as one of the leading political cartographers in the United States, is the author of a number of atlases of the United States Congress (entry 204). The Confederate States of America had a governmental organization patterned after that of the United States with a Senate and House of Representatives. The Confederate congresses met during the Civil War, 1861–1865. Districts were created, elections were held, and the members debated and voted on matters governing the Confederacy. Atlases of the Civil War period have all been military atlases. As with all of the Martis atlases, this one is focused on the political geography of the Confederate congress. There are 45 full-page maps: 43 in color, which provide details of the elections and roll-call voting. All research on the governance of the Confederacy needs to include this reference work.

485. Land Campaigns of the Civil War. Paul Calore. Jefferson, NC: McFarland, 2000. 272p. ISBN 0-7864-0323-3.

A chronological, campaign-by-campaign, military analysis gives attention to the role each campaign played in the greater scheme of the war. The focus in the work is on strategy and military successes and failures. There are maps, an appendix, a bibliography and an index.

Also published by McFarland, is *Land Battles of the Civil War, Eastern Theatre* by Bruce H. Stewart, Jr. In chronological order are descriptions of each battle, infantry, artillery, and cavalry, and the names of the commanding and senior officers. The work begins with the first battle at Fort Sumter, South Carolina, on April 12, 1861, considered to be the beginning of the war, and ends with the surrender of Joseph E. Johnston to General William T. Sherman on April 26, 1865. Minor skirmishes and all action in Florida and west of the Mississippi river are excluded.

There are two works with the same title, which treat the major battles of the war, published closely together. In *Great Battles of the Civil War* (Macmillan, 1988), John Macdonald puts forth the thesis that terrain plays a large role in the operations of a military campaign. To illustrate this point, Macdonald selected 17 major Civil War campaigns and constructed three-dimensional landscape models via computer mapping of the geographical features of the battle sites. Troop movements are marked to show the effects of the terrain on the action. The maps are accompanied by text, graphs of troops and losses, and other illustrations. The interesting analysis using modern computer technology makes this a unique tool among Civil War reference works. It should be of interest to students, historians, and military history buffs.

The other publication with exactly the same title, *Great Battles of the Civil War* (Beekman, 989) treats 36 of the most important Civil War battles through descriptive narratives illustrated with reproductions of chromolithographs from the late nineteenth century by Louis Kurz and Alexander Allison. In addition, there are diagrams, sidebars, and photographs that further illustrate the battles and facts about them. This attractive volume presents an overview of the Civil War through the narrative on the major battles.

486. The Language of the Civil War. J.D. Wright. Westport, CT: Oryx Press: 2001. 296p. ISBN 1-57356-135-5.

The Language of the Civil War contains words that originated or were in use during the Civil War. America's language changed as well as history because of the Civil War. In standard dictionary arrangement, this work is a unique compilation of 4,000 slang, nicknames, military jargon and terminology, idioms, colloquialisms, and other expressions. The origin and meaning of terms such as Buttermilk Rangers, jackstraws, Nassau bacon, pumpkin slinger, and "stand the gaff" are included in the entries that focus primarily on everyday camp life, military hardware, and military organization. Many of the terms and phrases are no longer in use, but many are also expressions that have changed in meaning over the years. The unique reference work is illustrated with 50 photographs and drawings. It will be useful to students, researchers, and enthusiasts alike.

487. Microbes and Minie Balls: An Annotated Bibliography of Civil War Medicine. Frank R. Freemon. Cranbury, NJ: Fairleigh Dickinson University Press/Associated University Presses, 1993. 253p. ISBN 0-8386-3484-2.

The emphasis in this bibliography is on military medicine. The entries are divided into two main sections each alphabetical by author. The first section lists primary sources of books and articles written by Civil War doctors, nurses, and hospital attendants. Important contemporary medical publications and some diaries of wounded or hospitalized soldiers are included. The second section includes secondary sources of books and articles that deal directly with Civil War medicine, works that discuss aspects of medical care during the period, and descriptions of the health of key figures. An introductory essay on the nature of Civil War medicine and the descriptive annotations contribute greatly to an understanding of the state of medicine at the time. The bibliography updates and expands the coverage of earlier standard bibliographies on the Civil War. There is an index.

488. Naval Campaigns of the Civil War. Paul Calore. Jefferson, NC: McFarland, 2002. 240p. ISBN 0-7864-1217-8.

Naval campaigns of the Civil War are presented in a chronological arrangement, which allows for ready reference on specific engagements. An overview of the events preceding the war is presented. The maritime problems of both sides at the beginning of the war, their attempts to overcome these problems and the victories and failures of both sides are presented. The maps are an important aspect of the explication of the strategies and battles. There is a glossary, a bibliography, and an index. Calore is also the author of *Land Campaigns of the Civil War* (entry 485).

The overview of the naval campaigns is complemented by *Warships of the Civil War Navies* by Paul H. Silverstone (Naval Institute Press, 1989). This is the first reference work that treats all of the vessels that participated in the naval forces during the Civil War. The work provides a comprehensive listing that includes detailed descriptions and brief war records. The vessels are divided into four categories: U.S. Navy warships, U.S. revenue cutter service, U.S. coast survey, and the Confederate States Navy. The Confederate section is divided geographically, and the federal sections are divided by size and mode of propulsion as well as type of duties. The descriptions include name, builder, construction date, dimensions, tonnage, machinery, armor, service record, later history, and other details. There is a list of shipbuilders and an index by ship name. The book is amply illustrated with photographs and drawings. Silverstone has brought a considerable amount of information together into this volume, which is a definitive reference on the naval vessels of the Civil War. It is useful for all researchers seeking information on ships of the period.

A more limited work by Louis S. Schafer, *Confederate Underwater Warfare: An Illustrated History* (McFarland, 1996) explores the South's superiority in underwater weaponry. More Union ships were destroyed by torpedoes than by all other means combined. The work by Schafer is the first detailed history ever of the South's development and deployment of both offensive and defensive underwater weaponry. The work includes many photographs of actual salvaged Confederate mines.

489. Supplement to the Official Records of the Union and Confederate Armies. Janet B. Hewett, Noah Andre Trudeau, and Bryce A Suderow, eds. Wilmington, NC: Broadfoot Publishing, 1998. 12 v. ISBN 1-56837-275-2.

The 128-volume set *The War of the Rebellion: The Official Records of the Union and Confederate Armies,* popularly referred to as the *OR,* has been mentioned in numerous annotations in this section on the Civil War. Broadfoot Publishing has been the major firm producing modern monumental reference works dealing with the Civil War period. The *Supplement* is projected to be a 100-volume set when completed. There are four distinct parts to the overall titles and these are separately numbered and sold: part 1, records; part 2, records of events and itineraries; part 3, correspondence; part 4, files of the US. Secret Service. The *Supplement* adds thousands of records to the original *OR* plus other materials that relate to but were not part of the original *OR.* For the monumental task of the *Supplement,* many historians, genealogists, librarians, archivists, and others have spent years searching through newspaper and other microfilm, archives, and other repositories for documents and related materials that were not included in the original *OR.* Part 1 of the Supplement consists of 10 volumes with a two-volume index. Volumes 1–7 follow the format of the original *OR* and contain newly found records and reports on military engagements of all types written by officers on both sides during the war as well as accounts written after the war. Volumes 8–10 include longer more specific text such as a 400-page history of the U.S. Signal Corps, 1861–1865. The index volumes provide access to battles, person, and subjects. A cumulative index is planned for the entire 100-volume set. When completed, the *Supplement* will greatly enlarge the universe of primary documents collected and made available for research. As far as is known there are no plans to produce an electronic version of the work.

490. The Union Army 1861–1865: Organization and Operations. Volume I: The Eastern Theater. Volume II: The Western Theater. Frank J. Welcher. Bloomington, IN: Indiana University Press, 1989. v. 1: 1,065p. ISBN 0-253-36453-1. v. 2: 1,088p. ISBN 0-253-36454-X.

The organizational history of the Union's four military divisions, 26 departments, 13 field armies, and other subdivisions forms the core of this reference work. The set gives a complete account of all Union military divisions, departments, and subunits, including geographical boundaries and important dates. It makes it possible to track the activities of a specific unit. Information given includes the date of creation and the composition of each unit; changes in organization and commanders; and dates of the end of the unit. Details of personnel and maneuvers are also provided. Half of the first volume, on the Eastern Theater, deals with battles and campaigns, giving itineraries of all major units. Volume 2 includes extensive name and unit indexes for the set. This work contains much of the information in Dyer's *Compendium of the War of the Rebellion* (entry 477) but does not completely replace it. The modern work will be a core source for military historians and buffs of the Civil War.

The microform collection, *Regimental Histories of the American Civil War* (Proquest/UMI) when completed, will contain 3,000 titles, including state adjutant generals' reports; rosters; published memoirs, letters, and diaries; prisoner of war accounts and other personal narratives; biographical sketches; and other documents. The collection includes materials from the U.S. Army Military History Institute at Carlisle Barracks, the Huntington Library, and the Newberry Library. Another microfiche collection published by Proquest/UMI is *Pamphlets of the Civil War*. The emphasis in this collection of 1,758 titles is on the issues and attitudes that led to the conflict. The collection is accompanied by its own guide.

Biographical Sources

491. Biographical Dictionary of the Union: Northern Leaders of the Civil War. John T. Hubbell and James W. Geary, eds. Westport, CT: Greenwood Press, 1995. 683p. ISBN 0-313-20920-0.

Issued by the same publisher as the *Biographical Dictionary of the Confederacy* below, this work provides an introduction to the lives of over 800 individuals associated with the Union cause in the Civil War. The list is comprehensive for major figures, political leaders, and selective for others. Military leaders are selected for specific contributions to the Union cause, and include most of those who were at least division commanders. The signed entries are by leading historians. In addition to the usual biographical facts, the entries are evaluative and provide an interpretative assessment of the biographees' activities. Although biographical information on many of the individuals can be found in other tools, the entries are evaluative and place the individual in context. The entries make fascinating reading. Each biography contains a list of the best resources on that individual to consult. Thus this work makes an excellent starting point for research. There is a bibliography with full citations to many other biographical resources. The index lists all individuals mentioned in the work whether or not they have a separate entry. The work is a useful addition to standard biographical tools.

The *Biographical Dictionary of the Confederacy* by Jon L. Wakelyn (Greenwood Press, 1977) was published almost 30 years before the same title for the Union. Approximately 650 individuals who played prominent roles—political, military, economic, and social—in the Confederacy are profiled in this biographical work. The information is drawn from other published biographical sources, although these are not indicated. In addition to the biographical sketches there is a computer analysis of 72 variables from information in the biographies. Wakelyn analyzes the quantitative information in four chapters at the beginning of the work. There is a bibliography and an index. Five appendixes show 1) general mobility before and after the Civil War; 2) principal occupations; 3) religious affiliation; 4) education; and 5) pre- and postwar political party affiliations. The biographical information on Confederate commanders does not supercede that of other works, including *Generals in Grey* by Ezra Warner (entry 492n). This dictionary is a good one-volume reference work on prominent individuals in the Confederacy. It is suitable for use by students, researchers, and the general public.

492. The Confederate Governors. W. Buck Yearns, ed. Athens, GA: University of Georgia Press, 1985. 291p. ISBN 0-8203-0719-X.

The role of the governors of the 13 Confederate states during the war is approached through biographical essays. All but 2 of the 15 men who served in office during the war were born in the South; most were young lawyers with political experience. Most of those elected early in the war years were Democrats, but as the war wore on Whigs and Unionists were elected to office in some states. The immense problems faced by the state governments are apparent: feeding the civilian population and supplying troops; overcoming serious financial difficulties; dealing with the Confederate government; maintaining home defense; and numerous others. This book brings together discussions of the kinds of problems faced by the Southern states during the war and the responses to those problems. The editor concludes that the governors effectively aided the war effort. The volume forms an excellent political history of the states of the Confederacy traced through the men who led during that difficult time. A bibliography comes at the end and an index. The work can be used both as a biographical reference work and as a scholarly treatment of the subject by students and researchers.

Yearns was also involved with the *Biographical Register of the Confederate Congress* (Ezra J. Warner and W. Buck Yearns, LSU Press, 1975). The Confederate Congress is not heard of often because it was only in existence during the war years and did not play a large role in the military conduct of the war. Nonetheless, the biographies of its 267 members collected into one volume do expand the amount of established reference information on the Confederacy. Many of the men who served in the Confederate Congress had been U.S. Congressmen prior to the war. The biographies contain all the information the authors were able to find through extensive research, but some of the figures remain relatively obscure in spite of the effort. The work contains four appendixes that furnish information on the sessions of the Confederate Congress, standing committees, membership, and maps of the Occupied Confederate Territory, 1861–1864. A bibliography of sources used to compile the biographical information completes the volume. This biographical work is rather specialized and will probably only be used by researchers seeking information on the Confederate Congress or individuals who served in that body.

Ezra Warner also produced two well-known biographical titles that are still classics in Civil war studies: *Generals in Blue: Lives of the Union Commanders* (LSU Press, 1964) and its earlier companion volume, *Generals in Grey* (LSU, 1959). Warner spent years researching the two biographical works, contacting descendants and searching family records and newspapers files, to establish facts about the lives of 425 Confederate and 583 Union generals. The biographies contain sound opinions and analysis as well as biographical facts. The two works have not been surpassed or replaced by any subsequent reference publications and are still the most useful for serious research.

Another biographical work is *Civil War Generals: Categorical Listings and a Biographical Directory* (Greenwood Press, 1986). This volume features a conspectus arrangement of listings by rank, date of birth and death, college, and vocation before and after the war. There is also a listing by battle of those killed, with dates. Following the listings are four-line biographical sketches. This work does not contain as much information as do the Warner titles. The presentation of the information makes it more of a quick reference source, but the Warner titles are to be preferred for serious research.

493. Leaders of the American Civil War: A Biographical and Historiographical Dictionary. Charles F. Ritter and Jon L. Wakelyn, eds. Westport, CT: Greenwood Press, 1998. 465p. ISBN 0-313-29560-3.

The concept of this "dictionary" is not that of the usual biographical work. It is a selective biography of only 47 men and women who are perceived to have been "leaders" in some way. It includes many of the great leaders from both sides of the war, but also civilians, businessmen, manufacturers, and even literary figures. The book provides an overview of their career and the war's impact on the rest of their lives. The difference in this work from most biographical sources is that it provides an assessment of the reputation of the individuals throughout history. Not only are the persons' influences during the war period assessed, but their legacy and how they have been perceived since then are examined. The evolution of scholarship and the views of modern historians are discussed. The work includes an introductory essay on the writing of biographical history. The majority of the entries are written by the editors, reputable historians of the Civil War, both of whom have other reference works to their credit. The entries average around 10 pages each with bibliographies at the end. The work is very readable and is a good starting point for student research.

A similar selective biographical work is *The Civil War 100: A Ranking of the Most Influential People in the War between the States,* by Robert Wooster (Citadel Press/Carol Publishing Group, 1998). The order in this book is from the most to the least influential. The ranking is that of the authors, a professor history at Texas A & M University in Corpus Christi. Each brief biographical entry includes a portrait. An introduction to the volume is a brief history of the Civil War period. There is a chronology, six pages of appendixes, and an index. Perhaps the most valuable aspect of this work is that the author includes individuals of negative influence and others who would not make most lists of major figures of the period.

While the publication year of this work is 2000 the *Encyclopedia of Civil War Biographies* by James M. McPherson (Armonk, NY: M.E. Sharpe, 2000. 3v.) is not a new biographical work, but a republication of 528 biographical sketches of Civil War figures culled from the *National Cyclopedia of American Biography* by noted Civil War historian James M. McPherson. The *Cyclopedia* began publication in 1888 and did not cease until 1984. The biographies in this *Encyclopedia* appeared between 1890 and 1910, for the most part. Many of the individuals were still living when their sketches were published. Thus, the sketches are not critical, and in some cases are inaccurate. They do not reflect recent scholarship and do reflect the politics and culture of the late nineteenth century. The individuals included are almost entirely male military and political figures. The set brings together biographies scattered throughout the *Cyclopedia.* It is interesting to see the reputation of those included at the time the sketches were written. The work is useful for researchers who are knowledgeable about the era.

494. Locating Union & Confederate Records: A Guide to the Most Commonly Used Civil War Records of the National Archives and Family History Library. Nancy Justus Morebeck. North Salt Lake, UT: Heritage Quest, 2001, 152p. ISBN 0944931898. **Roster of Confederate Soldiers 1861–1865.** Janet B. Hewett, ed. Wilmington, NC: Broadfoot Publishing, 1995, 1996. 16v. ISBN 1-56837-306-6. **Roster of Union Soldiers 1861–1865.** Janet B. Hewett, ed. Wilmington, NC: Broadfoot Publishing, 1997. 12v. ISBN 1-56837-344-9.

Broadfoot Press has provided two comprehensive sets for locating information on individuals who fought in both armies in the Civil War, edited by Janet Hewett. The sets are transcribed from National Archives microfilm reels containing the rosters of soldiers. The set for the Union Army is about twice as large as that for the Confederacy. The organization of the set for the Confederacy is one alphabetical sequence and thus the set forms an index to the compiled rosters, which are by military unit, in the national Archives. This index provides the basic information for each soldier—state, rank, military organization, and company—under the form of the name that appears in the roster. There is an introductory essay to the set, which provides further sources for finding and identifying soldiers. The set for the Union is organized by state and then alphabetical within states. The printed rosters provide means of comparison and research that were extremely difficult to impossible with the reels of microfilm. Because of the number of volumes, the sets are expensive but should be owned by libraries in institutions in which there is considerable Civil War or genealogical research.

A subset of the *Roster of Union Soldiers* transcribed from the microfilm group M589 comprises a two-volume set of registers of African American soldiers. The set has been sold separately as *The Roster of Union Soldiers, 1861–1865: United States Colored Troops.* The two-volume set is an alphabetic roster of nearly 200,000 African Americans who served as volunteer Union soldiers in the U.S. Civil War. Also listed are about 7,000 white officers who served with the "colored" units.

495. Who Was Who in the Civil War. Stewart Sifakis. New York: Facts on File, 1988. 766p. ISBN 0-8160-1055-2.

Biographies of approximately 2,500 individuals, both military and civilian, are contained in this *Who Was Who.* The essay biographies concentrate on the individual's wartime activities and accomplishments but also follow through during the postwar period. The biographies are lively and interesting, often quoting humorous comments made by or about the individual. Some entries give references to other sources for more information. Illustrations from the period are interspersed throughout the volume. There is a selective critical bibliography, a list of illustrations (with sources indicated by codes), and a glossary of place names. One appendix contains a chronology of Civil War battles and events, and the other gives a list of Union officers thanked by the U.S. Congress. There is an index that includes occupational titles, lists each side's participants by rank, and cites references to places and events.

Facts on File has published two volumes extracted from *Who Was Who in the Civil War;* the titles are *Who Was Who in the Confederacy* (1988) and *Who Was Who in the Union* (1988). The duplication makes it unnecessary for libraries to own the individual volumes, but inquirers can use either the one-volume or the two-volume formats, as both contain the same information.

THE FRONTIER AND INDIAN WARS (1860–1890)

From 1860 to 1890, the United States military engaged in war after war with the indigenous peoples of the western United States. Although numerous treaties recognized the rights of individual tribes, the U.S. government often did nothing to stop settlers from expanding into Indian territory. The reaction of the various tribes varied; some fled, some attempted to peacefully coexist, but many fought against the loss of their homelands and traditional way of life. It was inevitable given the superior numbers, organization, and technology of the United States that they would be overcome. But the Indian resistance was often skillful, heroic, and tenacious, and there were notable victories along the way. The Battle of the Little Bighorn is the legendary event midway through the period and the one entry in this section is for that conflict. Further treatment on the subject of the frontier wars can be found in "The Native American Experience" in chapter 6.

496. Custer and the Battle of the Little Bighorn: an Encyclopedia of the People, Places, Events, Indian Culture and Customs, Information Sources, Art and Films. Thom Hatch. Jefferson, NC: McFarland, 1997. 229p. ISBN 0-7864-0154-0.

The body of literature relating to General George Armstrong Custer is voluminous. The author of this reference work is a Custer fan whose purpose in compiling the work was to assist readers by providing one comprehensive resource on the entire career of Custer and others on both sides of his last battle. The book is arranged alphabetically and covers people, places, social, political, cultural, and historical events of the times. Military topics, campaigns, battles, equipment, and terminology take into account recent research on the battle. Plains Indian customs and culture, including drawings and oral histories, are covered. Entries include cross-references, maps and illustrations, and suggestions for further research. In one entry, "Motion Pictures and Videos Relating to Custer and Little Bighorn," there are over 40 movies and videos listed. There is an appendix, "Custer Civil War Chronology and Battle Summary." The work summarizes scholarly research as well as covering much of the popular literature, fiction, movies, and art relating to the topic. There is an extensive index. The work broadly covers an era in U.S. western history and makes a useful starting place for research on that time period.

SPANISH-AMERICAN WAR AND PHILIPPINE-AMERICAN WARS (1898–1902)

The Spanish-American War was America's shortest war, lasting only eight months. It propelled the United States onto the world stage as an international and colonial power with the acquisition of the Philippines, Puerto Rico, and Guam. Conversely, Spain lost its remaining colonial territories in the Caribbean and the Pacific. The role of the press emerged as "yellow journalism," a term for the manipulation of public opinion in the United States to favor the short war. A number of new reference works were issued in the latter 1990s in connection with the centennial of, what then Secretary of State John Hay called a "splendid little war."

497. Encyclopedia of the Spanish-American and Philippine-American War. Jerry Keenan. Santa Barbara, CA: ABC-CLIO, 2001. 467p. ISBN 1-57607-093-X.

The entire period of the two wars with details of all the campaigns and principal battles are covered in this work. In an A-Z arrangement, brief biographies are provided of key military and political figures from the United States, Spain, Cuba, and the Philippines. The role of the press in manipulating public opinion to favor the war; the complex maneuvering by both sides during the Paris peace negotiations; and the aftermath of the war in the Philippines and the Sulu archipelago are all dealt with. There are a bibliography, a chronology, and an index.

Another reference work that treats both wars is *The War of 1898 and U.S. Interventions 1898–1934: an Encyclopedia* (Garland, 1994). This work covers the longest span of time among the reference works on the Spanish-American and Philippine wars. A new title is given to the Spanish-American War because the war in Cuba had been largely won by the Cuban revolutionaries before U.S. intervention, hence the title Spanish-Cuban/American War. The term Philippine War has also been replaced by "Philippine Insurrection." Over 700 detailed mini-essays, of which approximately 400 are biographical, are written by 130 contributors who offer interpretations of events, strategies, and tactics. Maps, a glossary, and bibliographical references are included. This work is valuable for the extended time period it includes and for adding additional viewpoints to the study of that period.

498. The Spanish-American War: An Annotated Bibliography. Anne Cipriano Venzon. New York: Garland, 1990. 255p. (Wars of the United States, v. 11; Garland Reference Library of the Humanities, v. 1,120.) ISBN 0-8240-7974-4.

The entire time period of the Spanish-American War, extending to 1902 through the U.S.–Philippine conflict, is covered in this selective bibliography of over 1,000 items. It contains English-language source materials written between 1898 and 1986, including scholarly monographs, periodical articles, dissertations, personal accounts, War and Navy Department reports, and other government documents. Fiction, poetry, and music are included but not annotated. Only printed source materials are cited in the bibliography, but there is a section on special collections for further research. The entries are organized into topical chapters. Several chapters are devoted to public opinion on the issues raised by the war, such as expansionism and anti-imperialism. The bibliography is useful for students, scholars, and general readers.

499. The Spanish-American War: A Historical Dictionary. Brad K. Berner. Lanham, MD: Scarecrow, 1998. 443p. (Historical Dictionaries of War, Revolution, and Civil Unrest, no. 8). ISBN 0-8108-3490-1.

Timed to coincide with the year of the centennial commemoration of the Spanish-American war in the United States, Spain, and Cuba, this reference work covers the war in all aspects. It begins with a chronology followed by an alphabetical arrangement of 1,000 entries cover the involvement of Spain, Cuba, the Philippines, and Puerto Rico along with the United States. The famous incidents and scandals such as the investigation of the Maine, the "yellow press," and the "Embalmed beef scandal" are all covered. The war strategy of the United States is highlighted covering major battles, correspondents, military leaders, military units, and specific data on the Spanish and American navies. There is in-depth coverage of the post-war period including the Armistice Protocol and the treaty of Paris, which sealed the transfer of colonial possessions from Spain to the United States. It covers the wide-ranging political and cultural significance of the Spanish-American war in entries written by 96 historians and specialists. The work contains a 26-page bibliography topically arranged. There are no maps and no index although the entries are cross-referenced.

A similar but less comprehensive work is Donald Dyal's *Historical Dictionary of the Spanish American War* (Greenwood Press, 1996), which also lacks maps. It includes 700 entries with bibliographies for each entry, a chronology, a bibliographic essay, and a subject index.

WORLD WAR I (1914–1918)

There are many associations and societies that encompass both world wars, probably because the two conflicts were waged within one generation of each other and were fought on some of the same terrain, with the German adversary in common. Groups specifically focused on the first World War are the Veterans of World War I of USA (c/o Muriel Kerr, PO Box 8027, Alexandria, VA 22306-8027, (703) 780-5660), Widows of World War I (c/o Helen Green, 324 SW Gregory, Burleson, TX 76028, (817) 295-1658), World War I Overseas Flyers, and Allied Airborne Association (c/o Frank Juliano, 117 Milton Ave., Staten Island, NY 10306, (718) 979-1950). The National Ladies Auxiliary to Veterans of World War I of the U.S.A. was found in 1953 and has 10,000 members (c/o Opal Petersen, Natl. Sec. Treas., 767 SW Fourth St., Rm. 101, Forest Lake, MN 55025-1547, (651) 982-1646).

The First World War has been eclipsed in history by the magnitude of the Second World War. There have been a few reference works published in recent years that focus on World War I.

500. The American Field Services Archives of World War I, 1914–1917. L.D. Geller, comp. Westport, CT: Greenwood Press, 1989. 87p. (Bibliographies and Indexes in World History, no. 16). ISBN 0-313-26794-4.

This slim volume describes the collections of the archives of the American Field Service, a voluntary medical organization that operated in France from 1914 to 1917, at which time it became part of the U.S. Army. The volume contains an essay on the American Field Service and the sources in the archives, followed by descriptions of over 50 archival collections. An appendix contains box and folder lists. There is a name and subject index. The small volume is attractively illustrated with over 50 photographs from the AFS archives. A grant from the National Historical Publications and Records Commission contributed to the completion of the bibliography. Students and scholars of World War I will want to explore the research materials contributing to perspectives on the conduct of the war in France, Franco-American relations, and the contributions of the leaders and volunteers of the American Field Service to the war effort.

501. Army Uniforms of World War I: European and United States Armies and Aviation Services. Andrew Mollo. Poole, England: Blandford Press, 1977; distr. by Sterling Publishing, 1986 printing. 219p. ISBN 0-7137-1928-1.

The illustrations in this work are drawings based on actual uniforms or photographs, resulting in consistency and accuracy in the details depicted. The only pieces not illustrated are the various insignia, which are only described in the text. The uniforms included are from the U.S. and European forces and are arranged by country. The accompanying text covers detailed aspects of the uniforms and traces the changes in type and design throughout the war. The work is of interest to all military enthusiasts as well as historians.

502. Atlas of World War I. 2nd ed. Martin Gilbert. New York: Oxford University Press, 1994. 164p. ISBN 0-19-521075-1; 0-19-521077-8pa.

The first edition of this atlas has been revised and updated with five new maps. There are 164 black-and-white maps with brief narratives covering all facets of the war and the immediate postwar period. One of the strengths of this atlas is the statistical data provided, such as the number of soldiers in the U.S. Army by state. The maps are grouped in sections for land, air, sea, global affairs, and the war's aftermath. In addition to battle maps there are topical maps giving detailed economic and political coverage such as food riots in Germany. There is a detailed index and a bibliography. The work is an ideal reference to keep near when doing reading or research on the period.

In *Great Battles of World War I,* by Anthony O. Livesey (1989), 18 major battles are presented in three-dimensional maps constructed through computer graphics. The book is a comprehensive history of World War I with photographs, paintings, and drawings in addition to the maps. The text is accompanied by sidebars focusing on weaponry, uniforms, ships, planes, and notable persons. The work illustrates the horrors of the trench warfare and the tactics that resulted in the high casualty rate (over 8 million killed). The work can serve as a reference source or as supplemental reading for students.

503. Chronicle of the First World War. Randal Gray and Christopher Argyle. New York: Facts on File, 1990–1991 2v. ISBN 0-8160-2139-2 (v. 1); 0-8160-2595-9 (v. 2).

Every aspect of World War I, military, political, and international, is tracked in this two-volume chronology. Volume 1 spans the period from before the assassination of Archduke Ferdinand in 1914 to 1916. Volume 2 continues through 1917 to the end of the war in 1918 and the finalization of the peace process in 1921. The volumes present a day-by-day record of the war accompanied by critical analyses of events. Each volume is illustrated with maps and contains a foreword, a glossary, tables, statistics, a bibliography, and an index. Volume 2 contains a biographical section of over 100 key figures in the war. The source is scholarly and can be used for quick reference or read vertically as an overview of the war.

Almanac of World War I (University of Kentucky Press, 1998) by David Burg and L. Edward Purcell also is a chronology. There are five chapters, each devoted to a year of the war. Each chapter begins with an analysis of the events of that year. There follows a day-by-day account of the events of the year subdivided by locations where the most important events occurred. The work has a military emphasis with considerable analysis of the strategy and tactics of specific battles. It is attractively formatted with inserts on specific topics. There are biographical sketches on key figures. The volume contains a bibliography and an index. The work is useful for the analysis provided and as a summary of the war years.

504. The United States in the First World War: An Encyclopedia. Anne Cipriano Venzon, ed. Hamden, CT: Garland, 1995. 830p. (Military History of the United States, v. 3; Garland Reference Library of the Humanities, v. 1205.) ISBN 0-8240-7055-0.

This one-volume work is designed to be a comprehensive, but quick reference for information concerning all aspects of U.S. involvement in World War I. The time period is from the preparation prior to military entry into the war through the signing of the Armistice, which ended it. The signed, alphabetical entries are by 200 specialist authors. Attention is paid to the role of women, African Americans, and volunteers. Because the majority of the time period was not actually spent in military engagement in Europe, the work covers both the civil and military aspects of the war. Topics of political, industrial, and moral support of the war and organizational and individual opposition to it are covered. Military coverage includes sketches of important figures and individual histories of the major army divisions. Also covered are foreign leaders and foreign relations. There are six maps but no other illustrations. The bibliographies accompanying the entries only have a small number of sources. In that respect the work is most useful as an information source and not as a starting place for further research. There is a name/subject index. The coverage of the time period and the issues is thorough.

A similar work is *Dictionary of the First World War* (St. Martin's, 1995) by Stephen Pope and Elizabeth-Anne Wheal. This work contains a 15-page insightful introduction, a monthly chronology of major battles and events, and 25 maps. There are 1,200 informative entries. The strength of the work is its coverage of the global aspects of the conflict. Entries are devoted to the events in India, Asia, and the Middle East, the non-Western front. Social topics such as alcohol and pacifism also receive attention. Although the two works are similar, the topics are covered in somewhat different perspectives.

505. World War I. Neil M. Heyman. Westport, CT: Greenwood Press, 1997. 257p. (Greenwood Press Guides to Historic Events of the Twentieth Century). ISBN 0-313-29880-7.

More an overview than an informational reference volume, this work is an excellent beginning point for student research. It has an introduction by the author, a chronology of events, and a clearly organized map showing the sequential changes in European borders 1919–1937. There are seven chapters that examine various aspects of the war and its aftermath. The last chapter provides links between the war and the impact of the outcomes upon the remainder of the century. One feature of the work, which makes it an excellent resource for students, is the inclusion of the text from many primary documents such as speeches, letters, newspaper accounts, and personal diaries. There is a 25-page annotated bibliography, a glossary of terms, and an index. Although not suitable for use as the only source on World War I, this work makes an excellent introduction to the subject.

Also intended primarily for students, is the *Grolier Library of World War I,* an eight-volume encyclopedia: "The Causes of the Conflict, 1914"; "The Race for the Sea, 1915"; "The Lines are Drawn, 1916"; "The Year of Attrition, 1917"; "The U.S. Enters the War, 1915–17"; "The Eastern Front, 1918"; "A Flawed Victory"; and "1919–39, the Aftermath of the War." The set is highly illustrated with maps and photographs. There are sidebars with biographical sketches, quotes from letters and diaries. The entries are cross-referenced to related topics. The emphasis in the set is on the causes of the war ranging back to 1878 and its effects up to 1939. It provides insights into social history, literature, and medical and technological advances of the period. A section called "what if" provokes further thought on alternatives that could have affected the future differently. Each volume contains indexes to the set, a glossary, and a bibliography. This is an excellent, authoritative resource for students.

506. World War I Aviation Books in English: An Annotated Bibliography. James Philip Noffsinger. Metuchen, NJ: Scarecrow, 1987. 305p. ISBN 0-8108-1951-1.

This bibliography of over 1,600 items is arranged in one alphabetical sequence by author. Not all entries are annotated, but the bibliography is fairly comprehensive for monographic works on World War I aviation, including rare editions. The subject matter of the titles cited ranges from technical aspects of the aircraft to personal memoirs and biographies of the famous pilots and other personalities of the period. The work is attractively illustrated, and there is a subject index. The bibliography partially updates that of Myron J. Smith, *World War I in the Air* (Scarecrow, 1977), but does not replace it, because the Smith work covers a wider variety of source materials. It has an aviation chronology for the war years and a list of Aces by country, ranked by number of "kills." Both bibliographies will be of interest to World War I historians, aviation historians, and enthusiasts.

A broader work in scope is by A.G.S. Enser, *A Subject Bibliography of the First World War: Books in English, 1914–1987* (Brookfield, VT: Gower, 1990). This bibliography of monographic works includes personal memoirs. It has a topical arrangement, but there are author and anonymous title indexes. A list of subject headings eases access to the volume's contents.

507. World War I Reference Library. Gale Group. 2001. ISBN 0-7876-5475-2. **World War I Almanac.** 2001. ISBN 0-7876-5476-0. **World War I Biographies.** 2001. ISBN 0-7876-5477-9. **World War I Primary Sources.** 2001. ISBN 0-7876-5478-7.

Gale has published a Reference Library on each of the major U.S. wars of the twentieth century designed as an introduction to the period for students. Each set contains an almanac, biographies, and primary sources. The *World War I Almanac* contains 15 chapters beginning with the European background to the war, the causes of U. S. involvement, the Espionage and Sedition acts, and the evolving military arsenal and tactics. The *Biographies* volume includes all key figures of the period, military and political. The volume of *Primary Sources* includes the full text or excerpts from 20 diaries, speeches, letters, journals, and memoirs. There is a cumulative index to the set. The reference is a good place to begin research on the period of World War I.

508. World War I Songs: A History and Dictionary of Popular American Patriotic Tunes, with Over 300 Complete Lyrics. Frederick G. Vogel. Jefferson, NC: McFarland, 1995. 530p. ISBN 0-89950-952-5.

A complete reference on songs of the World War I period, this work is divided into three parts. The first part contains essays dealing with different topics reflected in the popular music and how the music related to the mood of the country. The essays cover the period before the war up through WWII. Part 2 lists all WWI songs published in the United States with information on lyricist and composer. Part 3 gives the complete lyrics to over 300 songs of the period. Black-and-white reproductions of sheet music covers enliven the book.

An extensive index lists song titles, composers, lyricists, publishers, subjects, and key words in the songs. This work is the starting place for research on songs from the World War I period.

*509. World War I: Trenches on the Web. Available: http://www.worldwar1.com.

Developed and maintained since 1996 by a private individual with an avid interest in World War I, Mike Iavarone, this Web site points to many other Web resources with information on the period. The site features a "reference library" which offers quick access to original documents, a war atlas, photo archives, statistics, artwork, books, reviews, and more. An "exhibit" section contains digital images of primary sources, a chronology of the war, battle maps, and other materials. There are links to other sites of World War I materials, including bibliographies, booksellers, and not-for-profit organizations. Not strictly for research, the site is valuable for the breadth of information it gathers together.

WORLD WAR II (1941–1945)

In the Second World War fighting began on much the same terrain as in World War I, but the technology of weapons, airplanes, and sea craft was much advanced. Because many people in Europe and the United States still had memories of the earlier war, the second war was entered very reluctantly. Once the United States was committed, however, the war became global; it was fought on all continents except Australia. The Cold War that followed lasted for four decades. The 50th anniversary of the United States' entrance into World War II was observed in 1991.

The global scope of World War II has occasioned the formation of many societies and organizations, some by type of military unit, some by geographical region. There are still many veterans of the Second World War living, and the history of that conflict will be preserved through video records, which had just reached a level of sophistication sufficient to capture the reality of war.

The American Committee on the History of the Second World War, now titled the World War II Studies Association (c/o Mark Parillo, Dept. of History, Kansas State University, Eisenhower Hall, Manhattan, KS 66506-1002, (785) 532-0374), is a small organization (300-plus members) composed of academic and government historians and others interested in promoting historical research on all aspects of World War II. The organization meets annually in conjunction with the American Historical Association and publishes a semiannual *Newsletter* that includes book reviews and emphasizes archival and bibliographical resources.

Many popular works on aircraft, ships, tanks, artillery, and the like have been published. Only a few such recently published works are described in this section. The majority of the reference works in this section are for scholarly research.

510. Biographical Dictionary of World War II. Mark M. Boatner, III. Novato, CA: Presidio Press, 1996. 733p. ISBN 0-89141-548-3.

Although a number of biographical dictionaries of World War II figures have been published, Boatner's is the most extensive to date having 1,000 entries. *A Biographical Dictionary of World War II* by Tunney (St. Martin's, 1972), a standard work, has 540 entries that cover only the war years. Similarly, *Who's Who in World War II* by Mason (Little,

Brown, 1978; repr. Oxford, 1994) contains 527 entries confined to the war period. Boatner, author of numerous historical works, selected the individuals to be included by counting the number of citations to the person in indexes. The coverage is evenly balanced between the major countries and nationalities that participated in the war. The coverage of Russian officials and officers is particularly good. Significant military and nonmilitary figures, persons from the arts, and civilian victims are included. The sketches are written in a lively style. In addition to the biographical sketches, there is a glossary, which provides background mini-articles cross-referenced to the biographies. The work is the definitive biographical tool on the period and supplements current encyclopedias on the war.

Who's Who in World War II by John Keegan (Oxford University Press, 1995) is a small volume suitable for students. It contains more than 300 brief sketches of the most important figures in the global war.

Political Leaders and Military Figures of the Second World War: A Bibliography (Brookfiled, VT: Dartmouth Publishing/Ashgate Publishing, 1996) by Steven D. Chambers provides both brief biographical information and a bibliography of books for leading figures of the World War II era. Each entry consists of a brief one- or two-page biographical introduction followed by a selectively annotated bibliography. Only well-known figures are included and the bibliography is limited to monographs. The work is useful as a beginning place for student research, but contains information that can be found elsewhere.

511. The Biographical Dictionary of World War II Generals and Flag Officers: the U.S. Armed Forces. R. Manning Ancell and Christine M. Miller, comps. Westport, CT: Greenwood Press, 1996. 706p. ISBN 0-313-29546-8.

Almost 2,400 biographical entries are arranged in six chapters by branch of service. The compilers claim to have found basic information on 99 percent of the officers who served in World War II through searching a large number of official government records and archives. The information for each officer includes place and date of birth, education, military career from start to end, decorations and awards, and date and place of death. Two appendixes of birthplaces by state and birth date by years and service are included along with an alphabetical index of all biographees. The information is presented without commentary and there are no illustrations. The work is an excellent starting point for genealogists or those researching the pertinent aspects of service during World War II.

512. The D-Day Encyclopedia. David G. Chandler and James Lawton Collins, eds. New York: Simon & Schuster Academic Reference Division, 1994. 665p. ISBN 0-13-203621-5. Also available as a CD-ROM product.

This work was issued to mark the 50th anniversary of D-Day, June 6, 1994. The *Encyclopedia* contains 400 essays written by more than 150 contributors, either outstanding military leaders, or academics. The work is heavily illustrated containing over 400 photographs and drawings, with original maps specially commissioned for the volume. The organization is topical with a comprehensive index. Every aspect of the invasion is covered in great detail. The CD-ROM contains the complete text of the printed encyclopedia with an accompanying teacher's manual. Menus and pop-ups within articles offer further explanation or guide the reader to other resources on the topic. The encyclopedia is an excellent resource for the study of the invasion of Europe by the Allied Forces.

513. Destroyers of World War II: An International Encyclopedia. M.J. Whitley. Annapolis, MD: Naval Institute Press, 1988. 320p. ISBN 0-87021-326-1.

All destroyer-class ships in existence during the time period 1939–1945 for all nations, including completed and constructed vessels, are recorded in this encyclopedia. The arrangement is alphabetical by country and then by class of destroyer. Technical data are given for the class, displacement, length, beam, draught, machinery, and so on. The class is then described in three categories: design, modifications, and service. There is a short introduction and history for each country's vessels. A historical essay on torpedo boats/destroyers is at the beginning of the volume. Numerous photographs and drawings of individual ships illustrate the text. There is an alphabetical index of ship names. The encyclopedia is suitable for serious research by military historians and naval historians or others with a keen interest in World War II and naval battles.

Another work published by the navel Institute Press is *U.S. Army Ships and Watercraft of World War II* by David H. Grover (1987). Although the subject of this work would seem somewhat specialized, it certainly is not small. The U.S. Army had over 127,000 naval vessels of various types in operation during World War II, nearly twice as many as did the Navy. This was not a fleet of battleships but rather a miscellany of ships needed for various chores—tugboats, hospital ships, tankers, transports, and communication ships. Each chapter in the work is devoted to a particular class of ship with data and facts such as dimensions, tonnage, build, engines, and builder. The postwar fate is also given. A glossary, bibliography, and index to the volume are presented. The work is attractively illustrated with photographs. The little-known subject makes this work valuable to those interested in naval history and World War II, students and researchers alike.

A more specialized work is *Hospital Ships of World War II: An Illustrated Reference to 39 United States Military Vessels* (McFarland, 1999). Of the 39 ships only one was designed to be a hospital ship. The others were existing ships that were converted to bring home thousands of wounded American and Allied soldiers. U.S. Army and Navy ships were used as well as civilian vessels. Extensive information is given on the entire life of the ships: deck plans, commissioning documents, namesakes, personnel, wards, and visiting celebrities. There are an index and a bibliography.

514. The Historical Atlas of World War II. John Pimlott. New York: Henry Holt, 1995. 224p. ISBN 0-8050-3929-5.

Two World War II historians have contributed to this atlas with an international perspective on the military course of the war. The atlas is divided into five sections, each with an essay on the period. The major battles and campaigns are traced in 100 color topographically detailed maps showing major unit movements. The volume includes a chronology and numerous black-and-white photographs. There are general and place-name indexes.

515. The Holocaust and World War II Almanac. Peggy Saari and Aaron Maurice Saari. 3v. Detroit: Gale Group, 2001. ISBN 0-7876-5018-8.

Designed for the beginning researcher, this three-volume set includes more than 100 biographical profiles, over 600 illustrations and maps, and selections from primary sources. Volume 1 covers the period from the end of World War I up to the beginning of World

War II reviewing the conditions and ideologies of that time which set the stage for World War II, including Nazism in Germany, Fascism in Italy, militarism in Japan, and isolationism in the United States. Volume 2 covers the war period, both the European and Pacific theaters, as well as the Holocaust. Volume 3 contains the biographies of more than 100 figures of the era. There are appendixes on Jewish victims, the Nuremberg war crimes trials, the Tokyo trials, and films related to the Holocaust. The volumes are plentifully illustrated with photographs, political cartoons, and maps. The set forms an excellent starting point for research.

516. The Hutchinson Atlas of World War II Battle Plans: Before and After. Stephen Badsey, ed. Chicago: Fitzroy Dearborn, 2000. 275p. ISBN 1-57958-265-6.

The "Before and After" in the title refers to the approach used in this work, which contains analyses of 21 major battles in the European theater in World War II from the fall of France in 1940 to the Battle of Berlin in 1945. The original battle plans are compared with maps showing how the battles were actually fought. The battles are divided into seven categories on armored blitzkriegs, amphibious landings, slogging matches, air power, the war at sea, airborne assaults, and city battles, with three battles in each. An introductory essay, "The Strategy of World War II," describes wider events, placing battles into a context so that their origins and outcomes can be better understood. Each entry covers the dates of the battles, lists the armies and commanders involved, provides a chronology, an analysis of the battle, and suggestions for further reading. The work is an excellent research tool for the battles covered of use to students and historians.

The essential facts and a concise summary of 52 of the most important battles of World War II are given in *Battles and Battlescenes of World War II* (Macmillan, 1989). Air, land, and sea battles in Europe, Asia, and North Africa are included. Each entry contains factual information on date, location, object, opposing sides, casualties, and results. Each section contains a narrative about the battle and a list of suggested readings. Maps and photographs are provided for each battle. There is a chronological table at the end that gives data, location, opposing sides, and the nature of the battle. There is an index. This informative work should appeal to students and the general public.

War Maps: World War II, from September 1939 to August 1945, Air, Sea and Land, Battle by Battle by Simon Goodenough (St. Martin's Press, 1982) is an older atlas. The larger portion of the work, the first 140 pages, covers the European theater. The last 45 pages are devoted to the Pacific theater. There is an index to the maps at the end. In addition to the maps, there are explanatory text and photographs. The maps vary in scale, but the quality is high. This work will appeal to students, teachers, and librarians seeking a visual reference work to supplement other works on World War II.

517. Investigations of the Attack on Pearl Harbor: Index to Government Hearings. Stanley H. Smith, comp. New York: Greenwood Press, 1990. 251p. (Bibliographies and Indexes in Military Studies, no. 3). ISBN 0-313-26884-3.

The surprise attack on Pearl Harbor by the Japanese has been the subject of eight official inquiries by branches of the armed services and Congress. The reports of the hearings were published as the *Hearings before the Joint Committee on the Investigation of the Pearl Harbor Attack* (40 parts, Government Printing Office, 1946). In addition to the testimony, the volumes contain exhibits, charts, and illustrations prepared for the hearings. Although two indexes to congressional proceedings that include the Pearl Harbor hearings have been published—*Witness Index to the United States Congressional Hearings: 25th–89th Congress, 1839–1966* (Greenwood Press, 1974, microfiche) and *CIS U.S. Congressional Committee Hearings Index, Part V: 79th–82nd Congress, 1943–1952* (CIS, 1981)—there did not exist a separate satisfactory index to the Pearl Harbor investigations until the Smith work was published. The index references people, places, aircraft, ships, and events mentioned in the reports. A preface includes background information on the hearings and reports. The index makes the hearings and accompanying documents accessible to anyone seeking information on the events in the Pacific theater in World War II.

518. Oxford Companion to World War II. I.C.B. Dear and M.R.D. Foot, eds. New York: Oxford University Press, 1995. 1,343p. ISBN 0-19-866225-4.

Over 1,700 entries by 151 contributing historians fill this large encyclopedia. The exhaustive coverage includes military battles and campaign, biographies of leading figures, diplomacy, the home front, and the economic and social impact of the war. The entries run the gamut from brief explanations and identifications to in-depth, lengthy articles, some with bibliographies. There is a chronology and the work is illustrated with maps (some in color), charts, graphs, and photographs.

519. The Pacific War Encyclopedia. James F. Dunnigan and Albert A. Nofi. New York: Facts on File, 1998. 2v. ISBN 0-8160-3439-7.

This encyclopedia is a comprehensive overview of the war in the Pacific with Japan and the China-Burma-India theater as well. The two-volume set covers all sides of the war from many perspectives, including insights from Japanese military figures and civilians, women, and African Americans involved in or affected by the war. The majority of the entries concern the U.S.–Japan war. Weapons, warship classes, and aircraft types, brief unit histories, logistics, and political and strategic policy are included. Statistical data are provided in tables and boxes. There is a chronology of the Pacific War with lengthy month-by-month essays, one of the outstanding features of the work. There are an annotated bibliography and a name/subject index. Appendixes include a listing of present names for contemporary names and code words and names in use during the war. The authors, two distinguished military historians, have shared their expertise and viewpoints in writing the entries. As a single, comprehensive resource on the subject, this is an excellent reference work useful for any level of research.

The Pacific War Atlas, 1941–1945 (Facts on File, 1995 by David Smurthwaite) can be used along with the other works on the war in the Pacific. The major campaigns are presented in 65 maps. Reviews point out numerous errors in the text and the volume is not well indexed. It is useful only as an accompaniment to an authoritative text.

The War Against Japan, 1941–1945: An Annotated Bibliography by John J. Sbrega (Garland, 1989) is no longer current, but the broad coverage and excellent annotations make it still useful for research. There are over 5,200 citations to works published through 1987. Sources included are reference works, histories, biographies, articles, fictional works, official reports, and other government documents. The volume is organized into six chapters that follow the LC classification. Military matters make up a goodly portion of the work, but political, social, economic, and religious aspects of the Pacific war are well covered. The appendixes include a list of periodicals consulted; a directory of Japanese-American relocation centers; a chronology; and author and subject indexes.

Grolier has produced a CD-ROM, *Executive Order 9066: the Incarceration of Japanese Americans during World War II* (1997). The CD-ROM documents the internment of the approximately 120,000 people who were incarcerated by the United States government during World War II because of their ancestry. There are four main topical sections: a chronology, biographical profiles, subjects, and places.

520. The Southwest Pacific Campaign, 1941–1945: Historiography and Annotated Bibliography. Eugene L. Rasor. Westport, CT: Greenwood Press, 1996. 279p. (Bibliographies of Battles and Leaders, no. 19). ISBN 0-313-28874-7.

In the historiography, Rasor reminds readers that in one sense World War II began as early as 1931 in the East with the movement of the Japanese army into China. Part 1 of the work is a historiographical essay, a general survey and review of the works listed in part 2, providing critical analysis and placing the works in context and noting gaps in the literature. Part 2, the annotated bibliography of 1,500 entries encompasses popular and scholarly literature, memoirs and diaries, fiction, film, and art. The author index includes both page numbers for the historiography and entry numbers for the bibliography; the subject index includes only page numbers to the historiography. The bibliography makes an excellent supplement to other reference works.

A complementary work is *World War II in the North Pacific: Chronology and Fact Book* (Greenwood Press, 1994) by Kevin Don Hutchison. This work covers an area that did not have the military significance of the central and south Pacific. Hutchison, an amateur historian, has compiled an immense amount of detail into one volume. The sense of what it was like to be fighting in the harsh climate of the north toward the end of the war is conveyed. The arrangement is chronological with day-to-day records of the activities of the Allies and the Japanese, including the Soviet Union. There are maps, biographies of key figures, a bibliography, and appendixes.

521. U.S. Marine Corps World War II Order of Battle: Ground And Air Units in the Pacific War, 1939–1945. Gordon L. Rottman. Westport, CT: Greenwood Press, 2001. ISBN 0-313-31906-5.

The evolution and growth of the Marine Corps are studied in this complete reference source. In-depth background information on the units' functions, evolution, designation practices, tactical organization of combat units, and extensive statistical and technical data are given. Complete information is provided on all ground and air units in the Pacific with their evolution including dates in combat; location and code name of landing beaches; time of landing; island operation code names; date the island was declared secure; order of battle of the opposing Japanese units and their casualties; attached U.S. Army and U.S. Navy units; and much more. The work pulls together information formerly scattered through official documents and archives. It is the definitive resource for the study of the Marine Corps and the Pacific theater in World War II.

Rottman has also authored the *World War II Pacific Island Guide: a Geo-military Study.* (Greenwood Publishing Group, 2002). This work is organized by the islands that were taken from the Japanese. It is arranged regionally and chronologically according to when the islands entered the war so that the progression can be seen. Complete background information is provided on each island such as the physical characteristics, weather, health hazards, historical background, native population, natural resources, and military value and the island's postwar status. Japanese and Allied strategies and operations, military problems, military installations, key commanders and units, and brief battle descriptions are covered. The work will be essential to keep at hand when researching the Pacific theater.

522. World War II: An Encyclopedia of Quotations. Howard J. Langer. Westport, CT: Greenwood Press, 1999. 472p. ISBN 0-313-30018-6.

Over 1,500 quotations are provided from a variety of sources in this reference work, which is international in scope. The first 12 chapters contain quotations from individuals and are arranged by type of person quoted and then alphabetically by name. The remaining chapters cover subjects and are from movies, songs, coded military communications, and other anonymous sources. Biographical or contextual information is given on most entries so that those being quoted or the historical connection are established. An appendix lists quotations by category. There are indexes by subject and persons. The editor has compiled several other books of quotations from Native Americans and another on the Holocaust. Although many of the quotations are in standard reference works, this is an extensive work and there is merit in having the information for World War II in one volume.

523. World War II in Europe: An Encyclopedia. David T. Zabecki et al., eds. New York: Garland, 1999. 2v. (Garland Reference Library of the Humanities, v. 1254; Military History of the United States, v. 6.) ISBN 0-8240-7029-1.

This two-volume reference work is not designed to be a quick-reference source. It is organized into thematic parts rather than a straightforward alphabetical arrangement, making it a resource for reading. The work contains more data and fewer illustrations than most works of its kind. Over 1,400 signed entries covering new scholarship were contributed by 155 authors from eight different countries. The emphasis in the encyclopedia is the U.S. involvement in the European theater. Volume 1 is devoted to social and political issues and events. Volume 2 concentrates on military weapons and equipment, strategy, battles, campaigns, and operations. Five appendixes provide a chronology of events, tables of comparative ranks, a glossary of acronyms, abbreviations, foreign and military terms, and code names. There is a bibliography and two indexes: one of military units and warships and a general index. The work is recommended for serious students of U.S. history.

524. World War II Reference Library. Gale Group, 2001. ISBN 0-7876-3901-X. **World War II Almanac.** 2 vol. 2000. ISBN 0-7876-3830-7. **World War II Biographies.** 288p. 1999. ISBN 0-7876-3895-1. **World War II Primary Sources.** 222p. 2000. ISBN 0-7876-3896-X.

A "Reference Library" has been published by Gale Group for each of the wars of the twentieth century. As with the other similar sets, this one includes information and resources for students to use in beginning research and writing term papers.

The New Grolier Encyclopedia of World War II (1995) is an eight-volume set written for students at the middle school level. It is attractive and amply illustrated. The topical essays cover every aspect of the war and include biographical information, war stories, advances in technology, entertainment, and the Holocaust. It is an excellent reference work for students.

KOREAN WAR (1950–1953)

Often called the "forgotten war," the Korean War was a product of the post–WWII Cold War. Involving 1.5 million Americans, it was fought to contain Communism in a sort of proxy war by the United States against the Soviet Union and China under the auspices of the United Nations. The patriotism of World War II began to wane during the Korean conflict, which the U.S. military labeled as a "police action." The conflict brought about the partition of the Korean peninsula into North and South Korea. The Korean War is remembered by the Korean War Veterans Association (PO Box 10806, Arlington, VA 22210, (703) 522-9629), the Chosin Few (available at http://home.hawaii.rr.com/chosin), and Korean Veterans International.

Now 50 years after the conflict, renewed interest in the Korean War has resulted in new reference sources.

525. Encyclopedia of the Korean War: A Political, Social, and Military History. Spencer C. Tucker et al., eds. Santa Barbara, CA: ABC-CLIO, 2000. 3v. 1123p. ISBN 1-57607-029-8. Also available as an e-book.

Spencer Tucker is a noted historian, author or editor of 11 books on military and naval history. This three-volume encyclopedia delves into all aspects of the conflict, adding new perspectives based upon new information from Russian and Chinese archives. The 600 entries are written by 100-plus academic and military contributors. The work includes over 150 illustrations, 20 maps, and the text from 85 primary source documents. The entries cover the era of pre- and postwar Korea from both U.S. and Korean perspectives. There is a chronology of Korean history and a glossary. Volume 3 is devoted to primary-source documents never before gathered in one reference work. There are a general bibliography and an index. The encyclopedia is a definitive reference source.

526. The Korean War: An Annotated Bibliography. Paul M. Edwards. Westport, CT: Greenwood Press, 1998. 360p. (Bibliographies and Indexes in Military Studies, 10). ISBN 0-313-30317-7.

Similar in title and organization to Keith McFarland's 1986 bibliography, this recent work by Edwards serves to update the earlier work. The arrangement is similar with sections on broad topics and subdivisions. The alphabetical lists cover relevant books and articles up to 1997, as well as reports, theses, repositories, and document collections. Entries are primarily in English and annotations are brief but evaluative. There are author and subject indexes. The work is a bibliography and meant to be used as a reference work for research in conjunction with more descriptive and analytical dictionaries or encyclopedias.

The McFarland work, *The Korean War: An Annotated Bibliography* (Garland, 1986) lists over 2,300 English-language items dealing with the Korean conflict. Sources included are monographs, journal articles, government publications, personal accounts, and theses and dissertations. The work is divided into 23 topical chapters preceded by a chronology of the war. Topics covered include the background of the war and the U.S. decision to intervene, the home front, the U.S. Army in Korea, the United Nations and the war, the Truman-

MacArthur controversy, and a last chapter on analyses and consequences. A map of Korea is provided, and there are author and subject indexes. Although not an exhaustive bibliography, the work forms an overview of the subject. The bibliographies and the *Handbook* (entry 528) can be used in conjunction with each other. Together they provide good reference and beginning research coverage.

527. Korean War Almanac. Harry G. Summers, Jr. New York: Facts on File. 1990. 330p. ISBN 0-8160-1737-9.

The *Korean War Almanac* focuses on the United States and its military involvement in the Korean War. The work is divided into three parts. The first part, "The Setting," discusses the two Koreas. The second part is a chronology from June 25, 1950, to September 6, 1953. The largest portion of the work is the third section, "The Korean War A-Z," which contains 375 entries covering people, weapons and equipment, campaigns and battles, military terms, and political factors, issues, and events. Some entries provide references for further reading. The articles on weapons are very detailed. Biographical sketches cover the person's life, with an emphasis on the individual's role in the Korean War. There are 10 maps and numerous black-and-white photographs, as well as a selective bibliography and an index. The coverage in this work is not as balanced and objective as that of the *Historical Dictionary of the Korean War,* but its coverage of military terminology and technology and its illustrations and better maps make it useful as well. The two works complement each other.

528. The Korean War: Handbook of the Literature & Research. Lester H. Brune, ed. Westport, CT: Greenwood Press, 1996. 457p. ISBN 0-313-28969-7.

The *Handbook* provides a scholarly overview of the treatment of the Korean War and trends in historical writing about the conflict. The 23 chapters are each written by an academician. Part 3, "China, the Soviet Union, and the Korean War," describes recent research and how the release of Soviet and Chinese primary documents have altered previous interpretations. Each chapter has a bibliography and there are author and subject indexes.

The *Handbook* can be used in conjunction with an earlier reference also published by Greenwood, *Historical Dictionary of the Korean War,* edited by James I. Matray (1991). Approximately 500 signed entries cover prewar events, battles, strategies, documents, diplomacy, and truce talks. There are biographical sketches of government and military leaders from the United States, China, North and South Korea, and the USSR. Journalists and diplomats from other countries are also included. Cross-references and bibliographical references are given in the entries. There are 20 detailed maps of major battles and offensives placed in the front of the book. Statistical information on casualties, prisoners of war, lists of commanders, and so on are given in appendixes. There is a chronology and a selective topical bibliography. The purpose of the work is to contribute to an understanding of the issues surrounding U.S. involvement in the Korean War. The work is scholarly and has a detailed index. It can serve as a factual reference work or as a resource volume for serious study of the Korean War.

529. The Korean War Reference Library. Farmington Hill, MI: Gale Group, 2002. 2v. ISBN 0-7876-5573-2. **Korean War: Almanac and Primary Sources.** Sonia G. Benson and Gerda-Ann Raffaelle, eds. U*X*L Gale, 2002. 313p. ISBN 0-7876-5691-7. **Korean War: Biographies.** Sonia G. Benson, Gerda-Ann Raffaelle, eds. U*X*L Gale, 2002. 268p. ISBN 0-7876-5693-5.

Information and resources for the study of the Korean War are included in two volumes. The *Almanac and Primary Sources* volume covers the background of and issues related to the conflict in 13 chapters, starting with the Japanese occupation of Korea and ending with the armistice in 1953. The volume provides 12 full excerpts from primary sources of the period. The *Biography* volume includes approximately 25 entries on major figures of the war period. There is a list of additional sources for each biography and a detailed index for each volume. The set is designed for students and is illustrated with boxes highlighting special facts.

VIETNAM WAR (1957–1975)

The Vietnam War was long, controversial, divisive, and some say, a defining period in U.S. history. The Vietnam conflict was the first war in history to be covered on daily television news broadcasts. It is generally acknowledged that the immediacy of the news coverage had a large influence on the population back home. The long years of the Vietnam conflict involved a new generation that actively and sometimes vigorously questioned the motives of government in its conduct of foreign policy.

The Vietnam Veteran's Memorial has become one of the most frequently visited sites in Washington, D.C. The families and friends of those listed on the monument are organized into Friends of the Vietnam Veterans Memorial (520 N. Washington St., Suite 100, Falls Church, VA 22046-3538, (703) 525-1107). The organization seeks to ensure that the legacy of Vietnam is not forgotten and sponsors the Remember Them Project, which gathers biographical data and oral histories relating to persons listed on the wall (available at http://thewall-USA.com/). Other Web sites for the Wall are http://www.vietvet.org/thewall.htm, which has a gallery of photographs and stories of the Vietnam Veterans Memorial, and http://www.thevirtualwall.org/, "a digital, interactive legacy memorializing the men and women who gave their lives in Vietnam."

The Veterans of the Vietnam War, with 30,000 members, maintains a veterans locator service, POW/MIA listings, and collections of literature on Agent Orange and post-traumatic stress syndrome (available at http://www.vvnw.org).

Although U.S. involvement in Vietnam began before the term of President Kennedy in 1960, it did not end until 1975. The polarization of the U.S. citizenry over the Vietnam War has not truly receded into the historical past; the subject continues to provoke controversy and debate. Only in recent years has the Vietnam War begun to attain sufficient historical distance to become a subject for objective research. A number of reference works have been published for the purpose of assisting in historical research on the Vietnam conflict and its aftereffects.

530. America and the Indochina Wars, 1945–1990: A Bibliographic Guide. Claremont, CA: Regina Books, 1992. 286p. (New War/Peace Bibliographical Series, no. 1). ISBN 0-941690-43-1.

The Center for the Study of Armament and Disarmament of California State University, Los Angeles is responsible for the New War/Peace Bibliographical Series. The

United States was involved in three wars in Vietnam, Cambodia, and Laos. This bibliography concentrates on sources published since 1980, including books, periodical articles, and dissertations. The work reviews the history and background of the areas, the military conflicts, and the effect of the wars on life and politics in the United States during and after the wars. A reference chapter includes guides to library and archival collections and other useful reference works. The entries are not annotated except for an occasional one-line description. There are author and subject indexes and tables for war casualties and expenditures. The value of the bibliography lies in its coverage of literature published after the Vietnam War ended.

Louis A. Peake, the compiler of *The United States in the Vietnam War, 1954–1975: A Selected, Annotated Bibliography* (Garland, 1986), is a Vietnam-era Army veteran, not a librarian or bibliographer. The annotated bibliography of 1,667 English-language sources includes a number of useful features. One of these is a listing of accounts of the war by North Vietnamese. Another is the inclusion of films, art, and recordings. The bibliography is strong in references on the controversial issues and aftermath of the war. The organization is by topical chapters. A chronology and glossary are furnished. There are subject and author indexes, although they are somewhat inadequate.

A work with a narrower focus is *Air War in Southeast Asia 1961–1973: An Annotated Bibliography and 16mm Film Guide* by Myron J. Smith, Jr. (Scarecrow, 1979). Military strategy in the Vietnam War made heavy use of air strikes and other aerial technology, such as the spraying of herbicides. Although this bibliography is no longer current, it still pulls together, into one volume, sources on all aerial aspects of the Vietnam War. There are over 3,000 English-language sources covering the administrative and operational aspects of the air war for the 1961–1973 period. The majority of items are periodical articles. Studies from the Air War College and the Air Command Staff College are cited, as are popular sources. The films are primarily those produced by the military. There is a subject index that includes persons, aircraft, organizations, missions, and places. The variety of source material and the simple organization make this bibliography suitable for use by students and researchers.

531. Cultures in Conflict: The Vietnam War. Robert E. Vadas. Westport, CT: Greenwood Publishing Group, 2002. 230p. ISBN 0-313-31616-3.

The vast differences in cultures between the United States and Vietnam are examined in this work. A historical overview of the long period of the war includes a discussion of the Vietnamese and American ways of life. The author conducted many personal interviews. A wide selection of primary documents from both U.S. and Vietnamese combatants and civilians depict the meaning of the war. The documents are presented chronologically and thematically, moving from early motivations to war experiences and the shattered legacy left by the war. The work is unique and includes personal accounts from ordinary Vietnamese fighting with and against the United States. The text is illustrated with photographs. There is a chronology and a glossary. *Cultures in Conflict* is a series by Greenwood Publishing Group in which conflicts are seen through the eyes of ordinary men and women from both sides.

The New York Times' 20th Century in Review: The Vietnam War (2002, 2v.) also deals with the ideological struggles and cultural conflicts occasioned by the war. One of the works in the *New York Times' 20th Century in Review* series, the work traces the origins, the strategies, the successes, the failures, and the bitter legacy of the war for the United States, Vietnam, and the world. More than 600 articles, and 150 photos, news stories, essays, editorials and other articles that originally appeared in the *Times* are included. The set has an index.

532. Encyclopedia of the Vietnam War: A Political, Social, and Military History. Spencer C. Tucker, ed. Santa Barbara, CA: ABC-CLIO, 1998. 3v. ISBN 0-87436-983-5. Also available as an e-book.

Following the same format as the *Encyclopedia of the Korean War* (entry 525), this set includes documents, some never seen before. Spencer Tucker has also edited this three-volume work on the Vietnam War writing an introductory overview of Vietnamese history. Over 138 contributors wrote nearly 1,000 entries. The work contains 22 maps cover military, ethnographic, political, and geophysical information. After the entries in volume 2, there are a bibliography, a chronology, and a glossary. The third volume contains primary documents, including memos, letters, interviews, and speeches. The sources where each can be found as well as some Web sites for similar documents are also given. This set is the most comprehensive, scholarly resource for research into the period.

An earlier publication with the same title, *Encyclopedia of the Vietnam War* (Scribner, 1996) is a one-volume work edited by Stanley I. Kutler. The concise volume of 711 pages contains a chronology of Vietnam history from the seventh century to the present. The main body of the work consists of over 500 entries. Ten authoritative overview articles on political, social, and military aspects of the period, each with a bibliography, are included. Biographical articles include key figures from all sides. The treatment is objective with extensive descriptions of the leading Vietnamese participants and issues. The volume is amply illustrated with 210 black-and-white photographs and 13 maps. There is a bibliographic guide organized by subject and a detailed index. The work is useful for students in the amount of interpretative analysis provided.

The War in Vietnam is a resource intended for students. It does not deal with many of the more controversial issues of the conflict such as drug abuse by U.S. troops. There is a chronology of events and seven essays covering major aspects of the war and the consequences that followed. There are short biographies of key figures. Some primary documents are included. There are a glossary of terms and an annotated bibliography. The *Encyclopedia of the Vietnam War* and the earlier and *Dictionary of the Vietnam War* are superior publications.

533. MIAs: A Reference Handbook. Jeanne M. Lesinksi. Santa Barbara, CA: ABC-CLIO, 1998. 238p. (Contemporary World Issues). ISBN 0-87436-954-1.

One of the continuing issues since the Vietnam War has been the number of military personnel unaccounted for so many years afterward. This book contains an introductory overview of the MIA issue. There is a selected annotated bibliography, which does not cover the periodical literature on the subject. The up-to-date information on organizations concerned with the issue is one of the best features of the work. The other valuable feature is the large number of Internet sources covered. The work provides a good starting point for research.

534. Songs of the Vietnam Conflict. James Perone. Westport, CT: Greenwood Publishing Group, 2001. (Music Reference Collection, no. 83). ISBN 0-313-31528-0.

The political divisiveness of the Vietnam War spawned a much different kind of music than did the patriotism of the previous wars. The Vietnam War provoked anger, frustration, and rage, all of which is reflected in the songs of the period. The songs are divided into chapters on antiwar songs, pro-government songs, and songs dealing with the plight of the troops fighting the war. The author explores the relationship between the music of the time and the society within which it was written. Both well-known and obscure recordings are reviewed. There is a selected discography of the most notable recordings. The work provides a unique and important perspective on the popular music of a troubled time in U.S. history.

535. Vietnam: The Decisive Battles. John Pimlott. New York: Macmillan, 1990. 200p. ISBN 0-02-580171-6.

Another in the Macmillan military atlas series, this volume also features computer-generated three-dimensional maps. Seventeen key battles ranging from the French defeat at Dien Bien Phu in 1954 to the fall of Saigon in 1975 are depicted in two-page color spreads. In addition to the computer-generated maps, there are numerous diagrams, photographs, and drawings that further illustrate and relate to the battles. The volume contains a foreword written by Shelby L. Stanton. Military, political, and historical aspects of the war are covered in the notes accompanying the illustrations, and there is a military analysis of each battle. This work contributes to an understanding of the military conduct of the war and is a useful reference work for students and all others with an interest in the topic.

David B. Sigler has compiled a more-detailed and comprehensive account of military engagements, *Vietnam Battle Chronology: U.S. Army and Marine Corps Combat Operations, 1965–1973* (McFarland, 1992). This work traces more than 600 Army and Marine ground combat operations for the time period 1965–1973. The information given includes the dates, code names for the operation, geographical location, all military units involved, the objectives of the operation or targets, and casualties. In addition, there is a chronological list of operations according to command unit and an alphabetical listing by Army or Marine combat operation. One of the most useful features is a bibliography for each command unit that gives the National Archives record numbers for the Operational Reports. Name, subject, and military unit indexes conclude the volume.

536. Vietnam War Bibliography. Christopher L. Sugnet, John T. Hickey et al. Lexington, MA: Lexington Books/D.C. Heath, 1983. 572p. (The Lexington Books Special Series in Libraries and Librarianship). ISBN 0-669-06680-X.

Although this is a bibliography of the John M. Echols Collection at Cornell University, the number and depth of resources in the collection make the work a comprehensive bibliography for the Vietnam War. The sources span the mid-1940s to 1975, with the majority of sources concentrated during the period of heaviest military involvement. Over 4,000 of the more than 7,000 items in the Echols Collection are listed in the bibliography. Sources include books, pamphlets, manuscripts, documents, maps, serial titles, and archival and audiovisual materials. The sources are in English and foreign languages, including French and Vietnamese. The bibliography is computer produced and divided into three sections: a register, an index, and an appendix. The register is an alphabetical listing by title with basic bibliographical information such as date range, alternative titles, and call number/location within the Cornell libraries. The index is by authors, personal and organizational names, topics, and alternative titles. The appendix is a listing of acronyms and cross-references. The John M. Echols Collection is one of the largest and richest of primary- and secondary-source materials on the period of the Vietnam War. The bibliography will be useful to anyone engaged in scholarly research on the war in Southeast Asia.

University Microfilms has made available several microformat collections on the Victnam War. The first of these is *The Echols Collection: Selections on the Vietnam War.* The collection covers prewar and wartime history as well as the aftereffects of the war worldwide. It contains a variety of social and political commentaries, including views of anti- and pro-war factions, religious groups, and governments in the United States, Vietnam, and other countries. Another collection offered by Proquest/UMI is *The History of the Vietnam War,* which spans 25 years and includes 365,000 pages of material. Included are unclassified and declassified U.S. government documents; captured documents; prisoner of war interrogation reports; newspaper and periodical clippings from U.S., Vietnamese and other foreign newspapers; transcripts of speeches and press conferences; and propaganda leaflets and manuscripts by Vietnamese writers. These microform collections contain essential materials for research on the period of the Vietnam War.

537. Vietnam War Literature: An Annotated Bibliography of Imaginative Works about Americans Fighting in Vietnam. 3rd ed. John Newman et al. Lanham, MD: Scarecrow Press, 1996. 680p. ISBN 0-8108-3184.

A total of 1,370 entries for works written 1964–1995 are contained in the third edition of this bibliography. The concentration is on literary works. All types of creative writings, poetry, drama, fiction, and miscellaneous other imaginative writings are reflected in this growing body of literature about the war covered in the bibliography.

An earlier, similar bibliography is *Writing About Vietnam: A Bibliography of the Literature of the Vietnam Conflict* by Sandra M. Wittman (G.K. Hall, 1989). English-language works relating to the Vietnam experience by U.S. and foreign authors are listed in this bibliography of 1,734 citations. The bibliography is divided into 13 sections by literary format arranged alphabetically by author. The term "literature" is interpreted more broadly than in the Newman work. Dissertations and nonfiction narrative works are included. There are author and title indexes. The Wittman bibliography covers a broad range of sources, and the time span is from the French period up to latter 1980s. Both of these specialized bibliographies will be useful to general readers or researchers probing the psychological and sociological ramifications of the Vietnam War.

538. Vietnam War Reference Library. 1st ed., Kevin Hillstrom, Laurie Collier Hillstrom, and Diane M. Sawinski. Farmington Hills, MI: U*X*L Gale, 2001. 4v. ISBN 0-7876-4882-5. **Vietnam War: Almanac.** 307p. ISBN 0-7876-4883-3. **Vietnam War: Biographies.** 2v. ISBN 0-7876-4884-1. **Vietnam War: Primary Sources.** 244p. ISBN 0-7876-4887-6.

Another in the U*X*L series for students, the *Vietnam War Reference Library* gives comprehensive coverage to basic information about the topic. The *Almanac* provides a chronology from the beginnings in 1941 through the end of the war in 1975 with the fall of Saigon. Each of the 16 chapters contains a "Words to Know" and "People to Know" section, along with sidebars containing brief biographies, excerpts from memoirs and documents and interesting facts about issues and events. There are two volumes of biographies, some quite lengthy, on 60 people related to the war from all sides of the conflict. The *Primary Sources* volume contains 13 full texts or excerpts from a wide variety of sources including the media, screenplays, literature, speeches, and congressional testimony. All of the volumes conclude with a list of additional resources and a volume-specific index. A separate cumulative index is also provided with the set. Even though the level is for students, the set contains much reference information and would be useful for all levels of reader.

Another reference source is *Vietnam War Almanac* by Harry G. Summers, Jr. (Facts on File, 1985), which is similar to the *Korean War Almanac* (entry 527) by the same author. After an introductory essay about the war, there is a chronology. The main part of the book is an "A to Z" of persons, events, weapons, battles, and so forth. Every aspect of the war's history: military, political, social, diplomatic, and strategic aspects are covered. The volume is illustrated with 21 maps and more than 120 photographs. Summers, an infantry colonel who served in Vietnam covers controversial matters with respect to the U.S. armed forces and provides sensitive insights on the antiwar movements. The work is a standard reference source for readers at any level.

539. The War in Vietnam. Anthony O. Edmonds. Westport, CT: Greenwood Publishing Group, 1998. 192p. (Greenwood Press Guides to Historic Events of the Twentieth Century). ISBN 0-313-29847-5.

The books in this series are short works intended to serve both as a reference book and a history of the subject for students. The author, a professor of history, writes with an objective, nonjudgmental approach in analyzing various aspects of the war. There is a chronology followed by seven perceptive essays. There is a section of short biographies of key figures. The volume is completed with a section of primary documents, a glossary, and an annotated bibliography.

Another ready-reference work is *Historical Dictionary of the Vietnam War* by Edwin E. Moïse (Scarecrow, 2002). The work deals comprehensively with both military and political aspects of the war. Although the primary focus is on Vietnam and the United States involvement, the larger southeast Asia region, Laos, Cambodia, and the other countries are also covered. There is a chronology that traces the war from the early 1950s onward. The overview gives a brief discussion of the issues that continue to be debated among historians of the war. There is a bibliography, an index of names, and an index of operations.

An earlier similar reference work also published by Greenwood is *Dictionary of the Vietnam War,* edited by James S. Olson (1988). Brief entries with a few longer essays cover the people, legislation, military operations, and controversies of the U.S. involvement in Vietnam. Each entry includes references for further research. Two appendixes describe the population and minority groups of South Vietnam. Another appendix is a glossary of war acronyms and slang expressions. A selective bibliography, chronology, and maps of the Republic of Vietnam are also included. There is a name and title index, which includes names of aircraft, naval vessels, and weaponry. The dictionary is designed as a reference source for students and scholars.

THE PERSIAN GULF WAR (1991)

Shortly after the end of the war between the United States, its allies, and Iraq, reference works began appearing. The majority of them are non-scholarly and based upon published available source material. The conflict, although at the end of the previous century, probably does not yet have enough distance in time to be assessed from a longer historical perspective. The major reference works are covered in this section.

540. Encyclopedia of the Persian Gulf War. Mark Grossman, ed. Santa Barbara, CA: ABC-CLIO, 1995. 522p. ISBN 0-87436-684-4.

There were two works published with the same title, both receiving mixed reviews. The work by Grossman is based upon research in both primary and secondary sources and emphasizes the military. The narratives on weapons systems are detailed with a listing of sources for the information. There are a number of appendixes with table of casualties and other information about the countries involved in the war. One appendix is a list of slang definitions that are very helpful in reading the narratives on weaponry.

The other work with the same title by Richard Alan Schwartz (McFarland, 1998) provides a more balanced treatment of the war. The lengthy entries are arranged under alphabetical headings and cover people, places, events, weapons, operations, and other matters. There is an extensive chronology beginning with the overthrow of the Iraqi monarchy in 1958 through the aftermath of the war. The volume is illustrated with numerous pictures, maps, and portraits. There are a bibliography and an index. The Schwartz work is recommended as a supplement to other works on the subject.

541. Historical Dictionary of the Persian Gulf War 1990–1991. Clayton R. Newell. Lanham, MD: Scarecrow, 1998. 363p. (Historical Dictionaries of War, Revolution, and Civil Unrest, no. 9). ISBN 0-8108-3511-8.

Although the conflict in the Persian Gulf occurred in 1991, by the end of the decade there were already several reference works devoted to it. One of the most comprehensive is the *Historical Dictionary of the Persian Gulf War 1990–1991*. The author, who is a retired military officer, has endeavored to produce a reference work that would give the historical background to that area of the world. There is a chronology that begins in 1710 and covers many of the events which help to understand the modern context of the region. The main body of the work is an alphabetical arrangement of entries that define and describe the places, people, players, and military events. In addition to the entries there is an extensive bibliography divided into 35 topical categories covering political and military issues. Other sections of the bibliography list reference materials, book reviews, biographies, and other bibliographies. The full text of 40 primary documents are contained in three appendixes, including the United Nations resolutions and General Schwarzkopf's briefing of February 27, 1991. There are no illustrations or index, but there are extensive cross-references.

542. Operation Desert Shield/Desert Storm: Chronology and Fact Book. Kevin Don Hutchison. Westport, CT: Greenwood Publishing Group, 1995. 269p. ISBN 0-313-29606-5.

The time period covered in this work is from the middle of July 1990 to the end of April 1991. The emphasis is on military operations and events. A number of appendixes include names of casualties and those taken prisoner, tables of strengths of Iraqi units, and the order of battle for the U.S. and allied forces.

A similar work is Harry G. Summer's *Persian Gulf Almanac* (Facts on File, 1995). As per its title, this work is arranged chronologically. There is a brief historical background and discussion provides arguments on both sides. There are numerous photographs. Both of these chronologies make good companions to more extensive reference works.

Chapter 6
Social, Cultural, and Intellectual History

Of the historical divisions utilized in this guide, sociocultural and intellectual history furnishes the largest concentration of tools and resources. These study areas have undergone a great deal of review and examination in light of the heightened activity of the past few decades. Implications for scholars, students, librarians, and interested laymen are obvious in the numerous materials published on different topics and issues.

This chapter opens with a section on ideological trends and identifies reference sources dealing with the broad spectrum of sociopolitical thought, issues, movements, and trends from extreme right to radical left. Genealogy, the somewhat controversial auxiliary science, has been given equal footing with more established subfields and shares a section with immigration. This is followed by a look at works dealing with ethnic, gender, and racial influences, each of which is treated separately. The first edition of this reference guide was the first to deal with the gay/lesbian movement and to update coverage of works on the various ethnic minorities that contribute to our nation, and the current edition reflects that orientation. The diverse segments of our cultural and social existence are represented in our options and ultimate choices of religion, school, adherence to law and tradition, form of entertainment, and so on. Purposely excluded in this treatment, as was true of the first edition, are the fine arts (visual and musical), both popular and serious, and literature. The reader is advised to consult the several appropriate specialized guides in those subject areas.

A major resource of general nature is an internationally recognized organization in the field of cultural anthropology, The Human Relations Area Files, Inc. (HRAF; available at http://www.yale.edu/hraf/), which seeks to encourage and facilitate worldwide comparative studies of human behavior, society, and culture. Founded in 1949 at Yale University, HRAF is a financially autonomous research agency of Yale and produces two major collections (the *HRAF Collection of Ethnography* and the *HRAF Collection of Archaeology*) as well as encyclopedias and other resources for teaching and research. The homepage contains a link to the ethnography collection, which is itself linked to both the *Outline of Cultural Materials* and the *Outline of World Cultures*, serving respectively as subject guide and classification to HRAF publications. The major resource is the *Index to Human Relations Area File,* providing access to books, articles, documents and other relevant material.

Another useful tool of a general nature is *Sage Family Studies Abstracts* (1979–), which abstracts books, articles, documents, and other literature on a variety of topics relevant to family studies, marriage, gender issues, and employment among them. The emphasis is on current affairs, but historical writings are covered as well. Also of interest to the modern social historian is *Family Resources* (1970–), a database published by the National Council on Family Relations (available at http://www.ncfr.com). It is available through OVID and furnishes coverage of the psychosocial literature relating to family studies.

GENERAL SOURCES

543. American History and Culture: Research Studies by the National Park Service, 1935–1984. Alexandria, VA: Chadwyck-Healey, 1986. Microfiche.

Another of the monumental efforts by Chadwyck-Healey, now part of UMI, this microfiche source collection of more than 5,500 reports issued by the National Park Service over a 50-year period is valuable to scholars and serious students. Scope is extensive and covers three major areas: history, including oral history; archaeology and ethnology; and architecture and landscape, including interiors and artifacts related to the more than 300 national parks. Arrangement is geographical, with the country being divided into nine different regions. Reports vary in content and in depth of research; among them are identifications, descriptions, evaluations, and field studies of sites, furnishings, objects, and so on. Maps, photographs, drawings, and documents are given. Purchase of the complete set above ($24,000) includes *The Cultural Resources Management Bibliography* (*CRBIB*) on microfiche. *CRBIB* is an automated inventory of the reports issued by the National Park Service; the publisher's fiche edition furnishes access by location, subject, author, title, date, and category of study. This work is updated annually with the addition of current reports.

Recently, the publisher has had its immense collection of records placed on a single database, *ArchivesUSA,* available on the Web to subscribers only (available at http://archives.chadwyck.com). As of January 2001, it contained more than 118,000 archival collection records including over 50,000 from the *National Inventory of Documentary Sources (NIDS)* (entry 2n), over 79,000 from the *National Union Catalog of Manuscript Collection (NUCMC)* (entry 2n), and over 4,100 links to online finding aids. Directory information is supplied for 5,400 repositories with 2,200 links to repository home pages.

544. The American Family. Santa Barbara, CA: ABC-CLIO. 6v. 2000–2002.

Adolescence in America: An Encyclopedia. Jacqueline V. Lerner and Richard M. Lerner, eds. 2v. 2001. ISBN 1-57607-571-0. **Boyhood in America: An Encyclopedia.** Priscilla F. Clement and Jacqueline S. Reinier, eds. 2v. 2001. ISBN 1-57607-215-0. **The Family in America: An Encyclopedia.** Joseph M. Hawes and Elizabeth F. Shores, eds. 2v. 2002. ISBN 1-57607-232-0. **Infancy in America: An Encyclopedia.** Alice S. Honig et al., eds. 2v. 2001. ISBN 157607-220-7. **Girlhood in America: An Encyclopedia.** Dr. Miriam Forman-Brunell. 2v. 2001. ISBN 1-57607-206-1. **Parenthood in America: An Encyclopedia.** Lawrence Balter, ed. 2v. 2000. ISBN 1-57607-213-4.

This six-volume series of encyclopedic works treats the major component parts or features of the American family. Each volume provides a summary compendium identifying terms, personalities, events, and issues relevant to the role and dynamics of each element and its growth and development over centuries of U.S. history. This is accomplished through the presentation of several hundred articles treating a variety of relevant topics. Experts in the field have served as contributors. This is a unique work and should prove of value to a variety of users.

*545. American Journey Series. Woodbridge, CT: Primary Source Media (PSM), 1999. [CD-ROM].

This is an ambitious series of CD-ROMs providing treatment of landmark events within a wide spectrum of American history as recorded by eyewitnesses. PSM is part of the Gale Group and has spent the last 30 years developing an enormous archive of primary-source material. These disks, covering a variety of topics in social history provide a good introductory resource for college students supplying hyperlinks to essays, images, and documents such as treaties, eyewitness reports of events, legal opinions, official reports, and so forth. Exposition is supplied in the introductory sections. Each disk (topic) has a reputable editor with expertise in the subject. Topics in social history range from ethnic/gender groups (African-American Experience, Asian-American Experience, Hispanic-American Experience, Native American Experience Immigrant Experience, and Women in America, to Civil Rights, the Great Depression, and Westward Expansion.

*546. American Social Issues: An Interactive Encyclopedia. Santa Barbara, CA: ABC-CLIO, 1999. ISBN 1-57607-136-7. (CD ROM)

This electronic publication represents a useful source of information for a wide range of users from junior high school to college-level students, and is the second title issued by the publisher as an interactive encyclopedia (entries 594, 674, 838, 942, 1102). It surveys a variety of currently popular social issues in its 850 articles and provides access to primary-source material as well as informative narrative. Hypertext links are provided, one of which takes the user to eight extensive categories: labor, family, crime, discrimination, pacifism, environment, education, and sexuality. Entries treat a variety of topics in six divisions: biographies, documents, events, glossary, movements, and organizations. Included is a combination of images, video, narrative, audio clips, and hypertext links to additional material on the disk and to a related Web site from the publisher. Statistical tables are supplied as well. The work is relatively easy to navigate for successful access.

547. Encyclopedia of American Cultural and Intellectual History. Mary K. Cayton and Peter W. Williams. New York: Charles Scribner's Sons, 2001. 3v. ISBN 0-684-80561-8.

This is a comprehensive and up-to-date survey of American culture from the Puritans to Postmodernism, and provides treatment of all levels of culture. It furnishes another useful source for both high school and college students, and represents an enlightening vehicle for public library users. Included are such topics as Puritanism in the colonial era, the print revolution in the early republic, and slavery and race during the Civil War and Reconstruction, as well as modern cultural expression through books and film, success and consumerism in the economic order, and various cultural groups such as Asian Americans and Irish Americans. Coverage is of both high and low cultures, and focus is on both public and private ideologies with each article written by a scholar. There is liberal use of illustrations and boxed commentaries to facilitate study and understanding.

548. Encyclopedia of American Social History. Mary Kupiec Cayton et al., eds. New York: Scribner's, 1993. 3v. ISBN 0-684-19246-2.

Rather than emphasize isolated events and political phenomena, this work describes the processes by which people have defined their existence. Beginning researchers should find that the 180 essays furnish adequate depth and insight into the nature and composition of U.S. life from the precolonial period to the present. Essays vary from 8 to 16 pages and are organized into 14 topical segments covering such factors as social change, methodology, social identity, ethnic and racial subcultures, family history, and social problems. Included are maps, charts, and bibliographies. Each essay is written by an academician who has special interest or expertise in the topic. There is a comprehensive index to provide access. The entire text of this work is available in CD-ROM format along with several other Scribner's works in *Scribner's American History and Culture* (1998). Another effort from the same year, *Everyday Life: American Social History* (Macmillan Reference/Simon & Schuster, 1998) extracts selections from the *Encyclopedia*. It supplies a well-illustrated and concise approach.

A useful biographical dictionary published in the same year is *American Social Leaders: From Colonial Times to the Present* by James McPherson and Gary Gerstle (ABC-CLIO). This work treats 350 individuals who are recognized as leaders in the intellectual and social development in this country from the colonial times to the present day. Each entry contains a bibliography and in some cases pictures are supplied.

549. Encyclopedia of Social Issues. John Roth, ed. New York: Marshall Cavendish, 1997. 6v. ISBN 0-7614-0568-2.

Another useful compendium of contemporary social issues as they are represented in the American milieu is this multivolume treatment that includes lengthy topical articles of diverse nature such as animal research, U.S.–Cuban relations, gay and lesbian parenting, human reproduction, sex roles, medical ethics, and taxation. Included also are less detailed descriptions of subordinate issues, as well as organizations and personalities. Although the material is controversial in many cases, the articles are written in objective manner with the intention of providing information rather than advocacy. There are black-and-white photographs, charts, and graphs as well as tables to supplement the text.

Encyclopedia of Modern American Social Issues, edited by Michael Kronenwetter (ABC-CLIO, 1997) is a one-volume handy reference for students interested in the same area of study. Emphasis is on issues relating to twentieth-century social conditions, most of which continue as important concerns of the twenty-first century. Included here is a wide range of topics from abortion to welfare, as well as birth control, gun control, and acid rain. Historical context is furnished in some cases.

*550. Encyclopedia Smithsonian: American Social and Cultural History. Washington, D.C.: Smithsonian Institution, 1995–2000. Available: http://www.si.edu/resource/faq/nmah/start.htm.

From the great national museum of this country comes an important source enumerating bibliographies on various aspects of social history and providing links to information resources, exhibits, and collections of the Smithsonian. Beginning with an extremely useful "American History Timeline" under which one can click on elements of social life from the beginning to the present, the hot link outline then identifies "Art, Design, and Crafts," " Business and Consumer Culture," "Clothing, Costume, and Fashion," "Community Life," "Domestic Life," "Dance," "Film and Television," and more. Each of these divisions is subdivided into topics, all of which produce either a bibliography or graphics and narratives.

551. Growing Up in America: An Atlas of Youth in the U.S.A. Rickie Sanders and Mark T. Mattson. New York: Macmillan Library Reference, 1998. 291p. ISBN 0-02897-262-7.

Highly regarded for its extensive references and high-quality graphics is this award-winning source of information on young people in this country. Utilizing some 300 maps, graphs, and tables, this atlas provides visual awareness of the impact of key issues on this demographic group. Around 30 topics in health, race, immigration, crime, education, and poverty are examined in terms of their association with youth. Such aspects of the contemporary scene like runaways, homelessness, and AIDS are especially poignant when place into context with the tender age of their victims. As one might expect, there is the treatment of juvenile crime, teenage sex, and performance as students as well. An introduction is supplied for each section, along with an array of appendixes regarding minorities.

552. Index to America: Life and Customs Twentieth Century to 1986. Norma Olin Ireland. Metuchen, NJ: Scarecrow, 1989. 361p. (Useful Reference Series, no. 107). ISBN 0-8108-2170-2.

Best described as a popular bibliography of popular culture, this index has placed emphasis on titles that are common to most libraries. Included are articles from such publications as *People* magazine and various almanacs and handbooks, as well as recently published historical surveys and turn-of-the-twentieth-century writings. These focus on U.S. life and custom in all facets. Historical events are de-emphasized in favor of descriptions of family life, personalities, and social and political trends. The work has been criticized both for erratic coverage, with entries not always representing the most recent information within the framework of the stated time coverage, and for certain notable omissions. The author's earlier volumes in this series covered the seventeenth, eighteenth, and nineteenth centuries, and this one updates the coverage in *Index to America: Life and Customs, 20th Century* (1982). Arrangement is by subject, and the entire series should be considered more useful to the beginning student than to the serious inquirer.

553. Social Issues. Robert D. Benford. New York: Macmillan Library Reference/Simon & Schuster, 1998. 942p. (Macmillan Compendium). ISBN 0-02-865055-7.

Another useful encyclopedia for students from high school to college age is this collection of some 175 articles drawn from the *Encyclopedia of Sociology* (Macmillan, 1991) and from *Dictionary of American History* (Macmillan, 1995). It was thought that this would provide a necessary reference work for those especially interested in gaining insight into the social issues of the day. It provides focus on large-scale categories such as social institutions, social problems, social processes, and contemporary issues. Included within these areas are narratives on affirmative action, poverty, religious fundamentalism, inequality, crime, terrorism, drugs, abuse, and race and ethnic relations, among others. Taken from two fine sources, the signed entries are well written and informative. Arrangement is alphabetical and the work is well organized. Access is facilitated by a detailed subject index.

*554. SocioWeb: Your Independent Guide to Sociological Resources on the Internet. Mark Blair. 1995. Available: http://www.socioweb.com/˜markbl/socioweb/.

This independent guide has been maintained by Blair who has kept up with the field. (There is a notation that new listings had been added in late December 2001.) It serves as a directory of resources on the World Wide Web and has links arranged under 12 different categories. They are "Net Indexes & Guides," "Commercial Sites," "Giants of Sociology," "Journals and 'Zines," "Learning Sociology," "Sociological Theory," "Sociological Associations," "Sociology in Action," "Surveys and Statistics," "Topical Research," "University Departments," and "Writings." These divisions seem to serve their purpose well and users may choose to search the site by keyword or explore by category. It searches keywords in titles of the links and descriptions from the category listings. It represents a useful guide to the resources available.

555. This Remarkable Continent: An Atlas of United States and Canadian Society and Culture. College Station, TX: Published for the Society for the North American Cultural Survey by Texas A & M University Press, 1982. 316p. ISBN 0-89096-111-5.

The information used to construct the maps in this atlas is based on "detailed field surveys and interviews." The distribution of elements of culture and folklife, past and present, is depicted in 390 black-and-white maps. Topics covered include architecture, ethnicity, religion, language, food, politics, urban design, and leisure activities, presented with introductory material. The volume is more suitable for browsing than for searching for specific information, but it can be used as a supplementary source for data on ethnic groups, a study of regional patterns, and the geographic differences in attitudes of U.S. citizens. The first stage in the development of a comprehensive atlas by the society, it represents a unique source for scholars, students, and the general public. There is a bibliography of sources and an index.

IDEOLOGICAL TRENDS, ISSUES, AND MOVEMENTS

This country was created with a sense of pluralism that found strength in its diversity. In this section, one can find sources of information regarding philosophical orientations, sociopolitical movements and organizations, and trendy eras that have earmarked our past. For sources on the New Deal, see chapter 3, "Depression and Recession." For additional sources on civil rights, see section on "Ethnic, Racial, and Gender Influences" in this chapter.

The Center for Socialist History (available at http://www.gn.apc.org/csh) was founded in 1981 in Berkeley, California, to aid in the study of the U.S. Left. The institution has published its *Interbulletin* on an irregular basis since 1982. The Historians of American Communism (available at http://www.theaha.org), an organization of 165 members headquartered in Washington Depot, Connecticut, offers a quarterly newsletter. It can be accessed at the Web site of the American Historical Association as an affiliate. For advocacy of the U.S. right, the Intercollegiate Studies Institute (available at http://www.isi.org) was founded in 1953 and has more than 35,000 members. Currently operating out of Wilmington, Delaware, it has published the semiannual *Intercollegiate Review* since 1965.

GENERAL SOURCES

556. Encyclopedia of Modern American Extremists and Extremist Groups. Stephen E. Atkins. Westport, CT: Greenwood Press, 2002. 328p. ISBN 0-313-31502-7.

This is a unique source in terms of its focus on extremist politics and coverage of personalities, events, terms, and concepts from the period of the 1950s. There are 275 entries treating operatives and operations, both right wing and left wing, with decided emphasis on the past two decades. The extremist positions of the individuals and the organizations are described in well-written narratives identifying the radicalism in political, social, religious, and economic issues. Recent militia groups, cults, survivalists, and separatists are treated along with the traditional dissenters like the Ku Klux Klan. The work supplies bibliographies, photographs, and a chronology.

America in the Sixties: Right, Left, and Center, edited by Peter B. Levy (Praeger Paperback, 1998), is similar in its inclusion of diverse philosophies, and examines the frenzied period from the perspectives of liberals, new leftists, and conservatives. It enables the user to examine that period in a rich and full manner, providing a balanced treatment of key issues such as the Civil Rights Movement, Vietnam, the counterculture, and the women's movement. Included here are the arguments and manifestoes of both the Students for a Democratic Society and the Young Americans for Freedom, and the thoughts and words of a wide variety of individuals from Strom Thurmond to Hubert Humphrey to Jerry Rubin. There is a statistical profile given in the appendix, a bibliography, and an index.

557. From Radical Left to Extreme Right: A Bibliography of Current Periodicals of Protest, Controversy, Advocacy, or Dissent. 3rd ed., completely rev. Gail Skidmore and Theodore J. Spahn. Ann Arbor: Campus Publishers, 1987. 491p. ISBN 0-8108-1967-8.

The first edition of this work was compiled in 1967 by Robert H. Muller, at which time he mentioned the need for subsequent editions of a bibliography devoted to current periodicals of protest because of their ephemeral nature. The second edition was compiled by Muller along with Theodore and Janet Spahn in an expanded three-volume version issued between 1970 and 1976. This version identified 1,324 periodicals, as compared with 163 in the earlier edition. Some 280 periodicals were given full treatment, including name of editor, frequency, price, date of inception, circulation, and format. The third edition by Skidmore and Spahn processes the more recent material in the same manner, identifying 1,511 periodicals with 307 of them being given full treatment. Brief narratives or summaries for each title describe content and offer quotations. Entries are alphabetically arranged under various chapter headings, such as "Civil and Human Rights," "Peace," and "Libertarian." There are indexes providing access to titles, names, and opinions found in the narratives. Of importance is the cessation list for titles.

558. Social Movement Theory and Research: An Annotated Bibliographical Guide. Roberta Garner and John Tenuto. Lanham, MD / Scarecrow Press; Pasadena, CA: Salem Press, 1997. 274p. ISBN 0-8108-3197-X.

There is an introduction of more than 40 pages to open this work providing a fine descriptive analysis of the tenets of social movement theory and the historical perspective of research since the 1940s. The annotated bibliography is divided into three segments representing paradigm shifts with respect to social movements beginning with "The Irrational," embracing the negativity of the 1940s and 1950s and the McCarthy era in this country. This is followed by "The Rational," covering the more positive activity of the 1960s to change conditions represented by the period of Martin Luther King and the Civil Rights Movement, and finally by "The Deconstructive Movement" identifying the fragmentation of social structure of the 1970s to 1990s with the resulting backlash in producing a continued resistance and continuing racism. A name and subject index should prove helpful to college students and researchers alike.

559. Special Interest Group Profiles for Students. Kelle S. Sisung, ed. Detroit: Gale, 1999. 883p. (U.S. Government for Students). ISBN 0-7876-2794-1.

Of use to both high school and college students is this collection of 150 profiles of special-interest groups defined as "any organized group of individuals united together for a common cause that attempts to influence public policy." With such a broad-reaching definition, a diversified array of groups (right, left, and moderate) is included such as the American Library Association, the American Medical Association, Mothers Against Drunk Driving, and the Sierra Club. The work opens with an extensive chronology of American history. Entries are objective in style, run from four to six or seven pages in length, and are arranged alphabetically. Coverage begins with date of inception, number of employees, membership, and contact information. Descriptive narrative essays treat the group's mission, structure, functions, programs, and more. Current political issues are identified and illustrations, biographies, and graphs are provided in some cases.

PEACE, PROGRESSIVISM, AND REFORM

560. American Peace Writers, Editors, and Periodicals: A Dictionary. Nancy L. Roberts. New York: Greenwood Press, 1991. 362p. ISBN 0-313-26842-8.

A useful biographical dictionary that targets individuals associated with peace movements dating from the colonial era to modern times, this tool provides sketches of 400 writers and editors who attempted to enlighten their leadership to the issues of war and peace. The individuals selected for inclusion represent a wide range of interests, from well-known writers employed by mainstream publications to relatively obscure writers known only by readers of alternative periodicals published by church bodies and peace organizations. The entries are well done and informative and furnish personal information and descriptions of peace activities and of publications. Additional biographical sources are listed. In a work of this type, reviewers will question inclusions and omissions, but generally it should prove to be of substantial use to all inquirers. There is a chronology along with useful bibliographies of both peace publications and serious studies.

561. American Reform and Reformers: A Biographical Dictionary. Randall M. Miller and Paul A. Cimbala, eds. Westport, CT: Greenwood Press, 1996. 559p. ISBN 0-313-28839-9.

This is a useful biographical dictionary for college students and researchers in its in-depth coverage of leading reform movements and their advocates dating from the eighteenth century to the present. Treatment is given to 39 leaders who have left their mark on U.S. history. Arrangement is alphabetical beginning with Jane Addams and the settlement house movement and concluding with Frances Willard and temperance. All aspects of American reform are represented (antilynching, civil liberties, child welfare, labor, racial equality, theology, politics, feminism, education, pacifism, etc.). The detailed essays provide biographical information along with detailed historical analysis of the different movements.

American Reformers: A Biographical Dictionary edited by Alden Whitman (H.W. Wilson, 1985) is a more conventional source supplying just over 500 biographical essays of U.S. figures involved with reform movements dating from the seventeenth century to modern times. It represents a convenient package of useful information with treatment given to both the well known and the obscure. Entries range from 600 to 3,000 words and furnish dates, areas of reform, family background, education, and so forth, along with a summary of accomplishments. Photographs and bibliographies are included.

562. Anti-Intervention: A Bibliographical Introduction to Isolationism and Pacifism from World War I to the Early Cold War. New York: Garland, 1987. 421p. ISBN 0-8240-8482-9.

This extensive compilation of references gives annotations to about 1,600 monographs, periodical articles, essays, and dissertations; government documents are not covered, however. Beginning with the opposition to participation in World War I, the historical development of such resistance is traced to the late 1950s and the defeat of isolationism as a viable policy. The work is divided into five chapters: general works; World War I; the period from World War I to the 1950s; opinion-making elements; and ideological groups and leaders. Although the organization of this tool is excellent, the annotations are not consistent in length and utility. Some are too truncated to be viable, others nonexistent. Because material on these subjects is elusive, however, the work should be examined by all levels of inquirers.

563. Dictionary of American Temperance Biography: From Temperance Reform to Alcohol Research, the 1600s to the 1980s. Mark Edward Lender. Westport, CT: Greenwood Press, 1984. 572p. ISBN 0-313-22335-1.

This is a useful biographical dictionary consisting of about 375 entries of men and women considered to be activists in the temperance movements since the colonial period. The entries are written in three segments, beginning with brief summaries of life and achievements, followed by essays of one to two pages on the subject's involvement with temperance, and concluding with bibliographies of up to six works by the biographees and up to six works about them. Selection of the individuals is somewhat arbitrary, with no criteria for inclusion listed, but those included appear to merit consideration because of their activism or their intellectual productivity. Most of them are of historical importance, with relatively little representation of contemporary individuals responsible for the recent resurgence of the issue. Access is provided by an index of subjects, names, and organizations.

564. Peace Archives: A Guide to Library Collections of the Papers of American Peace Organizations and of Leaders in the Public Effort for Peace. Marguerite Green, comp. and ed. Berkeley, CA: World Without War Council, 1986. 66p.

This brief guide was created as a result of a historical program initiated in 1980 by the World Without War Council, the purpose being to analyze the peace movement in this country since 1930. This particular effort identifies documents and manuscripts held by approximately 30 major archive collections in this country. Included in each entry are the name of the curator, specific collections on the topic, types of services available, and services offered to donors and contributors. Although the guide has been termed of limited value by reviewers because of minimal information provided about the quality of each collection covered, it facilitates the search for such material and merits consideration by any researchers. Included in the appendix is a listing of 70 additional collections; there is a bibliography of search guides and manuals.

THE LEFT AND DISSENT

*565. Alternative Press Index: An Index to Alternative and Radical Publications. College Park, MD: Alternative Press Center, 1969–. ISSN 0002-662X.

Of interest to social historians and now available in CD-ROM, and on the Web through NISC (available at http:www.altpress.org/api.html), the *Alternative Press Index* has been in operation for over 30 years. It is issued on an annual basis with quarterly updates, and is the leading index of leftist or radical literature furnishing coverage of the pertinent articles from 380 periodicals. It includes listings of monographs, reviews, and essays; coverage embraces the environment, women's issues, anarchy, and the gay/lesbian movement, among other things. The Alternative Press Center issues the print version.

Similar coverage is given in **The Left Index: A Quarterly Index to Periodicals of the Left,* published since 1982 by The Left Index of Santa Cruz, California. This work indexes some 120 left-wing periodicals, both U.S. and foreign, on a variety of subjects, issues, and topics. Book reviews are listed separately. Now it is available on the Web through Political Research Associates with monthly updates (http://www.nisc.com).

566. Biographical Dictionary of the American Left. Bernard K. Johnpoll and Harvey Klehr, eds. Westport, CT: Greenwood Press, 1986. 493p. ISBN 0-313-24200-3.

A well-conceived and well-developed tool consisting of nearly 400 biographical essays, the work succeeds in providing a cross-section of leading personalities treated within the ideological context of their time, place, and milieu. About 50 contributors, mostly young scholars, have been utilized, provoking some justifiable criticism of certain inequities, imbalances, and omissions. Regardless, the essays are informative and well researched for the most part, and they furnish an excellent perspective on the U.S. Left through all its practitioners (e.g., socialists, communists, anarchists). The essays range in length from less than one page to nearly eight pages, reflecting the relative stature of the individual. Dates, personal and professional background, political affiliations, and activities are covered; sources for further study are listed. The work concludes with appendixes that attempt to qualify or categorize some of the data reported and a useful index.

567. The Citizen Action Encyclopedia. Richard S. Halsey. Phoenix: Oryx Press, 2001. 416p. ISBN 1-57356-291-2.

Issued at the tail end of the year 2000, this work represents the most recent compendium of information on the history of activism of U.S. citizens in the past century. There are some 300 entries with cross-references along with some illustrations treating a diverse array of social issues (animal welfare, homelessness, feminism, the religious right, and more). With such a comprehensive coverage of personalities, organizations, and developments from both the Left and the Right, this work will be used by both students and advocates. It supplies adequate background of the struggle that ultimately resulted in various degrees of social change through legislation, political success, and/or social mobility.

568. Encyclopedia of American Activism, 1960 to the Present. Margaret B. DiCanio. Santa Barbara, CA: ABC-CLIO, 1998. 322p. ISBN 0-87436-899-5.

Although there is some coverage given to activism on the part of the Right and certain reactionary groups like the Neo-Nazis and various militia movements, the bulk of the material treats left-wing activism. There are nearly 200 entries, arranged alphabetically, describing movements, organizations, events, personalities, and issues associated with dissent. They vary in length from a paragraph or two to several pages but generally supply adequate detail on the topics. As one might expect, the antiwar movement of the 1960s is prominent as is the environmental movement of the 1990s. One is able to find such individuals as Cesar Chavez, Malcolm X, and Tom Hayden; events such as the Native American Alcatraz occupation; issues such as civil rights and the sexual revolution; and organizations such as the Symbionese Liberation Army. Of course, topical inclusion is highly selective and many deserving subjects have been omitted.

569. Encyclopedia of the American Left. 2nd ed. Mari Jo Buhle et al., eds. New York: Oxford, 1998. 1024p. ISBN 0-19-512088-4.

The second edition continues to represent one of the few comprehensive works on the subject of the Left in U.S. society. Over 300 contributors have provided 650 articles describing major events, important personalities, institutions, and sources of information. Included here are the Sacco and Vanzetti trial as well as the Black Panther Party and Leonard Peltier. Defining the Left as that segment of society that has sought changes in the economic, political, and cultural systems, the work provides the student and inquirer with an informative introduction to ideological study. The period covered begins with 1870 and extends to the present day. Entries are full and detailed for the most part and provide insight into the topic; a bibliography is given at the conclusion. A special feature is a glossary of terms and acronyms, and access is furnished by a name-subject index.

Louis Filler, a prolific author of conservative persuasion, has authored an interesting and informative biographical work, *Distinguished Shades: Americans Whose Lives Live On* (Belfry, 1992). Fifty-six men and women of the mid-eighteenth to mid-twentieth century, largely of liberal and progressive belief (reformers, politicians, feminists), are revealed through detailed three- to five-page biographical sketches.

570. The Radicalism Handbook: Radical Activists, Groups, and Movements of the Twentieth Century. John Button. Santa Barbara, CA: ABC-CLIO, 1995. 460p. ISBN 0-87436-838-3.

In this case, the radicalism is of leftist to left-wing nature and the main text of the work provides page-length identification and lucid description of some 380 personalities of the past century. By way of introduction, there is an opening essay treating radicalism in this time period along with biographical coverage of nearly 40 personalities who operated prior to that time. Following the biographical coverage, there is a brief but well-considered treatment of the various radical groups and organized movements. Personalities and organizations run a wide spectrum from those who are very familiar and well known to those who are quite obscure. Entries provide bibliographic references for further reading and are of use to undergraduate students. Also of interest are several appendixes classifying the various subjects treated in the entries. An index provides access.

571. Voices from the Underground. Ken Wachsberger, ed. Tempe, AZ: Mica's Press, 1993. 2v. ISBN 1-879-46103-X.

This is an interesting and informative collection of histories of several underground newspapers and serves as a research guide for those attempting to find information on the underground press. The work begins with a history of the alternative press and examines the counterculture through personal narratives of 27 contributors who describe their experiences in the business. Included here are selections from such publications as *Fifth Estate, Great Speckled Bird, Guardian, Fag Rag,* and more. Along with the selections are expository essays seeking to enlighten the user. Volume 2 supplies a useful guide to the Vietnam era of dissent. There is an annotated bibliography of the underground press of that time, a guide to directories of special collections on social movements, and an essay on preservation of the underground press of the Vietnam period in microform.

THE RIGHT AND EXTREMISM

572. Censorship in America: A Reference Handbook. Mary Hull. Santa Barbara, CA: ABC-CLIO, 1999. 233p. (Contemporary World Issues). ISBN 1-57607-057-3.

This work supplies a useful introduction to current issues of censorship through a brief but informative historical survey and chronology of events and happenings that help the user place such developments in perspective. Emphasis is on the broad application of censorship in its coverage of such areas as music, art, and politics with treatment given to the various concerns regarding the Internet. Biographical coverage of personalities, descriptions of court cases, and identification of landmark documents are provided in analytical manner enabling the user to gain insight into the nature of the issue and the controversies surrounding it. There is a concise but useful glossary along with bibliographies of a variety of sources, both print and electronic. An index provides access.

573. The Concise Conservative Encyclopedia: 200 of the Most Important Ideas, Individuals, Incitements, and Institutions that Have Shaped the Movement, a Personal View. New York: Free Press Paperbacks, 1996. 318p. ISBN 0-684-80043-8.

As the former literary editor of the *National Review,* the author comes well prepared to describe the full spectrum of conservative thought as it relates to ideas, institutions, and historical events. This he has done in an enlightening collection of 200 provocative and informative, albeit brief, articles. Terms, concepts, and personalities are arranged in alphabetical order and provide awareness of the development of conservative thought from its origins to the present day. Major avenues of study dealing with economic, social, political, and spiritual issues are presented in clear fashion from their beginnings to modern trends and developments. Entries contain cross-references and quotations on the topic from conservative thinkers; they examine such diverse topics as ancient influences from the Greeks and Romans, Jewish contributions, and the impact of Christianity.

Biographical Dictionary of the Extreme Right Since 1890 by Philip Rees (Simon & Schuster, 1991) is a well-written compilation of biographical sketches covering the influential right-wing conservatives of the twentieth century.

574. The Conservative Press in Eighteenth- and Nineteenth-Century America. Ronald Lora and William H. Longdon, eds. Westport, CT: Greenwood Press, 1999. 401p. (Historical Guides to the World's Periodicals and Newspapers). ISBN 0-313-31043-2.

Following a detailed introduction presenting a historical survey of conservatism in the country during this time, this work treats 38 journals developed between 1787 and 1879, supplying historical descriptions in the form of well-constructed individual profiles identifying each journal's conservative themes. Omitted here are daily newspapers and all but a few significant weekly publications. Instead, emphasis is placed on serials with less frequency, especially monthly and quarterly publications. The heavy concentration of nineteenth-century products with only a few dating from the earlier period is indicative of the conditions attending such publication during the early years. Each entry is arranged in chronological order within its thematic category such as "political journals." Each entry contains a bibliography, notes on indexing, and availability.

The Conservative Press in Twentieth-Century America, published by the same authors in the same year, utilizes the same format in treating 65 periodicals dating from the late nineteenth century to the present. Categories include "the libertarian press" and "extreme rightist publications" among others.

575. Dictionary of American Conservatism. Louis Filler. New York: Philosophical Library, 1987. 380p. ISBN 0-8022-2506-3.

This one-volume dictionary of conservative thought is an interesting and even "lively" information piece, the intent being to provide a definition of concepts both past and present. Included are the "visible personalities," "symbolic slogans and ideas," and representative figures rather than a comprehensive or in-depth examination. As a result, the tool has been reviewed as lacking a balanced viewpoint. Filler, a prolific historian-writer of conservative orientation, seems to enjoy the process of creating reference books to espouse his philosophy: Gun control is defined as a "cause generally identified with liberals"; within the entry on abortion, one learns that "freedom of choice" is a euphemism for "legalization of abortion." Arrangement of entries is alphabetical, and length varies from a brief paragraph to more than a full page for certain individuals, such as Ronald Reagan, and broad topics.

A companion work is the author's *A Dictionary of American Social Change* (Krieger, 1982), which is an update of a 1963 publication with a slightly different title. Topics range from "abolitionism" to "Zoar Society." Most are treated concisely; like Filler's other works, it leaves no doubt of the author's sociopolitical stance.

576. The Ku Klux Klan: An Encyclopedia. Michael Newton and Judy Ann Newton. Hamden, CT: Garland, 1991. 639p. (Garland Reference Library of Social Science, v. 499.) ISBN 0-8240-2038-3.

This short-entry encyclopedia furnishes informative factual descriptions of several sentences in length, rather than broad-based interpretive analysis. It is a convenient tool, with alphabetical arrangement of entries designed to enlighten students to the nature and activity of what has been described as the "world's oldest terrorist organization." There are references within each entry to sources used by the authors, sources that have themselves been compiled as a bibliography at the back of the volume. These for the most part represent secondary sources of a popular rather than scholarly nature, such as wire service articles from newspapers (with an emphasis on the *New York Times*), magazines, and books of general interest. There is a brief, interesting history of the organization provided in the preface; listings of groups, individuals, and geographical entries are given at the beginning in place of an index.

577. The Ku Klux Klan: A Bibliography. Lenwood Davis and Janet L. Sims-Wood, comps. Westport, CT: Greenwood Press, 1984. 643p. ISBN 0-313-22949-X.

This is the second major book-length bibliography on the Klan and serves to complement the coverage by William Harvey Fisher (see below). Davis and Sims-Wood have produced a rather selective but generous listing of nearly 9,800 entries organized by sections covering major works, books, and pamphlets; dissertations and theses; KKK material; and government documents. Included are references to speeches of Klansmen and articles from *Kourier Magazine,* the *New York Times,* and regional newspapers. Although the work has been criticized for omitting materials from Jewish and other ethnic presses, it represents an important source for both students and researchers. There is a directory of archival repositories in the appendix. An author index furnishes access.

William Harvey Fisher's *The Invisible Empire: A Bibliography of the Ku Klux Klan* (Scarecrow Press, 1980) was the initial bibliography of large proportions, furnishing several thousand entries arranged under nineteenth- and twentieth-century divisions. No newspapers are treated, but coverage is given to subdivisions by form—dissertations, manuscripts/archives, government documents, monographs, and periodical articles. Annotations are brief. There are author and subject indexes.

578. Right Minds: A Sourcebook of American Conservative Thought. Gregory Wolfe. Chicago: Regnery Books, 1987. 245p. ISBN 0-89526-583-4.

In response to the surge of conservative thinking that has emerged over the recent decades comes this bibliographic guide prepared under the auspices of the *National Review* through Regnery Books. There is a foreword by William F. Buckley, Jr., who provides tribute to the conservative cause and praises the volume for its success in representing the essence of conservatism. The first part of the tool furnishes a bibliography of such writing organized under 22 subject headings such as "Education" and "The Welfare State." Part 2 renders a biographical dictionary of 75 leading conservatives from the beginning of the republic to 1985. The author serves as the editor of a conservative periodical, and in certain cases the application of the label "conservative" to some of the individuals named is questionable. Nevertheless, the volume serves the needs of both scholars and students, who profit from the final section, which identifies publishers, special collections, journals, and so on.

579. Unity in Diversity: An Index to the Publications of Conservative and Libertarian Institutions. Carol L. Birch, ed. Metuchen, NJ: Scarecrow, 1983. 263p. ISBN 0-8108-1599-0.

Prepared under the auspices of the New American Foundation, a conservative research firm, this work provides indexing to the periodical and monographic literature issued by the organization and 14 others of similar mind (among them the American Enterprise Institute for Public Policy, Cato Institute, and Hudson Institute). Publications date from between 1970 and 1981, thus providing a fairly intensive survey of conservative thought over this limited time period. The value of the work lies in its uniqueness, for most of these items have not been indexed by other services. Entries are arranged alphabetically by author under subject headings taken primarily from *Public Affairs Information Services* (*PAIS*). The work has been criticized for inconsistency or inadequacy of cross-referencing and for limitations of the selective subject index. The author index is detailed and includes editors, compilers, and contributors.

COMMUNISM AND ANTI-COMMUNISM

580. Communism and Anti-Communism in the United States: An Annotated Guide to Historical Writings. John Earl Haynes. New York: Garland, 1987. 321p. ISBN 0-8240-8520-5.

As the editor of the "Newsletter of Historians of American Communism," Haynes is well qualified to prepare this bibliography of over 2,000 items on the topic. The bibliography is divided into 37 major categories, such as "Schismatic Communist Movements" and "Right-Wing Anti-Communism and McCarthyism"; in many cases, these are subdivided into smaller categories. The detailed table of contents identifies these categories and subcategories, encompassing a variety of subjects. Included are books, periodical articles, and even some dissertations. The period covered is primarily from the beginning of U.S. Communism in 1917 to the decline of the American Communist Party in the mid-1950s and should provide both scholars and students with useful materials. There is an author index, but no subject index is provided. The introduction is most useful in describing the periods of writing and providing perspective.

581. Encyclopedia of the McCarthy Era. William K. Klingman. New York: Facts on File, 1996. 502p. ISBN 0-8160-3097-0.

Probably overdue in its coming is this reference work on that peculiar period of American history when the anti-Communist sentiment rose to fever pitch and sent many people in the arts and in government into forced isolation. The nature of that era is presented through 280 articles alphabetically arranged treating personalities, events, and issues. Emphasis is placed on the biographical treatment; a good estimate is that two-thirds of the articles deal with individuals of varying impact. Key figures such as Whittaker Chambers, Alger Hiss, and Joe McCarthy, himself, merit several pages and detailed observations while less influential people such as Morton Kent are given several paragraphs. To supplement the articles in the main text, there are useful aids such as a chronology beginning in 1919 and ending in 1960. Numerous appendixes supply transcripts of HUAC (House Un-American Activities Committee) hearings as well as texts of important documents. Illustrations are provided in many entries. There is a useful bibliography, and an adequate index.

COMMUNAL SYSTEMS

582. American Communes 1860–1960: A Bibliography. Timothy Miller. New York: Garland, 1990. 583p. (Sects and Cults in America Bibliographic Guides, v. 13; Garland Reference Library of Social Science, v. 402.) ISBN 0-8240-8470-5.

One of the publisher's two titles on communes issued during 1990, this work covers a period of 100 years normally considered a hiatus in communal development. Miller has shown that this is not true and furnishes excellent coverage in his identification of over

3,000 books, chapters, articles, theses, and dissertations. Entries are arranged alphabetically by community name and follow two general sections of bibliographies and reference works. Communities are both religious and secular in nature; each is given a brief description and historical treatment. Sections are subdivided by type of source material. Both primary- and secondary-source material is given. A comprehensive name index furnishes access.

The other Garland effort of the same year is Philip N. Dare's *American Communes to 1860: Bibliography,* which identifies over 1,900 works covering the early period of communal development to the onset of the Civil War. Structure and arrangement is similar to that of its counterpart above, although this volume has received more criticism for omissions in coverage and failure to explain its selectivity.

583. Dictionary of American Communal and Utopian History. Robert S. Fogarty. Westport, CT: Greenwood Press, 1980. 271p. ISBN 0-313-21347-X.

As editor of the *Antioch Review* with a background in the research of communal history, Fogarty was especially well prepared to develop this work. It has been limited to communal existence from 1787 to 1919 and provides both biographical and historical descriptions of the notable and noteworthy. The biography section contains about 150 sketches of individuals prominent in the founding and development of communes, or utopias, as they were called. Each sketch concludes with a bibliography of the individual's writings and a list of additional source materials. The other major segment furnishes historical passages describing nearly 60 communal societies, along with lists of sources. Criteria for selection are described in the preface to the work, and the introduction furnishes an overview of communal existence. A useful feature in the appendix is a listing of 270 communes. Access is provided by a name index.

584. Encyclopedia of American Communes, 1663–1963. Foster Stockwell. Jefferson, NC: McFarland, 1998. ISBN: 1-57607-181-2.

The development of communes, or utopian communities, with strong bonds to all residents in North America began in the seventeenth century and has continued to this day. This work treats more than 500 of these communities founded on the basis of political or religious ties over a period of 300 years. The work opens with an introduction explaining the nature of the commune and its importance in American history. The main text consists of alphabetically arranged entries providing interesting and informative profiles of each development. Included in each entry are the locations and dates of operation along with founding personalities, belief systems, ideologies, and activities. Also treated are the endings or dispositions of the communes. Entries include cross-references to those communes that shared the same site during different time periods. Illustrations are supplied, appendixes provide useful listings, and a detailed index provides access.

BIRTH, DEATH, ETC.

See also section on *The Female Experience* in this chapter.

585. The Disability Rights Movement: From Charity to Confrontation. Doris Z. Fleischer et al. Philadelphia: Temple University Press, 2001. 312p. ISBN 1-566-39812-6.

This work, about one of the movements that became visible in the modern era, contains a chronology beginning in 1817, but focuses on the time of Franklin D. Roosevelt to the present. It is not a reference book in the real sense but can be used in the reference department to provide awareness of the social context in which the rights of people with disabilities have become a significant part of the story of this country. Individual chapters treat such topics as groundbreaking legislation, technology, and de-institutionalization thus expediting the search for specific information. Much attention is given to the Americans with Disabilities Act. Numerous interviews provide a solid basis for this important study.

The Disability Rights Movement by Fred Pelka (ABC-CLIO, 1997) is a reference book in the true sense, supplying nearly 500 entries examining court cases, landmark laws, personalities, historical events, issues, and topics. These entries are alphabetically arranged for easy access and contain cross-references. Further support is provided through a detailed chronology. The work contains illustrations, and will prove helpful to a variety of users.

586. Encyclopedia of Birth Control. Vern L. Bullough. Santa Barbara, CA: ABC-CLIO, 2001. 349p. ISBN 1-57356-255-6.

It is interesting to note that two very similar sources with identical titles appeared in the same year. The controversy continues long after *Roe* v. *Wade* has become part of American history. Bullough's effort supplies entries alphabetically arranged that examine the nature and historical development of birth control in English-speaking countries. Various perspectives are presented from a variety of viewpoints (anthropological, biological, economic, feminist, political, and psychological). Such concerns as use of the pill and distribution of condoms, along with leading personalities and milestone events are treated in a clear and lucid manner. Contraception in various cultures is described with emphasis on Western institutions and developments.

Encyclopedia of Birth Control by Marian Rengel (Oryx Press, 2001) is a second resource treading the same ground. The work is comprehensive in nature and treats a variety of topics of international concern also with clarity. There are more than 200 entries in which information regarding biology, anatomy, methods of birth control, and leading personalities is given. One is able to examine the nature of issues and their controversies, and is made aware of religious perspectives as well as legal issues.

587. Margaret Sanger and the Birth Control Movement: A Bibliography, 1911–1984. Gloria Moore and Ronald Moore. Metuchen, NJ: Scarecrow, 1986. 211p. ISBN 0-8108-1903-1.

Normally, in a literature guide of this type, there is a purposeful attempt to avoid including materials on a single individual. In this case, however, the birth control movement is inextricably linked to Ms. Sanger's life, as is apparent in the organization of this extensive bibliography. More than 1,300 items, most of them annotated, are arranged chronologically by year from 1911 to 1966, the year of Ms. Sanger's death. The following sections contain materials written between 1967 and 1984. Sanger's own writings precede those of others in the 1911–1966 segment. Materials are varied and include monographs, periodical articles, newspaper articles, pamphlets, dissertations, and even novels. Annotations tend to be brief but useful. Additional coverage includes listings of special collections of relevant material, legislative bills, and hearings. The work represents an earnest attempt to include all materials available through academic or college libraries.

588. Pro-Choice/Pro-Life Issues in the 1990s: An Annotated, Selected Bibliography. Richard Fitzsimmons and Joan P. Diana, comps. Westport, CT: Greenwood Press, 1996. ISBN 0-313-29355-4.

The first issue appeared as *Pro-Choice/Pro-Life: An Annotated, Selected Bibliography, 1972–1989* by the same compilers (Greenwood Press, 1991). Its continuation is evidence of the unending contentiousness of the issue. Included here are monographs, articles, ERIC documents, dissertations, and court decisions from 1990 through 1994. There are over 1,500 entries by main entry representing the importance of this issue to the American public. Annotations point out the complexity of the issue and the degree to which it excites the interests and emotions of a polarized public. It is comprehensive in its inclusion of viewpoints and represents a wider range of resources than does the work listed below. Annotations are objective and summarize the content of the articles.

Abortion: A Reference Handbook by Marie Costa (ABC-CLIO, 1996) is now in its second edition and continues to profile groups and individuals associated with both sides of the controversy. This will serve as a useful resource for high school and college students in its provision of objective research material. There are biographical sketches, identification of laws and policies, and a chronology of events beginning with Ancient Greece. In addition, there is an annotated bibliography and useful filmography along with data on public opinion, the psychological impact of abortion, Internet resources, and Supreme Court cases.

589. The Right to Die Debate: A Documentary History. Marjorie B. Zucker, ed. Westport, CT: Greenwood Press, 1999. 336p. (Primary Documents in American History and Contemporary Issues). ISBN 0-313-30522-6.

Considered to be a well-balanced primary source of documents on the controversial matter of the right to die in this country, this work provide a well-considered selection of 138 government documents, court cases, statements from religious groups, and especially poignant personal narratives. Each document is preceded by an exposition of its nature in helping high school and college students understand the arguments put forth. Ideas and emotions are dynamic on this issue from one generation to the next and these changes are seen in the content of the documents, which range in age from the colonial period to the present. Arrangement of documents is by section divisions representing definitions of death, care of the dying and euthanasia before and after 1952, advance directives, role of the courts, and assisted suicide.

THE ENVIRONMENT

590. The ABC-CLIO Companion to the Environmental Movement. Mark Grossman. New York: ABC-CLIO, 1994. 445p. ISBN 0-87436-732-8.

Beginning its coverage at the end of the first quarter of the seventeenth century this work supplies some 400 interesting and informative articles on the key issues, events, and personalities associated with the environmental movement in this country. Aimed at the less sophisticated user, the work includes pieces of legislation and organizations relevant to the struggle to preserve the environment. Emphasis is, as one might think, on twentieth-century developments, although such well-known figures as Henry David Thoreau are treated along with more contemporary individuals like Theodore Roosevelt and Rachel Carson. There are a comprehensive chronology and a useful bibliography; a good index concludes the effort.

The Sierra Club Green Guide: Everybody's Desk Reference to Environmental Information by Andrew Feldman (Sierra Club Books, 1996) furnishes topical coverage of leading information sources through 1,200 entries organized by chapters. Stylized format for each chapter begins with an abstract of the topic followed by lists of relevant sources that include organizations, online services, and Web sites along with print materials. Access is aided through cross-references found in the entries along with the index.

591. American Environmental Leaders: From Colonial Times to the Present. Anne Becher et al. Santa Barbara, CA: ABC-CLIO, 2000. 2v. ISBN 1-57607-162-6.

This is a highly interesting and well-written biographical dictionary treating some 350 personalities associated with the study, debate, and activism associated with the environment. Coverage is comprehensive in its inclusion of individuals over the past 300 years. Most of the well-known figures are included such as Rachel Carson, John Muir, Wallace Stegner, and Henry David Thoreau, but it is believed by many that the real value of the work lies in the treatment given to the more obscure figures. The author is an environmental writer and has selected her subjects carefully, providing a broad array of individuals including writers, politicians, health-food advocates, entertainers, and ordinary citizens turned activists by the abuses of their environment. Entries range from two to three pages and include brief bibliographies, and in some cases photographs. The work finds a ready audience of high school and college students as well as the general public.

592. Encyclopedia of Environmental Issues. Craig W. Allin, ed. Hackensack, NJ: Salem Press, 2000. 3v. ISBN 0-89356994-1.

A well-received source of information due to its comprehensive and thorough coverage supplied through 475 well-written and detailed articles, this work appeals to a variety of users from students through practitioners and activists. Articles range from 500 to 3,000 words and provide adequate treatment of important events, personalities, legislation, and key issues and subjects (geology, genetics, engineering, etc.). Arrangement is alphabetical, and the work is enhanced with the inclusion of special features such as nearly 200 photographs and 100 charts, graphs, and tables. The work is considered to be an outstanding contribution in its capacity to provide a real understanding of the issues surrounding the environment. There is a glossary and several appendixes, which include a timeline of environmental legislation. Access is provided through a well-constructed index.

593. Environmental Law Handbook. 16th ed. Thomas F.P. Sullivan, ed. Rockville, MD: Government Institutes, 2001. 811p. ISBN 0-86587-820-X.

This work continues to provide up-to-date information on the basic factors and features of environmental law. Contents are organized into 16 chapters that provide an overview and background material as well as exposition of the laws in this country designed to protect public safety and health, as well as the environment. Early chapters present general information regarding the basic elements of the laws, their enforcement, and the liability associated with their violation. Aspects of pollution treated in subsequent chapters are clean air, clean water, safe drinking water, solid waste, toxic substances, and more. Separate chapters are given to the National Environmental Policy Act of 1969, and to the Pollution Prevention Act establishing this as national policy. Other chapters treat safety in the work place, and the community's right to know.

*594. The Environmental Movement in the United States: Interactive Encyclopedia. Santa Barbara, CA: ABC-CLIO, 2000. ISBN 1-57607-250-9. [CD-ROM]
Another of the highly successful interactive encyclopedias from the publisher (see entries 546, 674, 838, 942, 1102), this effort examines the movement from its beginning to the present day. It provides useful historical perspective through the inclusion of some 600 topics grouped alphabetically under six broad categories. The categories are simple in concept but provide awareness of the range of coverage; they are biographies, documents, events, glossary, movements, and organizations. Access is established in several ways through use of a subject index, category search, timeline, and even a search by theme in which key avenues are provided: community action, conservation versus preservation, environmental activism, health issues, land use, natural resources, and wildlife conservation. Media searches produce audio and video clips, photographs, and tables. Like other works in this series, coverage is thorough and of interest to a wide variety of users encompassing high school students, the intended audience, but embracing undergraduates and adults as well.

GENEALOGY AND IMMIGRATION

In the past, genealogy as an auxiliary study has been held suspect by historians as a relatively undisciplined "popular" exercise in self-fulfillment. More recently, however, following the success of Alex Haley's *Roots,* with its systematic methodology, and the broadened focus on social history, there has been greater acceptance in many (but not all) quarters of the potential utility and historical value of genealogical inquiry.
Prior to beginning the task, the investigator needs to become acquainted with the study through use of genealogy handbooks and manuals listed here. It is also important to consider the services and products offered by the Genealogical Department of the Church of Jesus Christ of Latter-Day Saints (available at http://www.lds.org) in Salt Lake City, Utah, as well as the various commercial distributors of genealogical products. The Church, through sale of its Family Search product line, offers both World Wide Web and CD-ROM access to various files, the most important being *The Family History Library Catalog,* which lists and describes the vast holdings in Salt Lake City. Many local church branches have the equipment to conduct searches for patrons. The Genealogical Publishing Company has been a leading publishing house, and The American Genealogical Lending Library (now Heritage Quest Lending Library) in Bountiful, Utah, has been an important supplier offering several useful publications such as the *AGLL Catalog.* Now titled **Heritage Quest Microform Catalog,* it is in CD-ROM and represents a powerful resource tool containing over 250,000 titles of source documents available on microfilm, microfiche, or CD-ROM.
The National Genealogical Society of Arlington, Virginia, has 17,000 members and was founded in 1903. It has published the *National Genealogical Society Quarterly* since 1912. The organization's catalog is available online at http://www.ngsgenealogy.org.

The Immigration and Ethnic History Society (available at http://www.iehs.org) originally of Chicago, Illinois, was founded in 1965 as the Immigration History Group by scholars interested in the study of human migration, especially immigration to the United States and Canada. Membership is made up of historians, economists, sociologists, and others interested in research in the field of immigration history and has remained at 900 or so. The society presents awards to outstanding books, articles, and dissertations on immigration or ethnic history. It continues to publish *Journal of American Ethnic History* quarterly, and *Immigration and Ethnic History Newsletter* on a semi-annual basis.

GENERAL SOURCES: ELECTRONIC

Guides

595. The Genealogist's Virtual Library: Full-Text Books on the World Wide Web. Thomas J. Kemp. Wilmington, DE: Scholarly Resources, 2000. 268p. ISBN 0-8420-2865-X.

The author serves as a librarian and archivist with strong interest in genealogy and has authored several books in the past on the topic. With the growth of the Internet, there has been an increase in the number of books and journals available in full on that medium. This print guide is a genealogical bibliography dedicated to those resources. In this work, the titles are organized into three categories: family histories, local histories, and general research subjects. The listing of sources represents the use of the Web in the truest and best sense for information work, because many of the titles date from the nineteenth and early twentieth centuries and are no longer available in print format. Although, the claim is that access to the sites is free of charge, one will find many instances in which a fee is required to utilize the links provided at these sites. This work is also available with an accompanying CD-ROM that provides the links to the Web sites.

596. Instant Information on the Internet: A Genealogist's No-Frills Guide to the 50 States & the District of Columbia. Christina K. Schaefer. Baltimore: Genealogical Publishing, 1999. 86p. ISBN 0-8063-1608-X.

Serving as an introductory vehicle for using the Internet in genealogical searching, this work has a ready-made audience. It furnishes a representative collection of Web sites providing genealogical information of general nature, complete with URLs and descriptive narrative of the contents and coverage. Hundreds of sites offering information on genealogical sources and search routines are included, although it is a small sample of the total population. Arrangement is alphabetical by state and includes sites containing vital records, descriptive and analytical narrative, and more. Included are state departments of vital records, important research libraries and archival collections, and historical societies. Additional segments identify Web resources furnishing local indexes, electronic documents, and databases.

Sources on the World Wide Web and on CD-ROM

*597. American Genealogical-Biographical Index to American Genealogical, Biographical and Local History Materials. Fremont Rider, ed. Middletown, CT: Godfrey Memorial Library, 1952–2000. v. 1–200. (In progress).

AGBI originally began as a card file of names from genealogies held by several cooperating libraries back in the mid-1930s. Since that time it has been published in book format as the *American Genealogical Index* over a 10-year period from 1942 to 1952 (48v.), when it was superceded by the present title. Through it all, Fremont Rider, the eclectic, enterprising, and somewhat eccentric librarian at Wesleyan University guided its fortunes. Although Rider died in 1962, his work goes on with the work carried on by the *Family History Center* (see entry 599). Volume 200 was published in 1999 with additional supplementary indexes issued in 2000. The intent is to furnish a comprehensive index to names in published family genealogies that are not themselves indexed. The index is a comprehensive index of names drawn from thousands of sources, and is available in CD-ROM as well as print. Currently one is able to search the index on the Web through *Ancestry.com* search engines.

*598. Cyndi's List of Genealogy Sites on the Internet. Cyndi Howells. Available: http://www.cyndislist.com.

Ms. Howells has furnished researchers and hobbyists more than 100,000 links to genealogy resources on the World Wide Web, making it the largest and most comprehensive of its kind. She has managed to update it on a weekly basis, making it a most dynamic resource. As one might have thought, there is a large array of categories from which the user can choose ranging in content from "Mailing Lists" to "Female Ancestors" leading to a vast array of Web sites from a broad range of organizations and individuals. Several indexes are furnished to aid access.

Cyndi's List is hosted by *RootsWeb* (available at http://www.rootsweb.com) produced by Genealogical Data Cooperative. *RootsWeb* bills itself as "the Internet's oldest and largest genealogy site" and serves as host to several thousand genealogical Web sites, 22,000 mailing lists, and 175,000 message boards. It contains interactive guides, and various resources for researching family histories. It offers a "surname list" of one million names with dates and locations as well as e-mail addresses to contact others working on the same name.

*599. FamilySearch—Internet. The Church of Jesus Christ of the Latter-day Saints. Salt Lake City, Utah. Available: http://www.familysearch.org.

As the most active collector of genealogical material over the years, the Church has amassed the largest collection in the world. The Family History Library, established in 1894, and its 3,400 Family History Centers located in 75 countries and territories, provide access to 2.2 million microfilm rolls, 742,000 microfiche, 300,000 books, and 4,500 periodicals of value to genealogical research. Each month over 4,000 microfilm rolls and 700 books are added. Microfilming is being carried out in more than 40 countries. Recently, the Web site has become a functional search tool; and one is able to search various files; the "Ancestral File," a compilation of genealogies, "International Genealogical Index" for vital records data from various sources, "Social Security Death Index" and more.

*600. Immigration History Research Center: Guide to IHRC Collections. Immigration History Research Center, University of Minnesota. Available: http://www1.umn.edu/ihrc.

Previously issued as a Greenwood publication edited by Suzanne Moody and Joel Wurl in 1991, the new Web site has been expanded to include more collections. The guide enumerates the holdings of the Immigration History Research Center (IHRC) created at the University of Minnesota to remedy the oversight apparent in U.S. libraries' failure to collect certain ethnic materials. There is a strong emphasis on Central and East European culture, although southern Europe is also represented. In all, there are 24 different national groups ranging, alphabetically, from Albania to Ukraine, with Jewish immigration also being treated. There is a separate segment for each group for which the holdings of IHRC are described. Included in these collections are manuscripts, newspapers, monographs, and serials. Emphasis is given to the period just prior and subsequent to the turn of the century, a period for which the causes of immigration are examined and experiences are recorded. The online catalog is easily navigated and full information is given regarding the operation and accessibility of IHRC.

A rich source for scholarship is the full-text database to begin appearing on the World Wide Web in 2003 as *North American Immigrant Letters, Diaries, and Oral Histories* from Alexander Street Press. It will be available as a series of offerings each treating a different ethnic group. The first four units will cover Jewish immigrants, Italian immigrants, German immigrants, and Irish immigrants. Like other titles from Alexander Street (entries 702n and 1136n), it will be offered through annual subscription or one-time purchase. Each unit will contain 20,000 pages of material with much of it being published for the first time.

*601. Index to U.S. Marriage Record, 1691–1850. Bountiful, Utah: Heritage Quest, 1997. [CD-ROM].

Another of the useful CD-ROM sources issued by the publisher is the comprehensive listing of marriage records over a period of more than 150 years from the colonial era to the mid-nineteenth century. Included here are more than 500,000 marriages conducted in 17 states. Entries supply names of both bride and groom along with date of marriage and county and state. There is an introductory section for each state describing the history of its settlement and a useful exposition of requirements for recording marriages during the relevant years. A useful feature is an index of the million names in order to expedite the search. The reference use of this tool is obvious for those interested in family history, and, happily, the technology appears smooth and efficient. A brief print manual is supplied to aid in installing and using the system.

*602. Local History and Genealogy Reading Room, Library of Congress. Washington, D.C. Available: http://www.loc.gov/rr/genealogy.

The collection was established as early as 1815 with the purchase of Thomas Jefferson's personal library and currently represents one of the premier collections of both U.S. and foreign genealogical holdings. The Web site is useful in describing the composition of the collection and its vast array of resources and supplies directory information, and identification of regimental histories as well as bibliographies and guides. In the introductory segments, the site provides instruction to the beginning researcher; most important, it furnishes a link to the Library's online search system to ascertain individual titles.

Genealogical Research at the National Archives—Genealogy Page of the National Archives and Records Administration (available at http://www.archives.gov/research_room/

genealogy/index.html) provides similar information in preparing researchers for a visit to one of the facilities. It describes the Archives' collections of census, immigration, and military records. In its early stages of construction as a Web site at the time of access, coverage is given to information regarding research facilities, online information, policy issues, publications, workshops and courses, and resources on the World Wide Web.

*603. My Family.Com, Inc. Provo, UT: My Family. Com. Available: http://www. myfamilyinc.com.

A major network for searching family and genealogical connections on the World Wide Web, the recently created corporate structure owns and operates three major Web sites; MyFamily.com, *Ancestry.com,* and *FamilyHistory.com,* and gives access to *RootsWeb.com* (see entry 598n). MyFamily.com is a password-protected site that permits families to post news, create family albums, conduct chats, and maintain a calendar of events. It also furnishes software to update family trees.

Ancestry.com (available at http://www.ancestry.com) is a major force in genealogy research, offering 3,000 searchable databases containing information on one billion names. There are several hundred monumental sources including such tools as the "*Periodical Source Index*" (PERSI) indexing thousands of relevant periodicals, the "*Social Security Death Index*" allowing for search of people's death dates, and *World Tree,* a huge database of family trees furnished by contributors. *FamilyHistory.com* (available at http:// www.familyhistory.com) supplies message boards for the exchange of information by those engaged in genealogical research. These are useful in identifying surnames, geographic areas, and research topics.

GENERAL SOURCES: PRINT

604. The Abridged Compendium of American Genealogy: First Families of America. Genealogical Encyclopedia of the United States. Frederick A. Virkus and Albert Nelson Marquis, eds. Baltimore: Genealogical Publishing Co., 1987. 7v. ISBN 0-8063-1171-1.

This work was begun in 1916 in response to the need for evidence to prove citizenship lineage for those applying for jobs in war-related or war-sensitive organizations, agencies, and firms. The final volume appeared in 1942, at a time when it was again necessary for some to obtain this sort of proof. Bearing a 1970 copyright date, the title was reprinted with a new foreword by noted genealogy writer P.W. Filby. It represents an extensive listing of first families (earlier rather than most prominent), with information having been gathered mostly from people born in the second half of the nineteenth century, describing their earlier lineage. This is not a "vanity" publication: Much was discarded by the editors, and an attempt was made to verify the dates. Entries appear as biographical narrative and identify the degree of descent from particular ancestors. There is a name index to provide access.

605. The American Census Handbook. Thomas J. Kemp. Wilmington, DE: Scholarly Resources, 2000. 580p. ISBN 0-842-02924-9.

The author is a well-known genealogical writer who has designed a comprehensive and valuable source meeting the needs of genealogists, but useful to all searchers. The Handbook presents the most complete listing of published census indexes ever compiled and is a necessary bibliographic resource for any collection. Arrangement is directory-fashion and in a state-by-state approach; thousands of useful resources are identified in chronological order by census year. Not only indexes, but census abstracts, and census reproductions are included as well. Authors, publishers, and dates of published materials are given, and within states, citations to county-wide indexes and abstracts are supplied in thorough fashion. Both print and electronic resources (online databases and Web sites) are included with sources of general nature as well as those targeting specific population and ethnic groups.

606. American Immigrant Cultures: Builders of a Nation. David Levinson and Melvin Ember, eds. New York: Macmillan, 1997. 2v. ISBN 0-02-897208-2.

The editors have developed an excellent source of information regarding the immigrant experience in this country by covering 161 nonindigenous ethnic groups who currently reside in this country. Many of the groups are rarely examined in works of this kind; coverage of such cultures as the Amish, Cape Verdean, Cham, Garifuna, Hmong, Hutterites, Indos, and Russian Molokos, among others makes the work especially useful. Alphabetically arranged from Acadians to Zoroastrians, the entries consist of a descriptive essay for which much of the content is drawn from primary research in the social sciences. These are signed by the contributors and furnish group names, features, historical accounts of immigration and settlement as well as background in country of origin, housing, marriage, religion and more. There are cross-references to group names.

607. American Immigration. Danbury, CT: Grolier, 1999. 10v. ISBN 0-7172-9283-5.

This multivolume encyclopedia provides a comprehensive and easy-to-understand but useful treatment of the nature of immigration and its impact on American history that will suit the needs of students from the middle grades through high school, and possibly undergraduates. Volume 1 furnishes a general overview of the activity from its beginning some 400 years ago to the current time, and volume 2 gives a detailed historical account of Ellis Island. The remaining volumes examine different topics, issues, terms, and cultural groups in alphabetical sequence from "Abolitionist Newspapers" in volume 3 to "West Indians" in volume 10. Included in the entries on ethnic groups are historical background information including reasons for their relocation to the United States, relevant statistics, description of the reception they received in this country, and current status.

608. American Naturalization Records, 1790–1990: What They Are and How to Use Them. 2nd ed. John J. Newman. Bountiful, Utah: Heritage Quest, 1998. 127p. ISBN 1-877677-91-4.

This is another useful and comprehensive source of genealogical information from one of the leading publishers in treating a period of 200 years. Considered by most users to be an indispensable tool, this work represents an update and revision of the first edition completed 13 years earlier. The author is an archivist with many years of experience in dealing with the difficulties of the naturalization process. He is a frequent lecturer to genealogical societies at all levels, and is considered and expert on the use of court records in genealogical research. This work enumerates and explains the types of records and the differences in naturalization law and its impact on the documents in the period following

1906 as compared to the earlier years. Also included are those special records of aliens serving in the military or purchasing land before attaining citizenship.

609. America's Best Genealogy Resource Centers. William Dollarhide and Ronald A. Bremer. Bountiful, Utah: Heritage Quest, 1998. 139p. ISBN 1-877677-90-6.

Considered by some of its users as the best directory of its kind, this work enumerates various facilities containing genealogy resource collections for research on family history. The lead author, Dollarhide, is a specialist in the field and has served as a writer for Heritage Quest in Bountiful, Utah, and is the founder of the bimonthly journal, *Genealogy Bulletin,* now published by Heritage Quest. He serves as lecturer, and has contributed a number of articles and monographs to the field. As a result, he is well-qualified to address the topic and together with his colleague, Bremer (also a lecturer in genealogy), has compiled a useful listing of research facilities at local, state, regional and national levels. The text opens with the top ten genealogy research centers in the country; this is followed by the best centers in each state. Subsequent chapters identify regional branches of the National Archives and vital statistics office of each state.

The Library: A Guide to the LDS Family History Library, edited by Johni Cerny and Wendy Elliott (Salt Lake City: Ancestry, 1988) is still useful as a print guide to the collections and services offered through the Church of Jesus Christ of Latter-day Saints (LDS), its monumental library in Salt Lake City, and the numerous branch libraries. In this work, the United States is divided into 10 regions, for which information is given concerning historical background, migration, and settlement. Various records are described (census, court, church, cemetery, etc.). Charts and checklists are furnished with the data for each region. The remainder of the world is covered through a series of 14 different essays in which Europe is treated most thoroughly. Africa and South America are both represented, making the guide a valuable starting point.

610. Ancestry's Red Book: American State, County & Town Sources. Rev. ed. Alice Eicholz, ed. Salt Lake City: Ancestry, 1992. 858p. ISBN 0-916489-47-7.

Designed as a guide to family research in each of the 50 states and Washington D.C., this useful manual continues in the same vein as the previous edition in issued in 1989. Additional records have been included in the state-by-state coverage. Descriptions are furnished of the various genealogical records (census, land, probation and court, tax, cemetery, church, military). Local history is covered, and collections are identified and located in libraries and historical societies. Useful charts are provided, along with location of county and town records and earliest date of extant primary sources. Records of immigration are enumerated, including those important to Native American inquiry. There is a useful introductory section in the beginning and a good detailed index along with bibliographical references at the end. The previous edition received mixed reviews with reports of many errors. It appears that the errors have been corrected in this edition with more attention to detail, and the title should prove useful to anybody searching for genealogical information in a particular state or county.

Printed Sources: A Guide to Published Genealogical Records by Kory L. Meyerink (Ancestry, 1998) serves a dual purpose as a guide to sources of information for genealogical research, and as a bibliography of useful titles. The difference here is that Meyerink chooses to emphasize the utility of secondary published materials such as encyclopedias, histories, periodicals, biographies, etc. In this respect, it should prove useful to genealogical researchers at all levels of expertise. The introduction provides insightful recommendations for utilizing the material.

611. Atlas of American Migration. Stephen A. Flanders. New York: Facts on File, 1998. 214p. ISBN 0-8160-3158-4.

Especially useful for the undergraduate is this well-designed and esthetically attractive atlas identifying various stages of migration of ethnic groups to and within the United States. It is a product of careful research and provides successful integration of text with the various graphics. In total, there are more than 150 maps, charts, and photographs serving to enhance the extensive narrative. The work is divided into 10 chapters beginning with a general overview of migration of groups in this country, followed by treatment of different time periods and groups from pre-Columbian times in chapter 2 to the flight to the suburbs after 1945 in chapter 10. Both instances of forced migration in our history, that of the Native Americans' trail of tears, and that of migration in chain of African American slaves receive separate chapters. The text is supplemented with sidebars, statistical data, and chronologies.

612. Compendium of Historical Sources: The How and Where of American Genealogy. Rev. ed. Ronald A. Bremer. Bountiful, Utah: AGLL, Inc., 1997. 914p. ISBN 1 877677 15 9.

This is a comprehensive source of information that has earned accolades from reviewers and users for the amount of information it contains. It is divided into three major sections; 1) nuts and bolts of genealogical research, which contains information of basic nature in terms of conducting a search 2) records, that provides listings of places to go and sources to use in locating records of all kinds (census, immigration, naturalization, passenger lists, insurance, military, and more, and 3) special topics, that treats supplementary sources and additional pertinent information including a list of major genealogical periodicals, repositories, museums, place-names, and more. There is an extremely useful glossary of terms and expressions that supplies abbreviations and terms of legal significance that one may encounter in genealogical research. To provide access, there is a well-constructed and extensive table of contents, supported by a less detailed index.

*613. The Complete Book of Emigrants in Bondage, 1614–1775. Peter Wilson Coldham. Baltimore: Genealogical Publishing Co., 1988. 920p. ISBN 0-8063-1221-1.

This is a comprehensive listing of names of individuals who were forcibly sent by judicial action from England to this country from the early seventeenth century to 1775. Crimes range from petty theft and indebtedness to more serious felonies. Following an introductory essay on the history of transportation from 1615 to 1775, coverage is based on the conviction list of the various British judicial districts or circuits for example, "London, 1656–1775," and volume 8, "Northern Circuit, 1665–1775." More than 50,000 names are arranged alphabetically and this effort represents the largest listing of immigrants to the U.S. colonies prior to the Revolutionary War. Entries include the date of sentencing, the name of the ship, and in some cases indication of the nature of the crime and/or place of arrival. This work is a revised edition of the author's *Bonded Passengers to America* issued five years earlier by the same publisher. In 1996. the complete contents of this revised version along with another Coldham effort (see entry 614) were issued on CD-ROM.

Another work, not so extensive, is Marion J. Kaminkow's *Original Lists of Emigrants in Bondage from London to the American Colonies, 1719–1744* (Magna Carta, 1967), which identifies nearly 7,300 people who were sent to this country for assorted crimes and misdemeanors.

*614. The Complete Book of Emigrants, 1607–1660. Peter Wilson Coldham. Baltimore, MD: Genealogical Publishing Co., 1988. 600p. ISBN 0-8063-1192-4.

This work targets British emigration to the Americas during a limited time segment of the seventeenth century and furnishes a listing of 15,000 available names. There is duplication of certain information previously published by Hotten (entry 639) and in other public records. Coldham has examined over 30 archival sources such as those issued by the British Public Record Office in producing this listing. The names are limited to English only and do not include Irish or even Scottish or Welsh families. When available, information concerning age, family relationships, status and ship are included for each entry. Because much of the emigration record has been lost through the years, Coldham's energetic effort represents a great asset to those who conduct such studies. Arrangement of entries is chronological, with access provided by a name index. Continuing this work are three additional volumes by Coldham; *The Complete Book of Emigrants, 1661–1699* (1990), *The Complete Book of Emigrants, 1700–1750* (1992), and *The Complete Book of Emigrants, 1751–1776* (1993) With these three efforts, an additional 80,000 names are furnished in the same manner as in the initial work. In 1996, the complete contents of this set along with the above "*Bondage*" publication (see entry above) were issued in CD-ROM format by Broderbund Software as **The Complete Book of Emigrants, 1607–1776 & Emigrants in Bondage, 1614–1775.*

American Migrations 1765–1799: The Lives, Times, and Families (Genealogical Publishing, 2000) is a more recent work by Coldham scrutinizing a short chaotic period during the Colonial era beginning with the time of the Stamp Act in which the author identifies names of families that migrated from America, generally due to their political posture as Loyalists. The author studied the records of the American Claims Commission which include letters, depositions, affidavits, etc. of claimants. Some 15,000 individuals are identified in nearly 6,000 claims filed.

*615. Dictionary Catalog of the Local History and Genealogy Division. New York Public Library, Local History and Genealogy Division. Boston: G. K. Hall, 1974. 18v. ISBN 0-81610-784-X. **Supp. 2v.** 1974.

This is one of the major resource tools for both local history and genealogy based on the extensive holdings of the New York Public Library. G.K. Hall, publisher of important library catalogs, produced this multivolume access tool in the mid-1970s to cover the material cataloged by the library through the end of 1971. Since that time, the materials have been listed in the Library's *Dictionary Catalog of the Research Libraries.* Since 1976, these materials have been supplemented on an annual basis in the Library's *Bibliographic Guide to North American History* (entry 38n). The 20-volume work (which itself includes a two-volume supplement of local history) bears the unmistakable design of the G.K. Hall company and is simply a reproduction of the catalog cards of items in this collection. About 100,000 titles were identified in the original 20 volumes. The work is available in microfilm as well.

Materials acquired and cataloged since 1971 are best accessed through "CATNYP" the Library's online catalog. Presently there is a conversion project to capture older material. The online catalog can be accessed through a link from the genealogy section's Web site "Genealogical Research at The New York Public Library" (available at http://www.nypl.org/research/chss/lhg/research.html).

616. The Dictionary of American Immigration History. Francesco Cordasco, ed. Metuchen, NJ: Scarecrow, 1990. 784p. ISBN 0-8108-2241-5.

The editor has been a prolific bibliographer in a variety of fields but most frequently in ethnic studies. In this dictionary, various ethnic groups are described, along with personalities, organizations, societies, topical themes (such as pluralism), legislation, and unions. It is a product of large proportions, with over 90 contributors from this country, Canada, and the United Kingdom. There are more than 2,500 entries, arranged alphabetically and varying in length from a single paragraph to several pages depending upon the importance of the subject. Brief bibliographies are furnished at the end of the entries. American Indians as a group have been excluded from coverage because of extensive treatment given in numerous other publications. Certain omissions occur (such as gypsies). There is a brief but useful introduction that describes immigration policies in this country for a period of 100 years beginning with the 1880s. There is no index.

The Immigrant Experience: An Annotated Bibliography by Paul D. Mageli (Salem, 1991) furnishes a selective listing of books and articles, largely of a popular nature, that should prove useful to the student or interested layperson. Annotations are detailed, and coverage is given to various ethnic groups and time periods beginning with the mid-nineteenth century.

617. Encyclopedia of American Immigration. James Ciment. Armonk, NY: M.E. Sharpe, 2001. 4v. ISBN 0-7656-8028-9.

A comprehensive and well-constructed source of information, this work provides a survey of immigration developments in this country beginning with the early colonial period and running to the present day. Entries treat immigrant groups, issues, eras and time periods, and related factors of social, legal, political, and economic consequence. Information is culled from a variety of sources (INS records, U.S. census, and departments of the government, contents are organized under four sections; immigration history, issues, various groups by geographical origin, and finally, full-text documents. Numerous illustrations consisting of historical and contemporary photographs enhance the text.

The second edition of *The Ellis Island Source Book* by August C. Bolino (Kensington Historical Press, 1990) edition updates the earlier version recognized as the most extensive and comprehensive survey of materials relating to Ellis Island in print form. Originally undertaken as part of the Ellis Island restoration effort, it was necessary to visit major cities affected by ethnic immigration (Pittsburgh, Chicago, Cleveland, and others) in order to gain perspective on existing material. Locations of existing material on Ellis Island are given that include government agencies at various levels, church records, ethnic presses, and documents from various fraternal groups and social clubs. The bibliography contains books, articles, and dissertations. Also of importance to the modern researcher in examining the Ellis Island records is the Web site maintained by the *American Family Immigration History Center* (available at http://www.ellisislandrecords.org). Here one can examine ship manifests of immigration and commentary with access by personal name and year of arrival.

618. Genealogical & Local History Books in Print: Family History Volume. 5th ed. Marian Hoffman, comp. and ed. Baltimore, MD: Genealogical Publishing, 1996–1997. 4v.

Vol. 1. Family History, 1996. 477p. ISBN 0-8063-1513-X.

Vol. 2. General Reference and World Resources, 1997. 375p. ISBN 0-8063-1538-5.

Vol. 3. U.S. Sources and Resources: Alabama—New York, 1997. 574p. ISBN 0-8063-1536-9.

Vol. 4. U.S. Sources and Resources: North Carolina—Wyoming, 1997. 530p. ISBN 0-8063-1537-7.

    First issued in1975, this work has appeared every two to three years as *Genealogical Books in Print,* and is regarded as the most important bibliographical source in the field. The fifth edition has been issued in four volumes, each serving as a useful tool in providing awareness of available materials for purposes of inquiry, a marketing device for authors and publishers, and an ordering tool for librarians, researchers, and collectors. Entries are arranged by subject and furnish bibliographic information and, in some cases, annotations. Recent editions greatly expand the coverage of the early efforts, and reflect the growing interest in the field. Volume 1 lists family genealogies with an index of family names while Volume 2 supplies sources of adoption, census, and church records, and more on an international basis. The *Sources and Resources Volumes* furnish U.S. coverage by region and by state. Listings are based on data submitted by publishers; therefore, coverage is not complete, but it still represents one of the very important sources of bibliographic information in the field.

619. Genealogical Encyclopedia of the Colonial Americas: A Complete Digest of the Records of All the Countries of the Western Hemisphere. Christina K. Schaefer. Baltimore: Genealogical Publishing, 1998. 814p. ISBN 0-8063-1576-8.

    The ambitious goal of this work is to provide awareness of colonial history and genealogical sources from the time of European colonization up to the American Revolution. As a result, numerous sources of information are supplied. Treatment is given to colonies founded by Spain with another chapter given to colonies founded by other European countries including England. The 13 original colonies along with Maine and Vermont are given detailed treatment with sources given for each town and county. There is another section given to other states with settlements prior to the Revolution in which sources are provided for an additional 18 states. Subsequently, there is coverage of colonial sources found in European countries, as well as foreign records found at the Library of Congress. An index serves to provide access to these numerous records.

620. Guide to Genealogical Research in the National Archives of the United States. 3ʳᵈ ed. Anne B. Eales and Robert M. Kvasnika, eds. Washington, D.C.: National Archives and Records Administration, 2000. 411p. ISBN 1-88087-521-7.

Divided into four major sections, this work is a revised and expanded version of a publication which began in 1969, and was later revised in 1985. As before, it describes groupings of records in the National Archives in terms of their content and access. Since there are 11 regional facilities located in all regions of the country except Hawaii, all researchers may make use of these holdings on microfilm. Treatment is given to population and immigration records, census holdings, passenger lists, and naturalization records. Military records are furnished in a separate section which details service in the various branches; coverage is given to volunteers and pension files, and more. There is a useful inclusion of records of different population segments at time of war in which minority activity is recorded. Additional files include records of land claims, court proceedings, and cartography. There is a useful introductory segment on the value and limitations of government records for genealogy; issues of general organization of records, existence of special programs at the National Archives, and the use of finding aids are treated in useful manner. Appendixes provide various listings, and access is furnished through a detailed index.

621. The Library of Congress: A Guide to Genealogical and Historical Research. James C. Neagles and Mark C. Neagles. Salt Lake City: Ancestry, 1990. 381p. ISBN 0-916489-48-5.

This is a useful print resource to guide the user through a vast array of materials in the national library related to genealogy. It is not limited to those materials in the Local History and Genealogy Reading Room, but examines the utility of various divisions and catalogs of LC in conducting such research. It provides an introduction to the entire library, identifies the categories of research and publication; and describes nearly 3,000 source publications by state and by region. An index is included at the end.

One of the great efforts to enumerate genealogical sources in a single library is *Genealogies in the Library of Congress: A Bibliography,* a two-volume effort edited by Marion J. Kaminkow (Magna Carta Book Company, 1972). It identifies some 20,000 English and U.S. family histories. This includes all listings in the Library's "Family Name Index" in which both published and unpublished genealogies, arranged by family surname and representing various countries of origin are listed. Supplements were issued in 1977 and 1987 covering genealogies added through 1986. Numerous cross-references facilitate use of these Kaminkow volumes. *Genealogies Cataloged by the Library of Congress Since 1986: With a List of Established Forms of Family Names and a List of Genealogies Converted to Microform Since 1983* (Library of Congress, 1991) continues the coverage through mid-1991 with over 10,000 family-name entries and more than 22,600 cross-references. Kaminkow's *A Complement to Genealogies in the Library of Congress: A Bibliography* (Magna Carta Book Company, 1981) identifies genealogies found in 45 libraries, excluding the Library of Congress. Also treated are supplements, corrections, and new editions. About 20,000 entries are furnished. A complementary resource is P. William Filby's *Directory of American Libraries with Genealogy or Local History Collections* (Genealogical, 1988) identifying library collections and services throughout the U.S. and Canada. Arrangement is alphabetical by state or province.

622. The 1997 Genealogy Annual: A Bibliography of Published Sources. Thomas J. Kemp. Wilmington, DE: Scholarly Resources, 1999. 368p. Ann. ISSN 1090-7440.

This is a useful serial bibliography identifying a variety of resources published in genealogy during a single year. The first issue covered the year 1995 and was published in 1996, the second issue for 1996 was published in 1998, and the third for 1997 appeared in 1999. The work was planned as an annual publication, but at the time of this writing, the 2000 issue has not appeared. It represents a comprehensive source in its inclusion of genealogies, local histories, dissertations, source materials, and new journal titles as well. Formats are varied with books, videos, serial publications, and CD-ROMs. The sources are organized into three major categories; family histories that represent the bulk of the works identified, guides and handbooks providing reference assistance, and genealogical sources by state in which the material is organized by county.

623. Passenger and Immigration Lists Bibliography, 1538–1900: Being a Guide to Published Lists of Arrivals in the United States and Canada. 2nd ed. P. William Filby and Dorothy M. Lower, eds. Detroit: Gale, 1988. 324p. ISBN 0-8103-240-6.

This is the most recent edition of a work first issued in 1981 and supplemented in 1984. It supercedes these efforts by including all the lists in the two earlier volumes and adding 750 others. This bibliography is a real asset to those undertaking the challenge of genealogical investigation or immigration history. All told, there are over 3,300 published sources here. Arrangement is alphabetical by author; entries include full bibliographic description as well as informative annotations describing the content and value of the work in question. There is a detailed index that provides access to topics (e.g., "Illinois Arrivals") and is subdivided by such elements as nation of origin.

Filby's *Passenger and Immigration Lists Index: A Guide to Published Arrival Records of 500,000 Passengers Who Came to the United States and Canada in the Seventeenth, Eighteenth, and Nineteenth Centuries* was issued in 1981 followed by annual supplements providing an important index of names taken from passenger lists. Arrangement is alphabetical and includes age, date and place of arrival, source list, symbol/page number, and names and relationship of accompanying passengers. The supplements have increased the coverage considerably with the cumulated three-volume set titled *Passenger and Immigrant Lists Index: A Guide to . . . 3,430,000 Immigrants Who Came to the New World between the Sixteenth and Mid-Twentieth Centuries.* This was published in 2000 as was a later issue, *"Part I, 2001 Supplement."*

624. Refugees in America in the 1990s. David W. Haines, ed. Westport, CT: Greenwood Press, 1996. 467p. ISBN 0-313-29344-9.

This represents an update and rewriting of Haines's earlier work, *Refugees in the United States: A Reference Handbook* (Greenwood Press, 1985). It is a broad-based reference tool designed to cast light on the refugee problem in this country as it has unfolded over the past 35 years. The current effort is an attempt to draw attention to the changed conditions regarding the refugee situation. This new perspective from a scholar who has studied the issues and problems over an extensive period of time makes the new title an unusual and desirable resource for social historians interested in tracing contemporary influences. The new data is based on recent surveys and examines the situation of 14 groups including Afghans, Cubans, Ethiopians, and Iranians with respect to legislation, public opinion, and perceptions. Haines was formerly associated with the Federal Refugee Resettlement Program and has brought expertise to the study of the history, background, and problems in refugee life.

625. The Researcher's Guide to American Genealogy. 3rd ed. Val D. Greenwood. Baltimore: Genealogical Publishing Co., 2000. 662p. ISBN 0-8063-1621-7.

This guide was established as the premiere text on U.S. genealogy with its first edition in 1973, and continued its dominance with the second edition in 1990. The third edition continues as a thorough, understandable, and exceptionally informative manual explaining the location and utilization of existing records. There is excellent treatment and analysis of various records with new sources and access techniques carefully and clearly described. Search strategies are enumerated with the incorporation of the new technology available on the World Wide Web. Exposition of family history is furnished and family historians are identified. Classes of records are described in detail, as in the earlier versions. Bibliographies have been updated, and it still serves as one of the best sources of initial inquiry for both the beginner and the specialist.

The Complete Idiot's Guide to Genealogy by Christine Rose and Kay G. Ingalls (Alpha/Macmillan, 1997) and *The Complete Idiot's Guide to Online Genealogy* by Rhonda R. McClure (Alpha/Macmillan, 2000) in combination provide formidable competition to Greenwood as a resource for the beginner. As part of the popular series that has captured the attention of the American public in recent years, these works identify the basic techniques of searching out information and the relevant sources to search. Tips are furnished with respect to searching and record-keeping, development of family tree charts and use of online programs. With respect to the importance of the computer in genealogical research today, the latter work addresses major concerns of a range of inquirers from the novice to intermediate and in some cases, the sophisticated searcher.

626. Shapers of the Great Debate on Immigration: A Biographical Dictionary. Mary E. Brown. Westport, CT: Greenwood Press, 1999. 322p. (Shapers of the Great American Debates, no. 1) ISBN 0-313-30339-8.

Being the first volume of a series, it provides evidence of the historical importance and wide-ranging interest in the questions and controversies surrounding immigration as an issue. Designed primarily for the use of upper-level high school students and undergraduates, this work examines the lives and careers of 20 important people (shapers) who by their leadership, gained prominence in their advocacy of a point of view. Leadership was demonstrated in various ways such as legislative or executive leadership, writing, and organizing in behalf of their side of the issues. Arrangement is chronological by date of birth beginning with Thomas Jefferson, born in 1743, and concluding with John Tanton, born in 1934. Included among the advocates are such diverse personalities as Booker T. Washington, Theodore Roosevelt, Henry Ford, and Cesar Chavez. Essays range from 10 to 20 pages, and contain a picture, summary, and bibliography of each personality.

627. The Signers of the Declaration of Independence: A Biographical and Genealogical Reference. Della G. Barthelmas. Jefferson, NC: McFarland, 1997. 334p. ISBN 0-7864-0318-7.

Due to its narrow focus, this work presents a convenient vehicle for examining the lives and careers of that notable group of individuals who severed the ties with Great Britain, thus ending the colonial period of our history. There were 56 signers along with the Secretary of the Continental Congress for whom information is supplied. The work is well written, although the genealogical information is not always easy to follow. Entries for each personality are divided into three major sections in a stylized manner that adequately conveys the major points to users. First there is biographical coverage that includes the individual's role or participation in the Revolution. Then, there is a section of auxiliary information treating such elements as physical appearance, personal stories, and current memorials. The final segment provides genealogical awareness of the lineage through several generations. A picture accompanies each entry.

628. The Source: A Guidebook of American Genealogy. Rev ed. Sandra H. Luebking and Loretto D. Szucs, eds. Salt Lake City: Ancestry, 1997. 846p. ISBN 0-916489-67-1.

This title has been revised after 13 years of excellent service to genealogical researchers at all levels of expertise. It is structured more as a reference guide than as a manual of genealogy practice and continues the previous format with three major sections. First are the sources of records (family, home, cemetery, marriage, divorce, business, prison, military). Part 2 treats the published sources (directories, newspapers, genealogical tools), while part 3 enumerates special resources related to ethnic influences (immigrant origins, Spanish and Mexican records, as well as those of blacks, Asian Americans, Jewish Americans, etc.). In all, there are 23 chapters from the earlier edition, all of which have been updated or completely revised. In addition, there are two new chapters relevant to the current practice; one on twentieth-century research, the other on family history research. Also useful are the frequent illustrations of documents and sources.

629. They Became Americans: Finding Naturalization Records and Ethnic Origins. Loretto D. Szucs. Salt Lake City, UT: Ancestry, 1998. 294p. ISBN 0-916489-67-1.

From one of the leading genealogical publishing houses comes this basic tool designed to meet the needs of a variety of users. The importance of naturalization records to family history is obvious in their capacity to identify locations of residential areas and towns of early ancestors as well as immigration dates and names of ships that brought them to this country. Alternative records are examined with examples provided. The author presents an array of information regarding various records in covering time periods from the earliest days of immigration and relocation to activity in the twentieth century. The work is written well and is enhanced with suggestions for additional searching possibilities. Also treated is historical awareness of ports of entry, and an index provides access.

From the same publisher and issued the same year is *Printed Sources: A Guide to Published Genealogical Records* by Kory L. Meyerink. It serves as another basic source in serving as a guide to the array of numerous and varied print sources including compilations and syntheses of original data utilized in genealogical research. The work opens with an introductory chapter describing basic research considerations, followed by sections on sources of background information, finding aids, original records, and compiled records. Appendixes furnish listings of material in CD-ROM format, major libraries, and publishing houses.

630. Touchstones: A Guide to Records, Rights, and Resources for Families of American World War II Casualties. Ann B. Mix. Bountiful, UT: AGLL, 1996. 133p. ISBN 1-877677-72-8.

One finds this to be a specialized source limiting its coverage to resources useful to those searching out information on World War II combatants. As an enthusiastic amateur genealogist, the author brings a great deal of emotion and enthusiasm to her task, if not correct syntax. That said, it is of value due to its content, and supplies comprehensive coverage with respect to the identification and securing of records of various types. Annotations of sources are informative and serve to describe the major points in terms of utility and value. The book is divided into sections treating military records, burials, medals, repositories, and more, and materials on prisons and prisoners as well as persons who have disappeared are furnished.

631. United States Immigration: A Reference Handbook. Willard Miller and Ruby M. Miller. New York: ABC-CLIO, 1996. 304p. (Contemporary World Issues). ISBN 0-87436-845-6.

Another of the vital issues treated in this publisher's series, the matter of immigration is handled in a format and manner useful to undergraduate students. The work is divided into chapters with the first half of the book furnishing an in-depth narrative of the history of immigration in this country in chapter 1, and a detailed chronology enumerating the key events and legislative developments spawning the laws and regulations in place today in chapter 2. This legislation is examined in an entire chapter devoted to the topic. Along with that, there is a directory of the many organizations, societies, and agencies that deal with various aspects of the activity, and a useful annotated bibliography of books, articles, and documents as well as audio-visual materials. Interesting issues such as illegal immigration, racial tension, and economic differences are examined. There is a glossary and a good index to provide access.

632. U.S. Immigration and Naturalization Laws and Issues: A Documentary History. Michael C. LeMay and Elliott R. Barkan. Westport, CT: Greenwood Press, 1999. 336p. (Primary Documents in American History and Contemporary Issues). ISBN 0-313-30156-5.

Opening with a detailed introductory essay examining the history of immigration policy from 1790 to 1996 in balanced manner, one is able to put current controversies and divisive issues into perspective within the framework of American the social milieu through time. More than 100 documents are organized chronologically under one of four parts beginning with the colonial period to 1880 when admission and entry was unrestricted. This is followed by the period 1880 to 1920 in which immigration was not restricted, but naturalization was limited, then by the period 1920 to 1965 in which immigration reform was implemented and restrictions were put in place. Finally, the contemporary period, 1965 to 1996 is treated in terms of the effect of policies within an age of globalization. The documents are well chosen and represent a wide array that includes court cases, presidential proclamations, Congressional commentary, and statements from various sociopolitical groups.

Illegal Immigration in America: A Reference Handbook, edited by David W. Haines and Karen E. Rosenblum for the same publisher in the same year, furnishes a timely examination of this controversial topic. Divided into four parts or sections treating "Concepts, Policies, and Numbers," "The Migrants and Their Work; "The Responses," and "Illegal Immigration in Perspective," the work treats illegal entry of various kinds from Latin America and Mexico, Europe, and Asia. The work is well constructed, balanced, and up-to-date in its treatment of a highly emotional issue. Remedies range from acceptance and legalization to withdrawal of economic support and forced return to their previous country of residence.

MULTICULTURAL SERIES

633. Ellis Island Series. New York: Holmes & Meier, 1991–2000. **Branching Out: German–Jewish Migration to the United States, 1820–1914.** Avraham Barkai. 1994. 269p. ISBN 0-8419-1152-5. **Distant Magnets: Expectations and Realities in the Immigrant Experience, 1840–1930.** Dirk Hoerder and Horst Rossler. 312p. ISBN 0-8419-1302-1. **Faith and Family: Dutch Immigration and Settlement in the United States. 1820–1920.** Robert P. Swierenga. 1996; repr. 2000. 362p. ISBN 0-8419-1319-6. **Ties that Bind, Ties that Divide; 100 Years of Hungarian Experience in the United States.** Julianna Puskas. 2000. 444p. ISBN 0-8419-1320-X. **Voices from Southeast Asia: The Refugee Experience in the United States.** John Tenhula. 1991. 247p. ISBN 0-8419-1110-X.

This series examines the immigrant experience of different ethnic groups and identifies the impact they have had on societal existence in this country. Drawn from a variety of records including customs passenger lists, census data, and emigration records, the authors are well prepared and well qualified to present comprehensive and accurate accounts of immigration and social life. The volumes are generally divided into chapters treating immigration patterns, religion, employment, political orientation, and statistical data, and conclude with a bibliographic essay and an index.

634. Genealogy Sourcebook Series. Paula K. Byars, ed. Detroit: Gale, 1996. 4v. ISBN 0-8103-8541-4. **African American Genealogical Sourcebook.** 244p. ISBN 0-8103-9226-7. **Asian American Genealogical Sourcebook.** 280p. ISBN 0-8103-9228-3. **Hispanic American Genealogical Sourcebook.** 224p. ISBN 0-8103-9227-5. **Native American Genealogical Sourcebook.** 219p. ISBN 0-8103-9229-1.

According to the publisher, this series is edited by Byars who has coordinated the work of experts in compiling and presenting useful information. These works are designed to serve as starting points for research into the genealogy of four major minority groups in this country. Therefore they are stylized in format and content and to some degree in presentation and have become familiar vehicles to users of this series. Volumes treat several major categories of information through use of chapters beginning with a grouping of background essays introducing users to historical information and giving practical advice regarding the utility of existing records and searching procedures for the particular group. There are a listing of a wide range of resources and a directory of libraries and archival collections of value. Of note is the excellent listing of organizations at both state and federal level that provide assistance in searching family history. Indexing is thorough furnishing access through author, title, organization, and subject.

635. Oryx American Family Tree Series. Phoenix: Oryx Press, 1996. **A Student's Guide to African-American Genealogy.** Anne E. Johnson and Adam M Cooper. 170p. ISBN 0-89774-972-3. **A Student's Guide to British American Genealogy.** Anne E. Johnson. 168p. ISBN 0-89774-982-0. **A Student's Guide to Chinese American Genealogy.** Colleen She. 168p. ISBN 0-89774-980-4. **A Student's Guide to German American Genealogy.** Gregory Robl. 168p. ISBN 0-89774-983-9. **A Student's Guide to Irish American Genealogy.** Erin McKenna. 168p. ISBN 0-89774-976-6. **A Student's Guide to Italian American Genealogy.** Terry C. Brockman. 168p. ISBN 0-89774-973-1. **A Student's Guide to Japanese American Genealogy.** Yoji Yamaguchi. 192p. ISBN 0-89774-979-0. **A Student's Guide to Jewish American Genealogy.** Jay Schliefer. 192p. ISBN 0-89774-977-4. **A Student's Guide to Mexican American Genealogy.** 192p. George R. Ryskamp. ISBN 0-89774-981-2. **A Student's Guide to Native American Genealogy.** Barrie E. Kavasch. 192p. ISBN 0-89774-975-8. **A Student's Guide to Polish American Genealogy.** Carl S. Rollyson. 192p. ISBN 0-89774-74-X. **A Student's Guide to Scandinavian American Genealogy.** Lisa O. Paddock and Carl S. Rollyson. 168p. ISBN 0-89774-978-2.

The "student" referred to in the titles ranges from the middle school grades to undergraduate level and embraces interested adults as well. The series represents a highly stylized introductory resource to 12 different ethnic groups in this country. It is clear that interested users must proceed to more detailed sources if they wish to do comprehensive and intensive research. All items in the series were published during the same year and represent similar coverage in terms of genealogical information. Each of the titles covers the basics of search techniques and resources in enabling users to collect data, evaluate primary-source materials, and conduct interviews. There are annotated listings at the end of every chapter, and computer resources are examined along with census information.

AFRICAN AMERICAN

636. African American Genealogy: A Bibliography and Guide to Sources. Curt B. Witcher. Round Tower Books, 2000. 217p. ISBN 0-964-39253-4.

This recent entry among the increasing number of resources in the African American experience provides a useful source for those interested in family history. It supplies a number of sources, some of which are essential, although obscure in expediting the search for information. It is the unusual listings such as the one on individual planters in the South that may unlock some of the doors to enlightenment in this regard. The work is organized into several sections regarding the search such as essential points for both beginners and experienced researchers and practical advice in tracing African American roots. There is an extensive bibliography arranged by ancestral places of residence, which should prove useful. Additional listings include those dealing with Southern plantation records.

637. Black Genealogy. Charles L. Blockson and Ron Fry. Upper Saddle River, NJ: Prentice-Hall, 1977; repr. Baltimore: Black Classic Press, 1991. 232p. ISBN 0-933121-53-9.

This is considered a classic work and has served as a major source of information in searching family history of African Americans. It furnishes the inquirer with a well-chosen compilation of sources necessary to trace African ancestry. Although it is not as detailed in some respects as the Rose and Eicholz volume below, there are many useful features. Especially noteworthy are the listing of important newspapers and the directory of research resources identifying information centers both in the United States and elsewhere. There is helpful information on how to conduct the search in the introductory chapters.

Black Genesis by James Rose and Alice Eichholz. (Gale, 1978) is an annotated bibliography helping to create interest in black ancestry and focus on research that helps reclaim or retrace that part of history. There are two major sections. Part I contains seven chapters, including "Oral History" and "War Records." Part II presents a survey of the United States, the West Indies, and Canada, in which state, regional, and local records are identified. These include records of federal origin and cemetery, church, military, personal, and slave records. There is a list of projects that need to be done. Annotations are brief but informative.

Ethnic Genealogy: A Research Guide by Jesse Carney Smith (Greenwood Press, 1983) is another early entrant in multicultural genealogy and facilitates the search for information pertaining to the family life of American Indians, Asian Americans, black Americans, and Hispanics. This serves as a manual for conducting such searches and provides helpful listings of the various resources and records.

BRITISH

638. Immigrants from Great Britain and Ireland: A Guide to Archival and Manuscript Sources in North America. Jack W. Weaver and DeeGee Lester, comps. Westport, CT: Greenwood Press, 1986. 129p. ISBN 0-313-24342-5.

This is the first volume of another Greenwood series and offers a listing of archival resources in various repositories on this continent as they relate to the Anglo-Irish experience. English, Welsh, Scottish, and Irish immigration manuscripts, unpublished and relatively obscure in most cases, are identified through institutional responses to questionnaires on their holdings. The centers listed represent just about every state in the United States and every province in Canada. Some repositories are uncertain about how much they own of the Anglo-Irish culture. Entries furnish name of source, address, phone number, hours and accessibility, and availability of photoreproduction. Brief descriptions are included, and arrangement is alphabetical under state or province, then city, then repository. Much effort has gone into this work, and although there are notable omissions, its value is evident.

639. The Original Lists of Persons of Quality; Emigrants; Religious Exiles; Political Rebels; Serving Men Sold for a Term of Years; Apprentices. . . . John C. Hotten, ed. Repr. Baltimore: Genealogical Publishing Co., 1996. 580p. ISBN 0-8063-0605-X.

This monumental effort has been a major aid for investigation since its initial publication in 1874 and is one of the best-known sources. Hotten employed the public records of the Chancery and the Exchequer to create a listing of names representing a wide range of individuals who emigrated to American plantations from Great Britain during the years 1600–1700. As stated in the extensive subtitle, in addition to "persons of quality" there were emigrants, religious exiles, political rebels, indentured servants, apprentices, "children stolen," and "maidens pressed." Entries include ages, localities of origin, and names of the ships whenever possible.

Over 100 years later, the work was supplemented by James C. Brandow, who edited *Omitted Chapters from Hotten's Original Lists . . . Census Returns, Parish Registers and Militia Rolls for the Barbados Census of 1679/80* (Genealogical Publishing Co., 1982). Hotten's rather surprising omission of Barbados records was brought to light and corrected by Brandow, who scoured the registers, rolls, and landholder lists to produce the names of an additional 6,500 persons. This is quite important, because many of those who arrived in Barbados later relocated in this country.

GERMAN

640. Germans to America: Lists of Passengers Arriving at U.S. Ports, 1850–. Ira A. Glazier and P. William Filby, eds. Wilmington, DE: Scholarly Resources, 1988–. v. 1–64 (in progress). ISBN 0-8420-2279-1.

In recent years, there has been much more interest in the publication of tools to aid the investigation of German immigration. Glazier and Filby have produced a large-scale effort that reached its 64th volume in 2000. The intent was to supply complete passenger lists beginning with the year 1850 to continue through the late 1960s. Entries furnish age, gender, trade or occupation, place of origin, and destination of most but not all passengers from Germany who arrived in any of the major ports in this country. A name index furnishes access to the proper list. Each volume covers approximately one year of passenger listings; volume 65 (1893–1894) is soon to be issued.

A complementary effort is *German Immigrants: Lists of Passengers Bound from Bremen to New York 1842–1867 with Places of Origin,* compiled by Gary J. Zimmerman and Marion Wolfert (Genealogical Publishing Co., 1985–1988) in three volumes. About 100,000 names are given of those who arrived through the well-traveled route of Bremen to New York. The work is of value because of its focus on an elusive time period.

HISPANIC

641. Finding Your Hispanic Roots. George R. Ryskamp. Baltimore: Genealogical Publishing, 1997. 290p. ISBN 0-8063-1517-2.

For those Americans of Spanish or Latin American descent interested in family history, this work is an important source. It is the most comprehensive manual on Hispanic ancestry to date and provides excellent exposition of basic records including birth and baptismal names characteristic of Hispanic culture. The author is an academic historian and experienced genealogist and writer. He presents clearly the techniques of research including description and explanation of methods to trace Hispanic immigrants in U.S. government records, church records, census, and military records. Of value are the segments describing computer searches and use of the family history centers. There is a good bibliography of carefully selected sources for additional information. Illustrations are furnished, and a general index provides access.

642. Hispanic Surnames and Family History. Lyman D. Platt. Baltimore: Genealogical Publishing, 1996. 349p. ISBN 0-8063-1480-X.

Platt has put together what amounts to the most extensive bibliography of Hispanic family histories to date, and in so doing has identified the geographical distribution of these names throughout Latin America and the Hispanic United States. The content of the work has been divided into several segments, the first of which is an account of the origin, historical development, and frequency or commonality of some 1,500 names. Following is a directory of information centers and agencies in this country and others that furnish information on Hispanic surnames. Of most importance is the previously mentioned bibliography of more than 1,800 family histories published in the United States and Latin America. There are cross-references to the 1,500 surnames treated in the first section, enabling users to continue their genealogical search. Several appendixes analyze relevant content in the 1980 census and in three published works on the topic.

JEWISH

643. The Encyclopedia of Jewish Genealogy. Volume I: Sources in the United States and Canada. Arthur Kurzweil and Miriam Weiner, eds. Northvale, NJ: Jason Aronson, 1991; repr.1996. 226p. ISBN 0-87668-835-0; 1-56821-998-9 (pbk).

With the growing interest in family origins, the more specialized manuals that deal with problems specific to an ethnic or racial group have become increasingly important. To the Jewish people, family study has always been a major interest, and location of records has been an important task. This recent entry is the first of what is projected to be a three-volume work. In this volume, there are three major chapters: immigration and naturalization; U.S. institutional resources arranged by city; and Canadian resources arranged by city. The second chapter, in directory fashion, first by state, then by city, identifies and describes the collections and resources of a variety of institutions (libraries, cemeteries, synagogues, funeral homes). Canada is treated in similar fashion by province, then city. This volume describes immigration and naturalization records and identifies passenger and steamship listings. Volume 2 was projected to cover sources for the rest of the world, and volume 3 to provide a topical approach.

An interesting source from the same publisher is *A Dictionary of Jewish Names and Their History* by Benzion C. Kaganoff (1996) who examines the derivations of Jewish names with respect to their beginnings in biblical, occupational, and regional influences. Nearly 4,000 names are treated in alphabetical sequence.

644. Jewish Immigrants of the Nazi Period in the U.S.A. Herbert A. Strauss, ed. New York: K.G. Saur, 1978–1997. 6v. ISBN 0-89664-026-4.

This set represents a large-scale, ambitious project designed to provide access to documents and secondary sources that trace the immigration and resettlement in this country of German Jews fleeing the Nazi menace. It is sponsored by the Research Foundation for Jewish Immigration and issued as a six-volume work. Its composition is volume 1, *Archival Resources* (1978), compiled by Steven W. Siegel; volume 2, *Classified and Annotated Bibliography of Books and Articles on the Immigration and Acculturation of Jews from Central Europe to the USA since 1933* (1981), compiled by Henry Friedlander et al.; volume 3, part 1, *Guide to the Oral History Collection of the Research Foundation for Jewish Immigration* (1982), compiled by Joan C. Lessing; volume 3, part 2, *Classified List of Articles Concerning Emigration in Germany* (1982), compiled by Daniel R. Schwartz; volume 4, *Jewish Emigration from Germany 1933–1942 (1992) compiled by Herbert A. Strauss;* volume 5, *The Individual and Collective Experience of German-Jewish Immigrants, 1933–1984* (1986), compiled by David Rohrbaugh; and most recently, volume 6, *Essays on the History, Persecution and Emigration of the German Jews* (1997), again compiled by Herbert A. Strauss, which provides a social and communal history of Jewish immigrants. The work is valuable for its full and detailed scholarship and is a must for this type of inquiry.

FEMALES

645. Immigrant Women in the United States: A Selectively Annotated Multidisciplinary Bibliography. Donna R. Gabaccia, comp. New York: Greenwood Press, 1989. 325p. (Bibliographies and Indexes in Women's Studies, no. 9). ISBN 0-313-26452-X.

This bibliography updates the Cordasco volume treated in the paragraph below. A more comprehensive effort, this one identifies more than 2,000 items (books, journal articles, dissertations) of a scholarly nature dealing with the subject of immigrant women and their daughters born in this country. Chapters focus either on format/type, such as "Bibliography" or "General Works," or on topical elements ("Migration," "Family," "Work," etc.). There is a useful introduction in each chapter, and many of the entries are annotated. Arrangement is alphabetical by author within the chapters. The entries are accessible through no less than four indexes, which cover authors, persons, groups, and subjects.

The earlier bibliography, by Francesco Cordasco, *The Immigrant Woman of North America: An Associated Bibliography of Selected References* (Scarecrow, 1985), furnishes 1,190 entries, some annotated, drawn from a variety of books and journals. These examine the female experience in immigration history. There are six broad categorical headings, both form/format ("Bibliography" and "General References") and topical ("The Workplace" and "Political Encounters"). The material is accessed by both subject and author indexes.

ETHNIC, RACIAL, AND GENDER INFLUENCES

Since the 1960s, there has been a real interest in ethnicity and national origins, which has inspired the production of an array of trade and reference publications on the topic. Authors, editors, and publishers have both followed and encouraged the public interest in the awakening of pride within ethnic, racial, and gender segments of U.S. society during the past 30 years. This focus is in keeping with the emphasis on such societal factors in modern historiography. Following a slight lapse of enthusiasm for the subject during the late 1970s, there has been a renewed interest in the 1980s and 1990s with the country's growing commitment to the promotion of multicultural studies and appreciation of its cultural diversity.

A current abstracting service of interest is *Sage Race Relations Abstracts* (Sage, 1975–) that is issued quarterly and abstracts books, periodicals, essays, and pamphlets relating to both U.S. and European happenings. Occasionally, historical topics are treated.

GENERAL SOURCES

This subsection treats the more generic or comprehensive sources, such as those on racism in general or those covering more than one ethnic group. Works having a more specific focus, be it ethnic, racial, or gender-based, are treated in listings for each of those particular groups. Included in this general subsection are materials that are pertinent to other areas such as the study of immigration, addressed in the previous unit of this chapter. The same is true of "Law and Crime" treated in a subsequent unit of this chapter, and of areas covered in chapter 3, "Economic History."

646. Affirmative Action: A Documentary History. Jo Ann O. Robinson, ed. Westport, CT: Greenwood Press, 2001. 464p. (Primary Documents in American History and Contemporary Issues). ISBN 0-313-30169-7.

Another well-executed source from the publisher's series designed to meet the needs of high school and undergraduate students, this work furnishes background texts of significant documents relevant to the struggle for affirmative action. The nature of the controversy is revealed through documents both pro and con; they have been selected in careful manner. The work opens with an introductory essay and chronology enumerating developments and important events with respect to considerations of race, gender, and physical disability.

Affirmative Action: A Bibliography by Joan Nordquist (Reference and Research Services, 1996) is number 41 of the *Contemporary Social Issues* series from the publisher. Like others in the series, the bibliography is concise but well constructed and useful in enabling the researcher or serious student to discover important resources. Arrangement is topical in 13 chapters addressing the debate regarding the wisdom of affirmative action policies, attitudes surrounding the issue, elements relating to employment, legal issues, and government policy with separate consideration of gender and of race. Sources include titles from feminist literature, social, political, and philosophical works of small presses, mainstream publications, and those of activist organizations. A more recent resource from the same series is *Affirmative Action: A Reference Handbook* by Lynne Eisaguirre (1999) complementing the Nordquist bibliography with excellent narrative. Designed to meet the needs of a wide and varied audience, the handbook supplies brief but lucid identifications, expositions, and descriptions in objective manner.

647. The Almanac of Women and Minorities in American Politics 2002. Mart Martin. Boulder, CO: Westview Press, 2001. 409p. ISBN 0-8133-0918-7.

This work updates the earlier edition published in 1999 and provides coverage through the year 2000 in identifying minority personalities who have been elected or appointed to government posts. Coverage is expansive and extends through all branches of state and federal government. Similar in format and presentation to the earlier work, the current effort contains six major sections each of which is given to a specific group and its participation in the business of government. Included here are women, African Americans, Hispanics, Asian Americans, Native Americans, and gays and lesbians. A seventh section presents important milestones or "firsts" and in some cases includes instances relevant to local governance. The work is conveniently packaged and facilitates quick reference to specific facts regarding minority office-holders both past and present.

648. Atlas of American Diversity. Larry H. Shinagawa and Michael Jang. Walnut Creek, CA: Altamira, 1998. ISBN: 0-7619-9127-1.

With the increased emphasis in the recent past regarding ethnic and cultural influences and the impact of different groups on the American landscape, several published resources have targeted population patterns and migrations of these peoples. Based on the

1980 and 1990 censuses, the authors have produced a work that treats the whole array of cultures from different parts of the globe and their population distributions in this country. More than 200 maps are given with charts and graphics to illustrate the stories of these peoples. The work examines residential distributions as well as family patterns, and numerous demographics (ages, occupations, incomes, crime, and housing choices among others). Of interest is the history of their immigration as well as migration within the country.

649. The Color of Words: An Encyclopaedic Dictionary of Ethnic Bias in the United States. Philip Herbst. Yarmouth, ME: Intercultural Press, 1997. 259p. ISBN 1-877864-42-0.

Herbst has created a unique and valuable reference source providing identifications, descriptions, and sources of origin of several hundred words and phrases pertinent to the study of racism and ethnic bias. Included here are slur and slang words, epithets, stereotypes, and other expressions generally associate with bias or prejudice. A useful element is the treatment of common phrases such as "Native American" and "politically incorrect" to clear up commonly held misconceptions. The scope of the work embraces bias against peoples in comprehensive manner in addressing the terminology pertinent to African Americans, Asians, Hispanics, Jews, and a number of European immigrant groups. Entries supply definitions, etymology, and usage along with social background and societal implications.

650. Dictionary of Race and Ethnic Relations. 4th ed. Ernest E. Cashmore and Ellis Cashmore. London: Routledge, 1996. 412p. ISBN 0-415-15167-8.

The first edition of this useful work was issued in 1984 and was recognized for its coverage of both British and U.S. racial relations. Both the second and third editions were similar to the first in utilizing the talents of distinguished group of experts in providing in-depth articles (essay-length in most cases) on major figures and sociological elements related to the study of ethnic influences. The current effort follows in the same vein with treatment given to theories and concepts as well as individuals, for which much of the material has been rewritten or updated. Many topics have been added, with dramatic changes evident in media reporting and mass perception of such events as the O.J. Simpson trial and the continuous attacks on affirmative action. There is a scholarly introduction with respect to key elements in race relations in the 1990s. The book is useful to the student of U.S. history in its inclusion of British sentiment. An index is provided.

*651. DISCovering Multicultural America: African Americans, Hispanic Americans, Asian Americans, Native Americans. Detroit: Gale Research, 1996. [CD-ROM]

Another source providing coverage of the cultural and ethnic history of the four major minority groups in this country, it has the power of interactive multimedia approach to enhance learning for students at levels ranging from junior high school to college undergraduate. A major effort, it is heavily illustrated with 1,500 photographs and offers some 2,000 entries furnishing biographical coverage of personalities. There are another 2,500 historical and topical descriptions describing relevant events, court cases, treaties, speeches, and more. Treatment is accorded to 500 places serving as ethnic landmarks. In addition, there are 350 documents of historical importance and 200 statistical charts, graphs, and tables, and audio and video clips. The technology and searching systems appear be usable and flexible enough to satisfy the user.

652. Encyclopedia of Minorities in American Politics. Jeffrey D. Schultz et al., eds. Phoenix, AZ: Oryx Press, 2000. 2v. (The American Political Landscape Series). ISBN 1-57356-129-0.

This is a detailed and thorough work in two volumes treating a vast array of issues pertinent to the study of the four major minority groups with respect to their involvement in the politics of this country. Volume 1 contains two sections, African Americans and Asian Americans, and volume 2 covers Hispanic Americans and Native Americans. Each section opens with an introductory essay of historical nature. In all, there are nearly 2,000 entries furnishing biographical coverage of personalities, relevant court cases, important events, a variety of political organizations, and numerous movements. Certain entries furnish survey-length treatment of important and complex issues such as immigration. Entries have cross-references and a bibliography of print and nonprint sources. Several appendixes provide supporting material such as speeches and copies of important documents. A comprehensive index furnishes access by name, title, and subject.

653. The Ethnic Press in the United States: A Historical Analysis and Handbook. Sally M. Miller, ed. New York: Greenwood Press, 1987. 437p. ISBN 0-313-23879-0.

Although not as comprehensive as the earlier work by Wynar and Wynar (below), which covers 63 ethnic groups, this more recent effort furnishes in-depth historical analysis. Scholarly, essay-length articles contributed by ethnic studies specialists describe the newspapers of 27 different ethnic groups. Included are both the better-known and the more obscure newspapers. The editor from the staff of the *Pacific Historian* regards the ethnic press as the "best primary source for an understanding of the world of non-English-speaking groups in the United States." Prior to World War I, there were as many as 1,300 foreign-language newspapers in this country; the decline was brought about by immigration restrictions. Essays treat the background of each ethnic group and the cultural-political atmosphere contributing to the origin and development of its publications. Bibliographies are provided; there is an index of subjects, titles, and names.

The second edition of *Encyclopedic Directory of Ethnic Newspapers and Periodicals in the United States* by Lubomyr R. Wynar and Anna T. Wynar (Libraries Unlimited, 1976), albeit old and needing of revision at this point in time, is still useful for its breadth in treating 63 ethnic groups. It gives background information on nearly 1,000 different serial titles. Arrangement is alphabetical within the 51 sections, and entries are separated by languages employed (English or native/bilingual). Entries give dates, frequency, circulation, subscription rate, and scope of each publication, plus addresses and phone numbers of editors. Statistical information is found in the appendix, and an introductory essay explores the nature of the ethnic press

654. Gale Encyclopedia of Multicultural America. 2nd ed. Jeffrey Lehman and Robert von Dassanowsky, eds. Detroit: Gale Group, 2000. 3v. ISBN 0-787-63990-7.

This is a revision of the earlier work edited by Judy Galens and published five years earlier. It has been expanded to three volumes from two and having added approximately 50 more culture groups to the 101 in the first edition. It continues as an excellent work for youngsters from junior high school level and up, and will find many willing users among college undergraduates. Descriptive narrative regarding the history and culture is presented in the form of detailed essays on each group represented from Acadians to Yupiats in alphabetical order through the three volumes. Coverage is given to the history of each group, its acculturation and assimilation, and to social issues and dynamics affecting its people. Religion, employment, economics, traditions, and politics are treated. The essays conclude with bibliographies of relevant books and a listing of museums and research centers.

Gale Encyclopedia of Multicultural America: Primary Documents, edited by Lehman in two volumes for the same publisher (1999), serves as a supplementary source or companion to the one above. The focus is on primary documents of relevance to the cultural groups and includes letters, articles, cartoons, photographs, interviews, speeches, Web sites, legislation, songs, and more. Each group is treated as a separate entry that opens with a brief history on origins and relevant foreign policies.

655. Guide to Information Resources in Ethnic Museum, Library, and Archival Collections in the United States. Lois J. Buttlar and Lubomyr R. Wynar, comps. Westport, CT: Greenwood Press, 1996. 369p. (Bibliographies and Indexes in Ethnic Studies, no. 7) ISBN 0-313-29846-7.

Seventy American ethnic groups are treated in this directory that seeks to identify and describe institutional collections of value. Nearly 800 museums, libraries, and archives are identified and arranged alphabetically under ethnic groups. Entries supply name of institution, type, address, phone, and fax number, as well as sponsoring organization, personnel, contact person, founding date, scope, publications, staff, and so forth. Data was furnished through responses to questionnaires or use of secondary sources, even though the usual number of inaccuracies will be found to exist, directories of this type are extremely useful to a wide range of users.

Genre and Ethnic Collections: Collected Essays, edited by Milton T. Wolfe and Martin S. Murray (JAI, 1996) was issued as volume 38 (pp. 217–467) of *Foundations in Library and Information Science.* It identifies library collections and examines the development of ethnic collections, ethnic literature, and minority authorship in this country.

*656. Hatewatch: Combating and Containing Online Bigotry. (tolerance.org) Southern Poverty Law Center. Available: http://www.hatewatch.org.

One of the leading advocacy organizations standing for the rights of all peoples, the group has grown in size and influence from an inauspicious beginning. Hatewatch is now part of the Southern Poverty Law Center's tolerance.org. The group follows the affairs of major hate groups in this country and issues reports of their activity. The Web site is dynamic and changing and offers much useful information. Included here are full-text articles reproduced from leading U.S. newspapers. There are sections on "Tolerance Watch," "Do Something," and "Dig Deeper"; "hatebooks online" leads to full-text versions of printed materials espousing extremist points of view.

657. Making it in America: A Sourcebook on Eminent Ethnic Americans. Elliott R. Barkan, ed. Santa Barbara, CA: ABC-CLIO, 2001. 448p. ISBN 1-57607-098-0.

This is a comprehensive biographical dictionary attempting to be as inclusive of as many ethnic groups as possible and to embrace a good proportion of women and also of occupations. As a result, approximately 90 racial, ethnic, and national groups are represented ranging from the traditional (Italian Americans, Irish Americans, etc.) to the more recently classified minorities such as Hawaiian Americans and Jewish Americans. The work is politically correct and in addition to careful representation of females, there is a definite attempt to include people of color. As a result, it is highly selective in its choice of 400 personalities selected on the basis of their symbolism of the American dream in terms of their successful adaptation and contribution to society. Many of these individuals are not well known, but their stories are of interest and of value in the weaving of the American fabric.

658. Multicultural Resources on the Internet: The United States and Canada. Vicki L. Gregory et al. Englewood, CO: Libraries Unlimited, 1999. 366p. ISBN 1-800-237-6124.

This is a useful directory of Web sites relevant to multicultural study, especially for U.S. and Canadian users. All are in the English language although there are some that are multilingual in nature. The work is organized into 14 chapters, the first of which serves to provide an introductory essay to the nature and composition of the work. Subsequent chapters treat different cultural groups and are the work of different specialists. Each chapter opens with an introduction of varying length; annotations tend to be brief. Chapter 2 is given to comprehensive sites covering more than one culture, followed by chapters supplying Web sites relevant to the study of Native Americans, African Americans, Hispanic Americans, Asian Americans in general, Chinese Americans, Japanese Americans, Asian Indian Americans, Jewish Americans, Middle Eastern Americans, French Canadians, Cajuns and Creoles, and Hawaiian Americans.

Multiculturalism in the United States: A Comparative Guide to Acculturation and Ethnicity by John D. Buenker and Lorman A. Ratner (Greenwood Press, 1992) provides a comprehensive treatment of both the traditional immigrant cultures from various parts of Europe and the more recent arrival of Latin Americans, as well as the Native Americans. Chapters succeed in providing informative profiles of individual cultures written by scholars in their own areas of expertise. As is the case with most multiauthor works, there is a certain inconsistency both in style and treatment but both students and researchers should profit from the description of major institutions for each tradition. Each chapter has a full bibliography for further examination. A more recent effort is *Multiculturalism in the United States: Current Issues, Contemporary Voices* edited by Peter Kvisto and Georgianne Runblad (Pine Forge Press, 2000). This work identifies the thoughts and commentary of various peoples regarding issues of acceptance, adaptation, ethnic conditions, and race relations in adjusting to a pluralistic society.

659. A Nation of Peoples: A Sourcebook on America's Multicultural Heritage. Elliott R. Barkan, ed. Westport, CT: Greenwood Press, 1999. 583p. ISBN 0-313-29961-7.

This is a highly acclaimed source of information on 27 cultural groups demonstrating the multicultural makeup of our nation. Following an introductory essay on America as a nation of various peoples, the groups are described in detailed essays alphabetically arranged by either an individual group or a geographical region with treatment of several cultures. Beginning with coverage of African Americans by general editor Barkan, and concluding with West Indians/Caribbeans by Philip Kasinitz and Milton Vickerman, the *Sourcebook* presents such stories as those of American Indians, Hawaiians, and South Asians as well as those of various European and Middle Eastern cultures among others. The essays are well written by authors who are specialists and scholars qualified to describe immigration history, settlement patterns, religious issues, cultural impact, and degree of assimilation. It represents a useful source for serious students and inquirers. The index has been criticized for certain inconsistencies in supplying cross-references for some groups and not others.

660. Peoples of the World: North Americans: The Culture, Geographical Setting, and Historical Background of 37 North American Peoples. Joyce Moss and George Wilson. Detroit: Gale, 1991. 441p. ISBN 0-8103-7768-3.

Designed more for the layman and high school or undergraduate student rather than the practicing historian, this recent work provides an excellent overview of the people who have inhabited the North American continent. As such, it will be in great demand for a variety of needs associated with the new emphasis on multicultural elements within our society. Beginning with the early inhabitants who came prior to the European settlements, the book enumerates a mix of native cultures, including three lost cultures as well as 34 current groups. Entries profile these peoples and emphasize the human dimension in terms of their cultural achievements. In so doing, they provide an excellent awareness of the continent as a melting pot of diverse cultural composition. Maps and illustrations accompany the text and help to illustrate the cultural movements.

661. Race and Crime: An Annotated Bibliography. Katheryn K. Russell et al., comps. Westport, CT: Greenwood Press, 2000. 192p. (Bibliographies and Indexes in Ethnic Studies, no. 8). ISBN 0-313-31033-5.

The major author is an academic who with the collaboration of doctoral students has produced this comprehensive bibliography of crime associated with various ethnic groups. The introduction explains the intent to dispel stereotypical assumptions and establishes the importance of studying such relationships in scientific manner. Coverage is given to works issued between 1950 and 1999 and includes books, articles, essays from books, dissertations, government documents and Web sites. The work is divided into three segments the first of which is race-specific and entries are categorized under five groupings; whites, Native Americans, Asian Americans, Hispanics, and African Americans. The second part treats general race research and crime, and the final section enumerates several important Web sites for documents. Annotations are detailed and informative. The work is indexed by author and by subject.

662. Racial and Ethnic Diversity: Asians, Blacks, Hispanics, Native Americans, and Whites. 3rd ed. Ithaca, NY: New Strategist Publications, 2000. 782p. ISBN 1-885070-27-6.

Another of the sources dealing with the ethnology and population characteristics of the four major minority groups in the United States, this is a convenience tool targeted to an audience of market researchers and decision makers in the realm of public policy. The emphasis is on the reporting of statistical summaries of characteristics and factors of population, economics, education, and consumerism of each of the different groups. Data is largely drawn from reports of government agencies: Census Bureau, Bureau of Labor Statistics, and the National Center for Education. Information is current up to 1999, and heavy use is made of the 1990 census. Some 60 charts treat statistical data from various surveys.

Each group is treated in a separate chapter with narrative summaries provided by the authors, and tables are provided.

Of similar nature is *The Official Guide to Racial and Ethnic Diversity: Asians, Blacks, Hispanics, Native Americans, and White* by Cheryl Russell (New Strategist Publications, 1996) also targeted to the needs of market analysts and depending upon census publications in its reporting of demographic characteristics through statistical summaries. A useful feature is the inclusion of data on attitudes toward racial and ethnic groups gathered through the 1994 General Social Survey questionnaire.

663. Racial and Ethnic Relations in America. Carl L. Bankston. Pasadena, CA: Salem Press, 2000. 3v. ISBN 0-89356-629-2.

The goal of this comprehensive effort is to provide a reliable and objective source of information in presenting facts and figures regarding the most important topics, occurrences, and issues relevant to the study of ethnic relation in this country and in Canada. In all, there are 900 entries, alphabetically arranged throughout the three volumes. They vary in length and in type of coverage and range from 200 word definitions of relevant terms to lengthy survey articles of 2,500 words or more providing cultural and historical treatment and analysis of the various cultural groups (Japanese Americans, Jewish Americans) or of theoretical topics such as "cultural pluralism." Essays generally contain cross-references and brief annotated bibliographies, and many are accompanied by photographs. In addition, the work contains a number of charts and timelines, and features a general chronology of events and a brief biographical section treating leading personalities. Name and subject indexes help provides access.

664. Racism in Contemporary America. Meyer Weinberg, comp. New York: Greenwood Press, 1996. 838p. ISBN 0-313-29659-6.

This volume joins the compiler's *Racism in the United States: A Comprehensive Classified Bibliography* (Greenwood Press, 1990) as another major contribution to bibliography on this topic. Both efforts provide comprehensive lists of references to titles with brief annotations in some cases. The current work adds 14,671 citations, with few duplications of the 10,000 items treated in the first publication. Each effort contains more than 80 subject divisions under which entries are alphabetically arranged. Sexism, anti-Semitism, gender, and extreme nationalism are included, with most emphasis given to African American issues. Materials include books, articles, monographs, hearings, and dissertations. There are listings of bibliographies in each topical area. Both efforts have been criticized for incompleteness (no listings of electronic resources for one thing), but with such an extensive listing of titles, both works are considered major assets to serious inquiry. There is an index of authors but not of subjects.

Another source is *Discrimination and Prejudice: An Annotated Bibliography* compiled by Halford H. Fairchild and others (Westerfield Enterprises, 1991), which identifies books, articles, and dissertations in five separate bibliographic segments: Afro-Americans, American Indians, Asian Americans, Hispanic Americans, and a multiethnic listing.

665. The State Atlas of Political and Cultural Diversity. William Lilley et al. Washington, D.C.: Congressional Quarterly, 1997. 298p. ISBN 1-877864-42-0.

From one of the leading publishers of reference sources dealing with the U.S. government comes this analytical tome providing awareness of proportional population distributions of 15 major "racial, ethnic and ancestral groups" among more than 6,700 state legislative districts. These groups are identified by the authors as having disproportionate political power due to their numbers within certain state districts. Such data is the result of laborious research matching census group block data in the 1990 census to existing Senate and legislative districts within the states. It is both interesting and important to find out that some districts are composed of more than 50-percent representation by a single ethnic group. Such characteristics as average household income, college education levels, and numbers of social security recipients are given for districts with large proportions of the groups in question. Although much of the data is significant information, one might wonder at the reason for the attempt to show that certain nonwhite minority groups (due to their residential cohesiveness) have profited politically at the expense of older white cultures that have been assimilated and have dispersed throughout the country.

666. Statistical Handbook on Racial Groups in the United States. Tim B. Heaton et al. Phoenix: Oryx Press, 2000. 360p. (Oryx Statistical Handbooks Series). ISBN 1-57356-266-1.

Heaton and his associates have drawn upon a variety of government sources and surveys, including the 1990 census, to furnish both high school and college students an array of statistical data and analyses of important topics as they relate to the racial groups in this country. Statistical comparisons are provided regarding educational goals, employment, leisure pursuits, marital life and family, political participation, sex and contraception, religion, health issues, and more. More than 400 charts are supplied in presenting such data. The work is divided into major sections such as "Demographic Context," "Education," and "Economics and Employment" with subsections addressing topical factors like "age and sex" as part of demographical coverage, "dropouts" under education, and "poverty" within the economics category. There is an excellent index providing access to the large array of statistics in the work.

*667. UXL Multicultural CD. A Comprehensive Resource on African Americans, Hispanic Americans, and Native North Americans. Detroit: UXL/Gale, 1997. [CD-ROM].

Another of the UXL/Gale CD-ROM products designed to meet the needs of youngsters from junior high school to early adulthood at the college level, this useful source provides quick and easy access to a broad range of information on the three most studied cultural groups in the United States. It endeavors to furnish a complete picture of the historical background and current development of the three groups through its provision of 3,400 entries that cover more than 500 influential and important personalities, as well as events, activities, and relevant cultural aspects of daily life. Such topics as civil rights, the media, fine arts, education, sports, and more are included. There are useful graphics to enhance learning with the inclusion of 900 photographs and maps. The work comes complete with a print teacher's guide to aid its use in the classroom.

668. Voices of Multicultural America: Notable Speeches Delivered by African, Asian, Hispanic, and Native Americans, 1790–1995. Deborah G. Straub. New York: Gale Research, 1996. 1372p. ISBN 0-8103-9378-6.

Another compilation or anthology of important speeches, these works are issued with some degree of regularity by reference publishers to meet the needs of high school and college undergraduate students. The current effort is of value to the comprehension of racial and ethnic relations in its provision of the complete text of more than 230 speeches by members of the targeted ethnic minorities over a lengthy historical period. Selection of the speeches to be included was determined with the help of an advisory board; these speeches were drawn from periodical and newspaper accounts, archival collections, government publications, and biographical sources. They range in popularity from the memorable "I have a dream" speech of Martin Luther King to relatively obscure reflections on the plight of farmworkers and the internment of Japanese Americans. All are of historical interest and value, and generally are accompanied by photographs and brief bibliographies. Several indexes aid access by subject and purpose, category, ethnicity, and keyword.

669. We the People: An Atlas of America's Ethnic Diversity. James P. Allen and Eugene J. Turner. New York: Macmillan, 1988; Reprint, New York: Macmillan/Free Press, 1998. 315p. ISBN 0-02-901420-4.

As a work seven years in the making, this cultural atlas is the product of a happy union of the two geographers, Allen as a specialist in immigration and Turner as an expert in computer mapping. The data are arranged by ethnic group and are taken from the 1980 census. Presentation is excellent thanks to the use of 115 maps, most of which are in color. Nearly 70 racial and ethnic groups are treated, their movements and distributions charted from 1920 to 1980. Subsections are given to the coverage of special groups, such as Catholic and Protestant Irish, Sephardic Jews, and Chinese from Vietnam. Accompanying text of about three pages for each group describes settlement patterns and reasons for locating in certain geographic locales. Indexes of ethnic population and place provide access to the content.

CIVIL RIGHTS

670. Civil Rights Decisions of the United States Supreme Court: The 19th Century. Maureen Harrison and Steve Gilbert, eds. San Diego: Excellent Books, 1994. 239p. (Civil Rights Decisions Series). ISBN 1-880780-04-6.

This is a selection by the authors of what they consider to be the most significant civil rights cases of the century. The narrative presents the actual decisions in the cases as represented by the official text of the majority opinion. Some editing is apparent in the use of brackets following the original text where exposition is thought to be necessary. References are made to the text in the *United States Reports.* Supplementing the primary text is a concise history of the case, listing of Supreme Court justices and bibliography of additional readings. In this time period, coverage is given to decisions relating to African Americans, Native Americans, and Chinese Americans.

Civil rights Decisions of the United States Supreme Court: The 20th Century issued by the same editors for the same publisher in the same year, follows the same pattern or format. For this time period, coverage is given to decisions affecting Japanese Americans and again to those concerning African Americans.

671. Civil Rights in America: 1500 to the Present. Jay A. Sigler. Detroit: Gale, 1998. 710p. ISBN 0-7876-0612-X.

This is a well-constructed exposition of the emergence of civil rights in this country providing accurate historical perspective in its treatment of the experiences of different racial, religious, and ethnic groups. The country was founded on the principles established in English common law as a prerogative of all men. Articles are informative and in-depth and are written by the author and other contributors. The work is divided into 18 signed chapters beginning with the origins and limits of American rights followed by identification of rights enjoyed by Americans in the twentieth century. Subsequent chapters treat different ethnic groups (African Americans, Asian Americans, Hispanic Americans, and Native Americans) as well as immigrant experiences of various European, Asian, and Middle Eastern cultures. Nonethnic rights (voting and education) are addressed as well as the more current issues of employment rights and housing rights. Court decisions are described and enumerated, personalities are examined in each chapter, and the entries are enhanced through illustrations and bibliographies.

672. Civil Rights in the United States. Waldo E. Martin and Patricia Sullivan, eds. New York: Macmillan Reference, 2000. 2v. ISBN 0-02-864765-3.

This represents a narrower scope than the entry above in its emphasis on the Civil Rights Movement of the 1950s and 1960s, and its intent to furnish the most recent scholarship available to a wide-ranging audience. In so doing, it serves as a thorough examination of that most important period in providing over 700 articles arranged alphabetically from A to Z. The editors are academics who have coordinated the efforts of more than 300 contributors representing a variety of viewpoints. Earlier history and roots of the movement are included beginning with the close of the Civil War and subsequent issues such as the conditions of women and gays and lesbians are addressed. Coverage is given to personalities, movements, historical periods, issues, and topics of varying importance. An interesting approach is the inclusion of entries for each state in which civil rights elements particular to that state are covered.

673. The Civil Rights Movement. Hackensack, NJ: Salem Press, 2000. 2v. (Magill's Choice). ISBN 0-89356-169-X.

Drawing from previous publications, this work provides a useful historical overview of the Civil Rights Movement as it impacted African Americans with examination of issues, events, personalities, and legislation. Intended for a less-sophisticated audience ranging from high school to undergraduate students, it examines the history of the struggle by African Americans in attempting to achieve equality of opportunity. Arrangement is alphabetical with entries treating a variety of topics from the abolitionist movement to the Voting Rights Act. Bibliographies and additional suggestions are given for most entries. Court cases are described in lucid manner and there is a separate section containing biographies of important individuals. Also in the appendixes is a useful timeline of events. Illustrations are included, and a detailed subject index concludes the work.

Intended for the same audience is another work by the same name. *The Civil Rights Movement* by Peter B. Levy (Greenwood Press, 1998) is a well-written narrative of the Movement divided into six essays beginning with overview and exposition of its origins. Also treated are activism and resistance in Mississippi, the legal process and affirmative action, the Movement's legacy, and the leadership role of women. There is a chronology dating from 1857 to 1996, as well as a section of biographies of 20 important leaders. Excerpts from several primary documents are provided as is a bibliography.

*674. The Civil Rights Movement in the United States: Interactive Encyclopedia. Santa Barbara, CA: ABC-CLIO, 2000. ISBN 1-57607-252-5. [CD-ROM].

Another of the publisher's interactive encyclopedias (entries 546, 594, 838, 942, 1102), this work provides an opportunity to examine the topic in a variety of ways. Articles are intended to convey an understanding of social and political ramifications of this important aspect of American history. There are more than 500 entries providing awareness of personalities, organizations, issues, events, and relevant documents. One is able to choose a topic and follow the links to related biographical coverage, documentary source material, charts, photographs, and voice and video clips. There is a timeline section with events organized by date, and a media section identifies available audio-visual material. Also, there is the capacity to connect to the companion Web site in which one is able to access additional links to related Web sites and manual-type information such as how to write a biography. This should be especially useful for the high school student.

675. The Encyclopedia of Civil Rights in America. David Bradley and Shelley F. Fishkin, eds. Armonk, NY: M.E. Sharpe, 1998. 3v. ISBN 0-7656-800-9.

Considered to be a major reference source of information, this work supplies coverage of the subject through 700 articles of varying length. There is an emphasis on rather lengthy survey articles of broad topics such as historical events and key issues. These articles generally are subdivided into smaller sections to expedite reference work. Also included are relatively concise articles on such topics as court cases, relevant organizations, and biographical sketches of a wide range of personalities. The articles contain cross-references and there are a number of illustrations. Arrangement is alphabetical, and articles are signed by the contributors who are well qualified to address their topics. Appendixes contain a number of items including a chronology dating from 1619 to 1997, an enumeration of court cases, and various listings. There is a general index as well as an index of court cases.

676. Human Rights in the United States: A Dictionary and Documents. Rita C. Cartwright and H. Victor Conee. Santa Barbara, CA: ABC-CLIO, 2000. 2v. ISBN 1-57607-109-X.

This represents a comprehensive treatment of the topic as it has evolved in this country in providing 240 dictionary entries covered in the first volume, and should be of use to a wide audience. Entries supply definitions and explanations with cross-references to related entries in the volume and run from one to two paragraphs to one to two pages in length. Each entry contains a description of significance of the term along with references to pertinent documents and court cases. Following the entries, volume 1 begins the "Documents" section and offers 26 of the 59 documents included in this work as part of the human rights landscape in the United States. The documents are organized under six divisions such as "U.S. Documents"; each document is profiled with information concerning its subject, official citation, and type along with commentary and a Web location. Volume 2 completes the collection of documents and supplies a topical bibliography and an index.

THE ASIAN EXPERIENCE

Compared to the other ethnic influences on this country, the Asian American experience had suffered from neglect and lack of documentation. This neglect has persisted longer than it did in the case of European ethnic minorities, who did benefit from a surge of interest in ethnicity during the 1970s. With the relatively recent focus on multiculturalism, however, reference tools on Asian Americans have begun to appear. Our rationale for arrangement of entries gives primacy to racial and ethnic factors as the primary criteria in organizing these chapters. Therefore, in this section one will find resources on the female experience, education, demography, the law, and labor that are relevant to Asian American history. The Chinese Historical Society of America (available at http://www.chsa.org/htm) was founded in 1963 in San Francisco and has several hundred members. Although it is small in size, it is quite active in conferences and programs; it has published *Chinese America: History and Perspectives* on an annual basis since 1980.

General Sources

677. The Asian American Encyclopedia. Franklin Ng, ed. New York: Marshall Cavendish, 1995. 6v. ISBN 1-85435-677-1.

The editor is an anthropologist who has put together a well-qualified group of contributors to produce the first encyclopedia of its kind. The work provides some 2,000 entries in alphabetical sequence examining the history, events, culture, personalities, organizations, and major publications as well as topics and issues of current interest. The work represents a well-structured and intensive treatment, giving special emphasis to the six largest groups (Chinese Americans, Filipino Americans, Japanese Americans, Asian Indian Americans, Korean Americans, and Vietnamese Americans) especially with respect to lengthy historical treatment. Following the last entry in volume 6, there are several special features; a chronology dating from 1521 to the time of publication, directories of organizations, museums, libraries, and so forth, college programs, and media, along with a useful bibliography.

Another bibliographic work by Joan Nordquist for the *Contemporary Social Issues Series* (see entries 646n, 681, 873, and 950) is *Asian Americans: Social, Economic and Political Aspects: A Bibliography* (Reference and Research Services, 1996) was issued in 1996 as number 42. It is a compact work identifying several hundred books, periodicals, dissertations, and so forth, categorized into major subject divisions representing economic and employment conditions.

*678. Asian-American Experience On File. Carter Smith and David Lindroth, eds. New York: Facts on File, 1999. 160p. ISBN 0-8160-3696-9.

This is a useful work designed to serve the needs of a wide range of users from junior high school to the college undergraduate level. Similar to other titles from the publisher, it is bound in a three-ring notebook and organized in chronological sequence in the first five chapters. Chapter 1 covers the history of initial immigration activity, describing the politics, conflicts, and upheavals in Asia. It also explains social conditions in the United States in the nineteenth century. Chapter 2 examines the Chinese communities in detail; Hawaiian plantation life is treated with respect to the role of Chinese, Japanese, and Filipino workers. Chapter 3 covers the first half of the twentieth century and the arrival of Koreans, Indians, and Filipinos and the legislation designed to control the growing number of Oriental arrivals. Chapter 4 examines the period of the Cold War in terms of its effect on Asian Americans from mid-century to 1974, and chapter 5 studies the new surge of immigration from 1975 to the present. The final chapter provides an overview of social contributions in the arts, business, cooking, and the martial arts.

679. Asian American Reference Library. Detroit: U*X*L/Gale, 1996–1997. 5v. ISBN 0-8103-9685-8. **The Asian American Almanac: A Reference Work on Asians in the United States.** Susan Gall and Irene Natividad, eds. 1995. 834p. ISBN 0-8103-9193-7. **Asian American Biography.** Helen Zia and Susan B. Gall, eds. 1995. 2v. ISBN 0-8103-9687-4. **Asian American Chronology.** Deborah G. Baron and Susan B. Gall, eds. 1996. 173p. ISBN 0-8103-9692-0. **Asian American Voices.** Deborah G. Straub. 1997. 240p. ISBN 0-8103-96769.

Another of the comprehensive sets by Gale examining the culture and history of an American ethnic group, the volumes can be purchased individually or as a set. Designed to appeal to users from middle grades to college level and adulthood, the titles supply a near complete source of reference information regarding Americans of Asian and Pacific Island descent. Each volume is edited by an expert in the field and represents an authoritative and solid piece of work. The *Almanac* treats 15 different groups and provides descriptive narrative on issues, events, and personalities. The *Biography* contains biographical essays of 130 important personalities from all areas of endeavor. The *Chronology* provides information on events and personalities relevant to 20 groups arranged by year from 11000 B.C.E. to 1995 C.E. The *Voices* volume contains full and excerpted speeches, sermons, orations, poems, testimony, and more with descriptive introductions.

680. Asian-American Studies: An Annotated Bibliography and Research Guide. Hyung-Chan Kim, ed. Westport, CT: Greenwood Press, 1989. 504p. ISBN 0-313-26026-5.

This is a fine bibliography of nearly 3,400 items drawn from a variety of sources such as newspapers, periodicals, books, and dissertations dealing with Asian Americans. Many of the entries furnish informative annotations. An introductory essay on research precedes the listings. There are 13 chapters covering historical perspectives and 14 chapters dealing with contemporary existence. This bibliography serves the needs of historical inquiry with respect to a variety of topics. Historical chapters cover such issues as community, justice, and religion. There is good coverage of the Japanese internment. These chapters are subdivided by format and medium (books, periodicals, theses). Creative writing is purposely excluded because it is covered in another recent source. There is a detailed subject index. This is one of several works by Kim for Greenwood (see entries 680, 683, 684, and 694).

New Visions in Asian American Studies: Diversity, Community, Power edited by Franklin Ng et al. (Washington State University Press, 1994) is a compilation of 20 essays presented at a conference held in Honolulu the previous year that examines the culture of

Asian Americans. Included are expositions of history, literature, language, and women's studies relevant to Asian Americans and indigenous Hawaiians.

681. The Asian American Woman: Social, Economic & Political Conditions, a Bibliography. Joan Nordquist, ed. Santa Cruz: Reference and Research Services, 1997. 72p. (Contemporary Social Issues: A Bibliographic Series, no. 48) ISBN 0-937855-94-4.

Another brief but useful bibliography from the publisher's series, that despite its brevity supplies titles of publications covering a full range of the important sociopolitical issues confronting the Asian American woman in this country. The content is timely and efforts have been made to bring the sources up-to-date as of time of publication. There are about 725 entries categorized into 20 major subject divisions, the first seven of which treat the Asian American population groups. The remaining categories represent broad topical issues such as education, economic conditions, employment, health, feminism, sex roles, and so forth. The publications are recent and include books, pamphlets, government documents, dissertations, and articles from books and periodicals.

682. Columbia Guide to Asian American History. Gary Y. Okihiro. New York: Columbia University Press, 2001. 323p. (The Columbia Guides to American History and Cultures). ISBN 0-231-11510-5.

The author is an academic specialist in Asian American studies and has developed a useful bibliographic guide to complement the coverage given in the entries above. Since publication of *Asian American Studies: An Annotated Bibliography and Research Guide* by Kim (entry 680), there has been a considerable body of historical literature that is identified and described in this work. In keeping with the pattern developed for this series, it provides a concise but informative history and chronology of important dates and events relevant to Asian Americans. Also included are descriptions of historical periods and selective treatment of a variety of controversial issues such as the situation of Asian American internment during World War II. Historiography is examined at length and listings of print, electronic, and film resources are supplied.

683. Distinguished Asian Americans: A Biographical Dictionary. Hyung-Chan Kim. Westport, CT: Greenwood Press, 1999. 430p. ISBN 0-313-28902-6.

No editor has done more to preserve the legacy of Asian Americans than has Kim who has edited a number of publications issued by Greenwood (see entries 680 and 684) This most recent effort supplies biographical treatment of 166 personalities, both foreign and native born who have had an impact on this country. Included here are Chinese, Japanese, Korean, and Filipino as well as South Asians and Southeast Asians. A good source for high school students as well as more serious inquirers, the individuals are selected not only for their outstanding accomplishments, but for their inspirational stories as well. They represent all areas of endeavor: sports, politics, education, acting and performance, science, labor, and more. Entries are alphabetically arranged and are detailed in composition, ranging from two to three pages. In some cases, photographs are supplied and there are listings by field of endeavor in the appendixes.

Distinguished Asian Americans Series from Greenwood Press will make its appearance on November 30, 2002. The first offering is *Distinguished Asian American Political and Government Leaders* by Don T. Nakansishi and Ellen D. Wu. It represents the first biographical dictionary of Asian American elected officials, political appointees, and judges, and even extends to the inclusion of activists. Nearly 100 personalities are treated, all of whom have left their mark on the politics of this nation from 1950 to the present. The second title in this series is *Distinguished Asian American Business Leaders* by Naomi Hirahara, and is the first biographical dictionary to treat business people of Asian American heritage. Nearly 100 individuals are profiled thus affirming the pattern or framework for this series. The education and careers of successful people representing a variety of business fields are given along with references for additional reading.

684. A Legal History of Asian Americans, 1790–1990. Hyung-Chan Kim. New York: Greenwood Press, 1994. 0-313-26026-5.

This is the another work by Kim for Greenwood (entries 680 and 683). In this effort, he describes in clear fashion the development of immigration laws relating to Asian Americans in this country from 1882 to 1990. The first three chapters provide a historical survey of immigration history prior to the arrival of the Asians; the remaining five chapters supply an overview and analysis of the various elements of restrictive legislative practices, modifications, and court cases to eliminate racial discrimination in the quest to become naturalized citizens.

Dictionary of Asian American History is Kim's earliest Greenwood product, published in 1986. It remains a useful general source of information found in nearly 800 entries dealing with all aspects of Asian American history. Entries describe major events, personalities, places, and ideas "that have left indelible marks," and run from a few lines to two pages; many have lists of additional readings and cross-references. Both individual and collective experiences of the major groups are treated. In addition, there are 15 thematic essays from 4 to 15 pages in length. The first seven essays cover histories of particular groups in the United States (Chinese, Japanese, and Southeast Asians). The other essays are topical (immigration law, justice, politics, economics, education, mental health, literature, and popular culture). There is a chronology, a selective bibliography, and a useful detailed index.

685. Notable Asian Americans. Helen Zia and Susan B. Gall, eds. Detroit: Gale, 1995. 468p. ISBN 0-8103-9623-8.

Fifteen ethnic groups compose the Asian American experience treated in this informative and entertaining biographical dictionary that contains 250 articles on notable Asian Americans, both living and dead. Considered an outstanding reference source by experts, the work provide sketches ranging from one to three pages in length, and is designed to meet the needs of students from junior high school to college level. Essays are well written and informal in style; many have been developed from personal interviews with the personalities. Included here are diverse professions and trades consisting of physicists, farmers, politicians, entertainers, and more. The essays are divided into sections and furnish personal and career information, along with treatment of important successes and achievements. Several indexes provide access by occupation, ethnic group, and subject.

Chinese

686. The Chinese Americans. Benson Tong. Westport, CT: Greenwood Press, 2000. 248p. (The New Americans Series.) ISBN 0-313-30544-7.

The author is an academic historian and has provided a brief but comprehensive history of the Chinese, the first Asian group to arrive in the United States. The work is designed to meet the needs of students from high school to the college undergraduate level, and it succeeds well. The work is divided into eight chapters, the first of which contains basic historical background information on the Chinese culture from the mid-seventeenth century through the first decade of the twentieth century. Tong describes the language, philosophy, religion, and politics under the dynasty and places the departure of large numbers to this country in understandable context. The following five chapters furnish chronological coverage of the American experience with emphasis on the second half of the twentieth century. Chapter 7 examines the Chinese in the visual and performing arts, and chapter 8 examines social identities with sections on gangs, homosexuality, interracial marriage, and more. There is a bibliography, a few photographs, and an index.

687. The Island: Poetry and History of Chinese Immigrants on Angel Island, 1910–1940. Him Mark Lai et al. San Francisco Study Center, 1980. repr. Seattle: University of Washington, 1999. 174p. ISBN 0-295-97109-6.

The first and second reprint editions were by the initial publisher; the third and this one, the fourth reprint, are handled by the University of Washington. It is an important work because it preserves the poetry and brief narratives of those unfortunate individuals detained on Angel Island between the years of 1910 and 1940. The poetry speaks volumes of the thoughts and emotions of its creators during the holding period, and was taken from the walls of the barracks for the most part. Along with the collection of quotes, the work serves as informative social history in describing not only such events as the voyage but also impressions of the new homeland. As one might expect, the emotions are varied and the expression is honest in providing the reader with a perspective of the past.

The Chinese-American Heritage by David M. Brownstone (Facts on File, 1988.) is a well-written, heavily illustrated treatment of Chinese American history intended for young adults. Asian Americans have been slow to assimilate into mainstream United States and this work serves to help us understand the history and cultural background of early Cantonese immigrants. Living conditions in their homeland are described, as are their early experiences in the United States beginning with the period of the Gold Rush, when discrimination and prejudice were at their peak. The work ends on a positive note with the easing of immigration laws and lessening of racial tensions. There is a useful bibliography, and an index locates specific topics.

688. Of Orphans and Warriors: Inventing Chinese-American Culture and Identity. Gloria H. Chun. New Brunswick, NJ: Rutgers University Press, 2000. 208p. ISBN 0-8135-2708-2.

Written in a simple, straightforward manner, Chun provides a compelling history of Chinese Americans in the twentieth century that reads like a popular novel with a strong focus on personalities. In so doing, she provides brief but informative summaries of developing influences in furnishing analytical interpretations of the culture through different periods. The work is divided into five major chapters beginning with the Chinese American experience in the 1930s, indicative of Chun's intent to examine the sociological conditions surrounding the lives of the children and grandchildren of the initial settlers. Chapter 2 describes the World War II era, and chapter 3 examines the challenges found as residents and citizens of the United States at the time the mother country was turning communist. Chapters 4 and 5 explain and interpret the reformulation of Chinese American identity following the War. The effort concludes with a bibliography for additional reading, and an index.

689. The Taiwanese Americans. Franklin Ng. Westport, CT: Greenwood Press, 1998. 163p. (The New Americans). ISBN 0-313-29762-2.

With their origins in old China, several national groups are becoming part of the American landscape. Those descended from the Nationalist Chinese represent the peoples of Taiwan who are more numerous in the United States than either those from Hong Kong or those from Singapore. This is a unique reference source in its focus on the Taiwanese rather than the Chinese as a people. The work is divided into four major segments, the first of which provides an informative introductory essay on Taiwan, its land, people, customs, and historical development. This is followed by sections on early immigration and the immigrant conditions, adaptation to life in the United States, and finally, the current situation with respect to the evolving conditions of an American identity. Photographs enhance the text, and appendixes provide biographical treatment of several significant individuals, and statistical tables.

Japanese

690. Encyclopedia of Japanese American History: An A-to-Z Reference from 1868 to the Present. upd. ed. Brian Niiya, ed. New York: Facts on File, 2001. 446p. (Facts on File Library of American History). ISBN 0-8160-4093-1.

The first edition of this work was issued in 1993 under a different title, and was heralded as a real asset to the literature of Asian American studies. The current effort updates and expands that work in providing new insight and additional interpretation based on more recent research and inquiry. The work begins with an introductory section providing a brief but well-conceived historical overview written by the respected Issei politician, Daniel K. Inouye. This is followed by a second historical account of the Japanese in this country by the scholar, Gary K. Ohiro (entry 690n), along with a detailed and comprehensive chronology. The main text is described in the title and represents an alphabetical treatment of some 400 entries contributed by more than 30 specialists in the field describing personalities, legal decisions, events, terms, and so forth. Each entry contains a reading list and about 100 photographs enhance the text.

*691. Executive Order 9066: The Incarceration of Japanese Americans During World War II. Danbury, CT: Grolier, 1997. [CD-ROM].

Designed for the use of junior high school to high school students, this work provides an examination of relevant issues and factors of one of the dark periods of our history when native-born Americans along with aliens who were not permitted to gain citizenship were forced to liquidate businesses and personal possessions for a forced relocation to internment camps on the basis of their ethnic origins. The CD is narrated by motion picture and television actor, Pat Morita, and is organized into four sections treating "Chronology," "Profiles," "Topics," and "Places." The chronology begins in the year 1882 with passage of the Chinese Exclusion Act and continues with subsequent restrictive legislation offering newsreel footage, commentary, and photographs. Profiles contain the stories of six famous Japanese Americans who were interned. Topics document 10 areas or issues including the attempt to gain redress of the wrongs, while places examine the internment facilities in graphic fashion.

Japanese American Internment During World War II: A History and Reference Guide by Wendy Ng (Greenwood Press, 2002) provides high school and college undergraduate students with a useful source of information on that notoriously dark period in American history. The work contains biographical sketches of significant personalities along with the text of 10 key documents (including Executive Order 9066 above). There are personal narratives of those interned, a glossary of terms, and a chronology, as well as an annotated bibliography print sources and important Web sites.

692. The Issei; The World of the First Generation Japanese Immigrants, 1885–1924.
Yuji Ichioka. New York: Free Press, 1988; repr. 1990. 317p. ISBN 0-029-32435-1.

Developed as a labor history, this work also serves to help the reader understand the social and political obstacles facing the early Japanese immigrants in this country. That these obstacles dictated the type of labor chosen by these immigrants is clear in their inability to join unions. Even more important is the disenfranchisement from the political process inherent in their status as aliens. The work is carefully researched using contemporary sources of the time such as early Japanese immigrant newspapers in presenting the story of the Japanese immigration to this country and the subsequent treatment accorded them by self-serving labor contractors and shrewd businessmen who needed their services. Real perspective is provided perhaps for the first time in this work.

A Buried Past: An Annotated Bibliography of the Japanese American Research Project Collection is an earlier bibliographic effort compiled by Ichioka and others (Berkeley, CA: University of California, 1974). It is a catalog of the collection held by the UCLA Research Library regarding Japanese government primary-source materials relating to Japanese immigration and resettlement in the United States. It consists of 1,500 documents and records of various types organized under 18 different subjects. These categories include "history," "education," and "poetry," as well as "religion," "economics," and "society." Also included is a useful segment on "wartime internment." Each category opens with an introductory historical summary providing an overview of the listings on the issue. The work was undertaken as a special project of the Asian American Studies Center at the university. There is a general introduction examining the status of publications on the topic.

Koreans

693. The Korean Americans. Won Moo Hurh. Westport, CT: Greenwood Press, 1998. 190p. (The New Americans). ISBN 0-313-29741-X.

Designed to meet the needs of high school students and general readers, the work is of value to college undergraduates in ethnic studies courses. The author is a respected writer and authority and he summarizes historical, sociological, economic, and cultural development placing emphasis on their adaptation to life in this country. The work is divided into four major sections, the first of which examines the culture and heritage of the Korean people. Part 2 furnishes historical coverage regarding their immigration to the United States, and part 3 provides detailed description of their adaptation and adjustment to American society. An interesting and informative perspective is given in part 4 in the author's emphasis on the unique characteristics of the group and its impact on the American social milieu.

Wayne Patterson has recently published *The Ilse: First Generation Korean Immigrants in Hawaii, 1903–1973* (University of Hawaii Press, 2000). The year 1903 is important in this case because it marks the beginning of organized Korean immigration to Hawaii. The first chapter treats the arrival of the first Korean immigrant group of barely 100 males, most of them single, who were to contract for labor jobs in competition with the Japanese and Chinese workers. It is a fine social history that examines all aspects of the early Korean existence in Hawaii, treating religion, education, community organization, and ending with an epilogue of the post-war years.

694. The Koreans in America, 1882–1974: A Chronology and Fact Book. Hyung-Chan Kim and Wayne Patterson, comps. and eds. Dobbs Ferry, NY: Oceana, 1974. 147p. (Ethnic Chronology Series, no. 16). ISBN 0-379-00513-1.

The editors are prolific contributors to the literature of Asian Americans and have compiled this brief chronology and handbook as a unique contribution to the history of Korean Americans. There is no attempt to be exhaustive, merely a desire to furnish an additional aid to the few that exist. The work consists of three major sections, beginning with the chronology that identifies in sequence the events and activities involving Koreans in the Hawaiian Islands and the continental United States over a period of 90 years. The second segment, treating documents, creates a little confusion because it is not limited to source documents but includes reprints of journal articles and an unpublished paper by Professor Kim. The third section furnishes a selective bibliography on the topic. Although criticized for omissions in the chronology and typographical errors, the work is useful to students and beginning researchers. There is a name index to provide access.

In 1993, Patterson and Kim issued a very brief slightly revised update with the same title (albeit without dates) as part of the *In America* series through Lerner Publications. Coverage in this 64-page history is from 1903 to the present, and it is designed to appeal to youngsters in the middle grades.

Filipinos

695. Filipino Achievers in the USA & Canada: Profiles in Excellence. Isobello T. Crisostomo. Farmington Hills, MI: Bookhaus, 1996. 369p. ISBN 0-931613-11-6.

Divided into three parts, this is the first biographical dictionary devoted to Filipino Americans as a response to their growing numbers. The first part is a general survey history of Filipino migration to North America from 1763 to the present. This is an important segment for its examination of sociological issues. Part 2 is the main text providing in-depth biographical essays of some 70 carefully selected individuals who have achieved a high level of success. These essays are classified by profession into eight categories such as "Arts and Culture," "Law and Jurisprudence," and "Science and Technology," and then arranged alphabetically. Part 3 supplies briefer biographical sketches of an additional 29 significant people. Personalities were first nominated, and then selected by a panel of judges on the basis of achievement and success. Photographs accompany the entries in part 2, and some in part 3. The work is indexed by name and by subject.

696. The Filipino Americans. Barbara M. Posadas. Westport, CT: Greenwood Press, 1999. 190p. (The New Americans). ISBN 0-313-29742-8.

Like others in this series (entries 686, 689, 693, 699, and 880), this is a well-constructed informative guide history of the immigration, settling, and adjustment of the more recently arrived groups of people. Filipinos make up the second-largest Asian American ethnic group following the Chinese, but have generally been neglected in terms of the literature. The author is an academic specialist and has produced an important source of information on the practices, traditions, issues, and conditions of life of this group. The work is organized into nine chapters with primary focus on the years subsequent to the mid-1960s. The nature of the Filipino identity, socio-economic status, and value system is documented in understandable manner appealing to a wide-ranging audience. The text is enhanced by photographs and statistical tables, as well as a glossary, and bibliography.

Others

697. Arab American Biography. Loretta Hall and Bridget K. Hall. Farmington, MI: U*X*L /Gale, 1999. 2v. ISBN 0-7876-2953-7.

This is a unique biographical dictionary in its treatment of Arab Americans who have not received coverage in reference sources of this type. As part of the U*X*L division of Gale, it is intended for an audience ranging from the middle grades to senior high school and undergraduate level. Entries provide dates, place of birth, an informative biographical sketch, photograph, and biography of 75 notables whose ancestry can be traced to any of the Arab States. They describe a diverse array of personalities who include political figures, entertainers and sports people, business leaders, scientists, theologians and others who have distinguished themselves in their line of endeavor. A glossary and chronology are given, and the several indexes provide access by occupation and country of origin as well as name and subject.

698. Armenian American Almanac: An Encyclopedic Guide to Armenian Organizations, Churches, Print & Non-Print Media, Libraries. 3rd ed. Hamo B. Vassilian, ed. Glendale, CA: Armenian Reference Books, 1995. 496p. ISBN 0-931539-09-9.

In the western part of Asia, in an area shaped by the influence of the Persians and the Turks, lies the ancient region of Armenia from which many Americans have original roots. The work is a substantial directory of a range of personalities, organizations, media activities, and educational institutions categorized in seven broad divisions or parts. These are further subdivided into sections and arranged by state. Entries vary in length, some providing fuller information than others. The first major division provides a general directory that contains organizations, churches, newspapers and periodicals, libraries, schools, bookstores, publishers, and so forth. This is followed by divisions listing financial aid to those of Armenian descent, Armenian American professionals accessed by profession, markets that carry Armenian food, more than 1,100 Armenian names, a telephone directory of 63,000 names that includes addresses, and a final division containing a 50-page bibliography of relevant books in English.

699. The Vietnamese Americans. Hien Duc Do. Westport, CT: Greenwood Press, 1999. 148p. (The New Americans). ISBN 0-313-29780-0.

Another of the popular histories in this series, this effort examines the social and economic conditions in which Vietnamese Americans have found themselves beginning with their arrival in this country in numbers. The author is a former refugee who begins the six-chapter narrative with an introductory narrative of Vietnam and its culture in chapter 1, followed by a useful examination of Vietnamese immigration history in chapter 2. Chapter 3 furnishes an exposition of the issues in the Vietnamese American community, and chapter 4 addresses employment and education trends. Analysis of adjustment to American life and lifestyles is seen through the eyes of both parents and children within the community, and not unexpectedly, represents diverse viewpoints. Conflicts are shown to exist leading in many cases to unfortunate conditions of dropping out of school and anti-social behavior.

THE BLACK EXPERIENCE

Only a few reference tools were recognized as standard sources on blacks and African Americans until the 1960s and 1970s, when such publications were encouraged by the increased interest in social responsibility and racial pride. Mainstream authors and publishers found ready markets in libraries and bookstores. Small black publishing houses emerged during this period, but they encountered difficulty in producing their materials in supplies adequate to market them effectively. If there had been a slight decline in proportions in the 1980s–1990s with trade publishers giving increased attention to both the female experience and the gay/lesbian experience as part of their "alternative" programs for publishing, this condition has changed today with increasing publication of books dealing with the black experience. Reference book publishing has remained steady with both bibliographic and textual information sources continuing to be in strong demand. Electronic access has been made available in many cases.

Included in this section are books, databases, and Web sites on various topics, occupations, and issues treated elsewhere in this guide. Our rationale remains the same in giving primacy to the racial and ethnic factors as the primary criteria in organizing these chapters. Therefore, here one will find resources on the following topics and elements as they relate to African American history: the female experience, education, religion, urban studies, demography, ideological trends, business, and labor. Exceptions are the resources on black genealogy, which are found in the "Genealogy and Immigration" section previously in this chapter, and those on blacks in film, which are found in the section on "Popular Culture: Entertainment, Recreation, Sports," later in this chapter. For materials on the Ku Klux Klan, see "Ideological Trends, Issues, and Movements" in this chapter. For works on desegregation, see "Education" in this chapter.

One of the oldest organizations in the field of black studies is the Association for the Study of African American Life and History (available at http://www.asalh.com), headquartered in Silver Spring, Maryland. Founded in 1915, it has over 2,000 members and in 1916 began issuing the quarterly *Journal of Negro History* (now the *Journal of African American History*).

General Sources

700. The African-American Atlas. Rev. ed. Molefi K. Asante and Mark T. Mattson. New York: Macmillan, 1998. 251p. ISBN 0-0289-7021-7.

This is the revised and updated edition of an earlier work, *The Historical and Cultural Atlas of African Americans* by Asante and Mark T. Mattson (Macmillan, 1991; repr.1996). Like the earlier issue, the current effort is attractive in format and treats the black experience in the United States from the period of the slave trade to 1996. African origins are examined as well. Arranged in chronological sequence, the work gives encyclopedic treatment to important periods in African American history that have shaped the culture, heritage, and people of today. The story of the barriers and obstacles to full participation in the American dream is facilitated by the well-designed maps accompanied by clear and lucid text. Illustrations and graphics (photographs, diagrams, and charts enhance the value of this resource as a learning aid for students from high school to college level. The two editors have again produced a useful and reliable source.

A similar publication is *Atlas of African-American History* by James Ciment (Checkmark Books/Facts on File, 2001) in its provision of well-conceived maps covering a historical time span. Beginning with the first chapter on Africa and African heritage, it identifies important events, places, and sites and includes biographical information of major figures from a variety of professions and gives statistical data in tracing historical developments through the 1990s. As part of the publisher's series of historical atlases, Jonathan Earle has authored *The Routledge Atlas of African American History* (Routledge, 2000). Like the others, it is a well-conceived work providing full color maps and informative commentary along with chronologies, and more.

701. The African American Encyclopedia. 2nd ed. Michael W. Williams et al. Tarrytown, NY: Marshall Cavendish, 2001. 10v. ISBN 0-7614-7208-8.

This is a major revision of the six-volume effort published six years earlier, and represents a significant source of information on all aspects of African American life. It contains nearly 3,600 entries of which nearly half have been updated and revised in some way. Nearly 350 specialists served as contributors; much of the revision has been extensive and involved complete rewriting along with the incorporation of new topics making the work a new encyclopedia. Entries vary in length from several paragraphs to several pages in the case of survey essays on issues and societal phenomena. Entries are well written and are enhanced by relevant listings and tables placed in proximity to the narratives. Topical coverage is not limited to the United States but includes treatment of African roots and areas of Latin America and the West Indies. Several bibliographies provide additional sources for study.

*702. African American History & Culture: An On-Line Encyclopedia. New York: Facts on File, 1999. Available: http://www.fofweb.com/subscription.

This effort was published initially in CD-ROM and placed on the Web in 1999. This is a slightly expanded and updated source. It has been considered to be a useful work for students from junior high school to college level. It draws from other sources from the publisher such as *The Biographical Dictionary of African Americans* (1999), *Encyclopedia of African-American Heritage* (entry 718), *Facts on File Encyclopedia of Black Women in*

America (entry 751n) among others. In so doing, it presents a comprehensive survey of the culture, history, and continued progress of Black people in this country in its offering of 184 primary documents dating from 1662 to the present day. From the main menu, one is able to key on various categories of study (encyclopedia, biographies, maps and charts, photographs, and a timeline with 2,000 entries, along with the full text of 13 history books, as well as the historical documents. In addition there is a reconstruction of "W.E.B. DuBois's Exhibition of the American Negro" as it was presented at the 1900 World's Fair in Paris.

Located at the same Facts on File Web site is a related source, *African-American Experience on File On-Line* providing a database of narratives and graphics treating and array of topics organized under six chronological categories following an introduction supplying background information. The six remaining categories treat the periods 1492–1820, 1821–1865, 1866–1900, 1901–1945, 1946–1969, and 1970–present.

703. The African-American Odyssey: Combined Edition. Darlene C. Hine et al. Upper Saddle River, NJ: Prentice Hall, 2002. 704p. ISBN 0-13-097796-9.

Initiated as a two-volume text for African American history courses at the undergraduate level, the current effort combines the two volumes and serves well as a reference history in its survey of the historical development of the African American experience. The story is organized into 23 chapters falling under six major parts or sections. Part 1 contains 5 chapters beginning with African existence and ending with conditions in this country up to 1820. Part 2 provides 5 chapters on slavery and related issues prior to the Civil War, followed by 3 chapters examining the Civil War and failure of Reconstruction to 1877 in part 3. Part 4 contains 4 chapters on white supremacy up to the 1920s; part 5 describes the impact of the Depression and the World War II period up to the 1950s in 3 chapters. The contemporary period ("The Black Revolution") is treated in 3 chapters in part 6. A CD accompanies the narrative along with a companion Web site for instructional purposes (http://www.prenhall.com/hine).

Another significant source for scholarship from Alexander Street Press (entries 600n and 1136n) is *Black Thought and Culture,* to be issued in 2003 as a database on the World Wide Web in two parts, the first of which treats North America. This part contains approximately 30,000 pages of monographs, essays, articles, speeches, and interviews written by important black leaders from the earliest times to 1975. Much of the material has not been accessible in the past and represents the work and thoughts of a wide array of personalities from W.E.B. DuBois to Jackie Robinson. Part 2 will cover Africa.

704. African American Quotations. Richard Newman. Phoenix: Oryx, 1998. 504p. ISBN 1-57356-118-5.

This quotation handbook contains more than 2,500 quotations from more than 500 individuals, making it the largest collection of its kind. With few exceptions such as John Brown, and Shakespeare (interestingly enough), they have been the words of black Americans and represent a large range of topics and personalities. As one might guess, they vary considerably in length from witty one-liners to a full paragraph. Predictably, major contributors are Martin Luther King, Jr., Malcolm X, and W.E.B. DuBois, but one can find such popular figures as Oprah Winfrey and Tupac Shakur as well. The quotations are numbered and arranged under topical categories such as civil rights movement, despair, evil, Harlem, racism, spirituality, and so forth. Speakers are identified with dates and occupations for each quote. Three indexes supply access.

Contemporary Quotations in Black by Anita King (Greenwood Press, 1997) provides access to the words of contemporary African Americans and black Africans as well. More than 1,000 quotations from a variety of personalities (athletes, journalists, teachers, politicians, and so forth) are culled from magazines and newspaper articles.

705. African American Reference Library. Detroit: Gale Group. 1994–. **African American Almanac.** 8th ed. Jesse C. Smith and Joseph M. Palmisano, eds. 1999. 1360p. ISBN 0-7876-1750-4. Ann. **African American Biography.** Phyllis Engelbert. 7v. in 4. 1994–2001. ISBN 0-7876-3563-4 (v. 7). **African American Breakthroughs: 500 Years of Black Firsts.** Jay P. Pederson and Jesse C. Smith. 1995. 280p. ISBN 0-8103-9496-0. **African American Chronology.** Deborah G. Straub. 1994. 371p. ISBN 0-8103-9231-3. **African American Voices.** Deborah G. Straub. 2v. 1996. ISBN 0-8103-9497-9.

Another of the fine Gale series that may be purchased as separates or in a set is this complete treatment of the African American experience for junior high school to college-level students. The current *Almanac* (formerly *The Negro Almanac*) has a long history and now as part of this set, is an annual publication examining a wide range of issues and events both current and historical. Currently, it contains 29 subject areas (religion, black nationalism, civil rights, etc.) and includes a chronology and excerpts from court cases. The *Biography,* was first issued in 1994 in four volumes furnishing biographies of 300 notables. Since then it has been supplemented periodically with additional volumes, each treating 20 new personalities, and updating previous sketches from earlier issues. *Breakthroughs,* as its name implies is a chronology with brief explanations of important events in Black history in a variety of areas that are designated as "firsts." The *Chronology* is an excellent listing of events (not limited to "firsts") beginning with the discovery of America in 1492, and running to the present day. *Voices* presents a fine collection of speeches by African Americans representing a variety of issues and topics along with introductory narrative and brief biography of speakers.

706. Africana: The Encyclopedia of the African and African American Experience. Kwame A. Appiah and Henry L. Gates, eds. New York: Basic Civitas Books, 1999. 2144p. ISBN 0-465-00071-1.

The authors are distinguished academics at Harvard University who collaborated to produce this comprehensive encyclopedia of the black experience, fulfilling the vision of W.E.B. DuBois expressed some 90 years earlier. Emphasis is on events, issues, and topics associated with the African American culture and history, but the work embraces every area in which black people have lived including European and Asian countries and the entire realm of Latin America. Naturally, every aspect related to political, social, and cultural developments of blacks in Africa is examined. More than 3,000 articles of varying length contributed by 400 scholars are presented in treating, events, trends, sites, movements of various kinds, art, business, religion, ethnic groups, organizations, countries, and a full range of prominent personalities from DuBois to Michael Jordan.

There are 12 lengthy featured essays by acclaimed scholars on such topics as the "Harlem Renaissance." Illustrations and graphics accompany many of the articles. There is no index.

707. Afro-Americana: A Research Guide to Collections at the University of California at Berkeley. Phyllis Bischof. Berkeley: General Library and the Department of Afro-American Studies, University of California, 1984. 76p. **Supp.** 1988. 20 leaves.

A convenient and informative guide, and its supplement identifying the resources of the University related to the black experience, these works survey the various branches and departments, including the Bancroft Library. It provides useful information regarding the locations and essential character of the resources. Operations and procedures are described in order to expedite access. Also covered is the online catalog, *MELVYL* (available at http://www.melvyl.ucop.edu), with suggestions and recommendations for its use, and descriptions of relevant periodical indexes. Subject headings from the card catalog are enumerated, and a list of dissertations that utilized the collection is given. There is a list of reference materials, followed by an author-title index. Bischoff's *African American Theses and Dissertations 1907–1990* (University of California African, 1992) provides a record of achievement in higher education by this minority group and is important in documenting such progress during the twentieth century.

The Amistad Research Center's *Author and Added Entry Catalog of the American Missionary Association Archives, with Reference to Schools and Mission Stations* (Greenwood Press, 1970) is a standard listing of primary-source materials in this area. Now located at Tulane University, the center offers a wide variety of documents in its catalog of over 100,000 items, most of which relate to correspondence. Because of its traditional concern over "the Negro problem," the Amistad Center has amassed a fine collection of items of historical importance on such aspects as the Underground Railroad. For specific item from this collection, one may use the Tulane online catalog, *Tulanet Voyager* (available at http://voyager.tcs.tulane.edu).

708. Bibliography of African American Leadership: An Annotated Guide. Westport, CT: Greenwood Press, 2000. 279p. (Bibliographies and Indexes in Afro-American and African Studies, no. 41). ISBN 0-313-31314-8.

This scholarly bibliography was designed aid research into the nature of leadership, in this case focusing on both personalities and issues of the African American community. It is comprehensive in terms of formats with representative books, articles, unpublished theses as well as unpublished papers, and audio-visual sources. Some 2,000 entries provide brief annotations, most of which refer to biographical studies with a smaller share going to the treatment of broad social issues regarding the nature of broad social issues regarding leadership of black persons. These are arranged under six major divisions; "Critical Studies and Appraisals," "Local Leadership Studies," "Ideologies and Social Movements," "Selected Bibliographic Materials," "Selected Leadership Organizations," and "Selected Audio & Visual Media Resources." Access is aided by an index of names and organizations.

709. Black Americans in Autobiography: An Annotated Bibliography of Autobiographies and Autobiographical Books Written Since the Civil War. Rev. and exp. ed. Russell C. Brignano. Durham, NC: Duke University, 1984. 193p. ISBN 0-8223-0559-3.

This is a revision and expansion of a 1974 bibliographic effort by Brignano that targets autobiography with a historical perspective. Of use to students and researchers at all levels, the work is divided into two major sections. The first part, "Autobiographies," lists volumes that cover significant amounts of the authors' lives, whereas the second part, "Autobiographical Books," contains listings of diaries in journals, collections of essays, eyewitness accounts, personal experiences, and so forth. Annotations are well written but brief, and bibliographical information is accurate for each entry. In the old tradition of bibliographies intended to aid scholarship, library locations are given by symbol for up to 10 libraries. Several useful indexes are furnished that provide access through various points: occupation, organization, institution, geographical location, chronological sequence by first date of publication, and title.

710. Black Biography, 1790–1950: A Cumulative Index. Randall K. Burkett et al., eds. Alexandria, VA: Chadwyck-Healey, 1990. 3v. ISBN 0-89887-085-2.

As the access tool of a large-scale microfiche project described below, this extensive index to nearly 300 biographical dictionaries and collective biographies covers more than 30,000 names. Because of its high price ($900), the index and its parent sourcebook (see below) will be purchased only by those agencies serving the needs of serious inquirers. Many of the titles indexed are of historical importance, as publication dates range from 1790 to 1950. Entries are organized alphabetically and provide name, gender, birth date, birthplace, death date, occupation, religion, biographical source, and location of illustrations. Volume 3 serves as both a bibliography and summary index volume that classifies the entries by birthplace, religion, occupation, and gender.

Black Biographical Dictionaries, 1790–1950 (Chadwyck-Healey, 1987) is the major microfiche source providing copy of all 300 biographical works. It represents an enormous project, with a correspondingly high price of about $5,500 at time of publication. A product of some 20 years in the making, it furnishes a highly valuable aid to scholarship and education.

711. Black Heritage Sites: An African American Odyssey and Finder's Guide. Nancy C. Curtis. Chicago: American Library Association, 1996. ISBN 0-8389-0643-5.

A useful directory of sites important to those interested in African American history in both this country and in Canada, this work provides a comprehensive guide for travelers and students of history. Major sites include such places as Frederick Douglass's grave in Rochester, New York, and the Delta Blues Museum in Clarksville, Mississippi, but many relatively obscure sites and those not limited to the black experience are treated as well. Arrangement is directory fashion, by region, then state and city. Each region is introduced with historical essays describing its association to the black experience. One is able to determine that the western states, with the exception of California, have not preserved many of their historical sites compared to the rest of the country. Entries furnish introductory narrative, address, telephone number, access policy, fees, and dates and times of operation. Together with Cantor's *Historic Landmarks of Black America* (see entry 720) and Beth

Savage's *African American Historic Places* (Preservation Press, 1994), this work helps to create a comprehensive inventory.

712. Black History: A Guide to Civilian Records in the National Archives. Debra L. Newman, comp. Washington, D.C.: National Archives Trust Fund Board, 1984. 379p. ISBN 0-911333-21-5.

The print guide, which has been described as a "roadmap" to the National Archives' holdings on what has been called "civilian" records, represents a time saver to researchers in the field. The materials are summarized and described and include textual, photographic, and audiovisual resources of over 140 federal agencies (Bureau of the Census, Customs, Department of Commerce, Coast Guard, etc.). A history of each agency is given, and its relevance to the black experience is examined. The records are identified by record group number. Descriptions of holdings are by necessity brief, but access is measurably aided by the inclusion of a detailed index that specifies names, sites, ships, and so on and sharpens the focus on events and occurrences. The researcher should not hesitate to use this tool to find information on either an individual or a broad topic. The Web site supplies links to an array of collections bibliographic graphic, and narrative.

713. Black Leaders of the Nineteenth Century. Leon Litwack and August Meier, eds. Urbana, IL: University of Illinois, 1988. 344p. (Blacks in the New World Series). Repr. Champaign, IL: University of Illinois, 1991. ISBN 0-252-06213-2.

Composed of 16 chapters, each by a different scholar (one of the chapters is coauthored), this is a valuable title for both students and researchers. Most of the chapters cover a single individual of large stature, such as Harriet Tubman (examined by Benjamin Quarles), Frederick Douglass (by Waldo E. Martin, Jr.), and Nat Turner (by Peter H. Wood). A collective biography is represented by two chapters on Reconstruction leaders. The essays are well written and full and include pictures.

Part of the same series is the earlier work by Litwack and Meier, *Black Leaders of the Twentieth Century* (University of Illinois, 1982). Fifteen major leaders are treated individually in scholarly essays written by different historians. Covered are such illustrious and at times controversial figures as Booker T. Washington, Malcolm X, Marcus Garvey, Mary McLeod Bethune, and, of course, Martin Luther King, Jr.

714. Black/White Relations in American History: An Annotated Bibliography. Pasadena, CA: Salem Press and Lanham, MD: Scarecrow Press, 1998. 189p. (Magill Bibliographies). ISBN 0-8108-3389-1.

The author is an academic and provides a basic introduction to useful sources of information for learning and scholarship from high school to college level in this annotated bibliography restricted to race relations between blacks and whites in this country. The focus is on monographs published from 1944 to 1996, the bulk of which were issued between 1970 and 1990. In all, some 700 entries supply a broad sweep of the African American experience in supplying historical and sociological studies. Coverage ranges from the time of the slave trade to the great struggles for civil rights. The entries are grouped into 10 chapters covering distinctive phases such as Reconstruction and areas of historical endeavor such as local studies. Annotations are well written although brief, and examine the author's perspective and in some cases, the influence or impact of the title. Author and subject indexes are furnished.

715. Chronology of African-American History: Significant Events and People from 1619 to the Present. 2nd ed. Alton Hornsby, Jr. Detroit: Gale, 1997. 720p. ISBN 0-7876-0492-5.

This is the second edition of a chronology originally published in 1991 and slightly expanded in 1995. It remains a useful resource for inquirers at all levels. There is an informative introduction examining the history of black Americans from their African origins to the present day. Of interest is an analysis of the effects that each U.S. president has had on black society in the United States. The chronology spans a period of more than 400 years, with a 50-percent increase in coverage of events from the fifteenth through the twentieth centuries. Entries are annotated briefly but effectively; and are organized under different six different chapter headings representing different periods of history. Appendixes furnish excerpts from various documents, speeches, and laws, which have been enumerated in the chronology, as well as statistical tables and lists. There is a lengthy bibliography and an index, as well as more than 180 photographs and illustrations.

Another excellent chronology is *Black Saga, The African American Experience: A Chronology* by Charles C. Christian and Sari Bennett (Boston: Houghton, Mifflin, 1995) and reprinted by Counterpoint Press in 1999. It is a comprehensive and well-researched historical survey treating people, places, and events from 1492 to the present time. Most helpful is a decade-by-decade overview of political and social developments.

*716. Dictionary Catalog of the Schomburg Collection of Negro Literature and History. New York Public Library. Boston: G.K. Hall, 1962. 9v. **1st supp.** 1967. 2v. **2nd supp.** 1972. 4v. **3rd supp.** 1976. 2v. **Ann. supp.** 1976–.

G.K. Hall produced another of its valuable catalogs of notable library collections with its coverage of the famous Schomburg Collection of the New York Public Library. The initial issue provides copy of catalog cards arranged alphabetically by author, title, and subject of some 36,000 bound volumes of materials of international scope on the black experience both historical and contemporary. The three supplements furnish additional materials cataloged subsequent to publication of the basic edition. The *Bibliographic Guide to Black Studies* (Schomburg Center for Research and Black Culture, G.K. Hall, 1976–) is an annual update of the Schomburg catalog beginning with the year 1975, thus continuing the earlier works. Arrangement of entries is similar to those publications. For quick access to specific titles, go to the Schomburg Web site (available at http://www.nypl.org/research/sc/scm/marb.html) and use the online catalog, CATNYP. Also, in 2000 the publisher issued a CD-ROM, **Black Studies on Disc 2000: Catalog of the Schomburg Center for Research in Black Culture at the New York Public Library and G.K. Hall's Index to Black Periodicals.* Thus with a single CD-ROM, there is unlimited access not only to this major catalog of resources but to more than 10 years' cumulation of article indexing and abstracts from leading scholarly and popular periodicals.

The *Dictionary Catalog of the Jesse E. Moorland Collection of Negro Life and History* (Moorland-Spingarn Research Center, Howard University, G.K. Hall, 1970; supp., 1976, 3v.) is a basic catalog of this famous collection. It consists of references to over

100,000 books, pamphlets, periodical titles, theses, compositions, clippings, and pictures on the black experience, with special emphasis on the slave trade and abolition. A three-volume supplement was issued in 1976 and listed additions to the book collection but not manuscripts, music, or photography. Further description of the collection is available at the Web site (available at http://www.founders.howard.edu/moorland-spingarn).

717. Encyclopedia of African-American Culture and History. Jack Salzman et al., eds. New York: Macmillan Library Reference /Simon & Schuster, 1996. 5v. ISBN 0-02-897345-3. **Supp. 1,** 2000. 471p. ISBN 0-02-865441-2.

This is a highly acclaimed comprehensive source of information for students at the undergraduate college level and beyond on the black experience in this country from the seventeenth century to the present day. It has been utilized by the publisher as the basis for developing several subsequent resources. There are more than 2,200 signed entries of varying length contributed by 600 authorities. Emphasis is placed on the biographical treatment with coverage of more than 1,500 personalities from all areas of American life. Topical examination is adequate in describing events, organizations, sociopolitical and cultural developments, business enterprises, movements, and more. Especially noteworthy are the 40 monographic essays surveying contributions to the various fields of endeavor. The work is especially strong in its coverage of the cultural, economic, political, and intellectual influences over the past 100 years or so. Illustrations are included, and appendixes supply statistical and categorical listings. *African-American Culture and History: Supplement 1* by Greg Robinson and Thaddeus Russell (2000) serves as an enlargement of the set in supplying entries examining additional topics not treated initially as well as updates to some of the earlier articles. **African American Culture and History CD-ROM* was issued in 1999 containing the entire text with new and updated articles as well as graphics from another publication.

A print offshoot of the initial work and supplement in one volume is *African American Culture and History: A Student's Guide* by Salzman and James S. Haskins (2000) furnishing a modification and rewriting to make it more useful to students at high school and grade school level. This was preceded in 1998 by Salzman's *Macmillan Compendium: African-American History,* which offered a selected grouping of biographies and essays drawn from the *Encyclopedia.*

718. Encyclopedia of African-American Heritage. 2nd ed. Susan Altman. New York: Facts on File, 2000. 353p. ISBN 0-8160-4125-3.

A well-designed, interesting work intended to suit the needs of students from junior high school to high school level, it can be used by undergraduates and interested adults for quick identifications as well. Entries are brief, ranging from 150 to 200 words in most cases, providing description of personalities, events, ethnic groups, political developments including movements and organizations, and much information relevant to African origins. In this regard, entries are supplied for individual African countries and tribes, and African issues are addressed when relevant to African American culture. In treatment of broad topics such as "education" or "slavery," the entries are of greater length and are more satisfactory for serious inquiry. Cross-references are included in the entries, as are bibliographies in some cases. A general bibliography and an index conclude the effort.

719. Guide to African American and African Primary Resources at Harvard University. Barbara A. Burg et al. Phoenix: Oryx Press, 2001. 304p. ISBN 1-57356-339-0.

This recent title serves as both a guide and directory to more than 800 holdings in the vast research collections located in 22 libraries at Harvard University. It represents the first effort to provide an inventory of the Harvard collection with respect to the focus on African American materials, and should be of value to the researcher and serious student. Burg is a research librarian at Widener Library, and is familiar with the needs of this type of audience. Included here are artifacts, diaries, letters, manuscripts, deeds, maps, oral histories, photographs, political posters, sheet music, works of art, and more. Entries are arranged alphabetically describing the holding and giving its library location. An index aids access. As a print resource, it is a throwback to an earlier time when such tools were published in abundance. That the authors chose to use this format rather than a Web site or electronic database is evidence of the continued convenience of such items in print.

720. Historic Landmarks of Black America. George Cantor. Detroit: Gale, 1991. 372p. ISBN 0-8103-7809-4.

Of interest to both students and scholars, this much-needed travel book covers historical landmarks and monuments important to the black experience in this country. These sites are listed in the publisher's *African American Almanac* (entry 705n), but Cantor furnishes descriptive commentary for each landmark varying in length from one paragraph to one page. The author is a journalist who brings excellent form and style and combines a subtle sense of humor with good, informative summaries. Included are details regarding the site's importance, plus information on location and access. The 300 entries are arranged in directory fashion, first by region, beginning with the Midwest; then alphabetically by state; then by city. All types of sites are represented: birthplaces, battlefields, cemeteries, and so on. There is a chronology and a lengthy bibliography, as well as an index of proper names.

*721. The Kaiser Index to Black Resources, 1948–1986. Brooklyn: Carlson, 1992. 5v. ISBN 0-926019-60-0. Available: http://biblioline.nisc.com/scripts/login.dll?BiblioLine.

Another of the valuable access tools based on the magnificent collection at the Schomburg Center is this comprehensive five-volume print guide to selected periodical holdings spanning a period of nearly 40 years. Over 150 periodicals covering the black experience in all its facets are treated, thus furnishing scholars, students, and interested laypersons with a wealth of information. The effort was supported by a grant from the National Endowment for the Humanities and the Aaron Diamond Foundation and represents the enormous effort expended in converting the great card file to publication format. The file was started as a reference tool of answered questions, with full indication of the periodical source material that provided the answers. Over the 40-year period, the file grew to the 174,000 items in this work, having been codified, edited, and organized during the mid-1980s. Arrangement is alphabetical by Library of Congress subject headings. A CD-ROM edition is planned for the future. The *Index* is available on the Web as the **Black Studies Database* through NTIS "Biblioline."

The *Index to the Schomburg Clipping File* (Chadwyck-Healey, 1986–1988) also was made possible by an NEH grant and furnishes access to this extraordinary resource, which now is available on microfiche. Here one is able to locate through a topical approach the facts, personalities, and events preserved by librarians of the past over a period of 50 years, from 1924 to 1974. Arrangement of the index is alphabetical by topic. Source material is preserved in over 9,500 microfiche and is available from the publisher as *Schomburg Clipping File, Part I, 1924–1974* ($20,000). *Part II, 1975–1988* ($17,000) contains 4,500 microfiche, for which an index is in preparation.

722. The New York Public Library African American Desk Reference. New York: John Wiley, 1999. 606p. ISBN 0-471-23924-0.

Sponsored by the Schomburg Center for Research in Black Culture at the library, the work offers students at all levels a wealth of information on a variety of issues and topics. Coverage is divided into 19 topical chapters, in which one is able to find charts, tables, chronologies, and graphics as well as descriptive historical narratives. Such aspects as civil rights, religion, health, business, science and technology, arts, sports, and more are examined. Each chapter is filled with facts, many of which are placed in attractive sidebars, and contains biographical sketches of important personalities and photographs. Chapters conclude with a list of sources (books only) for further reading. An adequate general index provides access.

Black Firsts by Jesse C. Smith (Gale, 1999) is a more generic work in its presentation of details regarding some 3,000 significant "firsts" involving personalities, places, and events in the history of black people.

723. Organizing Black America: An Encyclopedia of African American Associations. Nina Mjagki, ed. New York: Garland, 2001. 768p. ISBN 0-8153-2309-3.

A comprehensive directory of nearly 575 organizations, both historical and contemporary, this work represents a useful source of information for a wide-ranging audience. Entries vary in length from a paragraph or two to several pages, and furnish descriptive narrative regarding the origins and historical development and decline (if applicable) of the groups and identify goals, personalities, membership, and achievements. Treatment is given to associations established by African Americans, interracial organizations serving the interests of African Americans, and other groups working in their behalf such as societies and national committees. All large organizations and groups from international to regional are included whether or not well known as long as there is evidence of significant impact. Entries contain brief bibliographies for additional reading.

724. Who's Who Among African Americans. 14th ed. Detroit: Gale, 2001. 1334p. ISBN 0-7876-3635-5.

Now published by Gale, this work continues *Who's Who Among Black Americans* (8th ed., Shirelle Phelps and William C. Matney, eds., 1994/1995). It remains an important ongoing publication. This biographical dictionary of black U.S. figures has been issued periodically since its initial edition in 1976. Since Gale took control, it appears to be on a biennial basis. Criteria for inclusion in the latest edition have not changed and emphasize the attainment of elective and appointive office or distinctive achievements in "meritorious" careers. Biographical sketches are based on information from the personalities themselves through questionnaires. The title has been important in the past inasmuch as African American achievement had not been documented very well up to the present time except for sports figures. Relatively few of the entries are covered in *Who's Who in America* (entry 62n). There are both geographic and occupational indexes.

A much earlier, now historical, publication is *Who's Who in Colored America: A Biographical Dictionary of Notable Living Persons of Negro Descent in America* (Burckell, eds. 1–7, 1927–1950). Even earlier coverage is provided by *Who's Who of the Colored Race: A General Biographical Dictionary of Men and Women of African Descent,* first published in 1915 and later reprinted by Gale in 1976. These are similar to the newer work in terms of coverage of contemporary professionals and the type of access to the entries.

Slavery

725. African American Frontiers: Slave Narratives and Oral Histories. Alan Govenar. Santa Barbara, CA: ABC-CLIO, 2000. 551p. ISBN 0-87436-867-7.

The author, an academic who has done work for the Smithsonian Institution among others, opens with an introductory historical survey examining the origins and subsequent developments and changing conditions of slavery on this continent. Maps are furnished that identify proportions of freed persons and slaves in a state-by-state comparison beginning with the latter part of the eighteenth century. The main text contains a collection of first-person accounts of individual black Americans beginning with a grouping of 15 slave narratives dating from 1703 and including such notables as Harriet Tubman as well as lesser-known personalities in the first section. This is followed by another collection of seven narratives from the WPA Federal Writers Project of the 1930s. Finally, and possibly most important, because most of them have not been published previously, is the section of 47 oral histories taken from archival collections or through personal interviews. The result is a successful representation of life from the time of slavery into the twentieth century that serves the needs of students at all levels. Each narrative contains biographical data and some are illustrated. Two bibliographies conclude the effort.

*726. American Slavery: A Composite Autobiography. Westport, CT: Greenwood Electronic Media, 2000. Available: http://www.slavenarratives.com.

This is considered to be an authoritative collection of WPA slave narratives available by subscription in an online searchable database on the World Wide Web. These narratives were collected by field-workers for the Federal Writers Project between 1936 and 1938, and the Library of Congress compiled transcripts of the more than 2,300 interviews conducted in 17 states (some 10,000 typed pages). Professor George Rawick assembled the collection for publication in 17 volumes by Greenwood in 1972, and organized the entries by state in which the interview was held. Later, Howard Potts provided an enormous service by utilizing the indexed collection to furnish an index by state of birth rather than location of the interview for *A Comprehensive Name Index for The American Slave* in 1997. The Web site provides access to the entire range of interviews presented in Rawick's first series along with relevant materials, links, and Potts's index.

727. Dictionary of Afro-American Slavery. Upd. ed. Randall M. Miller and John D. Smith, eds. Westport, CT: Praeger, 1997. 892p. ISBN 0-275-95799-3.

This is an updated edition of a 1988 work by two leading authorities who collaborated to produce a valuable reference source synthesizing the best scholarship on the various considerations regarding slavery. Both students and researchers find it useful for the full treatment given the nearly 300 topics contributed by over 200 qualified specialists, beginning with the first English settlement and closing with Reconstruction after the Civil War. The current effort supplies a new introduction and the entries continue to embrace the social, institutional, intellectual, sociological and political aspects of slavery. Entries treat broad subjects, such as the slave trade and abolition, as well as topics of specific interest, such as conditions in a particular city or state. The bibliography has been revised and updated, and there is a well-constructed chronology. A detailed subject index provides good access.

728. Slavery in America: From Colonial Times to the Civil War, an Eyewitness History. Dorothy Schneider and Carl Schneider. New York: Facts on File, 2000. (Eyewitness History series). 464p. ISBN 0-8160-3863-5.

As is true of many of the publisher's offerings, this work is intended to serve the needs of a wide range of students from junior high school to undergraduate level. It represents a form of documentary history that provides eyewitness accounts supported by descriptive and expository narratives in examining the nature and impact of slavery on people's lives dating from the African beginnings in the fifteenth century to the Civil War period in this country. Entries are arranged into 12 topical chapters, providing a chronological sequence ("slave life," "runaways," "argument over slavery," etc.) to the study of the primary-source material. Chapters begin with a historical overview followed by a chronology prior to introducing the eyewitness account. Three appendixes furnish listings of 45 related documents, 200 biographical sketches, and a glossary of terms. There is an extensive bibliography and an index.

729. Slavery in the Courtroom: An Annotated Bibliography of American Cases. Paul Finkelman. Washington, D.C.: Library of Congress, 1985. 312p. ISBN 0-8444-0431-4.

This is a valuable guide to the holdings of the Library of Congress related to the question of slavery and the law. While serving as the Jameson Fellow at the Library, Finkelman was moved by the discovery of numerous uncataloged pamphlets on fugitive slave cases stored in the Law Library. This discovery led to extensive research on approximately 30,000 cards on the library's Trial Collection. Because there is no subject access to this collection, Finkelman has performed an important service for students and researchers of both legal and social history with respect to this topic. Organized into seven major chapters (e.g., the "Slave in a Free Jurisdiction" and "Abolitionists in the South"), materials date from 1772 to the beginning of the Civil War. The guide covers most important considerations. Also included are a "Table of Cases," lists of pamphlets and illustrations, a select bibliography, and an index.

Education

730. Education of the Black Adult in the United States: An Annotated Bibliography. Leo McGee and Harvey G. Neufeldt, comps. Westport, CT: Greenwood Press, 1985. 108p. ISBN 0-313-23473-6.

An interesting and unique coverage of nearly 370 books, articles, and dissertations proves useful to beginning researchers and students in helping to trace the history of black adult education from the precolonial days to the present. There are five major sections to the work, under which the annotated entries are alphabetically arranged. The first part, "Pre-Civil War (1619–1860)," covers education on the plantation and the influence of the Quakers; the next deals with "Civil War and Reconstruction," in which government responsibility and illiteracy are treated; the third segment, "Separate but Equal, 1880–1930," covers the withdrawal of federal protection and the beginnings of segregated education; and the fourth section examines "The Modern Era, 1930–," which has witnessed the renewal of federal intervention. Part 5 includes items not fitting into the classified arrangement of the others. There are subject and author indexes.

731. Encyclopedia of African-American Education. Faustine C. Jones-Wilson et al. Westport, CT: Greenwood Press, 1996. 575p. ISBN 0-313-28931-X.

A useful reference source in its comprehensive historical coverage of important developments and pertinent issues relating to the education of black people in this country, it examines an array of topics dating from the eighteenth century to the present. Some 200 contributors have supplied several hundred entries ranging from one to two pages in length. They are arranged alphabetically and furnish informative descriptions of personalities, organizations, universities and colleges, laws and legal decisions, sites, and events of significant impact. Local or regional information is included along with data of national consequence. Each entry concludes with a bibliography, and the work concludes with a general bibliography and an index.

African Americans and ROTC: Military, Naval and Aerospace Programs at Historically Black Colleges, 1916–1973 by Charles Johnson, Jr. (McFarland, 2002) provide a narrower and more unique historical account on the military training offered in historically Black colleges during the twentieth century. Origins of these programs are examined and their evolutionary development is described.

Civil Rights, Nationalism, Protest, and the Law

732. Afro-American Nationalism: An Annotated Bibliography of Militant Separatist and Nationalist Literature. Agustina Herod and Charles C. Herod. New York: Garland, 1986. 272p. (Canadian Review of Studies in Nationalism, v. 6; Garland Reference Library of Social Science, v. 336.) ISBN 0-8240-9813-7.

This annotated bibliography furnishes more than 600 books and articles published subsequent to 1945 on the little-understood theme of black nationalism. The work is useful to both students and researchers because of its comprehensive nature and substantial annotations. Beginning with the legacy of the Free Negro prior to the Civil War, the work provides historical coverage to the present time through a sequence of 10 sections representing different chronological periods. There are also sections on religious black nationalism (where one will find references to works on Malcolm X, among others) and "Garveyism." There is an author index, but the work would have profited from better subject access.

On Malcolm X specifically, there are two important bibliographies dating from the mid-1980s: *Malcolm X: A Selected Bibliography* (Greenwood Press, 1984), compiled by Lenwood Davis, the prolific bibliographer of African Americana, and Timothy V. Johnson's *Malcolm X: A Comprehensive Annotated Bibliography* (1986), a Garland endeavor. The first work identifies over 1,150 books and articles on Malcolm X, along with brief annotations. The Johnson compilation, as its title implies, is more thorough, yet both titles suffer from lack of currency. It is likely that these bibliographies will soon be updated, supplemented, or superceded, particularly in view of new interest in the subject elicited by Spike Lee's explosive 1992 motion picture *Malcolm X*.

733. Encyclopedia of African-American Civil Rights: From Emancipation to the Present. Charles D. Lowery and John F. Marszalek, eds. New York: Greenwood Press, 1992. 658p. ISBN 0-313-25011-1.

From Greenwood Press comes this new dictionary of the fight for civil rights, the product of the effort of two historians from Mississippi State University. There are over 800 articles, each averaging just under a page in length, covering all important elements and considerations of the 100-year-long struggle. Entries describe personalities, events, court cases, organizations, and important legislation. Arrangement is alphabetical and furnishes easy access to the specific topic treated. There are cross-references to related articles and useful bibliographic references for additional reading. Enhancing the text are numerous illustrations, both photographs and drawings, designed to further the reader's comprehension. The work opens with a foreword by David J. Garrow, winner of the 1987 Pulitzer prize for his work on Martin Luther King, Jr., who describes this encyclopedia as a rich and valuable source even for senior scholars.

734. Equal Protection and the African American Constitutional Experience: A Documentary History. Robert B. Green, Jr., ed. Westport, CT: Greenwood Press, 2000. 342p. (Primary Documents in American History and Contemporary Issues). ISBN 0-313-30350-9.

Another title in the series of compilations of important documents designed for the use of students from high school to college level, this work treats 177 primary sources of all kinds supplies a broad overview of the topic. The documents are arranged into five sections in chronological divisions and include a variety of messages relevant to the concept of equal protection under the law as established in the period of the Revolution and expressed in the Constitution. Documents range from letters of Paul (50–60 B.C.E.) to the court case of *Wessman* v. *Gittens* in 1998. Through these carefully selected items (Supreme Court decisions, state laws, statutes, transcripts of speeches, and excerpts from books), one is able to comprehend the stresses and tensions underlying the implementation and enforcement of equal protection in such areas as housing, education, and the military. An index aids access to specific documents.

735. A Guide to Research on Martin Luther King, Jr., and the Modern Black Freedom Struggle. Comp. by staff of the Martin Luther King, Jr., Papers Project. Stanford, CA: Stanford University Libraries, 1989. 185p. (Occasional Publications in Bibliography Series, no. 1). ISBN 0-911221-09-3.

This is the first of what is anticipated to be a multivolume effort of the Martin Luther King Papers Project. It began as an access tool to materials housed at the Center for Non-Violent Social Change in Atlanta, which itself is part of a larger database maintained at Stanford University. Included are listings of books and articles, most scholarly but some popular, as well as dissertations, theses, government documents, reference works, and audiovisual materials. Microform materials and manuscripts are included as well. Brief annotations are provided. All works by King are included when readily accessible, along with representation of other materials on the movement as well. Access to the database at Stanford University is now possible through the Internet (http://www.stanford.edu/group/King).

A comprehensive and thorough effort is *The Malcolm X Encyclopedia* edited by Robert L. Jenkins (Greenwood Press, 2002) providing more than 500 essays testifying to the impact of the life and work of Malcolm in the arena of civil rights, religion, politics, and so forth. There are more than 70 contributors representing a broad array of the social sciences (education, history, philosophy, etc.) who supply interpretation of Malcolm's influence as seen through their own discipline.

736. Racial Violence on Trial: A Handbook with Cases, Laws, and Documents. Christopher Waldrep. Santa Barbara, CA: ABC-CLIO, 2001. 311p. (ABC-CLIO's on Trial Series.) ISBN 1-57607-244-4.

Although the title might infer more general coverage, the work is focused on the historical experience of African Americans and the manner in which court litigation has helped to shape cultural values and perspective in this country. There are four major chapters, the first of which is an introduction to the issues, events, and individuals relevant to comprehension of the controversies. This is followed by a brief but informative historical account of the social and political elements involved in the second chapter, followed by a more thorough treatment of factors with coverage given to such events as the Colfax Massacre and Scottsboro, as well as to the NAACP and to due process in chapter 3. Chapter 4 examines the impact and legacy of these phenomena and interprets the results in reviewing additional court cases and tragic events. In addition, there are biographical sketches, a chronology, a table of cases, an annotated bibliography, and a listing of Internet sources.

Family, Community, Statistics

737. African-American Community Studies from North America: A Classified, Annotated Bibliography. Fred J. Hay. Hamden, CT: Garland, 1991. 234p. (Applied Social Science Bibliographies, v. 5; Garland Reference Library of Social Science, v. 420.) ISBN 0-8240-6643-X.

This classified bibliography of community studies performed on the black community from the 1890s through the 1980s is of value to social historians and serious students. The methodology of the "community study" invokes ethnographic and sociological premises in documenting the nature and social conditions relevant to race and culture. This work includes both sociological studies and those less-systematic inquiries more representative of "folklorist" traditions. A variety of source materials (some relatively obscure) is presented: books, theses, dissertations, bulletins, and reports. Entries are organized by decade beginning with the 1890s and should be useful for historical inquiry. Annotations are detailed and describe population, education, economics, and religion, among other things. There are cross-references to related subjects; the specialized classified scheme is described in a separate chapter.

738. The Black Family in the United States: A Revised, Updated, Selectively Annotated Bibliography. Lenwood G. Davis, comp. New York: Greenwood Press, 1986. 234p. ISBN 0-313-25237-8.

Professor Davis has been compiling bibliographies on the black experience for many years, and with this effort he has furnished a revision of a 1978 publication for research and study in social history. This bibliography gives 725 annotated entries of books, articles, and dissertations written over the 25 years prior to its publication. Entries are classified by format in four divisions (major books, books, articles, and dissertations), then by topical subdivisions covering such elements as slavery, children, adoption, abortion, poverty, sickle-cell diseases, and stress. Some of these have been added since the original effort. Annotations are detailed and run about a paragraph for each. An author-subject index furnishes access.

A more comprehensive title (although not fully annotated) is *Black American Families, 1965–84: A Classified Selectively Annotated Bibliography,* edited by Walter R. Allen et al. (Greenwood Press, 1986). It appears as number 16 in the series "Bibliographies and Indexes in Afro-American and African Studies" and contains over 1,100 entries (about one-fourth annotated) of books, journals, and dissertations published during the vital 20-year period. Indexing is excellent, with a keyword index of titles, classified subject index, and coauthor index.

739. Historical Statistics of Black America. Jesse C. Smith and Carrell P. Horton, comps. and eds. Detroit: Gale, 1995. 2v. ISBN 0-8103-8542-2.

A massive compilation of historical information on blacks in North America, this work contains more than 2,000 tables derived from government publications and published African American sources. Tables provide statistical data ranging from the colonial period to 1975. They are organized into 19 alphabetically arranged chapters of topical nature beginning with "agriculture" and ending with "vital statistics," and including "business," "crime and justice," "education," "labor and employment," and so forth. Each chapter is divided into sections treating various elements, issues, and topics. Within these sections are the tables providing statistical comparisons along with charts and brief narrative expositions. There is a diverse array of statistical data in terms of significance, impact, and value within the chapters presenting tabular coverage of sports records to number of lynchings. Indexes are by subject and by year.

The compilers have issued a one-volume companion to complement the coverage of the above work. *Statistical Record of Black America,* now in its fourth edition (Gale, 1996) furnishes more than 1,000 tables, graphs, charts, and listings of statistical data on the status and conditions of contemporary black Americans from 1975 to the present day. Data is culled from a wide range of governmental sources and from private or commercial publications, and organized into 16 broad topical chapters.

740. The Social and Economic Status of the Black Population in the United States, 1790–1978: An Historical View. U.S. Bureau of the Census. Washington, D.C.: U.S. Department of Commerce, Bureau of the Census, 1979. 271p. (Current Population Reports, Special Studies Series P–23, no. 80.) SuDoc No. C3.186:P23/80.

Derived from government census reports, this useful source of historical statistics covers a period of nearly 200 years. Black population changes and characteristics are shown clearly with the use of graphs, charts, and tables, accompanied by historical overviews for each area covered. The major segment, the first of a two-part arrangement, presents historical trends from 1790 to 1975. The second part illustrates recent trends from 1975 to 1978. This source is valuable for all historical inquiries because it summarizes the societal changes that have marked the black population since the adoption of the Constitution: income levels, employment characteristics, housing, voting, and so on. The appendixes furnish definitions, explanations, and sources. There is a detailed table of contents but no index; therefore the researcher must study the organization of the tool to expedite its use.

Creative Arts, Athletics, Professions

741. African American Criminologists, 1970–1996: An Annotated Bibliography. Lee E. Ross. Westport, CT: Greenwood Press, 1998. 108p. (Bibliographies and Indexes in Afro-American and African Studies, no. 36.) ISBN 0-313-30150-6.

This bibliography is designed to represent the research and publications of black American criminologists and is intended to make public the little-publicized writing activity of black Americans who are engaged in fighting crime. It is especially important at a time when much publicity is being given to the disproportionate numbers of African Americans held in prisons. The work opens with a reprint of a published article coauthored by Ross and a colleague examining the realities and challenges faced by African American criminologists; this is followed by the main text consisting of abstracted works of publications (limited to four) of each criminologist who responded to the author's request. They are generally from professional journals but include books and government sources. Doctoral dissertations are listed in an appendix.

742. African-American Sports Greats: A Biographical Dictionary. David L. Porter, ed. Westport, CT: Greenwood Press, 1995. 429p. ISBN 0-313-28987-5.

With the contributions of more than 40 sports writers and historians, Porter has put together an extraordinary work in term of its comprehensiveness and focus. Included here are alphabetically arranged and biographical sketches of 166 athletes, coaches, and administrators, both male and female, representing a wide spectrum of both team and individual sports. Both the present and the past are treated with profiles on personalities like Satchel Paige and Jack Johnson included along with Shaquille O'Neal and the irrepressible Michael Jordan who spans different generations with case. Each entry is signed, well written in an easily comprehensible style, and covers family and educational background as well as career achievements and awards in such endeavors as football, baseball, basketball, tennis, golf, boxing, wrestling, and more. Appendixes furnish useful listings.

Historical Dictionary of African Americans in Sport by David K. Wiggins (M.E. Sharpe, 2002) is the most recent biographical dictionary of African American sports notables supplying more than 400 entries of men and women selected in their areas of endeavor. Included also are tournaments, leagues, organizations, and associations that are relevant to the topic. Both professional and amateur sports of all kinds are treated with both well-known and more-obscure figures included. Sports range from baseball and football to golf, tennis, and sports car racing in presenting comprehensive coverage of the sports world.

743. Blacks in the Humanities, 1750–1984: A Selected Annotated Bibliography. Donald F. Joyce, comp. New York: Greenwood, 1986. 209p. (Bibliographies and Indexes in Afro-American and African Studies, no. 13.) ISBN 0-313-24643-2.

The compiler has been an active contributor to African American history and has produced a unique source in terms of its scope. It covers leading black personalities and their contributions over a wide range of the humanities and creative arts spanning a period of over 200 years. The humanities are defined broadly to include art, music, drama, literary criticism, linguistics, philosophy, science, history, and even library science. Coverage is provided for over 600 monographs, journal articles, and dissertations, offering both students and researchers well-selected and carefully developed listings. Annotations range from brief to very full; entries have been taken from numerous sources (bibliographies, indexes, union lists, encyclopedias, biographical dictionaries, catalogs, textbooks, etc.). Access is provided by both subject and author/title indexes of comprehensive nature.

Joyce recently issued a sequel to this title, *Rooted in the Chants of Slaves, Blacks in the Humanities, 1985–1997: A Selected Annotated Bibliography* (Greenwood Press, 1999). The second effort employs a similar pattern to that of the initial offering and supplies more recent sources providing needed documentation of the great strides that have been made in the 12 years since publication of the original work.

744. Blacks in the American Armed Forces, 1776–1983: A Bibliography. Lenwood G. Davis and George Hill, comps. Westport, CT: Greenwood, 1985. 198p. (Bibliographies and Indexes in Afro-American and African Studies, no. 3.) ISBN 0-313-24092-2.

Another of the Davis bibliographies is this thorough and well-designed treatment of the black experience with respect to military service. This has been an elusive topic in the past, and the relatively recent effort is welcomed by both students and researchers. The major coverage of the book is in the first of two segments, which contains 10 chronological sections with each one covering a war or campaign. Entries are arranged alphabetically within these sections; no annotations are given, although they would have been useful. The range of coverage is from the American Revolution to the small wars following Vietnam. The second segment is auxiliary in nature and furnishes four appendixes: "Black American Generals and Flag Officers," "Ships Named for Black Americans," "Black Soldiers in Films" and, finally, one containing documents from World War I.

African American Recipients of the Medal of Honor: A Biographical Dictionary, Civil War through Vietnam War by Charles W. Hanna (McFarland, 2002) profiles 87 individuals awarded the Medal of Honor. Entries describe the acts of valor and heroism and are organized under categories relating to the particular wars. There is an appendix providing numbers of awards by war and battle along with a bibliography and an index.

745. Distinguished African Americans Series. Westport, CT: Greenwood Publishing Group. 1996–. **Distinguished African American Dancers and Choreographers.** Richard Newman. 2002. 344p 1-57356-260-2. **Distinguished African American Political and Governmental Leaders.** James Haskins. 1999. 328p. ISBN 1-57356-126-6. **Distinguished African American Religious Leaders.** Quinton H. Dixie. 2002. 344p. ISBN 1-57356-239-4. **Distinguished African American Scientists of the 20th Century.** James H. Kessler et al. 1995. 382p. ISBN 0-89774-495-3. **Distinguished African Americans in Aviation and Space.** Betty K Gilbert et al. 2002. 336p. ISBN 1-57356-218-1.

This recent, well-conceived series of biographical dictionaries began in 1996 with publication of the work on scientists, then came the effort on political and government leaders in 1999. The other three all were issued or are to be issued in 2001–2002. The series titles are stylized in their inclusion of 100 men and women both living and dead who were contributors to their field of endeavor. Some are well known by the public, others are relatively obscure. The style and language are clear and comprehensible to students from junior high school to college age, and the writing is free of bias. Coverage generally begins with birth and death dates, indication of educational institutions and degrees, and current position. Narratives examine the individual's life from childhood through career highlights. Photographs are included and appendixes contain helpful listings.

746. Freedom's Lawmakers: A Directory of Black Officeholders During Reconstruction. Rev. ed. Eric Foner. Baton Rouge: Louisiana State University, 1996. 298p. ISBN 0-807-12082-0.

A comprehensive source of specialized nature is Eric Foner's most recent effort furnishing brief biographical coverage of just over 1,500 officials in both the North and South during the period following the Civil War. Offices range from constables to congressmen and represent the degree of social change that was taking place following the Civil War from 1865 to 1877. The author is a respected authority of liberal orientation who had undertaken extensive research in presenting the commonalities and differences in the backgrounds ranging from freeborn to slave origins of those who assumed these responsibilities. Entries are arranged in alphabetical sequence and when complete, furnish dates of birth and death, state, free or slave status at birth, occupation, property ownership, military service, mulatto status, literacy status, service in elected office, and very brief biographical sketch. Several indexes supply access by state, occupation, office, and more.

Less comprehensive and more focused is *Black Congressmen During the Reconstruction: A Documentary Sourcebook,* edited by Stephen Middleton. It provides biographical coverage of the two black senators and 19 black representatives holding those elected offices during the period of Reconstruction. Along with the biographical narratives are excerpts from documents helping to clarify the roles played by these individuals and their interests and activism with respect to various legislative endeavors such as the attempt to make lynching a federal offense.

747. The Harlem Renaissance: A Historical Dictionary for the Era. Bruce Kellner, ed. Westport, CT: Greenwood Press, 1984; 476p. Repr. New York: Methuen, 1995. ISBN 0-416-01671-5.

This excellent information tool describes an era of excitement, self-awareness, and creative expression as it developed around the black population of Harlem from 1917 to 1935, when the first riot occurred. Kellner and seven other contributors, mostly university professors, have furnished over 800 signed entries that range from a few lines to two pages in length. Coverage is given to personalities, books, periodicals, newspapers, groups, associations, musical comedies, and significant places associated with those dynamic years. As one would expect, the period embraced various types of people (politicians, educators, and clergy, as well as poets, artists, and especially musicians and entertainers). Separate chronologies of events, books, and plays are presented in the appendixes, along with a listing of serial publications and even a glossary of Harlem slang. The work concludes with a substantial bibliography and good analytical index. It remains the most comprehensive reference source on the topic, and furnishes some of the material found in the more recent but less sophisticated work, *Harlem Renaissance* by Kelly K. Howes (U*X*L/Gale, 2001). Howes provides a useful overview of the period including biographies of 15 major figures designed to appeal to youngsters.

The Harlem Renaissance: An Annotated Reference Guide for Student Research by Marie E. Rodgers (Libraries Unlimited, 1998) is a more recent effort but serves as a complementary vehicle to the above work especially for students from junior high school through senior high school, but also of use to those at the undergraduate level. It is a bio-bibliography inasmuch as it furnishes brief biographical sketches of important contributors to a variety of fields (art, music, dance, sports, film, and literature) and follows with annotated bibliographies of books, articles, and even videos. The work is organized into 20 chapters such as "women" and "literature" containing alphabetically arranged entries.

Business and Labor

748. Black Labor in America, 1865–1983: A Selected Annotated Bibliography. Joseph Wilson and Thomas Weissinger, comps. and eds. New York: Greenwood Press, 1986. 118p. (Bibliographies and Indexes in Afro-American and African Studies, no. 11.) ISBN 0-313-25267-X.

Another of the Greenwood publications, this work identifies nearly 600 books, pamphlets, government documents, private studies, and collections of papers. The more significant entries receive full annotations; in other cases, annotations are brief or nonexistent. They are arranged alphabetically by main entry. One can only conjecture about the omission of journal articles, but one suspects that the purpose was to provide a focused perspective regarding the monographic literature. Also excluded are sources that do not have the black worker as the central theme and certain occupational categories, such as athletics and the military. Although the production is shoddy in some respects (titles arranged alphabetically by first words, *including* the article adjectives; omissions; inconsistencies; and typographical errors), there is an obvious need for the content. Indexing is provided by a title index and a subject index.

Black Business and Economics: A Selected Bibliography by George H. Hill (Garland, 1985) is number 267 of the publisher's series, *Garland Reference Library of Social Science,* supplies entries for over 2,650 books, dissertations, theses, government documents, and articles from journals, newspapers, and magazines covering black capitalism and ownership, employment, and economic mobility in the corporate world. The purpose is to provide researchers and students with references to both published and unpublished materials written over the past 100 years with most of the material dating from the 1960–1980 period. Sixteen chapters present such topics as banking, capitalism, income, insurance, organization, and clubs.

749. Encyclopedia of African American Business History. Juliet E.K. Walker, ed. Westport, CT: Greenwood Press, 1999. 721p. ISBN 0-313-29549-2.

The author is an academic historian and has produced a unique reference work in its focus on business and entrepreneurship within the black experience. A comprehensive and cogent analysis of attendant conditions and leading personalities is provided through some 200 signed entries from over 100 contributors presenting individual biographies, topical essays, and descriptive commentaries regarding African American involvement in various industries. Coverage is comprehensive and an excellent chronology highlights developments over a period of time beginning in the seventeenth century and running through the 1990s. Entries are alphabetically arranged and vary in length from less than a page for some biographies to 18 pages for expositions of such endeavors as "international trade enterprises" or "women business enterprises." Biographies examine the person's business activities and the degree of success in their conduct; all entries conclude with a bibliography. A detailed index provides access.

750. The History of Black Business in America: Capitalism, Race, Entrepreneurship. Juliet E.K. Walker. New York: Macmillan Library Reference/Simon & Schuster, 1998. 482p. (Twayne's Evolution of Modern Business Series.) ISBN 0-8057-1650-5.

This is a well-received source of information on the historical dimensions of black business in this country and provides a comprehensive coverage dating from the days of slavery in seventeenth-century Africa to the present day. Treatment is chronological and the very early slave trade is placed in the perspective of the beginnings of black entrepreneurship. The author is an academic historian who provided a carefully developed history utilizing an array of primary and secondary sources examining all related elements and characteristics to business development and growth. Such aspects as discrimination, government policies, cultural traditions, and societal upheavals such as wars are described as part of a continuous and continuing challenge (as well as opportunity) to achieve success in the business enterprise. Contemporary conditions are examined as well as historical events, and current issues are interpreted with regard to future directions. A detailed index provides excellent access to topics, themes, names, and so forth.

Gender Influences

751. Black Women in America: A Historical Encyclopedia. Darlene C. Hine et al., eds. Bloomington, IN: Indiana University Press, 1994. 2v. ISBN 0-253-32774-1.

Widely acclaimed at time of publication, this work represents a comprehensive biographical dictionary and directory as well in presenting just over 800 entries treating significant personalities in terms of their influence at both the national or regional/state/local levels, and important organizations as well. Biographical coverage composes the bulk of the main text as one would expect, but information on organizations, institutions, and topical coverage broadens the work beyond that of a simple biographical dictionary. Entries are of moderate size and many include pictures of families as well. Women of diverse occupations and professions are treated; astronauts, musicians, politicians, doctors, bankers, and even maids and people of the trades.

Facts on File Encyclopedia of Black Women in America edited by Hine and Kathleen Thompson (Facts on File, 1997) is a reworking and updating of the above title in 11 volumes and is intended for a less sophisticated audience. Some entries from the earlier work are incorporated without change, however, and the photographs are the same. In all, some 950 entries are furnished; following chapter 1 treating the early years from 1617 to 1899, the volumes are organized in topical fashion with individual volumes covering areas of endeavor (education, religion, arts and entertainment, science, and so forth. Volumes open with a chronology and arrange the entries in alphabetical order. The work is well suited to the needs of both high school and undergraduate students. *Black Women in America* by Joe Kraynak is now in its second edition (Macmillan Library Reference, 2001) and is less comprehensive and inclusive than either of the above titles. As part of the Macmillan Profiles series, it supplies biographical profiles (sketches) of 176 African American women from the eighteenth century to the time of publication. They represent a variety of occupations—arts, science, entertainment, politics, and so forth—and range from a few paragraphs to a few pages in length. Few of the entries are unique to the work, the remainder being drawn from the publisher's *Encyclopedia of African-American Culture and History* (see entry 717). Photographs and a glossary of terms are useful special features for an audience that begins with the middle grades and extends to high school level.

752. Black Women Scientists in the United States. Wini Warren. Bloomington, IN: Indiana University Press, 2000. 366p. ISBN 0-253-33603-1.

The author is an academic in the field of American studies and has prepared this reference work as an outgrowth of her dissertation. She begins the work with an introductory essay examining the published material on black women in critical manner.

Her effort is carefully researched and well documented in its coverage of more than 100 black females in all areas of scientific endeavor. Entries are alphabetically sequenced and vary in length, running from one paragraph to several pages depending upon the impact of the figure. They include individuals both living and dead, and furnish footnotes that in some cases are annotated. Fields of inquiry include anatomy, anthropology, astronautics, medicine, pharmacology, physics, and so forth. An appendix lists publications by many of the women treated, and indexes provide access by discipline and by name.

753. Early Black American Leaders in Nursing: Architects for Integration and Equality. Althea T. Davis. Boston: Jones & Bartlett, 1999. 243p. (National League for Nursing series). ISBN 0-763-71009-1.

This work contains biographical essays on three major figures, born in the nineteenth century, who were influential in elevating black females to full participation in the profession of nursing through their efforts to upgrade education and employment levels. The lives and careers of Mary Eliza Mahoney (1845–1926), Martha Minerva Franklin (1870–1968), and Adah Belle Samuels (1870–1943) are treated in depth in detailed and informative essays. Essays are well written and important to students of ethnic black history. All of these women have been admitted to the Nursing Hall of Fame and serve as role models for African American females aspiring to a career in the field. Appendixes are important to historians for their inclusion of photographs and facsimile documents pertinent to the National Association of Colored Graduate Nurses from 1908 to 1951.

754. Notable Black American Men. Jesse C. Smith, ed. Detroit: Gale, 1998. 1365p. ISBN 0-7876-0763-0.

Editor Smith has modeled this work after her previous successful effort, *Notable Black American Women* (see entry 755) and supplies the user with 500 biographical sketches running from one to five pages each. Entries are alphabetically arranged and similar in content to those in the earlier work. Personalities are diverse in nature and represent various stages of familiarity and renown, some being very prominent and others obscure. Relatively recent figures have received emphasis with half of them still alive, deceased within the past two decades, or having made their contributions in the past 50 years at the time the work was published. Approximately 400 photographs are included to enhance the narratives.

The African American Male: An Annotated Bibliography compiled by Jacob U. Gordon (Greenwood, 1999) is part of the publisher's series titled Bibliographies and Indexes in Afro-American and African Studies. It serves as a comprehensive bibliography in its presentation of 900 books, book chapters, monographs, articles, and dissertations issued from 1855 to 1998. About half of the entries are annotated with emphasis given to titles published in the 1990s. Arrangement is under broad topics such as civil rights and sports. It has been criticized for emphasis on contemporary figures and for editorial mistakes such as misspellings.

755. Notable Black American Women. Jessie C. Smith, ed. Detroit: Gale, 1992–1996. 2v. ISBN 0-8103-4749-0 (v. 1); 0-8103-9177-5 (v. 2).

This is an interesting and useful source of information on the lives of black females born between 1730 and 1958 and who achieved stature. They represent all areas of endeavor and include businesswomen, artists, political activists, educators, scholars, and professionals, with decidedly less emphasis given to sports figures. They range from those of monumental historical significance (Sojourner Truth, Harriet Tubman, Mary McLeod Bethune) to the notables of today (Whoopi Goldberg, Maya Angelou, Rosa Parks). Also included are the more obscure but equally worthy individuals in every historical period. The first volume treats 500 personalities, and Book 2 adds another 300 names. With the resources of Fisk University at her disposal, librarian Smith and her advisory board were able to select an interesting and wide-ranging group of people. Pictures are included for a number of the personalities, who are alphabetically arranged.

Science, Technology, and Medicine

756. African American Firsts in Science and Technology. Raymond B. Webster. Detroit: Gale, 2000. 462p. ISBN 0-7876-3876-5.

This is a comprehensive work in the field of history of American science and technology in its treatment of 1,500 contributions by black people. All areas of science and technology are included from biological breakthroughs to agricultural improvements to developments in clock making and physics. Various milestones including honors, awards, and appointments are included. The entries are organized under eight broad topical categories representing general fields of endeavor such as medicine (the lengthiest segment) and agriculture. Entries are brief, ranging from 50 to 100 words but generally are well written and informative. They furnish descriptions of the achievement as well as biographical and educational data along with citations for up to five publications containing additional information. Photographs are furnished for about 100 contributions, and the work concludes with a general bibliography and several indexes.

757. Health of Black Americans from Post Reconstruction to Integration, 1871–1960: An Annotated Bibliography of Contemporary Sources. Mitchell F. Rice and Woodrow Jones, Jr., comps. Westport, CT: Greenwood, 1990. 206p. (Bibliographies and Indexes in Afro-American and African Studies, no. 26). ISBN 0-313-26314-0.

This annotated bibliography is meant to complement an earlier effort by the compilers that covered the more recent literature (1970s and 1980s) on the health of U.S. blacks. The historical effort furnishes nearly 600 entries, most of which are references to journal and periodical literature written over a span of 90 years. Entries are organized under three major chronological periods, beginning with post-Reconstruction to the early twentieth century (1871–1919), followed by the 1920–1950 period (which provides the bulk of the cited entries), and concluding with the 1950–1960 period. Entries are arranged alphabetically and numbered sequentially within each division. Annotations are well developed and detailed; they vary from a paragraph to nearly a full page. There is a fine introductory essay on health and working conditions of blacks from the time of slavery; both author and subject indexes furnish access.

758. Notable Black American Scientists. Kristine M. Krapp, ed. Detroit: Gale, 1998. 349p. ISBN 0-7876-2789-5.

A useful biographical dictionary describing the lives and careers of 250 African American scientists, both male and female, this work is designed to meet the needs of students at all levels and general readers as well. Entries are arranged in alphabetical order and run an average of two to three pages in length. Like other works by the publisher, it is carefully researched and highly informative with useful headers furnishing personal data such as birth and death years, and major field of work. Personal information is given along with career developments and achievements with respect to theory development, experimentation and research projects, and of course, any discoveries, inventions, or patents granted. There is a personal statement and selective bibliography as well. One helpful special feature is the provision of definitions of unfamiliar scientific terms within the appropriate entry or in parentheses. Photographs are supplied as is a timeline. Three indexes furnish access by master name and subject, field of specialization, and gender (see also entry 745n).

Journalism and the Press

759. African American History in the Press, 1851–1899: From the Coming of the Civil War to the Rise of Jim Crow as Reported and Illustrated in Selected Newspapers of the Time. Richard C. Schneider, ed. Detroit: Gale, 1996. 2v. ISBN 0-8103-9555-X.

The subtitle clearly indicates the coverage of this large compilation of particular use to college-level students and faculty. It contains more than 1,200 articles and editorials as well as 470 illustrations drawn from 13 American newspapers in large cities, especially New York. Most heavily used is *Harper's Weekly* followed by the *New York Times*. Beginning with an illustrated report of the enforcement of the Fugitive Slave Act of 1851, the articles are arranged in chronological sequence on a year-by-year basis. Each year is presented as a separate chapter opening with an introductory survey or overview of the year written by a historian, and one is able to perceive the changes in attitudes toward African Americans through time. Nearly 475 illustrations enhance the text, and an index facilitates access.

760. African American Newspapers and Periodicals: A National Bibliography. James P. Danky et al., eds. Cambridge, MA: Harvard University Press, 1999. 740p. ISBN 0-674-00788-3.

Danky, the serials librarian at the University of Wisconsin, has long been involved in the production of catalogs, bibliographies, and anthologies relating to the press and to the literature of minority and alternative groups. He has utilized the extensive periodical holdings at the University in compiling these works. This is his latest effort and represents a thorough and comprehensive documentation of the existence of some 6,500 American newspapers addressing the African American community. Social historians gather much of their data from the issues of such periodicals expressing the opinion, commentary, and interpretation of what are now historical events. They range in age from the earliest publication of this type, *Freedom Journal* in New York City in 1827 to those who are operating today. Arrangement is alphabetical by title and directory-type information such as addresses, subjects, holdings, details of editorship, subscription rates, frequency, and so forth are supplied. Several useful indexes provide access.

Religion

761. Directory of African American Religious Bodies: A Compendium by the Howard University School of Divinity. 2nd ed. Wardell J. Payne, ed. Washington, D.C.: Howard University Press, 1995. 382p. ISBN 0-88258-184-8.

From the Howard University School of Divinity comes this fine directory of black religious groups in the United States. The church historically has been a strong influence on the lives of African Americans, and the *Directory* furnishes an alphabetical listing of some 1,000 significant religious bodies beginning with coverage of Black Primitive Baptists. The work opens with a useful introduction followed by essays on four major Christian groups (Baptists, Methodists, Pentecostals and Catholics). The main listing of entries includes Jews and Muslims, and many relatively obscure bodies such as the final entry for Yoruba Village of Oyotunji. Entries supply brief historical surveys and treatment of religious traditions as well as addresses, names of contacts and key personnel, membership figures, and publications. They also contain cross-references; an additional useful feature is a glossary of terms.

762. Encyclopedia of African and African American Religions. Stephen D. Glazier, ed. New York: Routledge, 2001. (Religion and Society series). 452p. ISBN 0-415-92245-3.

This is the second publication in the series, provides comprehensive coverage in treating the religious history and development in both the African and African and African American cultures. There are 145 signed entries supplied by 70 international scholars examining religious movements, churches, beliefs, practices, and events along with the provision of interpretive commentary on the role and impact of these traditions on their society. Although much of the coverage is given to religion in the United States, a real strength of this work lies in its anthropological orientation embracing the culture of Africa and the diaspora outside this country. The entries are detailed enough to be of value to sophisticated users, and many are full essays in examination of religious influences in North America, South America, and Central America. They contain bibliographies and generally serve to clarify the complexities and commonalities of the religious traditions of diverse peoples. A general bibliography concludes the effort.

364 / Social, Cultural, and Intellectual History

Regionalism

763. The Black New Yorkers: The Schomburg Illustrated Chronology, 400 Years of African American History. Howard Dodson et al. New York: John Wiley, 2000. 470p. ISBN 0-471-29714-3.

Not only those interested in New York influences and developments, but those examining the complete nature of the black experience as well, will find this timeline chronology an important resource in identifying important events and developments in that locale from 1525 (explorations of Esteban Gomez) through the year 1998. Although the focus is on the New York region with its rich and varied tradition embedded with the contributions of Native Americans in the areas of religion, politics, entertainment, and so forth, the timeline does include the very significant and notable historical events and dates regardless of where they occurred. Entries are brief with one sentence describing the event; there are many black-and-white photographs. In addition there are appendixes furnishing useful listings of influential personalities, a bibliography, and an index.

764. Blacks in the American West and Beyond—America, Canada, and Mexico: A Selectively Annotated Bibliography. George H. Junne, Jr. Westport, CT: Greenwood Press, 2000. 686p. (Bibliographies and Indexes in Afro-American and African Studies, no. 40). ISBN 0-313-31208-7.

This is a comprehensive bibliography in keeping with the author's definition or interpretation of what constitutes the West. Here it is regarded as the continental states west of the 98th degree longitude and brings in Arkansas, Iowa, and Missouri. The region referred to as "beyond" in the title encompass Mexico and Canada due to patterns of migration from those countries. There are 43 sections including those on special topics that include buffalo soldiers, black women, lynching, and so forth, although geographical sections are predominant. The work is comprehensive in its inclusion of materials and one is able to find references to books and monographs, book chapters, articles, dissertations, reference sources, films, and videos as well as black newspapers. Annotations are found in relatively few entries, and explanatory narrative is included only when the title is not descriptive of content. Indexing is furnished by subject as well as by author and title.

765. A Narrative Bibliography of the African American Frontier: Blacks in the Rocky Mountain West, 1535–1912. Roger D. Hardaway. Lewiston, NY: Edwin Mellen Press, 1995. 242p. (Studies in American History, v. 9.) ISBN 0-7734-8879-0.

Treating a little-understood aspect of the activity of blacks in the western regions of this country (Arizona, Colorado, Idaho, Montana, Nevada, New Mexico, Utah, and Wyoming). This work identifies and describes sources that date this activity back to the sixteenth century when the first slave, Estevanico, passed through the area. The descriptive narrative is organized into 15 chapters beginning with general studies. Succeeding chapters treat both personalities like Estevanico and historically significant topics such as the buffalo soldiers, slavery, Mormon relations, mining, Lewis and Clark Expedition, and so forth. The bibliography identifies some 50 books and 150 articles from 62 journals, and describes them in thorough fashion. Several indexes provide access by name, journal title, state, and subject.

THE EUROPEAN EXPERIENCE

In terms of documentation through the reference literature, European Americans benefited from the resurgence of interest in ethnic studies brought on by the expansive spirit of the 1960s and 1970s. The 1970s and 1980s witnessed an output of reference tools (many of which were singular in nature) furnishing bibliographic and/or historical coverage of minority Americans of various European persuasions. Commonly, the author or editor was of ethnic extraction, served as a librarian or professor, and produced a work on his or her tradition. These sources are still utilized because the 1990s were less productive, with a decline in materials examining European heritage. It is clear that certain traditions, such as those of Germany, Ireland, and Italy, have received disproportionate coverage. It is hoped that with the recent, more vigorous pursuit of multicultural studies, much of the aging material dating from the 1970s on European American groups will be updated, and new material will be issued. In keeping with our policy of utilizing racial and ethnic factors as the most important criteria governing organization of this work, this section contains resources on religion, education, and journalism that are relevant to European American history. Entries in this section are organized under regional categories.

General Sources

*766. The American Bibliography of Slavic and East European Studies (ABSEES). Aaron Trehub, executive ed. Urbana, IL: University of Illinois at Urbana Champaign. Available: http://gateway.library.uiuc.edu/abseees.

This excellent bibliographic resource has been in operation since 1956 under the auspices of the American Association for the Advancement of Slavic Studies (AAASS), having received financial assistance from various organizations and foundations including the National Endowment for the Humanities (NEH) and the Center for Russian and East European Studies at the University of Pittsburgh. In its current location at the University of Illinois, it continues to provide bibliographic records of scholarly studies relevant to Eastern European issues, culture, and identity. Included are references to books, articles, book chapters, dissertations, government publications, and online resources produced in both Europe and North America. It is available to educational institutions and libraries by subscription for an annual fee.

767. American Ethnic Groups. The European Heritage: A Bibliography of Doctoral Dissertations Completed at American Universities. Francesco Cordasco and David N. Alloway. Metuchen, NJ: Scarecrow, 1981. 366p. ISBN 0-8108-1405-6.

This is an extremely useful source to scholars and serious inquirers who wish to utilize the work of doctoral students or determine the state of the literature with respect to dissertations. There are more than 1,400 dissertations identified that have attempted topical treatment of the European heritage in this country, interpreted broadly to include any element of the U.S. ethnic experience. Entries are annotated and arranged in chapters under two major headings: "Western and Northern Europe" and "Central, Southern, and Eastern Europe." Nations or regions are treated, as are subsections on multigroup studies, emigration/immigration, and history, among others. Jewish people are considered under "European Jewry" as a special category defying geographic classification. There are some limitations in the omission of certain titles and needed cross-references. Author and subject indexes furnish access.

Central/Eastern Europe

The Finnish-American Historical Society of the West (www.finamhsw.com) was founded in 1962 and has about 400 members. Headquartered in Portland, Oregon, it offers a periodic historical monograph series as well as quarterly newsletter.

768. Guide to the American Ethnic Press: Slavic and East European Newspapers and Periodicals. Lubomyr R. Wynar. Kent, OH: Center for the Study of Ethnic Publications and School of Library Science, Kent State University, 1986. 280p.

This is a unique effort in terms of its content and its focus on the Slavic and East European press. The author is a bibliographic specialist in the area of ethnic studies and has compiled what amounts to the first annotated encyclopedic directory of currently operating newspapers and journals representing the interests and viewpoints of Americans of Slavic or East European descent. The value of this enterprise to social historians is unmistakable: The ethnic press has furnished much of the record regarding the customs, traditions, and socioeconomic status of these groups. There is an introductory essay that covers the nature of the Slavic and Eastern European presses; the entries are well developed and furnish information on sponsorship, editors, language, frequency, circulation, and price. The work concludes with an appendix of useful statistics, followed by a geographical and title index.

Slavic Ethnic Libraries, Museums, and Archives in the United States: A Guide and Directory by Wynar and Pat Kleeberger (Chicago: Association of College and Research Libraries, 1980) treats the Slavic American experience. Although most of the institutions are covered in the more recent work above, there is value in the detailed chapter-by-chapter coverage of 14 Slavic American groups. Entries provide similar information to those of the more comprehensive work above. Each chapter opens with a brief introductory description of the important institutions.

769. Polish American History and Culture: A Classified Bibliography. Joseph W. Zurawski. Chicago: Polish Museum of America, 1975. 218p.

Riding the wave of ethnic consciousness developing in the early 1970s came this 1975 bibliography of over 1,600 English-language entries related to Polish Americans, the single largest Slavic community in this country. There have not been a great many attempts at controlling the literature on the impact of Eastern or Central European cultures, and this tool was definitely needed for study. It was not intended to be a definitive work but rather was meant to cover a wide range of topics, for which a representative group of titles is provided (some annotated). Even so, it is of use to both students and scholars beginning their study. Topics of interest to the social historian are Polish American history, as well as the segments on political, cultural, social, and economic life; separate chapters are given to creative expression, such as one titled "Polish-American Poetry." An author index furnishes access.

770. The Romanians in America and Canada: A Guide to Information Sources. Vladimir Wertsman. Detroit: Gale, 1980. 164p. ISBN 0-8103-1417-7.

Another reported "first" is this annotated guide to informational materials concerning Romanian Americans. This resource joins with the author's chronology and fact book, published in 1975, and supplies needed material on the Romanian influence. The guide covers titles of general reference, humanities, and social sciences. There are several directory-type listings of organizations, periodical titles, churches, and research centers representing Romanian American culture and history. There are over 900 annotated entries of relevant books and periodical articles from both English- and Romanian-language presses. Annotations vary in size from very brief to ample. This tool will suit the needs not only of undergraduates and beginning researchers but also of the general public. Access is provided through three indexes: title, name, and subject.

771. Ukrainians in Canada and the United States: A Guide to Information Sources. Aleksander Sokolyszyn and Vladimir Wertsman. Detroit: Gale, 1981. 236p. ISBN 0-8103-1494-0.

This is a useful directory to various types of information sources pertaining to Ukrainians, who number an estimated 2 million–plus in the United States and more than 600,000 in Canada. This publication, as is true of others covering Eastern or Central European groups, is unique in dealing with a national influence that had largely been ignored. The guide has over 1,000 annotated entries representing both the historical and contemporary perspectives. It is divided into several major segments broadly covering general reference works, immigration and settlement, culture and heritage preservation, education, and social structure. There is a directory of organizations, churches, and other institutions. Included in the bibliography are books, articles, dissertations, and pamphlets. The content is indexed by author, title, and subject.

Ukrainians in North America: A Biographical Directory of Noteworthy Men and Women of Ukrainian Origin in the United States and Canada, edited Dmytro M. Shtohryn (Association for the Advancement of Ukrainian Studies, 1975) provides biographical treatment to this group of people who have not received much coverage in the literature. Entries furnish personal and professional data on 1,800 individuals, from movie stars to nuclear scientists living at the time of publication. Inclusion was decided on the basis of individuals' position of responsibility; scientific, scholarly or professional work; cultural, social, or political involvements; and past achievements. There is a segment with several entries covering individuals who died during the preparation of the work (1973–1975).

772. Who's Who in Polish America. 1996–1997 ed. Boleslaw Wierzbianski et al., eds. New York: Bicentennial Publishing; distr. Hippocrene Books, 1996. 571p. ISBN 0-7818-0010-1.

The first issue of this directory was in 1943; it was reprinted by Arno Press in 1970, and only recently has it been updated. The publisher is an active influence in and contributor to Polish American culture and issues a Polish language newspaper and a monthly English language magazine on Polish American interests. Therein, lies the motivation to document the existence of influential Polish American citizens. The current edition treats nearly 2,000 Americans of Polish descent who were judged to be distinctive by the criteria utilized by Marquis Who's Who in its respected series of biographical dictionaries. Biographical information was submitted by the personalities in response to a questionnaire, therefore coverage is limited to those who were willing to cooperate. Entries identify date and place of birth, address, family, education, career data, publications, memberships, honors, and more.

Northern/Western Europe

The Swedish-American Historical Society (available at http://www.swedishamericanhist. org) is located in Chicago and has a membership of nearly 1,200. Founded in 1948, it has published the *Swedish American Historical Quarterly* since 1950. The Swiss-American History Society, whose Web site can be accessed as an affiliate of the American Historical Association (available at http://www.theaha.org) is also based in Chicago. It was begun in 1927 and has 375 members. Since 1965, it has published its *Review,* which now appears three times a year. The American Irish Historical Society (available at http://www.aihs.org) of New York City was founded in 1897 and has issued *The Recorder* since 1901. Since 1985, it has appeared twice a year.

773. Dutch Americans: A Guide to Information Sources. Linda P. Doezema. Detroit: Gale, 1979. 314p. (Gale Information Guide Library; Ethnic Studies Information Guide Series, v. 3.) ISBN 0-8103-1407-X.

This offering comes from Gale Press and from the solid effort of the author, a librarian of Dutch descent who extended her master's thesis into the development of an excellent bibliographic guide. The work furnishes 800 annotated entries for both students and researchers. It represents a unique source, the first of its kind on Dutch Americans who, like other groups in this country, were finally documented in some fashion during the 1970s. The period covered spans nearly 300 years from the growth of commerce in the 1660s to the migrations of the twentieth century following World War II. There are four major chapters, the first two listing reference works and general works. The other two divide into historical periods and are subdivided by topics such as religion, sociology, politics, and language. Annotations are brief. The work contains author, title, and subject indexes.

774. The Encyclopedia of the Irish in America. Michael Glazier, ed. South Bend, IN: University of Notre Dame Press, 1999. 988p. ISBN 0-268-02755-2.

This is a comprehensive source of information on Irish Americans in its attempt to treat every significant person, place, or thing related to Irish life in this country. Nearly 250 contributors have provided some 1,000 entries with enough detail and descriptive data to satisfy most needs. As the first work of its kind, it is an important source of information on the Irish influence, especially in regard to the biographical coverage of some 500 Irish American personalities including clerics, entertainers, politicians, artists, writers, businesspeople, and more. In addition to biographies, entries examine topics and issues with lengthy treatment of such elements as Irish immigration, theater, and education. All states are treated, as are many cities. Brief bibliographies and 300 photographs add to the value of the coverage that spans a period of some 400 years.

From the publisher's *Material Culture Directory Series* is Susan K. Eleuterio-Comer's *Irish-American Culture: A Directory of Collections, Sites and Festivals in the United States and Canada* (Greenwood Press, 1988). It describes the holdings of nearly 100 museums, libraries, historical societies, and archives responding to a questionnaire. It locates over 40 historical sites and festivals relevant to Irish American traditions. The introduction provides a brief history.

775. German-American Relations and German Culture in America: A Subject Bibliography, 1941–1980. Arthur R. Schultz. Millwood, NY: Kraus International, 1984. 2v. ISBN 0-527-71572-7.

This is the most respected and most comprehensive effort at bibliographic control that has appeared since Henry A. Pochman's standard 1953 work (see below). Schultz's volume has nearly 21,000 entries, many annotated, of books, articles, dissertations, manuscripts, collections, and unpublished works; it continues the Pochmann coverage. Drawn particularly from the annual bibliographies appearing in *The American German Review* and *German Quarterly* between 1942 and 1971, the book covers writings on every aspect of German influence in this country and Canada. The work is divided into 12 segments covering philosophy, sociology, culture, history, and so on. Indexing amounts to over 100 pages and identifies authors, editors, reviewers, places, and other topics.

Pochmann's *Bibliography of German Culture in America to 1940* (Kraus International, 1982), was recently corrected and revised by Schultz, who now has furnished us with an indispensable guide. The revised edition contains nearly 5,000 addenda and hundreds of corrections. The two publications now serve as companion volumes.

776. The German Language Press of the Americas, 1732–1968: History and Bibliography. 3rd rev. ed. Karl J.R. Arndt and May E. Olson. München: Verlag Dokumentation, 1976–1980. 3v. ISBN 3-794-03422-8.

This book represents an update and expansion of what amounts to a historical and bibliographic directory of large proportions and of great importance to historical inquiry. Volume 1, *History and Bibliography, 1732–1968* (1976), originally appeared in 1961 and in 1965 as *German-American Newspapers and Periodicals, 1732–1955*. Volume 2, *History and Bibliography, 1732–1968: Argentina . . .* and 16 other countries, was issued in 1973. These comprehensive volumes furnish bibliographic listings with essential data on every German-language newspaper or periodical ever published in the Americas. The first volume for the United States lists the presses by state, then city or town; volume 2 organizes the countries of Central and South America alphabetically from Argentina to Venezuela. Both volumes have title indexes, and provide access by holding libraries; they furnish historical narrative regarding the various presses and their publications. Volume 3, *German-American Press Research from the American Revolution to the Bicentennial* (1980), contains 23 essays written in German on the history of German journalism in the Americas.

777. Guide to Swedish-American Archival and Manuscript Sources in the United States. Chicago: Swedish-American Historical Society, 1983. 600p. ISBN 0-914819-00-3.

Sponsored by the Swedish-American Historical Society, this bibliographic guide developed from a survey funded by the National Endowment for the Humanities is concerned with the materials on Swedish immigration and acculturation in this country. Nearly 130 U.S. libraries and archives are listed, first by state, then by city; file holdings (both personal and organizational), histories, and photographic materials are described. A total of 30 states are represented, although the major bulk of the material (over 1,200 of the approximately

3,100 items) comes from Augustana College or from the closely linked Swenson Swedish Immigration Research Center. Entries furnish brief, informative narratives; cross-references are supplied. This work has found broad acceptance among wide varieties of researchers and interested inquirers. Access is provided by an index of proper names.

778. Guide to the Archival Materials of the German-Speaking Emigration to the United States After 1933. John M. Spalek and Sandra Hawrylchak, eds. Charlottesville, VA: University Press of Virginia, 1978–1996. 3v. in 5 parts. ISBN 3-907820-92-4.

This guide is the result of a long-term project aimed at locating the existence of papers and manuscripts of about 1,000 prominent German-speaking intellectuals who arrived in this country after 1933 following the Nazi rise to power. That year marked the beginning of a general exodus from Germany of creative people who felt stifled and constrained by the political climate (Arendt, Brecht, Einstein, Mann, Schönberg, etc.). The editors have provided a real service in making accessible a wealth of material by such important contributors to U.S. society. Arrangement of entries is alphabetical by name. Entries identifying estates held by libraries and private collections are reported and described briefly in terms of status and conditions. Materials are listed and classified by symbols. There are appendixes of names for which little or no information has been found and of material that has changed location.

779. Immigrants from the German-Speaking Countries of Europe: A Selective Bibliography of Reference Works. 2nd ed. Margrit B. Krewson. Washington, D.C.: Library of Congress, European Division, 1991. 76p. ISBN 0-8444-0715-1.

The author is a specialist with the European Division of the Library of Congress and has produced bibliographic works of interest to both area and social history. At the same time, they serve as finding lists for the Library of Congress collection. This effort is a revision and expansion of *Germanic People in the United States,* a 1983 publication, and is the most recent title to deal with the German tradition in this country. There are separate sections for Austria, Germany, and Switzerland, all of which have been subject to a variety of influences affecting their German "character." Although less provincial in terms of origin, an interesting culture such as that of the Pennsylvania Dutch has been categorized only under "Germany." There is an introduction covering patterns of migration, which has been criticized for omitting ethnic Germans from Eastern Europe.

780. The Irish Experience in New York City: A Select Bibliography. New York: New York Irish History Roundtable/ Syracuse: Syracuse University Press, 1995. 130p. ISBN 0-8156-8121-6.

New York has played a major role in the life and times of the Irish in this country, and this brief volume is useful in its presentation of an array of research materials both published and unpublished relevant to the Irish American influence in that city. The work is divided into six sections, the first of which examines the state-of-the-art of Irish American bibliographical coverage today. Section 2 serves as a directory of some relevant holdings of theses and dissertations by libraries in New York, while section 3 furnishes brief annotations of unpublished theses and dissertations. Section 4 treats published sources with references to *Dissertation Abstracts International* for those derived from dissertations, and section 5 lists audio-visual material. Section 6 lists additional theses and dissertations that have not been seen by the authors or (unfortunately) not included in the indexes.

More comprehensive in its scope of coverage is Patrick J. Blessing's *The Irish in America: A Guide to the Literature and the Manuscript Collections* (Catholic University of America, 1992). This useful source is a bibliography of print material representing scholarly studies, memoirs, literature, and criticism, and includes theses and dissertations. It also serves as a directory of manuscript collections arranged by state, and by Federal agency.

781. Research Guide to the Turner Movement in the United States. Eric L. Pumroy and Katja Rampelmann, comps. Westport, CT: Greenwood Press, 1996. 358p. (Bibliographies and Indexes in American History, no. 33). ISBN 0-313-29763-0.

The compilers of this work have performed a service in helping to document the Turner movement that began in the late 1840s and early 1850s with the arrival of German immigrants to this country. By the turn of the century the movement was flourishing with 40,000 members belonging to about 300 sociocultural societies that served as community centers for German Americans and were tied to the American Turnerbund. With assimilation of ethnic groups in the twentieth century, the Turners declined as did similar organizations of other ethnic groups. The guide opens with an introductory essay describing the history of the Turner movement in the United States. Subsequent chapters identify existing publications and records both for the national organization and for the local units, and enumerate the movement's influence on physical education within the American Gymnastic Union. Books, articles, and research studies are listed in the final chapter. Several appendixes furnish helpful listings.

782. The Scotch-Irish: From the North of Ireland to the Making of America. Ron Chepesiuk. Jefferson, NC: McFarland, 2000. 182p. ISBN 0-7864-0614-3.

The Scotch-Irish formed the largest ethnic group immigrating to this region in the early years except for the English, and by the time of the Revolution they numbered 250,000 residents or about one-tenth of the total population. Their tradition in the old country stemmed from an emigration to Ireland by Scottish Presbyterians in the seventeenth century to form the Ulster Plantation. Their tale is of interest to historians and genealogists and this work provides detailed descriptions of the arrival and settlement within this country. Of interest is the description of life in the old country in their treatment by English overlords, the exposition of reasons for their relocation, and analysis of their hopes and expectations in terms of what they hoped to find in the new country.

Southern Europe

The American Italian Historical Association (available at http://www.mobilito.com/aiha), headquartered at the University of Rhode Island in Providence, was founded in 1966 and has 430 members. It has published *Italian Americana,* a semiannual journal, since 1974.

783. Basque Americans: A Guide to Information Sources. William A. Douglass and Richard W. Etulain. Detroit: Gale, 1981. 169p. (Ethnic Studies Information Guide Series, v. 6.) ISBN 0-8103-1469-X.

Another product of the recent increased interest in ethnic studies is this bibliographic guide to materials on Basque Americans. The authors (both experts on Basque culture) were assisted in their effort by the work of seven contributors who produced the 413 entries. The sources are drawn primarily from the holdings of the Basque Collection at the University of Nevada in Reno. Basques have been misunderstood and ignored in the literature for reasons relating to their almost total agrarian/shepherd existence, largely in the U.S. West; their avoidance of metropolitan centers; and their lack of literary productivity. As a result, the present work represents a unique and valuable tool. Divided among 16 sections, some topical, such as "History in U.S.," a few by form, such as "Bibliographies and Reference Works," the entries are annotated in an evaluative manner. There is a subject index, although it is somewhat lacking in detail.

784. A Bibliographic Guide to Materials on Greeks in the United States, 1890–1968. Michael N. Cutsumbis. Staten Island, NY: Center for Migration Studies, 1970. 100p.

This brief work received little attention at the time it appeared, at the onset of the revival of ethnic interest in this country. Very little has been done on Greek-American culture; this bibliography was sponsored by the Center for Migration Studies. The tool is well planned and well executed, with entries organized under 12 chapter headings, most of which are related to form and format: "Books by Greeks in the United States," "Articles," "Publications Dealing with the Greek Orthodox Church," "Unpublished Works," "Serials Currently Published," "Fraternal Publications," "Manuscript Collections," and so on. No annotations are given, but location symbols are provided for many of the entries. Although quite selective in the titles chosen, this resource provides a good perspective of representative publications of every type.

785. The Italian American Experience: An Encyclopedia. Salvatore J. LaGumina et al., eds. New York: Garland, 1999. 735p. (Garland Reference Library of the Humanities, v. 1535). ISBN 0-8153-0713-6.

On of the few references sources on Italian Americans to come out in recent years is this compendium developed by four editors and 166 contributing scholars. It is a comprehensive effort that includes brief biographical sketches of Italian Americans, both living and dead, who have influenced American society in some way. These range from the very prominent and popular (Robert De Niro, Madonna, Mario Cuomo) for whom photographs are generally supplied in separate entries, to less familiar personalities who may be treated in a general categorical entries such as "Politics" or "Movie Actors and Actresses." There is a wide array of people from the creative arts, professions, trades, and vocations among those included. More important, however, are the lengthier essays on topical areas treating arts, history, religion, sports, science and technology, and so forth. There are detailed expositions of the part played by Italian Americans in political organizations, labor unions, and business enterprises.

786. Italian-Americans and Religion: An Annotated Bibliography. 2nd ed. rev. and enl. Silvano M. Tomasi and Edward C. Stibili. New York: Center for Migration Studies, 1992. 365p. ISBN 0-9934733-52-X.

This annotated bibliography has expanded considerably since its first edition in 1978. It provides a listing of various types of documents and secondary publications treating the religious experience of Italian Americans. Of most interest to scholars and historians are the materials supplied in the section devoted to primary-source documents. In this section, one is able to utilize a directory-type listing that enumerates locations and describes the content of a number of depositories and archival agencies holding various resource materials. The secondary sources include bibliographies, serials, dissertations, histories of various parishes, and books and articles. Hundreds of entries are given, and annotations are provided of varying size and depth. In general, they are useful in determining the nature of the work. The immigrant tradition has not been examined in the major religious bibliographic works of the past, so both scholars and students will need to consult this one when beginning their studies. The index furnishes entry numbers of listed materials.

787. The Portuguese-Americans. Leo Pap. Boston: Twayne, 1981. 300p. (The Immigrant Heritage of America). Repr. Boston: Portuguese Continental Union of the United States, 1992.

This is another important title by Pap (see entry 787), furnishing a unique comprehensive survey-history of a little-understood and relatively undocumented minority in the U.S. milieu. Beginning with the initial contacts of the Portuguese in the days of exploration, Pap describes their immigration and settlement from the periods of colonization to modern times. Emphasis has been placed on the earlier movements as compared to the post-1965 period. Immigrant life and conditions are revealed in an interesting and enlightened manner; economic factors, religious influences, newspapers, organizations, and civic groups are explained. The work has been criticized for not being vigorous enough in its interpretation of some of the dynamics involved in the more recent treatment of immigration history (e.g., social mobility, assimilation) although these aspects are described. The description of immigrant communities is especially revealing. An excellent bibliography accompanies the text.

Pap's earlier bibliographic effort, *The Portuguese in the United States: A Bibliography* (Center for Migration Studies, 1976) and supplemented in 1989, was the first of its kind. It furnishes about 800 entries treating books, articles, doctoral dissertations, and master's theses. Supplements have appeared in an annual, *Essays in Portuguese Studies* published under the auspices of the University of New Hampshire's International Conference Group on Portugal. The titles cover Portuguese in the United States as well as those in Portugal, from the period of exploration to the present day. There is no author index.

THE FEMALE EXPERIENCE

The past 20 years have seen many changes in the role and position of women in U.S. society. The struggle over the Equal Rights Amendment crystallized much of the dualism surrounding women's employment, rights, and status as a whole; as well as the latent fears of both males and females when such issues were "pushed." Since then, the agenda has been well publicized regarding spouse abuse, parity in the sexual act, and health issues through the efforts of such forces as the National Organization of Women. The rise of social consciousness in the 1960s and 1970s led to an increased production of books concerning women's issues. Since the 1970s, mainstream publishers have increased their activity regarding the social conditions and social conditioning relevant to the U.S. woman. At the same time, small female publishing houses have come into operation. Reference book publishers have been quick to respond with a continuing production of a variety of sources.

Reference tools included here embrace many areas covered elsewhere in this work; the rationale being that, following race and ethnicity, gender is the criterion of primary importance. Therefore, one will find books in this section on the following topics as they relate to the female experience in U.S. history: politics, ideological trends, education, labor, science, social welfare and philanthropy, sports, religion, and the military. Exceptions are found in the case of women in cinema and in radio and television, for which entries are found in the section titled "Popular Culture: Entertainment, Recreation, Sports," later in this chapter. *Women's Studies Abstracts* is a quarterly abstracting service of periodical articles and books relevant to women's studies. There is a history section that includes various sources, most often those pertinent to the United States. It is published by Rush Publishing and has operated since 1972.

The National Women's History Project (available at http://www.nwhp.org) of Santa Rosa, California, was founded in 1977 and maintains a staff to promote women's history. It publishes *Women's History Resource Catalog* on an annual basis.

General Sources

788. American Women: Who They Are & How They Live. Editors of New Strategist Publications. Ithaca, NY: New Strategist, 1997. 400p. ISBN 1-885070-08-X.

Although intended to provide insight into the mind, activity, expression, and progressive development of American females for purposes related to business success in terms of successful marketing, there is much useful data for students in women's studies and in history. It represents a reporting of market research focused on women born in this country subsequent to World War II, and is presented through nine chapters providing statistical tables along with brief descriptive narratives. Much of the information has been culled from government sources, and the nine chapters examine are indicative of important characteristics or categories: attitudes, education, health, income, labor force, living arrangements, population, spending, and wealth. Historical data are included with indications of changing conditions through time. Each table is labeled with the original source from which the statistics were taken.

789. The American Women's Almanac: An Inspiring and Irreverent Women's History. Louise Bernikow. New York: Berkley, 1997. 388p. ISBN 0-425-15616-8.

The author produced this work in association with the National Women's History Project and credits the feminist activity in women's history in the past 25 years for the substance that she is able to present. The source is divided into nine chapters, each disposed toward a feature or element in celebrating the life of a modern woman. Chapters represent categorical topics: politics, the female body, the female body in motion, the female mind, writers and artists, entertainers, media, domestic life, and work. Each chapter opens with a descriptive narrative on the topic, and follows with facts, quotes, and anecdotes in treating personalities, events, and issues. Many photographs provide insight and illustrate points made in the text. There is a general bibliography of some value, along with an epilogue to provide a summary. An index helps to provide access.

Almanac of American Women in the 20th Century by Judith F. Clark (Prentice-Hall, 1987) is a chronology and handbook on U.S. women of the past century. Coverage begins with January 1900 and extends to the time of publication in 1987. Narratives and expositions that range from a half-page to a full page in length are interspersed with the dated listings. Most essays are biographical in nature, but some deal with social issues such as child care. The work is divided into nine chapters, each of which deals with pertinent events that happened during a single decade. Emphasis is given to women who have contributed to societal change rather than those active in the arts or the professions, and entries are classified by categories such as popular culture, science, and ideas/beliefs.

790. Atlas of American Women. Barbara G. Shortridge. New York: Macmillan, 1987. 164p. ISBN 0-02-929120-8.

A most welcome source is this recent atlas designed to illustrate important data concerning demographics, employment, education, social roles and relationships, health, and crime. Based on the 1980 census data and other sources, the work clearly indicates the contrasting conditions that prevail in different parts of the country. There are nearly 130 maps, which in many cases are accompanied by charts and diagrams. Textual narrative is detailed and well developed in terms of comparative analysis. An interesting point of coverage is the section on women's sports. This work was one of several that appeared at the same time, all bearing feminist orientation. Both students and scholars of recent social history will find it of value in studying the various distributions presented. There is a bibliography and an index.

A more current source is one by Sandra Opdycke and comes as part of the publisher's series of historical atlases. *The Routledge Historical Atlas of Women in America* (Routledge, 2000) examines both general developments and trends, as well as specific events in the history of women in this country. Maps, charts, and descriptive commentary are divided into five chronological periods with thematic divisions beginning with the era prior to 1800 ("Breaking Old Ties") and ending with the period, 1965 to the present ("Redefining Women's Place").

791. Biographies of American Women: An Annotated Bibliography. Patricia E. Sweeney. Santa Barbara, CA: ABC-CLIO, 1990. 290p. ISBN 0-87436-070-6.

Especially useful to the student or beginning researcher is this recent annotated bibliography of nearly 1,400 biographies of 700 U.S. women from various fields. Entries are arranged alphabetically by personal name. Obviously, there will be some inequity in number of titles listed for the various subjects; Eleanor Roosevelt has nearly 20 items, whereas others are limited to only one. The number of listings a woman has, of course, represents her importance as perceived by writers rather than a bias on the part of the author of this work. Publications vary widely and include many of the offerings of the popular literature as well as those from university presses and even doctoral dissertations. To have been included, the biography must have been at least 50 pages long; annotations are brief but evaluative. There is an appendix of biographies by profession and an author/title index.

Portraits of American Women: From Settlement to the Present by G. J. Barker-Benfield and Catherine Clinton (St. Martin's, 1991) is a highly selective and detailed collective biography of only 25 women from different historical periods and representing different ethnic groups. Arrangement is under historical period, and a portrait accompanies each sketch. There is no index.

792. Columbia Guide to American Women in the Nineteenth Century. Catherine Clinton and Christine A. Lunardini. New York: Columbia University Press, 2000. 331p. (Columbia Guides to American History and Cultures). ISBN 0-231-10920-2.

The authors are highly regarded for their expertise in the topic of this work, having conducted research and contributed books and articles in the past. With the publication of this effort, they have produced a successful introductory bibliographic guide for the comprehension and understanding of lives and activities of American females during the period under investigation. They open with an introduction that supplies a historiographical essay presenting a survey of the literature; then provide chapters of topical nature treating such areas as economy, households, labor, and sociopolitical strata of suffrage and reform. There are a segment of encyclopedic nature furnishing definitions of key terms and brief sketches of important personalities, political movements, organizations, and legislation. A chronology precedes a bibliography of additional sources, both primary and secondary.

793. Encyclopedia of Women in American History. Joyce Appleby et al., eds. Armonk, NY: M.E. Sharpe, 2002. 3v. ISBN 0-7656-8038-6.

This comprehensive work represents an excellent combination of historical survey, detailed encyclopedia, and documentary history. Designed for students at high school level and above, the volumes each treat an expansive historical period: 1585–1820, 1820–1900, and 1900 to the present. Each volume opens with a historical account and thematic essays on significant issues and developments during the period. This is followed by several hundred alphabetically arranged entries on personalities, developments, events, legislation, and more. The volumes contain primary-source material and documents as well as statistical charts, graphs, and illustrations.

The Encyclopedia of Women's History in America by Kathryn Cullen-DuPont (Facts on File, 1996) treats women's history from colonial times to the present in and is also a combination of encyclopedia and documentary history. The first part is similar to, although not as inclusive, as the *Handbook of American Women's History* (see entry 796) containing some 500 alphabetically arranged entries. These describe personalities, important events, legislation, organizations, movements, places, and issues such as "pregnancy discrimination" pertinent to the theme. Extensive appendixes contain the complete texts of 34 significant documents (the Constitution, *Roe* v. *Wade,* etc.) dating from the mid-seventeenth century to 1992. A detailed index provides access.

*American Women's History (available at http://www.fofweb.com/) is a subscription database available on the Web from Facts on File. It is a comprehensive encyclopedia treating the period from the fifteenth century to the present and is culled from more than 40 of the publisher's sources. There are five divisions from which the user may access the material; biographies, subjects, historical documents, image gallery, and maps and charts. There are links within entries leading to additional relevant information. One criticism is that the complete text is not provided for most of the historical documents.

794. The Female Experience in Eighteenth- and Nineteenth-Century America: A Guide to the History of American Women. Jill K. Conway et al. New York: Garland, 1982. 290p. (Garland Reference Library of Social Science, v. 35.) ISBN 0-8240-9936-2. Repr. Princeton: Princeton University Press, 1985. ISBN 0-6910-0599-0.

This is a fine selective bibliography of real value to beginning researchers and serious students in its coverage of both private and public lives of U.S. women over a span of two centuries. Much of the strength of the work lies in its organization of books, articles, and dissertations (both primary and secondary sources) into broad subject categories; each of these is furnished with an excellent introductory essay describing and interpreting important events and developments. These categories are "U.S. Culture and Society," "Industrialization," "Women's Work and the Transformation of the Household," "The Cultural Roles of Middle-Class Women," "Women's Religious Life and the Reference Tradition," and "Biology and Domestic Life." These chapters are subdivided by topic (family life, legal status, social work) or format (diaries, travel accounts, etc.). There is an author index.

Another selective bibliography is *Victorian American Women 1840–1880: An Annotated Bibliography* by Karen R. Mehaffy (Garland, 1992), issued as volume 1,181 of the Garland Reference Library of the Humanities series. The middle-class woman of the period is the subject of the work, and coverage includes books, articles, and other publications dealing with social and family life. Unfortunately, there is no index, and access is dependent upon the table of contents.

795. Great Lives from History: American Women Series. Frank N. Magill, ed. Pasadena, CA: Salem Press, 1995. 5v. ISBN 0-89356-892-9.

Another of the Magill biographical compendia, this is the sixth set in the "Great Lives" series of sets, multivolume works that provide a comprehensible source of information for students at high school and undergraduate levels. There are 409 entries for women of varying levels of achievement and diverse areas of endeavor. Included here are visual and performing artists, writers, diplomats and politicians, scientists, businesswomen, and others spanning a period from colonial times to the present. Entries run about 2,000 words and begin with summary data identifying birth and death dates, category of achievement, and a brief description of the person's major accomplishment. The essay is divided into several segments beginning with a brief biographical sketch in "early life." This is followed by a more detailed treatment of "life's work," and finally a very brief "summary." Concluding each profile is a short annotated bibliography. Volume 5 supplies a timeline by birth date and indexes by name and by career.

796. Handbook of American Women's History. 2nd ed. Angela Howard and Frances M. Kavenik, eds. Thousand Oaks, Sage Publications, 2000. 724p. (Garland Reference Library of the Humanities, v. 696.) ISBN 0-7619-1635-0.

This one-volume handbook, edited by Ms Howard, was first issued in 1990 and designed to provide quick and easy-to-gather information on women's history for students and beginning researchers. The new edition has addressed some of the inconsistencies in style and organization of entries, and the work continues its success in furnishing basic information in easily digestible manner. It is a comprehensive effort with entries alphabetically arranged and providing brief exposition of a variety of events, people, issues, organizations, books, jobs, ideas, and laws. There are 142 new entries in the total of 922, with many new contributors. For each entry there is a brief bibliography for additional reading which now includes a few Web sites. Coverage is of popular culture and the arts as well as politics and social issues of weighty concern. The entries, although brief, are well developed for the most part, and informative in supplying useful background data. Coverage is selective and there is some unevenness in the treatment of various topics. There is a general index.

797. The History of American Women's Voluntary Organizations, 1810–1960: A Guide to Sources. Karen J. Blair. Boston: G.K. Hall, 1989. 363p. (G.K. Hall Women's Studies Publications.) ISBN 0-8161-8648-0.

This is a well-constructed, annotated bibliography of books and articles culled from a number of standard indexing sources. It is useful for historical studies in its sharp focus on women's voluntary organizations recognized by the author-historian as being vital to both personal and political change. Arrangement of the nearly 700 entries is alphabetical by author; there is a symbol for each entry indicating its coverage of one of 13 classes representing either charitable or socially active organizations involved in patriotism, temperance, peace, suffrage, racial awareness, religious causes, and so on. Trade unions have been excluded. The annotations are thorough and provide both information and critical interpretation. There is a brief bibliography of sources used. A detailed index provides access by subject and name of association.

798. Index to American Women Speakers, 1828–1978. Beverley Manning. Metuchen, NJ: Scarecrow, 1980. 672p. ISBN 0-8108-1282-7. **Supp.** 1989. 620p. ISBN 0-8108-2122-2.

This unique bibliographic product provides a real boost to women's studies and documentation of the female experience in the United States. The author, an academic librarian, has examined a variety of sources—anthologies, documentaries, histories, published conference proceedings, government documents, and periodical—in an attempt to identify and locate speeches given by U.S. women. More than 3,000 speeches are listed from 225 sources. Virtually none of these were listed either in *Speech Index* or *Vital Speeches,* which as indexing tools, have not been prone to include women's contributions. The expansive coverage of this 150-year period makes this tool an important asset for social historians and serious students. The speechmakers range from the very famous (Susan B. Anthony and Bella Abzug) to the now obscure. Author, subject, and title indexes are furnished.

The supplement, also by Manning, titled *We Shall Be Heard: Speeches by American Women, 1978–1985,* continues the coverage.

*799. North American Women's Letters and Diaries: Colonial to 1950. Alexandria, VA: Alexander Street Press, 2001. Available: http://www.alexanderstreet2.com/NWLDlive.

Designed to grow in size to the equivalent of 150,000 print pages with quarterly supplementary additions, this database was issued containing about 50,000 pages of material. In early 2002, it will have grown to some 80,000 pages. It represents the very latest innovative approach in reference source production and is part of the publisher's series (entries 462, 600n, 1166n). It can be acquired through payment of a one-time fee for perpetual access or through annual subscription. The work will expand and grow through material selected by the editorial board with contributions and suggestions from its users. Culled from several hundred sources (published and unpublished diaries, journal articles, pamphlets, newsletters, monographs, and conference proceedings) the very personal writings and reflections of both the historically famous (Phyllis Wheatley, Gertrude Stein, Dolly Madison, etc.) and of the average women of different time periods present a vivid picture of their lives and aspirations. As it continues to grow, it has become the largest collection of this material ever compiled.

800. Notable Women in American History: A Guide to Recommended Biographies and Autobiographies. Lynda G. Adamson. Westport, CT: Greenwood Press, 1999. 540p. ISBN 0-313-29584-0.

This is a companion publication to Adamson's *Notable Women in World History* issued by Greenwood the same year. It follows the same format as the other, this time identifying biographical publications treating 500 American women from the colonial period to the time of publication. The females represent some 100 fields and professions ranging from celebrity actresses to religious missionaries and must have met the three selection criteria. First, they must have lived in this country and if born elsewhere had become naturalized citizens; second, they must have enriched the lives of other Americans; and third, they must have had a biography or an autobiography published since 1970. Entries are arranged alphabetically and contain brief biographical information, followed by up to five annotated citations to primary and secondary biographical sources. Appendixes furnish listings by year of birth, field of endeavor, and ethnicity.

801. The Reader's Companion to U.S. Women's History. Wilma Mankiller et al. New York: Houghton Mifflin, 1998. 696p. ISBN 0-395-67173-6.

This effort by Mankiller, Gloria Steinem, and others seeks to provide awareness and understanding of the conditions, societal and health issues, moral codes, and accomplishments relevant to the history of American females. The final product represents the efforts of more than 300 contributors instructed to research their topics and render brief evaluations of their impact. There are 400 entries treating such diverse elements as marriage, breeding, divorce, privacy, spirituality, ethnic and racial groups, religion, eating disorders, and more. There has been some criticism over uneven coverage given to certain topics, opinionated viewpoints, lack of bibliographies in many cases, and selection of entries, but there is general agreement that the work furnishes a wealth of information on the main theme.

802. A Shared Experience: Men, Women, and the History of Gender. Laura McCall and Donald Yacovone. New York: New York University Press, 1998. 387p. ISBN 0-8147-9683-4.

This work is unique to this section in that it serves as a vehicle promoting an agenda that would include men in a broadened definition of women's history. It is felt that by focusing on similarities and not only the differences of the lives led by men and women that the truth be told. The "shared experience" needs to be understood, but rarely has this been attempted. The result is a collection of 14 essays examining issues and conditions attendant to historic developments regarding the male role in society and the sharing of interests, issues, and problems of females. Essays are varied in nature and examine a variety of historical conditions; contributions of Southern women to Whig politics, fraternal love of Victorian men, sexual relationships among male settlement house reformers, gender equality in marriage, education, problems of freed slaves, and more.

803. Statistical Handbook on Women In America. 2nd ed. Cynthia M. Taeuber, comp. and ed. Phoenix: Oryx Press, 1996. 354p. ISBN 1-57356-005-7.

This is a welcome source of convenience compiling much elusive data from publications of the government and various private organizations. It follows the same format of the first edition issued five years earlier in its organization of data under several major divisions or parts. The first section treats demographics, followed by employment and economic status, health, and social characteristics. These sections open with a useful introductory essay highlighting and summarizing the important elements regarding the information collected. Data is presented in the form of statistical tables and furnish a complete picture of the modern female. Race and ethnicity are also treated. Although emphasis is on the period 1988 to 1995, historians will welcome the many comparisons provided in the representation of data over several decades, even to the turn of the century.

804. Through a Woman's I: An Annotated Bibliography of American Women's Autobiographical Writings, 1946–1976. Patricia K. Addis. Metuchen, NJ: Scarecrow, 1983. 607p. ISBN 0-8108-1588-5.

Nearly 2,225 autobiographical publications of U.S. women are identified in annotated listings arranged alphabetically by the author. All materials cited are at least 25 pages long and were issued during a 30-year period. This work serves to supplement Louis Kaplan's *Bibliography of American Autobiographies* (entry 55n), which covers autobiographies of both males and females published through 1945. Entries in the present work appear to be readily available in U.S. libraries and represent various literary forms—autobiographies, journals, letters, diaries, travel narratives, and memoirs. Annotations are brief but informative as to content, and cross-references are used to identify name variations and synonyms. Given in each entry are the writer's birth and death dates, when known, as well as complete bibliographic information. An author index categorizes the writers by occupation, whereas subject and title indexes furnish easy access.

805. U.S. Women's Interest Groups: Institutional Profiles. Sarah Slavin, ed. Westport, CT: Greenwood Press, 1995. 645p. (Greenwood Reference Volumes on American Public Policy Formation). ISBN 0-313-25073-1.

This is a useful directory and guide to nearly 200 organizations. It opens with an informative summary and overview of the major concerns and focus of activity of women's groups and the nature their political activity. Organizations selected for inclusion in the guide met at least one of the following criteria: have a connection to women, limit membership to women, serve specific women's interests, represent a traditional women's role, or take positions on issues of importance to women. Included in the mix are religious and ethnic groups. Data primarily are from responses to questionnaires, but also are culled from interviews and publications. Entries present profiles containing a wide variety of information; origin and developmental history, structure and funding, policy concerns and tactics, along with publications, and additional bibliography. Cross-references are given.

806. Women in Particular: An Index to American Women. Kali Herman. Phoenix: Oryx, 1984. 740p. ISBN 0-89774-088-2.

This is a useful index to sketches of U.S. women. The sketches appear in more than 50 biographical dictionaries, ranging from *Notable American Women* (Harvard University Press, 1971) to the *Slavonic Encyclopedia* (Associated Faculty Press, 1969). More than 15,000 women are treated, and access is aided by a noteworthy array of classification approaches. First, there is a field and career index, which is divided into areas of endeavor, such as education or fashion and etiquette. This segment represents the bulk of the volume. Second, there is an index by religious affiliation, followed by a third index by racial and ethnic background and a fourth by geographic location. Names are listed in all applicable indexes in chronological fashion. Entries furnish name, date, career information, religion, workplace, and residence, as well as references to biographical dictionaries. There is a final alphabetical index, which is comprehensive to the work. The author, now known as Kali Tal, has a personal Web site in which she provides introductory information to this work and links to her other publications (available at http://www.kalital.com).

807. Women in the First and Second World Wars: A Checklist of the Holdings of the Hoover Institution on War, Revolution, and Peace. Helena Wedborn, comp. Stanford, CA: Hoover Institution, Stanford University, 1988. 73p. (Hoover Press Bibliography Series, v. 72.) ISBN 0-8179-2722-0.

From the Hoover Institution on War, Revolution, and Peace comes this brief catalog of its holdings as of 1987 on women's history as it relates to the two World Wars. There are nearly 400 entries for each war representing both printed and archival holdings, although no correspondence is included. Because the organization has a noteworthy collection on various issues relevant to social change, it is important to the historian that access tools are being developed. Two catalog listings are provided, the first one covering the period 1914–1918, the second listing materials between 1939 and 1945. Entries are organized in classified manner using Library of Congress subject headings. The format presents a slight problem with no table of contents. The lack of specificity in some of the Library of Congress terms is disconcerting, but the search results are worthwhile.

808. Women in U.S. History: A Resource Guide. Lyda M. Hardy. Englewood, CO: Libraries Unlimited, 2000. 344p. ISBN 1-56308-769-3.

Linking the documentation of women's history to subsequent efforts in research and education, the author furnishes a work targeted to the needs of a wide audience ranging from middle school level to college and adult. It is a comprehensive annotated bibliography treating a variety of source materials general histories, reference works, biographies, as well as videos, documentaries, posters, and Web sites. The volume is organized into six parts or sections, the first three of which provide listings of resources by subjects useful in the examination of the contributions of women within the social fabric. The last three parts provide essays on historiography of women in this country, theory and methodologies relevant to women's history, and education in women's studies in which the integration of women's studies into the curriculum is addressed. Indexes supply access by author, title, and subject.

Journal of Women's History Guide to Periodical Literature, compiled by Gayle V. Fisher (Indiana University Press, 1992) furnishes a listing of over 5,500 articles relevant to women's history culled from 750 journals. About 75 percent of the entries concern women in this country.

809. Women Remembered: A Guide to Landmarks of Women's History in the United States. Marion Tinling. New York: Greenwood, 1986. 796p. ISBN 0-313-23984-3.

This is an interesting and useful directory of more than 2,000 sites—monuments, parks, memorials, homes, workplaces—of historically important contributors to women's history in this country. Women chosen for inclusion made an impact on society through either their performance of heroic deeds or their participation in historic events. Bystanders (wives, daughters) are excluded, as are living individuals. Of real value are the brief but well-developed biographical essays for each entry. Locations are given and accessibility is described, along with hours of opening. There are indicators of the subject's inclusion in *Notable American Women* (Harvard University Press, 1971). Entries are organized under five regional divisions, then by state, city, and personal name. Only those sites open to the public are treated. There are listings classified by occupations, a chronology of dates, a brief bibliographic narrative, and a personal name index.

810. The Women's Atlas of the United States. Rev. ed. Timothy H. Fast and Cathy C. Fast. New York: Facts on File, 1995. 246p. ISBN 0-8160-2970-9.

This edition is similar in format and treatment to the first edition published in 1986, and again is organized into seven sections representing topical coverage; "demographics," "education," "employment," "family structure," "fertility and health," "criminal behavior," and "political activity." Notable by its absence is coverage of union activity, lesbian presence, and physical disability. Maps (with lively titles) and sometimes, opinionated descriptive narratives are utilized to furnish statistical representation under each of these standard sections and provide a graphic analysis of conditions. There is an introductory segment on reading maps, and an appendix contains tables that summarize the data found in the maps. Concluding the work is a bibliography for the maps, and suggestions for additional reading. An index provides access.

811. Women's Diaries, Journals, and Letters: An Annotated Bibliography. Cheryl Cline. New York: Garland, 1989. 716p. (Garland Reference Library of the Humanities, v. 780.) ISBN 0-8240-6637-5.

This annotated listing of nearly 3,000 primary-source writings by women (mainly Americans, but also heavily representative of French and British thought) is of importance to both scholars and students. Other parts of the world receive far less treatment; for example, Africa has a total of seven entries. Entries describe private writings, mainly letters, diaries, journals, and travel accounts, mostly in the English language. There is a wealth of historical background on an array of topics such as divorce, religion, slavery, and the arts, enabling a slice of female life to be placed in historical perspective. There is an introductory segment describing the use of letters and diaries and problems in editing. Entries are then arranged under form and type divisions (e.g., critical works, anthologies, letters). It is indexed by authors, subjects, locations, and titles.

812. Women's History Sources: A Guide to Archives and Manuscript Collections in the United States. Andrea Hinding et al., eds. New York: Bowker, 1979. 2v. ISBN 0-8352-1103-7.

This two-volume set is considered to be one of the most important contributions to research and scholarship on the history of U.S. women in the last 20 years. It represents an immense undertaking and is the product of several years' effort. Funded by a large grant from the National Endowment for the Humanities, a survey was conducted of nearly 7,000 archives and manuscript repositories regarding their holdings of primary-source materials related to women's history. From the survey and subsequent fieldwork, nearly 1,600 repositories were selected offering more than 18,000 collections in their charge. These collections are composed of personal papers, correspondence, diaries, photographs, organizational records, and oral history tapes, most of which had never been documented. Volume 1 is the main volume and lists the entries arranged alphabetically by state and city. The collection is described in terms of document type, size, date, access, and content. Volume 2 is an index volume providing both subject and geographic access in detailed fashion.

A useful supplementary source is the more recent *Women in the West: A Guide to Manuscript Sources* by Susan Armitage and others (Garland, 1991). This directory identifies the holdings of numerous collections and archives of varied size that document the history of women in the U.S. West over a period of 300 years beginning in 1610.

813. Women's Reference Library series. Detroit: Gale, 1996–. **Women's Almanac 2002.** Doris Weatherford. Phoenix: Oryx Press, 2002. 376p. ISSN 1529-5311. **Women's Reference Library: Women's Chronology, a History of Women's Achievements.** Susan B. Gall and Peggy Saari. 362p. ISBN 0-7876-0660-X. **Women's Reference Library: Prominent Women of the 20th Century.** Peggy Saari. 1996. 4v. ISBN 0-7876-0646-4. ***Women's Voices: A Documentary History of Women in America.** Lorie J. McElroy, ed. Detroit: U*X*L/Gale, 1997. 2v. ISBN 0-7876-0663-4.

This series of volumes follows a similar pattern to others in the publisher's series offering a comprehensive treatment of an ethnic or gender group useful to students from middle grades and junior high school on up. *Women's Almanac* is designed to be a biennial publication and provides an array of information relating to recent news and developments, women's issues, statistical indicators, and brief biographical and career descriptions of significant women throughout history. A timeline is a worthwhile feature.

Women's Chronology traces significant events in women's history from 4000 B.C.E. to 1997 with two timelines showing women's achievements and also parallel world events in their examination significant milestones. *Prominent Women of the 20th Century* is a biographical dictionary furnishing coverage of the lives and careers of 200 prominent women of varied ethnic origins. Scientists, politicians, social activists, athletes, and artists are included among others. *Women's Voices* supplies students with the writings of significant females over the past 200 years. Included here are 32 full-text documents dealing with a variety of women's issues along with introductory narratives and commentary giving analyses of their impact.

*814. Women's Studies Encyclopedia. Rev. and exp. ed. Helen Tierney, ed. Westport, CT: Greenwood Press, 1999. 3v. ISBN 0-313-29620-0.

The first edition of the *Encyclopedia* was issued some 11 years earlier and was acclaimed as a landmark success in bringing a feminist orientation within a historical context in furnishing definitions and descriptive narratives of women's contributions in all fields of endeavor and aspects of life. The current effort is the work of 400 contributors and consultants, and provides expanded coverage in certain needed areas such as violence against women, women in public life, and women in various countries, although emphasis is clearly on the United States. The essay on rape is completely rewritten and the bibliography expanded. New entries have been added where needed. Format has changed considerably from the initial effort with alphabetical arrangement of entries replacing the broad topical approach. The work is available in CD-ROM format that makes use of hyperlinks to related topics.

*815. Women's Studies on Disc 2000. New York: G.K. Hall/Macmillan, 2000. ISBN 0-7838-8879-1. [CD ROM].

Another of the electronic sources from the publisher, the current effort provides a single database for serious inquirers created from the contents of four earlier titles. Designed to be updated on an annual basis, this initial offering includes a 10-year cumulation of *Women's Studies Index* producing more than 60,000 articles and book reviews in over 125 periodicals since 1988, over 16,000 entries from the two volumes of *An Index to Women's Studies Anthologies* by Sara Brownmiller and Ruth Dickstein; some 1,200 titles from Barbara Ryan's *The Women's Movement: References and Resources,* and nearly 1,500 serials from *Women's Periodicals and Newspapers From the 18th Century to 1981* by James P. Danky (G.K. Hall, 1982). The work facilitates access to a wealth of materials, the bulk of which were published in the 1980s and 1990s.

Politics

816. American Political Women: Contemporary and Historical Profiles. Esther Stineman. Littleton, CO: Libraries Unlimited, 1980. 228p. ISBN 0-87287-238-6.

Although the emphasis of this biographical dictionary is on the current scene in U.S. politics at the time of publication, there is an attempt to provide a historical perspective. Inclusions are Jeannette Rankin, Dianne Feinstein, Pat Schroeder, and Bella Abzug. It is selective to be sure, only furnishing 60 biographical sketches of women who operated at various levels of government, from city mayors to congresswomen and presidential advisers. Both students and researchers of recent history will appreciate the lengthy treatment given to women, most of whom served during the 1970s. The sketches are generally two to three pages long. Selected speeches are also included, as are bibliographies for additional reading on each subject. There is a general bibliography, and several useful appendixes provide listings of women in various key positions.

817. Biographical Dictionary of Congressional Women. Karen Foerstel. Westport, CT: Greenwood Press, 1999. 300p. ISBN 0-313-30290-1.

A useful introductory chapter opens the work with a historical description of the conditions that women have faced and in getting elected and then getting top-level committee appointments. The entrenched prejudice and sexism present hurdles to overcome, but indeed have not prevented them from influencing legislative directions. Also in this chapter, there are two charts, one furnishing names of females who have chaired full congressional committees, and the other indicating the number of women who have served as representatives or senators since 1917. Entries are alphabetically arranged and vary in length from several paragraphs to several pages. They focus primarily on the career progression and achievements of some 200 personalities with little attention given to family or background. Some of the entries contain anecdotes to provide a fuller understanding of the individuals. There is a bibliography and indexing is by name and subject.

818. Encyclopedia of Women in American Politics. Jeffrey D. Schultz and Laura van Assendelft, eds. Phoenix: Oryx Press, 1999. 354p. (The American Political Landscape Series). ISBN 1-57356-131-2.

As the first work in the publisher's series, it represents a comprehensive source of information on the involvement and participation of women in the American political process from colonial times to the present. Opening with a substantial introductory essay describing the historical development and progress along with demographics, the main text is composed of more than 700 entries alphabetically arranged. They vary in length from a single paragraph given to biographical entries to several pages given to important concepts or issues. Biographical treatment is given to every woman elected or appointed to Federal office, and many at the state and local level as well. Contributors are 56 academic scholars who furnished narratives of pertinent aspects including movements, legislation, case law, and more. A useful special feature is the timeline covering the past century and a half.

The Almanac of Women and Minorities in American Politics by Mart Martin (Boulder, CO: Westview Press, 1999) is not limited to women but includes racial minorities and gay/lesbian participation. Each group is treated in a separate chapter in this comprehensive source. Like others, the chapter on women opens with a chronology, and then provides a descriptive narrative of political accomplishments and progressive development. Statistical tables identify voting percentages; additionally, there are a roster of political accomplishments and biographical sketches of major figures.

819. From Suffrage to the Senate: An Encyclopedia of American Women in Politics. Suzanne O. Schenken. Santa Barbara, CA: ABC-CLIO, 1999. 2v. ISBN 0-87436-960-6.

The author has published other titles on the topic, and in this case has produced a comprehensive source of information furnishing nearly 700 alphabetically arranged entries beginning with a biographical sketch of Grace Abbot and ending with an identification and explanation of the YWCA. Coverage is from precolonial times to the present and descriptive narrative is given for various aspects relevant to political activity of females. These include significant personalities, events, key court cases, organizations, legislation, and important issues. Entries vary in size from one-paragraph identifications to two-page expositions of especially important issues, and conclude with brief bibliographies. The table of contents supplies topical categorical of entries, and the appendixes contain historical documents, statistical listings of women in public office, and a chronology. The work concludes with a general bibliography and an index.

820. Modern First Ladies. Nancy K. Smith and Mary C. Ryan, ed. Washington, D.C.: National Archives and Records Administration, 1989. 184p. ISBN 0-911333-73-8.

Written for a popular audience, this work is designed to trace the evolution of the position of first lady throughout the twentieth century. As bureaucracy has grown, so has the "office" of the first lady, resulting in a large staff generating considerable documentation. This guide covers documentary materials available for research on 14 first ladies. They are treated in essays that survey their activities and place them in the historical context of their respective presidential administrations. Edith Roosevelt, Helen Taft, Ellen Wilson, and Edith Wilson are grouped in one essay because their papers are all in the Manuscript Division of the Library of Congress. The others, ranging from Lou Henry Hoover to Nancy Reagan, each receive a separate chapter. This basic guide is useful as a starting point for further research.

Two more recent works are *American First Ladies: Their Lives and Their Legacy,* edited by Lewis L. Gould (Garland, 1996) and *First Ladies: A Biographical Dictionary,* Dorothy Schneider and Carl Schneider (Facts on File, 2001). In *American First Ladies,* for each first lady there is a portrait, a chronology of her life, an evaluation of her place in developing the role of first lady, precedents set, important news coverage and scholarly writings, her own writings, and the location of her personal papers and other manuscript sources. Each account presents the problems and controversies, and gives a sense of personality. The subject index is exhaustive. The Facts on File title includes 56 black-and-white photographs, a bibliography, chronologies, and an index.

821. Women and the American Left: A Guide to Sources. Mari J. Buhle. Boston: G.K. Hall, 1983. 281p. (G.K. Hall Women's Studies Publications). ISBN 0-8161-8195-0.

This annotated bibliography on the role of women and the U.S. Left identifies nearly 600 entries concerning the "woman question" written over a period of 110 years from 1871 to 1981. Entries represent books, articles, and pamphlets and include biographies, autobiographies, fiction, plays, and poetry. The question as to what role women could play in furthering the cause of the working class while pushing their agenda for liberation is addressed in a variety of ways through these materials. Entries are organized under four time periods relevant to the U.S. Left, 1871–1900, 1901–1919, 1920–1964, and 1965–1981, then subdivided by form and format. Annotations are full and detailed, describing the scope and content of the documents chosen; they range from one paragraph to a full page. Full bibliographic data is given. There is a dictionary-style index combining authors, titles, and subjects for easy access.

822. Women in Modern American Politics: A Bibliography 1900–1995. Washington, D.C.: Congressional Quarterly, 1997. 414p. ISBN 1-56802-133-X.

This is comprehensive in its inclusion of writings issued throughout the twentieth century, but is limited to books, book chapters, and periodical articles. It does not treat government documents, audio-visual materials, newspaper articles, or electronic resources. There are 6,000 citations organized efficiently into broad subject categories to political involvement at various levels ("Movement and Advocacy," "Participation in Voting," "Political Theory," "Public Institutions," etc.) which themselves are subdivided into smaller subsections or subtopics. This facilitates the search for relevant items and helps to isolate sources on such issues as "abortion rights," "affirmative action," and "sex discrimination." About 2,000 of the citations represent publications issued since 1980, providing evidence of increasing awareness and political involvement in recent years.

823. Women in the United States Military, 1901–1995: A Research Guide and Annotated Bibliography. Vicki L. Friedl, comp. Westport, CT: Greenwood Press, 1996. 251p. (Research Guides in Military Studies, no. 9). ISBN 0-313-29657-X.

Compiled by a librarian, this work could serve as a model research guide. In the introductory chapter, "Conducting Research," Friedl gives an outline of steps to follow in conducting research and a guide to sources of information on women in the armed forces. The compiler combed online databases, online catalogs, journal indexes, bibliographies and dissertation indexes. Popular reading is excluded, but the scholarly resources covered include books, research reports, conference papers, archival materials, government documents and journal articles. Also included are student papers from the service schools and interviews, in journals, diaries, biographies, and histories. The 857 full bibliographic, annotated entries are organized into military units, subjects, time periods, and types of publications. The majority of the entries are for publications in the last 20 years. The annotations are evaluative. There are indexes by author, title, and subject. Appendixes cover archival resources, women's military organizations, a chronology of women's service from 1901 up to the Gulf War, and a listing of Web pages. The work is thorough. Recommended for all libraries serving students and researchers.

Although intended to be a general work, *Women and the Military: An Encyclopedia* by Victoria Sherrow (ABC-CLIO, 1996) is almost entirely devoted to women in the U.S. military. The alphabetic organization includes over 400 entries for individuals, events, laws, court cases, organizations, wars, and the military branches. The introduction surveys women's contributions to military operations throughout history. Articles are cross-referenced and provide citations for further reading. There are photographs, a bibliography, and an index.

824. Women of Congress: A Twentieth-Century Odyssey. Marcy Kaptur. Washington, D.C.: Congressional Quarterly, 1996. 256p. ISBN 0-87187-989-1.

In describing the degree of participation by women at federal legislative levels, the author (a congresswoman) has made it clear why this source was published. Fewer than 200 females have served as senators and representatives at the time of publication and there has been little documentation of their lives and careers. She furnishes detailed profiles of 15 of those personalities organized under three chronological periods. Coverage begins with the period from 1917 to World War II and treats such individuals as Jeannette Rankin; this is followed by World War II to the 1960s (the greening age) and supplies coverage of Margaret Chase Smith and others. Finally she examines the modern period with such lawmakers as Shirley Chisum and Pat Schroeder. Each section is given a historical overview summarizing the struggles and achievements during that time. Entries provide useful perspective of these 15 females in examining their lives, careers, issues and points of view. The final segment of the work supplies charts and tables of brief biographical and career data of all the women who have served in Congress.

825. Women Patriots of the American Revolution: A Biographical Dictionary. Charles E. Claghorn. Metuchen, NJ: Scarecrow, 1991. 519p. ISBN 0-8108-2421-3.

The information contained in this dictionary is brief for most of the entries. There are short biographical sketches for 600 women and a separate section listing another 4,500, with references to the sources in which they are mentioned. The work seems to include all women not classified as Loyalists for which *any* information was found, rather than those who were truly patriots. The main biographical sketches include the state in which the woman lived and the source of the information, indicated by a code to sources explained in a table at the front of the work. This work is useful for students and researchers for the number of names and the references to information sources it contains.

Education, Professions, Trades

826. American Women Historians, 1700s–1900s: A Biographical Dictionary. Jennifer Scanlon and Shaaron Cosner. Westport, CT: Greenwood Press, 1996. 269p. ISBN 0-313-29664-2.

This is a comprehensive biographical dictionary in its treatment of 200 female historians in this country over a span of 200 years. Selection of personalities for inclusion was based on their influence or accomplishment in the field determined by their publications or acknowledged contributions to the development of their field of inquiry. Entries are fairly uniform in size ranging from one to two pages in length and providing standard biographical and career information (family, education, employment, achievements, and so forth and close with a bibliography both by and about the individual. Various types of careers are treated such as academic historians, writers of popular history, biographers, and administrators, with all fields of history represented. There is an understandable emphasis on those who study U.S. history. Some photographs are included, and a detailed index facilitates access.

827. American Women Managers and Administrators: A Selective Biographical Dictionary of Twentieth-Century Leaders in Business, Education, and Government. Judith A. Leavitt. Westport, CT: Greenwood, 1985. 317p. ISBN 0-313-23748-4.

Included in this biographical dictionary are sketches of over 225 women who held prominent positions in business, education, or government. In addition to giving credit to women who were "first" to serve in their capacities, the book lauds those who have been recognized for major accomplishments in their fields of management or who founded businesses and educational institutions. The sketches are brief but informative and include bibliographies of materials both by and about the subject. Arrangement of entries is alphabetical; there appears to be a good balance of early leaders such as Jeannette Rankin and contemporary figures such as Elizabeth Dole. Sketches of current personalities may well include quotations on their style of management taken from the returned questionnaires. A list of "firsts" appears in the appendix; both a bibliography and an index are furnished.

828. Historical Dictionary of Women's Education in the United States. Linda Eisenmann, ed. Westport, CT: Greenwood Press, 1998. 552p. ISBN 0-313-29323-6.

Targeted to a wide audience ranging from researchers and scholars to students and laypersons, this well-constructed and useful work focuses on the history of women's education. The intention is to place emphasis on the social trends, describe the diversity among various societal groups of females, and treat education in a broad sense through examination of both formal and informal activities. There are 245 entries, signed by more than 100 contributors with coverage given to the examination of important events, personalities, organizations, and movements relevant to historical development of education of women. Entries are arranged alphabetically, average about two pages in length, and contain bibliographies. Special features include a substantive introduction, a timeline of important events, bibliography, and list of contributors. A well-designed index provides access.

829. Historical Encyclopedia of American Women Entrepreneurs: 1776 to the Present. Jeannette M. Oppedisano. Westport, CT: Greenwood Press, 2000. 312p. ISBN 0-313-30647-8.

This is a useful source of information on some 100 women who achieved in a variety of business enterprises and influenced the economic system at different levels ranging from national to local impact in both the private and public sector. Covering a period from 1776 to the present time, biographical sketches of the famous (Jane Addams, Elizabeth Arden, Mary Baker Eddy, Mary McCloud Bethune, Oprah Winfrey, etc.) as well as the not so famous (Ninnie Baird, Molly Haley, Helen Schultz, etc.) are presented in a readable and interesting manner. Sketches average from two to four pages in length and examine the backgrounds and careers of businesswomen, educators, social scientists, economists, and others. Emphasis is placed on their personal and business philosophies, perseverance and hard work, creative genius, and philanthropic efforts. A detailed index furnishes access to names, organizations, and businesses.

830. Women in Agriculture: A Guide to Research. Marie Maman and Thelma Tate. New York: Garland Publishing, 1996. 308p. ISBN 0-8153-1354-3.

This work identifies and describes more than 700 sources of information on women in agriculture. Emphasis is on the United States but coverage is international with respect to events, personalities, and issues treated. Sources vary in depth and in scholarly endeavor with the inclusion of books, journals, dissertations, and electronic resources, most of which were issued between 1985 and 1995. Data is organized into sections representing such categories as historical studies, sexual division of labor, education, and women's role in agricultural economic development. The authors are reference librarians who selected their sources on the basis of accessibility to students and teachers. There are separate sections on French-language sources, bibliographies, and relevant journals.

Women's Work in Britain and America from the Nineties to World War I: An Annotated Bibliography by Mary D. McFeely (G.K. Hall, 1982) supplies an annotated listing of more than 500 books (including fiction), pamphlets, essays, and periodical articles published between 1890 and 1980. Included here are writings on the subject of women's work in both England and the United States during a brief historical period preceding World War I. The bibliography is divided into two major sections, one for each country, providing useful resource material for comparative study. Major considerations are treated such as work in shops, factories, social organizations, and agencies.

Suffrage, Feminism, and Liberation

*831. Documents from the Women's Liberation Movement: An On-Line Archival Collection. Durham, NC: Duke University Special Collections Library. Available: http://scriptorium.lib.duke.edu/wlm.

This is a useful Web site providing full-text copy of a selection of documents from the Duke University Special Collections Library relating to the origins of the Women's Liberation Movement in the early 1960s and late 1970s. The documents were selected in 1997 by a professor at the university teaching a course in "Social History of the American Woman" with the help of two colleagues from other institutions. Organization is under eight subject categories: general and theoretical; medical and reproductive rights; music; organizations and activism; sexuality and lesbian feminism; socialist feminism; women of color; and women's work and roles. Keyword searching is also possible. In addition, there are links to a few related sites. There is a statement informing the user that the Special Collections Library continues to acquire materials on the topic.

832. Historical and Multicultural Encyclopedia of Female Reproductive Rights in the United States. Judith A. Baer, ed. Westport, CT: Greenwood Press, 2002. 270p. ISBN 0-313-30644-3.

The most recent reference source on one of the most controversial and important issues facing women today, the work is edited by a political science professor and is designed to meet the needs of college-level students and their instructors. The nature of this issue is examined in the introductory pages examining the range of claims with respect to the implications of the right to decide whether, when, and how to bear children. Contributors are respected authorities, for the most part academics, who were solicited to examine the various political, legal and cultural aspects. Topics are alphabetically arranged and the entries treat such elements as age, class education, health, religion, and of course, child-rearing practices. Treatment is given to the experience of females of minority racial and ethnic groups in separate articles. It represents an important source of information in the area of women's studies

833. A History of the American Suffragist Movement. Doris Weatherford. Santa Barbara, CA: ABC-CLIO, 1998. ISBN 1-57607-065-4.

The author is an academic in women's studies and has performed a valuable service in producing what amounts to a reworked, condensed, and revised edition of the original six-volume history by Elizabeth Cady Stanton, *History of Women's Suffrage, 1848–1920* (repr. Ayers, 1979). The Stanton work has long been considered the official history of the movement in providing a collection of autobiographical accounts by numerous suffragists. As initially written, however, it is not well organized and is wanting in terms of accessibility. Weatherford provides readers with a well-written coherent history telling the "fascinating story of the struggle for suffrage" and acknowledges that it supplies only a fraction of the details available in the Stanton effort. At the same time, it enlarges the scope by beginning the coverage in 1637. The important thing is that it presents the thoughts of the suffragists themselves in clear and lucid manner. It is important now, as it was then, to examine the ideas and activities of Stanton, Susan B. Anthony, and other pioneers.

834. Significant Contemporary American Feminists: A Biographical Sourcebook. Jennifer Scanlon. Westport, CT: Greenwood Press, 1999. 361p. ISBN 0-313-30125-5.

A useful effort by an academic in women's studies, the work serves to identify leading feminists of our time in its focus on "second-wave" activists. Fifty personalities (all female) were chosen for inclusion by a panel in this highly selective initial title, leaving open the possibility of subsequent works. The women are diverse in their career patterns but deemed to have been influential, and include such personalities as Ruth Bader Ginsburg, Gloria Steinem, and Judy Chicago. Entries are signed and alphabetically arranged with enough detail to provide substantive information. Each entry concludes with a selective bibliography by and about the individual. A bibliography of significant titles on second- and third-wave feminism is furnished at the end, along with a detailed index.

835. Women and Feminism in American History: A Guide to Information Sources. Elizabeth Tingley and Donald F. Tingley. Detroit: Gale, 1981. 289p. (Gale Information Guide Library; American Government and History Information Guide Series, v. 12.) ISBN 0-8103-1477-0.

With coverage given to works on suffrage, equality, and activity promulgating action necessary for women to obtain their rightful status, this annotated bibliography aims to provide access to sources of information relevant in a historical or contemporary context. Entries to books and collections are arranged in 22 chapters under three major divisions. The first part covers general resources such as manuscript collections, biographical directories, and periodical titles, whereas the second segment furnishes chapters on historical periods through the 1920s. The third section contains topical chapters regarding the status of women as well as their societal role and impact. The tool will be helpful to the student and nonspecialist with its ample listings of book titles. Annotations are brief. Author, title, and subject indexes furnish access.

836. Women and Sexuality in America: A Bibliography. Nancy A. Sahli. Boston: G.K. Hall, 1984. 404p. (G.K. Hall Women's Studies Publications.) ISBN 0-8161-8099-7.

This annotated bibliography contains nearly 1,700 entries under 15 topical chapters covering such issues as "Children and Adolescents," "Sexual Dysfunction," "Lesbians," "Psycho-Analytic Views," and "Adolescent Sexuality," The purpose is to document the changing perspective of female sexuality as expressed in the professional literature of this country during the nineteenth and twentieth centuries. Each chapter opens with a brief historical description, which is then followed by the annotated entries. Entries identify books drawn primarily from the social and behavioral sciences (history, sociology, psychiatry, and medicine). Then follow listings of periodical titles representing the same disciplines. This work is useful for both students and beginning researchers who wish to study trends from a historical perspective. Both an author/title index and a subject index assure access.

837. The Women's Liberation Movement in America. Kathleen Berkeley. Westport, CT: Greenwood Press, 1999. 225p. ISBN 0-313-29875-0.

The work serves as an introductory critical history of the movement in this country from World War I to the 1990s, but opens with a chronology of events that takes the user a little closer to the present up to the Clinton-Lewinsky matter. This is followed by a descriptive essay explaining the Movement. Following that is the main text, well organized and divided into six major sections furnishing narrative chronological coverage. The history begins with a view from the past in which the seeds of feminism emerged prior to the twentieth century. The remaining segments represent a coherent account of the suffrage movement, addressing the demand for equal rights, emergence of the Women's Liberation Movement in the 1960s, progressive activity surrounding the Equal Rights Amendment, the feminist agenda, and backlash from the political Right. The history concludes with an epilogue regarding the future. Special features are a biographical section treating 13 key figures, a selection of 15 documents, a glossary, and bibliography.

*838. The Women's Movement in the United States: An Interactive Encyclopedia. Santa Barbara, CA: ABC-CLIO Interactive, 1999. ISBN 1-57607-135-9. [CD-ROM].

This is the first of the publisher's interactive encyclopedias (see entries 546, 594, 838, 942, and 1102) providing access to an accompanying Web site, and is designed to facilitate the search for information by students of all ages. They are then able to organize the information and utilize it for their schoolwork. This title supplies some 700 articles of varying length covering the topic from colonial times to the present. Entries treat various aspects including specialized movements such as abolition, events like the "Triangle Shirtwaist Fire," court cases, organizations, major publications and pieces of legislation, relevant definitions. Advantages of the CD-ROM format enable the user to key into images, audio and video clips, primary-source documents, and more.

Science, Technology, and Medicine

839. American Women in Science, 1950 to the Present: A Biographical Dictionary. Martha J. Bailey. Santa Barbara, CA: ABC-CLIO, 1998. 455p. ISBN 0-87436-921-5.

This volume supplements and extends Bailey's *American Women in Science: A Biographical Dictionary* (ABC-CLIO, 1994) in which biographical treatment was furnished for 400 career women who began their career in the sciences prior to 1950. The current effort is similar in structure and format, providing biographical and career coverage of more than 300 female scientists either born since 1920 or who had begun their careers subsequent to 1950 and have careers represented by either the National Academy of Sciences or the National Academy of Engineering or who had contributed to their fields in nontraditional ways. This extends the scope to include sociologists and others from popular or pseudo-scientific areas, although the bulk of the entries treat scholars and writers. The work opens with an introductory essay providing an overview of significant issues. Entries are alphabetically arranged and supply full name, dates of birth and death, profession, education, career history, and marital status along with a one-page documented biographical sketch.

840. American Women in Technology: An Encyclopedia. Linda Zierdt-Warshaw et al. Santa Barbara, CA: ABC-CLIO, 2000. 384p. ISBN 1-57607-072-7.

This is a useful source of information for students at the high school and college undergraduate level in providing biographical sketches of more than 300 women along with various subject areas in science and technology. Designed in part, to encourage females to consider the possibilities of careers in these male-dominated fields, the *Encyclopedia* corrects any misconceptions that may exist. Biographical coverage is of a wide range of personalities engaged in professional pursuits from the eighteenth century to the present day. Entries also treat various technology disciplines, associations, laboratories, awards and numerous related topics, and vary in length from a half page or less to three pages. Each one contains a brief bibliography for further reading. Appendixes supply tables of award-winners, inductees to the Women's Hall of Fame, and more. There is a general bibliography that includes articles and Web sites along with books.

841. Ladies in the Laboratory? American and British Women in Science, 1800–1900: A Survey of Their Contributions to Research. Mary R. Creese and Thomas M. Creese. Lanham, MD: Scarecrow Press, 1998. 452p. ISBN 0-8108-3287-9.

This well-written work is a combination of biographical reference source and social history of female contributions in two countries during the nineteenth century. It is organized into three major parts; the "life sciences," "mathematical, physical, and earth sciences," and the "social sciences, " and supplies chapters covering individual disciplines. Inclusion of the social sciences broadens the concept of science to include those who worked in anthropology and in psychology. Using the *Catalogue of Scientific Papers 1800–1900* (Royal Society, 1914–1925), the authors identified 680 females from both the United States and the United Kingdom. The style of presentation is that of continuous narrative that includes biographical sketches ranging from a few paragraphs to several pages emphasizing career and professional lives within each discipline. Of great value is the extensive bibliography furnishing citations to the works of all 680 women.

A Biographical Dictionary of Women Healers: Midwives, Nurses, and Physicians by Laurie Scrivener and J. Suzanne Barnes (Oryx, 2002) supplies biographical sketches of 240 women identified as healers and providing services in this country and in Canada. Some of these people were formally trained in the sciences and others practiced the art over a span of time beginning with the colonial period and continuing to the present day. Each entry contains a bibliography for additional reading.

842. Women in the Scientific Search: An American Bio-Bibliography, 1724–1979. Patricia J. Siegel and Kay T. Finley. Metuchen, NJ: Scarecrow, 1985. 399p. ISBN 0-8108-1755-1.

This title attempts to furnish information on an array of U.S. female scientists spanning a period of 250 years. It should be noted that only a few of the more than 150 women covered date back to the eighteenth century. Arrangement of entries is chronological under scientific discipline (anthropology, archaeology, biochemistry, zoology). Brief biographical sketches are furnished that appear to be accurate and well developed. There are a number of omissions, which is to be expected of a work of this type. Included with all entries is a bibliography of works about the subjects (not by them), making this more of a tool for the undergraduate than the scholar. An annotated section of general biographical works introduces the listings.

Journalism and the Press

843. American Women's Magazines: An Annotated Historical Guide. Nancy K. Humphreys. New York: Garland, 1989. 303p. (Garland Reference Library of the Humanities, v. 789.) ISBN 0-8240-7543-9.

Designed to expedite research and inquiry, this recent annotated bibliography is viewed by its author as an introductory compilation of writings about women's magazines. Nearly 900 entries are presented here, drawn from nearly 30 indexes and abstracting services. Entries are arranged alphabetically in one of the two major divisions: alternative and mainstream publications. Articles for mainstream newspapers were purposely excluded; only periodicals in the English language are covered. The time span ranges from the later nineteenth century to the late 1980s. Alternative publications are subdivided into sections on earlier magazines for women's rights and on feminist periodicals from the 1960s on. Mainstream publications are classed as nineteenth-century ladies' magazines, twentieth-century women's magazines, women's pages in newspapers, and romance/confession magazines. Annotations are brief but informative; there is a subject index.

844. Women's Periodicals in the United States: Social and Political Issues. Kathleen L. Endres and Therese L. Lueck, eds. Westport, CT: Greenwood Press, 1996. 529p. (Historical Guides to the World's Periodicals and Newspapers.) ISBN 0-313-28632-9.

The editors have provided an excellent service in their preparation of two useful companion guides giving detailed profiles of 76 women's periodicals addressing social and political conditions issued during the period 1835 to 1984 in this country. These were judged to be significant and selection was based on frequency of mention in reputable publications such as reference books and histories as well as historical reputation of editors, and the popularity of the periodical itself. A number of titles were excluded due to their relatively quick demise. Entries are signed and arranged alphabetically, and supply carefully researched descriptions of the history, editorial orientation, and affiliation to any organizations. They run from 3 to 12 pages in length and include data on title changes, editors, and circulation. An appendix gives a chronology of the titles included.

One year earlier, the editors had produced a work of similar nature and part of the same series as the title above. *Women's Periodicals in the United States: Consumer Magazines* (Greenwood Press, 1995) profiles 75 women's consumer magazines of popular nature published from the nineteenth century to the present. Titles vary in substance and in orientation ranging from "Barbie" meant for a children's audience to *Ms. Magazine,* but does not treat titles of the women's movement.

845. Women's Press Organizations, 1881–1999. Elizabeth V. Burt, ed. Westport, CT: Greenwood Press, 2000. 348p. ISBN 0-313-30661-3.

As a topic rarely covered in the historical reference literature, this directory of nearly 40 women's press organizations is a welcome addition to any reference collection serving the needs of journalists or researchers in women's studies. Organizations are treated in alphabetical sequence from "American Women in Radio and Television, 1951–Present" to Women's Press Organizations of Missouri, 1996–Present." They range from large groups with national membership to smaller units of regional, state, or local importance. Not all the organizations are still in operation. The beginning year for organizations of this type was 1881, and they have enjoyed a rich history. Each entry is authored by a different contributor, and contains a historical essay regarding the origins of the group, membership details, activities, issues, and achievements. Footnotes are provided and there is a summary of important facts. The work concludes with a chronology, a bibliography, and an index.

Race and Religion

846. Encyclopedia of American Women and Religion. June M. Benowitz. Santa Barbara, CA: ABC-CLIO, 1998. 466p. ISBN 0-87436-887-1.

An award-winning reference source, this work provides a comprehensive view of the role and impact of females in different religious groups, established mainstream and less familiar denominations as well as quasi-religious groups Included here are Episcopalians, Shakers, Jews, Native American tribes, witches, and so forth. There are more than 300 entries arranged alphabetically, furnishing biographical sketches, issues, events, and topics. Personalities differ widely and represent a diverse array of women such as Shirley MacLaine, Tammy Faye Baker, and Harriet Tubman. Topical entries treat issues like abortion and birth control, movements like feminist theology, and organizations like the Young Women's Christian Association. Photographs are included in many cases, and each entry furnishes cross-references to relevant sources. There is a chronology and useful general bibliography, and an index provides access.

847. Women of Color in the United States: A Guide to the Literature. Bernice Redfern. New York: Garland, 1989. 156p. (Garland Reference Library of Social Science, v. 469.) ISBN 0-8240-5849-6.

One of the products of the recently awakened interest in people of color is this listing of over 630 entries on the experience of the non-Caucasian female. The work contains four major divisions covering Afro-American women, Asian American women, Hispanic American women, and Native American women. Included are books, articles, chapters, and dissertations published since the mid-1970s. Each of the four chapters begins with a summary of the available literature, which should prove useful to serious inquirers. These are followed by subdivisions based on form and format (e.g., bibliographies, life histories, etc.). There are topical segments as well (history and politics, literature and the arts). Emphasis is placed on scholarly contributions, and only those popular works deemed significant are included. Both author and subject indexes are furnished, the latter providing good access to the various topics.

848. Women Religious History Sources: A Guide to Repositories in the United States. Evangeline Thomas et al., eds. New York: Bowker, 1983. 329p. ISBN 0-8352-1681-0.

This is a useful guide and directory to the collections and archival repositories of nearly 575 women's religious communities in this country. Arrangement of entries is by state, then by city. Entries furnish location and holdings information obtained through a survey funded by the National Endowment for the Humanities, which took four years to complete. Of real value is the brief but informative historical description of each religious community. Coverage is given to those female devotees identified as sisters or nuns in the Catholic, Orthodox, and Episcopal churches and to the deaconesses in the Lutheran, Methodist, and Mennonite churches. There is a useful glossary as well as a 16-page bibliography. Appendixes furnish a chronological listing of founders, with references to appropriate entry. There is a main-entry name index.

Law and Crime

849. Encyclopedia of Women and Crime. Nicole H. Rafter, ed. Phoenix: Oryx Press, 2001. 392p. ISBN 1-57356-214-9.

As the first comprehensive reference book treating the relationship of women to crime, both as victims and perpetrators, this is a groundbreaking encyclopedia designed to meet the needs of college-level students, instructors, attorneys, officials, and researchers. Although the coverage is international in scope, emphasis is on the United States. The volume supplies 240 signed entries contributed by more than 200 authorities that examine crime, victims and victimology, policing, courts, and the legal process. Entries cover issues and individuals from the nineteenth century to the year of publication; they vary in length from a single paragraph to several pages and are arranged alphabetically. Included are the earliest accounts of criminal acts to the most recent issues, and treatment is given to an array of topics such as "aggression," "elderly victims," and "shoplifting," as well as personalities like Lizzie Borden and Ma Barker. Large topics like "battered women and self-defense" are examined through separate essays for various countries allowing for international comparisons. Of value is the "Topic Finder" enabling the user to retrieve all relevant entries. Indexing is by subject and by name.

850. Feminist Jurisprudence Emerging From Plato's Cave: A Research Guide. Frances S. Holland. Lanham MD: Scarecrow Press, 1996. 193p. ISBN 0-8108-3141-4.

This annotated bibliography is the first of its kind in furnishing students and scholars with an excellent starting point for their research or inquiry into the topic of feminist jurisprudence. It examines and evaluates some 200 print publications of various types (books, journals, newsletters, etc.) issued from 1976 through 1993. The first two chapters provide introductory material. Chapter 1 supplies information pertinent to the development of research strategies (listings of keywords, databases, major authors, etc.) and chapter 2 furnishes definitions of feminist jurisprudence in giving the basics of major feminist theories. Entries treating the publications follow organized under pertinent topics (religion, family, politics, criminal, etc.). Entries provide useful data on the publications relating to their scope, depth of coverage, and dates, as well as cross-references. An index aids access.

851. Women's Rights on Trial: 101 Historic Trials. . . Frost Knappman. Detroit: Gale, 1997. 478p. ISBN 0-7876-0384-8.

In recent years, publishers have become more interested in relationships between the law and various life practices of females. Each entry of this useful effort opens with the major facts (plaintiff, defendant, lawyers, dates, verdict, and sentence) accessible at a glance in boxed sidebars. This is followed by a narrative essay of 1,000 to 2,000 words examining the conduct and events of the proceedings, appellate rulings, and impact. Just over 100 trials involving women from colonial times to the 1990s are organized under six broad topical divisions; crimes of conscience and nonconformity; crime and punishment; rights and responsibilities of citizenship; reproductive rights; marriage, parenting, and divorce; and women at work. Included are the Salem witch trials, *Roe* v. *Wade,* and the Tailhook scandal among others, all of which set legal precedents within their times.

Sports and Entertainment

852. The All-American Girls Professional Baseball League Record Book: Comprehensive Hitting, Fielding, and Pitching Statistics. W.C. Madden. Jefferson, NC: McFarland, 2000. 294p. ISBN 0-7864-0597-X.

Subsequent to the motion picture, *A League of Their Own* (1992) there has been a growing interest in professional baseball as played by women during the 1940s and 1950s. The author is a former newspaper editor and journalism who, earlier, had authored a biographical dictionary of these female athletes (see below), and more recently has contributed this book of records to add to others published by McFarland. Both individual and team records are enumerated in this effort that begins with a history of the league. Also included are team rosters, and the detailed treatment of statistics regarding fielding, hitting, and pitching records of all women who played in the league during its 12-year history. Photographs of important events and key players are included. An index furnishes access.

Madden's earlier work, *The Women of the All-American Girls Professional Baseball League: A Biographical Dictionary* (McFarland, 1997) now serves as a companion to the title above. Profiles of more than 600 women of the 700 who played in the league are given. Such data as date and place of birth, height, weight, position, team, active seasons, and career statistics precede biographical treatment describing the entry to the league, career highlights, and life after baseball. Photographs are included.

853. American Women in Sport, 1887–1987: A 100-Year Chronology. Ruth M. Sparhawk et al., comps. Metuchen, NJ: Scarecrow, 1989. 149p. ISBN 0-8108-2205-9.

Providing a quick overview of the achievements of U.S. female athletes since the Victorian period, this first-of-its-kind chronology is divided into four periods. These periods are determined by the social perspective toward women engaged in sports: the pre-organizational era, 1887–1916; the organizational years, 1917–1956; the competitive period, 1957–1971; and, finally, the Title IX period, 1972–1987. Entries are arranged chronologically within each time period for which names and accomplishments are enumerated. The gradual changes from individual to group or team competition can be studied in terms of their social acceptability. Included are large numbers of individuals and their feats; they range from very famous figures such as Babe Didrikson Zaharias and Billie Jean King to obscure and all-but-forgotten heroines for a day. Included is a bibliography for further reference and inquiry. There are indexes by name and by sport.

854. Celebrating Women's Coaches: A Biographical Dictionary. Nena R. Hawkes and John F. Seggar. Westport, CT: Greenwood Press, 2000. 312p. ISBN 0-313-30912-4.

Although not free of stylistic errors, the work provides a useful addition to areas dealing with either physical education or women's studies in its unique focus on female coaches. This career endeavor has long been ignored even if coverage of women in athletics has improved. This biographical dictionary presents profiles of 42 contemporary women coaches in an array of sports from lacrosse to basketball, selected because of their success or through recommendations from other female coaches. Information was gathered through telephone interviews and responses to questionnaires. Entries are detailed and run several pages in length, and provide adequate coverage of personal and career backgrounds in their examination of the formative years, sport participation and playing career, and coaching and their decision to become a coach. But most telling is the exposition of the individual's coaching philosophy and her perception of changes in athletes.

855. Encyclopedia of Women and Sport in America. Carol A. Oglesby et al., eds. Phoenix: Oryx Press, 1998. 384p. ISBN 0-897-74993-6.

This is a comprehensive treatment furnishing insight into the historical background, impact, organizations, events, individual sports, and issues as well as important personalities. It is an extraordinary source in its provision of opinion commentary as well as factual description. Opinion essays examine controversial matters such as the role of the media, and provide the viewpoints of the authors (sports educators, writers, scientists, athletes, etc.) and are printed on gray paper. Entries are alphabetically arranged and signed in some cases by their contributors. They are presented in informal manner for easy reading and include about 140 biographical articles of leading athletes over the years. Designed for the benefit of users from junior high school age to adulthood, this work is well illustrated and furnishes a useful bibliography.

Encyclopedia of Women and Sports by Victoria Sherrow (ABC-CLIO, 1996) is similar to the above work in its focus on the United States and supplies nearly 600 well-written entries on people, events, and individual sports. Included are teams, court cases and legislation, accomplishments, and feats. It opens with an introduction and furnishes cross-references and photographs within the entries, and a bibliography at the end.

856. Funny Women: American Comediennes, 1860–1985. Mary Unterbrink. Jefferson, NC: McFarland, 1987. 267p. ISBN 0-89950-226-1.

About 80 female performers, mostly from the twentieth century, are given generally good biographical coverage. Entries vary from less than a full page to seven pages in length. Comedy routines had their origins in the days of stage and vaudeville; such performers are well represented here, including Fanny Brice, Mae West, and Sophie Tucker. Those who made their impact on radio, television, and film are not neglected, and there is ample coverage of the familiar funny ladies of today, such as Goldie Hawn and Lily Tomlin. The work is divided into eight chapters, beginning with the early days of radio and finishing with a segment on rising stars. Several of these rising stars, like Whoopi Goldberg and Elayne Boosler, have since achieved success. There is an index of personal names, titles, and awards.

THE HISPANIC EXPERIENCE

Like other ethnic groups, Hispanic Americans have received increased documentation in the trade literature since the 1970s. Reference sources and bibliographic tools also seem to have kept pace in the recent decade. One of the tools (entry 866) defines Hispanics in terms of a pure Spanish origin. In this section, Mexican Americans are treated separately as are Puerto Ricans and Cuban Americans. General sources are described first. As is the case for other groups, race and ethnicity are the most important criteria in the organization of this work. One finds resources on the female experience, education, and social activism relevant to Hispanic American history. Exceptions are the resources on genealogy, that are found in the "Genealogy and Immigration" section previously in this chapter, and those on Hispanics in cinema found in the section titled "Popular Culture: Entertainment, Recreation,

Sports," later in this chapter. For related material on Puerto Rico and its people, see chapter 2, "Regional History," under "Territories and Dependencies."

Since 1978, *Hispanic American Periodicals Index* (*HAPI*) has been issued through the UCLA Latin American Center (available at http://www.isop.ucla.edu/lac) on an annual basis. Now available online, it identifies historical topics at times but emphasis is on current conditions in Latin America. Some 400 journals are indexed, many of which cover Hispanics in the United States.

The Hispanic Society of America (available at http://www.hispanicsociety.org) addresses both history and culture and was founded in 1904 in New York City. There are some 400 members today.

General Sources

857. Atlas of Hispanic-American History. George Ochoa. New York: Checkmark Books/ Facts on File, 2001. 214p. (Facts on File Library of American History). ISBN 0-8160-3698-5.

The author is a prolific writer and specialist in the area, and has produced a comprehensive source of information for students and others. Following an introduction, the content is divided into nine chapters in chronological sequence. They cover origins and roots of Hispanic America, the Spanish period, emergence of the new world culture, the impact of manifest destiny, transitional period, the World Wars, La Raza Unida and civil rights, changing community, and finally the current conditions. These different periods are examined through nearly 80 maps as well as photographs, illustrations, and chronologies enhancing the narrative and providing insight into the complex political and social history. One is able to understand the many influences that have enriched the culture. Major personalities, migrations, events and such controversial issues topics such as Puerto Rican statehood, labor rights, and the Zoot Suit Riots are described.

858. Census Records for Latin America and the Hispanic United States. Lyman D. Platt. Baltimore: Genealogical Publishing, 1998. 198p. ISBN 0-8063-1555-5.

Of use to both historians and genealogists, this work provides a comprehensive inventory and directory of some 4,000 census records located in Latin America and the United States. Included for coverage are Spanish North America, Central America, South America, and parts of the United States. Records date back to the sixteenth century to the early twentieth century with emphasis on the period from the 1760s to the 1820s. Mexico is most detailed and includes the records from three southwestern states that were part of Mexico at the time. Florida and Louisiana receive separate coverage. Entries furnish name of locality and province, country, year, and a reference number to the repository or archive where the census or its microform copy can be found.

859. Chronology of Hispanic-American History: From Pre-Columbian Times to the Present. Nicolas Kanellos and Cristelia Perez. Detroit: Gale, 1995. 427p. ISBN 0-8103-9200-3.

A useful source for college undergraduates and adults with an interest in the topic, this is work supplies comprehensive chronological treatment of events, personalities, and places of importance to Hispanic American history over an extensive time period. It opens with a segment on regional histories furnishing exposition of the geographical areas of Hispanic America, and follows with a concise historical outline. The chronology is then presented in 11 chapters under four time periods beginning with prehistory to 1492 and ending with the modern period of 1899 to 1995. A wide variety of information is given in various aspects of life and culture such as agriculture, economics, literature, music, politics, religion, spots, and so forth. A section on significant documents is a valuable special feature as is a glossary of terms. There is a general bibliography, and information is accessed through category and subject indexes.

860. Dictionary of Hispanic Biography. Joseph C. Tardiff and L. Mpho Mabunda, eds. Detroit: Gale, 1996. 1011p. ISBN 0-8103-8302-0.

A well-constructed comprehensive biographical dictionary, this work supplies information on a wide array of notable individuals from Latin America, Spain, and the United States who made their contributions from the time of the fifteenth century to the present day. Emphasis is on those who lived during the twentieth century who receive 70 percent of the total coverage. Entries are alphabetically arranged, and supply detailed biographical essays of men and women who achieved in all areas of endeavor. Careers include those in art, business, education, entertainment, journalism, politics, religion, science, sports, and so forth. Selection was made by the editors with advice from a panel of six members. Entries vary in length from one to three pages, and each includes a bibliography of writing by and about the person. Photographs accompany some of the essays, and indexes supply access by occupation, nationality, and subject.

861. Encyclopedia of Latin American History and Culture. Barbara A. Tenenbaum et al., eds. New York: Scribners's/Simon & Schuster Macmillan, 1996. 5v. ISBN 0-684-19253-5.

A good example of the heightened interest in producing reference sources on Latin American history in the past decade, this is the work of some 850 contributors who have supplied over 5,000 articles to make this a comprehensive and valuable source for students from high school to college level. Organization of entries is alphabetical, beginning with volume 1, and treatment is given to a large number of personalities representing various careers and achievements as well as to a variety of topics relevant to the historical and cultural study of life in Latin America. Latin American countries receive fullest description with lengthy survey essays. Biographical coverage is not as extensive, but all such entries contain at least 100 words highlighting the lives and achievements of notable people. There is a listing of source materials in all entries. A good feature is the inclusion of many photographs and graphics throughout. Volume 5 contains a detailed index, and lists both the biographies included in the work and the contributors.

Latin American Lives from the same publisher (1998) is derived from the above title and simply represents a less-inclusive work in furnishing some 3,000 of the entries exactly as they appeared. Designed for a younger and less sophisticated audience, listings of bibliographic sources are omitted in the entries. There is both a general index and an index of broad subject categories.

862. Hispanic-American Experience on File. Carter Smith III and David Lindroth. New York: Facts on File, 1999. 160p. (Ethnic Minorities in America Series). ISBN 0-8160-3695-0.

Another product from Facts on File issued in the familiar loose-leaf binder–style, this title is of value to both teachers and students at the high school and college undergraduate levels who utilize graphic resources in their work. It supplies hundreds of visual resources such as maps, graphs, photographs, illustrations, and more on pages that can be removed and photocopied. Following an introductory segment, the work is divided into five historical periods, "Spanish and Mexican Settlement in North America" (1565–1835), "Manifest Destiny and Hispanic America" (1863–1900), "The Early 20th Century" (1901–1945), "La Raza Unida" (1945–1974), and "Hispanic America Today" (1975–present). A final section, "Hispanic American Cultural Contributions," furnishes an overview. There is a bibliography that includes Web sites and an index.

The work is mounted on a Web site as *Hispanic American Experience on File On-Line* (available at http://www.fofweb.com/subscription). It is available to subscribers only.

863. Hispanic American Reference Library. Detroit: U*X*L/Gale, 1995–1997. 5v. **Hispanic American Almanac.** 2nd ed. Nicolas Kanellos, ed. 1996. 884p. ISBN 0-8103-8595-3. **Hispanic American Biography.** Rob Nagel and Sharon Rose, eds. 1995. 2v. ISBN 0-8103-8595-3. **Hispanic American Chronology.** Nicolas Kanellos and Bryan Ryan, eds. 1996. 195p. ISBN 0-8103-9826-5. **Hispanic American Voices.** Deborah G. Straub, ed. 1997. ISBN 0-8103-9827-3.

Another set in the popular U*X*L/Gale series (entries 679, 697, and 813) providing comprehensive treatment of the social and cultural life of an ethnic group for benefit of students at all levels, these works serve an important purpose. The *Almanac* furnishes a survey and overview of Hispanic civilization and culture through 14 chapters covering the periods of Spanish exploration, immigration, family structure and religion, employment, and achievements in sports and in the arts. The *Biography* supplies alphabetically arranged profiles of 100 personalities representing all areas of endeavor, both living and dead. The *Chronology* provides a timeline of important events and personalities arranged by year and date. It enumerates social, political, cultural, and educational contributions, and is rich in graphics and photographs. *Voices* supplies the text of full and excerpted speeches, orations, poems, and other words of 17 Hispanic American activists, politicians, attorneys, and other public figures. Biographical information is given followed by the selected texts.

864. Hispanic Firsts: 500 Years of Extraordinary Achievement. Nicolas Kanellos. Detroit: Gale, 1997. 372p. ISBN 0-7876-0517-4.

This may well be intended to be part of the Gale series above, since the author appears to have presented a similar if more restrictive coverage in his recognition of "firsts" associated with the lives of Hispanic Americans from the early sixteenth century to 1997. Like *Hispanic American Almanac* (entry 863) it is divided into 14 areas of endeavor: the arts, business, education, film, government, labor, literature, media, military, performing arts, religion, science, sports, and theater. The work opens with an introductory section, a calendar of "firsts," and a timeline. Entries are concise and are somewhat uniform in length, ranging from one to two paragraphs, with some enriched by photographs. "Firsts" vary in signifi-

cance from little-known or forgotten and decidedly trivial sports events to major accomplishments. There is a bibliography, and two indexes supply access by year, and by subjects
and names.

**865. The Hispanic 100: A Ranking of the Latino Men and Women Who Have Most
Influenced American Thought and Culture.** Himilce Novas. New York: Citadel Press/
Carol Publishing, 1995. 495p. ISBN 0-8065-1651-8.

This is a valuable and detailed source for students from junior high school to college
level on the lives of 100 Latinos who have most influenced the life and culture of the United
States. Coverage of personalities extends from those born in the eighteenth and nineteenth
centuries to the present day, although there is emphasis on the contemporary period. The
work is unique in that entries are arranged in order of significance of the impact or influence
that the individual has demonstrated on American life and culture; it begins with Cesar
Chavez and ends with Elizabeth Pena, the actress. This rating system is based on the degree
to which the people met three criteria; trailblazer status, legendary regard, and far-reaching
recognition. Applications and measurements of achievement of these criteria were evaluated
by the author. Entries are detailed and treat the career, contributions, and awards, and in
some cases, family and private life. Photographs are included. A name index completes the
volume.

866. The Hispanic Presence in North America from 1492 to Today. upd. ed. Carlos M.
Fernandez-Shaw et al. New York: Facts on File, 1999. 416p. ISBN 0-8160-4010-9.

Originally written in Spanish by the former Spanish consul-general in Miami and
published as *Presencia Española en los Estados Unidos* (Cooperación liberoamerica
[Spain], 1987), it was first translated into English in 1991. Comprehensive in scope, the
work furnishes both students and scholars with a one-volume history of Spanish influence
in the United States. Each state with a sizable Hispanic population is treated in separate
chapters; and the country is divided into regional coverage. The effort represents another
area of inquiry in U.S. history assumed by Facts on File in its design to provide coverage
of the cultural heritage of the various U.S. ethnic groups. In this work, the term "Hispanic"
is applied to *influences* emanating from Spain, rather than Spanish-speaking *peoples*. The
Spanish role in U.S. history is described in the introductory section or part; this is followed
by six sections each devoted to a region of the United States (e.g., "Atlantic Coast" states
in part 2). Useful listings of officers, missions, historical societies, associations, festivals,
readings, and more are given in the appendixes along with a chronology and an index.

867. Hispanic Resource Directory. 3rd ed. Alan E. Schorr, ed. Juneau, AK: Denali Press,
1996. 493p. ISBN 0-938737-33-3.

This is a comprehensive source in term of its extensive coverage of local, state,
regional, and nationwide associations and organizations as well as research centers, libraries,
museums, diplomatic offices, publications, and other resources and agencies relevant to
Hispanic life and culture. Eighteen chapters enumerate these categories, under which more
than 8,000 entries are listed. Organization is under topical headings, then by state in alphabetical sequence in each chapter. To merit inclusion the units must have met three criteria:
provide services to Hispanics, furnish demographic data about Hispanics, and have largely

Hispanic membership. Entries contain the customary directory-type data and supply name, address, telephone number, and contact person; there is additional information on research centers, libraries, museum, and so forth. Three indexes furnish access.

868. Latino Americans. Judy Culligan, ed. New York: Macmillan Library Reference/ Simon & Schuster, 1999. 465p. (Macmillan Profiles). ISBN 0-02-865373-4.

This is a selective biographical dictionary in its inclusion of 180 distinguished Latino Americans, both male and female, who achieved success from the sixteenth century to the present day. The series is designed to appeal to users of all ages beginning at the junior high school level in its presentation of clearly written biographical profiles derived from sophisticated titles in the Macmillan Reference collection and updated as needed. Both Latin Americans and U.S. citizens are included and a diverse group of people is described from early Spanish explorers to Jennifer Lopez. Entries are alphabetically arranged and furnish timelines and quotations relevant to the understanding of the personalities along with bio-graphical narrative. They vary in length from one paragraph to several pages. Useful special features are the definitions of key terms in the margins as well as a separate glossary in the back. Several indexes provide access.

869. The Latino Encyclopedia. Richard Chabran and Rafael Chabran, eds. North Bell-more, NY: Marshall Cavendish, 1996. 6v. ISBN 0-7614-0125-3.

This work has had mixed reviews due to its attempt to include everything and any-thing related to the lives of Latin Americans in the United States. Entries are alphabetically arranged and contain descriptions of personalities, events, cultural groups, legislation, sites and locations, and definitions of terms deemed to be useful to understanding the culture. In this regard, there are events and activities treated because a segment or portion of the par-ticipants were Latino, and terms are defined because they describe commonly eaten foods. Also such non-Latino happenings as Vatican II are treated. Following the final entry in volume 6, there are appendixes furnishing a timeline identifying an array of societal events ranging from sports to religion and dating from 1000 B.C.E. to 1994. Several useful bibli-ographies are supplied as is a thorough and detailed index.

870. Notable Latino Americans: A Biographical Dictionary. Matt S. Meier et al., eds. Westport, CT: Greenwood Press, 1997. 431p. ISBN 0-313-29105-5.

This is a useful source of information for high school and college students as well as interested adults in its presentation of the lives of 127 distinguished Hispanics with ties to the United States. A variety of individuals are included such as visual and performing artists, educators, entertainers, sports figures, and scientists among many others, all of whom have achieved success in their fields of endeavor. Many are politically active and the bi-ographies treat the struggles and frustrations they have encountered. Entries are alphabeti-cally arranged and furnish detailed essays ranging from a single page to three pages. Bib-liographies and in some cases, photographs, are included. The work is indexed by career or activity, and by ethnic origin.

The Biographical Dictionary of Hispanic Americans by Nicholas Meyer (Facts on File, 1997) was published the same year and overlaps the coverage of personalities to a large extent. It is intended for a younger audience beginning with junior high school and treats the lives and careers of 200 individuals from the time of Ponce de Leon to the present day. Entries are well written, interesting, and brief, averaging a page or less. Bibliographies are supplied for each entry, and photographs are given for some. A general bibliography and a general index conclude the effort.

871. Statistical Record of Hispanic Americans. Marlita A. Reddy, ed. Detroit: Gale, 1993. 1173p. ISBN 0-8103-8962-2.

The work utilizes the definition supplied by the U.S. Census Bureau to define U.S. residents of Hispanic descent as those "of Mexican, Puerto Rican, Cuban, Central or South American or other Spanish-speaking culture or origin, regardless of race." It supplies statistical information culled from a number of government sources such as *Statistical Abstracts of the United States* (entry 122) as well as private and public sources in presenting a complete statistical portrait of Hispanic Americans in tabular form. Nearly 930 tables are organized into separate chapters dealing with various general aspects of life and culture (demographic trends, mental illness, family, health, law, health care, and more). There is a detailed index providing access.

872. Who's Who Among Hispanic Americans 1994–1995. 3rd ed. Amy L. Unterburger and Jane L. Delgado, eds. Detroit: Gale, 1994. 990p. ISSN 1052-7354. Bienn.

As the third and what appears to be the final of three editions of this biennial work issued between 1990 and 1994, it supplies more than 11,000 entries containing brief biographical information on prominent living Hispanics who reside in this country. There is an informative introductory forward describing the Hispanic population. The main text contains profiles of figures representing a variety of professions and careers, and personalities are widely distributed through all geographic areas of the United States. One is able to identify influential figures in medicine, labor, government, and so forth, who were selected due to their professional achievements or their civic contributions. Several indexes provide access by occupation, geographic location, or ethnic heritage.

Females

873. Latinas in the United States: Social, Economic, and Political Aspects, a Bibliography. Joan Nordquist, comp. Santa Cruz, CA: Reference and Research Services, 1995. 80p. (Contemporary Social Issues: A Bibliographic Series, no. 40). ISBN 0-937855-78-2.

This is another of the brief bibliographies in the series compiled by Nordquist for the publisher. Emphasis is placed on the current or recent literature in its inclusion of a wide range of publications: books, book chapters, pamphlets, articles, and even government documents and dissertations. Nearly 1,000 citations are arranged in 20 categories, most of which represent subject divisions relevant to the lives of females, ranging from health and medical care, economics, or religion to sex roles, lesbianism, or violence. The initial category treats general sources and those that examine specific countries. Bibliographies and directories are found in the final segment. All entries represent English-language titles, and there are no annotations. The work is not indexed that hinders quick reference to specific authors or titles.

874. Latinas of the Americas: A Source Book. K. Lynn Stoner. New York: Garland, 1989. 692p. (Garland Reference Library of Social Science, v. 363.) ISBN 0-8240-8336-1.

Ms. Stoner has made a real contribution to both study and research of the female experience within the Americas with this excellent resource. More than 3,000 studies, both published and unpublished, are organized under 15 different chapter headings. All but two of them are topical in nature. Such subjects as history, health, demography, household and family studies, religion, and urban/rural development are treated. Two segments deal with anthologies and bibliographies exclusively. Each chapter is prepared by a different specialist or scholar, and each opens with a bibliographical essay providing an overview of the subject and the works cited; these are followed by listings of entries without annotations. Coverage is given to studies on Hispanic women in this country as well as those in the various parts of Latin America. The work is indexed by author, country or region, and subject.

875. Notable Hispanic American Women, Books I and II. Eva M. Neito et al., eds. Detroit; Gale, 1993–1998. ISBN 0-8103-7578-8 (BkI); 0-7876-2068-8 (BkII).

Together the two volumes furnish biographical sketches of more than 500 Hispanic American women who achieved a level of prominence from the eighteenth century to the present. Emphasis is placed on contemporary personalities and one is able to examine the lives and careers of notable actresses, scientists, politicians, artists, businesswomen, and others. The framework is similar to that of *Notable Black American Women* (entry 755), and selection of personalities was determined by members of an advisory board of knowledgeable professionals familiar with the Hispanic American community. Entries are signed by the 49 contributors and vary in length from 500 to 2,500 words. There are photographs of the more highly prominent, and information regarding life, education, career, achievements, and successes is presented in readable style.

Mexican Americans

876. Bibliography of Mexican American History. Matt S. Meier, comp. Westport, CT: Greenwood, 1984. 500p. ISBN 0-313-23776-X.

Covering materials written between 1842 and 1982, this must be considered the most comprehensive of all bibliographies of English-language publications on Mexican Americans. As such, it has value for historians and beginning researchers, furnishing 4,500 entries representing both primary and secondary sources. Students at the secondary school level will also find it beneficial. It begins with a chapter on general works; then follow five chapters on chronological periods, beginning with the colonial era and ending with the 1980s. Finally, three topical chapters cover labor, civil rights, and culture. Within these chapters, there are subdivisions based on formats (books, dissertations, articles, etc.). Annotations are given for more than two-thirds of the entries; these are brief and average one or two sentences in length. Both author and subject indexes are furnished.

877. Dictionary of Mexican American History. Matt S. Meier and Feliciano Rivera. Westport, CT: Greenwood Press, 1981. 498p. ISBN 0-313-21203-1.

Through a combination of the efforts of the two authors, both academicians, as well as 30 contributors, this work furnishes quick access to information on people, places, events, and organizations that have influenced Mexican American history. Although coverage begins with the sixteenth century, emphasis is given to mid-to-latter nineteenth-century and twentieth-century developments. About 1,000 entries are furnished that vary in length from a few lines to several pages, depending on the perceived importance of the topic. The intention is to furnish a useful source for students at all levels. There are a few compromises on the inclusion of popular figures such as Trini Lopez. Articles are not signed, although contributors are listed in the preface. Also included are a bibliography, chronology, glossary, list of journals, statistical tables, and maps. An index is furnished to aid access.

878. Encyclopedia of the Mexican American Civil Rights Movement. Matt S. Meier and Margo Gutierrez. Westport, CT: Greenwood Press, 2000. 293p. ISBN 0-313-30425-4.

This is a well-constructed source of information by two experts on the topic of Mexican American history, and presents up-to-date and accurate information on an array of topics including well-developed presentations of both highly profiled and relatively obscure personalities, lucid exposition of legislation and court decisions, somewhat brief examination of concepts and issues, events, and organizations. Entries are arranged alphabetically and vary in length from one paragraph to two pages. Generally, they are less than a page, but do furnish cross-references and bibliographic references at the end. Appendixes provide special features such as a chronology, acronyms, text of significant documents such as the U.S. Bill of Rights and the Treaty of Guadalupe Hidalgo, notes on Spanish pronunciation, and a general index.

879. The Mexican American: A Critical Guide to Research Aids. Barbara J. Robinson and Joy C. Robinson. Greenwich, CT: JAI, 1980. 287p. (Foundations in Library and Information Science, v. 1.) ISBN 0-89232-006-0.

This represents a major effort in furnishing sources of information on the Mexican American tradition, an effort for which the authors are well prepared by virtue of their positions as a Latin American bibliographer and a professor of history. The bibliography furnishes nearly 670 titles of books, book chapters, articles, pamphlets, dissertations, and documents that are placed within 17 chapters divided into two major divisions, "General Works" and "Subject Bibliographies." General works include chapters on bibliographies, guides, and biographies, whereas subjects include history, education, and labor. Annotations are of the critical nature and are useful in evaluating significance. Emphasis is given to twentieth-century writings, especially the 20 years prior to 1978, the cutoff date.

Mexican Americans: An Annotated Bibliography of Bibliographies by Julio A. Martinez and Ada Burns (R&E Publishers, 1984) is a compact volume considered to be supplementary to the above work. Selection of bibliographies is concentrated in the period following the coverage of the earlier work beginning with 1978 for the most part. Annotations provide both descriptive and evaluative information.

880. The Mexican Americans. Alma M. Garcia. Westport, CT: Greenwood Press, 2002. 192p. (The New Americans.) ISBN 0-313-31499-3.

This concise, but informative work, examines the historical development of the Mexican American population from their beginnings in Mexico to their immigration and relocation to various parts of the United States. Included in the account are descriptions of their culture and traditions along with identification of the demographics, political involvement, and ongoing struggle to achieve full participation in the workings of this country. Chapters treat border problems as well as the relations between this country and Mexico. Emphasis is placed on the contemporary period dating from the period of immigration reforms over the past 40 years.

Mexican American Biographies: A Historical Dictionary, 1836–1987 by Matt S. Meier (Greenwood, 1988), historian and frequent contributor to the literature of the Mexican American. Meier gives biographical coverage of 270 *prominentes* ranging from sports figures to politicians ranging from the mid-1830s to the 1980s. About 75 percent of the personalities are contemporary figures, the remainder being the more frequently covered historical personalities. Entries are arranged alphabetically and vary in length (dependent to some degree on the amount of available information). Emphasis is placed upon accomplishments, preparation, and training rather than family or marital details. Appendixes list individuals by state and by field of endeavor. There is no index.

Cuban Americans

881. The Cuban Americans. Miguel Gonzalez-Pando. Westport, CT: Greenwood Press, 1998. 185p. (The New Americans series). ISBN 0-313-29824-6.

A source of information for high school and undergraduate-level students as well as interested adults, this work is another in the publisher's well-received series examining the conditions and historical developments surrounding immigration and their settling in this country. The style of writing is personal in tone and it is not difficult to determine the author's orientation regarding the chaotic events that spurred the major wave of immigration during the Castro ascendancy. Political history from the period of Spanish colonization to the early twentieth century is presented followed by chapters on the immigration, development and growth of Cuban American communities, economic conditions, political orientation and active participation. The work is well written in furnishing the users with understanding of the complexity of the issues surrounding this Cuban Americans and their adaptation to life in this country. Special features include photographs, statistical representations, listing of notable exiles, and a bibliography.

882. Cuban and Cuban-American Women: An Annotated Bibliography. K. Lynn Stoner and Luis H.D.S. Perez, comps. and eds. Wilmington, DE: Scholarly Resources, 2000. 189p. ISBN 0-8420-2643-6.

This impressive bibliography provides a unique focus on females of a seldom-documented Latin American group in both the country from which they or their parents originated and in their current home country, the United States. It furnishes some 1,600 annotated entries describing the contents of a variety of resources for the student or scholar (monographs, journals, newspaper articles, etc.) of great value to the study of Cuban and Cuban American women. Emphasis is on twentieth century materials but date from 1868 to the time of publication. The work is organized into two major parts or sections, the first of which treats archival and secondary sources in Cuba. The second section identifies sources in the United States such as histories of the exile years, family histories, literature, studies of issues such as employment, education, literature, and so forth. Arrangement of entries is chronological by time period. Several indexes provide access.

883. Cubans in the United States: A Bibliography for Research in the Social and Behavioral Sciences, 1960–1983. Lyn MacCorkle, comp. Westport, CT: Greenwood, 1984. 227p. (Bibliographies and Indexes in Sociology, no. 1). ISBN 0-313-24509-6.

MacCorkle's research bibliography on Cuban Americans covers a 24-year period and is a real asset to scholars and serious students. It represents the initial effort of another of the Greenwood bibliographic series. Selection is limited to research studies as reported in journals, dissertations, government reports, conference papers, and miscellaneous other unpublished materials. The author has furnished about 1,600 entries, which are listed under several major categories: "Economics," "Education," "Public Administration," "Psychology," "Health," "Politics," "Sociology," and "Demography." These categories are well developed for use by researchers; the restrictions on content will discourage those with a desire for less rigorous literature. Although additional bibliographic work is needed to control the abundant popular literature, the present effort is a valuable contribution for historians at all levels. There is an author index to furnish access.

Puerto Ricans

884. Puerto Ricans and Other Minority Groups in the Continental United States: An Annotated Bibliography. Diane Herrera, ed. Detroit: Blaine Ethridge Books, 1979. 397p. ISBN 0-87917-067-0.

This is mostly a reprint of a 1973 effort by Ms. Herrera that focused solely on the Puerto Rican tradition and cited more than 2,150 books and articles published through the year 1972, primarily on the education of Puerto Rican children. For the present work, Francesco Cordasco, a prolific bibliographer of ethnic traditions, has added an introductory essay and some 300 titles on bilingual and bicultural education, only a few of which bear more recent imprint dates. The work retains its initial emphasis on the educational experiences of Puerto Ricans in this country. There is a peripheral and slight coverage given to Mexican Americans, blacks, Cuban Americans, American Indians, and Jews, but not enough to warrant a researcher's interest. A few of the sources furnish information on social and historical topics. There is an author index, but it does not include the supplementary Cordasco listings.

885. Puerto Ricans in the United States. Maria E. Perez y Gonzalez. Westport, CT: Greenwood Press, 2000. 186p. (The New Americans series). ISBN 0-313-29748-7.

Another title in the popular series from Greenwood, this work is designed to appeal to high school and college-level students as a well-written and interesting source of information on the immigration and adaptation to life in the United States. Beginning the coverage with the beginning of the twentieth century, the life and times of these people are examined and described in terms of their socioeconomic struggles and their challenges to overcome crime and violence and find gainful employment. The initial chapters furnishing a historical picture of life in Puerto Rico from the beginnings to the time of involvement with this country in the late nineteenth century. The bulk of the work describes the adjustment to the new environment through the years, and examines such issues as employment, housing, health care, the arts, sports, and more. Life in New York is presented in depth, warranted by its significance to the Puerto Rican culture. An appendix furnishes a tabular display of population growth in the United States from 1910 to 1990, a section of photographs enhances the coverage, and an extensive bibliography adds to the value.

THE NATIVE AMERICAN EXPERIENCE

The plight of the Native North American has received a great deal of news coverage since the 1960s. This coverage, in turn, has inspired a great deal of publishing by trade-book publishers, both mainstream and small press. Reference publishers have followed suit with bibliographic sources to control the increasing volume of literature, as well as information sources to furnish data and interpretation in convenient packages. In the past decade, we have witnessed an extraordinary interest on the part of both publishers and authors of reference material. Coverage spans the entire realm of American Indian life and addresses social ills, health problems, political involvement, and customs and traditions. History can be approached through study of individual tribes, cult of personality, or more generally through the development and progress of ideas and social response.

This section includes works on a variety of topics, some of which are addressed in more generic fashion elsewhere in this guide. As in the case of blacks, the racial/ethnic factor is considered dominant. Those issues examined here as part of the American Indian experience include those relating to education, law, the female experience, and medicine (science). For works relating to the treatment of American Indians in film, see "Cinema" under "Popular Culture: Entertainment, Recreation, Sports" in this chapter.

The American Indian Heritage Foundation (available at http://www.indians.org/aihf) Falls Church, Virginia, was founded in 1963 and has an extraordinarily large membership numbering more than 250,000. Contemporary concerns are foremost, but historical aspects are also treated in the quarterly newsletter. An important long-term goal is the establishment of a National Clearinghouse for American Indian Information. The Cherokee National Historical Society (available at http://www.powersource.com/heritage/) of Tahlequah, Oklahoma, has some 900 members and has operated since 1963. It issues a quarterly newsletter and administers the Cherokee Heritage Center.

General Sources

*886. The American Indian: A Multimedia Encyclopedia. New York: Facts on File, 1996. [CD-ROM].

This is the second effort by the publisher and represents an improvement and expansion of the earlier work issued in 1993. Like its predecessor, it combines several print reference sources in combination with the advantages offered by electronic format with the inclusion of sound, video, and numerous graphics and pictures. In presenting these special features with large bodies of text and expository narrative, the user is given a valuable reference source on the history and development of Native American life. Of real importance is the focus on the history and culture of individual tribes; also included are biographical sketches of significant figures, text of treaties and historic documents, and maps and timelines. Special features added to this edition are a directory of relevant cultural organizations, and a glossary of terms, as well as a survey of cultural folklore.

887. American Indian Quotations. Howard J. Langer, comp. and ed. Westport, CT: Greenwood Press, 1996. 260p. ISBN 0-313-29121-7.

This is a useful source of quotations, especially because the bulk of the entries are the words of Native Americans themselves. The work is divided into three segments beginning with an introduction, and followed by segments on "American Indian Quotations" and "Anonymous Quotations, Prayers, and Proverbs." Entries are placed in one of these categories and arranged chronologically under themes such as the land or spirituality. Some 800 quotations are furnished beginning with non-Indian reflections of missionaries, traders, and others dating from the mid-seventeenth century up to the Native American commentaries and ideological statements of the 1990s. Sources of the quotes are identified, and in 23 cases, photographs are given. Three indexes supply access by author, subject and keyword, and tribal affiliation.

*888. American Indian Resources: A Library of Native American Literature, Culture, Education, History, Issues, and Language. Will Karkavelas. Osaka University. Available: http://cobalt.lang.osaka-u.ac.jp/~krkvls/naindex.htm.

The compiler of this site is an academic who has copyrighted his work; he has provided a comprehensive and valuable resource for the study of the American Indian in furnishing the users this bibliography and directory. At the beginning, a link is given to evaluation criteria that should be followed when finding Web sites on this topic. Links leading to such resources as bibliographic listings, documentary, text, reviews, centers, organizations, and so forth are organized under categorical headings treating Native American life (studies, texts, culture, education, history, and representations, such as treatment of Native Americans in motion pictures), issues (law, environment, gaming, etc.), languages, literature, nations (includes home pages by state), and backgrounds to literature (historical treatment of cultural, spiritual, and artistic roots). A wealth of resources is found under each category, all of which contributes to the understanding of the topic.

American Indian History and Related Issues by Troy Johnson (available at http://www.csulb.edu/projects/ais) is another valuable Web site from an academic institution, California State University at Long Beach, which has the oldest continuous existing program for American Indian Studies in the country. This site furnishes links to a number of resources (artwork, photographs, video and sound recordings, and texts) relevant to the study of Indians of North America with special emphasis on the occupation of Alcatraz. There is another section on Indians of Central America and Mexico. In addition there are links to related Web servers and to tribes and their home pages.

889. American Indian Studies: A Bibliographic Guide. Phillip M. White. Englewood, CO: Libraries Unlimited, 1995. 163p. ISBN 1-56308-243-8.

Another of the useful literature guides from the publisher, this work identifies nearly 400 sources of information relevant to the study of Native Americans in North America. These sources were published from the 1970s to the mid-1990s, and are organized under chapters treating specific types of reference and research sources: literature guides, directories, bibliographies, periodicals, biographical sources, government documents, and microform materials. Most of these sources are targeted to the coverage of Native American life and culture, although the work includes more general sources with some coverage given to the topic. Designed to meet the needs of students from high school to college undergraduate level, entries describe the sources and in some cases furnish evaluative commentary. Bibliographies are listed by tribe, and detailed indexes provide access.

*890. American Indian Tribes. R. Kent Rasmussen, ed. Hackensack, NJ: Salem Press, 2000. 2v. (Magill's Choice Series.) ISBN 0-89356-063-4.

A useful resource for college-level students and instructors, this effort contains the essays published in an earlier work, *Ready Reference: American Indians* (Salem Press, 1995) with the addition of new material and in a revised format. There are two major parts or divisions, beginning with "Culture Areas" furnishing well-written essays on ten regions relevant to origins of the people; Arctic, California, Great Basin, Northeast, Northwest Coast, Plains, Plateau, Southeast, Southwest, and the Subarctic. These essays examine language groups and tribes and their relationship to the environment, culture, art, and language development, along with prehistory of the region. The second major part begins in the second half of volume 1 and continues through volume 2, treating tribal history, cultural development, demographic statistics, and so forth of 307 individual tribes beginning with Abenaki and concluding with the Zatopec. Appendixes furnish identification of gatherings, reservations, museums, organizations, and more. There are a timeline, mediagraphy that includes Web sites, and a bibliography. An index provides access.

891. American Indians. Harvey Markowitz, ed. Pasadena, CA: Salem Press, 1995. 3v. (Ready Reference series.) ISBN 0-89356-757-4.

This is a useful encyclopedia work examining a wide range of events, issues, cultural elements, and personalities relevant to the study of Native Americans. Included here are Inuits, Aleuts, and others from Meso-America and Canada. Coverage is both historical and contemporary, and the work is comprehensive in supplying more than 1,100 entries running from 200 to 3,000 words each. Cross-references are included and bibliographies are given in some cases. Photographs, maps, and charts appear throughout, and eight appendixes supply such features as listings of relevant organizations. There is a timeline, a detailed bibliography, and an index.

American Indian Biographies, also edited by Markowitz as part of the Magill's Choice series was issued in 1999, and like the publisher's *American Indian Tribes* (entry 890) most entries were drawn from *Ready Reference: American Indians,* a 1995 publication. Others were taken from the Salem's *Great Lives in History* series. Just over 20 entries were prepared especially for this work and they cover personalities from the twentieth century. The entries run up to five pages in length and average about a page in producing an adequate awareness of individuals from the seventeenth century to the present day.

892. Atlas of American Indian Affairs. Francis P. Prucha. Lincoln: University of Nebraska Press, 1990. 191p. ISBN 0-8032-3689-1.

The author, a well-known historian, has been a prolific writer on the Native American experience. This atlas opens with a brief preface, and then delivers nearly 110 large-scale black-and-white maps on a variety of themes. Maps are arranged by topics such as population, land cessions, reservations, the army, the Indian frontier, and agencies and other institutions. There is a segment of 10 maps by Rafael Palacios, reprinted from an earlier publication, covering the frontier and various army campaigns against American Indians. Narrative is slight and is offered in the introduction and in the historical notes, which are separated from the maps. Statistical data is furnished in tables. When appropriate, maps are targeted to regions rather than to the entire country. It is complementary to Waldman's *Atlas of the North American Indian* (entry 894).

893. Atlas of Indians of North America. Gilbert Legay. Hauppauge, NY: Baron's Educational Series, 1995. 95p. ISBN 0-8120-6515-8.

This is an attractive and well-designed atlas for use by students at the junior high school level and beyond. It contains more than 200 maps along with many illustrations in examining the history and present conditions of Native North Americans. Coverage is established through treatment of 10 distinct environmental areas that serve to provide the necessary linkage between cultural elements and the physical environment of Native Americans. Such basic essential factors as diet, dress, shelter, and family life, auxiliary factors like tools and technology, and enriching factors like art, religion, and sport represent adaptations to the physical forces that shape their world. The maps are clear and understandable, as is the concise textual narrative in treating the customs, dress, and village life.

894. Atlas of the North American Indian. Rev. ed. Carl Waldman and Molly Braun. New York: Facts on File, 2000. 385p. ISBN 0-81603-974-7.

Broader in scope and furnishing more textual narrative than does Prucha's *Atlas of American Indian Affairs* (entry 892), this work expands and updates the earlier edition issued in 1985. The work is comprehensive in nature providing not only an excellent atlas but also narrative treatment of history, culture, language, life of Native Americans. Organization continues to be topical and the work is still organized into seven broad divisions or chapters beginning with an introductory perspective on "Ancient Indians" and ending with an exposition of "Contemporary Indians." Narrative is extensive on these topics, and they are illustrated through a variety of improved maps and line drawings. The movements and migrations are presented clearly; with good coverage of the spread of Native American cultures into North America. Interpretation continues to be sound and clearly presented. Appendixes contain a general chronology and a listing of place names and societies. There is an expanded bibliography and the work concludes with a general index.

895. Bibliographical Series. Newberry Library. D'Arcy McNickle Center for the History of the American Indian. Bloomington, IN: Indiana University Press, 1976–. (In progress). ISSN 4200-4912.

This useful series began in the year of the bicentennial as *Newberry Library Bibliographical Series* in response to a need for better documentation of the life and culture of the American Indian. Beginning with an effort on historical demography, the series steadily produced a variety of titles completed by different scholars ranging from tribal-specific works on the Cherokees, the Delawares, and the Ojibwas, to volumes on more generic topics, such as sociology. The authority for the series changed several times but most commonly was regarded as the Newberry Library Center for the History of the American Indian, with publication being handled by Indiana University. The pattern for the series is an opening bibliographical essay followed by an alphabetical listing of all works cited in the essay. Two sets of recommended titles (for beginners and for basic library collections) complete the package, which generally runs about 100 pages or less. After the 29th issue, covering the Native American female experience, in 1983, the series was thought to have ended and was identified as a ceased publication by OCLC. Happily, the series was resurrected with new numbering as *D'Arcy McNickle Center Bibliographies in American Indian History* with subsequent publication of *Scholars and the Indian Experience: Critical Reviews of Recent Writing in the Social Sciences* by W.R. Swagerty in 1984 and *The Seminole and Miccosukee Tribes: A Critical Bibliography* by Harry A. Kersey, Jr. in 1987. Most recent is *Writings in Indian History 1985–1990* compiled by Jay Miller and others through the University of Oklahoma in 1995. The authority for the series is now known as the D'Arcy McNickle Center for the History of the American Indian.

896. Biographical Dictionary of American Indian History to 1900. Rev. ed. Carl Waldman. New York: Facts on File, 2001. 506p. ISBN 0-8160-4252-7.

The author is a historian who has produced a number of useful resources designed to meet the needs of popular rather than scholarly inquiry (entries 894 and 906). As a result it appeals to wide audience from junior high school level to adulthood. It represents a revision of the author's earlier publication, *Who Was Who in Native American History: Indians and Non-Indians from Early Contacts Through 1900* (Facts on File, 1990). Like its predecessor, coverage is almost equally divided between American Indian notables (chieftains, warriors, tribal leaders, etc.) and non-Indian personalities who influenced their history and culture. Coverage given to people such as George Washington and Andrew Jackson provides identification and description of their impact. More than 1000 personalities are treated in entries ranging from a single paragraph to two pages in length in describing tribal connections, contributions, and family ties. Cross-references are included. There is a detailed reading list and several indexes provide access.

897. Biographical Dictionary of Indians of the Americas. Gail Hamlin-Wilson. 2nd ed. Newport Beach, CA: American Indian Publishers, 1991. 2v. ISBN 0-937862-29-0. Repr. Library Binding, 1999.

As a small publishing house, American Indian Publishers of Newport Beach, California, has produced several multivolume sets that are considered to have value for the scholar and student. As with the output of other small publishers, its efforts are not always picked up by the general reviewing media. One of the recent titles is a two-volume biographical dictionary of Native Americans, both living and dead, who have had some impact on their tribe or nation. In many cases, these are notables and celebrities, such as the Tallchief sisters, Maria and Marjorie, who achieved international acclaim as prima ballerinas. Others have been obscured by time, such as Tarhe, the Wyandot chieftain who opposed Tecumseh. More than 2,000 individuals are covered in concise biographical sketches. Brief bibliographies are included whenever possible; there are over 900 pictures and a listing of variant names.

898. A Bookman's Guide to the Indians of the Americas: A Compilation of Over 10,000 Catalogue Entries with Prices and Annotations, Both Bibliographical and Descriptive. Richard A. Hand. Metuchen, NJ: Scarecrow, 1989. 750p. ISBN 0-8108-2182-6.

A recent effort that serves as both a bibliography and relative price guide to materials on Native Americans, this is a useful source of information for scholars and librarians as well as dealers and collectors. There are nearly 6,750 titles; additional copies of these titles are given also, which brings the total number of entries to 10,000. These items sell for at least $10 and were found through examination of 200 catalogs issued by 21 book dealers. Prices are quoted from the catalogs themselves, which furnish an accurate picture of only a limited time. The work is most valued as a bibliography and brings together books and monographs of interest and value to the study. Dates of imprints range from 1821 to 1985. There is a subject index to provide access.

899. The British Museum Encyclopedia of Native North America. Rayna Green and Melanie Fernandez. Bloomington: Indiana University Press, 1999. 213p. ISBN 0-253-33597-3.

Although of small size, this is an important and valuable source of information for college students interested in gaining insight into the history and culture of Native Americans. It is unusual because it considers the issues important to these peoples from their perspective, and examines an array of topics integral to the understanding of their past. Entries are well written and easily negotiated with related topics printed in bold type. Coverage is given to such diverse aspects as dams, clans, self-determination, diplomacy, tourism, Pocahontas, and so forth. Many illustrations enhance the descriptive narrative and represent both historical and contemporary art, culture, and personalities. Of value are the quotes and snippets within the text in pointing out the significance of the topic within the broad cultural fabric. The work also contains maps, listings of sources and credits, a general index, and an index of people.

900. The Cambridge History of the Native Peoples of the Americas. Volume 1, North America. Bruce G. Trigger and Wilcomb E. Washburn, eds. New York: Cambridge University Press, 1996. 2 parts. ISBN 0-521-34440-9.

The first volume of a scholarly and comprehensive three-volume history of Native Americans from the earliest times to the present examines the people of North America. The editors and 14 expert contributors furnish thorough and well-researched chapters beginning with a provocative view of history as seen by Native peoples. This is followed by treatment of their place in Euro-American historiography; archaeological chapters examine the hunting and agricultural elements in the early years leading to the initial contacts with Europeans in the sixteenth century. Of value are the chapters providing insight into the ethno-historical developments and life patterns characteristic of different geographical regions. Life on the reservation is described and part 2 concludes with the Native American renaissance of more recent times. Illustrations are well placed and useful, and chapters conclude with a bibliographic essay. Different editors cover *Mesoamerica* in volume 2 (2001), and *South America* in volume 3 (1999).

901. Chronology of American Indian History: The Trail of the Wind. Liz Sonneborn. New York: Facts on File, 2002. 384p. (Facts on File Library of American History). ISBN 0-8160-4052-4.

Similar in coverage and designed for the same audience as *Native North American Chronology* by Duane Champagne and Michael A. Pare (entry 902n), this work provides comprehensive coverage beginning with the year 25000 B.C.E and ending with the present day. Coverage of the early years from prehistory to the 1700s is based on archaeological records and treats the region of Central America. Subsequent to that period, the coverage is largely that of the relationships with first the English and then the colonials and later generations of U.S. residents. Coverage is chronological and arrangement is in chapters, each beginning with an introduction to the major issues or themes of the period. Included are photographs, quotations, and a glossary of terms. Narrative description is brief, but informative and should prove useful to a junior high to senior high school audience.

902. Chronology of Native North American History from Pre-Columbian Times to the Present. Duane Champagne, ed. Detroit: Gale, 1994. 574p. ISBN 0-8103-9195-3.

The editor is experienced in preparing reference sources on Native American life, and in this case has developed what he considers to be "the most comprehensive and sympathetic chronology about Native issues and events available today." The work opens with a historical overview of Native American culture, along with a timeline identifying historical Native American events, achievements, and places along with world developments. It is, indeed, expansive in its coverage, and the 10 chapters are organized into three historical periods beginning with Pre-1500, followed by 1500–1959, and 1960–1994. Selected tribal chronologies are given also, and the work contains short biographical sketches, excerpts from speeches, legal decisions, and an annotated bibliography.

Native North American Chronology, edited by Champagne and Michael A. Pare for U*X*L/Gale (1995), is a spinoff publication designed for younger audiences from junior high school to high school level. It is revised, shortened, and simplified but covers the same expansive period of time with particular focus on the twentieth century.

903. A Concise Dictionary of Indian Tribes of North America. 2nd rev. ed. Barbara A. Leitch. Algonac, MI: Reference Publications, 1991; repr. 1997. 646p. ISBN 0-917256-48-4.

This work begins with an introduction by well-known Native American author Vine Deloria. Considering that all of the articles in this useful handbook on individual tribes were the work of a single person, it represents an impressive effort. This is an update and revision of the earlier 1979 effort. It continues to provide several hundred articles on tribes, alphabetically arranged for easy access. The entries furnish extensive detailed narrative on the history, culture, language, rites, ceremonies, beliefs, and tradition of each group. The narratives are followed by brief bibliographies; there are illustrations that include both photographs and drawings from early books. Of use to students and beginning researchers are the several maps created by different contributors on language groups, culture groups, Indian communities, and regions. Scholarship and careful planning are evident. There is a glossary, and an index is furnished to aid access.

904. Encyclopedia of American Indian Contributions to the World: 15,000 Years of Inventions and Innovations. Emory D. Keoke and Kay M. Porterfield. New York: Facts on File, 2002. 384p. (Facts on File Library of American History). ISBN 0-8160-4052-4.

This is a unique work in its focus on the innovations and inventions discovered or created and used by Native Americans in their age-old struggle for survival. American Indians are treated in a broad sense with inclusion of indigenous peoples of Mesoamerica and South America as well as those of North America. There is an interesting and enlightening introductory section in which the authors describe the injustice of the usage of stereotypical labels such as "savage" or other pejorative terms giving the impression of an unskilled and unenlightened society. Entries identify and describe a wide array of inventions and creative applications and ascribe dates and tribal origins. To be included they were Indian innovations, used by Indian peoples, and had been developed early enough to have a history. There is a glossary, chronology, and bibliography, along with useful appendixes.

905. The Encyclopedia of Native American Biography: Six Hundred Life Stories of Important People, from Powhatan to Wilma Mankiller. Bruce E. Johansen and Donald A. Grinde Jr. New York: Henry Holt, 1997. 463p. (A Henry Holt Reference Book). ISBN 0-8050-3270-3.

This is the product of a great deal of research on the part of the two authors who are academic specialists in the area. The title indicates its inclusive nature in treating the lives of 600 personalities both historical and contemporary. Both celebrated and obscure individuals are described representing a variety of fields; art, literature, sports, politics, religion, military, and so forth. Both Native Americans and significant non-Indians, males and females, are presented from the Native American perspective in brief biographical sketches, in which quotations and in some cases, photographs and reading lists are furnished. Entries are well written and designed to appeal to a wide audience from junior high school level to adult. There are many references to the work by Dockstader (see below) and this effort may serve as an update in many respects with its treatment of contemporary figures.

Great North American Indians: Profiles in Life and Leadership by Frederick J. Dockstader (Van Nostrand Reinhold, 1977) is a true standard in the field in its presentation of 300 American Indians. Their lives span a period of 400 years up to the 1970s, but all were deceased at time of publication. Selection is broad and representative in identifying men and women judged to be of importance from the standpoint of Indians; entries are clear, concise, and informative. Photographs and illustrations add to the value of the work, and useful appendixes enumerate tribal divisions and give a chronology.

906. Encyclopedia of Native American Tribes. Rev. ed. Carl Waldman. New York: Facts on File, 1999. 312p. ISBN 0-8160-3963-1.

This one-volume encyclopedia has been revised after 11 years, and will continue to be appreciated by a variety of students from junior high school to undergraduate levels. It has changed little from the previous edition and furnishes easily digested, descriptive information on the culture, tradition, and history of over 150 different tribes of the United States, Canada, and Mexico. The author has served as an archivist for the New York State Historical Association and has produced a highly regarded atlas on the American Indian (entry 894). In this encyclopedia, entries for tribes are alphabetically arranged, and narratives vary in length from less than a page to several pages according to the size and historical impact of each group. Selection for inclusion of tribes was based on their historical significance and culture. Along with single tribes, certain classes of tribes, such as cliff dwellers, and language families have their own entries. There are over 300 color illustrations. Both the glossary and bibliography have been expanded over the earlier effort.

907. The Encyclopedia of North American Indians. Tarrytown, New York: Marshall Cavendish, 1997. 11v. ISBN 0-7614-0227-6.

Designed to appeal to the young user at the junior high school level and slightly above, the work will find favor among more sophisticated inquirers as well. As a multivolume work, it examines a wide array of topics, conditions, and development relevant to the life, history, and culture of Native North Americans and extends beyond the United States to include Canada, Mexico, Greenland, the Caribbean, Central America, and parts of South America. Some 1,700 entries, along with 1,400 illustrations, are alphabetically arranged throughout the first 10 volumes furnishing identifications, descriptions and expositions of individual tribal nations, key personalities, historical and contemporary events and issues, art, education, sports, and more. Sixty contributors, most of whom are Native American, have supplied well-researched articles ranging from a few paragraphs to several pages in length. Cross-references are included in the entries, and volume 11 contains several appendixes and indexes.

Encyclopedia of North American Indians, edited by Frederick E. Hoxie (Houghton Mifflin, 1996) is a well-conceived and well-executed one-volume source furnishing nearly 450 articles of varying length, with none exceeding 1,500 words. Of interest to a wide audience, entries supply 100 biographies of historical figures and 100 tribal descriptions along with a variety of events, terms, and overviews of historical topics and issues. Cross-references are included in the entries.

908. Ethnographic Bibliography of North America. George P. Murdock and Timothy J. O'Leary. 4th ed. New Haven, CT: Human Relations Area Files, 1975. 5v. ISBN 0-87536-205-2. **Supp. 1973–1987.** 1990. 3v. ISBN 0-87536-254-0.

The fourth edition, a five-volume effort, represents a computer-produced revision of a monumental and classic tool first issued in 1941. Considerable expansion of coverage in the areas of history, psychology, biology, and current Native American affairs, combined with an explosion of written material on Indians following publication of the third edition in 1960, contributed to the increased size. Listed are 40,000 entries, arranged geographically, with each volume covering a different geographic region. Entries represent books and articles; the introduction furnishes description of other types of sources, such as government publications, ERIC documents, dissertations, and maps. Nearly 270 different Native American cultures are treated, ranging from those in northern Mexico to the Eskimo in Alaska. This title is available through photocopy process from UMI Books on Demand.

Finally, there is a three-volume supplement, *Ethnographic Bibliography of North America, 4th Edition Supplement, 1973–1987,* by M. Marlene Martin and Timothy J. O'Leary (Human Relations Area Files, 1990), furnishing 25,000 more books and articles published during the indicated period. Citations represent all western languages; 21 more groups have been added. There is access by author and subject indexes; the work is also available on floppy disk.

909. Exploring Native North America. David H. Thomas. New York: Oxford University Press, 2000. 227p. (Places in Time). ISBN 0-19-511857-X.

Of interest to a wide-ranging audience from high school level to adult, this is a combination travel guide and well-researched historical survey of 18 sites significant to Native North Americans. Sites are chosen for their accessibility to the public and their importance to the history and culture of the people who utilized them. There is a well-

constructed and informative introductory essay treating the history of archaeological research of early North American peoples that precedes chapters devoted to each of the selected places. Each chapter supplies historical background of the site, and describes the life
and culture of its Native American residents. Sites vary in popularity from the famous (Mesa
Verde in Colorado) to the obscure (Cape Krusenstern in Alaska). The others titles in the
series are *Mesoamerica* and *Prehistoric Europe,* for which similar treatment is provided.

Guide to Ancient Native American Sites with 150 Sites in 30 States by Michael S.
Durham (Globe Pequot Press, 1994) is a compact work of about the same length as the
above title. It differs in that it sacrifices depth for breadth in its treatment of nearly 150
sites. Coverage is decidedly brief in terms of descriptive and historical narrative, information
is given regarding location, hours, and fees. Maps and illustrations are provided.

910. The Gale Encyclopedia of Native American Tribes. Sharon Malinowski et al., eds.
Detroit: Gale, 1998. 4v. ISBN 0-7876-1085-2.

This is a major reference work in its comprehensive and detailed examination of the
history and culture of some 400 tribal groups who reside or had resided in 13 different
sections or regions. The four volumes are developed with a regional focus in examining the
Northeast and Southeast; the Great Basin and Southwest; the Arctic, subarctic, Plateau, and
Great Plains; and the Pacific Northwest and California. Included in these volumes are parts
of Mexico and the Caribbean. With the exception of the Caribbean, Middle America, and
the Pacific Islands, each section is preceded by a detailed introductory essay describing the
background and common characteristics of people of that region. Entries on the tribes are
full and authoritative, with great care being taken to assure both accuracy and respect for
the topic. Included in the entries are biographical sketches, timelines, maps, illustrations,
and photographs in examining the history, culture, customs, and issues. Glossaries and
indexes are given in each volume.

**911. Guide to Native American Ledger Drawings and Pictographs in United States
Museums, Libraries, and Archives.** John R. Lovett, Jr. and Donald L. DeWitt, comps.
Westport, CT: Greenwood Press, 1998. 135p. ISBN 0-313-30693-1.

For the historian and serious student, ledger drawings are important in gaining a full
understanding of past events, mostly personal in nature since the artist is usually pictured
in the activity, as well as insight into Native American culture. Ledger art is so named
because in the early days, these pieces were generally created on animal skins that were
held in place by ledger or support forms. They were mainly the work of Native Americans
of the Great Plains, and this directory represents that dominance since most of the collections
identified are from those tribes. The volume opens with a useful historical overview and
analysis of ledger art. The main text is an institutional directory furnishing alphabetical
listing by state of some 100 public museums and archives containing collections ranging
from 5 pieces to 2,000 at the Smithsonian Institution. Entries identify artists, tribal affiliations, number of items, date, and thematic treatments or subjects of the art. There is an
annotated bibliography and a detailed index.

912. Guide to Records in the National Archives of the United States Relating to American Indians. Edward E. Hill, comp. Washington, D.C.: National Archives Trust Fund Board, 1982. 467p. S/N 022-002-00098-8.

Of real value to scholars and serious students is this guide, which facilitates the use of the magnificent holdings of the National Archives with respect to the American Indian. As such, it is a specialized effort supplementary to the more generic guide to the archives (entry 153) and is organized in similar fashion. Beginning with pre-federal records, it examines Indian treaties from 1789 to 1871, then covers the Bureau of Indian Affairs. From that point, there is a rather complex chronological coverage of U.S.–Indian affairs by different agencies. Entries describe these agencies in terms of their impact and their collections of records. Records vary and range from print narratives to photographs and maps. The work is indexed by subject, as well as by both personal and tribal names.

An additional research aid is *The American Indian,* published by the Archives in 1972, which furnishes a listing of important records available on microfilm. It is part of the *Select Catalog Series* (entry 153n).

913. Handbook of American Indians North of Mexico. Frederick W. Hodge. Washington, D.C.: U.S. Government Printing Office, 1907–1910. 2v. (U.S. Bureau of American Ethnology, Bulletin No. 30.) Reiss. Smithsonian Institution, 1912. Repr. New York: Pageant Books, 1959.

This two-volume reference work was originally issued as a two-part bulletin, then reissued by the Smithsonian Institution (see also entry 914 below) during the early years of this century. It remains the standard and classic volume on the subject of the American Indian. Since its first issue, it has been considered a beginning point for all serious research. It should not be neglected today, even though more recent material is available. All tribes north of Mexico are treated, including the Eskimo; inclusions are made for certain tribal affiliates that reside south of the border as well. Entries furnish brief descriptions of every linguistic stock, confederacy, tribe, subtribe, tribal division, and settlement known to have existed, as well as the origin of every name. Cross-references are liberally applied. Information is given regarding ethnic relations, history, migratory influences, culture, art, customs, and social institutions. Biographies of important leaders are included. References to additional sources create an invaluable aid to research.

914. Handbook of North American Indians. William C. Sturtevant, gen. ed. Washington, D.C.: Smithsonian Institution, 1978–2002. Dist. U.S. Government Printing Office. v. 4–13, 15, 17. (Projected 20v.)

Projected as a 20-volume set, this fine reference source represents a cooperative effort on the part of scholars and specialists to produce a work of permanent value. The series began in 1978 with the publication of three volumes. Progress has been slow and steady, with deliberate care being taken by Smithsonian Institution. There are 12 volumes to date, with another, volume 18, slated for publication in 2003. Each volume has an editor and multiple contributors of lengthy essays on the topics covered. Those sections covering tribal groups have segments on synonymies, identifying variant names by which the groups have been known. Each of the 700- to 800-page volumes concludes with a bibliography and an index. All are profusely illustrated. The plan for the set has the 20 volumes divided into three groupings. Volumes 1–4 are to furnish an overview of social-historical conditions. Of this group, only volume 4, *History of Indian-White Relations,* edited by Wilcomb E. Washburn (1988), is available. The second group is made up of volumes 5–15 and furnishes coverage of major cultural areas. Available are volume 5, *Arctic,* edited by David Damas (1984); volume 6, *Subarctic,* edited by June Helm (1978); volume 7, *Northwest Coast,* edited by Wayne Suttles (1990); volume 8, *California,* edited by Robert F. Heizer (1978); volumes 9–10, *Southwest,* edited by Alfonso Ortiz (1979, 1984); volume 11, *Great Basin,* edited by Warren L. D'Azevado (1986); volume 12, *Plateau,* edited by Deward E. Walker (1999); volume 13, *Plains,* edited by Raymond J. DeMallie (2001); and volume 15, *Northeast,* edited by Bruce B. Trigger (1978). Only one of the volumes in the third group, which is to cover technology, linguistics, and biography, is completed at this time; volume 17, *Languages,* edited by Sturtevant, the general editor. Volume 20 is to be the index volume.

915. History of the Indian Tribes of North America, with Biographical Sketches and Anecdotes of the Principal Chiefs, Embellished with Eighty Portraits from the Indian Gallery in the War Department at Washington. Thomas L. McKenney. Philadelphia: J.T. Bowen, 1848–1850. 2v. Repr. Kent, OH: Volair, 1978. ISBN 0-93148-012-4 (v. 1).

This monumental project completed between the years 1836 and 1844 is one of the real classics of the literature on American Indians. McKenney, as head of the Bureau of Indian Affairs from 1824 to 1830, was able to enlist aid and support in producing this work, which is described in the full title. It was published in two volumes, 1848–1850, after much trial and tribulation. McKenney begged, borrowed, and enticed both writers and graphic artists to participate, including his coeditor, James Hall. In the end, the effort met with little remuneration; the historical narrative and biographical sketches were all but forgotten in what was referred to as the "Great Portfolio" or "Indian Portrait Gallery." Those prints are especially valuable, the original volumes selling for thousands of dollars today. The work has been reprinted at various times and is available on microfilm. The 1978 reprint by Volair contains 120 portraits "from the Indian Gallery," which includes 40 more portraits than in the original printing.

In 1999, the United States Game Systems issued *Biographical Portraits of 108 Native Americans: Based on History of the Indian Tribes of North America* edited by Marc Newman. It represents an excellent and accessible abridgement of the original.

916. The Indian Tribes of North America. John R. Swanton. Washington, D.C.: Smithsonian Institution, 1952. 726p. (U.S. Bureau of American Ethnology, Bulletin No. 145.) Washington: Smithsonian Institution, 1995. ISBN 0-8747-4179-3.

Another of the excellent government publications regarded as an important tool in the field, this handbook of information on Indian tribes still provides useful information for present-day students and inquirers. It has been reprinted several times due to its value as a historical work. Of course, it should be augmented by more recent material, especially because its intent was to furnish all levels of inquirers with a "gazetteer of present knowledge." It was originally published in 1952, and coverage extended through the year 1944. Arranged in directory fashion, first by state, then by other countries on this continent, entries for each tribe give information on location, history, population, noteworthy circumstances, names and their meanings, villages, and so forth. The work is comprehensive in terms of its inclusion of Indian tribes; the bibliography is extensive and carefully developed. A special feature is the inclusion of four foldout maps of tribal territories. A detailed index completes the work.

917. Macmillan Encyclopedia of Native American Tribes. 2nd ed. Michael Johnson. New York: Macmillan Library Reference, 1999. 288p. ISBN 0-02-865409-9.

The first edition of this work was issued in 1994, and was regarded as a useful compendium of Indian life. The current effort is similar in format and treatment to the earlier publication; its scope is that of the four-volume *Gale Encylopedia of Native American Tribes* (entry 910) in its comprehensive coverage of 400 different tribes. Entries are brief but informative and supply historical and cultural overviews. The volume is organized into cultural regions, and then divided by linguistic groups. Illustrations have been integrated into the descriptive narrative in this edition resulting in an improved presentation over that of the initial work. Charts are used to identify language groups and tribes; maps are designed to appeal to the needs and interests of a wide audience. Appendixes supply listings of Web sites, museums, tribes, and more. Indexing is by tribal name.

918. Native America in the Twentieth Century: An Encyclopedia. Mary B. Davis, ed. New York: Garland, 1996. 832p. ISBN 0-8153-2583-5.

This is a unique and useful one-volume compendium, focusing on contemporary Amcrican (not Canadian) Indians and the conditions under which they live. There are over 300 signed entries furnished by experts in the field, 40 percent of whom arc of Native American descent. Entries are arranged alphabetically and run from less than a page to several pages in length. More than half of them treat individual tribal groups from the well-known Navaho to the obscure Hoh. Other entries contain survey-type overviews of broad topics such as art, economic conditions, health, educational policy, religion, and reservations. Especially interesting is the treatment given to the concept of Red Power and its impact on Indians today. Also included are various organizations, federal acts, and legal decisions. Entries contain useful bibliographies, and the work is enhanced through the presence of maps and photographs. A detailed index provides excellent access.

American Indians in American History, 1870–2000: A Companion Reader, edited by Sterling Evans supplies 17 essays by scholars and specialists addressing significant policies and relevant social issues (religion, environment, culture, gender concerns, and so forth. Essays are organized by time periods corresponding to those utilized in textbooks, and the work is a useful source for students at high school or college level.

919. Native American Bibliographies series. Metuchen, NJ: Scarecrow, 1980–. v. 1–. (Projected 20v.) ISSN 1040-9629.

This series began in 1980 with *Bibliography of the Sioux* by Jack W. Marken and Herbert T. Hoover and was projected as a 20-volume effort covering an array of topics and tribes. Since then progress has been steady, and the series has gained an excellent reputation for scholarly products. Comprehensiveness and depth compare favorably to the *Bibliographical Series* (entry 895) and other efforts that attempted similar coverage of specific tribes. Those volumes that are topical rather than tribal-specific are generally of the same high quality. Most volumes in the series list from one thousand to several thousand books, articles, government publications, newspaper items, and pamphlets, with the dates ranging from pre-colonial times to the present. Since then the series has continued and remains active in exceeding its projected total. It reached volume 26, *The Shawnee Indians: An Annotated Bibliography* by Randolph Noe in 2001. A complete listing of titles and authors can be identified through the series option in *WorldCat* (entry 14n).

920. A Native American Encyclopedia: History, Culture, and Peoples. Barry M. Pritz-ker. New York: Oxford University Press, 2000. 624p. ISBN 0-19-513897-X.

A useful source for students of all ages, this work is styled after an earlier work by Pritzker (see below). It examines the conditions surrounding the historical and cultural history of more than 200 Native American groups in the United States and Canada. It is organized into 10 geographic areas under which the entries for tribal nations are in alphabetical sequence. Tribal names are explained in terms of meaning and origin, and up-to-date information is given on the population, governance, economy, legal status, and land holdings along with historical accounts of key aspects. There are biographical sketches of important figures and excellent coverage of customs, dress, dwellings, and weapons. Some of the narrative is anecdotal in nature in retelling interesting and entertaining stories. This serves to bring history and culture to life for the user. Appendixes furnish useful listings of Alaskan Native Villages by Language, and Anca Village Corporations.

Pritzker's earlier work in two volumes, *Native Americans: An Encyclopedia of History, Culture, and Peoples* (ABC-CLIO, 1998) serves as a model for the more recent title above. Coverage is similar in content and in organization, although it has been criticized for difficulties in providing lucid distinctions between the past and the present. Volume 2 serves as the index and contains appendixes.

921. Native American Internet Guide. 2nd ed. Martha R. Crow. Nyack, NY: Todd Publications, 2000. 60p. ISBN 0-915344-88-2.

This represents a good attempt at producing what the author refers to as a genre Internet guide in its focus on a specific topic and its representation of useful Web sites. The result is a useful directory of some 1700 Native American organizations, businesses, and personalities organized under 28 categories. Categories include such topical designations and issues as computers, education, employment, law, social justice, and such elements of popular culture as radio, television, video, and so forth. Author Crow is Native American and has striven to provide authentic and accurate listings, but as one might expect, there are a number of nonworking links due to the lack of stability in cyberspace. Entries supply Web site location, phone number, and e-mail address and in some cases provide a descriptive annotation.

922. Native Americans: An Annotated Bibliography. Frederick E. Hoxie and Harvey Markowitz. Pasadena, CA: Salem, 1991. 325p. (Magill Bibliographies). ISBN 0-89356-670-5.

With the emphasis in the past few decades on eliminating stereotypes and the caricature-type formula from writings on American Indians, this product represents a useful and timely effort. It is an annotated bibliography of books and articles determined to be more genuine and truthful than most writings in their representation of events and conditions. In many cases, these works were aided in having Native American authors, collaborators, and contributors. Restricted to English-language material, most of which has been published since 1970, entries are organized into topical sections following the initial unit on general and reference works. There is a short segment on history, followed by sections on the various culture areas. Material tends to be scholarly rather than popular in nature. Annotations are descriptive of content. There is a personal name/author index.

923. The Native North American Almanac: A Reference Work on Native North Americans in the United States and Canada. 2nd ed. Detroit: Gale, 2001. 1472p. ISBN 0-7876-1655-9.

The first edition of this work was issued in 1994 and was designed to appeal to youngsters. The second edition represents a more sophisticated and more detailed treatment providing comprehensive coverage suitable to the needs of a wide audience ranging from high school to adult levels. Both historical and contemporary matters are examined in furnishing a comprehensive treatment of Native American life. Information is of varied nature, and one may find directory-type address and contact data including Web site URLs for numerous organizations and institutions such as archives, libraries, museums, and so forth, as well as historical descriptions of tribes and interpretations of tribal cultures. In addition, there are descriptions of religion, education, language, health, art, law and legislation and more. Maps and photographs complement the textual narrative and add to the utility of the work.

924. Native North American Firsts. Karen Swisher et al. Detroit: Gale, 1997. ISBN 0-7876-0518-2.

This is an entertaining as well as useful volume in its presentation of some 1,500 "firsts" in Native American history and culture. The work is organized under broad general topics (arts, crafts, and design, business, education, performing arts, etc.) that are arranged alphabetically. The entries then are listed in chronological sequence. Information was culled from a variety of sources such as standard reference works, biographical publications, and periodical articles as well as through solicitation and publicity placed in media targeted to appropriate audiences. Accomplishments and breakthroughs related to Indians in contiguous United States, Canada, and Alaska are included with slight coverage given to those of native groups in Mexico, Central America, and South America. In addition, there is a timeline, a calendar organized by month and date, and a bibliography. There is an index by year, as well as a general index.

*925. North American Indian & Eskimo Culture. South Dennis, MA: Quevillon Editions. [CD-ROM].

Available in CD-ROM format is the complete text of the Smithsonian Institution's four-volume set of Bureau of American Ethnology publications of 1879–1960. The sourcebook contains the text of 150 titles producing 8,500 plates, along with exposition and descriptive narrative on the culture of Eskimos and North American Indians. Anthropological discoveries are described; coverage is well developed and furnishes excellent in-depth information on nineteenth- and twentieth-century conditions and development. Insight is given into the lifestyles, legends, religious rites, art, and culture of these peoples. Included are relevant publications of the U.S. Geological Survey.

A similar CD-ROM product is *North American Indians,* available from Quanta Press of St. Paul, Minnesota. This title furnishes historical descriptions of Native Americans, including their tribal heritage, religion, family life, and customs. Material is derived from the U.S. Bureau of Ethnology.

926. Notable Native Americans. 2nd ed. Sharon Malinowski, ed. Detroit: Gale, 1995. 492p. ISBN 0-8103-9638- 6.

Opening with a scholarly and informative (yet interesting) introductory essay on the nature and complexities in establishing Indian identity, this biographical dictionary is useful in its emphasis on the inclusion of contemporary or twentieth-century personalities (many still living) who make up 70 percent of the total of 265 entries. Selection of individuals from all fields of endeavor was made with the assistance of an advisory board, and many of the contributors were Native Americans. Entries vary in length from one to four pages and contain reading lists and often furnish photographs. Special features include listings of figures by occupation, tribal affiliation, and surname, as well as brief descriptions of contributors. There is a detailed and comprehensive subject index.

Forthcoming from Greenwood in 2002–2003 are three titles from a new series, "Distinguished Native Americans" that will furnish in-depth sketches describing the lives and career achievements and analyzing the impact of some 100 notable current and historical personalities from different fields. *Distinguished Native American Spiritual Practitioners and Healers* by Troy Johnson, an academic specialist in the area, is slated to be the first issue in mid-2002. Following that will be *Distinguished Native American Political and Tribal Leaders* by Duane Champagne and Delia Salvatierra, later in the year. In early 2003, *Distinguished Native American Military Leaders* by Paulette Molin is due to be released.

927. Reference Encyclopedia of the American Indian. 9th ed. Nyack, NY: Todd Publications, 2000. 708p. ISBN 0-915344-89-0. Bienn.

Although useful, this work is misnamed; it is a directory rather than an encyclopedia. It remains a standard source in the field and generally has been issued on a biennial basis. It is unchanged in format and is divided into four sections, the first of which covers the United States (state by state) and the second treats Canada. In these two sections, one is able to find entries for reservations, tribal councils, associations, agencies, educational institutions and programs, museums, casinos, parks, events, and more. The third part furnishes a bibliographic listing of 4,500 relevant books, and the final segment supplies brief biographical sketches of 2,500 influential Native Americans.

Native Americans Information Directory is now in its second edition issued by Gale in 1998, five years after the initial effort. In a volume with half the number of pages as the above effort, it identifies more than 4,400 relevant resources in five sections treating United States, Alaska, Hawaii, and Canada, with a final section giving general resources. Much of the same information is given as in the work above.

928. Timelines of Native American History: Through the Centuries with Mother Earth and Father Sky. Susan Hazen-Hammond. New York: Perigee Books/Putnam, 1997. 332p. ISBN 0-399-52307-3.

A useful and comprehensive source written by a former academic, this work will find ready acceptance by students at high school and college undergraduate level. It provides an extensive chronology beginning with an entry "Before 20,000 B.C.," and ending with "2000 and Beyond." Coverage of actual events starts around 22,000 B.C. and finishes in 1996. Events are varied in nature and are enhanced with numerous sidebars containing pertinent quotations from speeches, excerpts from treaties, and interesting factual narratives regarding tribal history and customs. Biographical information is furnished as well. Coverage is broad and inclusive of some 500 tribal groups both prominent and obscure. A bibliography is given, and an index supplies access.

Wars

929. Encyclopedia of American Indian Wars, 1492–1890. Jerry Keenan. Santa Barbara, CA: ABC-CLIO, 1997. 278p. ISBN 0-87436-796-4.

A model of objective treatment, this work provides a useful and informative coverage of campaigns, battles, and wars that were fought due to the conflict between the new western culture and the values and customs of American Indians. Some 450 entries describe an array of topics such as individual tribes, concepts, issues, policies, treaties, sites, weaponry, and personalities. Both familiar and obscure topics are treated. Entries contain cross-references to readings listed in the bibliography at the end. Personalities are diverse and both significant Native Americans involved in the battles as well as relevant white authorities, military personnel, and settlers are identified and their lives described. Illustrations enhance the effort, although certain entries would profit from more-detailed narrative than they were given. In general, it is a satisfactory source that appeals to a wide audience.

930. A Guide to the Indian Wars of the West. John D. McDermott. Lincoln: University of Nebraska Press, 1998. 205p. ISBN 0-8032-8246-X.

A useful source in its examination of the issues and challenges faced by both the soldiers and their Indian enemies in waging war in the trans-Mississippi West beginning in the 1850s, the guide is authored by national park administrator and historian. Then, as now, there were differing ideas within the body of the American people about the wisdom of carrying on the war effort, and these controversies affected the soldiers and soldiering then as they do now. The arguments, issues, and varying perspectives of both sides are identified and summarized in logical fashion and one is able to perceive the difficulties in pursuing these struggles. Treatment is given to the material culture, approaches to warfare, background issues, clothing, philosophy, and religion. Also comparisons are given of the similarities and differences between Native American tribes, and treatment of the battles as portrayed in art and motion pictures. The second part of the work is the directory by state to relevant historic sites.

931. Indian War Sites: A Guidebook to Battlefields, Monuments, and Memorials, State by State with Canada and Mexico. Steve Rajtar. Jefferson, NC: McFarland, 1999. 330p. ISBN 0-7864-0710-7.

This is a comprehensive guide and directory to hundreds of battles in which the enemies were Native Americans on one side and Caucasians on the other. This would include engagements such as those in the Civil War and in the War of 1812 in which Indians participated on the side of one of the armies involved. Hundreds of battles are identified beginning in 1513 with the landing of Ponce de Leon and ending in 1915 with the Yaqui War. They range from minor skirmishes to major battles and are arranged state by state in chronological sequence. Entries supply a brief description of the struggle, identification of the larger war of which it was a part, dates, locations, memorials, and a list of sources keyed to a bibliography of 425 items. Indexes are given to battles and to place names.

Indian-White Relations

932. A Bibliographical Guide to the History of Indian-White Relations in the United States. Francis P. Prucha. Chicago: University of Chicago, 1977. 454p. ISBN 0-226-68476-8.

Prucha, a noted bibliographer-historian and expert on the history of Native Americans, made this excellent contribution to research and study. More than 9,700 entries are furnished; these touch on every aspect of Indian-white relations, including those covering the British colonial period. Neither Canadian nor Spanish materials are given. Materials collected represent books, journals, periodical articles, pamphlets, and dissertations published through the year 1975. There are two major divisions. Part I offers a guide to source materials such as archives and government documents; part II represents the bulk of the text and furnishes a classified listing of materials in such categories as "Treaties and Councils," "Trade and Traders," and "Legal Relations."

The above title is supplemented by Prucha's *Indian-White Relations in the United States: A Bibliography of Works Published, 1975–1980* (University of Nebraska, 1982). Here, another 3,400 entries are furnished in the same style and organization of the earlier publication. Both volumes contain author and subject indexes.

933. Handbook of the American Frontier: Four Centuries of Indian-White Relationships. J. Norman Heard. Metuchen, NJ: Scarecrow, 1987–1998. 5v. (Native American Resources Series, no. 1.) ISBN 0-8108-1931-7 (v. 1).

As a first issue of a new series from the publisher, this superb five-volume work by a librarian and writer on Native Americans was developed to cover all aspects and considerations of Indian-white relations. It took 11 years to complete with each volume appearing at a different time. Each of the volumes treats a different region. Volume 1 examines the Southeastern Woodlands; volume 2 handles the Northeastern Woodlands; volume 3 covers the Great Plains; and volume 4 describes the far west. The final volume supplies a comprehensive index to the set, a chronology of Indian-white relations from 1513 to 1918, and a bibliography. The work is well constructed and is a useful resource for students and beginning researchers. Entries are alphabetically arranged and provide a surprising amount of detail on the tribes, leaders, explorers, traders, missionaries, battles, and events. They vary in length from a few sentences to a full page.

934. Images of the Other: A Guide to Microform Manuscripts on Indian-White Relations. Polly S. Grimshaw. Champaign-Urbana, IL: University of Illinois Press, 1991. 174p. ISBN 0-252-01759-5.

This recent bibliographic guide enumerates the holdings of 65 repositories for which collections have been reproduced and made available for purchase in microformat. They represent European perspectives on the American Indian and, as such, have value for both serious students and scholars of intellectual and social history. It has been noted that length of time of commercial availability varies considerably for the entries, and work is required in tracking down the present holders of some of the sets. Each entry is described at length, beginning with a history of the collection and its significance. Then follows enumeration of content, editorial strategies, and listings of guides and help aids. Even the legibility of the documents is covered. Sets are organized into several categories, such as reports, letters, treaties, and organizations, and coverage ranges from 1631 to the late 1970s. There are author and subject indexes.

935. Native American Testimony: A Chronicle of Indian-White Relations from Prophecy to the Present, 1492–1992. Peter Nabokov, ed. New York: Viking, 1991. 386p. ISBN 0-670-83704-0.

This sourcebook by a well-known social historian containing Native American commentary on the events of the past 400 years is of immense value to study and research. It opens with a foreword by Native American researcher and writer Vine Deloria, Jr., and constitutes an anthology of various types of primary source material found in autobiographies, government documents, and personal narratives. Uniquely, it presents a response from the perspective of the Native Americans to their life and times as shaped by their relationship with whites. It begins with the period of Columbus's exploration and progresses through the difficult years of war, retaliation, humiliation, and relocation, up to the present day and the attempts to redress earlier wrongs. The tales are poignant and effectively told through a good selection of documents, and commentary by the author is enlightening. This work was popular enough to issue a paperback edition in 1992.

Civil Rights and the Law

936. The ABC-CLIO Companion to the Native American Rights Movement. Mark Grossman. Santa Barbara, CA: ABC-CLIO, 1996. 498p. (ABC-CLIO Companions to Key Issues in American History and Life). ISBN 0-87436-822-7.

A useful compendium for students at the college level, this work provides a comprehensive examination of aspects, concepts, personalities, and documentary sources relevant to the movement to secure American Indian rights. Entries are alphabetically arranged and treat topics dating back to the early sixteenth century with Spanish law, but emphasis is placed on the laws, movements, events, documents, and trends relevant to and emerging out of existence in North America. Biographical treatment is given to reformers, Indian commissioners, Native American leaders, jurists, and legislators involved in the issues. A useful feature is the inclusion of excerpts from documentary sources (treaties, reports on massacres, proclamations, etc.) in presenting a vivid picture of reality. Pictures accompany some of the articles.

937. American Indian Law Deskbook. 2nd ed. Joseph P. Mazurek et al., eds. Boulder: University of Colorado, 1998. 520p. ISBN 0-87081-471-0.

The first edition was issued in 1993, and the work had been supplemented annually since then. The current effort incorporates the supplementary materials into the main text, and adds a thorough examination of the increasingly significant issues of tribal sovereignty. The work remains a collaborative effort of lawyers connected to the offices of the western states' Attorneys General, and represents a comprehensive treatise on Indian law. Users are given insight into the historical and legal framework behind the controversial and complex issues that govern the lives of American Indians. Chapters treat Federal law policy development, tribe and country issues, criminal law, and civil regulatory jurisdiction. Matters pertaining to such issues as gaming rights, child welfare, and environmental regulation are addressed within the chapters.

938. American Indian Legal Materials: A Union List. Laura N. Gasaway et al., comps. Stanfordville, NY: E.M. Coleman, 1980. (American Indians at Law Series). 152p. ISBN 0-930576-31-4.

In an attempt to control the elusive material on legal matters relevant to the Native American, the compilers have prepared a listing of over 4,500 entries held by libraries of 28 law schools, law firms, and governmental agencies. No annotations are given for the entries; arrangement is alphabetical by main entry, with each given a sequential entry number. Included are a variety of materials: monographic works on tribal codes, resolutions, constitutions, and so on. Quality of informational materials for the research of legal history varies widely, with many inclusions of novels as well as titles on education and on ethnology. Even so, the uniqueness of the content makes this an important resource for both scholars and students. There are three indexes to assure access by tribe, geography, or subject.

939. Encyclopedia of American Indian Civil Rights. James S. Olson et al., eds. Westport, CT: Greenwood Press, 1997. 417p. ISBN 0-313-29338-4.

As part of the increasing body of reference material issued in the recent past, this serves to focus on the issues of rights in the Native American quest for equality and equal protection under the law. Some 600 entries are furnished in alphabetical arrangement and examining a variety of events and significant personalities. Also included are organizations as well as court cases and legislation. The main text is preceded by a useful introductory essay enumerating and describing major issues. Entries generally are brief but range from a single paragraph to several pages in length. In most cases, they end with a selected bibliography for additional reading. Special features include a chronology of major landmarks in the history of Native American civil rights from 1781 to 1996 and numerous photographs. There are a listing of court cases and a detailed bibliography.

Civil liberties is one of the major issues examined in *American Indians and U.S. Politics: A Companion Reader,* edited by John M. Meyer (Praeger Publishers, 2002). This source supplies well-developed and cogent expositions and interpretations of major topics central to contemporary Native American life. Students at all levels are aided by treatments of such elements as Congress, the court system, campaigns and elections, political ideals, groups and interests, and more.

940. The Encyclopedia of Native American Legal Tradition. Bruce E. Johansen, ed. Westport, CT: Greenwood Press, 1998. 410p. ISBN 0-313-30167-0.

Considered to be an excellent source of information for students and inquirers in its presentation of a variety of topics and personalities relevant to the study of legal and political traditions as represented in the lives of Native American peoples, this source opens with an informative introduction providing thematic perspective. Entries are of varying length and are arranged alphabetically in examining diverse elements, generally containing cross-references and concluding with suggested sources. One is able to find information on treaties, legal decisions and court cases, acts of Congress, key figures (both Indian and non-Indian), and legal systems of individual tribes. There is topical treatment of issues, events and activities ("Indianizing," banishment, etc.). Contributors are professionals in academe or in jurisprudence with knowledge of the Native American experience. There is a general bibliography and an index.

*941. Native American Legal Resources. Marilyn Nicely. University of Oklahoma College of Law. 1997–. Available: http://www.law.ou.edu/indian/.

A valuable Web site for treatment of legal involvement and affairs of American Indians, it is the product of the long-held active interest and engagement of the University of Oklahoma College of Law. The first segment contains two important resources produced by the College, the first of which is the *American Indian Law Review.* This publication furnishes a directory, an index of articles, commentaries, and notes and indexes to authors and book reviews, subjects, tribes, and legislation statutes and treaties. The second is a major work, the *Native American Constitution and Law Digitization Project,* a cooperative effort with National Indian Law Library and various tribes. It supplies access to 22 tribal constitutions, six codes, texts on Indian land titles, documents relevant to the Indian Reorganization Act, summaries of recent cases, and more. The second segment or division gives links to additional resources such as tribal nation home pages, historical resources, legal resources, and so forth.

*942. The Native American Rights Movement in the United States: Interactive Encyclopedia. Santa Barbara, CA: ABC-CLIO, 2000. [CD-ROM].

Based on Mark Grossman's *The ABC-CLIO Companion to the Native American Rights Movement* (ABC-CLIO, 1996), this is another of the publisher's useful titles developed as an interactive encyclopedia (entries 546, 594, 674, 838, 1102). The printed work examines the history (beginning in the seventeenth century) and increasing emergence of the civil rights movement among Native Americans. Topics are arranged alphabetically and provide biographical sketches of significant personalities, both Indian and Caucasian, events, treaties, legal decisions, religious practices, acts, proclamations, and reports. Much of the data is drawn from primary sources issued by the government and significant wording and quotes are presented. Excerpts of reports furnish the true picture of the historical period, and its impact. The interactive encyclopedia reproduces the material in Grossman's effort and adds more to it in furnishing access to 500 topics. Video and audio-clips enhance the text and give evidence of the value of multimedia resources.

943. Native Americans and the Law: A Dictionary. Gary A. Sokolow. Santa Barbara, CA: ABC-CLIO, 2000. 278p. (Contemporary Legal Issues). ISBN 0-87436-877-4.

The author is an experienced attorney who has practiced before tribal courts and comprehends the complexities of Indian law. He has developed an important dictionary of terms used in the field for the non-lawyer who is challenged or unaware of the many nuances and obscurities relevant to legal judgments in cases involving Native Americans. To this end he supplies a comprehensive and useful introduction describing the history, scope, involvement, and participation as well as the future of Indian law. He defines Indian law as "determination of the rights and obligations that Indians, their tribes, non-Indians, and all levels of governments have toward one another." There are 250 entries arranged alphabetically and describing influential court cases, legislation, personalities, organizations, concepts, and relevant issues as well as terminology. The work concludes with tables of statutes and of cases, detailed bibliography, and comprehensive index.

Economics, Land, Statistics

944. The Encyclopedia of Native American Economic History. Bruce E. Johansen, ed. Westport, CT: Greenwood Press, 1999. 301p. ISBN 0-313-30623-0.

This is a unique source in its thematic treatment of economic conditions and relationships and their impact on the history of the Native American. The work consists of about 100 entries of varying length ranging from a paragraph to several pages covering a variety of aspects related to different Native American tribes and relevant issues in the United States, Canada, Mexico, and Guatemala. The work begins with an introductory narrative describing the lack of resources and continuous focused research in this area, and then furnishes alphabetically arranged articles treating diverse topics such as personalities, geographic locations, broad issues, organizations, and tribes. The economic traditions of the distant past are given as are the changes caused by contact with Europeans. Contemporary conditions on the reservations are examined, as are environmental influences and issues. Most entries contain references to additional sources.

945. Nations Within a Nation: Historical Statistics of American Indians. Paul Stuart. New York: Greenwood Press, 1987. 251p. ISBN 0-313-23813-8.

This recent compendium of historical statistics on American Indians is of use to both researchers and students. The information was drawn from an array of works published over the last 100 years, federal and state documents, books and monographs, articles, and reports. The author is a university professor in social work who has had an extensive professional interest in Native Americans and has prepared this volume as a statistical overview and starting point for scholarly research of the eight general areas into which the work is divided. These general topics are land holdings and climate, population, relocation (including urbanization), vital statistics (including health), government activities, health care, employment, and economic development. There are numerous tables and charts, primarily furnishing information from years subsequent to 1870. These are footnoted with additional references. There is an extensive bibliography of primary sources, and an index is also furnished.

946. Shapers of the Great Debate on Native Americans—Land, Spirit, and Power: A Biographical Dictionary. Bruce E. Johansen. Westport, CT: Greenwood Press, 2000. (Shapers of the Great American Debates, no. 2). 274p. ISBN 0-313-30941-8.

Designed to meet the needs of students at the high school and undergraduate levels, this work presents a fruitful examination of the overriding issue in Native American existence, that of land acquisition, ownership, and use. Following an introductory overview of the nature and importance of the topic, the contents of the work are divided into eight thematic chapters, chronologically sequenced, examining the lives and careers of influential personalities relevant to the chapter theme. The thoughts, belief systems, and personal philosophies of these individuals, both Native American and non-Indian, are described, and diverse viewpoints are presented. The first seven chapter themes represent topics of historical nature dating from the seventeenth through the early twentieth centuries. The final chapter, "Land Base and Reclamation of Culture, 1934–2000," supplies contemporary figures and their viewpoints. Chapters contain bibliographies, and a detailed index provides access.

947. Statistical Record of Native North Americans. 2nd ed. Gale Research Incorporated, ed. Detroit: Gale, 1995.

Among the vast array of statistical data related to contemporary Native American people in the continental United States, Alaska, and Canada, there is excellent coverage of historical elements. Included in the history segment are tables and listings of population estimates, migration, health issues such as epidemics, various demographics, and more. This is 1 of 12 chapters, and together with the coverage given to current cultural and social statistics relating to individual tribes, nations and families, population characteristics, economy and land ownership, social economy, education, legal status, environment, and so forth presents a complete compilation on this group of people. The 12 chapters treat broad subject areas, (history, family, etc.) and furnish some 900 charts, graphs, and tables on nearly 200 tribes. Data were collected from both primary and secondary sources as well as input from various organizations. A keyword index provides access.

Female Influences

948. A to Z of Native American Women. Liz Sonneborn. New York: Facts on File, 1998. 228p. (Encyclopedia of Women). ISBN 0-8160-3580-6.

This compact biographical dictionary examines the lives and achievements of 101 Native American women from the eighteenth century to the present day. There is emphasis on nineteenth- and twentieth-century personalities, with a third of them still living at the time of publication. The work opens with an introductory narrative providing exposition of the role played by Native American females. There is a good mix of personalities ranging from the well known to the obscure, and engaged in diverse endeavors such as art, education, the law, social activism, tribal politics, and more. Entries vary in length from one to four pages, some of which contain photographs. There is a bibliography and several indexes supply excellent access.

949. American Indian Women: A Guide to Research. Gretchen M. Bataille and Kathleen M. Sands. Hamden, CT: Garland, 1991. 423p. (Garland Reference Library of Social Science, v. 515; Women's History and Culture, v. 4.) ISBN 0-8240-4799-0.

This recent effort is considered to be the most comprehensive bibliography of scholarly and literary work by and about Native North American women. It furnishes nearly 1,575 items, both print and nonprint. Excluded are dissertations, pamphlets, children's literature, and any materials not in the English language. Annotations are brief and descriptive of content; many offer interesting and revealing facts related to the topic or the document. The entries are organized under eight different topical and form divisions, beginning with "Bibliographies and Reference Works." Following are "Ethnography, Cultural History, and Social Roles," "Policies and Law," "Health, Education and Employment," "Visual and Performing Arts," "Literature and Criticism," "Autobiography, Biography and Interviews," and "Film and Video." The work is indexed by time period, tribe, name, and subject and should serve the needs of both students and scholars.

950. The Native American Woman: Social, Economic, and Political Aspects. Joan Nordquist, comp. Santa Cruz, CA: Reference and Research Services, 1999. 67p. (Contemporary Social Issues: A Bibliographic Series, no. 56). ISBN 1-892068-10-9.

Another in the series of brief bibliographies on pertinent social issues by Nordquist for this publisher, this effort enumerates sources treating the world of Native American women. It is an extensive listing enumerating nearly 700 titles, and like others in the series includes books, book chapters, journal and magazine articles, as well as government documents, dissertations, and theses. The format is uniform to others in the series, and entries are organized into 15 categories, each of which is divided into listings for books, and those for articles. The entries are not annotated and are limited to published writings rather than unpublished narratives, as well as the scholarly research efforts. The work serves as a useful convenience tool for those with serious interest.

951. Native American Women: A Biographical Dictionary. 2nd ed. Gretchen M. Bataille and Laurie Lisa, eds. New York: Routledge, 2001. 396p. (Biographical Dictionaries of Minority Women). ISBN 0-415-93020-0.

The first edition of this work was published in 1993 and presented an important perspective of the lives and accomplishments of more than 230 females dating from the seventeenth century to the time of publication. The current effort is similar in style and format as well as style of presentation; like the earlier edition, many of the entries were contributed by Native American women. This is an expansion and updating of the earlier work. More than 60 contributors have been employed to provide a well-rounded and comprehensive treatment. Both living and deceased personalities are included, and much of the information from the former group was gathered from the individuals themselves. Following Bataille's useful introductory overview, entries are arranged alphabetically and contain listings of references. It remains a useful source for a wide audience.

Journalism and the Press

952. American Indian and Alaska Native Newspapers and Periodicals, 1826–1924. Daniel F. Littlefield and James W. Parins. Westport, CT: Greenwood Press, 1984. 482p. (Historical Guides to the World's Periodicals and Newspapers). ISBN 0-313-23426-4.

This is the first of three volumes issued by the authors over a period of two years and furnishes listings and holdings information for nearly 225 periodicals published by American Indians or Alaskan natives. It covers a span of nearly 100 years, from 1826 to 1924, and examines titles in depth, with entries running several pages in length. Entries are alphabetically arranged and contain general descriptions, information on indexing, library holdings, publication history, and editorship. There is a useful segment on titles known but not located. Appendixes furnish listings of titles arranged chronologically by publication date, state, and tribe. A general index of subjects includes persons, places, and topics.

The second volume was issued in 1986 and continues the coverage with an additional 500 newspapers and periodicals published between 1925 and 1970, and the third volume (also 1986) completes the coverage, adding another 1,000 titles published between 1971 and 1985. These efforts were aided by the contributions of more than 30 specialists for each volume.

953. Native American Periodicals and Newspapers, 1828–1982: Bibliography, Publishing Record, and Holdings. James P. Danky, ed. and Maureen E. Handy, comp. Westport, CT: Greenwood Press, 1984. 532p. ISBN 0-313-23773-5.

Issued during the same year as the first volume of Littlefield's and Parins's *American Indian and Alaska Native Newspapers and Periodicals, 1826–1924* (entry 952), this work drew favorable reviews for its more comprehensive nature in covering over 1,160 titles published over a 155-year period. Even with completion of the other (now three-volume) effort, this still remains a useful source of information that also should be used by inquirers at various levels. Entries tend to be brief but accurate and informative and furnish dates, frequency, editor, publisher, title variations, holding libraries, and availability in microform. The work is indexed extensively by subject, author, editor, publisher, geography, and chronology. Much of the material is held by the editor's library at the State Historical Society of Wisconsin, thus furnishing excellent resource material to develop this useful tool.

Religion

954. The Encyclopedia of Native American Religions. Rev. ed. Arlene B. Hirschberger et al. New York: Facts on File, 2000. 400p. ISBN 0-8160-3949-6.

The initial edition of this work appeared in 1991, and furnished entries of varying length examining ceremonies, rituals, and personalities (both Indian and non-Indian) associated with the religious observances of Native American peoples. Also included were sites involved in public disputes and litigation, but not the location of undisturbed sacred grounds. The current revised version continues in that vein but has expanded with the inclusion of court cases relating to environmental protection and increased coverage of litigation over preservation of sacred sites. The introduction describes the importance of traditional religions as the cohesive factor binding the various tribes through difficult times, and the significance of environmental influences is evident. Some 1,200 entries examine the traditions as well as the accommodations made necessary through European contact. An extensive bibliography is given.

Distinguished Native American Spiritual Practitioners and Healers by Troy R. Johnson (Oryx, 2002) supplies 100 biographical profiles of both famous and obscure spiritual leaders and healers. Personalities include both historical figures such as Geronimo and contemporary individuals who have devoted themselves to the healing arts. Entries furnish information regarding the lives, careers, and achievements of those selected for inclusion. There are recommendations for further reading and photographs of several of them. Appendixes contain listings by birth date and by tribal group or nation.

955. Encyclopedia of Native American Shamanism: Sacred Ceremonies of North America. William S. Lyon. Santa Barbara, CA: ABC-CLIO, 1998. 468p. ISBN 0-87436-933-9.

The author is an academic with real interest in the topic of Native American spirituality and religion, and the healing effects of strong belief systems. This is his second work in the subject area and represents a valuable source for serious inquirers. The focus is narrow in dealing with the manifestations of Shamanism, and entries are scholarly in nature and draw upon a body of research in anthropology. They vary in length from brief references to several pages and examine a variety of topics such as war medicine and ethnologists. The major emphasis in the main body of the text is the examination of specific beliefs and practices held by shamans. The subject index is important since it brings together the entries on individual tribes and broad topics.

Lyon's *Encyclopedia of Native American Healing* from the same publisher in 1996, is the initial effort and unique in its focus on shamanic healing qualities. Treatment is given to tribal cultures and origins of the belief systems. There are 15 maps furnishing locations of the tribal territories, and a bibliography relevant to the use of medicinal plants is given.

956. The Native American Sun Dance Religion and Ceremony: An Annotated Bibliography. Phillip M. White, comp. Westport, CT: Greenwood Press, 1998. 115p. ISBN 0-313-30628-1.

This is a unique source identifying 335 published works on the single most familiar of all Native American ceremonies. These are arranged by tribal name, then alphabetically by main entry. The source opens with a brief introduction explaining the significance of the Dance. The ceremony involves fasting and self-torture and has been observed by the Great Plains Indians (Arapaho, Blackfeet, Comanche, Cheyenne, Crow, Dakota, etc.) from the time of the early eighteenth century. Although outlawed by the government in 1904, it continued on a small scale until the mid-twentieth century when the practice regained its previous popularity. It requires the dancers to fix their gaze on the sun while dancing and blowing whistles. Included in the bibliographic coverage are dissertations and government publications as well as books and articles. No unpublished material is treated. The contents are indexed by author, tribe, and subject.

Regionalism

957. American Indian Archival Material: A Guide to Holdings in the Southeast. Ronald Chepesiuk and Arnold M. Shankman, comps. Westport, CT: Greenwood Press, 1982. 325p. ISBN 0-313-23731-X.

This directory of resources was compiled through responses to a mail questionnaire sent to institutions throughout the southeastern United States. From a total of 2,300 repositories in 11 states, there were just over 500 responses, the majority of them indicating that they held no archival or manuscript materials pertinent to the study of North American Indians. In addition to receiving 168 positive answers, the compilers were able to develop entries from secondary sources for six agencies that did not respond, producing a total of 174 archival centers. Although by no means complete, the listing is more comprehensive on the topic of native American materials than any previous effort. Entries are organized in directory fashion by state, then city, and furnish the expected information regarding the collections. Appendixes list both non-responding agencies and those reporting no holdings. There is a general index of names, places, and subjects.

*958. American Indians of the Pacific Northwest. University of Washington Libraries. Washington, D.C.: Library of Congress, 2000. (American Memory series). Available: http://memory.loc.gov/ammem/award98/wauhtml/aipnhome.html.

A well-constructed and useful Web site is maintained by the University of Washington in furnishing electronic access to its digital holdings drawn from its collection and those drawn from the collections of the Cheney Cowles/Museum/Eastern Washington State Historical Society in Spokane and of the Museum of History and Industry in Seattle. The digital collection was developed through support received from the National Digital Library Program administered by the Library of Congress. At this time, the collection contains over 2,300 photographs, and 7,700 pages of text relevant to the study of the American Indians in the Northwest Coast and Plateau areas. All aspects of life are treated such as housing, clothing, arts and crafts, education, employment, and so forth. Ten illustrated essays by specialists are furnished that cover several specific tribal groups and important issues.

959. An Annotated Bibliography of Northern Plains Ethnohistory. Katherine M. Weist and Susan R. Sharrock. Missoula, MT: Department of Anthropology, University of Montana, 1985. 299p. (Contributions to Anthropology, no. 8.) ISBN 0-916-29207-X.

This volume represents a real asset to serious inquiry on the Northern Plains Indians. It furnishes almost 700 annotated entries of primary sources (books, articles, and reports) on the pre-reservation period from 1690 to 1880. Because the amount of material covering the topic is massive in volume, inclusion was limited to titles written by authors present at that time and reporting their observations, regardless of publication date (some items date to the mid-1970s). Arrangement of entries is alphabetical by author; tribes covered include the Blackfoot, Gros Ventre, Assiniboine, Cree, Ojibwa, Crow, Cheyenne, and Arapaho. Full bibliographic data is given for each entry; annotations are ample and range from 100 to 150 words each. Included are lists of relevant secondary sources and of bibliographies on the subject. There is an index of names, tribes, and subjects.

960. Annotated Bibliography of the Literature on American Indians Published in State Historical Society Publications, New England and Middle Atlantic States. Arlene B. Hirschfelder. Millwood, NY: Kraus International, 1982. 356p. ISBN 0-527-40889-1.

This annotated bibliography furnishes a total of 1,182 articles derived from the issues of 37 journals and newsletters published by state historical societies from 11 New England and Middle Atlantic states. Materials both by and about American Indians are listed. Each journal is covered from its first issue to its final one or, if still operating, through its last full volume published during 1979. Although there is emphasis on tribes that lived in the area covered by Connecticut, Delaware, Maine, Maryland, Massachusetts, New Hampshire, New York, New Jersey, Pennsylvania, Rhode Island, and Vermont, other area tribes treated infrequently in those journals are included as well. Entries are arranged alphabetically and are accompanied by an ample annotation of descriptive nature. There are three indexes: by subject; by person, place, and title; and by Indian nation.

961. The Columbia Guide to American Indians of the Northeast. Kathleen J. Bragdon. New York: Columbia University Press, 2001. 276p. (Columbia Guides to American Indian History and Culture). ISBN 0-231-11452-4.

This is the second volume in a series designed to provide information and under-standing of Indian tribes in different parts of the country. The author is a professor of anthropology and has published other works on indigenous peoples. In this effort, she ex-amines the tribes of the northeastern United States and describes their history and cultural development beginning with the period prior to settlement by Europeans. The work is di-vided into four major sections, the first of which treats historical development, archaeology, and the issues surrounding cultural identity up to the present time. The second part provides a concise encyclopedia of personalities, issues, and events in alphabetical sequence, and the third section supplies a chronology. Part 4 contains a listing of sources with bibliographic entries as well as agencies and organizations.

The Columbia Guide to American Indians of the Southeast by Theda Perdue and Michael D. Green is the first volume in the series and set the pattern in presenting similar treatment and coverage of indigenous peoples of the southeastern United States beginning with the pre-Columbian period. Included here are the Cherokees and the Creeks as well as the early Mississippi Moundbuilder cultures.

962. A Guide to the Indian Tribes of the Pacific Northwest. Rev. ed. Robert H. Ruby and John A. Brown. Norman, OK: University of Oklahoma, 1986; repr. Pbk 1992. 289p. (The Civilization of the American Indian series, no. 173.) ISBN 0-8061-1967-5.

This is a slight revision and update of the 1986 issue. It continues as a general guide and encyclopedic work to more than 150 Indian tribes that either did reside or still reside in the Pacific Northwest region. It serves as a companion volume to a 1981 history by the same authors. The present effort furnishes an alphabetical approach, with entries varying in length according to the size or significance of the group. Illustrations are numerous and include both historical and recent photographic efforts. Cross-references are helpful in show-ing the relationship between tribes, and each entry ends with a list of suggested readings. Of interest to both students and beginning researchers, the tool furnishes information on historical traditions, customs, treaties, and population figures, among other things. There is a detailed index.

The companion work by the same authors, volume 158 in the *Civilization of the American* Indian series, is *Indians of the Pacific Northwest: A History* (University of Okla-homa, 1981; repr. 1988). It presents an excellent, well-constructed narrative, with emphasis on Indian-white relations over a period of 150 years, from 1750 to 1900. Included are maps and illustrations to aid comprehension.

THE GAY AND LESBIAN EXPERIENCE

The most recent struggle for fair treatment and equality is being waged by gay men and women who previously had concealed their sexual preferences and lived in fear of being detected. Beginning with a riot against the police in a Greenwich Village bar, the Stonewall Inn, in 1969, the past three decades have witnessed increasingly overt behavior among homosexuals, with public demonstrations of pride and strength. These demonstrations, not surprisingly, have met with both hostility and support from different quarters. All gay people do not agree, of course, on their social obligations or ethical roles, and some have felt victimized by an increasingly strident movement that has exposed or "outed" them despite their wishes to remain closeted. The television brouhaha over *Ellen* added further publicity and more recently, Rosie O'Donnell's decision to publicly announce that she is a lesbian was met with little shock and even less resentment. Americans have become more aware of the various issues that represent the focus or core of the struggle for fair treatment and acceptance. Even as legislators (such as those in Florida where O'Donnell resides) drag their feet, basic issues of health, employment, parenthood, and military service are now parts of public conscience and public record.

For the past decade, the trade literature has grown considerably in volume and has changed direction with respect to its more recent focus on homosexuality as an acceptable lifestyle. Liz McMillen's "From Margin to Mainstream: Books in Gay Studies" in *The Chronicle of Higher Education,* July 22, 1992, pp. A8–A13, is an example of publishing developments and the receptivity of mainstream publishers, especially university presses, to what has proved to be an extremely marketable topic. Series have been instituted by Oxford University, Duke University, New York University, and the University of Chicago, among others. Although reference publishing has not kept pace, its growth has been steady. In organizing our entries, the gender factor is secondary only to ethnic considerations; therefore works pertinent to gay and lesbian involvement in the law and politics will be found here rather than in other segments of this work treating legal and political influences.

The National Gay and Lesbian Task Force (available at http://www.ngltf.org) was founded in Washington, D.C., in 1973 and maintains an active program of lobbying, educating, and publishing. Some of the monographs provide historical insight.

General Sources

963. About Time: Exploring the Gay Past. Rev. and exp. ed. Martin B. Duberman. New York: Meridian, 1991. 480p. ISBN 0-452-01081-0.

The author is a well-known advocate, reporter, and historian of the gay experience who has put together an informative collection of both source materials and reflective essays furnishing a homosexual perspective. These pieces originally appeared in a 1986 publication, but here the set has been revised and in several ways augmented. The work is divided into three major segments, with the first part containing the original source material, which includes letters, excerpts from journals, and documents. The second section comprises reprinted material from Duberman's column from the *New York Native,* a periodical that since 1980 has been representing the gay viewpoint and advocating gay liberation. Finally, there is an extensive and useful bibliography of books and periodical articles covering a wide range of relevant topics in both the humanities and social sciences.

Another compilation, edited by Duberman and others, is *Hidden from History: Reclaiming the Gay and Lesbian Past* (New American Library, 1989). About 30 contributors have furnished scholarly essays on the homosexual experience from ancient to modern times in various parts of the world. Insight is given into the pattern of development that has led to the emerging awareness on the part of gay people in modern U.S. society.

964. An Annotated Bibliography of Homosexuality. Vern L. Bullough et al. New York: Garland, 1976. 2v. (Garland Reference Library of Social Science, v. 22.) ISBN 0-8240-9959-1.

This is the most extensive of the bibliographic efforts on the topic and furnishes nearly 12,800 books and articles representing coverage from various languages and subjects. Arrangement is by broad topical and format categories. Annotations tend to be brief and describe the content of most of the works included. Although the tool has been criticized for lack of expressed selection criteria, its breadth of coverage will assure its use by scholars and serious inquirers. Not only factual materials but also creative literary efforts and biographical works are enumerated. The strength of the work lies in its comprehensive nature and its employment of an interdisciplinary concept. The work is international in scope but gives ample coverage to U.S. issues and developments.

965. Completely Queer: The Gay and Lesbian Encyclopedia. Steve Hogan and Lee Hudson. New York: Henry Holt, 1998. 704p. ISBN 0-8050-3629-6.

Although not limited to homosexuality in the United States, there is an emphasis on American personalities as well as organizations, periodicals, and creative genres, while at the same time providing insight into the nature of the complex contemporary international subculture. The authors are New York-based and familiar with the interests of both homosexual men and lesbians and have represented those interests in balanced manner. There are some 500 well-written concise but informative entries arranged alphabetically and supplying carefully chosen bibliographies. About 250 photographs and illustrations enhance the narrative descriptions. There is a comprehensive detailed chronology dating from 12,000 B.C.E. through 1996, and useful listings of pseudonyms, gay literary award winners, and gay and lesbian detectives. Adequate indexing is supplied.

966. The Construction of Homosexuality. David F. Greenberg. Chicago: University of Chicago Press, 1988; repr. 1990. 635p ISBN 0-226-30628-3.

This is a cross-cultural comparative history of the nature of homosexuality and its impact on various societies and cultures. The author, a professor of sociology, begins his study with an examination of primitive tribes and clans, then traces developments through ancient and medieval periods and into modern times. He examines the character and structure of each time period and furnishes exposition of the nature of homosexual activity and the types of responses generated by each society. His examination is designed to explore why certain forms of homosexual practice emerged in the various cultures and to explain the types of attitudes that prevailed. Homosexuality, therefore, is treated to a unique type of scrutiny, providing opportunity for new interpretations within existing theories. It provides good background information to the scholar and researcher interested in U.S. studies.

967. Gay American History: Lesbians and Gay Men in the U.S.A., A Documentary History. Rev. ed. Jonathan N. Katz. New York: Meridian, 1992. 702p. ISBN 0-45201-092-6.

The work was originally issued in 1976, after which it was reprinted on several occasions. It has served as a documentary history of the gay presence in North America from the sixteenth century to the 1970s. Included here are complete and excerpted documents of various types: letters, journals, diaries, newspaper pieces, magazine and journal articles, reports, books, and interviews. The documents are arranged chronologically within six broad thematic sections: "Trouble" (early opposition/condemnation); "Treatment" (attempts at "curing" homosexuality); "Passing Women" (women who passed for men); "Native Americans/Gay Americans"; "Resistance"; and "Love." A feature of the new edition is an up-to-date 21-page bibliography of major texts for the study of lesbian and gay history in this country. The work remains one of the major sources of historical study.

The Rise of a Gay and Lesbian Movement by Barry D. Adam (Twayne, 1987) is a more comprehensive narrative history describing the social, economic, and political conditions associated with the rise of the movement on a global scale, from its seeds of origin in the French Revolution to its development in Germany in 1897, then its various phases in both Europe and the United States throughout the twentieth century. There are both lists of references and an annotated bibliography; the work places the U.S. gay movement within the perspective of a worldwide phenomenon.

968. Gay & Lesbian Biography. Michael J. Tyrkus, ed. Detroit: Gale, 1998. 515p. ISBN 1-55862-237-3. Robert B.M. Ridinger. New York: G.K. Hall/Simon and Schuster Macmillan, 1996. 487p. (Reference Publications on American Social Movements). ISBN 0-8161-7373-7.

This biographical dictionary is comprehensive in scope treating notable gays and lesbians from all time periods, cultures, and nationalities. There are 275 entries varying in length from several paragraphs to several pages, and written by freelance writers rather than specialists in the field of study. Selection of individuals was assisted by a six-member advisory board of librarians and writers representing the gay community. In examining the list of personalities, it is clear that emphasis has been placed on the inclusion of Americans and British nationals and literary figures, although artists, athletes, politicians, and others are present. Entries supply name, dates, and occupation at the outset, and provide a descriptive narrative on the person's role and influence in the gay and lesbian community. Lists of references are provided, as is a photograph when available. There is a general subject index to supply access.

969. The Gay and Lesbian Movement: References and Resources. Robert B.M. Ridinger. New York: G.K. Hall/Simon & Schuster Macmillan, 1996. 487p. (Reference Publications on American Social Movements). ISBN 0-8161-7373-7.

This is a comprehensive annotated bibliography providing more than 1,900 entries representing serious inquiry, research, and evaluative commentary relevant to the historical development of the international gay and lesbian movement. Entries representing monographs, popular and scholarly articles, and dissertations, are organized into three historical divisions. The initial period is 1864–1939 in which several publications are listed that treat the beginnings of the movement in Germany. The second period, 1924–1968, contains nearly 200 entries examining the awakening of the movement in the United States from its beginnings to the time of Stonewall. The bulk of the work, containing more than 1,600 entries, cover the post-Stonewall period, 1969–1993, in which the public marches and other overt acts brought attention to the issues. A detailed and comprehensive index is furnished.

970. The Homosexual and Society: An Annotated Bibliography. Robert B.M. Ridinger, comp. Westport, CT: Greenwood Press, 1990. 444p. (Bibliographies and Indexes in Sociology, no. 18). ISBN 0-313-25357-9.

This is a well-constructed, highly useful bibliography of articles and selected monographs published through 1987. Arrangement is under seven major realms "where homophobia has been expressed in coherent form: adoption and foster care, child custody, the military establishment, employment discrimination, censorship, religion, and police attitudes and actions." Nearly 860 entries are arranged chronologically under these issues, affording a convenient historical perspective. Entries date from the aftermath of the Stonewall Riots of 1969, generally considered to be the overt beginning of the gay liberation movement in this country. Articles are drawn primarily from three of the major journals of the gay community; *The Advocate, The Ladder,* and *The Mattachine Review,* as well as mainstream newsweeklies. Annotations are full and descriptive in content. There is an index of names and broad topics. Ridinger is a librarian and author of *An Index to the Advocate: The National Gay Newsmagazine, 1967–1982* (Liberation Publications, 1987).

971. Homosexuality: A Research Guide. Wayne R. Dynes. New York: Garland, 1987. 853p. (Garland Reference Library of Social Science, v. 313.) ISBN 0-8240-8692-9.

Containing more than 4,850 entries, this well-constructed annotated bibliography furnishes coverage of studies on various topics. Emphasis is given to history, psychology, sociology, and law, but also covered are an additional 20 categories such as language, politics, and anthropology. These categories are generally subdivided by more specific subtopics and furnish excellent access to needed material. There is a predominance of U.S. publications but also prominent German, Dutch, French, and Italian studies. Annotations are full and objectively describe content. The coverage is noteworthy for its balanced inclusion of studies relating to both past and current issues as well as U.S. and international influences. Also noteworthy are its interdisciplinary nature and its representation of all points of view. There is a name index and a subject index.

More recently, Dynes has served as principal editor for the two-volume *Encyclopedia of Homosexuality* (Garland, 1990), which gives a thorough look at issues, personages, and movements, with good historical emphasis.

972. Reader's Guide to Lesbian and Gay Studies. Timothy F. Murphy, ed. Chicago: Fitzroy Dearborn, 2000. 720p. ISBN 1-57958-142-0.

This is a useful bibliographic guide for serious inquirers to books, monographs, and periodical articles of scholarly nature primarily in English on a variety of topics relevant to gay and lesbian studies. Nearly 225 contributors have furnished more than 400 entries treating significant issues, personalities, historical periods, and topics of wide-ranging nature. Such aspects as regional studies are presented along with cultural phenomena specific to gay and lesbian life and lifestyle. Entries are arranged alphabetically, begin with a brief introduction to the subject, and supply bibliographic listings along with a summary overview and analysis of the secondary literature available. Sources identified in the bibliographies are described. A special feature is a thematic listing categorizing topics into broad subjects such as "African American culture", "AIDS", "education," "psychology," and so forth.

973. St. James Press Gay and Lesbian Almanac. Neil Schlager, ed. Detroit: St. James Press, 1998. 680p. ISBN 1-55862-358-2.

Considered by one reviewer to be "an outstanding reference title for gay and lesbian studies," this effort provides a comprehensive treatment of the topic in enough depth to satisfy the needs of a wide audience. In encyclopedic fashion, it examines factors and elements relevant to gay and lesbian life in this country with a pronounced emphasis on contemporary issues of the twentieth century. There are 23 chapters, most of which examine broad topical areas of study such as health, literature, politics, and so forth that in turn are subdivided by narrower subjects for study. There are biographical entries for 100 influential personalities. Special features are furnished in three chapters: a useful and detailed chronology dating from the 1940s to the 1990, identification and description of organizations, and both text and exposition of relevant documents. Some 200 illustrations enrich the textual narrative.

Civil Rights, the Law, Politics, and Gender Influences

*974. Bibliography: Lesbian and Gay History, Politics and Culture. Blanche W. Cook et al. New York: Hunter College. Available: http://maxweber.hunter.cuny.edu/polsc/ksherrill/biblio.html.

This is an excellent bibliography developed by instructors for a course they offer. It is organized into three major divisions each of which is then divided by narrower topics and furnishes books, periodical articles, and court decisions dating from the 1970s to the mid-1990s. The first major division is "The Historical Denial of Gay & Lesbian Experience" subdivided into sections treating "our closeted culture," "straightening the story," and "gays in the military." This is followed by the second part, "Civil Rights/Gay Rights/Human Rights" subdivided by "activists and agitators," "propaganda, political theater, performance, and writing," and "the role of law." The final segment is "Alternative Cultures/Counter Cultures Visions of Community Utopia/Revolution" and includes "families," "friendship networks and community building," and "acting up." It serves as a good starting point for a study in social and cultural history.

975. Creating Change: Sexuality, Public Policy, and Civil Rights. John D'Emilio et al., eds. New York: St. Martin's, 2000. 526p. ISBN 0-312-24375-8.

A useful source of information on the impact and progress of the gay and lesbian movement in the U.S. subsequent to Stonewall, this work offers a collection of essays by various participants and scholars. The essays are divided into three major categories treating presidential politics and government institutions, the gay legislative agenda, and the building of a viable advocacy movement. That so much has been accomplished in the past two decades while the country has been turning more conservative is a tribute to the active elements behind the movement who have understood the importance of developing strategies in the public policy arena. The effort represents a useful manual for social change and demonstrates the value of patience with cumulative incremental gain.

Creating a Place for Ourselves by Brett Beemyn (Routledge, 1997) is an earlier collection of 13 essays that serves as a precursor to the work above since it focuses on gay life in U.S. communities before Stonewall and spans a period from the 1920s to the 1960s. Contributors interviewed personalities and consulted written sources examining the gay communities in metropolitan areas such as San Francisco, New York, Chicago, Detroit, and Washington, D.C., among others. The story of their growth and survival provides an excellent introduction to the modern period dating from Stonewall.

976. Historical Dictionary of the Gay Liberation Movement: Gay Men and the Quest for Social Justice. Ronald J. Hunt. Lanham, MD: Scarecrow Press, 1999. 239p. (Historical Dictionaries of Religions, Philosophies, and Movements, no. 22.) ISBN 0-8108-3587-8.

The author is an academic who teaches a course in gay and lesbian influences, but in this work has restricted the focus to male homosexuals. The effort has been criticized for this restriction since many of the organizations identified and described provide services to both genders. Regardless, it is informative and useful to a wide audience due to its international coverage, beginning with a listing of acronyms followed by a comprehensive chronology spanning the period from 1864 to the 30th anniversary of Stonewall in 1999. The bulk of the work is the dictionary itself furnishing some 200 entries describing personalities, organizations, issues, publications, legislation, and activities relevant to the rights of homosexuals. Entries vary in length but average one page, and emphasize coverage of the twentieth century. There is an extensive bibliography, but no index is supplied.

977. Homosexuality and the Law: A Dictionary. Chuck Stewart. Santa Barbara, CA: ABC-CLIO, 2001. 429p. ISBN 1-57607-267-3.

This work has been carefully researched by the author who has presented solid information, much of it based on the findings and reports of studies carried out in fields such as sociology, psychology, and anthropology. The work opens with a detailed introductory essay presenting a historical overview of the gay rights movement from its beginnings to contemporary times following Stonewall. There are 112 entries alphabetically arranged, and providing detailed treatment of a variety of topics relevant to gay and lesbian life. These narratives supply information on such current concerns as "absurd sex laws," "gay scout leaders," "lesbian and gay families," and "sexual harassment in schools" as well as historical issues as "reparative therapy." The appendix furnishes a comprehensive directory of state and local laws, a listing of resources and services, and a table of statutes. The index supplies adequate access.

978. Lesbian Histories and Cultures: An Encyclopedia. Bonnie Zimmerman, ed. New York: Garland, 2000. 862p. (The Encyclopedia of Lesbian and Gay Histories and Cultures, v. 1.) ISBN 0-8153-1920-7.

Considered to be volume 1 of a two-volume encyclopedia (see work below), this is a landmark effort in its narrow focus on the issues and personalities representing the lesbian culture and history as distinctive in some respects from the conceptual, experiential, and societal orientation of males. Entries are arranged alphabetically and signed by an array of international contributors who are expert in the field. Entries vary in length from several paragraphs to several pages in their presentation of personalities, issues, events, organizations, broad topics, and so forth, and treat both the historical past and the present. Each entry contains a bibliography and cross-references to other entries to provide full coverage of such subjects as "activism," "adolescence," and the "media and popular culture." There are entries on various countries like "Zambia," affirming the international character of the work. A volume-specific index concludes the effort.

Gay Histories and Cultures: An Encyclopedia edited by George E. Haggerty and others (Garland, 2000) is volume 2 of the set and is similar in format in its presentation of the male homosexual culture. The articles are contributed by scholars and are concise but informative. Due to the selectivity of inclusion, the two volumes present a well-rounded, although not comprehensive, source of information on gay and lesbian life.

979. Sexual Politics, Sexual Communities: The Making of a Homosexual Minority in the United States, 1940–1970. 2nd ed. John D'Emilio. Chicago: University of Chicago Press, 1998. 258p. ISBN 0-226-14267-1.

The Chronicle of Higher Education review cited in our introductory narrative to this section describes D'Emilio's efforts to publish the first edition of this work (1983), the first published monograph on the history of gay life in the United States, and his gratefulness that the University of Chicago accepted it. Since then the market has exploded, and D'Emilio, an academic, has the services of an agent. This work examines the 30-year period prior to the Stonewall Riots in New York (1969) describing and interpreting the conditions that led to the emergence of gay liberation. The study began as part of the author's doctoral dissertation and is now recognized as a superb contribution, employing such records as personal letters, oral histories, and newspaper accounts. It examines both individual contributions and group efforts in order to place the movement within the context of other social developments. The second edition has a new preface and afterword that examines the conditions that led to publication of the book and the emergence of gay/lesbian historical writing. D'Emilio's compilation of articles, essays and lectures, *Making Trouble: Essays on Gay History, Politics, and the University* (Routledge, 1992), is divided into three segments: modern gay history in this country since World War I, response of the university to the emerging gay consciousness, and the struggle for social justice in the political realm.

Eric Marcus's book *Making History: The Struggle for Gay and Lesbian Equal Rights, 1945–1990: An Oral History* (HarperCollins, 1992) narrates the fight for homosexual rights up through very recent times through personal eyewitness accounts. *Before Stonewall: The Making of a Gay and Lesbian Community* by Andrea Weiss and Greta Schiller (Naiad, 1988) is a concise and well-developed popular history written by two principals involved in the making of an important documentary film of the same name. The formation of the gay subculture is described and its emergence explained.

SOCIAL WELFARE AND PHILANTHROPY

The question of philanthropy is associated with a variety of personal motivations on the part of the donor. These range from the self-serving to the altruistic. It is as important to study the motivations of the donors as they relate to the values and ideas of a group, class, or time period as it is to study the impact of the gifts on societal existence. Revisionist historians continue to probe these areas and furnish provocative theories about the giving of gifts and endowments on the part of both the private and public sectors. Regardless of the reasons for giving, such gifts benefit social welfare agencies and institutions. Closely related to the study of such social issues is the history of public works in this country.

Reference tools on these topics are not as abundant as one might have hoped. Additional sources relevant to this topic may be found in chapter 3, "Economic History," especially in the section on "Depression and Recession," which identifies sources on the Roosevelt era and New Deal measures.

Sociological Abstracts (1953–1992) is now a product of Cambridge Scientific Abstracts, and is no longer in print. It abstracts the periodical literature of sociology and related fields from 1,700 serial publications. Historical writings appear regularly. It is available online through the Internet, DIALOG, and in CD-ROM format through SilverPlatter.

The Public Works Historical Society (Chicago, Illinois) was founded in 1975 and has 850 members. It periodically publishes an *Essay Series* along with its quarterly newsletter, *Public Works History*. The Social Welfare History Group (SWHG) was founded in 1956 and has 260 members. It has operated out of the Michigan State University School of Social Work and meets in conjunction with the Council on Social Work Education. The SWHG offers an annual bibliography as well as a newsletter. Both groups have links to Web sites as affiliates of the American Historical Association (available at http://www.theaha.org).

980. American Philanthropy, 1731–1860: Printed Works in the Collections of the American Philosophical Society, the Historical Society of Pennsylvania, the Library Company of Philadelphia. Cornelia S. King, comp. New York: Garland, 1984. 529 col. (Garland Reference Library of Social Science, v. 183; Americana to 1860, v. 1.) ISBN 0-8240-9080-2.

Supported by a grant from the Mellon Foundation, officials of three Philadelphia libraries with major historical collections agreed on the development of a union catalog of historical materials on U.S. philanthropy as well as education (entry 990), natural history (entry 1077), and agriculture (entry 334n) covering a period of 130 years, from the colonial period to the onset of the Civil War. The work is of value to the scholar and serious student of history and other social science areas. This published catalog on philanthropy and the succeeding efforts in the other fields serve as excellent bibliographies. The effort on philanthropy furnishes over 3,700 entries of monographs, agency reports, and serial titles. Arrangement is alphabetical by authors of monographs and titles of serials, covering a wide range of social problems and remedial measures. Appendixes furnish a listing of institutions and a chronology of publications.

981. American Settlement Houses and Progressive Social Reform: An Encyclopedia of the American Settlement Movement. Domenica M. Barbuto. Phoenix: Oryx Press, 1999. 270p. ISBN 1-57356-146-0.

One of the significant social welfare movements was conducted from the late nineteenth to the early twentieth century and involved middle- and upper-class people in a concerted effort to provide assistance to the poor with much attention given to the plight of recently arrived immigrants. It was broadly based and addressed issues and concerns in various areas such as public health, politics, education, and living conditions in urban areas. There are 230 entries arranged alphabetically and providing brief but informative narrative of personalities, institutions that include all the major metropolitan settlement houses, events, organizations, summaries of influential publications, and legislation. The impact of labor unions and religious movements is examined. Numerous photographs and illustrations enhance the narratives.

982. The American Settlement Movement: A Bibliography. Domenica M. Barbuto. Westport, CT: Greenwood Press, 1999. 123p. ISBN 0-313-30756-3.

The author is an academic historian who has published a compendium in this area (entry 981) for which this bibliography serves as a companion. Following a brief introductory narrative describing the American Settlement Movement, there are 185 annotated entries divided into various categories relating to English antecedents, general surveys, settlement studies, biographical works, research and case studies, and reference sources. These are all secondary sources, and no periodical articles are included in the mix. Annotations are detailed and range from 150 to 300 words describing the content and analyzing the item's importance to serious inquirers. The work is indexed by author, title, and subject to provide good access.

983. Biographical Dictionary of Social Welfare in America. Walter I. Trattner, ed. New York: Greenwood Press, 1986. 897p. ISBN 0-313-23001-3.

This biographical dictionary of 330 deceased men and women active in the social welfare field from the colonial period to the present day should be of interest to students and beginning researchers. Entries are written by 200 specialists with expertise on the subject and are arranged alphabetically. Excluded here are the theoreticians, philosophers, donors, philanthropists in favor of the participants and practitioners. Similarly, labor leaders, feminists, and abolitionists are omitted. The field is defined loosely, with Cotton Mather and Benjamin Franklin included alongside Jane Addams. Entries are signed and furnish essay-length descriptions and analyses of the career and impact of each individual covered. There are selective bibliographies accompanying all entries. Appendixes contain a chronology and listing of subjects by place and year of birth. A subject index furnishes access.

984. Corporate Philanthropy: An Annotated Bibliography. David R. Farber and Susan M. Levy, comps. and eds. Chicago: Donors Forum of Chicago; Investor Responsibility Research Center, 1982. 58p. ISBN 0-317-52549-2.

This unique work focuses on corporate philanthropy; it should prove useful to scholars and researchers at various levels. It is an annotated bibliography of more than 350 items divided into 10 sections, beginning with an overview, then describing status, promotional efforts, types, and advice given, along with directories and general information on corporations. An academic with the University of Chicago's Project on the History of Philanthropy and Public Policy, Farber has produced an enlightening array of citations from a variety of sources—newspapers, journals, books, newsletters, research reports, magazines, and annual reports—issued between 1972 and 1981. Items listed explain how corporate philanthropy works, what has been said about it, and how to improve and promote it. There is a separate segment on philanthropy in Chicago and a listing of the Foundation Center's extensive collections.

Looking Good and Doing Good: Corporate Philanthropy and Corporate Power by Jerome L. Himmelstein (Indiana University Press, 1997) is an exposition of the nature of corporate philanthropy. Documentation is thorough and the work is informative in its treatment and manner in which corporations balance the profit motive with considerations of the social good. The concluding chapter examines the economic act with social and political dimensions.

985. From Poor Law to Welfare State: A History of Social Welfare in America. 6th ed. Walter I. Trattner. New York: The Free Press, 1999. 424p. ISBN 0-684-85471-6.

This title has been a standard and comprehensive history of social welfare in this country from the time it first was issued nearly 30 years ago. The new edition furnishes updated information on societal developments and the recent trends in social welfare. Bibliographic coverage is timely and useful. The work examines the various elements and issues relevant to the topic with coverage given to such topics as child welfare, social work as a profession, and public health. Scope of coverage is large beginning with colonial times and running to the time of publication during President Clinton's term. Chapters provide useful description and analysis of the impact of public policy, and the efforts to combat racism and sexism and to counter child abuse and homelessness.

986. Historical Dictionary of the Welfare State. Bent Greve. Lanham, MD: Scarecrow Press, 1998. 159p. (Historical Dictionaries of Religions, Philosophies, and Movements, no. 15). ISBN 0-8108-3332-8.

Another useful number in this well-received series from the publisher, its focus is on the welfare state and its evolution through time. Coverage of European countries and the Unites States receives emphasis in the author's purpose to examine the core concepts fundamental to the understanding of the concept and nature of the welfare society. The work opens with a chronology of social welfare of international proportions dating from the ancients to contemporary times. There are nearly 300 entries arranged alphabetically and furnishing brief descriptive narrative treating terminology, issues, concepts, institutions, historical and modern issues and developments, a few highly influential personalities, and so forth. Insights from various fields of the social sciences are presented. The bibliography is divided by topics.

987. Notable American Philanthropists: Biographies of Giving and Volunteering. Robert T. Grimm Jr., ed. Westport, CT: Oryx/Greenwood Press, 2002. 408p. ISBN 1-57356-340-4.

A unique biographical dictionary in its focus on those who were identified as significant American contributors to worthy causes and charitable organizations, the work includes those who gave of their time as well as those who provided substantial donations. There are 78 entries, some of which are composed of families such as the Rockefellers, producing a total of 110 individuals covered. Entries supply biographical essays describing early years, education, and career as well as philanthropic philosophy and activity. Archival sources are identified and bibliographic references are furnished.

Public Works History of the United States: A Guide to the Literature, by the Public Works Historical Society compiled and edited by Suellen M. Hoy and Michael C. Robinson (American Association for State and Local History, 1982) supplies books dissertations, dissertations, and journal articles dealing with the history of public works projects. The history of public works in this country is closely tied to social welfare, which is covered along with political and management considerations in these annotated references, although emphasis is on engineering and construction of public projects. Entries bear publication dates ranging from the nineteenth century to the 1920s and are organized into 14 segments treating various topics and subtopics (roads, streets, highways, railroads, highway traffic controls, mass transportation, etc.).

988. Social Welfare in America: An Annotated Bibliography. Walter I. Trattner and W. Andrew Achenbaum, eds. Westport, CT: Greenwood Press, 1983. 324p. ISBN 0-313-23002-1.

This is an excellent bibliography of more than 1,400 entries of all types of important materials of interest to scholars and serious students. Several major chapters divide the works; three were prepared by contributing specialists. An introduction provides perspective on the process and progress of social welfare. Chapter topics represent problems in the stages of human life: the care of infant and child, problems of youth, relief of domestic crises of adulthood, economic problems of adults, and coping with old age. The final chapter examines the need for a research agenda for the future. Each of the chapters is divided into a standardized sequence of syntheses, period pieces, and so forth. The subject index is especially useful in bringing entries together, because entries are duplicated in the sections when appropriate.

989. Welfare Reform: A Reference Handbook. Santa Barbara, CA: ABC-CLIO, 1996. 165p. (Contemporary World Issues). ISBN 0-87436-844-8.

Designed to meet the needs of students from high school to college level, this work furnishes insight into the development of social welfare initiatives and programs from their beginnings under Franklin Roosevelt in the 1930s to the time of publication. It traces the changes in orientation from the popular conceptions of those early days to the more current popular will to end social welfare in various ways. Significant developments and important events as well as policies, programs, speeches, reports, and legislation are described. Profiles are presented of advocates and adversaries in government from Roosevelt to Newt Gingrich, along with sketches of several influential citizens. Government agencies and other organizations are identified, listings of resources are given, and a glossary is provided. The work is a solid source of information on the topic.

EDUCATION; BOOKS, LIBRARIES, INFORMATION

EDUCATION

From its beginnings, this country has looked to its educational institutions as the means by which citizens better themselves to achieve the American Dream. Operating upon democratic principles designed to make allowances for delayed maturation, educators have shown no inclination to place students on different "tracks" at an early age in line with performance on examinations. Rather, the tendency has been to extend public education through the university levels in a nondiscriminatory manner. Following the dissent, protest, and riot period of the 1960s, the college campus has become relatively quiet; not much unrest was evident during the Gulf War, and the war against the Taliban inspired a unity of thought nationwide similar to the period of World War II. One obvious change, however, is that student voice in governance is a given in contemporary campus life and has become more of a factor in secondary and even elementary schools.

Prior to recent years, the majority of resources were bibliographic in nature, most of them being on higher education, where scholars tend to conduct their investigations. More recently, there has been an increase of informational compendia. Specific issues such as school prayer and desegregation of schools are treated, along with less volatile historical development. One of the leading current indexes of English-language materials is the *Education Index* published by the H.W. Wilson Company, one of the major index producers in this country. It has been issued since 1929 and now appears quarterly. Major emphasis is on the periodical literature, with over 300 titles covered, however, monographs, yearbooks, and reports are indexed as well. Historical topics are covered in some of the journals indexed. The tool is available on both CD-ROM (WilsonDisc) and online (WILSONLINE).

Two major sources are government-sponsored abstracting services, *Resources in Education (RIE)* and *Current Index to Journals in Education (CIJE)*, that began in 1966 and 1969, respectively. *RIE* identifies documents, and *CIJE* covers periodical literature. Both titles are issued through the U.S. Department of Education's Educational Resources Information Center (ERIC) and are available both in print and online formats where the two sources can be merged for convenient searching. The combined *ERIC* database is available in CD-ROM through various distributors.

The History of Education Society now working out of Slippery Rock University in Pennsylvania (available at http://www.sru.edu/depts/scc/hes/hes.htm) has operated since 1960 and has over 400 members. It has published *History of Education Quarterly* since 1961, and continues to hold an annual meeting with calls for papers. At the Web site of the American Council on Education (available at http://www.acenet.edu), one is able to find material on both the history of the GED and of Pell Grant funding by using the "search" option.

General Sources

990. American Education, 1622–1860: Printed Works in the Collections of the American Philosophical Society, the Historical Society of Pennsylvania, the Library Company of Philadelphia. Cornelia S. King, comp. New York: Garland, 1984. 354p. (Americana to 1860, v. 3.) ISBN 0-8240-8966-9.

Supported by a Mellon grant, this is the third of the four union catalogs of specific subject holdings of three major historical collections in the city of Philadelphia. The first covers philanthropy and was also compiled by Ms. King (entry 980). The other two were handled by another individual and covered agriculture (entry 334n) and natural history (entry 1077). The present effort, like others in the series, is an extremely useful bibliographic source of early printed materials in this country. There are nearly 4,900 entries representing pedagogical treatises, official publications of organizations, societies, institutions, and school systems issued over a period of nearly 140 years prior to the Civil War. Serial publications are included as well. Arrangement of entries is alphabetical, primarily by author. Appendixes provide valuable listings of institutions and organizations of various kinds. Neither textbooks nor dissertations or library catalogs are included.

A major project underway since 1987 is the *History of Education* microfiche collection (Research Publications), based on the extensive holdings of the Milbank Library, Teachers College at Columbia University. Expected to eventually comprise some 12,000 titles, the *History of Education* set reproduces the full text of monographs in the history and philosophy of education, classical educational treatises, general works in education, and obscure pamphlets and lectures published from the fifteenth through the nineteenth centuries, with significant coverage of U.S education. Examples include late nineteenth-century texts on "Special Kinesiology of Educational Gymnastics" and a "History of Tufts University." A printed *Guide to the Microfiche Collection* provides a detailed listing by fiche number but is of very little help for author/title/subject searches. Broad educational subjects are grouped together in "units" (e.g., psychology/philosophy of education, health education and gymnastics, U.S. universities). A subject index is anticipated.

991. Biographical Dictionary of Modern American Educators. Frederick Ohles et al., eds. Westport, CT: Greenwood Press, 1997. 432p. ISBN 0-313-29133-0.

This serves as a good companion to *Biographical Dictionary of American Educators,* edited by John Ohles for the same publisher in 1978. Whereas the earlier version contained more than 1,650 biographical sketches of individuals who had reached the age of 60, retired, or died by the year 1975, the current work treats 410 individuals born before January 1, 1935 or deceased. They were selected from names submitted by education agencies from all 50 states, and overlooked in the first work that contained only individuals who were prominent at either the national or state level in their roles as teachers, reformers, theorists, or administrators. The current effort contains biographies of those who made a contribution to some facet of education. Like the earlier work, there is purposeful inclusion of both genders as well as ethnic minorities. Entries provide information regarding the person's education, professional accomplishments, contribution or impact, and participation in professional associations and activities. Useful appendixes give listings by birthplace, state, and field of activity. Included also is a chronology of dates in American education, and the work concludes with a comprehensive index.

992. Biographical Dictionary of North American and European Educationists. Peter Gordon and Robert Aldrich. London: Woburn Press; distr., Portland, OR: International Specialized Book Services, 1997. 528p. (The Woburn Education Series.) ISBN 0-7130-0205-0.

Developed as a companion-piece to the authors' *Dictionary of British Educationists* (International Specialized Book Services, 1989), this biographical dictionary furnishes some 500 biographical sketches of educators from some 20 other countries. More than half the entries treat individuals from the United States followed by those from Germany, then from Canada, France, and so forth. Several countries (Bulgaria, Czech Republic, etc.) have only one representative. The work is historical in nature and inclusion is restricted to those who are no longer living and whose careers date primarily from 1800 onwards. Biographical sketches are relatively uniform, running a page in length and providing substantial bibliographies. Individuals were selected as predominant personalities involved in the field of education in their part of the world. Due to its uniqueness one should forgive the inevitable omissions and the multicultural imbalance.

993. Education Literature, 1907–1932. Malcolm Hamilton, ed. New York: Garland, 1979. 25v. in 12. ISBN 0-8240-3700-6 (v. 1). (Each volume has individual ISBN.)

Another useful tool for scholars and serious students is this large-scale facsimile reprint of the serial bibliographies from the U.S. Bureau of Education. The *Bibliography of Education* was published between 1907 and 1911, and the *Monthly Record of Current Education Publications* spanned a 20-year period of publication between 1912 and 1932. Included in these sources were books, proceedings, pamphlets, and periodical literature on education and related aspects at all levels. Over 700 periodical titles were covered during different periods; 44,000 entries are revealed. In some cases annotations were provided. Important here is the work done in unifying these serials; a separate volume now furnishes a comprehensive name and subject index to the entire work. This source affords a great advantage over the use of the original annual indexes, which were difficult and inconsistent and changed categories frequently from one volume to the next.

994. Encyclopedia of American Education. 2nd ed. Harlow G. Unger. New York: Facts on File, 2001. 3v. (Facts on File Library of American History.) ISBN 0-8160-4344-2.

The author is a former academic who has published widely in the field of education and has expanded and revised this useful comprehensive source of information following its initial publication in 1996. It continues to treat all aspects relevant to the history and development of American education. There are more than 2,000 entries, brief and well written, that treat both historical and current subjects. Arrangement is alphabetical throughout the three volumes and one is able to find coverage on such areas as educational movements, health issues, teaching methods, legal issues, and current topics as bullying, charter schools, distance learning, and so forth. Publications, educational organizations, sex education, tests, important personalities, programs, and more are included. Volume 3 supplies an extensive chronology of important milestones from the seventeenth century to the present day and a summary of important legislation and court decisions. There are a comprehensive bibliography and a detailed index.

A work of importance historically is the five-volume *A Cyclopedia of Education,* edited by Paul Monroe (Macmillan, 1911–1913; repr. Gale, 1968), which has served as a partial model for several subsequent works. Its emphasis is on education in this country. Both historical and biographical articles are included. An analytical index furnishes access to the signed articles. For a more theoretical coverage of education, see the *Encyclopedia of Educational Research* published by Macmillan under the auspices of the American Educational Research Association in four volumes and now in its seventh edition (2001). It provides thoroughly researched, signed articles covering topics ranging from academic freedom to high school driver education programs. Historians will be interested in the early editions of this work, which was first issued in 1941.

995. Historical Dictionary of American Education. Richard J. Altenbaugh, ed. Westport, CT: Greenwood Press, 1999. 499p. ISBN 0-313-28590-X.

This useful and compact treatment identifies and describes a variety of elements and factors relevant to education at the elementary and secondary levels (higher education is not treated). The work contains more than 350 entries arranged alphabetically and signed by the 130 expert contributors. Although brief, these narratives are well written and informative in their coverage of ideas, events, issues, agencies and organizations, court cases, educational theories, and so forth as they relate to the history of education from colonial times to the present. Important personalities include educators, philosophers, writers, and more. Entries furnish bibliographies as well as cross-references to sources that are identified in the general bibliography at the end of the volume. As one would expect of a one-volume work, there are omissions of various kinds, but generally this is a worthy source.

996. Who's Who in American Education: An Illustrated Biographical Dictionary of Eminent Living Educators of the United States and Canada. Ed. 1–23. Nashville: Who's Who in American Education, 1928–1968. Bienn.

This work represents an effort, now of historical importance, that ceased publication with its 23rd edition in 1968. It had been published since 1928, mostly on a biennial basis, and later incorporated a slight change in subtitle. The early editions cover many now-obscure figures who, during their time, played an active role in the educational process at all levels. There are many administrators of primary and secondary schools and systems, college and university faculty, and a variety of people in related fields, including public librarians and public relations executives.

For those professing an interest in more current history, there is a recent product of the same name (without subtitle), edited by Jeffrey Franz and Pamela R. Jones, that was intended as a biennial publication. The 1988–1989 inaugural edition (National Reference Institute, 1988) furnished 10,000 biographical sketches of personalities of reference interest. Marquis Who's Who published the fourth edition, 1993, but unfortunately the work ceased publication after the fifth edition, 1996–1997 (1995). Of continuing interest is the *Directory of American Scholars* with 24,000 entries of Americans and Canadians judged to be of merit in the ninth edition (Gale, 1999).

Higher Education

997. The American College President, 1636–1989: A Critical Review and Bibliography. Ann H.L. Sontz. Westport, CT: Greenwood Press, 1991. 176p. (Bibliographies and Indexes in Education, no. 10). ISBN 0-313-27325-1.

This recent effort is of value to both scholars and serious inquirers; it is the first bibliographic source on the subject in many years. Studies on college presidents have been numerous, and it is thought that the quality of such studies has improved in the past few decades. The work opens with a foreword by an academic, and then introduces the selection criteria. A bibliographic narrative is furnished, as are tables of statistics on the literature and on the presidents. The author hopes that the current emphasis on evolutionary historical process rather than personal contribution can be reassessed and balanced more equitably. Also, the administration of less-familiar institutions should be studied in terms of their socio-intellectual theories. Included are sections on background material, presidential biographies, and presidential works, which account for the bulk of the text.

998. American Universities and Colleges. 16th ed. Produced in collaboration with the American Council on Education. Hawthorne, NY: Walter de Gruyter, 2001. 950p. ISSN 0066-0922.

This work continues as one of the most useful directories of higher education with respect to its listing of institutions and is of real value to students, researchers, specialists, and librarians. Important to historians is the information given in each entry regarding each institution's origin and developmental history. Hundreds of colleges and universities receive good, informative descriptions. In addition, information is furnished regarding the school's calendar, organization, admission policy, degree requirements, fees, graduate work, financial aid, student life, sports, dormitories, library collections, and so on. There are numerous tables, charts, and listings. With the exception of the 14th edition (1992) that was issued after five years, the serial appears every four years in predictable manner.

999. Exploring the Heritage of American Higher Education: The Evolution of Philosophy and Policy. E. Grady Bogue et al. Phoenix: Oryx Press, 1999. 272p. ISBN 1-57356-310-2.

This is an interesting exposition of the history and politics associated with American higher education from its beginnings with the founding of the first college in the mid-seventeenth century to the present. The work is divided into 10 chapters in which the development of higher education is examined through identification of the policies, debates, and issues that have given it shape. Chapters treat such factors as institutional diversity, governance, accountability, student involvement, societal investment and return, and the position of athletics. The tone is upbeat and the authors, themselves educators, are able to demonstrate the societal gains of these investments, despite the fact that reforms are necessary especially in addressing current challenges regarding trust and accountability.

1000. A Subject Bibliography of the History of American Higher Education. Mark Beach, comp. Westport, CT: Greenwood Press, 1984. 165p. ISBN 0-313-23276-8.

In an earlier work, *A Bibliographic Guide to American Colleges and Universities* (Greenwood Press, 1975), Beach furnished a bibliography of books, articles, and dissertations that was unique in its focus on individual institutions. This more recent effort was designed as a companion volume rather than a supplement and provides a broad-based topical bibliography on the history of higher education. Again, he lists books, articles, and dissertations of consequence; arrangement of entries is alphabetical within classes or topics, which themselves are arranged alphabetically from "academic costume" to "zoology." None of these classes relate to specific colleges and universities; little duplication with the earlier effort is evident. Both scholars and students should benefit from this tool for its breadth and comprehensive nature.

Elementary and Secondary Education

1001. Private School Education in the U.S.: An Annotated Bibliography, 1950–1980. Alice H. Songe. Jefferson, NC: McFarland, 1982. 89p. ISBN 0-89950-045-5.

Of interest to inquirers at all levels is this selective annotated bibliography of the rarely documented private school. There are nearly 425 publications, arranged alphabetically under format divisions: books, monographs, and serials; government publications of both federal and state origin; journal articles; and doctoral dissertations. Publication dates cover a critical 30-year period, embracing the Supreme Court desegregation decision, *Brown* v. *Board of Education,* that gave visibility to the role of the private school in a pluralistic society. Annotations are brief but informative for most entries; they are excluded in the case of doctoral dissertations because *Dissertation Abstracts International* (entry 92) fills that need. Quality education and the differences in a private school environment compared to a public school environment have been important topics of argument and debate; these writings provide an excellent record of that controversy. Included is a list of associations concerned with private education; there are both author and subject indexes.

1002. Standards and Schooling in the United States: An Encyclopedia. Joe L. Kinchloe. Santa Barbara, CA: ABC-CLIO, 2001. 3v. ISBN 1-57607-255-X.

Kinchloe has put together a unique work that focuses on the development, impact, and future utilization of educational standards with the contributions of more than 50 qualified scholars. The contributed essays are arranged alphabetically and supply in-depth treatment of historical, cultural, social, psychological, and philosophical issues behind the development and implementation of these standards while at the same time examining the practical elements of politics and administration. The work opens with an important introductory essay by the author that enumerates basic concepts regarding the nature of future reform in education through re-examination of the issues and topics presented in the contributed essays. Topics include administration, curriculum, teacher certification, regulation of teaching, teacher education, individual curricular subjects (art, science, social studies, etc.), and more. There is a chronology, bibliography, and resource list.

Issues and Controversies

1003. From Brown to Boston: Desegregation in Education, 1954–1974. Leon Jones. Metuchen, NJ: Scarecrow, 1979. 2v. ISBN 0-8108-1147-2.

Of importance to both students and scholars, this two-volume annotated bibliography of critical studies on the topics of integration and segregation begins with the 1954 case of *Brown* v. *Board of Education of Topeka,* the landmark decision that outlawed school segregation in 1954. The work concludes with the 1974 *Miliken* v. *Bradley* case and the traumatic conditions in Boston at the time. The author, an education professor, and in volume 1 lists nearly 2,850 articles and about 440 books, each in separate sections by date of publication. In this manner the 20-year period is covered, with excellent perspective given on the quantity of publication with passing of time. Volume 2 lists over 1,750 legal decisions. Entries in both volumes are annotated in depth. Indexes provide access by author-title, case-legal issue, and by subject.

1004. Historical Dictionary of School Segregation and Desegregation: The American Experience. Jeffrey A. Raffel. Westport, CT: Greenwood Press, 1998. 345p. ISBN 0-313-29502-6.

The author is an academic who has participated in the process of school desegregation and has written widely on the topic; he opens the work with a helpful introductory essay. The work is comprehensive in its treatment with coverage with entries examining topics ranging from the eighteenth century to the mid-1990s. There are 270 entries, generally brief but well written and informative, covering an array of topics that include court decisions, personalities, concepts, events, terms, organizations, plans for desegregation, government agencies, and so forth. The narratives contain numerous cross-references and conclude with useful bibliographies. There is a chronology identifying important events over the period of time covered in the text, and a bibliographic essay as well as a bibliography.

1005. Religion in the Schools: A Reference Handbook. James J. Jurinski. Santa Barbara, CA: ABC-CLIO, 1998. 209p. ISBN 0-87436-868-5.

This is a source providing a narrow focus on one of the most controversial and divisive topics in education today. The interpretations given to the concept of separation of church and state, and interpretations given the right and freedom to pray are matters of historical record and have inspired emotionally charged argument and debate and continue to arouse and provoke heated sentiments. In addition to prayer in schools, coverage is given to the teaching of evolution and other issues, some of which have polarized communities through time. Designed to appeal to the layperson and interested inquirer, entries treat legal issues, personalities, court decisions, constitutional amendments, and furnishes historical background of key areas of conflict. There is a chronology and a useful bibliography.

1006. School Prayer and Other Religious Issues in American Public Education: A Bibliography. Albert J. Menendez. New York: Garland, 1985. 168p. (Garland Reference Library of Social Science, v. 291.) ISBN 0-8240-8775-5.

In 1992, a conservative Supreme Court followed the lead of previous, more liberal courts in its interpretation of the inviolable nature of the separation of church and state as it concerns school prayer. This bibliography of more than 1,600 books, periodical articles, law journal reviews, dissertations, theses, and newspaper articles represents a timely source for study and research of a powerful issue. Of the 21 chapters, 5 deal with the history, legal basis, and politics of school prayer, as well as arguments for and against. Others treat the Bible, celebration of Christmas, and moral education, among other subjects. Publications span 120 years, from the 1850s to the 1970s. The recent action on the part of the Court is a good indication of the multifaceted nature of the issue. There are an author index and a cursory subject index that focuses on geographic locales.

1007. Special Education: A Reference Handbook. Santa Barbara, CA: ABC-CLIO, 2001. 235p. (Contemporary Education Issues). ISBN 1-57607-274-6.

This is one of the few reference sources to examine the nature, development, and relevant factors associated with special education in America. As part of the broader perspective concerning societal responsibility and the gradual acquisition of civil rights by those whose circumstances warrant special treatment, the development of special education is placed within an appropriate context and one is able to appreciate the circumstances in its acceptance. The work is divided into eight chapters, the first of which supplies historical overview and treatment of the factors and issues pertaining to the acknowledgment of the need and active response to that need. Other chapters examine the law, advocacy, and politics while the concluding chapters contain a directory of organizations and a bibliography of print and electronic resources. There is a glossary of terms, and a useful index provides access.

BOOKS, LIBRARIES, INFORMATION

The American Library Association (available at http://www.ala.org) is the leading national professional association of librarians, the largest single group of information professionals. With its headquarters in Chicago and its membership of more than 25,000, it is a strong advocate for books, libraries, and literacy. The official journal of the Association is *American Libraries,* a monthly publication of news and events. Articles are brief and of the popular variety examining practical issues. ALA has divisions or specialized sections relevant to each of the various professional positions in libraries as well as those who serve different clienteles and in different types of libraries. These divisions generally publish their own journals that provide more research emphasis. Its Library History Roundtable is a small but active unit focused on the historical dimension. *Libraries and Culture,* a quarterly issued by the University of Texas, is the leading professional journal emphasizing historical research.

A small but vigorous organization is the American Society for Information Science and Technology (available at http://www.asis.org) operating out of Silver Spring, Maryland. It serves the interests of information professionals outside the library profession such as Web designers, computer programmers, system analysts, and so forth, as well as those librarians whose roles are primarily in the more high-tech areas. The Society has two major publications, the bimonthly, *Bulletin of the American Society for Information Science and Technology,* providing practical articles and news for practitioners, and *Journal of Information Science and Technology* that is issued 14 times per year and geared to research and theory.

1008. American Libraries Before 1876. Haynes McMullen. Westport, CT: Greenwood Press, 2000. 179p. (Beta Phi Mu Monograph Series, no. 6.) ISBN 0-313-31277-X.

McMullen is a longtime contributor and recognized expert in the field of library history; he examines libraries and their practices in this country prior to the pivotal year of 1876. In that year, the American Library Association was founded, becoming the first permanent professional organization for librarians in this country; *Library Journal* was issued for the first time as the official organ of the ALA; and the landmark state of the art report from the U.S. government was published as *Public Libraries in the United States of America.* Prior to the development of the profession in this manner there were over 10,000 social libraries addressing the needs of varied clienteles, some quite specialized in nature. In this work, the author examines the conditions of library development and decline in different regions of the country and identifies characteristics of population, economy, and administration that provide the means to comprehend and even predict success.

1009. A Handbook for the Study of Book History in the United States. Ronald J. Zboray and Mary S. Zboray. Washington, D.C.: Library of Congress, Center for the Book / New Castle, DE: Oak Knoll Press, 2000. 155p. ISBN 0-8444-1015-2.

The authors are academic historians with expertise in print culture history, dealing with the production, distribution, and utilization of books, and have collaborated to produce a useful and interesting source of information under the auspices of the Library of Congress Center for the book. The work serves as a manual for historical investigation in the area and is especially helpful to students and beginning researchers. The major portion of the guide is given to the segment on "How to Locate and Use Sources" in which the search strategies are treated under appropriate topical divisions. Various approaches and multidisciplinary techniques are identified and described. There is an extensive bibliographic section in which useful resources are categorized and enumerated, along with a listing of significant journals.

The revised and expanded edition of *Banned in the U.S.A.: A Reference Guide to Book Censorship in Schools and Public Libraries* by Herbert N. Foerstel of the Board of Directors for the National Security Archives (Greenwood Press, 2002) presents a rewritten, updated, and revised version of what has become a significant resource on book censorship in public institutions. Chapters treat such areas as the law of book banning and supply interviews with banned authors. Most important is the survey of banned books that includes annotated entries on the 50 titles most frequently challenged from 1996 to 2000, and the appendix listing of most frequently challenged titles and authors provided by the American Library Association.

1010. Historical Studies in Information Science. Trudy B. Hahn and Michael Buckland, eds. Medford, NJ: Information Today, 1999. 326p. ISBN 1-57387-062-5.

As librarians move into the electronic age, the ties to information science grow closer, and libraries benefit from the generation and emergence of modern information professionals who are schooled in the processing of data in ways that benefit the acquisition, organization, retrieval, and dissemination of information in a variety of formats. This is a collection of essays, most of which have been drawn from recent issues of several major journals in the field, by 25 contributors who are knowledgeable professionals. Coverage is given to various topics examining historical influences and personalities. The essays are organized under several sections: the career achievements of Paul Otlet, a nineteenth-century pioneer; a survey history of information projects over a span of 400 years; exposition of modern debates in the field; and examination of the theory behind information, The final section provides bibliographical information.

1011. Library History Research in America: Essays Commemorating the Fiftieth Anniversary of the Library History Roundtable. Andrew B. Wertheimer and Donald G. Davis, eds. Washington, D.C.: Library of Congress, Center for the Book, 2000. 279p. ISBN 0-8444-1020-9.

Published by special arrangement with the University of Texas Press, this work is a reprint of the Winter 2000 issue of *Libraries & Culture*. The title is indicative of the content in its presentation of a series of articles treating different aspects and serving as both a state of the art and to some degree a manual of procedure. In commemorating the 50th year of existence of LHRT, the small but active unit of the American Library Association and the editors, together with the efforts of 15 expert contributors, have produced a worthy source for the benefit of students and practitioners. Following an introduction by the editors, the articles are organized under five topical categories treating the critical approach, LHRT pioneers, new directions engaging multicultural applications among others, cognate fields examining archival history and historical bibliography, and finally a section focusing on the role and past activities of the LHRT.

RELIGION

This country has professed to be a nation under God; much of its real strength is thought to lie in its pluralistic outlook, which permits religious beliefs to be observed in a personal manner. Great care has been taken to preserve the right to free religious expression and to ensure separation of church and state. The Supreme Court has ruled in consistent fashion on this issue. With the election of George W. Bush, social and political conservatives have again raised the issue of school prayer and others that even now are being examined and debated in state legislatures.

The literature of religion is abundant, and reference sources continue to be published in great number. They examine both generic topics and specific issues, some of which remain controversial and deep-rooted. The religion section of our work is divided along the lines of the religious traditions that dominate Western society. Coverage is given to various titles that describe alternative faiths, both Christian and non-Christian, that embrace more-emotional sects, cults, and variant groups. Islamic American sources have been slow to appear unlike the prolific sources treating Judaism in this country.

One of the most interesting recent activities was *The Material History of America Project* undertaken by the Vanderbilt University Divinity School and supported by the Lilly Endowment from 1995 to 2001. The Project studied the history of American religion by focusing on material objects and economic themes. Its work and documentation can be examined at its Web site (available at http://materialreligion.org).

GENERAL SOURCES: CHRISTIAN AND NON-CHRISTIAN

1012. American Religions: An Illustrated History. J. Gordon Melton. Santa Barbara, CA: ABC-CLIO, 2000. 316p. ISBN 1-57607-222-3.

The author has been a prolific writer and creator of numerous reference sources in the field of religion, and in this work he presents a comprehensive history of religion and its practices for the past 500 years. In keeping with its title, the well-written entries are enhanced by more than 200 illustrations of various kinds (prints, maps, photographs, etc.). Following an introductory essay, the volume is organized into eight chapters developed around chronological themes, the impact of a generally tolerant American system of government is explained. In permitting religious practices and rites of worship of numerous denominations ranging from the traditional to the alternative, there is a unique environment for free expression that is unnerving to many observers. This work treats a wide range of belief systems, cults, movements, concepts, issues, conflicts, and controversies as well as important personalities. A bibliography is given.

1013. Atlas of Religious Change in America, 1952–1990. Peter L. Halvorson and William M. Newman. Atlanta: Glenmary Research Center, 1994. 226p. ISBN 0-914422-23-5.

Developed in similar style and format as two earlier editions published by Glenmary Research Center and covering the periods 1952–1971 (1978) and 1971–1980 (1987), the current effort continues the presentation of changes in size and locales of denominations in this country. In this case the period covered is more extensive and presents information from four data sets (1952, 1971, 1980, and 1990) collected from the national organizations representing the churches on 57 denominations that reported having more than 10,000 members in at least one of the data sets. There are 31 denominations covered in all four sets. More than 230 maps treat total adherents, changes over time, and shifts in population. Textual narratives describe the history of each denomination, and summarize current demographics.

1014. Church and State in America: A Bibliographical Guide. John F. Wilson, ed. New York: Greenwood Press, 1986–1987. 2v. ISBN 0-313-25236-X (v. 1); 0-313-25914-3 (v. 2).

Volume 1 covers the period of colonial existence through the early national period; volume 2 examines the Civil War period to the present. Each of the volumes of this important work furnishes 11 bibliographic essays prepared by young scholars (doctoral candidates and recent graduates) on the controversial issues of church and state. Essays are lengthy and examine various topics and philosophical interpretations. Chapters mainly cover historical periods, geographic divisions, or topical elements such as the Puritans in New England (volume 1) or Women and Religion from 1870 to 1920 (volume 2). Each of the essays is followed by an excellent listing of about 250 monographs, articles, and book-length bibliographies. Some of these listings are classified by topic; others are divided into primary- or secondary-source groups. The work is of substantial value to scholars and serious students.

1015. Contemporary American Religion. Wade C. Roof, ed. New York: Macmillan Reference USA/Gale, 2000. 2v. ISBN 0-02-864928-1.

This is a unique work in its focus on the contemporary conditions and perspectives surrounding various minor as well as major denominations. There are 500 entries arranged alphabetically and describing an array of topics relevant to the study and popular perception give to religion in the United States since 1965. Entries vary in length from half a page to certain individuals to survey-type essays of four pages given to treatment of African American religions. Written by scholars and specialists serving as contributors, they describe a diverse array of religious traditions, issues, influential personalities, controversial groups, cults, ritual practices, and belief systems that have been part of the religious history of our recent past. One is able to find descriptions of animal rights, God, school prayer, Billy Graham, Louis Farrakhan, and so forth. Numerous photographs enhance the text. A comprehensive and detailed index facilitates access.

1016. Dictionary of American Religious Biography. 2nd ed. Rev. and enl. Henry W. Bowden, ed. Westport, CT: Greenwood Press, 1993. 686p. ISBN 0-3132-7825-3.

Useful to both scholars and students, this retrospective biographical dictionary covers notable figures, from all time periods in this country, who died prior to July 1992. Included are religious leaders, philosophers, reformers, and controversial figures. Here one will find the Mathers, Cardinal Cushing, Martin Luther King, and Malcolm X, an interesting and well-designed mix of diverse personalities. The second edition supplies information on 550 individuals, an increase of 125 over the initial offering (1991), while also having revised and updated a majority of the original entries. Bowden is able to present the information in an unbiased manner and furnish a perspective respectful of the nation's pluralistic tradition. Each entry begins with a brief career overview and personal and educational data. Following this is a detailed narrative sketch giving both expository and evaluative commentary. A special attempt has been made to include women and minorities as well as dissidents from mainstream activity. Bibliographies that provide references by and about the biographee are included in each entry. There is a name and subject index.

A more specialized effort is *The Conversion Experience in America: A Sourcebook on Religious Conversion Autobiography* by James C. Holte (Greenwood Press, 1992). Holte furnishes in-depth treatment of religious conversions described by 30 Americans over a period of 350 years. Most are Protestant, but also represented are Roman Catholics, Black Muslims, and Shakers. Seven of these converts are female, and nine are from minority groups. The autobiographies are analyzed through descriptive narrative as well as critique and assessment.

1017. The Encyclopedia of American Religions. 6th ed. J. Gordon Melton. Detroit: Gale, 1999. 1243p. ISBN 0-8103-8417-5.

This title has achieved a prominent position with inquirers at all levels. The new edition covers nearly 2,400 religious bodies of all kinds (a 33 percent increase in coverage over the third edition [1989]). It treats religious bodies in a manner similar to that of its predecessors. There is comprehensive inclusion of Canadian groups, and categorical arrangement of religious families into 24 segments, each furnishing a concise essay that places groups into historical context and supplies references. Traditional denominations such as Lutheran, Reformed, Presbyterian, and Pietist-Methodist, are treated, along with more modern affiliations such as Communal, Metaphysical, Psychic, and New Age. Directory-type entries follow, providing information on the various religious bodies (history, development, organizational aspects, and periodicals published) as well as a bibliography and bibliographic notes. Additional coverage is given to unclassified churches. Several indexes (geographical, subject, master name, etc.) as well as a detailed table of contents supply excellent access.

Another useful tool is *An Encyclopedia of Religions in the United States: One Hundred Religious Groups Speak for Themselves,* edited by William B. Williamson (Crossroad, 1992). This work furnishes general information on founders, major leaders, doctrines, worship, and contributions to U.S. culture of various Judeo-Christian groups having at least 100,000 members. Additional bodies are treated in the appendixes.

1018. The Encyclopedia of American Religious History. Rev. ed. Edward L. Queen et al. New York: Facts on File, 2001. 2v. ISBN 0-8160-4335-3.

This is a comprehensive work, revised and updated from its initial edition in 1996. There are more than 800 entries alphabetically arranged treating all aspects of the history and development of religion in this country. Designed to appeal to the needs of high school and undergraduate students as well as interested adults, the work represents the efforts of three authors and eight contributors who have supplied interesting and informative narratives on a diverse array of topics. Included in the text are brief descriptions of personalities, denominations, organizations, issues, movements, and terminology. All religions and belief systems are addressed from Christianity to New Age and Native American religions; many of the entries are subdivided into narrower topics. Coverage is evenhanded, and is intended to give greater space to topics not covered elsewhere. Bibliographies are supplied and photographs are furnished in some cases. Two indexes facilitate access.

1019. Encyclopedia of Religion in American Politics. Jeffrey D. Schultz et al., eds. Phoenix: Oryx Press, 1999. 389p. (American Political Landscape Series). ISBN 1-57356-130-4.

This is a comprehensive treatment of the complex relationship between religious practice and political developments in this country over the past 200 years. The three editors have engaged the talents of 50 scholars who have contributed nearly 700 entries furnishing brief descriptive narratives. Coverage includes historical events as well as contemporary phenomena, and treats influential personalities, political movements, religious denominations, organizations, court decisions, and philosophical concepts. Entries are alphabetically arranged and tend to be brief with more-detailed treatment given to broad concepts such as "democracy" in explaining the significance of their relationship to religious practice. Appendixes supply copies of significant documents, a directory of organizations, and a chronology. Photographs and illustrations enhance the text.

1020. Encyclopedia of Religion in the South. Samuel S. Hill, ed. Macon, GA: Mercer University Press, 1984; repr. 1998. 878p. ISBN 0-588-X.

Students and beginning researchers of both religion and area history will find this treatment of religion in the South a useful starting point. The editor is a religion professor and has pooled the contributions of over 200 specialists in an encyclopedic one-volume work. There are more than 500 signed articles; nearly half of them furnish biographical sketches. Average length is a half-page, although there are 16 lengthy essays covering individual state histories originally written for a work published a year earlier by the editor. Bibliographies accompany most entries. Coverage is wide-ranging, from the history and ideology of over 50 denominations to the description of various organizations, movements, events, and activities. Most biographees are deceased and represent various stations of life, including politics and literature. An index is provided.

Bibliography of Religion in the South by Charles H. Lippy (Mercer University, 1985) is a useful comprehensive bibliographic source on the religions of the South. The author is a professor of history at Clemson University and has furnished a listing of 5,000 books, articles, monographs, essays, dissertations, theses, and recordings. Entries are placed into 22 chapters, each of which opens with a detailed scholarly bibliographic essay by the author. Bibliographic listings follow the essays and are arranged topically. The focus is primarily on Christianity and Judaism, with several chapters covering denominational traditions. Related cultural elements such as art, music, and literature are treated. No index is provided.

1021. Encyclopedia of Religious Controversies in the United States. George H. Shriver and Bill J. Leonard, eds. Westport, CT: Greenwood Press, 1997. 542p. ISBN 0-313-29691-X.

This is a comprehensive source of information on a single topic, and presents some 400 entries signed by 53 contributors who are specialists in the field. Treatment is given to a variety of subjects that include influential personalities such as Norman Vincent Peale and Jesse Jackson, ideas and doctrines such as predestination, organizations such as the Salvation Army, alternative groups such as the Branch Davidians, movements such as the Great Awakening, societal concepts such as academic freedom, and events such as the Scopes trial. Coverage is expansive beginning with the seventeenth century and continuing to the present in alphabetically arranged entries that vary in length from brief identifications of 250 words to full essay-type articles of 1,500 words. Each one supplies a brief bibliography, and there is a general bibliography at the end. A general index supplies adequate access.

The subject of religious conflict is examined in *Religious Conflict in America: A Bibliography* by Albert J. Menendez (Garland Reference Library of Social Science, v. 262, 1985). The author, having completed an earlier bibliography on church-state relations, then furnished this unannotated bibliography of religious conflict covering a period of history from the colonial era to the present. Various issues such as politics, cults, and the radical right are treated. All types of materials are included.

1022. Encyclopedia of the American Religious Experience: Studies of Traditions and Movements. Charles H. Lippy and Peter W. Williams, eds. New York: Scribner's, 1988. 3v. ISBN 0-684-18062-6 (set).

This three-volume encyclopedia is a throwback to an earlier period, when encyclopedias featured monograph-type essays of substance and depth. There are 100 essays averaging about 17 to 18 pages each; these are produced by young scholars writing in a clear and readable style. Each essay concludes with a summary paragraph and a bibliography of books and articles. Considered to be a product of excellent scholarship in terms of both breadth and depth of coverage, it explores both historical and contemporary conditions. Entries are organized into nine major segments dealing with approaches to religion, religious groups, religious movements, the arts, politics, and education, among other subjects. The work is exhaustive and includes coverage of most pertinent topics. It will serve as both a reference tool for students and scholars and an agreeable reading experience for those interested. There is an excellent detailed index.

1023. Historic Places of Worship: Stories of 51 Extraordinary American Religious Sites Since 1300. Paul D. Buchanan. Jefferson, NC: McFarland, 1999. 232p. ISBN 0-7864-0588-0.

This is an interesting and informative collection of profiles identifying and describing 51 religious sites located in the United States. Coverage is expansive and includes sites significant for their cultural, social, political, or architectural prominence. They represent a variety of faiths and doctrines; sites relevant to Jewish and Islamic culture as well as to various Christian denominations and other belief systems are examined. Arrangement is chronological and ranges from the pre-Columbian period with the kivas (social and cultural stone and wood structures) of the Anasazi Indians of the Southwest to the Chapel of Peace constructed in 1970. Entries are thorough in nature and run from 2,000 to 4,000 words treating background and significance and furnishing bibliographies, and in some cases pictures.

1024. New Historical Atlas of Religion in America. 3rd ed. Edwin S. Gaustad et al. New York: Oxford University Press, 2000. 464p. ISBN 0-19-509268-X.

Originally published in 1962, the current effort continues the excellent coverage and treatment of its predecessors. The work has been expanded and reorganized reflecting the complexity of American religious life in terms of increasing influence of Eastern religions and emergence of evangelical churches at the expense of mainstream Prostestantism. Native American and African American traditions are not overlooked. The atlas shows the expansion and development of religion in the United States from colonial times in the mid-seventeenth century to the present, with hundreds of full-color maps, charts, and diagrams. The emphasis is on Christianity, but other faiths are examined as well. The graphic material is integrated with descriptive narrative and tables to provide insight into the type of development that took place within church groups and denominations. One is able to follow the development of religious influence in terms of numerical distributions. There are separate indexes for authors and titles, places, and religious bodies, as well as for names and subjects.

*1025. On Common Ground: World Religions in America. New York: Columbia University Press, 2001. ISBN 0-231-12664-6. [CD-ROM].

This is the second issue of a work published in 1997 and was created out of the Pluralism Project conducted at Harvard University. It continues as an outstanding source of information on religious diversity in this country and serves the needs and interests of a serious audience college level and above. The work is divided into three major segments or divisions; "A New Religious Landscape," "America's Many Religions," and "Encountering Religious Diversity." The first division provides more than 400 entries identifying and describing a wide variety of religious centers in the United States. Treatment is given to churches, synagogues, and mosques. Also included is a nationwide directory to be updated when connected to the Pluralism Project. The second segment supplies a thorough history of 15 denominations in the United States. The third division examines the historical interactions and current issues relevant to religious diversity. Links are given to audio and video clips and the work makes excellent use of its multimedia format.

1026. Politics and Religion in the United States. Michael Corbett and Julia M. Corbett, eds. New York: Garland, 1999. 460p. ISBN 0-8153-3141-X.

This is a well-conceived history of encyclopedic nature in its treatment of the historical interactions between religion and politics throughout our past from the beginnings to contemporary times. It is divided into four major parts beginning with "Religion and History" in which the first four chapters examine the association from the early colonial period to the 1990s. This is followed by two chapters examining "Religion and the First Amendment." The third section contains three chapters dealing with "Religion and Public Opinion," and the fourth part offers two chapters on "Effects of Religious Influences in Politics." The exposition serves to place current issues within historical perspective. There is a Web site by the same title provided by the authors with links to relevant information (available at http://www.bsu.edu/web/jcorbett/relpol).

1027. Profiles in Belief: The Religious Bodies of the United States and Canada. Arthur C. Piepkorn. San Francisco: Harper & Row, 1977–1979. 4v. in 3. ISBN 0-06-066582-3 (v. 2); 0-06-066581-5 (v. 3–4).

When Piepkorn, a Lutheran scholar, died in 1973, he had prepared the copy for the first four volumes of what was to be a seven-volume work. These four volumes were published posthumously under his name. The first two volumes, on Catholicism and Protestantism, still are considered outstanding by scholars and students for their exposition of history, beliefs, statistics, liturgy, and practice. Volume 3, (*Holiness and Pentecostal*) and volume 4 (*Evangelical, Fundamentalist, and Other Christian Bodies*) were issued in one binding, with volume 3 approaching the level of quality associated with the earlier volumes. Although volume 4 displays less familiarity with the subject matter, when taken as a set the work represents an indispensable tool for scholarly inquiry.

For more up-to-date and less-detailed information on the denominations one may consult the Melton encyclopedia (entry 1017) and the old standard, *Handbook of Denominations in the United States* by Frank Spencer Mead. It is revised about every fifth year by Samuel S. Hill and is now in its 11th edition (Abingdon, 2001). There are brief descriptions of the history, doctrine, organization, and status of nearly 300 religious bodies; Web sites are included in this edition. Coverage is even and considered to be objective. *Religious Bodies in the United States: A Directory,* also by J. Gordon Melton (Garland, 1992), identifies and describes all religious groups operating in this country as of 1991. There are listings of periodicals for each of the bodies.

1028. Religion and American Law: An Encyclopedia. Paul Finkelman, ed. New York: Garland, 2000. 601p. (Garland Reference Library of the Humanities, v. 1548.) ISBN 0-8153-0750-0.

This is a comprehensive source of information regarding the complex and sometimes controversial relationship regarding the freedom of religion and religious practice under the law of the land. It is of serious nature but designed to appeal to a wide audience of interested laypersons, students, scholars, and practitioners. Entries run from one to five pages in length, and are written and signed by nearly 100 contributors who are scholars and academics. They are arranged alphabetically and treat a variety of themes and topics. Included are important Supreme Court justices, legal decisions, histories of religions and of churches, relevant documents, terminology, and topical coverage of such issues and phenomena as immigration and naturalization law and religion, school prayer, black Churches in the antebellum South, and so forth.

Somewhat less scholarly is *Religion and the Law: A Dictionary* by Christopher T. Anglim (ABC-CLIO, 1999) who opens with a detailed introductory essay furnishing historical background of the topic from its beginnings both in the Western world and in the United States. Emphasis is on constitutional influence and impact on the practice of religion. Entries furnish brief descriptions and identifications of legal cases and terminology. There are tables of cases and statutes, and the bibliography is thorough and detailed in its inclusion of monographs and articles from legal journals.

1029. Religious Leaders of America: A Biographical Guide to Founders and Leaders of Religious Bodies, Churches, and Spiritual Groups in North America. 2nd ed. J. Gordon Melton. Farmington Hills, MI: Gale, 1999. 724p. ISBN 0-8878-2. ISSN 1057-2961.

This recent effort by the prolific author represents a biographical dictionary of 1,200 personalities, Americans and Canadians who made their contribution subsequent to the Civil War. Coverage extends over a wide range of figures from both the traditional Judeo-Christian heritage and the alternative or fringe areas. Included are representatives of major religious bodies, ecumenical bodies, smaller traditions, and even those who proclaim themselves to be nonreligious. Minority figures, females, blacks, and Native Americans are listed in a purposeful attempt to be inclusive, a correction of the oversight of the previous edition. Although most of the entries are for deceased individuals, there is a good representation of living people such as Pat Robertson, Jesse Jackson, and Billy Graham. Entries furnish birth and death dates, birthplaces, and religious affiliations, and a well-developed biography. Reading lists are included. There is an appendix of religious affiliation classifying the subjects into various groups. A comprehensive index identifies individuals, organizations, and publications.

1030. Religious Seminaries in America: A Selected Bibliography. Thomas C. Hunt and James C. Carper. New York: Garland, 1989. 231p. (Garland Reference Library of Social Science, no. 539). ISBN 0-8240-7732-6.

This represents the completion of a trilogy, the first two volumes of which covered religious schools and religious universities, respectively. Sixteen specialists from the world of academe furnished these chapters, which vary in quality and consistency and cover a wide range of seminaries. Books, articles, dissertations and masters theses, even mimeographed reports and photocopied materials are included among the total of nearly 1,150 items. Following an introductory chapter on seminaries and civil government, coverage is given to Baptist, Catholic, Christian Church, Church of the Brethren, Episcopal, Hellenic, Independent, Jewish, Lutheran, Nazarene, Presbyterian, Reformed, Seventh-Day Adventist, United Church of Christ, and United Methodist denominations. The chapter on independent seminaries covers several denominations but omits others, such as the Quakers. Annotations vary in length but generally are brief. The work is indexed by author and subject.

1031. Religious Sites in America. Mary E. Snodgrass. Santa Barbara, CA: ABC-CLIO, 2000. 508p. ISBN 1-57607-154-5.

This is an interesting directory and guide to 160 notable places of worship throughout the United States. They represent a good distribution of American religious sites at the time of publication, since all are actively engaged in religious practices. Sites are selected from all 50 states and include the major traditions as well as alternative systems of belief and ritual. Entries treat cathedrals, churches, synagogues, temples, tabernacles, and so forth but also examine geological formations such as mountains and parks. Entries are arranged alphabetically and describe the site in terms of its significance and history as well as current activity. Religious practices are explained and contact and access information is given. There is a glossary as well as an extensive bibliography that includes electronic sources. A thorough and detailed index provides access.

1032. The Routledge Historical Atlas of Religion in America. Bret E. Carroll. New York; Routledge, 2000. 144p. (Routledge Atlases of American History). ISBN 0-415-92137-6.

This useful and attractive historical atlas is designed to appeal to a wide audience with the idea that in viewing maps, the distribution of migrations, periods of expansion, resettlement and relocation, and immigration patterns, one is able to comprehend the formation, expansion, and in some cases, decline of various religious groups over time. The work begins its coverage with Native American belief systems, for which both hunting regions and agricultural regions are shown; it then proceeds to European entry and treats both Spanish and English influences with particular emphasis on the impact of early English settlers on the development of Protestantism. Coverage is given to the later arrivals of Catholic immigrants during the past two centuries, and even more recently to the impact of

Jewish, Islamic, Hindu, and Buddhist refugees. The final section examines the futures of modern influences such as contemporary fundamentalism and Scientology. A chronology is provided, as is a general bibliography.

1033. South Asian Religions in the Americas: An Annotated Bibliography of Immigrant Religious Traditions. John Y. Fenton. Westport, CT: Greenwood Press, 1995. 241p. (Bibliographies and Indexes of Religious Studies, no. 34). ISBN 0-313-27835-0.

This is a unique source in its focus on the literature treating South Asian religions as practiced primarily in the United States and Canada, but also in Central America, South America, and the Caribbean Islands. The religious practices of people from India, Pakistan, Bangladesh, and so forth represent such traditions as Hinduism, Islam, Christianity, Judaism, and more. There is a total of 925 entries that include books, articles, reference sources, and printed bibliographies published in countries of the Americas. Organization of the work is in five chapters, the first of which examines the state of the study of these South Asian traditions, while the second chapter furnishes listings of bibliographic publications in both print and electronic format. The final three chapters supply listings by country for the United States and Canada, and by geographical area for the others.

ALTERNATIVE FAITHS: CHRISTIAN AND NON-CHRISTIAN

Alternatives to mainstream and established religion are common to this country and for years have represented the pluralism associated with life in the United States. Both Christian and non-Christian belief systems (both emotional and cerebral) have thrived and continue to thrive. In some cases, like the Shakers, their numbers are down to a precious few, but practices are still observed. In general, there is a feeling that religious rights should be observed; when these beliefs run contrary to public law, there is much controversy and debate about the constitutionality of the issues. The Unitarian Universalist Historical Society of Boston (available at http://www.uua.org/uuhs), founded in 1978, has several hundred members and publishes an annual, *Journal of Unitarian Universalist History* (formerly its proceedings) and newsletters. The Evangelical and Reformed Historical Society and Archives of the United Church of Christ (available at http://www.erhs.info) was founded in 1863 and operates out of Lancaster (Pennsylvania) Theological Seminary. It has over 1,500 members and publishes a newsletter as well as archival bibliographies.

1034. American Evangelicalism: An Annotated Bibliography. Norris A. Magnuson and William G. Travis. West Cornwall, CT: Locust Hill, 1990. 495p. ISBN 0-933951-27-2. **Supp.** 1997. 273p. ISBN 0-933951-68-X.

This bibliography and the Blumhofer and Carpenter entry below appeared at the same time and cover much of the same ground. This one is the more extensive, however, with twice the number of books and articles. Even so, there is a surprising lack of duplication in areas touched by both works, such as "The Bible." There is emphasis on monographic literature over periodical articles in this work. Also, there is a greater focus on the literature of evangelicalism rather than literature on the topic of evangelicalism. Although this effort is primarily focused on the twentieth century, the nineteenth century is surveyed as well. Annotations are brief, and there is an author index. Magnuson and Travis produced a supplement, *American Evangelicalism II: First Bibliographical Supplement, 1990–1996* in

1997 that identifies more than 1,500 entries for the seven-year period of coverage. Annotations are well written and informative in each work.

Twentieth Century Evangelicalism: A Guide to the Sources by Edith L. Blumhofer and Joel A. Carpenter (Garland, 1990) is another offering of the Garland Reference Library of Social Science (volume 521). More selective than the above effort, it serves as a useful complementary vehicle, with a helpful introductory segment and a good subject index. Annotations are slightly longer than those of Magnuson and Travis. Another useful tool, *Holy Ground: A Study of the American Camp Meeting* by Kenneth O. Brown (Garland, 1992), furnishes good bibliographical coverage of the literature as well as an informative history of the camp meeting, which originated in the South during the late eighteenth and early nineteenth centuries.

1035. Biographical Dictionary of American Cult and Sect Leaders. J. Gordon Melton. New York: Garland, 1986. 354p. (Garland Reference Library of Social Science, v. 212.) ISBN 0-8240-9037-3.

This useful biographical tool was developed in response to a clear need for material on leaders of divergent, nonmainstream groups. Both scholars and students should profit from the focus on what have come to be called alternative religions. Melton has provided comprehensive coverage of 213 founders and major leaders of U.S. cults and sects. Coverage is limited to deceased figures. A sect is considered to be a group in protest of the mainstream church, and a cult is defined as a more radical new spiritual option. Some of the groups have become mainstream, such as the Mormon Church. The biographies are well written and informative, numbering from 300 to 500 words in length and including bibliographies by and about the individual. Appendixes provide classification by tradition, birthplace, and religious influences. A good general index is given.

1036. Cults in America: A Reference Handbook. James R. Lewis. Santa Barbara, CA: ABC-CLIO, 1998. 232p. (Contemporary World Issues Series.) ISBN 1-57607-031-X.

This is a well-designed and informative source of information on what may be called alternative faiths in American society. Entries are organized into chapters that examine various types of cults, such as the chapter on "Controversial Groups and Movements" containing narratives on Satanism as well as the Krishnas. Entries are informative and treat each cult in detail; they provide a historical description of the origin and development of the cult and its belief system. Important personalities are identified and their role and influence explained. Special features include an extensive chronology beginning with the mid-eighteenth century in which important events and various facts are enumerated. There is a directory of relevant organizations with Web sites included among the other address information. The list of sources includes videotapes as well as books and articles. A detailed index furnishes access.

1037. The Encyclopedia of Cults, Sects, and New Religions. James R. Lewis, ed. Amherst, NY: Prometheus Books, 2001. 775p. ISBN 1-573-92888-7.

In response to the growing interest, and in some cases indignation, to the conduct of cult worship, this work furnishes a comprehensive treatment of such groups. Following a useful introduction explaining the meaning of cults and sects as being neutral rather than negative in nature, more than a thousand cults and sects are identified and described. The broad interpretation of these terms to include less-common denominations such as the Amish might be questionable. Entries tend to be brief ranging from one to three paragraphs in length, although greater detail is given to controversial movements. Groups are identified and described in terms of their origin and development throughout the history of this country.

Similar in nature, although somewhat more pejorative in tone, is *Encyclopedia of Cults and New Religions: Jehovah's Witnesses, Mormonism, Mind Sciences, Baha'I, Zen, Unitarianism* by John Ankerberg and John Weldon (Harvest House Publishers, 1999). It complements the work above since it sacrifices breadth for depth in treating only 60 religious movements in about the same number of pages. Entries are of varying length ranging from one page given to Krishnamurtri Foundation to more than 80 pages describing the Jehovah's Witnesses.

*1038. Encyclopedia of Mormonism: The History, Scripture, Doctrine, and Procedure of the Church of Jesus Christ of the Latter Day Saints. Daniel H. Ludlow, ed. New York: Macmillan, 1992. 4v. ISBN 0-02-879605-5.

This is a detailed and comprehensive compendium of the Mormon Church edited by a prominent professor of religion. Entries are well written and organized under five major topics: history of the Church; scriptures of the Church; doctrines of Mormonism; organization of the Church; and practices of Church members in society. Controversial topics such as feminism, abortion, and racism are treated in a frank and forthright manner, although doctrinal concepts may be difficult to grasp. There is an optional fifth volume that contains the sacred scriptures of Mormonism. Contributors to the encyclopedia are religious scholars of various affiliations. The CD-ROM version is available through Infobases of Orem, Utah; it does not contain the sample Mormon hymns.

The Presidents of the Church: Biographical Essays, edited by Leonard Arrington (Deseret Books, 1986), is a biographical dictionary primarily useful for students who are interested in pictures and biographical descriptions of the life and times of the 13 men who have served as head of the Church of Jesus Christ of Latter-Day Saints, the major arm of the Mormon faith. Beginning with Joseph Smith and ending with Ezra Taft Benson, who served as the secretary of agriculture under Dwight Eisenhower, biographies furnish highlights of each man's career and provide a human focus on their accomplishments. The tool's importance to scholarship is somewhat limited because of its failure to supply footnotes to source material. This work replaces the 13th edition of the same title completed in 1994.

1039. Encyclopedic Handbook of Cults in America. Rev. ed. J. Gordon Melton. Hampden, CT: Garland, 1992. 407p. (Garland Reference Library of Social Science, v. 797.) ISBN 0-8153-1140-0.

This informative handbook of alternative religions has been revised and expanded since the second edition in 1986. Melton, long an authority on religion in U.S. life and founder of the Institute for the Study of American Religion, has continued to produce an objective compendium of information. Especially useful are the introductory essays defining cults and their opponents in the United States. Coverage is given to 33 different groups ranging from the more established Rosicrucians to the more recent and publicized movements such as Unity School, Unification Church, and Krishna units. Each group is described in terms of leading figures, belief systems, organizational structure, and controversies. Bibliographies are provided. A name index and a detailed table of contents facilitate access.

1040. A Guide to the Study of the Pentecostal Movement. Charles E. Jones. Metuchen, NJ: American Theological Library Association and Scarecrow, 1983. 2v. (ATLA Bibliography Series, no. 6.) ISBN 0-8108-1583-4.

This is another of the interesting and important bibliographies produced through the increased desire to cover the writings on various denominations. The Pentecostal movement developed out of an emotional conviction that at times discouraged scholarly inquiry. This two-volume effort, authored by a religious scholar and librarian, presents a unique listing of more than 6,000 books and articles from a variety of sources and representing various languages. Many denominations are treated within a broad-based definition of Pentecostalism. Historical narrative is included with respect to churches, schools, associations, and missionary agencies. The emphasis is on U.S. Pentecostalism, but foreign movements are covered as well. This work is important to inquirers at various levels, ranging from student to scholar. A helpful directory is included as a special feature. Several indexes furnish adequate access.

1041. Historical Dictionary of Mormonism. 2nd ed. Davis Bitton. Lanham, MD: Scarecrow Press, 2000. 310p. (Historical Dictionaries of Religions, Philosophies, and Movements, no. 32.) ISBN 0-8018-3797-8.

The Mormon religion, founded in 1830 in this country, has expanded from its North American presence and is now growing substantially in other parts of the world, most notably in South America, Asia, and Africa. This work includes religious activities in different regions of the world while also providing awareness of historical development, events, personalities, and specialized terminology of the faith. Following a chronology and an introductory essay, entries are arranged alphabetically in the main text categorized as "Dictionary." Of particular interest are the entries treating specific periods in Mormon history. Entries vary in length from a single paragraph to several pages. Several appendixes enhance the work in covering church presidents, temples, the Family proclamation, the Relief Society Declaration, and quotations. An extensive bibliography is given.

1042. Historical Dictionary of the Shakers. Holley G. Duffield. Lanham, MD: Scarecrow Press, 2000. 288p. (Religions, Philosophies, and Movements, no. 28.) ISBN 0-8108-3683-1.

The author is an academic specialist in the field of Shaker studies who has provided a comprehensive source of information on the history and development of the alternative religious group in this country from the time of its initial arrival in New York Harbor in 1774 to the present day. At its height just prior to the Civil War, the Shaker population reached only 6,000; since that time the number has steadily declined and today it has only six members residing in New Gloucester, Maine. The religion has had an inordinate impact on U.S. religious history in view of its slight population figures, and its central tenets are well known and are part of the doctrine of other more populous denominations. Included within the belief system are such principles as nonviolence, communal existence in a utopian culture, economic independence and self-reliance, celibacy, and separation of males from females. Entries treat personalities, events, beliefs, communities, living conditions, and so forth. There is a chronology along with several appendixes and a detailed index.

1043. Jehovah's Witnesses: A Comprehensive and Selectively Annotated Bibliography. Jerry Bergman, comp. Westport, CT: Greenwood Press, 1999. 368p. ISBN 0-313-30510-2.

The author is an academic and specialist in the study of Jehovah's Witnesses, and has been a prolific writer in the past. The current effort updates and expands his earlier bibliography, *Jehovah's Witnesses and Kindred Groups: A Historical Compendium and Bibliography,* published by Garland in 1984. It is similar in arrangement and organization to the earlier work but is more comprehensive in its attempt to identify every publication by and about Jehovah's Witnesses and the Watchtower Society. These include books, articles, and reports that vary in terms of scholarly or popular intent, and span a period of nearly 200 years from nineteenth century to 1999. Following a useful and informative introduction describing the history and development of the religion, there are nearly 10,000 entries arranged under chapters treating issuing body or types of literature. Included here are official publications of the Society; books, manuscripts, tracts; periodical articles; and so forth.

1044. Mennonite Bibliography, 1631–1961. Nelson P. Springer and A.J. Klassen, comps. Scottdale, PA: Herald, 1977. 2v. ISBN 0-8381-1208-3.

This is a useful bibliography of writings of all types on the Mennonites. It represents a comprehensive listing of more than 28,000 books, periodicals, pamphlets, dissertations, Festschrift, symposia, and conferences, and even includes individual articles from encyclopedias and periodicals. Book reviews are also identified. U.S. Mennonites can trace their beginning to both the Swiss and Dutch wings of Anabaptism, which developed in Switzerland in the sixteenth century. It embraced parts of Germany and spread to the United States through various groups such as the Amish and the Hutterites. Volume 1 of this work covers the international aspects of the Mennonite faith, with volume 2 targeting its presence in North America. Entries are arranged under various topics as they fall under geographical divisions. There are indexes to author, subject, and book review.

1045. Modern American Popular Religion: A Critical Assessment and Annotated Bibliography. Charles H. Lippy. Westport, CT: Greenwood Press, 1996. 250p. (Bibliographies and Indexes in Religious Studies, no. 37.) ISBN 0-313-27786-9.

This is a well-constructed and useful annotated bibliography designed to meet the needs of serious inquirers, both students and scholars in examining the nature, composition, and role played by popular religion in the twentieth century. An introductory essay examines the essence of popular religion and whether it is defined as folk religion, common religion, or invisible religion. Eleven chapters contain nearly 560 entries some of which are categorized under such topical chapters as evangelicalism, fundamentalism and the religious right, radio and televisions ministries, and so forth, and others placed under format or type of resource chapters such as survey works, reference works, and so forth. Emphasis is on Christianity although New Age sources are included. Annotations are detailed and describe secondary sources, mostly book and book chapters, but periodical articles, theses, and dissertations as well.

Lippy's *Twentieth-Century Shapers of American Popular Religion* (Greenwood Press, 1989) is a welcome tool for both scholars and students because of its detailed biographical essays on leading figures, both living and dead, representing some form of "popular" religion. Religions of this type focus on a charismatic leader and utilize (or exploit) the media. Television evangelists of today along with the capable spokesmen of the past are included but coverage is highly selective, limited to just over 60 men and women representing this unique U.S. experience. Included here are leaders such as Mordecai Kaplan, Harvey Cox, Marcus Garvey, Amy Semple McPherson, Malcolm X, and Pat Robertson. Others have been included for their influence, such as Sinclair Lewis for his *Elmer Gantry*. Entries include an evaluation, critical summary, and bibliography.

1046. A Mormon Bibliography, 1830–1930: Books, Pamphlets, Periodicals, and Broadsides Relating to the First Century of Mormonism. Chad J. Flake, ed. Salt Lake City, UT: University of Utah, 1978; repr. 1995. 825p. ISBN 0-87480-016-1. **Supp.** 1989. 413p. ISBN 0-87480-338-1.

This work serves a dual role as both an important scholarly bibliography and a union catalog of various printed materials relating to the Mormon faith during its first hundred years. Included here are the formats enumerated in the title; excluded are specific articles, manuscripts, maps, and prints. There are over 10,000 entries representing the holdings of nearly 200 libraries. Arrangement is alphabetical by author in the manner of the *National Union Catalog* (entry 46). Entries provide bibliographic identification as well as symbols indicating library locations. The lack of a subject index is one drawback to its use as a convenient tool by scholars and serious students.

The supplement compiled by Flake and Larry W. Draper, *A Mormon Bibliography, 1830–1930: Ten Year Supplement* (University of Utah, 1989) is organized in the same manner and furnishes listings of additional citations covering the same time period. Rare materials available in over 40 libraries are identified. Currently Peter Crawley is working on *A Descriptive Bibliography of the Mormon Church* issued by the Religious Studies Center of Brigham Young University. Volume 1, treating the period 1830–1847, was published in 1997.

1047. New Religious Movements in the United States and Canada: A Critical Assessment and Annotated Bibliography. Diane Choquette, comp. Westport, CT: Greenwood Press, 1985. 235p. (Bibliographies and Indexes in Religious Studies, no. 5.) ISBN 0-313-23772-7.

This annotated bibliography furnishes comprehensive coverage of more than 700 writings from the 1960s and 1970s on a variety of alternative faiths: Eastern religions, New Age and spiritualist sects, and the occult, as well as Christian variants (Jesus People and the People's Temple). This is another in the Greenwood series designed to cover various faiths and is of use to scholars, students, and serious laypeople in its focus on both scholarly and popular literature. Entries represent books, periodical articles, dissertations, conference papers, unpublished works, and some audiovisual materials. Annotations are descriptive and sometimes critical. Arrangement of entries is by category or type (e.g., reference works, types of scholarly studies, popular titles). Many of these sections are subdivided by subject.

Entries are alphabetically arranged within these categories. There is a general index of authors, titles, and subjects that furnishes good access to content.

1048. Shaker Literature: A Bibliography. Mary L.H. Richmond, comp. Hancock, MA: Shaker Community; distr. Hanover, NH: University Press of New England, 1977. 2v. ISBN 0-87451-117-8.

Mother Ann Lee arrived in this country in 1774; subsequently, 18 Shaker communities were founded at different times. The Shakers as a religious group have most certainly attracted attention of both scholars and popular writers to a degree disproportionate to their relatively small number in U.S. religious history. This title provides an excellent bibliography with introductory essays. About 4,000 entries are divided into two volumes. The first volume furnishes over 1,700 entries and covers material by Shakers. Volume 2 covers material *about* Shakers. Included in the two volumes are references for books, parts of books, pamphlets, periodical articles, broadsides, almanacs, catalogs, advertisements, leaflets, and notices. Library locations are furnished. Of great interest is the segment on court decisions in volume 1 and the anti-Shaker tracts listed in volume 2. The annotations are useful in describing content. There is an index of titles and joint authors.

1049. Studies in Mormon History, 1830–1997: An Indexed Bibliography. James B. Allen et al. Champaign: University of Illinois Press, 2000. 1168p. ISBN 0-252-02565-2.

Described by the publisher as a monumental work, this comprehensive, well-conceived bibliography has received similar ratings from its reviewers. Allen and his co-authors are respected scholars and prolific contributors to the literature of the Mormon church, and in this effort they have attempted to include every English-language publication of substantive value in providing comprehension of the history and development of the church from its beginnings to the current age. Thousands of books, journal articles, dissertations and theses, and reports of diverse nature are identified in works ranging from popular and personal narratives to serious inquiry. Stories of pioneers and biographical treatment of significant personalities are part of the mix. A useful special feature is an extensive topical guide to relevant social science literature. Access is facilitated by author and topical indexes.

CHRISTIAN MAINSTREAM

The major current index of a general nature in religion, published by the American Theological Association is *Religion Index One,* published from 1953 to 1977 as *Index to Religious Periodical Literature.* Periodical articles and book reviews are covered in this semiannual publication issued by the American Theological Library Association. Emphasis is on English-language publications and on Protestant faiths, although other languages and religions are not excluded. The companion work is *Religion Index Two,* which has been issued since 1978 on an annual basis and indexes collective works by more than one author taken from anthologies, compilations, and other sources. Material of interest to the history of religion in the United States. routinely appears in both titles; both are available in electronic format as *ATLA Religion Database* on CD-ROM or through the World Wide Web. (See Introductory segment to "Protestant" section.)

General Sources

1050. Dictionary of Christianity in America. Daniel G. Reid et al. Downers Grove, IL: InterVarsity Press, 1990. 1305p. ISBN 0-8308-1776-X.

This is a massive and comprehensive volume that has been identified as a landmark in the field for its inclusive and thorough treatment of the topic. Some 2,600 entries, both historical and contemporary, are contributed by more than 400 specialists in the area of religious studies. Articles vary in length from several paragraphs to several pages and are signed and arranged alphabetically. They contain cross-references and give treatment to hundreds of personalities from Christopher Columbus to Ronald Reagan, significant institutions, denominations, events, traditions, issues, movements, ideologies, phenomena, and so forth. Bibliographies are included. Treatment is evenhanded, and especially well covered is the history of evangelicalism in this country.

Concise Dictionary of Christianity in America, by the same authors and issued by the same publisher five years later (1995), is a severe condensation of the original in cutting it down to one-quarter of its original size. This required the deletion of bibliographies and many of the lengthier essays, as well as reducing the length of most entries. About 50 new entries have been added. Despite its truncated nature, the work does represent an affordable purchase for brief identifications.

1051. Dictionary of Heresy Trials in American Christianity. George H. Shriver, ed. Westport, CT: Greenwood Press, 1997. 511p. ISBN 0-313-29660-X.

A useful resource in the study of Christianity is this examination primarily of heretical personalities and in some cases seminaries engaged in Christian worship in this country. The editor is an academic scholar and prolific contributor to the literature on the topic for several decades. In this work, he has utilized the talents of more than 40 specialists in the field who have served as contributors in supplying 50 entries treating significant trials, including the Salem witch trials, over a span of 200 years dating from the colonial period to the 1990s. Most trials cover breeches of faith in various Protestant denominations, although two involve Catholics. Entries are arranged alphabetically and provide serious and cogent analyses and interpretations in essays that average about 4000 words. In addition to selective reading lists for each entry, the work concludes with a general bibliography and subject index.

Catholic

The *Catholic Periodical and Literature Index* is the leading current index of books and articles pertinent to Catholicism. Routinely it cites writings useful to the study of the history of Catholicism in this country. It is published quarterly and indexes more than 150 periodicals. Book reviews are included as well. Initially two separate publications, it has been issued since 1930 by the Catholic Library Association (available at http://www.cathla.org) in Haverford, Pennsylvania; the present title was adopted in 1968.

The American Catholic Historical Association (available at http://www.research.cua.edu/acha) was founded in 1919 and is headquartered at Catholic University of America in Washington, D.C. It has over 1,000 members and issues the *Catholic Historical Review* on a quarterly basis. The United States Catholic Historical Society first appeared in 1884 and has more than 1,200 members. It currently operates out of New York City, and has issued a quarterly journal, *U.S. Catholic Historian,* since 1980.

1052. Dictionary of American Catholic Biography. John J. Delaney. Garden City, NY: Doubleday, 1984. 621p. ISBN 0-385-17878-6.

A useful tool for quick answers to questions from all types of inquirers, this biographical dictionary lists 1,500 deceased personalities who have made a noteworthy contribution to the Catholic Church and/or to this country. Coverage represents a long time span, from the period of exploration to the present or recent past. Both men and women are treated in entries that are concise but well developed and carefully researched. As one might expect, the majority of the entries represent church people at various levels, but a good proportion of laypersons are included as well. Such people as Bing Crosby, Arturo Toscanini, Babe Ruth, and John F. Kennedy demonstrate the scope and breadth of coverage. No bibliographies are furnished with the entries, an omission that does limit its value to scholarship.

1053. Documents of American Catholic History. John T. Ellis, ed. Wilmington, DE: Glazier, 1967–1987. 3v. ISBN 0-894-53611-7 (v. 1).

The author has been one of the most respected historians of the Catholic Church in the United States for the past 35 years, having produced a concise historical survey the same year the original edition of this work came out in 1956. In the revised two-volume edition published in 1967 by H. Regnery, the first volume contained source material dating from 1493 to 1865 and volume 2 continued the coverage to 1966. What was offered was interesting documentary material showing the full flavor of Catholic existence. Included are laws, charters, papal documents, and so on, as well as John Adams's perception of a mass he attended, comments of Mr. Dooley on various issues, and poetry by Joyce Kilmer. The most recent edition offers a reprint version of the earlier two-volume effort, along with a new third volume covering the years 1966–1986.

1054. Encyclopedia of American Catholic History. Michael Glazier and Thomas J. Shelley, eds. Collegeville, MN: Liturgical Press, 1997. 1567p. ISBN 0-8146-5919-5.

A highly useful work is this comprehensive source offering more than 1,200 entries treating various aspects and personalities of significance to Catholicism in the United States over a span of 500 years, with up-to-date coverage of the present day. Entries are signed and vary in length from less than a page to several pages depending upon the breadth of the topic. Numerous contributors have authored the well-researched and well-written articles that supply biographical sketches of missionaries, other clerics, influential laymen, explorers, and so forth as well as descriptions of various groups, historical periods, events, institutions, and church phenomena. Of real value are the detailed essays on Catholicism in each state. Photographs are supplied throughout. Arrangement is alphabetical, and many entries contain bibliographies. An index completes the work.

1055. A Guide to American Catholic History. 2nd ed., rev. and enl. John T. Ellis and Robert Trisco. Santa Barbara, CA: ABC-CLIO, 1982. 265p. ISBN 0-87436-318-7.

The principal author has been one of the more prolific recorders of the U.S. Catholic experience for the past three decades (see entry 1053 above) and revised the initial edition of this work some 23 years after its issue in 1959. The more recent effort furnishes an annotated bibliography of more than 1,250 entries, of which nearly 500 are newly added. The majority of the 800 original entries have been retained, with little revision evident. Both monographic and journal literature are treated along with dissertations; issue and publication dates run to 1979. Arrangement of entries is by classes covered in various chapters, some of which are very pertinent to the needs of social historians. The segment on manuscript depositories, once considered useful to the needs of scholarship, has been eliminated. There is a comprehensive index to subjects, authors, and titles.

Protestant

The major indexing tool, initially established with a Protestant perspective, but now much more universal, is *ATLA Religion Database* published by the American Theological Library Association (available at http://www.atla.com) of Chicago, IL. The database version incorporates three separate print indexes and furnishes identification of 350,000 articles, 150,000 essays from anthologies, and 350,000 book reviews. It is available both on the World Wide Web and in CD-ROM from SilverPlatter. One is able to identify items relevant to the study of religious history dating from 1949.

Many of the Protestant denominations have a historical society or association promoting research and publication. For example, the Southern Baptist Historical Society was formed in 1938 at the Southern Baptist Theological Seminary, and from 1951 to 1995 functioned as an auxiliary of the Historical Commission of the Southern Baptist Convention of Nashville, Tennessee. It became an independent organization in 1995 and in 2001, changed its name to the Baptist History and Heritage Society (available at http://www.baptisthistory.org) The organization has issued a quarterly journal, *Baptist History and Heritage,* since 1965. The American Baptist Historical Society (available at http://www.abc-usa.org/abhs) is the oldest Baptist historical organization in the country (1853) and is now headquartered in Valley Forge, Pennsylvania. It has published the *American Baptist Quarterly* since 1958. The Historical Society of the United Methodist Church (available at http://www.gcah.org/umhs/Default.html) was founded in 1988 and has over 1,000 members. Its quarterly journal, *Methodist History,* was started by the church in 1962.

1056. Dictionary of Baptists in America. Bill J. Leonard, ed. Downers Grove, IL: InterVarsity Press, 1994. 298p. ISBN 0-8308-1447-7.

This is a unique work in being a one-volume compendium describing the personalities, ideas, movements, institutions, societies, and various phenomena associated with the Baptist tradition in the United States. The work opens with a good exposition of the history and development of the Baptist influence in this country, and furnishes a reading list. Emphasis is placed on biographical data and the majority of the entries furnish coverage of major figures all deceased, much of the coverage being drawn from the *Dictionary of Christianity in America* (entry 1050). In treating individuals, entries give dates of birth and death, and describe life and career influences; they are contributed by some 100 scholars and specialists and are arranged alphabetically. Entries are evenhanded and informative, albeit concise, and run from a fourth to a half page. They contain bibliographies for further study.

1057. Dictionary of the Presbyterian & Reformed Tradition in America. D.G. Hart and Mark A. Noll, eds. Downers Grove, IL: InterVarsity Press, 1999. 286p. ISBN 0-8308-1453-1.

Following the same pattern as the *Dictionary of Baptists in America* (entry 1056), and a product of the same publisher, this work focuses on the Presbyterian and Reformed elements of Protestantism as did the other on Baptists. The editors are academics and specialists in the field who have been assisted by the contributed entries of numerous scholars. Emphasis is on coverage given to significant personalities and to various denominational groupings, but also treated are events, developments, ideologies, institutions, practices, and more. Following an informative introductory essay describing the historical development of Presbyterianism and the nature of its identity, there are some 400 entries, all of which are concise but useful in serving to identify the subject or topic. Like the entry above, much of the coverage is drawn from the *Dictionary of Christianity in America* (entry 1050), and bibliographical listings are furnished.

1058. Guide to the Manuscript Collections of the Presbyterian Church U.S. Robert Benedetto and Betty K. Walker. Westport, CT: Greenwood Press, 1990. 570p. (Bibliographies and Indexes in Religious Studies, no. 17.) ISBN 0-313-27654-4.

An excellent resource for scholarly study is this guide to the various manuscript collections available on the Presbyterian Church, U.S., the denomination founded in the South as the Presbyterian Church in the Confederate States of America in 1861. The principal author furnishes a brief, informative history and description of the nature and character of the unit until its 1983 merger with the northern factions into the present Presbyterian Church. Nearly 1,400 different collections are identified, most of which are located at the Department of History of the Presbyterian Church, U.S., in Montreat, North Carolina. Others are found in a variety of institutions, such as Davidson College. Arrangement of materials is by name of the person who developed the collection or created the materials. All types of source materials are cited, including diaries, correspondence, and photographs. A subject index is provided.

1059. Methodist Union Catalog, Pre-1976 Imprints. Kenneth E. Rowe, ed. Metuchen, NJ: Scarecrow, 1975–1994. v. 1–7. (Projected 20v.) ISBN 0-8108-0880-3 (v. 1).

This union catalog of the holdings of over 200 Methodist libraries in the United States and Europe has progressed steadily but slowly the initial volumes in 1975. The editor has served as the Methodist librarian at Drew University and is compiling what should become the standard bibliography of books, pamphlets, and theses on Methodism, as well as the writings of Methodists (even if not related to religious inquiry). Methodism is interpreted broadly here. Each volume furnishes between 6,000 and 7,000 entries, and arrangement is alphabetical by author. Publication dates start with the beginning of the movement in 1729 and continue up to the present day. There are six completed volumes thus far, and all bear a reputation for excellence in terms of comprehensiveness and adherence to high bibliographic standards. The sixth volume (1985) brought the alphabetical coverage through the letter "I," and most recently, volume 7 makes access possible through "J-Le." Symbols for locations of participating libraries accompany each entry. Index volumes are to be included to the entire set.

1060. A Presbyterian Bibliography: The Published Writings of Ministers Who Served in the Presbyterian Church in the United States During Its First Hundred Years, 1861–1961, and Their Locations in Eight Significant Theological Collections in the U.S.A. Harold B. Prince, comp. and ed. Metuchen, NJ: American Theological Library Association and Scarecrow, 1983. 452p. (ATLA Bibliography Series, no. 8.) ISBN 0-8108-1639-3.

An extremely useful source for scholars and serious students, this union list cites nearly 4,200 published works by ministers of the Presbyterian Church of the Confederate States of America and its successor, the Presbyterian Church in the United States. Historically, it represents an extremely important time following the disunion of the nation into warring camps and the division of the Presbyterian Church along those same lines. The holdings of eight theological libraries are treated here with references to relevant items in their collections. Arrangement of entries is alphabetical by author and furnishes a unique perspective on church development as seen by its majority. There is a subject index to provide access.

The *Bibliography of Published Articles on American Presbyterianism, 1901–1980* by Harold M. Parker (Greenwood Press, 1985) is the fourth entry of the Bibliographies and Indexes in Religious Studies series. It is another useful reference with which to identify nearly 3,000 articles in 17 library locations. Included here is material from natural and regional secular reviews; house organs of churches are excluded. A valuable topical index furnishes access.

JEWISH

The Jewish influence on the course of events in this country has been strong since the Revolutionary War. As they have done in other countries in which they settled and to which they migrated, the Jewish people have added immensely to the cultural, educational, business, scientific, and recreational achievement of the United States. This section lists sources that treat both the Jewish religion and the Jewish social tradition.

The *Index to Jewish Periodicals,* published by The Index in Cleveland Heights, Ohio, has been issued since 1963 and is the leading current index of Jewish periodical literature. It covers about 150 periodicals in the English language and includes book reviews. Material of interest to U.S. Jewish history appears on a routine basis. Beginning with volume 26 (1988), it changed from a semiannual to an annual publication. It can be purchased in print or CD-ROM format. There is a CD-ROM index available covering the period from 1988 through 1999.

The American Jewish Historical Society (available at http://www.ajhs.org) with offices in Waltham, Massachusetts, and New York City, was founded in 1892 and has more than 3,000 members. Its quarterly journal, *American Jewish History,* has been published since 1893. One of the society's most ambitious publishing projects was a five-volume history, collectively titled *The Jewish People in America* (1992), for which Henry L. Feingold served as general editor. Coverage of volume 1 begins with the first immigration of 23 Jews to New Amsterdam in 1654; succeeding immigrations are treated through volume 5, which covers the period subsequent to World War II. Jewish life in the United States is examined in depth from immigration through assimilation.

General Sources

1061. An American Jewish Bibliography: Being a List of Books and Pamphlets by Jews, or Relating to Them, Printed in the United States from the Establishment of the Press in the Colonies Until 1850. Abraham S.W. Rosenbach. Baltimore: American Jewish Historical Society, 1926. 486p. (Publications of the American Jewish Historical Society, no. 30). Repr. Mansfield Centre, CT: Martino Publishing, 1999. ISBN 1-57898-202-2.

The Rosenbach work has long been recognized as a standard bibliography relating to the study of U.S. Jewish history. It was issued in 1926 and remains a valuable source for research and scholarly inquiry. Originally a publication of the American Jewish Historical Society, it has since been reprinted. About 700 books and pamphlets are listed in chronological order and represent publications either by or about Jews from colonial times to 1850.

Two years after Rosenbach's death, there appeared a supplement: *Jewish Americana: A Catalogue of Books and Articles by Jews or Relating to Them Printed in the United States from the Earliest Days to 1850 and Found in the Library of the Hebrew Union College– Jewish Institute of Religion in Cincinnati* (American Jewish Archives, Monograph No. 1, 1954). Subsequently coverage was continued through Allan F. Levine's *An American Jewish Bibliography: A List of Books and Pamphlets by Jews or Relating to Them, Printed in the United States from 1851–1875, Which Are in the Possession of the Hebrew Union College– Jewish Institute of Religion Library in Cincinnati* (American Jewish Archives, Monograph No. 11, 1959).

1062. American Jewish History: Eight Volumes Bound in 13 Books. Jeffrey S. Gurock., ed. New York: Routledge, 1998. 8v. ISBN 0-415-91933-9.

This multivolume effort was sponsored by American Jewish Historical Society for which Gurock serves as chair. It is composed of more than 200 articles and book chapters treating life in this country as experienced by members of the Jewish faith. It represents a comprehensive history in chronological and thematic sequence through the eight volumes. Most of the articles are drawn from publications of the Society over the years. Volume 1 treats the beginnings with the colonial period and spans the period from 1654 to 1740; volume 2 examines the immigration of Central European Jews from 1840 to 1880; volume 3 (in three parts) describes life in this country for East European Jews from 1880 to 1920; volume 4 provides insight into Jewish life from 1920 to 1990; volume 5 (in three parts) examines the changes, transformations, adaptations, and compromises through time; volume 6 (in two parts) focuses on anti-Semitism in this country, while volume 7 presents the period of the holocaust and American response; volume 8 describes the Zionist movement and establishment of a national homeland.

1063. Conservative Judaism in America: A Biographical Dictionary and Sourcebook. Pamela S. Nadell. Westport, CT: Greenwood Press, 1988. 409p. (Jewish Denominations in America). ISBN 0-313-24205-4.

Conservative Judaism emerged in the nineteenth-century United States as a compromise between the almost total accommodation to modern U.S. life of the new Reform movement and the unwavering observance of Hebrew tradition of the Orthodox school. This biographical dictionary is first of a series from Greenwood Press and opens with three brief, informative essays on the history, ideology, and organization of Conservative Judaism. Institutions such as the Jewish Theological Seminary are identified and explained. The bulk of the work consists of biographical sketches of roughly 130 individuals considered to be leading figures of Conservative Judaism, most of them rabbis active in the movement. Entries furnish biographical information, evaluation of achievements, bibliography of the subject's writings, and references about them. Also included are a glossary of Hebrew terms, a bibliography, and appendixes listing names and dates. There is a detailed subject index.

1064. The Jewish Experience: A Guide to Manuscript Sources in the Library of Congress. Gary J. Kohn, comp. Cincinnati, OH: American Jewish Archives; distr. Hoboken, NJ: KTAV, 1986. 166p. (Monographs of the American Jewish Archives, no. 11.) ISBN 0-87820-014-2.

Another guide to the massive holdings of the Library of Congress pertinent to a specific topic, this title has proved of value to research and scholarly study. One may lament its failure to furnish critical analysis or even descriptive annotations, but in this case the identification and enumeration of such primary source material is justification enough for its issue and use. Arrangement of the tool is in three sections, beginning with a listing of over 130 collections in the library that contain some material on the topic. Second, there is a listing of about 300 individual collections containing papers of prominent Jews or corporate bodies. Finally, there is a topical listing that identifies papers on such subjects as the Holocaust. Entries furnish collection name, subjects, and location file number.

1065. Jewish Heritage in America: An Annotated Bibliography. Sharad Karkhanis. New York: Garland, 1988. 434p. (Garland Reference Library of Social Science, v. 467.) ISBN 0-8240-7538-2.

This relatively recent bibliography of nearly 325 books and 800 articles represents a good selection of both popular and scholarly literature. The author is the librarian of a community college in New York City and has culled his entries from nearly 90 journals spanning a period of over 60 years from 1925 through 1987. Selection was based on the significance of a topic and its treatment, with recognition of the need to present a balanced listing. Excluded are autobiographies, biographies, poetry, and fiction. Availability was a factor, with some emphasis on access through medium-sized libraries. Arrangement of entries is under seven broad categories, such as historical perspective and anti-Semitism, all of which are further divided by subcategories; books and articles are listed under topic. Descriptive annotations are lengthy. Author, title, and subject indexes are furnished.

American Jewish History: A Bibliographical Guide by Jeffrey S. Gurock (Anti-Defamation League of B'nai B'rith, 1983) is relatively compact work that was hailed as the first critical inventory of U.S. Jewish history in 30 years. The work is intended for all levels of users, from scholars to the general public, and features a guide to the titles considered most useful for examination of the major issues relevant to Jewish history in this country. It contains a series of brief but informative bibliographic essays that treat the basic introductory and reference titles concerning the topic from the colonial period to the present day. Special topics such as the Holocaust and Zionism are included.

1066. Jewish-American History and Culture: An Encyclopedia. Jack Fischel and San-ford Pinsker, eds. Hamden, CT: Garland, 1992. 710p. (Garland Reference Library of the Social Sciences, v. 429.) ISBN 0-8240-6622-7.

Reviewers consider this a groundbreaking work because it presents a well-designed, clearly written, comprehensive, one-volume source of information revealing the richness and depth of contribution of the Jewish people in the United States. Entries are alphabetically arranged and describe all aspects of life, including the arts, economics, history, the human-ities, the military, science, social institutions, organizations, and popular culture. Personal-ities are covered in liberal fashion. Entries range from brief sketches to detailed surveys and furnish not only description but also, in many cases, critical evaluation. Useful bibliogra-phies accompany most entries, enabling the reader to research the topic further. Contributors to the work are specialists in the field of Jewish studies and provide an enlightening and fair-minded exposition. Useful listings include Jewish Nobel Prize winners and libraries with extensive collections on the subject.

1067. Judaica Americana: An Annotated Bibliography of Publications to 1900. Robert Singerman. Westport, CT: Greenwood Press, 1990. 2v. ISBN 0-313-25023-5.

The author is a leading bibliographer in the realm of Jewish studies and in this work he has provided a rich and comprehensive source of information regarding published writ-ings on Jews and Judaism issued in this country from the colonial period to the beginning of the twentieth century. Sponsored by the Hebrew Union College-Jewish Institute of Re-ligion, the work contains some 6,500 entries representing books and articles that describe the history, culture, and societal relationships with Christians through the years. Volume 1 covers the period from 1676 to 1889, and volume 2 treats the significant and prolific decade from 1890 to 1900. Entries contain *National Union Catalog* symbols identifying library locations, and a thorough and detailed index supplies access.

Judaica Americana: An Annotated Bibliography of Publications from 1960–1990, edited by Nathan M. Kaganoff. (Carlson Publishing, 1995) also in two volumes presents similar coverage of nearly 7,500 entries culled from his numerous bibliographies that ap-peared in *Judaica Americana* published by the American Jewish Historical Society. Books and articles, both general and specialized and issued over a 30-year period, are supplied with brief annotations and content notes.

The Synagogue

1068. American Synagogue History: A Bibliography and State-of-the-Field Survey. Alexandra S. Korros and Jonathan D. Sarna. New York: M. Wiener, 1988. 247p. ISBN 0-910129-90-8.

Developed as a resource for both scholarly and popular inquiry, this bibliography of nearly 1,200 synagogue and community histories is arranged alphabetically by state. Syn-agogue histories are of different varieties and include separate publications, parts of larger community histories, periodical articles, chronicles, and even souvenir publications and pamphlets. The work opens with an introduction by a noted historian, Jonathan D. Sarna, and follows with a useful survey article by Daniel J. Elazar, raising important considerations pertaining to the development of the synagogue in the United States. Entries are subdivided by congregational and community history and furnish the usual bibliographic identification.

Brief annotations accompany some but not all citations. Special features include a separate bibliography on synagogue architecture as well as a selected listing of secondary sources. The work is of value because of the uniqueness of its content. An author index is provided.

1069. An Encyclopedia of American Synagogue Ritual. Kerry M. Olitzky and Marc L. Raphael. Westport, CT: Greenwood Press, 2000. 184p. ISBN 0-313-30814-4.

The authors are prolific contributors to the reference literature on American Judaism, and in this work describe the variety of rituals associated with the life of American Jews. Following an introduction analyzing the significance of ritualistic tradition to the Jewish people and general distinction of rituals in concert with custom and ceremony, entries are arranged alphabetically from "aliyah" to "yizkor." They provide exposition of the origins of the rituals in synagogue observation, their subsequent development, and their variation in the practice of various branches of the faith. Terms derived from Hebrew and Yiddish languages as well as those of English usage are defined.

Each entry contains a bibliography. An earlier work by the same authors is *The American Synagogue: A Historical Dictionary and Sourcebook* (Greenwood Press, 1996) in which selected synagogues representing all four movements within Judaism in the United States and Canada are described. Entries are about a page in length and provide good detailed coverage in their treatment of 350 synagogues with listings of their rabbis. History, development, architecture, and so forth of these synagogues are covered in entries that are organized by state.

Shul with a Pool: The "Synagogue-Center" in American Jewish History by David Kaufman (University Press of New England, 1999) is a highly readable and interesting historical account of the "shul" or synagogue emerging as social center in twentieth-century Jewish American communities. Amid the frustrations experienced by Jewish Americans in their efforts to gain acceptance and become part of the U.S. cultural and social fabric, the synagogue became an important societal force in its capacity to provide a supportive structure and friendly environment. The rabbi became increasingly active in promoting the social interests and events for members. The work is divided into seven chapters describing the center in the conduct of Jewish life from reformed to orthodox, its relationship to young peoples' associations, Hebrew school, seminary and so forth. The final chapter examines the synagogue-center movement of the 1920s. There is a chronology, and an index supplies access.

ISLAMIC

1070. The North American Muslim Resource Guide: Muslim Community Life in the United States and Canada. Mohamed Nimer, ed. New York: Routledge, 2002. 288p. ISBN 0-415-93728-0.

Unfortunately, there is little representation of Islamic American groups and personalities in the reference literature today. One of the few useful sources of information is this recent effort in providing both a guide and directory to the faith in this country. Included here are organizations in various communities, educational institutions, clubs and groups, media, and other elements in Islamic American life. Membership and contact information is included. An important feature is the descriptive narrative furnishing a brief history of the religion in this country as well as the graphic tables providing analysis of population statistics and the dramatic growth of the religion in recent years. There is an analytical account of the impact of the events of the past five years on Islamic American life and culture.

SCIENCE, TECHNOLOGY, AND MEDICINE

In American universities the history of science, as a cultural, philosophical, and intellectual pursuit, was formalized during the second decade of the 20th century with the active involvement of George Sarton. Today, the field remains a steady if not quite popular course of study for both graduate and undergraduate students and since 1913, has had a quarterly research and review journal publication, *Isis,* especially important for its annual bibliographic supplement (entry 1076). It is issued by the History of Science Society (HSS) of Worcester, Massachusetts (available at http://www.hssonline.org). Founded in 1924, the Society has an international membership of around 3,000 persons and institutions. It publishes book-length studies in its annual thematic journal, *Osiris* (1936–1968; 2nd ser., 1985–; ann./irreg.), and produces a quarterly *HSS Newsletter.* These publications are distributed through the University of Chicago Press. At the Web site, one is able to connect to links to graduate programs and centers of research in the history of science, and to search the online membership directory. The *HST Research Database* has 237,000 entries and is the definitive international bibliography in the field. This is available to members only.

The Society for the History of Technology (SHOT) (available at http://shot.jhu.edu), now operating at the Department of the History of Science, Technology, and Medicine at Johns Hopkins University, was founded in 1958 and has 2,000 personal members and 1,500 institutional memberships. The Henry Ford Museum in Dearborn, Michigan, is a sponsor and maintains the editorial office. The Society has published its journal, *Technology and Culture,* on a quarterly basis since its beginnings in 1958. At the Web site, one is able to search the cumulative index by issue from 1998 on. Operating in similar fashion with the support of Johns Hopkins is the American Association for the History of Medicine (AAHM) (available at http://www.histmed.org), formed in 1925. *Bulletin of the History of Medicine* has been the official quarterly journal since 1939. There are 1,200 members, and the Web site operates much like that of the Society for the History of Technology. There is a link to The College of Physicians of Philadelphia that maintains the archives of the Society.

This segment of our *Guide* contains those reference tools that are linked specifically to the history of American progress, development, and products in the broadly interpreted scientific arena. More international coverage can be gained by examination of works such as S.A. Jayawardene's *Reference Books for the Historian of Science: A Handlist* (Science Museum [London], 1982).

GENERAL SOURCES

The *General Science Index* is a current monthly index of periodical articles available in CD-ROM (WilsonDisc). It began in 1978 as a print publication from H.W. Wilson Company and began to offer its contents on CD-ROM in 1984. It is also available online through subscription to WilsonWeb (available at http://hwwisonweb.com), and is updated four times per week. Publications treating the history of science are included. Historical coverage is also given in the monthly CD-ROM publication *Science Citation Index,* available as a print publication beginning in 1961 from the Institute for Scientific Information. This massive ongoing index is available on the Web where it is updated on a weekly basis through subscription to *ISI Web of Science* (available at http://www.isiknowledge.com). It is also available through online distribution partners. *Science in America: A Documentary History, 1900–1939,* edited by Nathan Reingold and Ida H. Reingold (University of Chicago, 1981), provides useful and immediate access to source documents, such as correspondence, as well as descriptive narrative regarding issues, institutions, and individuals involved in U.S. science in the early twentieth century.

1071. American Men & Women of Science, 2000–2001: A Biographical Directory of Today's Leaders in Physical, Biological and Related Sciences. 21st ed. New York: Bowker, 2000. 8v. ISBN 0-8352-4344-3 (complete set).

This is one of the respected biographical dictionaries and represents coverage of more than 150,000 living scientists from every field from mathematics to public health and computer sciences. Historically, the publication has been important since its debut in 1906; "women" was added to the title after the 11th edition (1968). Early editions furnish useful biographical information of past achievers, many of whom are obscure today. The work enjoys an excellent reputation for maintaining a high standard with respect to invited entries; quality research or a significant and influential position is a requirement for inclusion. Information is supplied to the editorial staff through questionnaires returned by the biographees, producing entries on achievements and career developments. Publication has been irregular in the past, but since the 18th edition (1992) it has maintained a biennial publication pattern. A cumulative index to the first 14 editions was published in 1983.

1072. Biographical Index to American Science: The Seventeenth Century to 1920. Clark A. Elliott. Westport, CT: Greenwood Press, 1990. 300p. (Bibliographies and Indexes in American History, no. 16) ISBN 0-3132-6566-6.

This is a comprehensive biographical index prepared as a companion volume to the *Biographical Dictionary of American Science* (described below). It is extensive in its coverage and furnishes brief biographical entries for about 2,850 individuals representing a real cross-section of scientists from all disciplines over a period of 250 years. Entries are arranged alphabetically and furnish information regarding dates, field of activity, and occupation. References to various sources for further and more extensive biographical coverage are included as well. Sources used are biographical dictionaries, scientific journals, proceedings of associations, and collective biography. There is an index of scientists by subject field.

The *Biographical Dictionary of American Science: The Seventeenth Through the Nineteenth Centuries,* also compiled by Elliott (Greenwood Press, 1979), is a useful biographical dictionary of nearly 600 individuals who were not included in the *American Men & Women of Science* (entry 1071), as well as 300 who were. Entries run between 300 and 400 words. Appendixes furnish listings by birth date, birthplace, and education. An index is provided. The two Elliott titles are complementary to each other and are useful to inquirers at all levels.

1073. Early American Scientific and Technical Literature: An Annotated Bibliography of Books, Pamphlets, and Broadsides. Margaret W. Batschelet. Metuchen, NJ: Scarecrow, 1990. 136p. ISBN 0-8108-2318-7.

Considered one of the best historical bibliographies for its year of publication by a committee of the American Library Association's Reference and Adult Services Division, this selective, recent work supplies over 800 entries relevant to U.S. science and engineering published between 1665 and 1799. The natural and physical sciences are covered, as are medicine and technology. Entries represent primary-source material of use to scholars and serious inquirers and are arranged chronologically in three major sections covering medical titles, technical science titles, and physical science titles. Annotations are furnished in most entries, which are brief but informative. Most titles are included in the *Early American Imprint Series* (entry 34n), for which identification numbers are furnished. The work is accessed by both author and subject indexes, the latter of which has been criticized as being minimal in depth. A more intensive effort is the one by Harkanyi (entry 1078).

1074. A Guide to the Culture of Science, Technology and Medicine. Updated ed. Paul T. Durbin, gen. ed. New York: Free Press, 1984. 735p. ISBN 0-0290-7890-3 **(paperback).**

One of the few titles in this section not linked specifically to U.S. science is this outstanding guide underwritten by both the National Science Foundation and the National Endowment for the Humanities. It is an update of a 1980 effort. It consists of a series of nine essays, each accompanied by a set of bibliographic listings. The sections range from nearly 40 to nearly 70 pages in length, each written by a scholar in the field. Emphasis is given to the history of disciplines, with analyses of their methods, technologies, and relationships to other studies. Social and cultural values are examined, and the current conditions of the historical and philosophical disciplines are described with respect to their study of science, technology, and medicine. Meaning and relationship of values to science and technology are described extensively in the introductory section. More than 3,200 titles are furnished in the bibliography; scholars and serious students profit from the effort.

1075. The History of Science and Technology in the United States: A Critical and Selective Bibliography. Marc Rothenberg. New York: Garland, 1982–1993. 2v. (Garland Reference Library of the Humanities, v. 308, v. 815; Bibliographies of the History of Science and Technology, v. 2, v. 17.) ISBN 0-8240-9278-3 (v. 1); 0-8240-8349-0 (v. 2).

The author, a historian of science who previously edited the Joseph Henry papers at the Smithsonian Institution, is especially well qualified by experience and expertise to develop a survey bibliography of this type. He has done an excellent job in selecting the list of over 830 secondary sources from an initial pool of twice that number for volume 1 providing a modern perception of the discipline. Most references date between 1940 and 1980. Medicine is excluded as a topic. Entries represent books, articles, and dissertations and are arranged in several chapters covering bibliographies, special themes, physical sciences, biological sciences, social sciences, and technology. Entries furnish annotations, many of which are evaluative in nature, and will benefit inquirers at all levels. Both author and subject indexes provide access. Volume 2 continues the coverage with an additional 650 entries up to 1987.

1076. Isis: An International Review Devoted to the History of Science and Its Cultural Influences. Current Bibliography. Philadelphia: History of Science Society, 1913–. Ann. ISSN 0021-1753.

The major journal of international proportions began in 1913 with the efforts of George Sarton and today continues as the official quarterly journal of the History of Science Society. It publishes its first online issue in March 2002. The *Current Bibliography* (known until 1988 as the *Critical Bibliography*) is published at the close of each year as a supplement to *Isis,* and furnishes a comprehensive listing of secondary publications in the field (books, essays, journal articles, and reviews). The pattern generally has been to cover reference and general interest publications in the initial segment, followed by the various branches and periods of study. U.S. science is treated along with that of other nations. There is an index of names.

Retrospective bibliography is well served by the **HST Research Database,* available to members of the Society at its Web site. It is definitive in its identification of 237,000 publications and is maintained by the Research Library Group (RLG). Print publications include *Isis Cumulative Bibliography: A Bibliography of the History of Science Formed from Isis Critical Bibliographies 1–90, 1913–1965,* edited by Magda Whitrow (Mansell, 1971–1989, 6v.). This is supplemented by successive efforts edited by John Neu: *Isis Cumulative Bibliography, 1966–1975: A Bibliography of the History of Science Formed from Isis Critical Bibliographies 91–100, Indexing Literature Published from 1965 Through 1974,* (Mansell, 1980–1985. 2v.); *Isis Cumulative Bibliography, 1976–1985* (Mansell, 1989. 2v.), and *Isis Cumulative Bibliography,* 1986–1995 (Science History Publications, 1997. 4v.)

1077. Natural History in America (1609–1860): Printed Works in the Collections of the American Philosophical Society, the Historical Society of Pennsylvania, the Library Company of Philadelphia. Andrea J. Tucher, comp. New York: Garland, 1985. 287p. (Americana to 1860: Four Bibliographies of Printed Works in the Collections of Three Philadelphia Libraries, v. 4; Garland Reference Library of Social Science, v. 232.) ISBN 0-8240-8965-0.

This is the fourth volume in the series designed to provide commercial access to a union catalog of holdings in four subject areas of three great historical libraries in Philadelphia. It targets natural history, excluding anthropology. Included here are a wide variety of papers and publications of historic value, such as scientific reports, museum and society publications, travel logs, and broadsides. Organization of the work follows the pattern of previous volumes dealing with philanthropy (entry 980), agriculture (entry 334n), and education (entry 990). The Mellon Foundation, by providing an endowment for the original project, has furnished a real benefit to scholars and serious students, although it has been suggested that, for this particular subject, the holdings of the Academy of Natural Sciences should have been included. Arrangement of entries is by author; there are subject indexes.

1078. The Natural Sciences and American Scientists in the Revolutionary Era: A Bibliography. Katalin Harkanyi, comp. Westport, CT: Greenwood Press, 1990. 510p. (Bibliographies and Indexes in American History, no. 17.) ISBN 0-313-26547-X.

This is a comprehensive bibliography of about 5,100 entries on science and scientists in this country during its formative period. Publications were issued between 1760 and 1789 and represent a fertile yield for the scholar and serious student. Writers and authors were American colonists and U.S. citizens. Natural science as a branch of study was broadly interpreted to include such disciplines as mathematics and geology, as well as architecture and travel literature. Although the work is comprehensive in nature, certain categories or types of people were excluded: Canadians, émigrés, and immigrants who arrived after the middle of the century. There are several appendixes, including a chronology of accomplishments and listings of scientists by discipline. Brief annotations are given in some of the entries. For a more selective work, see the one by Margaret Batschelet (entry 1073).

MEDICINE

1079. American Nursing: A Biographical Dictionary. Vern L. Bullough et al., eds. New York: Garland, 1988–1992. v. 1–2. (Garland Reference Library of Social Science, v. 368, 684). ISBN 0-8240-8540-X (v. 1); 0-8240-7201-4 (v. 2). New York: Springer Publishing, 2000. (v. 3). ISBN 0-8261-1296-X.

Volume 1 of this biographical dictionary furnishes coverage of 177 U.S. nurses (175 female, 2 male) who are considered to have made an important contribution to the profession and were either deceased by 1988 or born prior to the year 1890. Volume 2 extends the coverage to those born between 1891 and 1915 or deceased between 1988 and 1991. Numerous contributors furnish lengthy biographical essays describing the biographees' career accomplishments and personal information and listing books and articles written by them. Also included is a bibliography. Indexes furnish access by decade of birth (before and beyond 1840), nursing school attended, special interest, or activities. This should prove useful to both researchers and students. Volume 3, from a different publisher, treats 132 American and Canadian personalities born prior to 1925 in much the same fashion as the preceding volumes. One drawback to the use of the set is the absence of a true comprehensive index to all volumes. In all, 512 women and 11 men are covered.

Similar coverage is given by Martin Kaufman in the *Dictionary of American Nursing Biography* (Greenwood Press, 1988), which treats 196 nurses who were historically important and died prior to January 31, 1987. Entries furnish basic biographical coverage such as education, contributions, and writings, with references supplied. There appears to be more emphasis on contemporary nurses here than in the Bullough effort, although 109 of the nurses are covered in both titles. Appendixes furnish listings by birthplace and specialty. Indexing is detailed.

1080. American Surgery: An Illustrated History. Ira M. Rutkow. Philadelphia: Lippincott-Raven, 1998. 638p. ISBN 0-316-76352-7.

The author is a surgeon and well-known, reputable historian of medical practice who perceived the need for documentation in his field. In this work he records the development of surgery in this country from its beginnings to the present day. The effort is divided into two major segments, the first of which presents a historical overview of American surgery with respect to economic, political, and societal developments ranging from Native American practices and the colonial period to the present day. The second section supplies a historical overview of the background and development of specific surgical procedures. The work is well illustrated with hundreds of pictures of individuals, events, and developments. It is organized into 12 eras or categories such as the Civil War, Native American Surgery, and so forth. There is an extensive bibliography.

An earlier work by Rutkow is a two-volume bibliographic effort, *The History of Surgery in the United States, 1775–1900.* The first volume (Norman, 1988) furnishes annotations to both primary and secondary book-length source material relevant to the development of surgery in this country. Included here are surgical monographs, textbooks, studies, and treatises published during a period of 125 years beginning with the Revolutionary era. More than 550 books are cited in eight chapters, each covering a different procedure from general surgery to neurosurgery. Annotations vary in length and may include not only content description but also biographical information on authors and illustrators, as well as printing history. Volume 2 (Norman, 1992) treats periodicals and pamphlet material, and supplies more than 1,400 entries issued during this period. Arrangement is similar to that in volume 1 with categorization under specialty.

1081. Bibliography of the History of Medicine. Bethesda, MD: National Library of Medicine, 1965–1993. 6v.

Once considered the leading U.S. serial bibliography on the history of medicine, it began in 1965 when the *Bulletin of the History of Medicine* (see introduction to "Science, Technology, and Medicine.") ceased publication. Its specific nature made it a real asset to serious inquiry in the field in bringing together journal articles and monographs from all over the world in various languages. Also included are symposia, congresses, and conference proceedings, as well as specific sections or parts of general monographs. Use of the print volumes is still helpful in searching pre-1993 material although a good portion of the total collection of monograph and serial titles in the National Library of Medicine's History of Medicine Division can be searched electronically on the World Wide Web through its search service, "LOCATOR*plus*" (available at http://www.locatorplus.gov). Most entries are drawn from *Index Medicus,* produced by the MEDLINE database.

The *Bibliography of the History of Medicine of the United States and Canada, 1939–1960* by Genevieve Miller (Arco Press, 1964; repr. 1979) is a compilation and consolidation of the bibliographies published annually from 1940 to 1960 in the *Bulletin of the History of Medicine.* After 1964, the bulletin ceased its publication of the bibliography.

1082. Dictionary of American Medical Biography. Martin Kaufman et al., eds. Westport, CT: Greenwood Press, 1984. 2v. ISBN 0-313-21378-X.

Considered a real contribution to the study of U.S. medicine, this work assumes the same title as the Kelly publication described below. The recent effort furnishes biographical coverage of more than 1,000 persons perceived to have made contributions to medicine or public health between the seventeenth and the twentieth centuries. Biographees were all deceased by the end of 1976. There is a conscious inclusion of blacks and women and a variety of occupations other than physicians; covered are nurses, administrators, educators, biochemists, even health faddists and patent medicine manufacturers. Entries are arranged alphabetically and furnish dates, geographical information, career information, family circumstances, education, and writings. Several appendixes offer various listings; the work is indexed.

The *Dictionary of American Medical Biography: Lives of Eminent Physicians of the United States and Canada from the Earliest Times* by Howard A. Kelly and Walter L. Burrage (Appleton, 1928) was originally issued in 1912, then again in 1920 under a different title. Biographies of more than 2,000 deceased physicians and surgeons from the colonial period to 1927 are provided. It has been reprinted on several occasions, most recently in 1978 by Longwood Press of West Newfield, Maine.

1083. The History of Science in the United States: An Encyclopedia. Marc Rothenberg. New York: Garland, 2001. 615p. ISBN 0-8153-0762-4.

The editor is a historian of science and technology who is prolific contributor to the professional literature in this area (entry 1075). In developing this single-volume coverage of scientific development in this country, he opens with an introductory essay on the nature of historiography of American science since World War II. There are 500 entries treating all aspects of science and its relationships to technology and medicine. They describe the contributions of personalities, organizations, institutions, and schools of thought dating from colonial times to the present. Entries tend to be brief, averaging a page in length but range from a paragraph or two to several pages in the case of broader topics. Brief bibliographies are included at the end of each entry. Contributors are specialists in the field of study who provide useful interpretations. A detailed analytical index provides access.

1084. 100 Years of American Nursing: Celebrating a Century of Caring. Thelma M. Schorr and Maureen S. Kennedy, eds. Philadelphia: Lippincott, Williams and Wilkins, 1999. 222p. ISBN 0-781-71865-1.

An interesting and appealing pictorial history created in honor of the centennial of publishing *The American Journal of Nursing,* coverage begins with the early years 1900–1913, and runs to the end of the century with treatment of the 1990s in anticipation of the millennium. The editors are members of the profession, and Ms. Schorr is a former editor of the *Journal.* This commemorative volume contains some 400 photographs and numerous anecdotes culled from the pages of the *Journal* in examining the relationship between progress in the field of nursing to societal and cultural developments. Such upheavals as war and the impact of scientific discovery represent some of the social changes that have raised the nursing profession to its more advanced and respected status today. Of real value are the commentaries provided by 16 members of the profession in helping the reader understand the impact and results of various noteworthy developments.

1085. Time to Heal: American Medical Education from the Turn of the Century to the Era of Managed Care. Kenneth M. Ludmerer. New York: Oxford University Press, 1999. 514p. ISBN 0-19-511837-5.

This is a provocative account by a significant medical historian on the nature of medical education and its development within the twentieth century. It is a continuation of the questions and interpretations presented in a previous effort published in 1985. Educational development is placed within the context of three historical periods beginning with the early years. Spurred by adoption of the Flexner Report, medical schools operated through allocation of time given to faculty for teaching students, conducting research of value to citizens, and providing medical services to those who could not afford it. In this era, the medical schools earned and gained the public's trust. The middle period witnessed a huge expansion of numbers to be taught that began to impact the learning environment and the time to provide beneficial services. Finally, there is the later or modern period in which educational decisions are dictated by economic considerations resulting in the erosion of quality education, leading to public disenchantment.

TECHNOLOGY AND ENGINEERING

1086. America in Space: An Annotated Bibliography. Russell R. Tobias. Pasadena, CA: Salem, 1991. 327p. (Magill Bibliographies.) ISBN 0-89356-669-1.

Like the other Salem Press Magill bibliographies, this work is intended for the less sophisticated inquirer and should serve both undergraduate and high school students needing material for term papers and reports. The strength of this work lies in its being recent and up-to-date in covering over 30 years of both technical and popular-interest publications of various types, including government documents. Annotations are well developed and furnish enough detail to describe and afford understanding of the work. Entries are arranged under several broad topical categories such as "Propulsion," "Manned Spacecraft," and "Earth-bound Support." Some limitations noted by reviews suggest a rather weak index in terms of providing access for less knowledgeable patrons. Even so, the bibliography should benefit those individuals.

1087. Engineers of Dreams: Great Bridge Builders and the Spanning of America. Henry Petroski and Edward Kastenmaier, eds. New York: Knopf. 1995. Repr. Vintage Books, 1996. 479p. ISBN 0-679-76021-0.

The author is a historian with special interest in technological development, and in this work he creates an interesting and well-developed historical account of the bridge-building activity of five major figures in this aspect of American innovation. Covering a period from the Civil War to the Depression, the work examines the efforts, successes, and failures of these men in developing their visions or dreams, promoting their projects to secure financing, and completing their bridges. The reader learns of James Eads (inventor of the diving bell that allowed construction of the bridge over the Mississippi River at St. Louis), Theodore Cooper and the unfortunate Quebec Bridge, Gustav Lindenthal and the Hell Gate Bridge, Othmar Ammann and the George Washington Bridge, and David Steinman and the Mackinac Bridge. The final chapter examines the reality of the achievement in terms of realization of the dreams after the necessary compromises were made.

1088. Great American Bridges and Dams. Donald C. Jackson. Washington, D.C.: Preservation Press, 1988. Repr. New York: John Wiley, 1995. 357p. (Great American Places Series.) ISBN 0-47114-385-5.

This attractive, well-illustrated work was developed by the National Trust for Historic Preservation as a guidebook to the most important extant bridges and dams from the nineteenth and twentieth centuries. The author, a technology historian, provides exposition of each site with respect to its place within the framework of technological development in this country. The book places emphasis on older structures but includes a full array of types and sizes. Three introductory essays describe the history of bridges and dams and offer a plea for increased attempts at preservation. Entries for individual sites are divided into six geographical regions, which are subdivided by state, then city in directory fashion. Brief narratives are furnished, with key details of construction highlighted in the margins. An index concludes the work, which should appeal to all levels of inquirers.

1089. The Historic American Engineering Record. Alexandria, VA: Chadwyck-Healey. (n.d.) 870 microfiche.

The Historic American Engineering Record (HAER) was created in 1969 as a joint undertaking of the Library of Congress, the American Society of Civil Engineers, and the National Park Service. Catalogs and other publications have generally been published under the auspices of the National Park Service. Recently, Chadwyck-Healey, in one of its large microfiche projects, has made available certain selected reports, along with illustrations documenting sites and structures throughout the United States. Included are over 20,000 pages of text and 24,000 photographs describing over 1,800 canneries, mines, railways, arsenals, breweries, dams, gristmills, bridges, and windmills; even a rocket launcher is treated. The entries were selected for their capacity to provide enlightenment in the development of U.S. technology and to furnish both historical descriptions and technical analyses. Arrangement of entries is alphabetical by place name under state, then county. Each state begins on a separate set of microfiche.

A brief history of the title and its process of documentation was issued by the National Park Service in *CRM* volume 23, no. 4 (2000) entitled "Historic American Engineering Record. Thirty Years of Documenting America's Technological History."

1090. Technology and American History: A Historical Anthology from Technology and Culture. Chicago: University of Chicago, 1997. 448p. ISBN 0-22671-027-0.

Following an introduction describing technology in the American context, the work consists of a collection of 15 essays drawn from the pages of *Technology and Culture,* the official journal of the Society for the History of Technology (see introduction to "Science, Technology, and Medicine") between the years 1963 and 1996. The work is of value to undergraduate students in its presentation of essays roughly in chronological sequence beginning with origins of American industry in the late eighteenth century, "Brandywine Borrowings from European Technology" by Norman B. Wilkinson and ending with the huge industrial systems of the 1980s and 1990s represented by "Momentum Shifts in the American Electric Utility System . . ." by Richard F. Hirsh and Adam H. Serchuk. The essays place technological innovation within societal context and describe the economic, cultural, and political forces that impact innovation and ultimately affect social values.

THE LAW AND CRIME

U.S. jurisprudence has long been the subject of scrutiny in terms of its fairness, application, and administration. Crime and its subsequent punishment have been examined in similar manner and recently has become a topic of increasingly volatile debate, especially as it concerns the death penalty. Included in this segment are those tools, primarily bibliographic, that may prove useful to the social historian interested in such issues.

The varied types of publications in the field of law include law reviews, scholarly journals, legal newspapers, and bar association publications. The online services *Westlaw (entry 224) issued by West Publishing) and *LexisNexis* (entry 11) part of the Reed Elsevier group, furnish both bibliographic and full-text information to federal and state case law for lawyers and legal researchers. For legal historians, the monthly index from the H.W. Wilson Company, *Index to Legal Periodicals,* should also prove beneficial. Dating back to 1908, it indexes several hundred periodicals from English-speaking countries. It furnishes access to authors, subjects, cases, and book reviews found in nearly 850 periodicals. Electronic access began in 1981 and is currently available through subscription to WilsonWeb where it is updated weekly and on CD-ROM through WilsonDisc, as well as in print.

A complementary work is *Index to Periodical Articles Related to Law,* a quarterly publication from Glanville Publishers that has been issued since 1958. It identifies in selective fashion important articles from journals not covered by the Wilson index. *Criminology & Penology Abstracts* (Kluger Publications, 1980–) began as *Excerpta Criminologica* (1961–1968) and from 1969 to 1979 was known as *Abstracts on Criminology and Penology* before finally assuming its present name in 1980. It is the premier international abstracting service for criminological studies. For more applied research on crime and the criminal, one should consult *Criminal Justice Abstracts* (Sage Publications, 1977–), available by subscription on the Web, and on hard disk. *Criminal Justice Periodical Index* indexed over 100 journals, newsletters, and law reporters on all types of crime before ceasing in 1998. It is available through DIALOG as a closed file from 1975 to 1998.

Related materials may be found in other segments of this *Guide;* constitutional history with its legal interpretations is found in chapter 2, "Politics and Government." Slavery both as a legal question and as an American phenomenon is treated elsewhere in this chapter, in the section on "The Black Experience" within the larger category of "Ethnic, Racial and Gender Influences."

The American Society for Legal History (available at http://www2.h-net.msu.edu/ ˉlaw/aslh_news/aslh.html) was founded in 1956 and has 1,100 members. In addition to a semi-annual newsletter, it publishes a series of book length monographs, *Studies in Legal History;* its three times yearly journal, *Law and History Review,* began in 1983.

GENERAL SOURCES

1091. American Judicial Proceedings First Printed Before 1801: An Analytical Bibliography. Wilfred J. Ritz, comp. Westport, CT: Greenwood Press, 1984. 364p. ISBN 0-313-24057-4.

This comprehensive bibliography furnishes listings of all judicial proceedings on record as having occurred prior to 1801. Included are law reports, trials, rules of court, and separate events for which something other than newspaper accounts was printed. Both primary- and secondary-source materials are included. The value of the effort lies primarily in the uniqueness of its coverage of the earliest years of U.S. jurisprudence prior to the adoption of the Constitution. Included also are English judicial proceedings relating to the colonies and U.S. reprints of European proceedings. There is an introduction, followed by an analytical section identifying references in over 65 bibliographic sources such as Evans (entry 34) and locations in over 100 libraries. Many of the materials are available in microform through the *Early American Imprints* project (entry 34n).

1092. Bloodletters and Bad Men: A Narrative Encyclopedia of American Criminals from the Pilgrims to the Present. Jay R. Nash. New York: M. Evans, 1995. 698p. ISBN 0-871-31777-X.

This is a work designed to appeal to the popular reading interests and is an update of the earlier version that was issued in 1973. It describes the most interesting, romantic, and macabre personalities associated with the perpetration of crime beginning with the colonial period and running to the present. The author has been criticized for historical inaccuracy in some cases, but he has provided a comprehensive survey of the topic and treats a variety of criminals and events ranging from petty theft to murder. One is able to find such well-known individuals as Al Capone, Jesse James, David Koresh, and John Wayne Gacy, along with obscure figures like Gretchen Baniszewski. There is an emphasis on men of the mafia in general. Most enlightening are the numerous photographs of criminals and crime scenes.

1093. Criminal Activity in the Deep South, 1700–1930: An Annotated Bibliography. A.J. Wright, comp. New York: Greenwood Press, 1989. 261p. (Research and Bibliographical Guides in Criminal Justice, no. 1.) ISBN 0-313-23798-0.

Initiating a new series for Greenwood Press is this bibliography focused on regional crime over a period of 140 years. The South has presented the world with a great enigma, being the most hospitable of regions yet capable of perpetrating violent inhuman acts to protect its way of life. Wright separates a good part of the South from this work, excluding crimes associated with slave revolts, Klan activities, Indian-white encounters, and military and labor violence. What is left is the general antisocial behavior found in any region or state (murder, robbery, etc.), here limited again to acts associated with economic gain. More than 1,250 entries are arranged alphabetically by author, and then organized by state and format (monographs, dissertations, theses, journal and newspaper articles). There are indexes by author, subject, and personal name.

1094. Criminal Justice in America, 1959–1984: An Annotated Bibliography. John D. Hewitt et al. New York: Garland, 1985. 347p. (Applied Social Science Bibliographies, v. 2; Garland Reference Library of Social Science, v. 271.) ISBN 0 8240-8813-1.

Focusing on the recent past, this annotated bibliography identifies over 800 books, articles, dissertations, and government documents in the field of criminal justice over a 25-year period. The work is organized under three major areas of inquiry: law enforcement, courts, and corrections. Each is covered in four chapters devoted to history, organization, process, and issues. Entries are placed within the proper segments and are given lengthy annotations describing their content. All users will profit from this work, including students, scholars, practitioners, and the general public. Coverage varies with each segment depending upon the availability of literature on the topics. The authors, academicians in sociology and criminal justice, were able to make good judgments in their selection of the "essential literature." There are indexes of personal names and of subjects.

1095. Crime and Punishment in American History. Lawrence M. Friedman. New York: Basic Books, 1993. 576p. ISBN 0-465-01461-5.

This is a comprehensive history of American response and reaction to crime and criminals beginning with the Salem witch trials and concluding with the acquittal of four police officers in Los Angeles for beating Rodney King. The author is a noted authority who has provided this exposition for popular rather than scholarly audiences. In doing so, he has furnished an informative examination of the activity of the criminal justice system and its changing nature through the years. In colonial times, immoral behavior was a criminal offense and required public demonstration of punitive nature, whereas such behaviors today, although not condoned, are not punished. The system has evolved and mirrors the cultural and ideological society in which it operates. Chapters cover a variety of issues such as victimless crimes, racial discrimination, juvenile crime, abortion, drugs, gambling, vigilantism, white-collar crime, and so forth. There is a useful bibliographical essay.

1096. Crime in America's Top-Rated Cities, 2000: A Statistical Profile 1979–1998. 3rd ed. Lakeville, CT: Grey House, 2000. 839p. ISBN 1-891482-84-X.

This is the third issue since 1995 in what is intended to be a biennial publication. In the current effort, one is able to obtain historical statistics on urban crime over a span of 20 years. In presenting data from 76 cities, an increase of 17 over the previous edition, it provides focus on what has been one of the most troublesome issues in the past 20 years in which the decline of the cities and many of their suburban areas has been well publicized. Cities were selected due to their high ratings as desirable places to live and in which to do business. Data is presented in charts, tables, and diagrams and each city is examined in terms of anticrime programs, risk, types of crime including hate crime, drugs and substance abuse, death penalty, laws, law enforcement, frequency of HIV positive among those arrested, and so forth. Unfortunately, there is little interpretation of the statistical data.

1097. The Encyclopedia of American Crime. 2nd ed. Carl Sifakis. New York: Facts on File, 2001. 2v. ISBN 0-8160-4040-0.

This serves as an update to the first edition published in 1982, and a revision that appeared in 1992. It continues as an interesting and useful reference book furnishing 2,000 entries on the topic of crime in the United States. Sifakis is a crime reporter who carefully researched the records and provides clear descriptions of people, events, reports, and organizations. Included are explanations of various crimes, historical treatment of different agencies, exposition of trials, and definitions of slang. Coverage varies in length and extends from the precolonial period to the present day. Individual biographies present a diverse group of criminals, detectives, lawyers, reporters, criminologists, and judges, beginning with some of the early Vikings. The first edition ended with John Hinckley, and the revision brought in such individuals as Jeffrey Dahmer, Sammy the Bull Gravano, and includes the O.J. Simpson trial among other new entries. There are numerous black-and-white photographs, charts, and drawings. Cross-references are furnished between entries, and the index provides access through subject and geographic headings.

Criminal Justice History (Meckler, 1980–) is an international annual devoted to the history of crime and criminal justice, particularly in their broader social, legal, and institutional contexts. It publishes research and articles on historiography, comparative and interpretive essays, conference assessments, book reviews, and reviews of the discipline and of current historical issues. Significant attention is given to the history and analysis of crime and criminal justice in the United States.

1098. Encyclopedia of American Prisons. Marilyn D. McShane and Frank P. Williams, eds. New York: Garland, 1996. 532p. ISBN 0-8153-1350-0.

This is a highly regarded compilation in which contributors have supplied nearly 200 separate essays on key personalities, significant prisons, topics such as riots, issues such as crowding, individual cases, terminology, and more. Arrangement is alphabetical and entries are written by prison and corrections experts, providing an overview of the history and development of incarceration in this country. The work opens with a brief historical chronology dating from 1773 to the early 1990s, and follows with the main text of entries. One should not make the mistake of using this source in an effort to obtain statistical data because all such material is imbedded within the narrative on the topic or issue. Instead, it should be considered an authoritative and reliable information source in examining factors relevant to penal institutions and incarceration.

Prisons in America: A Reference Handbook by Nicole H. Rafter and Debra L. Stanley (ABC-CLIO, 1999) provides information on the penal system. Although its intent is to be a practical guide to contemporary practices, there is a good historical survey of the system from the colonial period to the present. Issues and controversies are enumerated and the philosophical purposes of incarceration are examined.

1099. Great American Court Cases. Mark F. Mikula et al. Detroit: Gale, 1999. 4v. ISBN 0-78-762947-2.

This source examines more than 800 cases, organized by broad legal principle, for both state and federal courts, with Supreme Court cases receiving the bulk of the coverage. Designed for lay readers and students, this four-volume work is organized topically. The first volume on individual rights focuses on cases concerning the First and Second Amendment issues of privacy, press, religion, and the right to bear arms. The second volume on criminal justice presents cases about defendants' rights, criminal law and procedure, and capital punishment. The third volume covers equal protection and family law with cases involving affirmative action and sexual harassment. The last volume treats a combination of business and government and includes contracts, consumer protection, and Native American issues. Each volume begins with a short introduction to the particular areas of the law it covers and an explanation of the content, process, and procedure of the American legal system. Although most of the cases covered are twentieth-century Supreme Court cases, there are a few lower court cases and a few from the nineteenth century. Entries contain descriptions of each case with the legal citations and capsule fact boxes that list the party names, attorneys, and judges, as well as lists of related cases and brief summaries.

A similar work is the two-volume *Historic U.S. Court Cases: an Encyclopedia* (2nd ed. Routledge, 2001) containing 201 essays on cases judged to be historic by the editor, John W. Johnson. The two volumes are divided into five topical sections. Each essay begins with a factual background statement identifying the date, location, court, principal participants, and the significance of the case. Entries have bibliographies and there is an index of names.

1100. Great American Lawyers: An Encyclopedia. John R. Vile. Santa Barbara, CA: ABC-CLIO, 2001. 2v. ISBN 1-57606-202-9.

More than 50 lawyers, political scientists, historians, and other scholars have contributed to this two-volume work. There are full essays ranging from five to seven pages on the lives and cases of 100 notable American lawyers who have distinguished themselves in the courtroom from colonial times to the present. There are also shorter essays on other well-known figures, including women and minorities who have made contributions to the American legal system. Entries are arranged alphabetically and provide historical coverage with treatment given to such famous personalities as Lincoln, Hamilton, Adams, Henry Clay, and Johnny Cochran as well as to unknown figures. There is an extensive bibliography and suggested works for further reading.

Less comprehensive but more focused in its detailed treatment of 10 personalities who fought for social justice is *People's Lawyers: Crusaders for Justice in American History* by Diana Klebanow and Franklin Jonas. Most are well-known to the American public (Clarence Darrow, Louis Brandeis, Thurgood Marshall, etc.) but a few are relatively unfamiliar to student audiences. Chapters describe the lives, career developments, and achievements of attorneys who fought the good fight in both the nineteenth and twentieth centuries. Each chapter has an annotated bibliography and chronology relevant to the personality, as well as a summary of important cases.

1101. The Guide to American Law: Everyone's Legal Encyclopedia. St. Paul, MN: West, 1983–1985. 12v. ISBN 0-314-73221-1. **Ann. Supp.** 1990–. ISSN 1052-8253.

Because of its comprehensiveness and thorough coverage of the field, this work has been included here when others have been omitted. Considered the only guide of this size designed to explain legal concepts to laymen and non-jurists, it succeeds admirably in furnishing exposition of over 5,000 topics. Students of history profit from its inclusion of material pertinent to landmark documents, constitutional rights, and the famous trials of the past. There were numerous contributors to these volumes, and most of the articles are signed. Arrangement of entries (and volumes) is alphabetical, with each volume containing a detailed subject index. Heightening the interest and utility of this work for all its users is the inclusion of old prints, cartoons, and photographs. Since 1990, the title has received an annual supplement.

Historic U.S. Court Cases, 1690–1990: An Encyclopedia, edited by John W. Johnson (Garland, 1992), is a handy compilation of essays on important court cases tried over a 300-year period. There are more than 170 essays written by 80 specialists that identify major themes in U.S. history and law and probe the decisions. The work is useful to students of history, specialists, and even laypersons.

*1102. History of the American Legal System: An Interactive Encyclopedia. Santa Barbara, CA: ABC-CLIO, 2000. ISBN 1-57607-178-2. [CD-ROM].

The organization of this electronic reference tool is by eight legal topics: the amending process, appointment of federal judges, voting rights, constitutional interpretation, the Bill of rights, the federal judicial system, the Electoral College, and the relationship of civil rights and the U.S. Constitution. All of these have been topics for debate and discussion. Within each of the areas are data on individual court cases, documents, events, biographies, and organizations. Links are provided for related media sites The software is the same as other ABC-CLIO electronic products providing standard searching features. The entries provide coverage for the time period 1600–2000. The encyclopedia, like other interactive encyclopedias (entries 546, 594, 674, 838, 942), is designed to be used by students.

1103. The Oxford Companion to American Law. Kermit L. Hall, ed. New York: Oxford University Press, 2001. 640p. ISBN 0-19-512885-0.

This one-volume work is a comprehensive introduction to American law. Institutions such as the FBI, concepts such as torts, personalities such as Daniel Webster, issues such as affirmative action, definitions of terms such as paralegal, as well as events and cases that have shaped American law are covered in nearly 500 entries written by over 300 expert contributors. The development of American law and its role in structuring government at the local, state, and federal levels, plus the place of American law internationally are examined with respect to fundamental choices and decisions regarding preservation and protection of life and property as well as the practice of individual liberty. All practitioners and students of the law in the United States will have occasion to use this work.

1104. West's Encyclopedia of American Law. Farmington Hills, MI: Gale, 1998. 12v. ISBN 0-314-05538-X.

Available only in print format, this is an outstanding asset to the study of law in this country. It is the most comprehensive and authoritative encyclopedia on the legal system in the United States. There are more than 4,000 entries that provide an introduction to and brief exposition of important court decisions, references to pertinent statutes, and "in focus" essays of more detailed nature that supply added information of controversial issues. A table of cases should prove of value, and appendixes contain the text of seminal documents and speeches. The encyclopedia represents several years of effort.

Fair Trial Rights of the Accused: A Documentary History edited by Ronald Banaszak, Sr. (Greenwood Press, 2002) is another title from the publisher's *Primary Documents in American History and Contemporary Issues* series intended to provide high school and college students with the full text of significant documents on important issues or events. There are more than 60 documents selected to provide understanding of the evolution of trial rights beginning with English law and the colonial period and progressing to the present day. Various arguments are presented with different viewpoints on the rights of the accused.

CAPITAL PUNISHMENT

1105. Capital Punishment. Rev. ed. Harry Henderson. New York: Facts on File, 2000. 300p. (Library in a Book). ISBN 0-8160-4193-8.

This revised work is an up-to-date and comprehensive information source on the controversial topic and its history from the beginning of the eighteenth century to the present day. It reveals the nature of the controversy and examines the issues and arguments on both sides of the debate. The contents are presented in eight chapters beginning with an informative introduction to the debate and the moral and legal justification. Subsequent chapters treat the legal issues with respect to the circumstances involving its imposition; chronology of events from 1700 to 2000; biographical treatment of key personalities; glossary of terms; research guide that includes relevant Web sites; detailed annotated bibliography; and finally, a directory of organizations and agencies that includes their Web sites. Within these chapters all relevant arguments and factors are described in objective manner.

A recent publication with the same title is *Capital Punishment* by Raphael Goldman (Congressional Quarterly, 2002), part of the publisher's *Vital Issues Series* in which information on the topic is provided to enable the user to develop an informed opinion. The opening chapter defines the issues and furnishes perspective, and chapter 2 examines the constitutionality of the sentence as well as its applications. Subsequent chapters treat agencies, personalities, and organizations as well as trends. Appendixes supply a bibliography, a Web directory, policies, and more.

1106. Capital Punishment in America: An Annotated Bibliography. Michael L. Radelet and Margaret Vandiver. New York: Garland, 1988. 243p. (Garland Reference Library of Social Science, v. 466.) ISBN 0-8240-1623-8.

This is a listing of more than 1,000 publications in the English language reflecting the growing interest and debate on the topic. Emphasis is on the post-1972 period, and events of the 1970s to 1980s are covered well. Accessibility of material is one criterion for inclusion, and the books and articles are considered readily available in public and academic libraries. Annotations are brief and informative. Arrangement of entries is alphabetical by author as organized under three major format divisions: books and articles, congressional publications, and Supreme Court decisions. Newspaper articles have been purposely omitted because of what was perceived as a lack of accessibility. A subject index is furnished.

1107. Capital Punishment in the United States: A Documentary History. Bryan Vila and Cynthia Morris, eds. Westport, CT: Greenwood Press, 1997. 337p. (Primary Documents in American History and Contemporary Issues.) ISBN 0-313-29942-0.

This is a useful source of information on the historical background of capital punishment in this country beginning with the colonial era and running to the present day. Following a brief but well-conceived introduction, the work is organized into several chronological sections, each of which contains an exposition of trends and developments in that time period. The bulk of the text and the heart of the effort, of course, are the more than 100 documents selected by the editors and placed within each of the sections. Every document is preceded by a brief introductory narrative helping the user understand the context of its origin. Documents are of varied composition and include articles, book excerpts, position statements, court decisions, legislation, rulings, and more. There is a glossary and listings of capital offenses and of executions over a 400-year period.

1108. Encyclopedia of Capital Punishment in the United States. Louis J. Palmer. Jefferson City, NC: McFarland, 2001. 614p. ISBN 0-7864-0944-4.

The focus on this work is capital punishment and relevant factors in this country, but there are brief articles summarizing its practice or absence in 200 countries. The author is an attorney who has written on the topic in the past; in this work he provides a wealth of information in his coverage of every capital punishment decision rendered by the Supreme Court from the beginning to the end of the twentieth century, and on every justice who has furnished an opinion on capital punishment. Treatment is given to organizations, practice of the military, and capital prosecutions both significant and obscure. In addition there is examination of the impact of the sentence on various ethnic groups (African American, Asian American, Hispanic, and Native American), females, and on foreign nationals.

Encyclopedia of Capital Punishment by Mark Grossman (ABC-CLIO, 1998) is similar in scope and coverage to the above work. Coverage is international with emphasis on the United States, the only remaining Western nation to use the death penalty. Entries cover personalities, cases, methods of execution, and various issues from ancient times to the present.

MURDER, TERRORISM, AND VIOLENCE

1109. Lynching and Vigilantism in the United States: An Annotated Bibliography. Norton H. Moses, comp. Westport, CT: Greenwood Press, 1997. 441p. (Bibliographies and Indexes in American History, no. 34.) ISBN 0-313-30177-8.

A comprehensive bibliography treating the extra-legal or nongovernmental administration of justice and punishment to persons determined to be guilty without having been given a trial, the work provides identification of over 4,200 books, articles, and government documents, as well as unpublished dissertations and theses. They range in treatment from the scholarly to the popular and span a time period beginning with the mid-eighteenth century and run to the time of publication in the mid-1990s. The work is divided into chapters beginning with general studies, followed by four chronological chapters. The remaining chapters are topical in their coverage of the frontier West; antilynching bills, laws, and activists; literature and film; and finally, the visual arts. There is a well-designed index providing access by author and subject.

1110. Murder in America: A History. Roger Lane. Columbus: Ohio State University, 1997. 352p. ISBN 0-814-20732-4.

The author is an academic who has supplied a well-researched historical overview of murder in this country, the roots of which were begun in medieval England. In this era, murder was frequent and generally committed by pairs of men who robbed those in the lower classes. Punishment was public and severe, and with the English coming to America, such traditions were passed on. As the country grew in size and became multicultural, the incidence of murder increased and victims were represented in all classes of society. Societal mores changed through time with various fears and suspicions determining the value of human life. This varied with respect to position in the community, with Native Americans and blacks receiving less consideration or protection. Treatment is given to the phenomena of serial killing, gangland and gang violence, riots, and more.

1111. Murders in the United States: Crimes, Killers, and Victims of the Twentieth Century. R. Barri Flowers and H. Loraine Flowers. Jefferson, NC: McFarland, 2001. 226p. ISBN 0-7864-1037-X.

This work serves as a brief overview or survey of homicides committed in this country during the past 100 years. It is divided into three major sections, the first of which supplies decade-by-decade summaries of 53 of the most famous murders of the century, beginning with the assassination of President McKinley in 1901 and ending with the tragic incident at Columbine High School in 1999. Part 2 is arranged by name of criminal and contains 300 entries describing various murders; it identifies male, female, and juvenile perpetrators, and subdivides the content by such categories as outlaws, killers of celebrities, serial killers, and so forth. The final section treats significant victims such as John F. Kennedy and Marvin Gaye. There is a bibliography of print sources and Web sites.

Mass Murder in the United States by Ronald M. Holmes and Stephen T. Holmes (Prentice-Hall, 2000) provides a narrow focus on what they determine to be "mass murder" rather than serial killing for which the murderer becomes more familiar to the public. These incidents, which at one moment take the lives of several or more people, are on the rise, as we have recently seen with the event at the World Trade Center. The most notable killers of this type identified by the authors are Timothy McVeigh and Charles Whitman. There are 12 chapters, the second of which provides a history of mass murder in this country. Other chapters treat the various types of mass killers (disgruntled employees, family members, disciples, etc.).

1112. Terrorism. Harry Henderson. New York: Facts on File, 2001. 300p. (Library in a Book.) ISBN 0-8160-4259-4.

Terrorism is defined by the U.S. government as "premeditated, politically motivated violence perpetrated against noncombatant targets by subnational groups or clandestine agents" and it was not until recently that this country became aware and fearful of such dangers. At the time of publication, the Oklahoma City bombing was the worst incident on U.S. soil resulting in 168 deaths. Since then, of course, we have had the crises of September 11, 2001, making this a highly relevant source of information. The first section provides a useful overview and introduction to the topic in six chapters; the second part is a guide to research with three chapters containing a lengthy and detailed annotated bibliography, a chapter on research strategies, and a directory of 22 organizations. Appendixes offer relevant acronyms, statistics, state department terrorism designations, and a legislative summary of the antiterrorism measure of 1996.

1113. Terrorism in the Twentieth Century: A Narrative Encyclopedia from the Anarchist Through the Weathermen to the Unabomber. Jay R. Nash. New York: M. Evans, 1998. 468p. ISBN 0-87131-855-5.

Popular historian and storyteller Nash is well-known through his previous effort, *Bloodletters and Badmen* (entry 1092) and now presents an encyclopedic history beginning with the period of anarchists and the assassination of President McKinley at the turn of the century. Chapters are arranged chronologically and treat personalities, events, groups, and organizations. Terrorism of both the Left and Right is documented with chapters featuring the Ku Klux Klan as well as the 1960s malcontents. In between there are the rise of the Black Hand and various incidents, some quite sensational in nature. Of special interest is the 1980s chapter dealing with the assassination of Anwar Sadat, and coverage given to the Zodiac killer. As the title indicates, the work concludes with the story of the Unabomber. A chronology is provided as well as a number of photographs, glossary, and bibliography.

POLITICAL AND SOCIETAL ISSUES

1114. Encyclopedia of Organized Crime in the United States: From Capone's Chicago to the New Urban Underworld. Westport, CT: Greenwood Press, 2000. 358p. ISBN 0-313-30653-2.

Of interest to the general reader is this developmental history of organized crime in America from the mid-nineteenth century to the 1990s. There are more than 250 entries treating key personalities from Capone to Gotti, important events and activities, and various criminal organizations. The Mafia crime families and major figures are described, as are the leading minority street gangs. More distinctive is the inclusion of recently organized and publicized operations such as the Russian Mafia, Chinese Triads and Tongs, Colombian drug cartels, Dominican drug traffickers, Latin gangs, and Vietnamese American gangs. Entries are full and provide adequate information with cross-references to related topics and lists of suggested readings. In some cases, photographs and tables accompany the narratives. There is a well-constructed and useful general bibliography of various source materials both print and nonprint.

1115. Gun Control. Harry Henderson. New York: Facts on File, 2000. 297p. (Library in a Book). ISBN 0-8160-4031-1.

The author is a professional writer who has produced other expositions in this series (entries 1105 and 1112). In this work, he provides an objective and balanced, and as a result, an informative exposition of the controversy in U.S. society over the sale and possession of guns. It opens with a historical overview of the topic and continues with summaries of state and federal legislation. Relevant court cases are described in thorough manner supplying background, issues, and decisions. Terms are defined and personalities are identified. Relevant aspects are presented in legal and legislative context as well as criminological perspective. There is a comprehensive chronology dating from 1871 to the present day. Of real value is the section on conducting research that includes coverage of Web sites and the utility of search engines. There is a detailed annotated bibliography and a directory of organizations.

1116. Historic Preservation Law: An Annotated Survey of Sources and Literature. Gail I. Winson. Buffalo, NY: William S. Hein, 1999. 365p. ISBN 0-8377-1355-2.

This is a useful list of sources dealing with historic preservation law in the United States, and updates an earlier effort published by the National Trust for Historic Preservation in 1976. It opens with a well-conceived bibliographic narrative that identifies important topics and historical development of preservation law and significant sources on each aspect. The entire work serves as a literature review in tracing the development of such laws in this country as they relate primarily to preservation of worthy buildings, sites, and districts. Slight coverage is given to peripheral issues such as open space. The first segment is organized by subject (aesthetic regulation, tax incentives, conservation, etc.) and provides annotations on books in these categories. This is followed by a subject listing of articles and a chronology of legislation. An index provides ready access.

1117. Police Misconduct in America: A Reference Handbook. Dean J. Champion. Santa Barbara, CA: ABC-CLIO, 2001. 236p. (ABC-CLIO Contemporary World Issues Series.) ISBN 1-57607-599-0.

The author is an academic and prolific author in the field, who has provided this overview of questionable police action as an important element in maintaining public confidence and comprehension of legal ramifications. Various types of abuses are treated in seven chapters, the first of which provides an informative history of police misconduct from 1901 to the present. The bulk of the substantive text is presented in the second chapter that examines the issues and controversies including constitutional prerogatives, and provides examples of the manner in which abuses are committed. Abuses may be related to corruption, deviant behavior, and, of course, excessive force. Succeeding chapters supply a chronology, biographical sketches, relevant Supreme Court cases, and a directory of agencies and organizations. A glossary is provided along with an index.

Bryan Vila and Cynthia Morris, authors of *Capital Punishment in the United States* (entry 1107) have teamed up once again to produce *The Role of Police in American Society: A Documentary History* (Greenwood Press, 1999), another documentary history for the publisher's series (entry 1107). The work is divided into seven segments representing chronological periods beginning with the early seventeenth century and running to the present day. Documents placed in these segments are diverse in nature and include scientific studies, biographical pieces, legal decisions, and articles. One is able to comprehend the trends and changes that have taken place in police ethics and training through the messages borne by the various selections.

1118. The Tree of Liberty: A Documentary History of Rebellion and Political Crime in America. Rev. ed. Nicholas N. Kittrie and Eldon D. Wedlock, Jr., eds. Baltimore: Johns Hopkins University Press, 1998. 2v. ISBN 0-8018-5643-4 (v. 1). ISBN 0-8018-5811-9 (v. 2).

This documentary history supplies over 400 documents taken from a variety of sources and organized in 13 chapters through two volumes. Included here statutes, court decisions, pamphlets, broadsides, regulations, diaries, and speeches relevant to the study of political crime that has been interpreted to mean dissent, protest, rebellion, militancy, violence, and disobedience. Documents span a period of 600 years and are organized chronologically into 13 chapters beginning with coverage of the colonial period with the Treason Law of Edward III in 1352 and ending with the 1997 showdown between the federal government and the Provisional Government of Texas in 1997. Most documents are of contemporary nature dating since the onset of World War II, although one is able to find documents from most periods of our history. Various types of resistance are treated (social, political, religious, economic, gender-based, etc). Brief expositions are included for each document.

1119. The Watergate Crisis. Michael A. Genovese. Westport, CT: Greenwood Press, 1999. 197p. (Greenwood Press Guides to Historic Events of the Twentieth Century.) ISBN 0-313-29878-5).

This is another issue of the publisher's series attempting to cast light on one of the most influential events in our history. The author is an established expert on that era and has produced a readable and useful source of information. The work follows the stylistic pattern of the series and begins with a useful chronology that is followed by a historical treatment along with analysis. Watergate is seen as a landmark event that may have led to the estrangement of politicians from the press and inspired the type of scrutiny marked by frequent calls for special prosecutors. Also included in the work are biographical sketches of key personalities, selected documents, a glossary, and bibliography.

Watergate: An Annotated Bibliography of Sources in English, 1972–1982 by Myron Smith. (Scarecrow, 1983) remains a leading resource for the study of Watergate. More than

2,500 English-language publications representing both primary- and secondary-source material are identified and listed alphabetically. These were published over a span of 10 years tracing the revelations through newspaper accounts, books, articles, scholarly papers, government documents, dissertations, theses, and personal memoirs. There is a listing of video and sound recordings at the end. Entries are given annotations of varying length ranging from a sentence to a full paragraph. There is a chronology of events from 1972 to 1975, and a House Judiciary Committee report on the Nixon impeachment investigation.

JOURNALISM

The free press is one of the necessary ingredients to a free society. It is through the notable efforts of journalists that some of history's great scandals and governmental excesses have been brought to light and recorded. It thus serves as a watchdog and guardian at its highest level of societal service. Journalism is broadly interpreted here to reflect the various media by which information is disseminated, and includes the more sensationalistic disposition of tabloid publication. The history of U.S. journalism, both print and nonprint, offers a rich and varied study reflecting the diversity of the individual and of society.

The reference tools in this section represent that diversity, focusing on the events and especially on the personalities as covered in biographical sources. It is largely through the study of the lives of the more colorful, memorable, and often prominent and influential writers and reporters that Americans have come to appreciate its role as the fourth estate. Freedom of expression is of course dictated by editorial policy. Today, a number of indexes with which to search the content of newspapers, both print and online, are available.

The American Journalism Historians Association was founded in 1982 to advance the study of history of journalism and mass communication and has 400 members. It issues two quarterlies, *American Journalism* and *Intelligencer*. The Web site can be accessed through the affiliates section of the American Historical Association (available at http://www.theaha.org).

GENERAL SOURCES

1120. American Journalism History: An Annotated Bibliography. William D. Sloan, comp. New York: Greenwood Press, 1989. 344p. (Bibliographies and Indexes in Mass Media and Communications, no. 1). ISBN 0-313-26350-7.

This useful and convenient annotated bibliography furnishes scholars and serious students with a listing of more than 2,650 books and articles relevant to the history of both print and nonprint journalism. Selection was limited to those items perceived to be the most useful and includes biographies, histories, expositions, and other types of materials. Entries are organized chronologically under categories ranging from "The Colonial Press, 1690–1765" to "Contemporary Media, 1945–Present." Annotations vary in size from very brief to 150–200 words long. There is a miscellaneous segment at the beginning that treats general history from the colonial period to the present. Access is furnished by a general index of names, subjects, and titles.

1121. American Journalists: Getting the Story. Donald A. Ritchie. New York: Oxford University Press, 1998. 336p. ISBN 0-19-509907-9.

This is a well-conceived biographical dictionary of 60 American journalists from the colonial period to the present. There are editors, reporters, columnists, photographic journalists, printers, and broadcasters. Included in the mix are significant historical personalities like Ben Franklin, Horace Greeley, Thomas Nast, and Joseph Pulitzer, to contemporary figures such as Rupert Murdoch, Walter Cronkite, and Bernard Shaw. Coverage extends to those who are lesser known, and to females, minority figures, and to those who served the needs of specialized audiences such as Elias Boudinot, who founded the newspaper in the Cherokee language. Entries are thorough and are organized into chronological segments treating freedom of the press, technology, social critics, and modern journalism. Photographs are included.

1122. Biographical Dictionary of American Journalism. Joseph P. McKerns, ed. New York: Greenwood Press, 1989. 820p. ISBN 0-313-23818-9.

This handy biographical dictionary furnishes brief sketches varying from one to two pages in length of 500 men and women who were prominent in either broadcast or print journalism over a period of nearly 300 years, from 1690 to the present. Several of these individuals were still alive although at the tail end of their careers at the time of publication. The format emulates that of the *Dictionary of American Biography* (entry 60) and furnishes dates, summary of achievements, a biographical essay, and a bibliography of writings by and about the subject. Contributions by some 130 academicians are signed. As with other works of this type, one will find fault with some of the "popular" inclusions, but more likely the exclusions and omissions will generate interest or concern. Nevertheless, this resource is useful for inquirers at all levels.

1123. Encyclopedia of Twentieth-Century Journalists. William H. Taft. New York: Garland, 1986. 408p. (Garland Reference Library of the Humanities, v. 493.) ISBN 0-8240-8961-8.

A useful one-volume biographical dictionary, this work examines the lives of some 750 men and women who have achieved prominence in a variety of activities within the field of journalism during the twentieth century. Written in a popular style, the volume is eminently readable and should interest inquirers at all levels of interest and expertise. "Journalist" is here defined in a broad manner and includes such figures as cartoonists, photographers, broadcasters, and media managers as well as editors, reporters, and publishers. Just as diverse is the list of personalities, which includes George Will, Bob Woodward, Paul Harvey, Edward R. Murrow, Roger Ebert, Katherine Graham, and Hedda Hopper. Biographies vary in length from a few lines to several paragraphs.

1124. Guide to Sources in American Journalism History. Lucy S. Caswell, ed. and comp. New York: Greenwood Press, 1989. 319p. (Bibliographies and Indexes in Mass Media and Communications, no. 2.) ISBN 0-313-26178-4.

Issued as the second offering in the recent Greenwood series, this title has served as a guide to resources relating to the study of the history of U.S. journalism. The work is prepared under the auspices of the American Journalism Historians Association and opens with several essays on historiography; bibliographic works, including indexes, abstracts, and bibliographies; computerized databases; and oral history. The major segment of the tool furnishes a directory of the major repositories of archival and manuscript materials found in about 40 states, primarily in universities or historical agencies. Beneficial to scholars and serious students, it arranges entries alphabetically by state and furnishes brief descriptions and identifications. Included are names, addresses, phone numbers, hours, and holdings, with an indication of size of collections in linear feet and a brief exposition of subjects.

1125. Journalists of the United States: Biographical Sketches of Print and Broadcast News Shapers from the Late 17th Century to the Present. Robert B. Downs and Jane B. Downs. Jefferson, NC: McFarland, 1992. 391p. ISBN 0-89950-549-X.

Written by an eminent former librarian and library school dean, now deceased, this recently published biographical dictionary provides slightly more comprehensive coverage than does the related work, the *Biographical Dictionary of American Journalism* (entry 1122), with treatment of about 100 more personalities from both print and broadcast journalism. It contains 600 biographical sketches ranging from a few lines to two pages. Greater emphasis is given to the eighteenth- and nineteenth-century figures than to contemporary personalities. It is the inclusion of seventeenth- and eighteenth-century figures that is most useful to both scholars and students of history. The electronic media of today are covered in equitable fashion. There is an index of names, periodicals and newspapers, organizations, and subjects.

1126. Tabloid Journalism: An Annotated Bibliography of English-Language Sources. Gerald S. Greenberg. New York: Greenwood Press, 1996. 187p. ISBN 0-313-29544-1.

The author is a reference librarian who has produced a well-developed bibliography of more than 800 monographs, scholarly journals, magazines, trade articles, theses, and conference papers addressing the subject of sensationalism in journalism. Entries are annotated with brief summaries of their form and content. Supermarket tabloids have grown in popularity through the years just as steadily as has their criticism by scholars and analysts, therefore this work is of value to students in the area of communication and popular culture, as well as to those in journalism. Following an informative introduction, entries are organized into several chapters dealing with print journalism, television, legal implications, and finally, international perspectives. Access is supplied through subject and author indexes.

PRINT JOURNALISM

1127. American Magazine Journalists, 1741–1850. Sam G. Riley, ed. Detroit: Gale, 1988. 430p. (Dictionary of Literary Biography, v. 73.) ISBN 0-8103-4551-X.

This is the first volume of a selective three-part work that covers journalists who were productive over the 220-year period from 1741 to 1960. This first volume covers 1741–1850 and furnishes biographical essays of 48 individuals, most of whom have been treated in other volumes of this series and also in the *Dictionary of American Biography* (entry 60). The focus in the present work is on their magazine contributions; the biographical sketches are newly written by scholars and specialists. The essays are of considerable length, and extensive bibliographies are furnished.

American Magazine Journalists, 1850–1900, also edited by Riley (Gale; *DLB* v. 79, 1989), is the second issue of this set and furnishes 50 biographical sketches of writers. Entries follow the same format as that used in the previous effort and give lengthy coverage along with bibliographies. There is an informative expository essay on publishing trends relative to political, social, and economic developments of this time period. Photographs are included. *American Magazine Journalists, 1900–1960, First Series* (Gale; *DLB* v. 91, 1990) is the first of two volumes on this time period. Again, Riley serves as editor. Biographies and photographs of 37 editors and publishers of the twentieth century are furnished here in the manner of previous volumes.

1128. American Newspaper Journalists, 1690–1872. Perry J. Ashley, ed. Detroit: Gale, 1985. 527p. (Dictionary of Literary Biography, v. 43.) ISBN 0-8103-1721-4.

Similar to the coverage given magazine journalists in the previous entry is the treatment accorded newspaper journalists by Ashley for this *Dictionary of Literary Biography* (*DLB*) work. This is the first volume in terms of scope and coverage but the last one published. Like others in the series, it provides lengthy biographical sketches with critical interpretation rendered by scholars and specialists. Inclusion is highly selective, and bibliographies are furnished. Included here are 66 biographies of prominent contributors to newspaper journalism over a period of 180 years. Illustrations are provided.

American Newspaper Journalists, 1873–1900 (Gale; *DLB* v. 23, 1983) furnishes biographical essays of 42 individuals prominent during the fourth quarter of the nineteenth century. Included are such noteworthies as Samuel Clemens, Ambrose Bierce, and Joel Chandler-Harris. *American Newspaper Journalists, 1901–1925* (Gale; *DLB* v. 25, 1984) covers this burgeoning period of newspaper development with critical biographical essays of 47 personalities. Ring Lardner and William Randolph Hearst are among the group covered. *American Newspaper Journalists, 1926–1950* (Gale; *DLB* v. 29, 1984), the final volume on U.S. journalists, continues the pattern that has worked so well for the entire series, furnishing biographical and critical essays of the careers of 54 prominent journalists such as Heywood Broun, H.L. Mencken, and Ernie Pyle, who were dominant forces during the second quarter of the twentieth century. A new title by Ashley is American Newspaper Publishers, 1950–1990 (Gale, 1993). It is offered as volume 127 of the *DLB* series and provides similar coverage of notable publishers.

1129. Biographical Dictionary of American Newspaper Columnists. Sam G. Riley, ed. Westport, CT: Greenwood Press, 1995. 411p. ISBN 0-313-29192-6.

The author is an academic who has provided a comprehensive coverage of 600 columnists employed by newspapers in this country from the time of the Civil War to the present day. The columnists are those who are or were responsible for general interest-type columns and include political and humor writers, but not those associated with specialized columns on such topics as gardening, health, and so forth. Entries are arranged alphabetically and vary in size with the fame or popularity of the writer, who range from the giants in their field to those who wrote for local audiences. They generally run from a few sentences to several paragraphs and are limited to factual description. Included are birth and death dates, education, newspaper, career highlights and accomplishments, and description of their columns. A bibliography of sources utilized for this work is furnished.

1130. Newspapers: A Reference Guide. Richard A. Schwarzlose. New York: Greenwood Press, 1987. 417p. (American Popular Culture.) ISSN 0193-6859.

From Greenwood Press comes this unique bibliography on U.S. newspapers that should prove useful to both students and scholars interested in the history and development of the newspaper press. About 1,700 books and articles are identified through bibliographic essays organized into nine chapters covering reference sources, newspaper histories, newspaper work, production, social role, legal issues, technology, and so forth. Text focuses on the research value of the books and articles enumerated; essays are followed by listings of the publications in each chapter. All materials are in English and considered to be readily available in university libraries. The essays are well written and offer historical perspective on the role of the newspaper in U.S. society. There is a chronology, a listing of research collections, and an index of authors, titles, and subjects.

1131. The Nineteenth Century Photographic Press: A Study Guide. Robert S. Sennett. New York: Garland, 1987. 97p. (Garland Reference Library of the Humanities, v. 694.) ISBN 0-8240-8544-2.

Historically, the photographic press has played an important role in the documentation of U.S. history, especially since the period of the Civil War and the work of Matthew Brady. This concise guide is an important vehicle for research and study, providing focus on those early years and the coverage given to photography's emergence during that period. The journal literature of the years 1840–1899 is identified here, the intent being to include listings from every U.S. and European journal relevant to the study of photography. Coverage is selective rather than comprehensive. Although there are the usual number of omissions and technical flaws characteristic of a work of this type, it should be used by those with a serious interest. Entries are arranged chronologically under journal titles, which are organized alphabetically.

1132. The Power of the Press. Beth Levy and Denise M. Bonilla, eds. New York: H.W. Wilson, 1999. 187p. (The Reference Shelf, v. 71, no. 1.) ISBN 0-8342-0962-1.

The publisher's series is well-known through its multivolume coverage of a variety of social issues of concern to this country and to others. This volume examines the current topic through a compilation and presentation of some 20 articles and essays culled from a variety of sources. These are reflections of journalists about their profession and separate chapters embrace such topics as celebrity ethics, journalistic failures, and such concepts as freedom of the press. Of course, media scandals are covered as well. The initial chapter examines the perception of the media held by Americans, as well as the realities of the newspaper as a business entity, and recent trends in reporting.

Sourcebook of American Literary Journalism, edited by Thomas B. Connery (Greenwood Press, 1992) contains 35 essays by expert contributors on the personalities and styles of those influential writers who may be called literary journalists from the nineteenth century to the present. Included here are Mark Twain, Stephen Crane, Theodore Dreiser, Ernest Hemingway, and so forth. The essays provide commentary and exposition of their writing and supply examples. The editor furnishes briefer treatment of 19 additional figures. *The Journalist's Bookshelf: An Annotated and Selected Bibliography of United States Print Journalism* by Roland Wolsey (R.J. Berg, 1986), now in its eighth edition, excludes broadcast journalism and furnishes listings suitable to the general public. Entries are arranged under topical divisions.

BROADCAST JOURNALISM

1133. ABC News Index. Woodbridge, CT: Research Publications, 1986–. Quart. with ann. cum. ISSN 0891-8775.

A specialized index of importance to students and researchers of recent history in the field of journalism, this work identifies transcripts on microfiche available through *ABC News Transcripts* (Research Publications, 1986–), which gives complete transcripts of the important ABC news programs. *ABC News Closeup, Nightline, 20/20, World News Tonight,* and others are furnished on a quarterly basis from 1970 to the present. The Index furnishes quick access to content of transcripts also on a quarterly basis, with the fourth number issued as a hardbound annual cumulation. A 1970–1985 cumulated index was issued in two volumes in 1990. Arrangement is topical by Library of Congress subject headings, alphabetically arranged. Brief abstracts are given, along with dates, program, and fiche number. It furnishes access by name, subject, and program.

A similar publication is the *CBS News Index* (University Microfilms International, 1975–), a quarterly index with annual cumulations enumerating CBS news transcripts on microfilm. The monthly *Television News Index and Abstracts* (Vanderbilt Television News Archive, 1968–) indexes Vanderbilt University's massive videotape holdings (some 27,000 hours of broadcast time to date) of network evening news programs.

For some time, Journal Graphics, Inc., now of Portland, Oregon, has provided transcripts and/or videotape copies of over 160 news magazines and talk shows (such as CNN's *Crossfire* and *Larry King Live,* and ABC News's *20/20* and *Nightline*) as well as PBS, cable, and network documentaries (such as *Frontline* and *CBS News Special Reports*), some going back to 1968 and thus of great historical value. A very useful source providing access to Journal Graphics' vast and growing news/documentary archives is the *Transcript/Video Index* (Journal Graphics, Inc. 1991–; ann., with quarterly updates), also available online through the *CARL library consortium database, *LexisNexis, and *Dow Jones News Retrieval. Broadcasts are indexed under some 250 topic headings, such as "abortion" or "capital punishment"; abstracts of each program are also provided. There is a "topic alert service" that keeps customers informed of any new broadcasts covering a given subject. There are also specialty indexes covering newsworthy topics such as the environment, political/social issues, and banking and finance. Those wishing to order transcripts and/or video tapes or who wish further information on the service may call 1-503-790-9100 or fax 1-503-790-9043.

1134. Encyclopedia of Television News. Michael D. Murray, ed. Phoenix: Oryx Press, 1998. 336p. ISBN 1-57356-108-8.

The author is an academic with expertise in journalism history; he has compiled a comprehensive source of information to serve the needs of students and others interested in the development and operation of television news broadcasting. There is an increasing proportion of the American public preferring to get its news over television in the past decade, making this an important topic of investigation. The current effort contains over 300 entries arranged alphabetically and signed by more than 100 expert contributors. Included in the coverage are various personalities, significant issues, themes, and of course, specific programs. Some of the biographical sketches treat relatively unknown individuals who are not covered in other sources. Entries are brief but informative, and each one is accompanied by photographs. A general index supplies access.

1135. Special Edition: A Guide to Network Television Documentary Series and Special News Reports, 1980–1989. Daniel Einstein. Lanham, MD: Scarecrow, 1997. 870p. ISBN 0-8108-3220-8.

This volume continues the work begun in the initial publication, *Special Edition: A Guide to . . . 1955–1979* (Scarecrow, 1987). The earlier issue established a reputation for utility as a handbook supplying needed information to both researchers and students of recent history interested in the coverage and composition of network television documentaries and special reports over a period of 25 years. The current effort treats the following 10-year period in much the same manner. It is organized into three major divisions, the first of which covers network documentary series, the major segment constituting the bulk of the total. Also treated are network television news specials as well as special reports broadcast by major networks. Arrangement of entries is chronological within the groupings. Given for each entry are dates, titles, writers, directors, producers, and narrators, as well as brief descriptions of content. Over 7,000 individual programs and 120 series are enumerated. There are indexes of personalities and personnel, but the work suffers for lack of subject access. It is obvious that any future effort would do well to consider the inclusion of cable and possibly public broadcasting venues.

POPULAR CULTURE: ENTERTAINMENT, RECREATION, SPORTS

The many facets of popular culture and the entertainment arts have always represented an important consideration for civilized society. Modern cultural historians examine the impact and representative expression of these elements rather than the quality of the product. More recently, especially in this country, remuneration for sports personalities and entertainment figures has hit all-time highs and has somewhat distanced these heroes from the mainstream. The history of U.S. involvement with the various media has presented a fertile field for investigation, with the theater and the cinema being the chief interests of numerous scholars and popular writers.

This section opens with a segment on general sources that cover more than one medium or recreational art. Following are separate sections on radio and television; cinema; theater and stage; and, finally, sports and games. We have excluded from our coverage art, music, and literature; investigators are referred to the various literature guides, which consider these areas in more depth than would be permitted here.

The Popular Culture Association at Bowling Green (Ohio) State University was founded in 1964 and has 2,500 members. It has published the *Journal of Popular Culture* on a quarterly basis since 1967. The American Culture Association has issued *Journal of American and Comparative Culture* since 1978, also as a quarterly. Both organizations share a Web site through *H-Net Humanities Online* (available at http://www2.h-net.msu.edu/~pcaaca/).

*1136. The American Memory Project. Washington, D.C.: Library of Congress, 1999. Available: http://rs6.loc.gov/ammem/amhome.html.

The Library of Congress National Digital Library Program is a cooperative effort between the national library and other libraries and archives designed to preserve primary-source records of various kinds in digital format. The Web site currently offers more than 7 million items from over 100 historical collections. Included here are documents, manuscripts, soundbites, film clips, posters, sheet music, photographs, and so forth relevant to the telling of the American story. Links are provided to 13 categories of online collections ranging from "Agriculture" to "Technology and Applied Sciences." Those important to the study of popular culture are "Art and Architecture," "Performing Arts," "Recreation and Sports," and "Languages and Literature." Under "Performing Arts" one is able to find, among other things, some 13,000 images of play scripts and documents in the holdings associated with the Federal Theatre Project (entry 1204).

1137. American Popular Culture: A Guide to the Reference Literature. Frank Hoffman. Englewood, CO: Libraries Unlimited, 1995. 286p. ISBN 1-56308-142-3.

The author is an academic and frequent contributor to the reference literature of popular culture. In this work, he provides annotated listings of some 1,200 reference sources of all types organized into 13 chapters: general reference; mass media; performing arts; politics; popular history; popular music; religion and psychic phenomena; social phenomena; sports and recreation; special collections; societies and associations; and journals. Entries contain informative annotations describing scope and coverage and sometimes furnishing critical commentary. They run from 50 to 250 words, and are designed to meet the needs of students and others with a general interest.

Making its debut in the year 2002 is a new series from Greenwood Press, *American Popular Culture Through History,* providing individual titles by different specialists on various decades, developments, and movements relevant to art, music, film, literature, sports, and other elements of popular culture. The series is designed to provide high school and college students with more awareness of significant developments, trends, and personalities influencing the popular tastes and active interests of the American public. The first volume is *The 1910s* by David Burke who explores such phenomena as the Black Sox Scandal, introduction of the teddy bear, the initial hamburger, and so forth. Following that is *Westward Expansion* by Sara E. Quay, who examines the endless interest in the West with such icons as Levis, country-western music, Buffalo Bill, western movies, and so forth. *The 1900s* by Bob Batchelor treats the renewal of the Olympic Games, Gibson Girl, Tin Pan Alley, and more. *The New Nation* by Anita Vickers provides perspective on tavern life, partisan politics, and politically incorrect (and illegal today) spectator sports such as cockfighting and gander pulling. *The 1960s* by Edward J. Rielly furnishes insight into the popular culture emerging out of the struggle for civil rights, feminist influences, Bob Dylan, and so forth.

American Popular Culture: A Guide to Information Sources by Larry N. Landrum (Gale, 1982) was issued as volume 12 in the publisher's American Studies Information Guide Series. Nearly 2,200 books and a number of periodical articles are cited and annotated under form categories such as "bibliographies, indexes, and abstracts." These are subdivided by specific topics and appear with chapters on sports, music, theater, and so forth. The author served as a professor of literature and popular culture and was "selective and un-abashedly eclectic." Annotations vary in length from brief or nonexistent (subtitle only) to a full paragraph.

1138. Blacks in American Films and Television: An Encyclopedia. Donald Bogle. New York: Garland, 1988. 510p. (Garland Reference Library of the Humanities, v. 604.) Repr. New York: Simon & Schuster, 1989. Repr. New York: Simon & Schuster, 1989. 0-671-67538-9.

The author is regarded as a reputable historian of blacks in the entertainment industry, and with this volume he offers a critical interpretation on the manner in which black char-acters have been developed in some 260 films and more than 100 television series, motion pictures, and specials. More than 100 black performers and directors are profiled, their careers examined and contributions evaluated. Arrangement of entries is alphabetical, thus precluding the establishment of a historical perspective such as might have been provided in a chronological arrangement. As part of the Garland humanities series, the work provides useful information and provocative commentary for students, scholars, and the interested public. There is a bibliography of additional readings and numerous illustrations, as well as a comprehensive index to furnish access.

1139. Colonial America on Film and Television: A Filmography. Jefferson, NC: Mc-Farland, 2001. 267p. ISBN 0-7864-0862-6.

The author is a Swedish physician and obvious fan of American motion pictures, who has thoroughly researched the topic of the colonial period and its treatment in cinema and television series. He has provided a comprehensive survey and description of some 160 films and television series set in the time period from the founding of the first European settlement to the War of 1812. The work is thorough in its coverage, beginning with an introductory historical survey of the colonial period with frequent references to films and television series in their treatment of specific events and personalities. The filmography then is arranged alphabetically by title of each film and series. Entries supply synopses, names of actors, running time, excerpts of critical commentary, production information, and com-mentary. In some cases, there are photographs of movie scenes.

1140. Encyclopedia of 20th-Century American Humor. Alleen P. Nilsen and Don L.F. Nilsen. Westport, CT: Greenwood Publishing Group, 2000. 376p. ISBN 1-57356-218-1.

A well-conceived and serious encyclopedic work in its treatment of humor, the effort succeeds in providing background and awareness of the history and development of humor in American life. The authors are academics who have examined the phenomenon in serious manner and its representation in various settings, forms, and formats in our society. There are nearly 100 broad-based entries, alphabetically arranged from "academic study of humor" to "wit"; they include such elements as "comic books," "children's television," "movies," and "ethnic humor." Such breadth offers opportunity for examination of related material within the various entries; they range in length from one to five pages. In general, they furnish adequate treatment of all material covered. There is a fine bibliography that includes scholarly expositions as well as joke books.

1141. From Elvis to E-Mail: Trends, Events, and Trivia from the Postwar Era to the End of the Century. Paul Dickson. Darien, CT: Federal Street, 1999. 401p. ISBN 1-892859-09-2.

This is an entertaining and informative chronology of events and personalities associated with the historical development of American culture and social history from the end of World War II to June 1999. Presentation is in timeline fashion with organization by year and month; all manner of events are featured along with brief interpretive commentary. The author is a prolific writer and storyteller who has selected a limited number of entries for every year. We learn of home run records being set, television shows being introduced, and motion pictures being released along with interesting and sometimes important developments in technology and in politics, as well as various fads, trends, and trivial occurrences. Special features include identifications of bumper sticker slogans, catch words and phrases, and statistics of interest.

1142. Greenwood Guide to American Popular Culture. M. Thomas Inge and Dennis Hall, eds. Westport, CT: Greenwood Press, 2002. 4v. ISBN 0-313-30878-0.

This work represents the most detailed and comprehensive guide to popular culture to date, and presents a series of essay-length chapters on each form, genre, or theme of current or historical importance (amusement parks, computers, fashion, popular religion, etc.). These are arranged alphabetically and coverage within chapters is in historical sequence allowing the user to examine the evolutionary development of these elements within the American milieu over time. Bibliographic essays of critical nature are supplied to provide an overview of the most important sources of information that include reference works, bibliographies, histories, critical studies, and significant journals. Resource centers and important collections are identified in each subject area. The work is well illustrated with numerous photographs that enhance the descriptive narratives. It serves to update and expand the second edition of Inge's three-volume *Handbook of American Popular Culture* (Greenwood Press, 1989).

Popular Entertainment Research: How to Do It and How to Use It by Barbara J. Pruett (Scarecrow, 1992) identifies and describes resource centers, library collections, journals, and databases of importance to the researcher and student. Along with descriptions, suggestions are provided for gaining access to and utilizing resources and for conducting research.

1143. Hispanics in Hollywood: A Celebration of 100 Years in Film and Television. Luis Reyes and Peter Rubie. Santa Monica, CA: iFilm Publishing, 2000. 592p. ISBN 1-58065-02-2.

The authors are insiders in the film and television industry and write from a solid background in dealing with those associated with the profession. They have produced a useful survey of 400 films and television shows along with proper credits, production information, plot synopses, and critical commentary. Following a useful and informative introductory history of the Hispanic presence in popular culture, there are two separate sections for film and for television productions (includes series, miniseries, and full-length motion pictures). They are arranged alphabetically and precede a separate section covering the two major heroes, Cisco Kid and Zorro, in terms of television and film treatment over the years.

A final and important segment serves as a biographical dictionary treating the careers of significant personalities dating from the earliest days of the industry to the present.

1144. Image as Artifact: The Historical Analysis of Film and Television. John E. O'Connor, ed. Malabar, FL: Krieger, 1990. 344p. ISBN 0-89464-312-6.

The author is a film historian and professor who has developed a useful manual for scholars and serious students on methodology for the utilization of moving images (films and television programs) as historical documents and artifacts. These elements of popular culture furnish a rich source of documentation and are capable of supporting a body of critical scholarship that can enhance the understanding of social history. The work is divided into five chapters, the first two of which lead with an introduction and describe data collection on the contents, production, and reception of a moving-image document. Chapter 3 consists of four frameworks for perceiving the moving image, each of which is examined in essays by three contributing historians. These different types of inquiries are discussed in terms of methodological concerns in working with evidence. The final chapters offer a case study and an introduction to visual language. Both a bibliography and an index are supplied.

1145. Mass Media: A Chronological Encyclopedia of Television, Radio, Motion Pictures, Magazines, Newspapers, and Books in the United States. Robert V. Hudson. New York: Garland, 1987. 435p. (Garland Reference Library of Social Science, v. 310.) ISBN 0-8240-8695-3.

This chronology is beneficial to both students and scholars of the mass media because it divides the coverage between the media's dual roles: entertainment and information. Organization of the work is by divisions of 16 chronological periods, beginning with 1638–1764 and concluding with 1973–1985. Within the periods the entries are arranged chronologically by medium (books, broadsides, pamphlets, radio, and television). Entries vary in length from a few lines to a few paragraphs and enumerate various events, along with their key figures and sites. Exposition is furnished on the importance of the happenings, which include the founding of publications, the release of movies, court cases, and technical advances. The work begins with an informative history of mass media and a listing of "firsts," along with references to where they are treated in the chronology. There is a detailed index.

1146. The New Encyclopedia of American Scandal. George C. Kohn, ed. New York: Facts on File, 2001. 455p. (Facts on File Library of American History.) ISBN 0-8160-4225-X.

Because the element of scandal is a favorite topic in American popular culture, the editor has seized the opportunities presented in the events of the past decade to update and expand the initial edition published in 1989. The current effort contains some 450 entries (an increase of 100 over the first edition) covering a variety of significant incidents of notoriety, breaches of faith, and violations of ethics, propriety, or law. Perpetrators and episodes represent all sectors of the American milieu (arts, business, entertainment, politics, religion, etc.), and range from the early seventeenth century to the present day with emphasis on the past 100 years. Included in the updated effort are President Clinton (of course), Heidi Fleiss, Newt Gingrich, O.J. Simpson, and the Bobbits, who join the earlier examples (Donner party, Presidents Jefferson, Jackson, and Harding, Karen Silkwood, etc.). Entries provide adequate exposition and treatment of the events and figures.

1147. Performing Arts Biography Master Index: A Consolidated Index to Over 270,000 Biographical Sketches of Persons Living and Dead, as They Appear in Over 100 of the Principal Biographical Dictionaries Devoted to the Performing Arts. 2nd ed. Barbara McNeil and Miranda C. Herbert, eds. Detroit: Gale, 1982. 701p. (Gale Biographical Index Series, no. 5.) ISBN 0-8103-1097-X.

This is a convenience tool derived from the massive coverage of *Biography and Genealogy Master Index* (entry 57). Beginning as *Theatre, Film, and Television Biographies Master Index* (Gale, 1979), the new title expanded and increased coverage, more than doubling the number of entries. The number of biographical dictionaries indexed was increased in similar fashion, from about 40 to over 100 sources. Entries are alphabetically arranged and provide coverage of personalities representing a wide spectrum of the performing arts (theater, film, television, classical and popular music, dance, puppetry, magic). Entries furnish dates of birth and death and references to the biographical dictionaries (including page numbers). The biographical sources are considered readily available in library collections, making this a practical reference tool for both students and researchers in need of background information on significant and obscure entertainers.

A work of wider scope but less comprehensive is *American Cultural Leaders: From Colonial Times to the Present* by Richard Ludwig and others, to be published by ABC-CLIO in 1993. The work is not limited to performing artists but includes painters, architects, writers, and so on. Over 350 individuals are treated in narratives ranging from 500 to 1,500 words.

1148. St. James Encyclopedia of Popular Culture. Tom Pendergast and Sara Pendergast. Detroit: St. James Press, 1999. 5v. ISBN 1-55862-405-8.

A useful and comprehensive source of information on popular culture, the work contains more than 2,700 entries providing descriptive narrative of a wide range of activities, personalities, developments, and phenomena that have become ingrained in the American milieu. Entries are signed by contributors and vary in length from those providing brief descriptions and identifications of 150 words or less to survey essays of 3,000 words. They are organized under broad categorical subjects such as film, music, television and radio, and so forth. One is able to find entries on such diverse elements as aerobics, the AARP, Sputnik, Winnie the Pooh, Fay Wray, *The Mary Tyler Moore Show,* and so forth. The work is profusely illustrated with some 1,250 photographs, and a comprehensive bibliography. Volume 5 concludes with a general index, category index, and time frame index by decade.

1149. Sourcebook for the Performing Arts: A Directory of Collections, Resources, Scholars, and Critics in Theatre, Film, and Television. Anthony Slide et al., comps. New York: Greenwood Press, 1988. 227p. ISBN 0-313-24872-9.

This is a comprehensive directory in terms of its coverage of a wide spectrum of the performing arts (television, radio, theater, and film), yet it is selective in its inclusion of entries. The work is divided into three major sections, the first two making up the bulk of the total text. The first section lists institutions and their collections. These entries are arranged alphabetically by state and indicate the usual directory information (name, address, telephone number, and description of collection). The second section furnishes brief biographical coverage of various personalities associated with the study (historians, librarians, etc.). The final section gives a brief listing of addresses of various participating units, agencies, and organizations, such as journals, book publishers, bookshops, studios, and production companies. There is an index to entries covered in the first two sections.

1150. The Stars of Stand-up Comedy: A Biographical Encyclopedia. Ronald L. Smith. New York: Garland, 1986. 227p. (Garland Reference Library of the Humanities, v. 564.) ISBN 0-8240-8803-2.

Comedy and humor retain an important position within the realm of popular culture, and the study of such performance receives continual attention among scholars and students. This biographical coverage of stand-up comedians furnishes useful information for all inquirers. More than 100 individuals and comedy teams are covered. Arrangement of entries is alphabetical and performers vary considerably. Included here are Groucho Marx, Lily Tomlin, and Bob Hope, as well as Lenny Bruce, Tom Lehrer, and Eddie Murphy. The performers represent a wide array of entertainment modes and gained their reputations through motion pictures, radio, and/or television. Entries provide illustrations, dates, recordings, television appearances, films, biographies, and books written by subject. Essays are informative and cover background, philosophy, and brand of humor in well-written two- to three-page formats.

1151. Variety Obituaries: Including a Comprehensive Index. Chuck Bartelt and Barbara Bergeron, proj. eds. New York: Garland, 1988–1995. 15v. ISBN 0-8240-0835-9 (v. 1).

From Garland Press comes this multivolume compilation of obituaries and related articles of entertainment figures as they appeared in *Variety* over a time span of more than 80 years. The work is of real value to researchers and serious students. Arrangement and format are similar to that of *Variety Film Reviews,* and entries appear in chronological sequence. Volume I contains obituaries published between 1905 and 1928. Much of the material originated as news stories and editorials rather than as obituary listings. Personalities from all aspects of entertainment are represented, ranging from performers to business employees in fields from the circus to television. No photographs are included. Volume II is an index to the first 10 volumes and completes a set covering the years 1905–1986. The work continued with separately indexed volumes on a biennial basis: volume 12 covered the period 1987–1988; volume 13, 1989–1990; volume 14, 1991–1992; and volume 15, 1993–1994. No issues have appeared since the publication of volume 15.

Jeb H. Perry has authored *Variety Obits: An Index to Obituaries in Variety, 1905–1978* (Scarecrow, 1980) for those who have *Variety* on microfilm and need only an index to the material.

1152. War and American Popular Culture: A Historical Encyclopedia. M. Paul Holsinger, ed. New York: Greenwood Press, 1999. 470p. ISBN 0-313-29908-0.

This encyclopedic work is organized into 13 chapters, chronologically arranged from colonial wars with Native Americans beginning in the sixteenth century to coverage of the military subsequent to 1975. Each chapter is introduced by an informative essay describing the period; this is followed by entries describing significant cultural achievements and events, personalities, specific productions, and other societal elements. The focus is on the nature of the popular culture and the impact of the wars and their treatment in art, literature, motion pictures, plays, radio and television, posters, comic books, and so forth. Coverage is especially full for the more recent periods from the time of World War II, but there is detailed examination of the Revolutionary War and Civil War cultural developments as well. Both the introductory essays and the individual entries contain brief reading lists, and a section of photographs enhance the text.

RADIO AND TELEVISION

Reviews of television shows of historical interest may be found in a recent publication, *Variety Television Reviews, 1923–1988: The First Fifteen Volumes of the Series Including a Comprehensive Index,* edited by Howard H. Prouty (Garland, 1989–1991, 15v). This set consists of reviews as they appeared in *Daily Variety* out of Hollywood, California, from 1946 to 1960 (v. 1–2) and *Variety* out of New York from 1923 to 1988 (v. 3–14). Volume 15 is an index. The series continues as *Variety and Daily Variety Television Reviews* on a biennial basis, with volume 16 (1992 publication) covering the reviews of 1989–1990. For related works on news broadcasting, see the "Journalism" section in this chapter.

Academy of Television Arts & Sciences (available at http://www.emmys.com/) is the national organization responsible for the awarding of Emmys for notable television presentations. The organization is in the process of creating an archive and to this end has conducted 260 interviews with notables as of March 2002. Currently, there are a few listings available as well as news and notes on the Web site.

General Sources

1153. Radio and Television: A Selected, Annotated Bibliography. William E. McCavitt. Metuchen, NJ: Scarecrow, 1978. 229p. ISBN 0-8108-1113-8. **Supplement One: 1977–1981.** 1982. 155p. ISBN 0-8108-1556-7. **Supplement Two: 1982–1986.** 1989. 237p. ISBN 0-8108-2158-3.

The initial bibliography furnishes 1,100 items, mostly books, written over a time span of 50 years, from 1926 to 1976. Comprehensive coverage is given to all areas of broadcasting activity, with entries arranged under broad subject categories such as history, society, regulations, and audience, along with format categories such as annuals, periodicals, and bibliographies. The organization tends to be a weakness, as certain subjects seem to be scattered throughout rather than integrated as a unit. This problem is lessened somewhat by the inclusion of cross-references. Annotations vary in length and quality, with many entries not given any description at all. There is an author index.

The first supplement was completed by McCavitt in 1982 and furnished an additional 500 entries organized under 27 categories representing the literature from 1977 to 1981. *Supplement Two: 1982–1986* was compiled by Peter K. Pringle and Helen H. Clinton and identifies an additional 1,000 publications listed under six major categories.

Radio

1154. Encyclopedia of American Radio, 1920–1960. Luther F. Sies. Jefferson City, NC: McFarland, 2000. 904p. ISBN 0-7876-0452-3.

An extensive survey of a limited period, considered by the author to be the Golden Age of radio, the work concludes with the beginning of the ascendancy of television as the primary home entertainment medium. The 40-year period is handled in comprehensive fashion in providing nearly 29,000 alphabetically arranged entries covering radio personalities of all types (performers, announcers, musicians, vocalists, commentators, auxiliary personnel, etc.) as well as specific programs and types of programming. Descriptions are brief for the individuals but are in-depth for the topical matter such as sports broadcasting and black radio. There are helpful cross-references, chronology, and detailed bibliography.

The Encyclopedia of American Radio: An A-Z Guide to Radio from Jack Benny to Howard Stern, edited by Ron Lackmann also was issued in 2000 by Facts on File as a revision of a 1996 publication, *Same Time Same Station.* It contains over 1000 entries treating all significant radio programs, characters, sponsors, storylines, and stations that carried them. Although, there are two-thirds fewer entries than the work above, the scope is broader in bringing radio up to the present day. Appendixes supply listings of clubs, conventions, and current stations that offer vintage programs.

1155. Lux Presents Hollywood: A Show-by-Show History of the *Lux Radio Theatre* and the *Lux Video Theatre, 1934–1957.* Connie Billips and Arthur Pierce. Jefferson, NC: McFarland, 1995. 729p. ISBN 0-89950-938-X.

One of the major series on radio was the Lux Radio Theatre that ran for 23 years; it was joined by a television counterpart, Lux Video Theatre, which began in 1950 and concluded that same year in 1957. These one-hour programs were adaptations of motion pictures and were carefully designed to appeal to a home audience. This work represents a thorough and comprehensive record of those performances with entries organized in chronological sequence and giving name of production, cast, date, source or basis of screenplay, network affiliation, plot description, and information on the motion picture version. One is able to determine time slot, announcer, studio, and, of real interest, the intermission guests who were some of the leading personalities in Hollywood at the time. Appendixes supply listings of archives and sources of memorabilia.

The CBS Radio Mystery Theatre: An Episode Guide and Book to Nine Years of Broadcasting, 1974–1982 by Gordon Payton and Martin Grams, Jr. (McFarland, 1999) is similar in concept to the above work. In this case, it provides a record of the popular daily show that ran for nine years. Brief identification and plot description of all 1,400 programs in the series is given along with dates of broadcasts and rebroadcasts, list of performers, and writers. In some cases there are interesting commentaries and stories. There is a brief but informative history of the series, and appendixes contain information on the spin-off series for children, as well as the short-lived revival of the series in 1998.

1156. Radio: A Reference Guide. Thomas A. Greenfield. Westport, CT: Greenwood Press, 1989. 172p. (American Popular Culture.) ISBN 0-313-22276-2.

Another of the Greenwood issues in the *American Popular Culture* series, this bibliographic guide should prove useful to students and researchers at all levels. Over 500 books, articles, dissertations, and monographs are treated in bibliographic essays divided among chapters relating to the history of radio (in which both stations and networks are examined), more specifically of music, drama, comedy, news, sports, and advertising. Important personalities are also treated within the various topical segments as leaders of their genre. The guide is well organized and carefully developed to meet the needs of both undergraduates and more serious investigators. The essays are readable and informative; the concluding bibliographers for each chapter were carefully selected. Also included are listings of organizations, serial publications, indexing services, and important collections. There is a corporate index of names, titles, and subjects.

1157. Radio Drama: A Comprehensive Chronicle of American Network Programs, 1932–1962. Martin Grams, Jr. Jefferson City, NC: McFarland, 2000. 288p. ISBN 0-7864-0051-X.

The publisher has been active in the production of resources in this area, and this work takes its place with the others of its kind (entries 1154, 1158). It is a useful and comprehensive listing of some 300 program series aired by the major networks over a 30-year period. The research has been thorough in culling the material from newspapers, script files, and network records as well as personal documentation of those who served as directors of the series. Entries for series are arranged alphabetically and supply brief histories, broadcast dates, and time slots of individual programs. Credits for cast members are provided as are those for direction, writing, and musical performance. Most of the popular series of the time are represented (Superman, Sam Spade, etc.) with some notable exceptions such as the Lone Ranger. There is a detailed index of personal names.

1158. Radio Programs, 1924–1984: A Catalog of Over 1800 Shows. Vincent Terrace. Jefferson City, NC: McFarland, 1999. 399p. ISBN 0-7864-0351-9.

This work is an update and expansion of an earlier publication by Terrace, *Radio's Golden Years: The Encyclopedia of Radio Programs, 1930–1960* (A.S. Barnes, 1981). It employs the same style and format with alphabetical arrangement of entries providing identification of cast members, plot, announcers, music, sponsors, network information, and length and date of broadcasts, as well as openings and closings of series. This format had been adopted by the author in the 1979 work, *Complete Encyclopedia of Television Programs.* Since that time he has been active in documentation of the latter medium, and the current effort is unique in that it marks a return to his coverage of radio. It should become a standard tool in its coverage of more than 1,800 nationally broadcast programs, and a valued resource for identification purposes. A name index provides access.

Television

1159. Encyclopedia of Television: Series, Pilots, and Specials. Vincent Terrace. New York: Zoetrope, 1985–1986. 3v. ISBN 0-918432-69-3 (v. 1).

Vincent Terrace is a well-known writer in the field, known for his reference sources (entries 1158 and 1160). This three-volume effort furnishes a comprehensive listing of more than 7,000 television series, pilots, experimental programs, and specials over a period of nearly 50 years. The guide provides plot summaries, cast information, number of episodes aired, networks, running times, syndication, and cable information. Also included are songs, vocalists, and musicians associated with production. Volume 1 covers the period 1937–1973; volume 2 examines the period 1974–1984; and volume 3 is the index giving access by names of individuals.

An earlier work by the author that helped establish his reputation in the field is *The Complete Encyclopedia of Television Programs, 1947–1979* (Barnes, 1979, 2v), which itself was a revision and second edition of an earlier work covering the period 1947–1976. The more recent effort gives comprehensive coverage of information regarding television programs for a period of more than 30 years. A name index furnishes access.

A more recent work of greater scope is *Les Brown's Encyclopedia of Television* (Gale, 1992), now in its third edition. Brown has furnished 800 entries treating performers, programs, and events in alphabetical order. The publication originated in 1977 as the *New York Times Encyclopedia of Television* and subsequently has been revised and expanded.

1160. Fifty Years of Television: A Guide to Series and Pilots, 1937–1988. Vincent Terrace. Cranbury, NJ: Cornwall Books; distr. Associate University Presses, 1991. 864p. ISBN 0-8543-4811-6.

Another of Terrace's efforts (see also entries 1158 and 1159) is a comprehensive directory of more than 4,850 television series and pilots that ran between 1937 and 1988. Included here are entertainment series, experimental programs, and pilots (even those that were not aired). Excluded are mini-series, television movies, daytime serials, specials, and sports and news programs. Entries are arranged alphabetically and include the information normally associated with the author's handbooks: one- or two-sentence plot descriptions, type of program (e.g., comedy, western), cast lists, producers, dates, running times, networks, syndication, and cable information. Much of the information was gathered through viewings of the programs rather than release information furnished in press releases or *TV Guide*. The work should prove useful to inquirers at all levels because of its breadth and comprehensiveness. There is a selective index of performers.

Screen Gems: A History of Columbia Pictures Television from Cohn to Coke, 1948–1983 by Jeb H. Perry (Scarecrow, 1991) is a more specialized source that begins with a brief corporate history. The work then furnishes listings of series with descriptions, pilots, and specials produced by Columbia Pictures. Cast listings are provided, along with a chronology of premieres and cancellation dates.

1161. Performers' Television Credits, 1948–2000. Jefferson, NC: McFarland, 2001. 3v. ISBN 0-7864-1041-8.

This work has been praised by reviewers as a superlative and detailed effort designed to provide researchers, librarians, and serious inquirers with historical identification of television appearances of thousands of performers over a period of more than 50 years. It represents 15 years of research resulting in the most complete and comprehensive work of its kind. The author, a well-known syndicated columnist for Gannett news service, has organized the entries alphabetically by stage name with a cross-reference from the original name. Entries supply date and place of birth, death date, and brief description of the performers' most popular roles, awards, writing or directing activity, and so forth. The bulk of the effort is the exhaustive listing of credits for all types of appearances on television shows both as a regular and as a guest with the exception of such events as parades and award shows in which little performance was required.

1162. Television, A Guide to the Literature. Mary B. Cassata and Thomas Skill. Phoenix, AZ: Oryx Press, 1985. 148p. ISBN 0-89774-140-4.

This is a bibliographic essay divided into three segments, each of which was initially published in *Choice* (January, February, and April 1982). More than 450 publications are identified and described in the three sections. The introductory "Test Patterns" furnishes historical perspective, general efforts on communication, and reference tools; "The Environment" treats the research concerned with various processes and influences of television, news, politics, and service to youth; and "Directions" furnishes coverage of the industry, its criticism and collected works. Because the work unfolded in separate segments, these sections retain separate identities rather than standing as a synthesized examination of the field as a whole. Nevertheless, both students and scholars find it useful in helping to define segments of the field in which they are interested. The work is indexed by author, title, and subject.

1163. Total Television: The Comprehensive Guide to Programming from 1948 to the Present. 4th ed. Alex McNeil. New York: Penguin, 1996. 1251p. ISBN 0-14-024916-8.

This is another comprehensive source of information covering network programming over a period of nearly 50 years. It features complete listings of every series that has been nationally broadcast on any of the networks, cable operations, or in syndication, as well as special programs, game shows, motion pictures, and more. Data regarding principal actors, running time, and so forth are supplied for over 5,400 daytime and evening series. Entries are of varying length from a paragraph or two to several pages in the case of major shows with great impact such as *All in the Family*. Entries are alphabetically arranged from *ABC Afternoon Break* to *Zorro and Son*. The work is intended for serious inquirers at all levels of sophistication, and provides useful features such as listings of Emmy and Peabody award winners and Nielsen's top 20 rated shows for each season. A comprehensive index provides access.

1164. Tube of Plenty: The Evolution of American Television. 2nd rev. ed. Erik Barnouw. New York: Oxford University, 1990. 607p. ISBN 0-19-506483-6.

This work was originally issued in 1975, reprinted with additions in 1977, and first revised in 1982. Written by one of the leading scholars and historians of the industry, it continues to offer one of the most useful survey histories of the communications revolution. The author has diligently and capably recorded the changes within the social fabric and related them to developments within the broadcasting industry. In more recent years we have seen the decline of the major networks and the expansion of cable and pay-television, with emphasis on specialized audiences such as those for MTV.

Much of the intellectual foundation of this work was derived from the author's scholarly three-volume *History of Broadcasting in the United States* (Oxford University, 1966–1970). This massive work is a merger of three separate publications that combine to form an in-depth retrospective. Coverage begins with volume 1, *A Tower of Babel,* which treats the beginnings of the industry up to Roosevelt's first inauguration in 1933. *The Golden Web* is the title of the second volume, which examines the next two decades, and volume 3, *The Image Empire,* covers the period from 1953 through the Eisenhower years to the moon landing.

1165. Women and American Television: An Encyclopedia. Santa Barbara, CA: ABC-CLIO, 1999. 513p. ISBN 0-87436-970-3.

This is a welcome source of information on the roles that women have played as stars of television. There are more than 400 entries furnishing biographical sketches of actresses and other female television personalities. Also included in the coverage are all programs that lasted more than six months, as well as selected topics including media innovations, important events, government rulings, and so forth. Entries are alphabetically arranged and vary in length from a few paragraphs on *Gidget* to two pages on *The Mary Tyler Moore Show.* They are written within a feminist orientation and in the case of lengthier articles, furnish analysis and interpretation of the program and its impact on the depiction of women. Format is appealing with the inclusion of sidebars that supply definitions and additional brief descriptions of topical nature. Following the main text, there are useful listings of award winners, and other significant individuals. A bibliography precedes the index.

CINEMA

Motion picture reviews published in the *New York Times* are provided in *New York Times Film Reviews, 1913–1968* (New York Times, 1970, 6v). Since then it has been updated on a biennial basis, with the most recent issue published in 2002 and covering the years 1999–2000. *Variety* reviews are found in *Variety Film Reviews, 1907–1980* (Garland, 1983. 16v). Publication continued on a biennial basis through R.R. Bowker, and later through Garland until it ceased publication in 1995. Since then, Variety has published an annual *Variety Movie Guide* supplying comprehensive coverage of more than 8,000 films. Additionally, there is a comprehensive two-volume index by Patricia K. Hanson and Stephen L. Hanson titled *Film Review Index* (Oryx, 1986–1987) that identifies substantial reviews from a variety of sources on films considered important to film researchers. Coverage extends from 1882 to 1985. *Magill's Survey of Cinema* was issued on an annual basis by Salem Press for many years, and now continues as *Magill's Cinema Annual* through St. James. It is a yearly review of motion pictures furnishing lengthy and detailed treatment

*Academy of Motion Picture Arts and Sciences (available at http://www.oscars.org) provides information regarding news and events of the Academy and is especially useful in it coverage of Oscar award winners both past and present. It contains a searchable database for that purpose. *The American Film Institute* (available at http://www.afi.com) is the leading organization for the conduct of educational programs and preservation practices regarding film. Information concerning actors, directors, and others can be found on the Web site as well as listings of AFI 100s (stars, movies, etc.).

General Sources

1166. American Film Studios: An Historical Encyclopedia. Gene Fernett. Jefferson, NC: McFarland, 1988; repr. 2002 310p. ISBN 0-7864-1325-5.

Identified as a *McFarland Classic,* this remains a useful source for its historical treatment of the origins and development of U.S. film studios of varied nature and importance. Coverage is given not only to the major studios but to the more obscure as well. More than 60 studios are covered, with informative, well-developed narratives furnishing clear and revealing insight and perspective regarding the various studios treated. Emphasis is given to the early years, with many modern studios being omitted. Entries cover major personalities of all types (actors, producers, directors, and owners), promotional literature, and photographs. Coverage varies in length from one page to several pages in presenting information regarding the nature and composition of the studios. Both scholars and students benefit from the treatment. There is a detailed name index to assure access.

American Film Scripts Online (2001) is another of the full-text online sources from Alexander Street Press (entries 462, 600n, 799) designed to provide researchers, serious students, and practitioners with primary-source material. This work contains more than 1,000 film scripts authorized for inclusion through rights agreements with film studios. The work can be accessed through script considerations such as interior scenes and close angles as well as themes, personalities (playwrights, directors, etc.) and titles. Like others from the publisher, it is available on the Web through purchase or subscription.

1167. Cinema Year by Year 1894–2000. Robyn Karney and Joel W. Finler, eds. New York: DK Publishing, 2000. 975p. ISBN 0-7894-6118-8.

A lavish and comprehensive illustrated history of the cinema from its beginnings to the present, this work serves as an update to what has been a biennial production, formerly titled *Chronicle of the Cinema.* It is a detailed and well-received work and the editors are prolific contributors to the literature of the motion picture industry. The chronicle format treats events and personalities in chronological sequence, reporting the facts in newspaper fashion in using the present tense. Articles are informative and describe the topics in clear and concise fashion. The work is enhanced by more than 3,000 illustrations that include movie stills, posters, candid photographs, and studio portraits. In addition, there are special features treating various aspects of cinema history such as the silent era, the new wave, and the independent movie.

1168. Encyclopedia of American Independent Filmmaking. Vincent LoBrutto. Westport, CT: Greenwood Press, 2002. 360p. ISBN 0-313-30199-9.

Although the topic and study of independent filmmaking is a significant element in scholarship today, the activity is not a recent phenomenon but has been part of the cinema since its beginnings. This work supplies alphabetically arranged entries describing filmmakers, important films, genres, industry issues, and approaches utilized over the years in cinema production. This separation from corporate Hollywood is a commendable status today, and represents what many consider a needed independence in producing works of artistic merit. Along with informative narrative of topics, bibliographic references are furnished for additional reading and study.

Film: A Reference Guide by Robert A. Armour (Greenwood Press, 1980) presents a bibliographic essay giving a well-organized systematic examination of popular U.S. films from the nineteenth century to the present. Nearly 1,500 English-language books are identified and arranged under 11 chapter headings (film history, criticism, production techniques, genres, major actors, and individual films, etc.). As part of the publisher's *American Popular Culture* series, the volume places emphasis on popular U.S. fare, with description accorded to individual titles through a bibliographic narrative. Bibliographic listings follow in each chapter. Coverage is comprehensive in terms of time periods and topics treated. There are indexes by author and subject to provide access.

1169. Film Composers in America: A Filmography, 1911–1970. 2nd ed. New York: Oxford University Press, 2000. 534p. ISBN 0-19-511473-6.

This is a comprehensive effort intended to identify every composer of music for film of every kind (feature-length motion pictures, shorts, cartoons, documentaries, and more). Some 20,000 titles are covered in this work that is organized by name of composer. Under each composer is listed the films in which he contributed in chronological sequence. The work is important in identifying authorship of film scores, and serves to provide a comprehensive catalog of such work for each composer. It is carefully researched and based on years of experience and painstaking research utilizing manuscript scores and cue sheets rather than screen credits. No biographical information is given. As one might expect, a variety of musical influences in composition is represented from composers of serious concert music to composers of popular music.

1170. Filmography of American History. Grant Tracey. Westport, CT: Greenwood Press, 2002. 352p. ISBN 0-313-31300-8.

A source with wide appeal for a variety of audiences, this work identifies 200 recommended films that enhance the study of American history. Especially fruitful in its coverage of social history, the work provides provocative narratives or brief essays on each title in such areas as the Great Depression, immigration, multicultural elements and concerns, and female influences, as well as the more traditional representation of wars and political developments. Documentaries are included along with better-known Hollywood fare, and analysis is given of varied and diverse film treatments of historical figures and events. These differences are dependent to some degree on the era in which the films were created, and the user is able to understand the logical influence of social forces behind the production.

1171. History of the American Cinema series. Charles Harpole, gen. ed. New York: Scribner's, 1991–. v. 1–6, 8–10 (in progress.) ISBN 0-684-18413-3 (v. 1).

This projected 10-volume history, edited by an academic, covers the story of the cinema from 1895 to 1989 and lacks only volume 7 to complete the effort. The work represents a massive effort, with individual volumes commissioned to individual scholars and historians in the field. All volumes treat a period of 10 years or so and are numbered sequentially. The series provides depth and critical perspective in analyzing the personalities and developments within the time periods. Volumes are detailed and include numerous illustrations of productions, advertisements, cartoons, and so on; they conclude with an index. The series was initiated for Scribner's Sons who seems to have made an agreement with the University of California for issuing the reprints. The most recent volume (8) was published by Macmillan. In order the volumes are: 1) *The Emergence of Cinema: The American Screen to 1907* by Charles Musset (1991, 1994); 2) *The Transformation of Cinema, 1907–1915* by Eileen Bowser (1991, 1994); 3) *An Evening's Entertainment: The Age of the Silent Feature Picture, 1915–1928* by Richard Koszarski (1991, 1994); 4) *Talkies; American Cinema's Transition to Sound, 1926–1931* by Donald Crafton (1999); 5) *Grand Design: Hollywood as a Modern Business Enterprise, 1930–1939* by Tino Balio (1995); 6) *Boom and Bust: American Cinema in the 1940s* by Thomas Schatz (1999); 7) not completed—to cover the 50s; 8) *The Sixties, 1960–69* by Paul Monaco (Macmillan, 2001); 9) *Lost Illusions: American Cinema in the Shadow of Watergate and Vietnam, 1970–1979* (2000); and 10) *A New Pot of Gold: Hollywood Under the Electronic Rainbow, 1980–1989* by Stephen Prince (1999).

1172. Hollywood Song: The Complete Film and Musical Companion. Ken Bloom. New York: Facts on File, 1995. 3v. ISBN 0-8160-2002-7.

Similar in style and format to an earlier work in musical theater (entry 1208), Bloom has produced a comprehensive source of information on just over 7,000 motion pictures for which songs or scores were written. It is not limited to the genre of "musicals" but contains all types of film. As one might think, the research was painstaking in nature and the author was able to access the cue sheets from the various studios in providing an exhaustive listing. The first two volumes list the films in alphabetical sequence and furnish identification of personalities responsible for the musical score, composers, lyricists, choreographers, producers, directors, screenwriters, cast, and the titles of each song written for the film. Volume 3 presents a year-by-year chronology beginning in the 1920s and running to 1990. There is a name index with identification of profession and a song index to quickly identify films for which song titles were written.

1173. The Illustrated Who's Who of Hollywood Directors. Volume 1: The Sound Era. Michael Barson. New York: Noonday/Farrar, Strauss & Giroux, 1995. 530p. ISBN 0-374-52428-9.

The author is an experienced historian of the popular-culture scene in this country and has provided a useful and informative history of the careers and achievements of Hollywood directors. The work profiles the contributions with entries given to 150 personalities who have worked in their craft between 1929 and 1995. There are two major segments, the first of which treats the leading or prominent figures, and the second or supplementary section dealing with lesser-known directors whose careers are described in briefer fashion. Essays generally begin with a survey or overview of the director's influence followed by a few paragraphs of biographical information. The major text then provides descriptive and evaluative opinion-type commentary on each of the director's films. There are photographs, both candid and posed of various figures.

1174. The New Historical Dictionary of the American Film Industry. Anthony Slide. Westport, CT: Greenwood Press, 1998. 266p. ISBN 0-810-83426-X.

This is an updated edition of Slide's *The American Film Industry: A Historical Dictionary* (Greenwood Press, 1986) in which he has expanded the coverage to 800 entries from the previous 600. It remains a unique source in its format as historical dictionary treating the development of the film industry in this country. The writing is smooth and the descriptions well developed, and cross-references are furnished. Focus is on the business end, with special attention given to business organizations, industrial techniques, and technology. Coverage is given to producing and releasing companies, film series, genres, organizations, and specific terms peculiar to the field. Entries vary in length from only a few lines to several pages and may include addresses and archival resources, as well as bibliographies in most cases. There is a general bibliography on film history, and a well-constructed index of persons, subjects, and organizations.

1175. The New York Times Encyclopedia of Film, 1896–1979. Gene Brown and Harry M. Geduld, eds. New York: Times Books, 1984. 13v. ISBN 0-8129-1059-1 (set).

Similar to the *New York Times Film Reviews* in format, this monumental collection of articles from the nationally read newspaper is arranged chronologically from 1896 to 1979. Included are all types of writings pertaining to motion pictures: news items, features, interviews, reports, and promotional pieces. As one might expect, reviews are studiously avoided so the other publication can retain its uniqueness in that area. Many illustrations are included, although the work has been criticized for the poor quality of the reproductions. Many subjects are covered, with a good proportion of the articles about personalities (producers, commentators, critics, news correspondents, and performers). There is an alphabetically arranged index volume providing access to the desired subject through identification of the month, day, and year the articles were published. During the 1990s, Garland Press has made individual volumes available on special order.

1176. 100 Years of American Film. Frank Beaver, ed. New York: Macmillan General Reference /Simon & Schuster, 2000. 840p. ISBN 0-02-865380-7.

The author is an academic who succeeds in furnishing a comprehensive source of information on the American cinema. Entries are alphabetically arranged and treat a variety of personalities (actors, directors, producers, critics and more) as well as important films, terminology, genres, organizations, topics, and so forth. Notable figures like John Ford and Mary Pickford are included but there is some criticism of such omissions as Spike Lee and John Cassavetes, thus making it difficult to understand the criteria for inclusion. Such technical subjects as "location shooting" are treated in detail. Much of the coverage, including that of a number of personalities, is presented in sidebars that seem to work well for the quotations from movies and about movies. Special features include listings of film facts and award winners as well as numerous photographs and a glossary.

1177. Silent Film Necrology. 2nd ed. Eugene M. Vazzana. Jefferson, NC: McFarland, 2002. 591p. ISBN 0-7864-1059-0.

The author was a specialist in the study of silent film who died shortly after completing this work. It is the second edition and doubles the size of the 1995 effort with the intent of being as comprehensive as possible in covering personalities on an international basis. By providing identification of dates of birth and death of 18,500 figures associated with production of silent films, the work is unique in terms of its breadth. Coverage is given to actors, directors, producers, composers, stuntmen and women, executives, camera persons, inventors, publicists, and others. Arrangement is the same as in the previous work with individuals listed in alphabetical sequence. In addition to dates, entries supply identification of real and married names, age at time of death, cause of death if known, type of employment, a list of film credits, and references to obituaries and other sources of information about them.

Genre and Topical Films

1178. American Political Movies: An Annotated Filmography of Feature Films. James E. Combs. New York: Garland, 1990. 173p. (Garland Filmographies, v. 1; Garland Reference Library of the Humanities, v. 970.) ISBN 0-8240-7847-0.

This is a useful tool for scholars and researchers who are interested in the thematic material examined or interpreted in motion pictures about politics. Such films, as well as those with purposeful political orientation, are treated, as are those that reflect on the political climate. Films are treated in nine chapters, eight of which generally follow a chronological sequence of coverage. The first chapter is most impressive, providing an overview and philosophical interpretation of film as a maker of popular opinion and political direction. The remaining chapters describe the involvement of politics in Hollywood fare from the early days to the 1980s. Interpretation is given to the various political orientations, with films being used as examples. The work concludes with a bibliography of books and articles and a filmography of some 350 "political" films. There is a subject index.

Picture This! A Guide to Over 300 Environmentally, Socially, and Politically Relevant Films and Videos by Sky Hiatt (Noble, 1992) examines films as propaganda and as instruments of social impact. Included are many titles that have been banned, blacklisted, and criticized for a variety of reasons. Such themes as morality, intolerance, and revolution are examined in this useful analysis.

1179. The Big Tomorrow: Hollywood and the Politics of the American Way. Larry May. Chicago: University of Chicago Press, 2000. 348p. ISBN 0-226-511626.

An interesting and provocative history of the American film industry by an academic, this work challenges suppositions of the inherently conservative representation of American life in the early years of sound film. He interprets Hollywood as producing motion pictures aimed at promoting an egalitarian society; he uses the leftist populism of Will Rogers, who he felt provided effective advocacy of FDR and the New Deal through the medium of film. Ascendancy of Jewish film moguls and the rise of independent studios maintained this thrust. This contrasts with the "lily white" depiction of the American milieu in the silent film era. This progressivism came to an end in the 1950s with the rise of McCarthyism and popular anti-Communist sentiment. The work is well researched and significant as revisionist history of this segment of popular culture.

1180. Doing Their Bit: Wartime American Animated Short Films, 1939–1945. Michael S. Shull and David E. Wilt. Jefferson, NC: McFarland, 1987. 198p. ISBN 0-89950-218-0.

Unique and useful coverage is provided both the film historian and the military historian on the production of animated cartoons related to World War II. In addition, this offering adds to the growing body of literature on animation, which has become a more popular study in recent years. The filmography of 271 entries gives title, distribution, company, date, producer, director, writer, animation personnel, and music director, as well as a plot synopsis. Cartoons are treated in serious manner: There is an informative and well-developed exposition of nearly 70 pages on the importance of this medium as an indicator of popular sentiment and a gauge of wartime attitudes. Several appendixes provide various listings, such as an index of featured characters and selected topics. An index to the filmography is furnished.

1181. Encyclopedia of American Film Comedy. Larry Langman. New York: Garland, 1987. 639p. (Garland Reference Library of the Humanities, v. 744.) ISBN 0-8240-8496-9.

Film historian Langman (see also entries 1182, 1183n, and 1184) has produced what purports to be the first one-volume encyclopedia of cinematic comedy. As one might expect, coverage is comprehensive but relatively brief. Included here are numerous performers, both individuals and teams, male and female, dating from the one-reelers of the second decade of this century to the films of the mid-1980s. Coverage is given not only to actors but also to directors and screenwriters, all of whom vary widely from one to another in terms of their success or impact. Also included are more than 150 comedy films representative of various styles and even entries for series, such as the Andy Hardy films. Entries vary from a few sentences to three pages in length and generally supply a brief filmography for each actor. There is a brief general bibliography; cross-references within entries furnish access in lieu of an index.

American Silent Film Comedies: An Illustrated Encyclopedia of Persons, Studios, and Terminology by Blair Miller (McFarland, 1998) supplements the above work in providing an alphabetical approach of entries of varying length of people, places, and events from approximately 1890 to 1930. There is a useful bibliography and the work concludes with an index. Another effort is *Quinlan's Illustrated Directory of Film Comedy Actors* by David Quinlan (Holt, 1992), which provides brief treatment of 300 film comedians, mainly U.S. and British. Entry length ranges from half a column (John Belushi) to three pages (Chaplin, Keaton); a filmography accompanies each entry. Stage and television contributions are described whenever applicable.

1182. Encyclopedia of American War Films. Larry Langman and Ed Borg. New York: Garland, 1989. 696p. (Garland Reference Library of the Humanities, v. 873.) ISBN 0-8240-7540-4.

Another of Langman's interesting and useful contributions is this comprehensive listing of some 2,000 U.S. films depicting wars in which this country was engaged. Entries are listed alphabetically by title and vary somewhat with the importance of the motion picture. Most entries furnish a brief plot summary or short review with some critical interpretation. The strength of this work lies in its breadth of coverage, and it appears to succeed in its purpose to treat every U.S. film of this genre, major and minor, made over a period of 90 years, from 1898 through 1988. All wars are represented, as seen in one of the appendixes, which links the wars to their related films. Also listed here are Oscar-winning films and a subject-arranged bibliography of film biographies.

A unique approach is taken by Mark Walker in *Vietnam Veteran Films* (Scarecrow, 1991), which covers motion pictures that include a Vietnam veteran among the characters. Plot summaries are given for 215 films, and genre classification is furnished (biker, vigilante, police, war, horror).

1183. From Headline Hunter to Superman: A Journalism Filmography. Richard R. Ness. Lanhah, MD: Scarecrow Press, 1997. ISBN 0-8108-3291-7.

This is a comprehensive listing of over 2,150 motion pictures that have portrayed journalists or represented the press in a significant manner. The author is an academic who has carefully researched the genre from the silent movie era to 1996, and has organized his work chronologically by year, then alphabetically by title. A broad survey essay precedes each decade. Included here are not only the important films of their day but grade B pictures, foreign contributions, and made-for-television movies. Plots are described and analyzed in careful manner and personnel are identified. Extensive narrative is given to the major films, with less exposition of minor efforts.

The Media in the Movies: A Catalog of American Journalism Films, 1900–1996 by Larry Langman (McFarland, 1998) covers the same ground but is more narrow in scope since it is limited to American film, and does not contain those made for television. Langman is a well-known filmographer (entries 1181, 1182, and 1184) who has identified more than 1,000 feature-length films and given them his standard treatment. Entries are alphabetically arranged and supply brief descriptive annotations of films that treat journalists of various types both print and nonprint along with date, running time, studio, director, screenwriter, producer, and cast members.

1184. A Guide to American Silent Crime Films. Larry Langman and Daniel Finn. Westport, CT: Greenwood Press, 1994. 384p. (Bibliographies and Indexes in the Performing Arts, no. 15.) ISBN 0-313-28858-5.

With this work, Langman, a prolific writer of cinema resources (entries 1181, 1182, and 1183n), and Finn began a string of reference books developed in similar style and format on the crime film as part of this series for Greenwood Press. This work focuses on the silent film era and identifies more than 2,000 such films. Arrangement of entries is alphabetical by title with each entry providing information on the production company, director, screenwriter, running time, and principal cast members, as well as brief description of the plot and historical commentary. Included in the interpretation of crime films are what are referred to as subgenres (cops and robbers, detectives, courtroom dramas, mysteries, etc.). It serves to provide a comprehensive record of these productions for serious inquirers as well as film buffs.

The work is continued by the authors' *A Guide to American Crime Films of the Thirties,* number 18 in the series and by *A Guide to American Crime Films of the Forties and Fifties,* number 19, both published in 1995. The former effort treats over 1,100 motion pictures released between 1928, the beginning of the sound era, through 1939. The latter title contains more than 1,200 films issued from 1940 through 1959. These sources focus on feature length movies but provide listings of serials and series related to crime and criminals in the appendixes. Photographs enhance the text in each case.

1185. Handbook of American Film Genres. Wes D. Gehring, ed. New York: Greenwood Press, 1988. 405p. ISBN 0-313-24715-3.

This offering covers the genres of U.S. film in more comprehensive fashion than does any previous publication. It identifies 18 different forms, organized under five broad divisions: action-adventure, comedy, fantastic, songs and soaps, and nontraditional. Within these divisions are chapters devoted to specific genres: adventure films, westerns, gangster films, film noir, social-problem films, screwball comedies, parodies, black humor, and so forth. Film scholars contribute informative essays giving definitions and historical perspective and identifying books and articles on the topic. Coverage of each genre tends to be well developed and insightful and concludes with a brief filmography of important productions of each type. There is an index of names, films, and titles drawn from the essays, filmographies, and publications. Although quality of coverage varies with the contributor, the work is useful to both students and scholars.

1186. Hollywood and American History: A Filmography of Over 250 Motion Pictures Depicting U.S. History. Michael R. Pitts, comp. Jefferson, NC: McFarland, 1984. 332p. (United States in Motion Pictures.) ISBN 0-89950-132-X.

This is a most interesting filmography in terms of content, because included in the definition of history is a wide range of influences representing various aspects of U.S. social and political development. The 250 entries are arranged alphabetically by title and enumerate the production company, date, running time, and color/b&w. Production credits are given for producers, directors, and screenwriters, followed by cast listings, then brief essays summarizing the films' historical context and plot, and, finally, critical interpretation. In many cases the commentaries extend to other, related films. Films represent a variety of themes, from wars to gangsters; in many cases the portrayals represent Hollywood versions rather than historically accurate ones. A conservative political leaning is evident in both inclusions and exclusions, as well as in the commentary. A general index of names, subjects, and titles furnishes access.

1187. Hollywood War Films, 1937–1945: An Exhaustive Filmography. . . Michael S. Shull and David E. Wilt. Jefferson, NC: McFarland, 1996. 482p. ISBN 0-7864-0145-1.

This is a well-researched and informative examination of the attitudes and degree of support for the war effort as determined by enumeration of numerous social factors and their presence in the cinema of this period. There are two major segments, the first of which covers the tense period from 1937, the rise of Hitler through 1941 and the attack on Pearl Harbor. Some 450 motion pictures are analyzed in their treatment of such elements as the military, pacifism, Jews, Germans, appeasement, isolationism, fascist organizations, and so forth. The second section presents the period from 1942 to 1945 from the attack on Pearl Harbor to the end of the War. In this section, there are more than 800 films analyzed for such expressions as those on Japanese American relocation, veterans, atrocities, female labor, and so forth. Entries identify directors, studios, release dates, genre, location, and supply codes based on their inclusion of any of the issues or themes identified. There are several informative appendixes reporting social and political bias, and a good bibliography.

1188. Political Companion to American Film. Gary Crowdus, ed. Chicago: Lake View Press, 1994. 524p. ISBN 0-941702-37-5.

Crowdus is the editor of the reputable critical film journal, *Cineaste,* and has drawn on the talents of many of his associates and fellow scholars and specialists to contribute 101 essays on various aspects examining the political nature of film and filmmaking. The essays are well conceived, articulate, informative, and even entertaining in their treatment of such social and political topics and issues such as Communism and anti-Communism, political assassination, blacklisting, gays and lesbians, Native Americans, African American influences, and so forth. In addition, there is commentary on individual personalities such as Woody Allen, Spike Lee, and Darryl Zanuck. Taking Crowdus's lead, the authors of the essays have provided a provocative and opinionated view in interpreting the political realities they cover. Entries conclude with a bibliography of important works for further reading.

1189. Radicalism in American Silent Films, 1909–1929: A Filmography and History. Michael S. Shull. Jefferson, NC: McFarland, 2000. 345p. ISBN 0-7864-0692-5.

This is another of Shull's efforts in the area of film genre (entry 1180, 1187); this work is well researched and the result is a product that meets the needs and expectations of serious inquirers on the changing treatment accorded radicalism over a period of 20 years. The work opens with monographic coverage of three periods in which the attitudes toward antiestablishment activity changed from encouragement and support in the period 1909–1917, to increasingly unfriendly portrayal with anti-Bolshevik elements in the 1918–1920 period, that continued with a wave of immigration from Eastern Europe in the 1921–1929 years. The filmography consists of 436 silent films and their portrayal of these influences. Arrangement is year by year and entries identify directors, release dates, and so forth, and provide synopses of plots, listings of biases or topics treated, and bibliography. There is a listing of important short films, and a comprehensive index.

Racial, Ethnic, and Gender Influences

1190. African American Films Through 1959: A Comprehensive, Illustrated Filmography. Larry Richards. Jefferson, NC: McFarland, 1998. 312p. ISBN 0-7864-0307-1.

This is a well-developed, carefully researched, and significant source of information on films of varied length having predominantly African American casts or featuring an African American as the lead actor. There are 1,324 entries representing films issued from 1895 through 1959 and include feature length motion pictures, short subjects, soundies (the antecedents of contemporary music videos), documentaries, and even trailers. Entries are arranged alphabetically by title and contain available information concerning production, direction, distribution, cast, date, genre, time, synopsis of plot, and references to sources of reviews. Of great value are the appendixes that list the films chronologically, and provide listings of credits for 1,800 well-known to obscure actors, 200 film companies, as well as producers and directors. Unfortunately, there is no bibliography.

1191. American Film Institute Catalog. Within Our Gates: Ethnicity in American Feature Films, 1911–1960. Alan Gevinson, ed. Berkeley: University of California Press, 1997. 1571p. ISBN 0-520-20964-8.

The catalogs from the American Film Institute are highly regarded as accurate comprehensive records of film production and presentation, generally for a single decade. This work spans a period of 50 years and focuses on those films that treat racial and ethnic experiences in this country. The work is inclusive in its coverage of some 2,500 feature-length motion pictures of varied consequence and origin ranging from blockbuster Hollywood fare to those from independent filmmakers and to those created by various organizations for particular ethnic or racial audiences including those in foreign languages. Entries are arranged alphabetically by title and contain production data, cast lists, genre identification, and detailed plot synopses. Five significant indexes identify films by title, subject, ethnic group, language, and personal names of varied personalities.

1192. The American Indian in Film. Michael Hilger. Metuchen, NJ: Scarecrow, 1986. 196p. ISBN 0-8108-1905-8.

Films with American Indians as characters have always been popular with the U.S. public. More recently there has been much criticism of the adverse treatment given these characters and the less-than-accurate portrayals accorded them. Hilger has furnished a filmography of motion pictures that included either Native American characterization or plot development of substantial proportion. Arrangement of entries is chronological, with the intent being to facilitate scrutiny of the changes occurring over time. There are four major chronological divisions, beginning with silent films and ending with the 1970s–1980s period. Entries provide title, distribution company, date, director, and plot summary, as well as quoted commentary of film reviewers regarding Indian characters. There are black-and-white illustrations. Access is furnished through indexes by actor name and by topic.

1193. Hispanics and United States Film: An Overview and Handbook. Gary D. Keller. Tempe, AZ: Bilingual Press, 1994; repr. 1997. 256p. ISBN 0-927534-40-1.

The first volume of a two-volume set, this work was reprinted at the time of publication of the second volume treated below. It is a compendium of information on the treatment of Hispanics in cinema, and is organized by thematic chapters arranged into chronological sequence. The first chapter is a general account of the depiction of race and ethnicity in motion pictures; this is followed by six chapters beginning with the effect of cultural factors on the depiction of minorities during the period 1903 to 1915 and concluding with the emergence Hispanic filmmaking in the United States in our time. The work analyzes film roles, actors, and types or genres of film relevant to the Hispanic experience. The bibliography is limited in view of the thematic matter.

A Biographical Handbook of Hispanics and United States Film (Bilingual Press, 1997) is the counterpart or sister publication and covers the careers of Hispanic personalities in the film world from 1894 to the present day. In listing the film credits for each of these individuals, the work represents the most complete record of its type. Entries are alphabetically arranged and supply what information is available; both given and stage names, dates of birth and death, birthplaces, awards, and so forth as well as a listing of film credits. The bibliography is detailed and comprehensive, thus correcting the shortcoming of the first volume.

1194. A Guide to Latin American, Caribbean, and U.S. Latino-Made Film and Video. Karen Ranucci and Julie Feldman, eds. Lanham, MD: Scarecrow Press, 1998. 361p. ISBN 0-8108-3285-2.

This guide identifies nearly 450 films and videos available in this country and covers Latin American nations as well as the United States. Entries are arranged by country of origin, then alphabetically by title. There are no cast lists but they identify original title and English translation, director, producer, running time, year, and furnish detailed synopses. These entries are especially useful to educators with inclusion of a section on "strengths and weaknesses" contributed by at least three reviewers or critics, as well as indication of suitable audience level and suggestion for introducing the film in teaching situations. Many entries contain supplementary reading lists. There are several indexes supplying access by subjects, distributors, Spanish and Portuguese titles, and English titles.

The Hispanic Image on the Silver Screen: An Interpretive Filmography from Silents into Sound, 1898–1935 by Alfred C. Richard, Jr. (Greenwood Press, 1992) examines the negative and demeaning portrayal of Hispanics by Hollywood over a period of 40 years. Coverage is given to over 1,800 films treating Hispanic issues, themes, and characters. Entries are listed chronologically and describe the film and its Hispanic connection. There are indexes by title, name of actors and actresses, subject, and country. The work was to serve as the initial volume of a projected set, but thus far it stands alone.

1195. Images in the Dark: An Encyclopedia of Gay and Lesbian Film and Video. Raymond Murray. New York: TLA Video Management, 1994. 573p. ISBN 1-880-70701-2.

This is a comprehensive filmography that also contains biographical treatment of 200 gay, lesbian, or bisexual directors, actors, writers, artists, and composers. Biographical entries are treated in the first three chapters and contain brief summaries of the individual's contributions to cinema, and information on his or her private life. This is followed by a listing of the person's film credits with date of release, running time, country of origin, and evaluative commentary. There is an emphasis on Anglo-Americans, but individuals from other countries are included. The remaining six chapters identify more than 3,000 films with gay or lesbian themes and are organized by type of audience appeal; "queer" denoting appeal to gays and lesbians alike, along with "gay," "lesbian," and "transgender." In addition there is a chapter on "cheesy" films, and the final chapter treats films with gays, lesbians, and transsexuals in secondary roles. There are many photographs, and indexing is detailed to assure access.

1196. Is that a Gun in Your Pocket?: Women's Experience of Power in Hollywood. Rachel Abramowitz. New York; Random House, 2000. 494p. ISBN 0-679-43754-1.

Author Abramowitz is knowledgeable of the Hollywood scene and as a writer for *Premiere* magazine has access to the rich and powerful. She provides a compelling narrative that has been labeled as a "combination oral history, cogent biography, and delicious gab-fest." She interviewed 150 women involved in the industry as executives, producers, and directors, and is able to furnish insight into the inherent narcissism, dedication, boundless energy, and drive that leads to success in that environment. Of course, there is price to be paid and the author documents the conflicts, self-doubts, and sacrifices. Beginning with the 1997 funeral of Dawn Steel, the studio head who died of a brain tumor, the work examines the lives and careers of powerful women such as Sherry Lansing, Sue Mengers, Barbara Streisand, Jodie Foster, and Polly Platt. The user is able to get a full picture of these personalities.

1197. Vishnu in Hollywood: The Changing Image of the American Male. David I. Grossvogel. Lanham, MD: Scarecrow Press, 2000. 225p. ISBN 0-8108-3767-6.

This is a brief but informative historical overview and exposition of the male movie hero, a product for which society must take its share of responsibility in its creation. Male heroes of the cinema were, and continue to be, projections of the American male; this work examines the changing nature of that social market and analyzes the psychological and sociological existence. Beginning with the strong, silent, and resourceful early western hero, William S. Hart, we are able to see his influence in the later development of John Wayne and Gary Cooper in contrast to the exotic appeal of Rudolph Valentino and Charles Boyer. Along with these men, there are the diverse personalities of Cary Grant, James Stewart, Spencer Tracy, Marlon Brando, and James Dean, all of whom served to provide the public with desired heroic images.

THEATER AND STAGE

Reviews of theatrical productions published in the *New York Times* can be located through *The New York Times Theatre Reviews, 1920–1970* (New York Times, 1971. 10v), with coverage continuing on a biennial basis ever since. Earlier retrospective coverage has been provided through a five-volume set published in 1976 covering the years 1870–1919. *The New York Theatre Critics Review* (Theatre Critics Review, 1940–1995) furnished copy of reviews as they appeared in a variety of New York newspapers and periodicals and even on television. Frequency varied through the years from weekly to monthly, and cumulative indexes were issued for 1961–1972 and 1973–1986. The work is continued by *National Theatre Critics' Reviews,* a semi-monthly publication.

The Theatre Historical Society of America (available at http://www. historictheatres.org) was founded in 1968–1969 and immediately began offering *The Marquee* as a quarterly journal. It also supplies members a quarterly newsletter and an annual special publication. It operates out of Elmhurst, Illinois, and has 1,000 members.

General Sources

1198. American Theatre Companies, 1749–1887. Weldon B. Durham. New York: Greenwood Press, 1986. 598p. ISBN 0-313-20886-7.

The first of a three-volume set on resident acting companies in the United States, this work covers a most interesting and creative period, 1749–1887. Included are P.T. Barnum's American Museum Stock Company and the Thalia Theatre Company, a prominent and successful German-language troupe in New York City. Coverage begins with the first important English-speaking company in the colonies and continues through the creation of the last company organized and managed in the style of the English playhouse. A total of 81 theater groups are treated. Entries provide dates and locations of operation, managers, description of artistic and business practices, performers, designers, technicians, and other information. An analytical description of the group's repertory and a bibliography of published and archival resources for further study are included. The excellent factual analysis makes this an important tool.

American Theatre Companies, 1888–1930, also edited by Durham (1987), is the second volume of the series and continues the first-rate coverage, with treatment of 105 more companies ranging over a span of 40-plus years. *American Theatre Companies, 1931–*

1986 (1989) completes Durham's effort on behalf of Greenwood Press, extending coverage an additional 55 years.

1199. Annals of the New York Stage. George C.D. Odell. New York: Columbia University, 1927–1949. 15v.

This massive set chronicles the period from 1699 to 1894 and remains the legacy of a single individual who persevered in the effort for more than 20 years. Unfortunately, Odell was to fall short of his goal of reaching the year 1900, but his scholarship, care, and attention to detail have enabled thousands of scholars, researchers, students, and critics to draw upon a wealth of well-organized information. Each volume proceeds in chronological sequence, covering a period of years (volume 1, to 1789; volume 2, to 1821; and so on). Included in the record are the actors, plays, theaters, critical commentary, and historical background of the period. Plays are identified along with cast listings and comments from contemporary critics and reviewers. Many portraits of now-obscure performers are included, for which access has been facilitated through the publication of the *Index to the Portraits in Odell's Annals of the New York Stage* (American Society for Theatre Research, 1963).

The Encyclopedia of the New York Stage, 1920–1930, edited by Samuel Leiter (Greenwood Press, 1985) in two volumes, is the first of a series designed to describe legitimate plays of every type produced either on or off-Broadway. The pattern of coverage identifies type, author, lyricist, director, opening date, and so on, along with plot description and critical commentary. Each title covers a decade. Subsequently, Leiter has furnished an additional two volumes: *The Encyclopedia of the New York Stage, 1930–1940* (issued in 1989) and *The Encyclopedia of the New York Stage, 1940–1950* (1992).

1200. Best Plays of 1894/1899–1989 and Yearbook of the Drama in America. New York: Dodd, Mead, 1920–1989. ISSN 0276-2625. 1990–. Ann.

This annual review of play production has been an excellent vehicle for keeping abreast of developments in the world of theater. Although the title has varied in the past, as did the frequency in the early years, it is now simply referred to as the Best Plays series, or "Burns Mantle" after its initial editor. Mantle provided retrospective coverage of the early years with two volumes: *1899/1909* (1944) and *1909/1919* (1933). These volumes identify plays and furnish lists of plays produced with date, theater, and cast. The annual began in 1920 under Mantle and, after his death in 1948, continued under others, who also completed the final retrospective volume, *1894/1989,* in 1955. The annuals furnished digests and descriptions of selected plays, including author, number of performances, theater, and cast. Various listings of actors, productions, awards, and statistics were offered. There are indexes of authors, plays, casts, and producers.

In 1990, the annual was renamed *The Burns Mantle Theater Yearbook* (Applause Theater Book Publishers), edited by Otis L. Guernsey and Jeffrey Sweet. Subsequently, the work retained its earlier name; the current issue is titled *Best Plays of 1999–2000* and is still edited by Guernsey (Limelight Editions, 2000). The series is now called *Otis Guernsey/ Burns Mantle Theatre Yearbook.* Guernsey's *Directory of the American Theater, 1894– 1971* (Dodd, Mead, 1971) is a convenient index to the series by author, title, and composer for a period of over 75 years.

1201. Cambridge Guide to American Theatre. Upd. ed. Don B. Wilmeth and Tice L. Miller, eds. New York: Cambridge University Press, 1996. 463p. ISBN 0-521-40134-8.

This is another of the excellent handbooks bearing the imprint of Cambridge University and provides encyclopedic coverage of personalities, plays, entertainment venues and topics relevant to the study of theater in this country. Some 2,300 entries are furnished by 80 specialists in the field; they are arranged alphabetically and provide brief but accurate description along with suggestions for further reading. A variety of elements are presented with the inclusion of circus, vaudeville, and burlesque along with mainstream theater. In addition, there are about 100 topical descriptions of elements such as Yiddish, African American, and Asian American ethnic theater, alternative gay and lesbian production, and theater in various cities. Both historical and contemporary subjects are examined and a biographical index contains more than 3,000 names. There is a lengthy bibliography.

1202. Cambridge History of American Theatre. Don B. Wilmeth and Christopher Bigsby, eds. New York: Cambridge University Press, 1998–2001. 3v. ISBN 0-521-47204-0 (v. 1); 0-521-65179-4 (v. 2); 0-521-66959-6 (v. 3).

This is a remarkable and well-developed set of historical accounts, each treating a period of time in chronological sequence. With the help of several specialists who contributed well-written and authoritative in-depth topical essays, the initial volume covered the period from the beginnings to 1870 and set the pattern for this stylized and important work. The volume opens with an informative introduction and is followed by a useful chronology identifying theater events within the context of social, political, and cultural developments from 1492 to 1870. The main text examines the world of theater in terms of actors and performance, playwrights, stagecraft, and so forth, with informative essays that include bibliographies. Volume 2 (1870–1945) followed the same pattern as did volume 3 (post–World War II to the 1990s). The work is both scholarly and entertaining.

1203. Catalog of the Theatre and Drama Collections. New York Public Library, Research Libraries. Boston: G.K. Hall, 1967–76. 51v. **Supp.** 1973. 3v. **Ann. Supp.** 1976–. ISSN 0360-2788.

Another of the important G.K. Hall efforts is this massive reproduction of the card catalog of the New York Public Library's outstanding collection of theater and drama materials established in 1931. This catalog has been published in several parts related to different components of the collection. Parts I and II were published in 1967. Part I, *Drama Collection: Author Listing* (6v.) and *Listing by Cultural Origin* (6v.), consists of 120,000 entries for plays published separately or in anthologies or even in periodicals. Part II, *Theatre Collection: Books on the Theatre,* has over 120,000 entries from over 23,500 volumes relating to all aspects of the theater (history, biography, acting, etc.). A 548-page supplement to part I and a two-volume supplement to part II were published in 1973. Part III, *Non-Book Collection,* was published in 30 volumes in 1975 and represents over 740,000 cards on such items as programs, photographs, portraits, and press clippings.

Coverage for parts I and II has been continued by an annual supplement, *Bibliographic Guide to Theatre Arts,* since 1976. This work lists materials newly cataloged by the New York Public Library, with additional entries furnished from the Library of Congress MARC tapes.

1204. The Federal Theatre Project: A Catalog-Calendar of Productions. Fenwick Library, George Mason University. New York: Greenwood Press, 1986. 349p. (Bibliographies and Indexes in the Performing Arts, no. 3.) ISBN 0-313-22314-9.

The Federal Theatre Project (FTP) was a product of the New Deal carried out through the WPA (Works Progress Administration). It was the only federally funded theater in this country and operated between 1935 and 1939, employing many professionals and helping young people to shape their careers. Hopes for a permanent national theater, unfortunately, were shattered by mounting criticism regarding the FTP's moral and political character. The materials from the project were housed in the archives of George Mason University's Fenwick Library on indefinite loan from the Library of Congress and remained in the archives section for 10 years between 1974 and 1984. This catalog calendar identifies nearly 2,800 individual productions, arranged alphabetically by title and including date and location of performance, theater, and name of director or choreographer. Materials in the collection are identified and indexed and include costume and set designs, play scripts, music, photographs, and programs, among other things.

Louis A. Rachow's *Theatre and Performing Arts Collections* (Haworth, 1981) surveys half a dozen of the important special collections in articles written by the curators or heads of the collections. Included are the Billy Rose Theatre Collection at the New York Public Library and the Library of Congress.

1205. Notable Names in the American Theatre. New and rev. ed. Clifton, NJ: J.T. White, 1976; repr. Gale Group, 1992. 1250p. ISBN 0-883-71018-8.

As the second edition of Walter Rigdon's *Biographical Encyclopedia and Who's Who of the American Theatre* (Heinemann, 1966), this work is useful although aging. Its nine major sections provide comprehensive coverage. Included are segments listing New York productions, 1900–1974, U.S. premiers, and U.S. plays abroad, listing title, author, date, and run. Also furnished are theater group bibliographies, New York theater buildings, and listings of awards. Important coverage is given to biographical bibliography, through references to books about theater personalities, and to necrology, through a comprehensive listing of deceased individuals from the colonial period to the present. The major segment is, of course, that on notable names, providing detailed biographical descriptions of then-living individuals (many of whom are now deceased). Actors, designers, producers, and writers of all levels of achievement are included. Gale Group published a slightly updated version of this work in 1992, calling it the third edition.

1206. The Oxford Companion to American Theatre. 2nd ed. Gerald M. Bordman. New York: Oxford, 1992. 735p. ISBN 0-19-507246-4.

This is the second edition of a specialized version of the Oxford Companion series, and it provides a comprehensive source of information on the U.S. theater. A continued strength is the biographical coverage of performers, playwrights, composers, librettists, choreographers, producers, managers, directors, and designers, as well as orchestrators, photographers, publicists, critics, scholars, and even architects. Represented in addition to the legitimate stage are various forms of live theater, such as minstrel shows and vaudeville. Unlike *The Oxford Companion to the Theatre* (Oxford, 1983), this volume covers individual plays, musicals, and revues. There are more than 3,000 entries providing production date, plot, summary, and commentary. The updated version adds personalities, groups, and plays appearing since the 1983 effort. Organizations, companies, unions, clubs, societies, periodicals, and newspapers are included, making this an extremely welcome resource for the specialist and layperson alike.

An abridged version was issued in 1987 by Bordman as *The Concise Oxford Companion to American Theatre* (repr. 1990). It eliminated about 280 pages of the original by deleting minor plays and personalities, retaining only the material of greater interest. It continues to serve well the popular good.

1207. The Tony Award: A Complete Listing of Winners and Nominees of the American Theatre Wing's Tony Award with a History of the American Theatre Wing. Upd. ed. Isabelle Stevenson and Roy A. Somlyo, eds. Portsmouth, NH: Heinemann, 2001. 224p.

This is an updated edition of the work issued last in 1994. Of interest to the historian are the essays describing the origin and development of both the Tony Awards and the American Theatre Wing, which founded the Tonys. These brief but informative expositions cover the major points in readable fashion. The major focus of the tool is a complete listing of recipients of and nominees for the Antoinette Perry (Tony) Awards over a period of 50 years, from 1947 to 2000. Arrangement of entries is chronological by year. All major categories of the awards are included in both the performance and technical operations. There are additional listings of regulations and theaters eligible for competition. There are indexes of winners of both regular and special category awards. First issued in 1975 by Arno, the title was continued by Crown Publishing with updates in 1980, 1984, 1987, and 1989. Since then, Heinemann has been the publisher.

The listings are also available at the official Web site of the *American Theatre Wing's Tony Awards* (available at http://www.tonys.org) by clicking on "Tony Archives."

Genre Theater

1208. American Song: The Complete Musical Theatre Companion. Ken Bloom. 2nd ed. New York: Schirmer Books/ Simon & Schuster, 1996. 2v. ISBN 0-02-870484-3.

Bloom has done for the song in musical theater what he accomplished for its treatment in Hollywood (entry 1172) in presenting a comprehensive factual record of song and performance. This updates and expands the initial edition published some 11 years earlier by going farther back to 1877 as his starting point and bringing the coverage to 1995. Nearly 4,900 musicals are identified with the inclusion of every Broadway, off-Broadway, and off-off-Broadway musical play during the period of coverage. In addition, there are resident theater productions that closed out of town before reaching Broadway, selected night club shows, nonmusical plays that contained songs, vaudeville, burlesque, and more. Some 42,000 songs are indexed along with nearly 60,000 personalities associated with them. Entries are arranged alphabetically by name of show and supply adequate identification of production facts and personalities.

1209. American Theatre: A Chronicle of Comedy and Drama. Gerald M. Bordman and Thomas S. Hischak, eds. New York: Oxford University Press, 1994–2001. 4v. ISBN 0-19-503764-2 (v. 1); 0-19-509078 (v. 2); 0-19-509079-9 (v. 3); 0-19-512347-6 (v. 4).

Initially planned as a three volume work, this detailed listing and well-constructed diary of events begins with the period 1869–1914 (volume 1), continues with 1914–1930 (volume 2), progresses to 1930–1969 (volume 3), and concludes with 1969–2000 (volume 4). The first three volumes have been edited by Bordman, whereas Hischak assumed responsibility for the final volume. The set provides a well-conceived and thorough documentation of American theater from the period following the Civil War to the present day. Presentation is year-by-year and coverage is essentially limited to New York theater. There is an introductory narrative furnishing a summary of major developments for each year, and this is followed by description of major plays in order of opening. Included here are brief biographies of significant personalities relevant to the plays described.

1210. Broadway, the Golden Years: Jerome Robbins and the Great Choreographer-Directors, 1940 to the Present. Robin E. Long. New York: Continuum Publishing, 2001. 312p. ISBN 0-8264-1347-1.

The author is a well-known critic and writer who obviously wanted to share his thoughts on the most successful choreographers in the business rather than produce a survey of personalities who had performed in that capacity. Six great choreographers are profiled with emphasis on Jerome Robbins who is featured in the title and receives three chapters of coverage. Also included are Agnes de Mille, Bob Fosse, Gower Champion, Michael Bennett, and Tommy Tune. The artists' careers are documented in thorough manner and analysis is provided of their impact, influence, and critical achievement. Long-utilized archival and personal written sources, as well as statements from critics and colleagues, reveal the stories and provide commentary. There is an epilogue to the work as well as a well-chosen bibliography, and detailed index.

1211. Chronology of American Musical Theatre. Richard C. Norton. New York: Oxford University Press, 2002. 3v. ISBN 0-19-508888-3.

Comprehensive and thorough, this well-researched set provides an extraordinary coverage of the musical theater in this country season-by-season beginning with the 1866–1867 period and concluding with the end of 1997. In addition, there is coverage of earlier musicals offered to the American public since the latter part of the eighteenth century. Entries identify more than 3,000 musical productions, and provide all the production information culled from playbills and opening night programs for musicals, operettas, revues, and so forth, that played on Broadway and off-Broadway. Data includes cast lists, dates of opening and closing, number of performances, songs and musical numbers in sequence, technical personnel, and more.

American Musical Theatre by Gerald Bordman, now in its third edition (Oxford, 2001) covers some of the same ground at about one-fourth the price. American musicals, operettas, revues, touring troupes, and one-person shows are chronicled season-by-season and show-by-show from the beginnings to the 1999/2000 season. There is descriptive and evaluative narrative as well as production data. The work is indexed by song titles as well as personalities and titles of shows.

Ethnic, Racial, and Gender Influences

1212. The African American Theatre Directory, 1816–1960: A Comprehensive Guide. . . Bernard L. Peterson, Jr. Westport, CT: Greenwood Press, 1997. 301p. ISBN 0-313-29537-9.

This work is a well-conceived and useful effort in providing a thorough and comprehensive directory of more than 600 professional, semi-professional, and college stage organizations, acting troupes, and significant theaters from the beginnings of black theater with the founding of the African Company in the early years of the nineteenth century to 1960. Entries are arranged alphabetically and vary in length from a single sentence to several pages. They identify dates, type of theater or group, and when possible plays performed, cast members, and directors. Many of these personalities are described in a follow-up work (entry below). The work opens with an introductory essay by Errol Hill that places black theater into historical perspective. Useful appendixes supply lists of theaters that have not been included as well as those that were, and listings by type.

Peterson's *Profiles of African Stage Performers and Theatre People, 1816–1960* (Greenwood Press, 2000) serves as a counterpart to the work above in supplying biographical sketches of 500 personalities associated with black theater over the years. Many of them were identified in the earlier work, and represent a variety of roles and positions (actors, choreographers, stage managers, etc.). Similarly there is a wide range of familiarity from those who remain famous to those who, today, are obscure and all but forgotten.

1213. African-American Performance and Theatre History: A Critical Reader. Harry J. Elam and David Krasner, eds. New York: Oxford University Press, 2000. 384p. ISBN 0-19-512725-0.

The editors are academics and well-known specialists in the topic who have selected a group of 14 scholars to join them as contributors in producing this critical anthology of essays treating the social, cultural, and political as impact, reception, and role of black performers and theaters in this country. The essays are organized into four major sections beginning with the category of social protest and representation. This is followed by the segment on cultural traditions and cultural memory, then by analysis of the mix of race and gender, and finally by interpretation of African American performance. The work as a whole provides needed insight not only into the history and culture of black theater, but the impact of race on the workings of society as a whole. A final section serves to provide a concluding summary with a roundtable discussion with senior scholars.

1214. Chicanas/Latinas in American Theatre: A History of Performance. Elizabeth C. Ramirez. Bloomington, IN: Indiana University Press, 2000. 188p. ISBN 0-253-33714-3.

The author has provided an absorbing and enlightening historical survey of the influences and societal forces that have shaped the development of Latin American theater and the part women have played in its reaching a position of prominence and acceptance in the United States. The work opens with an informative introductory essay providing an overview of Latin American drama and performance on the American stage. The main text is presented in six chapters beginning with its origins in the homeland. Following that is an analysis of the role of the Mexican Revolution in chapter 2, while chapter 3 treats social protest and political performance. This leads in to emergence of Latina performance in chapter 4, and to emergence of the Latina playwright in chapter 5. The final chapter examines current trends and an epilogue analyzes legacies and changing developments.

A specialized tool is *A History of Hispanic Theatre in the United States: Origins to 1940* by Nicolas Kanellos (University of Texas Press, 1990). The work describes the development of playhouses and theatrical groups in the United States, Spain, Mexico, and Puerto Rico from the nineteenth century through the first decades of the twentieth century.

1215. Yiddish Proletarian Theatre. Edna Nahshon. Westport, CT: Greenwood Press, 1998. 288p. ISBN 0-313-29063-6.

The author is an academic expert in the study of Jewish theatrical performance, and has produced a useful history and analysis of Artef, the major Yiddish theater company in the United States. As part of the New York theater scene from its inception in 1925 as a radical workers' theater group linked to the American Communist Party to its demise in 1940 with the signing of the Nonagression Pact between Russia and Germany, Artef was a leading voice and performing element in the Theatre of Social Consciousness; its move to Broadway in 1934 was indicative of its status as the single biggest factor in the city regarded as the capital of Yiddish theatrical performance. This work examines the heritage, traditions, artistic, ideological, and economic aspects of Artef's life within the context of political and cultural movements of the time, and serves as a mirror of the historical fabric of the American Left.

SPORTS AND GAMES

Because of the U.S. fascination for spectator sports, there are many almanacs, guides, statistical handbooks, and other information sources of a popular nature, many of which are issued periodically. Included here are representative sources that serve the needs of both popular and scholarly interests. *Sport Bibliography* (Human Kinetics Publishers, 1986–) is an annual listing of monographs, articles, and theses from all over the world. Of course, U.S. sport receives a good proportion of the coverage, and historical treatment is frequent. The bibliography is available online through DIALOG in a file of over 250,000 records. A similar effort on CD-ROM is *Sport Discus,* which identifies articles, monographs, dissertations, report, and proceedings on an international basis. Beginning in 1981, it draws from over 2,000 periodicals and furnishes abstracts for most entries.

The North American Society for Sport History (available at http://www.nassh.org) was founded in 1972 at Pennsylvania State University in University Park. It has some 900 members and publishes the *Journal of Sport History* three times per year.

General Sources

1216. Athletes and Coaches of Summer. New York: Macmillan Reference USA, 2000. 544p. (Macmillan Profiles). ISBN 0-02-865493-5.

From the publisher's series designed to provide biographical and career information of significant personalities (or events) for students from middle school through high school level, comes two sister publications dealing with sports figures of seasonal impact. This effort focuses on the summer sports and covers men and women associated with baseball, women's basketball, track and field, golf, boxing, auto racing, horse racing, and tennis. The work presents an interesting mix of individuals and includes broadcasters along with players and coaches and even great horses like Seattle Slew and Secretariat. There are 193 entries that vary in length from two to four pages and supply biographical narratives, career timelines, and photographs.

Athletes and Coaches of Winter (Macmillan Reference USA, 2000) is fashioned in the same manner and examines the lives and careers of 159 figures representing the major sports of basketball, football and hockey, as well as the less popular spectator sports of skiing and figure skating. There are single-page expositions of such significant events as the NBA finals, college bowl games, winter Olympics, and so forth.

1217. Biographical Dictionary of American Sports. Rev. ed. David L. Porter. Westport, CT: Greenwood Press, 2000. 2v. ISBN 0-313-31174-9 (v. 1). 0-313-31175-7 (v. 2).

Porter produced the initial volumes of this set in 1986 on baseball (entry 1229) and on football (entry 1240). They were followed by volumes on outdoor sports (see below) and on indoor sports including basketball (see below). Succeeding volumes acted as supplements and provided coverage of all sports on a three-year basis (1986–1989, 1989–1992, 1992–1995). They employed a similar format and when taken together treated some 3,000 important figures (athletes, coaches, administrators, etc.).The two volumes in the current effort add more than 600 personalities (only 30 of them are women) to the total. Entries average about a page in length and identify various figures in baseball, football, basketball, golf, swimming, auto racing, and more.

The *Biographical Dictionary of American Sports: Outdoor Sports* (Greenwood Press, 1988) describes figures in such competitive ventures as auto racing, golf, lacrosse, horse racing, skiing, soccer, speed skating, tennis, and track and field. About 520 major personalities are covered in brief biographical sketches. The initial volume on basketball, *Biographical Dictionary of American Sports: Basketball and Other Indoor Sports* (1989) includes a number of other indoor sports, some of minor significance to the U.S. viewing and cheering public. Of the nearly 560 personalities, more than half are basketball players, officials, and other notables. Representation also is given to bowling, boxing, hockey, swimming, weightlifting, diving, skating, gymnastics, and wrestling. These titles also are updated by the general source above.

1218. Encyclopedia of Ethnicity and Sports in the United States. George B. Kirsch et al., eds. Westport, CT: Greenwood Press, 2000. 544p. ISBN 0-313-29911-0.

This work opens with an introductory segment describing the process of assimilation of various sporting cultures into mainstream sports and defining the concept and treatment of ethnicity. It provides distinction between the mainstream sporting influences and activities brought over and established by the original British colonists and those traditions brought over by subsequent ethnic immigrants. The sporting activities of Native Americans, African Americans, Eastern Europeans and other immigrant cultures dating from the colonial times to the present are presented. Entries vary in length from half a page to several pages and treat racial and ethnic groups, ethnic games, mainstream sports, ethnic and racial institutions, and significant personalities. Each one concludes with a reading list. There is a general bibliography and detailed index to provide access.

1219. The Encyclopedia of North American Sports History. Ralph Hickok. New York: Facts on File, 1992. 516p. ISBN 0-8160-2096-5.

Games and sports have been an important part of human civilization since its beginnings. This comprehensive one-volume encyclopedia furnishes over 1,000 entries that include personalities, events, awards, stadiums, organizations, and other subjects pertinent to the history of sports on this continent. The work is of interest to inquirers at all levels; entries tend to be brief but informative, with baseball receiving the most coverage (some 3,000 words). In any one-volume effort of this type, the challenges will generally represent omissions of favorite personalities and scant coverage of favorite pastimes. Most interesting is the treatment given to the history and development of the various sports. There is a bibliography of several pages and many large photographs. There is a subject index to furnish access.

A recent work with a unique format is the *Atlas of American Sport* by John F. Rooney, Jr. and Richard Pillsbury (Macmillan, 1993). The title identifies regional differences in games played by Americans through maps by state, city, and zip code area. It also furnishes essays and photographs and shows both individual and team sports as they reflect American culture.

1220. Sports: A Reference Guide, 1980–1999. Donald L. Deardorff and Robert J. Higgs. Westport, CT: Greenwood Press, 2000. 361p. (American Popular Culture.) ISBN 0-313-30445-9.

Another of the entries from the Greenwood series on popular culture, this work furnishes a brief history of sports in the United States with emphasis on the past two decades. It serves as a companion effort to *Sports: A Reference* Guide by Higgs (Greenwood Press, 1982). The current effort contains 12 essays examining sports in cultural, social, legal, business, education, gender, and other contexts. The historian will especially appreciate coverage given to history of sports. Essays describe the scholarly and popular book literature and provide historical summaries of each topic. Each essay or chapter concludes with a bibliography, and description of periodicals that might be relevant. There is an index of subjects, authors, and titles.

A useful guide for both researchers and fans is *Sports Halls of Fame: A Directory of Over 100 Sports Museums in the United States* by Doug Gelbert (McFarland, 1992). The work is organized into three sections covering national halls, single-sport museums and multi-sport halls, and local attractions. There is a geographic listing and an index to facilitate access.

1221. Sports: The Complete Visual Reference. Francois Fortin. Willowdale, Ont: Firefly Books, 2000. ISBN 1-55209-540-1.

This is a comprehensive reference source in terms of its breadth of coverage and treatment of a wide variety of sports and sporting cultures and in its intent to provide awareness of the history, spectacle, and impact of sport on contemporary culture. Nearly 130 different sports are organized under 20 categorical headings (track and field with some 20 events, gymnastics with four activities, aquatic sports with 13, ball sports (small ball) with 7, ball sports (large ball) with 9, etc.). Each entry is two to three pages in length and supplies descriptive narrative, photographs and other visuals, and various facts in boxed format). Information regarding rules, strategies, training, unique challenges, and personalities of historical importance is presented in a manner designed to appeal to youngsters from junior high school through high school. A general index provides access.

1222. Sports Leagues and Teams: An Encyclopedia 1871–1996. Mack Pollak. Jefferson City, NC: McFarland, 1997. 716p. ISBN 0-7864-0252-0.

A comprehensive record book that provides data on leagues and their teams throughout the United States, this work treats all sports and all professional leagues regardless of their level of accomplishment. Sports vary from the vastly popular spectator sports; football, baseball, basketball, and moderately popular hockey, to the less frequently watched bowling, golf, tennis, lacrosse, soccer, softball, rodeo, volleyball, and so forth. Specialized leagues such as those currently or historically comprise women, African Americans, and seniors are included. Some 200 leagues are profiled with 3,200 teams. Chapters treat the sports individually and provide a brief history of each league in chronological order. Individual teams and their cities are identified and data regarding their names, playing field, championships won, and current status are given. Detailed indexes supply access.

The Olympics

1223. The Complete Book of the Summer Olympics: Sydney, 2000. David Wallechinsky. Woodstock, NY: Overlook Press, 2000. 928p. ISBN 1-58567-046-4.

Known for his compilation of listings and statistics in *The People's Almanac* (Bantam, 1978) and *The Book of Lists* (Morrow, 1980), Wallechinsky turned his attention to the Olympics in 1984, and since then has turned out a companion to these games in every year they have been played. These are published prior to the games being played that year, and therefore contain statistics, listings, and photographs for the games that run up to but not including the publication year. There is a highly informative introductory essay to the work describing the history of the Olympic games as well as the issues and controversies surrounding them. Treatment is given to every sport and entries present facts, figures, stories, anecdotes, and more in reporting the results of every event ever conducted; the rules for each competition are given.

The Complete Book of the Winter Olympics: Salt Lake City, 2002 (Overlook, 2001) is the companion effort and the reporting is done in the same manner. The work is strong on history, commentary, and insight, and like its counterpart, represents thorough and careful research.

1224. Results of the Early Modern Olympics Series. Bill Mallon. Jefferson, NC: McFarland, 1997–2000. v. 1–5. **The 1896 Olympic Games: Results for All Competitors in All Events, with Commentary.** 1997. (v. 1) ISBN 0-7864-0379-9. **The 1900 Olympic Games. . .** 1997. (v. 2) ISBN 0-7864-0378-0. **The 1904 Olympic Games. . .** 1999. (v. 3) ISBN 0-7864-0550-3. **The 1906 Olympic Games. . .** 1999. (v. 4) ISBN 0-7864-0551-1. **The 1908 Olympic Games. . .** 2000. (v. 5) ISBN 0-7864-0598-8. **The 1912 Olympic Games. . .** 2002. (v. 7) ISBN 0-7864-1047-7.

The series represents a comprehensive effort by the author who provides a thorough examination of the early days of the modern Olympic games. One more volume remains to be completed that will cover the 1920 events. Emphasis is on statistical data in enumerating sites, dates, events, athletes, and participating countries with reporting of results, but there is both analysis and commentary giving the user real insight into the debates, arguments, and controversies behind the conduct of the games each year. Events are listed alphabetically. The author is a physician and active enthusiast of the Olympic games, and is cofounder of the International Society of Olympic Historians (ISOH) (available at http://www.olykamp.org/isoh/). The Society publishes a journal three times per year, currently titled *Journal of Olympic History*.

1225. The Olympics: A History of the Modern Games. 2nd ed. Allen Guttman. Champaign/Urbana: University of Illinois Press, 2002. 214p. (Illinois History of Sports.) ISBN 0-252-07046-1.

In contrast to the entry above, this work supplies a compact one-volume history of the modern Olympic games from the 1896 events to the 2000 competition by a leading sports historian and writer. In this work, Guttman has updated the initial edition that ended with the 1988 Olympics. He continues his probing analysis and commentary in providing a social history in which the politics, economics, religious significance and personalities involved receive significant treatment along with the athletic events and their conduct. Scandals, questionable awarding of sites, drug influences, and increasing prominence of female athletes are presented as part of the mix. Apparently the modern games were revived with the idea of providing political messages. One is able to understand the importance of the games to political figures, and the ambitions and maneuvering taking place within the International Olympic Committee.

Baseball

1226. The Ballplayers: Baseball's Ultimate Biographical Reference. Mike Shatzkin et al., eds. New York: Arbor House/William Morrow, 1990. 1,230p. ISBN 0-87795-984-6.

The most comprehensive of the biographical works on baseball, this well-illustrated tool covers more than 6,000 players and managers and another 1,000 umpires, broadcasters, front office types, scouts, and so on. Also included are players from the Japanese, Mexican, and Negro leagues. There is excellent coverage given to historical figures—about 1,000 of the listed personalities date back to the nineteenth century. Entries are arranged alphabetically and offer biographical sketches varying in length from a few sentences to several pages. Sketches identify position, team, nickname, years of service, career statistics, and achievements. Awards, all-star selections, World Series performances, and other information of interest to baseball enthusiasts and researchers are also provided. The various contributors have signed their entries and are listed separately at the end.

1227. Baseball: An Encyclopedia of Popular Culture. Edward J. Rielly. Santa Barbara, CA: ABC-CLIO, 2000. 371p. ISBN 1-57607-103-0.

This is an unusual reference source in its focus on baseball as part of popular culture. In this regard, it examines a variety of current and historical topics: personalities, concepts, groups, events, phenomena, ballparks, and so forth that have had an impact on American society and culture. There are some 230 entries covering them in alphabetical sequence; they generally vary in length from 200 to 1,500 words, but provide even more extensive treatment of fundamental issues such as "women's baseball" and "night baseball." Personalities selected include players, owners, commissioners, authors, announcers, and more. Due to the cultural focus, such figures as Ernest Hemingway, Mark Twain, and Walt Whitman are included along with Babe Ruth, Roy Campanella, George Steinbrenner, and Sammy Sosa.

The McFarland Baseball Quotations Dictionary edited by David H. Nathan (McFarland, 2000) is an update of the editor's initial effort published a decade earlier. Quotes vary in terms of poignancy and humor, and are categorized by topic such as "attitude problems," Certain famous language abusers like Yogi Berra, Ralph Kiner, and Casey Stengel have their own sections. The work is indexed by name and by subject.

1228. Total Baseball: The Official Encyclopedia of Major League Baseball. 7th ed. John Thorn et al. Kingston, NY: Total Sports, 2001. 2600p. ISBN 1-930844-01-8.

This is considered by most users to be the most complete compendium of baseball information in terms of its thorough treatment of statistics, records, rosters, registers, histories, and most importantly, its enlightening essays. It is a massive work for which many expert contributors provided assistance. Several hundred biographical sketches are supplied along with detailed information on the changes that have taken place in the game since 1876, game summaries of every tie-breaking playoff game, and records of every player who participated in playoffs. More than 15,000 major-league and minor-league players are identified along with statistical treatment of their careers and in many cases, the stories behind them. An interesting feature of this edition is a special section on the history of the home run.

Baseball: The Biographical Encyclopedia edited by David Pietrusza and others (Total Sports, 2000) joins the work above as another massive effort by the publisher, this time in producing a comprehensive source focused on biographical coverage. Some 2,000 personalities of diverse nature are given short biographical sketches with career statistics along with photographs. Included are players, managers, executives, umpires, attorneys, sports writers, announcers, and others associated with the national pastime. Arrangement of entries is alphabetical, and coverage begins with the founding of what is now the National League in 1876 and extends to the present day. Several minor leagues are treated as well as a number of figures from the Negro League. Women's baseball is not treated, however.

1229. Biographical Dictionary of American Sports: Baseball. David L. Porter. Westport, CT: Greenwood Press, 2000. 2064p. ISBN 0-313-29884-X.

This is a three-volume expansion and revision of the author's previous work and replaces his coverage given to baseball in the initial volume in 1987, and in its supplements (entry 1217). Coverage embraces diverse personalities in treating 1,450 players, managers, coaches, executives, officials, administrators, writers, broadcasters, umpires, and more. There is excellent coverage given to the various leagues, both major and minor, including personalities from the Negro League as well as those from the women's league as well. Selection was made on the basis of the figure's impressive statistics or on his or her impact on the game. Entries provide adequate detail on careers, give information on family background as well as life after retirement, and conclude with good bibliographies. The index is well conceived and thorough.

1230. Minor League Baseball Standings: All North American Leagues Through 1999.
Benjamin B. Sumner. Jefferson, NC: McFarland, 2000. 714p. ISBN 0-7864-0781-6.

This is a comprehensive source of information on the standings and records of minor-league franchises from their beginnings to the end of the 1999 season. The work is organized chronologically by league with year-by-year enumeration of final standings, franchise rankings, and major-league affiliations for all teams. All minor leagues, current and historical, are included, some with very short runs like the Wisconsin-Illinois League in operation from 1908 to 1914. Information regarding entry and demise of teams is given for each year, as well as record by franchise and by affiliation. For leagues currently active, there is a listing of the franchise's 10 best and 10 worst seasons.

The second edition of *The Encyclopedia of Minor League Baseball,* edited by Lloyd Johnson and Miles Wolff (Baseball America, 1997) is a good complementary publication. Like the above work, it is thoroughly researched and provides league standings of all teams from 1884 to 1996. Franchise affiliations are given from the 1930s to the present. The work is organized into decades with a summary given for each 10-year period. In addition to season records, there are attendance records, and identification of league leaders in batting and pitching.

1231. No-Hitters: The 225 Games, 1893–1999. Rich Westcott and Allen Lewis. Jefferson, NC: McFarland, 2000. 418p. ISBN 0-7864-0722-0.

A good example of a reference source targeting a specific type of historical record and providing descriptive narrative regarding the particular event in which the record was set, this work has identified 225 no-hitters thrown by single pitchers over the course of a nine-inning game. The year 1893 marks the beginning of the period in which the distance from the pitcher's mound to home plate was set at 60 and a half feet. Entries provide description of the event and its circumstances along with a photograph of the pitcher for no-hitters completed in the major leagues and include the Federal League, but not the Negro League. Appendixes supply listings of combination no-hitters, those completed before 1893, and eight inning no-hitters.

Top Ten Baseball Stats: Interesting Rankings of Players, Managers, Umpires, and Teams by Bob Fulton (McFarland, 2000) is an interesting source in its inclusion of the top 10 record holders in a variety of categories. Because most record books limit themselves to the top performer, it is refreshing to be given data on the nine individuals who are next in rank. Listings include records for home runs, batting average, hits, stolen bases, no-hitters, fielding, managerial records, teams, and so forth. Of value is the analytical and descriptive narrative provided after each listing.

1232. The 100 Greatest Baseball Players of the 20th Century Ranked. Mark McGuire and Michael S. Gormley. Jefferson, NC: McFarland, 2000. 207p. ISBN 0-7864-0914-2.

John C. Skipper's *A Biographical Dictionary of the Baseball Hall of Fame* (McFarland, 2000) serves as a good complement to other biographical sources identified in this section. It is the work of baseball fans written for baseball fans and is meant to provide a subjective but defensible listing of a select group. Selection was made by judgment of the players' impact on their particular eras with the merits of their reputations weighed along with their statistics. Both Satchell Paige and Josh Gibson were included largely on their reputation and legend, because statistics were not carefully recorded by the Negro League. Entries supply basic data, statistical summaries, and evaluative commentary.

John C. Skipper's *A Biographical Dictionary of the Baseball Hall of Fame* (McFarland, 2000) is a convenience source bringing together basic biographical and career information and statistical summary of all members of the Hall of Fame in Cooperstown, New York. Entries are arranged alphabetically and span the entire membership up to and including the 1999 inductees. Hall of Famers include players, writers, broadcasters, managers, officials, umpires, and more.

1233. The Sports Encyclopedia: Baseball 2002. 22nd ed. David S. Neft et al. New York: St. Martin's Press, 2002. 787p. ISBN 0-312-27226-X.

Now in its 22nd edition, this annual publication continues to update the numerous records and statistics up to the time of publication. All types of statistics have been recorded with a complete enumeration of individual and team records, and identification of all record holders. The work begins with a chronologically arranged group of essays and sketches of interesting and significant events, stories, myths and developments such as an interesting account of the World Series in Chicago in 1906. Following that are the thorough and detailed listings of records of various kinds with season-by-season treatment of pennant winners, batting leaders, pitching leaders, no-hitters, awards, vital statistics, season and lifetime averages, and so forth. Coverage spans the 100-year period from 1902 to the time of publication with all teams and all players represented.

Basketball

1234. The Biographical History of Basketball. Peter C. Bjarkman. Lincolnwood, IL: Masters Press, 2000. 590p. ISBN 1-57028-134-3.

The author is well known as a prolific writer-historian of the topic; he has set out to correct current impressions that the game started with Larry, Magic, and Michael. The work is divided into chapters, the first four of which provide historical background and changing nature of basketball, both college and professional, and supply listings of significant personalities. The bulk of the text is presented in the next three chapters that provide biographical sketches of 500 important individuals representing various roles and responsibilities from players to executives over a span of more than 100 years. Names like Mikan, Russell, Robertson, and Lambert are reintroduced to fans along with the contemporary heroes. Entries are arranged alphabetically and supply biographical and career data of both popular and less heralded figures, both male and female. The final chapter broaches the question of the greatest player of all time in speculative fashion.

The fifth edition of *The Sports Encyclopedia, Pro Basketball* by David S. Neft et al. (St. Martin's Press, 1992) treats the first 100 years of the sport and represents a useful and handy digest of statistics and records, as well as a brief but informative historical summary. Coverage begins with the year, 1896, and continues through the 1991/1992 season. The work is organized into sections each with 10 years or so, and year-by-year chronologies are given. There are complete team rosters for every year along with individual leaders in every statistical category.

1235. College Basketball's National Championships: The Complete Record of Every Tournament Ever Played. Morgan G. Brenner. Lanham, MD: Scarecrow Press, 1999. 1036p. (American Sports History Series, no. 13.) ISBN 0-8108-3474-X.

This is a detailed and thorough source of information on the records of schools associated with championship play at the college level. Of most importance, of course, is the period of March madness when the NCAA (and others) conduct tournaments on a grand scale and capture the heart of the American public. Records are supplied for tournaments sponsored by eight collegiate associations that regularly send male and female teams to compete in the NCAA or the NAIA events, as well as those held by relatively small associations. Some 500 tournaments are included along with the less regarded national tournament conducted by the NIT (National Invitation Tournament). Major sections of the work treat the NCAA tournament, and a list of schools that have participated. Names of the coaches and won-lost records are given.

1236. The Sporting News Official NBA Guide. 1999–2000 ed. Mark Broussard and Brendan Roberts. St. Louis: Sporting News Publishing, 1999. 712p. ISBN 0-89204-618-X.

The Sporting News sponsors two major complementary sources in providing historical listings and statistics on professional basketball. The guide furnishes statistics of various kinds, the most comprehensive being team and individual year-end statistics for every team that has been in the NBA since its beginnings in 1947. Information is categorized under topic with entries giving team, schedules, rosters, detailed listings of game scores, team leaders, and more. Team histories are also provided. Additional coverage is given to the performance of the past season with award winners, all-star games, and more. A manual of current rules of the game is included.

The companion work by the same authors, *The Sporting News Official NBA Register* in the 1999–2000 edition (1999) primarily focuses on the past season and contains sections describing veteran players, individual career highs, game statistics, rookies, international players, and so forth. Head coaches are examined in terms of their careers, and there is a listing of the great coaches of the game who compiled 400 or more wins.

Football

1237. College Football Records: Division I-A and the Ivy League, 1869–1984. Jefferson, NC: McFarland, 1987. 198p. ISBN 0-89950-246-6.

This is a useful handbook of team records rather than individual achievements and furnishes listings of won-lost totals (and ties) for each of 111 Division I-A colleges and universities still active in the sport. Arrangement is by conference, under which the schools are listed alphabetically. Entries furnish the schools' nicknames, colors, location, and stadium with seating capacity. Also included are the years in which the football competition began, first year in the conference, and number of conference championships. Overall records are given, as are team versus team totals. Introductory information given at the beginning of the section for each conference includes founding date, charter members, overall records, and conference champions, year by year. Appendixes furnish a variety of summary listings, including bowl game records. There is an index of nondivision opponents; knowledge of conference affiliation is a prerequisite for use.

1238. NFL's Greatest. Phil Barber and John Fawaz. New York: DK Publishing, 2000. 160p. ISBN 0-789-45955-8.

More in the nature of a curiosity vehicle, this publication identifies the choices for a number of "bests." Included here are selections of the 100 greatest players, 25 greatest teams, 25 greatest games, and 25 biggest events. This is more than just a speculative vehicle, however, because the panel of judges is the current membership of the Pro Football Hall of Fame Selection Committee. The Committee considered the entire history of professional football in making their choices, and examined the records from the 1890s when Pudge Heffelfinger received $500 to the present day and its multimillion dollar salaries for the top stars. The mix provides the material for interesting and entertaining sources treating such top-drawer performers as Red Grange and Brett Favre and such outstanding teams as the '72 Dolphins and the '85 Bears.

1239. Pigskin: The Early Years of Pro-Football. Robert W. Peterson. New York: Oxford University, 1997. 256p. ISBN 0-19-511913-4.

This is an informative and well-developed history of professional football from its earliest days in the late 1890s when college players in the Ivy League were paid to play the game up to and including the 1958 championship game between the Baltimore Colts and the New York Giants. Coverage is provided in 12 chapters, the first of which provides an overview or summary introduction to the nature and state of the professional football world before the bonanza of television. Subsequent chapters are arranged chronologically from coverage of the beginning up to the dawn of the television era. Separate chapters describe the impact of Jim Thorpe, and the birth and development of the National Football League with such notables as George Halas and Red Grange. Other chapters treat such issues as black players, and periods such as the wartime era, and the post-war conditions.

1240. The Pro Football Bio-Bibliography. Myron J. Smith, Jr. West Cornwell, CT: Locust Hill, 1989. 388p. ISBN 0-933951-23-X.

Smith is known primarily as a prolific military bibliographer, particularly for his work on the U.S. Navy, but he changed directions here with his coverage of sports. For this work, he has identified articles from books, magazines, league publications, team yearbooks, and commercially published annuals, treating some 1,400 players, coaches, managers, and officials involved in professional football. Entries are arranged alphabetically by name with brief enumeration of career data (items, positions, years played) rather than personal information. Articles cited will furnish ample data for the researcher and serious inquirer as well as the football fan.

Smith's earlier work, *Baseball: A Comprehensive Bibliography* (McFarland, 1986) is a thorough and expansive effort that lists articles, monographs, government publications, theses and dissertations, yearbooks, and even literary efforts on the national pastime. Reference works are given, as are histories, studies, and so on. Baseball is treated comprehensively, from youth leagues and amateur status to the big leagues. There are author and subject indexes.

Biographical Dictionary of American Sports: Football by David L. Porter (Greenwood Press, 1987) examines the lives and careers of more than 500 gridiron personalities of various types. This work was issued as an update or supplement to the football-related parts of the general-purpose *Biographical Dictionary of American Sports* (entry 1217) issued originally in 1986. Appendixes include both collegiate and professional Hall of Fame members.

1241. The Sports Encyclopedia: Pro-Football, the Modern Era 1974–1998. 17th ed. David S. Neft et al. New York: St. Martin's, 1999. 640p. ISBN 0-312-20438-8.

As one of the volumes in the well-received series by the author (entries 1233, 1234n, and 1242), this work continues the tradition and furnishes a complete record of year-by-year coverage of a quarter century through the 1998 season and 1999 Super Bowl. It provides complete rosters of all teams and the scores of every game played during that time period. Individual players are given lifetime statistical treatment, and offensive and defensive leaders are identified. Description of great performances and significant events is given. Many key personalities are featured. The work continues the efforts in Neft's earlier publications, *Pro Football, The Early Years: An Encyclopedic History, 1895–1959* (rev. ed., Sports Products, 1987) and *Sports Encyclopedia: Pro Football, 1960–1989* (St. Martin's, 1989).

1242. Total Football II: The Official Encyclopedia of the National Football League. 2nd ed. David S. Neft and Bob Carroll. New York: HarperInformation, 1999. 1811p. ISBN 0-062-70174-6.

Matching the Herculanean effort of *Total Baseball* (entry 1228) and *Total Hockey* (entry 1245) is this comprehensive and thorough collection of data on professional football. Following the warm reception given the initial edition in 1997, the current effort maintains the same style and format. Since its beginnings, the NFL has been home to some 18,000 players (some of whom played only a single game). Statistics for each of these players is given along with informative historical accounts of championship teams, outstanding games and performances, and significant personalities. Every team is covered and complete rosters are provided along with draftees. Statistics were obtained from the League's statistical bureau along with information provided by the Hall of Fame.

Hockey

1243. Hockey All-Stars. Chris McDonnell. Willowdale, Ont: Firefly Books, 2000. 255p. ISBN 1-55209-542-8.

This is an entertaining, attractive, and informative compilation of biographical sketches and statistical data identifying all players selected as All-Stars by the Professional Hockey Writer's Association beginning with the 1930 season and running to the present day. It is profusely illustrated with photographs of each player in the 281 entries that are arranged alphabetically. Players have been chosen because of their outstanding performance through the years; their selection is not related to those who have played in the All-Star Game because there are a variety of reasons other than performance that have dictated some of those choices. Entries run about 350 words and describe career highlights, provide commentary, and identify relevant statistics.

A Century of Hockey Heroes: 100 of the Greatest All Time Stars by James Duplacey and Eric Zweig (Somerville House USA, 1999) is similar in style and appeal to a wide audience from the very young to the very old. It is limited to 100 of the all-time great performers from the early days to the present. Entries run about a page in length along with a full-page photograph of the individual. Both biographical narrative and statistical summaries are given.

1244. The National Hockey League Official Guide and Record Book 2002–2003. Dan Diamond. Chicago: Triumph Books, 2002. ISBN 1-572-43500-3.

With the growing interest in hockey in this country, there is an increased demand for works that parallel those in baseball, basketball, and football in their coverage of records, exploits, and season-by-season treatment. There is a recap of the past season for each team with scores of each game, club records, and complete schedule. This annual guide provides detailed historical statistics and indexes of retired players as well as examination of current prospects. Basic information on every player currently in the National Hockey League is furnished in adequate detail. Treatment is given to noteworthy achievements of the past along with numerous photographs. There is an analysis of the NHL draft making it a complete and useful resource.

Another effort is *The Sporting News Hockey Register: Every Player, Every Start,* by David Walton and Jeff Paur (McGraw-Hill, 2002). It focuses primarily on the past season (2001–2002) but provides a statistical record on a year-by-year basis. It contains sections treating each player in the NHL along with biographical narrative. Draft choices and European players are covered as well, and the careers of head coaches are described.

1245. Total Hockey: The Official Encyclopedia of the National Hockey League. Dan Diamond et al. eds. Kansas City, MO: Andrews McMeel Publishing, 1998. 1878p. ISBN 0-8362-7114-9.

Similar to the style and format of its sister publications in baseball (entry 1228) and in football (entry 1242), it represents a gargantuan effort in providing a thorough and comprehensive collection of data on the sport. Statistics, records, rosters, registers, histories, and enlightening essays are organized into several sections identifying treating the sport's historical beginnings, the NHL, other leagues, international games, the game's facets, and giving the detailed statistical biographical register. Another massive work for which many expert contributors provided assistance, the game is examined in careful and exhaustive manner and its changing nature described. Game summaries are given, records are furnished, and personalities are covered. As is true of the other works, the essays are informative and treat important issues and events in a comprehensible manner.

Wrestling

1246. Biographical Dictionary of Professional Wrestling. Harris M. Lentz, III. Jefferson, NC: McFarland, 1997. 383p. ISBN 0-7864-0303-9.

Unique in its focus on the wrestling profession is this biographical dictionary treating some 500 professional wrestlers both male and female, promoters, and managers spanning the twentieth century from the time wrestling was a true sport to the 1990s when it finally was acknowledged to be "sports entertainment." Entries are alphabetically arranged under best-known names with cross-references to real names and additional "stage" names. They identify dates of birth and death, place of birth, height and weight, and cover the time period, titles won, managers, tag team partners, major contests, and more. There is emphasis on American wrestlers although others are included.

Encyclopedia of American Wrestling by Mike Chapman (Leisure Press, 1990) establishes perspective outside the realm of current histrionics of professionals and emphasizes amateur wrestling, a truly competitive and taxing endeavor. The history and development of the sport in this country is revealed in various chapters dealing with U.S. champions in the Olympics, AAU National Freestyle Championships, United States Freestyle Senior Opens, Greco-Roman Nationals, Collegiate Nationals, Midlands Championships, Junior Nationals, and the Junior World Tournaments. Special awards are identified and nearly 80 members of the National Wrestling Hall of Fame are profiled. There is a concise bibliography but, unfortunately, no index.

1247. Wrestling Title Histories. 4th ed. Royal Duncan and Gary Will. Waterloo, Ont: Archeus Communications, 2000. 441p. ISBN 0-9698161-5-4.

With the rise in popularity in this form of what is now called sports entertainment attesting to the pre-ordained results in contemporary wrestling, it is refreshing to examine a source of historical information spanning the early time periods from the nineteenth century when professional wrestling, indeed, may have been a legitimate sporting event, to the present. The current edition represents a 60 percent increase in size over its predecessor, published five years earlier, and remains the most complete record of professional wrestling titles and title-holders. Data is presented in chapters within sections arranged by country with emphasis on U.S. titles. This section is divided by states, and champions are identified by name and nickname with the official title they held. Also given are the dates of winning the titles and the cities in which they won them. Coauthor Will maintains a Web site (available at http://www.garywill.com/wrestling/wresbook.htm) with useful links and leads to relevant pages and sites including his own "Deceased Wrestlers."

Golf

1248. Golf: The Legends of the Game. Alistair Tate. Willowdale, Ont: Firefly Books, 1999. 352p. ISBN 1-55209-435-9.

This is a well-designed and attractive volume with many excellent illustrations in which the lives and careers of 275 of the greatest professional golfers that have ever played the game. It is international in scope, although there is an emphasis on golfers who played in this country. The work spans a period of time beginning with the mid-nineteenth century with coverage given to Allan Robertson, the Scotsman regarded as the first true professional, and runs to the present day. Arrangement is alphabetical with entries supplying vital statistics, career achievements, and a brief summary essay. In addition, there are descriptions of important historical events and significant golf courses and holes. An important feature is the inclusion of the complete listing of major championships including the Ryder Cup.

1249. The Majors: In Pursuit of Golf's Holy Grail. John Feinstein. New York: Little, Brown & Company, 1999. 472p. ISBN 0-316-27971-4.

This is a well-written descriptive account of the competitions of a single year, 1998, and the thoughts, hopes, and aspirations of those who chase the elusive gold in winning a major tournament. What makes it suitable for inclusion here is the skillful weaving of historical fabric within the focus on the current era. Much as he did in his earlier work, *A Good Walk Spoiled* (Little, Brown, 1996) in which he documented the behind-the-scenes stories, disappointments, and exhilaration in the activities of the 1993–1994 period, Feinstein includes historical anecdotes and descriptions of the origins and subsequent development of the major tournaments along with his examination of the 1998–1999 season. It represents an informative observation of both the current and past highlights of the Masters, U.S. Open, British Open, and the PGA championships.

Billiards

1250. New Illustrated Encyclopedia of Billiards. Rev. ed. Michael I. Shamos. Guilford, CT: Globe Pequot Press, 1999. 336p. ISBN 1-558-21797-5.

This work updates the earlier effort issued in 1993, and continues as a comprehensive and authoritative historical exposition of the game. With a history dating back hundreds of years, the variations and changing nature of the game are presented in clearly written, interesting, and informative entries. Because the game is considered to be the third most popular participant sport in the country (following bowling and basketball) this source appeals to a wide audience. More than 2,000 entries and 200 illustrations supply interesting anecdotal coverage of the personalities, rules, records, particular shots, and terminology of all sports played with a cue. Appendixes furnish statistical data, and an extensive bibliography provides references to additional source material.

The Billiard Encyclopedia: An Illustrated History of the Sport by Victor Stein and Paul Rubino (Blue Book Publications, 1996) examines the history of the sport from its earliest precursors in ancient Egypt to the present. The work is well illustrated with hundreds of color plates, black-and-white photographs, and various graphics. Chapters cover personalities, events, manufacturers, and more.

Author/Title Index

The numbers in the index generally refer to item entry numbers. Additional sources mentioned in the annotations to the major entries (co-entries and minor entries) are indexed with the designation "n" following the entry number. Those authors and publications identified or described in the narrative of prefatory and introductory passages rather than within entries are indexed by page numbers preceded by "p." All sources available online or in CD-ROM format are preceded by an asterisk (*).

The following guidelines were used in alphabetizing index entries. Lengthy titles have been shortened in some cases. Arrangement is word by word. Names beginning with Mc or Mac or O' are treated as spelled. Acronyms, initialisms, abbreviations, and hyphenated word phrases employed in titles such as OHA, U.S., and Italian-Americans are treated as single words. Be sure to check listings under both United States and U.S. when in doubt. Numbers (including dates) when part of the title are arranged as though written in word form except when part of a chronological sequence or series. In such cases, the years or dates in the titles are arranged from earliest to latest in terms of coverage and scope.

Subject Index

Access is provided to the different themes, topics, and issues addressed by all entries (major, minor, and co-equal) wherever possible, as well as those covered in the introductory narratives to chapters, sections, and subsections. Specific titles described in those introductions are cited in the Author/Title Index. Numbers generally refer to entry numbers; page number references are preceded by a "p." Entry numbers of co-equal entries and minor entries described within the annotations of major entries are designated by an "n."